My Choice for Our Cover

This text has a tradition of highlighting the current President of the United States on the cover as a key representation of the power of public relations. We continue this tradition with President Barack Obama meeting the media—this photo expresses a lot about the practice of public relations in the 21st century.

First, effective public relations has become a primary responsibility for any leader, particularly the President of the United States.

Second, the President's press secretary (Robert Gibbs at Obama's side) is a trusted public relations advisor.

Third, the media now come armed, not with pencils and notebooks, but rather with cell phones and key pads, filing stories instantaneously on the Net.

Finally, even in these days of pervasive social media, building a solid and lasting relationship with the press still lies at the heart of the practice of public relations.

Fraser P. Seitel

THE
PRACTICE
of PUBLIC
RELATIONS

ELEVENTH EDITION

Fraser P. Seitel

Managing Partner, Emerald Partners

Senior Counselor, Burson-Marsteller

Adjunct Professor, New York University

Visiting Professor, Florida International University

Prentice Hall

Boston   Columbus   Indianapolis   New York   San Francisco   Upper Saddle River
Amsterdam   Cape Town   Dubai   London   Madrid   Milan   Munich   Paris   Montreal   Toronto
Delhi   Mexico City   Sao Paulo   Sydney   Hong Kong   Seoul   Singapore   Taipei   Tokyo

Editorial Director: Sally Yagan
Editor in Chief: Eric Svendsen
Acquisitions Editor: Melissa Sabella
Product Development Manager: Ashley Santora
Editorial Project Manager: Kierra Kashickey
Director of Marketing: Patrice Lumumba Jones
Marketing Manager: Anne Fahlgren
Senior Marketing Assistant: Melinda Jensen
Senior Managing Editor: Judy Leale
Project Manager: Becca Richter
Senior Operations Supervisor: Arnold Vila
Operations Specialist: Ilene Kahn
Creative Director: Christy Mahon
Senior Art Director: Janet Slowik
Art Director: Steve Frim
Interior and Cover Designer:
    Frubilicious Design Group

Manager, Visual Research: Beth Brenzel
Manager, Rights and Permissions: Zina Arabia
Image Permission Coordinator: Craig Jones
Manager, Cover Visual Research & Permissions:
    Karen Sanatar
Cover Photo:
    White House Photo by Pete Souza
Permissions Project Manager: Shannon Barbe
Media Project Manager, Editorial: Denise Vaughn
Media Project Manager, Production: Lisa Rinaldi
Supplements Editor: Kierra Kashickey
Full-Service Project Management:
    BookMasters, Inc.
Composition: Integra Software Services, Ltd.
Printer/Binder: Courier/Kendalville
Cover Printer: Coral Graphic
Text Font: 11/12 Apollo MT

Credits and acknowledgments borrowed from other sources and reproduced, with permission, in this textbook appear on appropriate page within text.

Library of Congress Cataloging-in-Publication Data

Seitel, Fraser P.
    The practice of public relations / Fraser P. Seitel.—11th ed.
        p. cm.
Includes bibliographical references and index.
ISBN-13: 978-0-13-608890-5 (pbk.)
ISBN-10: 0-13-608890-2 (pbk.)
    1. Public relations—United States.   I. Title.
HM1221.S45 2011
659.2—dc22

                                2009044076

10 9 8 7 6 5 4 3 2 1

Prentice Hall
is an imprint of

ISBN 10:   0-13-608890-2
ISBN 13: 978-0-13-608890-5

Gift   9/21/10

Dedicated to

Gene Weingarten, *Washington Post* columnist and avowed enemy of public relations, who lacked the courtesy to respond to four emails and one FedEx request for an interview for this book.

Nonetheless, I still love him.

Brief Contents

Contents

Part II   Preparation/Process

Part III   The Publics

Foreword

(Photo: Virgina Sherwood)

Opaque, confused, and inadequate communications by business and financial leaders characterized the 2008 financial crisis and the dizzying descent into global economic recession that followed. Unfortunately, their political brethren have not done much better in explaining what happened and what they are going to do about it. As a result all our institutions are under unprecedented stress and scrutiny.

As Fraser P. Seitel shows in the eleventh edition of his text, good public relations will not solve these problems, but the dissemination of principled policies by seasoned professionals will allow the rest of us to understand the basic issues and lead to the formulation of more appropriate and effective policies.

Regaining and maintaining public confidence is an absolute essential as we move forward. But saying it and doing it are two very different things. For students and even for professionals who have worked in the field for some *time, The Practice of Public Relations* is an excellent place to start. Seitel bridges the gap between theory and practice in a compelling and vivid way. His use of case studies, interviews, news photos, and other techniques, as well as his humorous and lucid text, brings the process brilliantly to life.

The latest edition also includes fascinating case studies about Barrack Obama's presidential campaign, the auto industry bailout, Pope Benedict's visit to the United States, and many others.

Leaders in the public, private, and not-for-profit sectors have learned from painful experience that they should rely on their public relations counselors for cogent advice on strategy and policy as well as communications. I learned to trust Mr. Seitel's instincts and abilities long ago when I was the chairman and chief executive officer of The Chase Manhattan Bank. I continue to rely on his advice to this day.

For those who are working to restore and enhance the capacity of our institutions and their leaders to deal honestly and effectively with the public, this book will provide useful and essential guidance.

—David Rockefeller

David Rockefeller is one of the most influential figures in the history of U.S. business, finance, and philanthropy; considered by many, "America's last great business statesman." Through four decades, Mr. Rockefeller served as an executive with The Chase Manhattan Bank, joining as assistant manager in the foreign department in 1946 and retiring in 1981, after 11 years as chairman and CEO. Over his 90+ years, Mr. Rockefeller has met hundreds of world leaders and traveled around the globe many times. Since his retirement, Mr. Rockefeller has continued to stay active, with wide-ranging interests and involvement in the fields of international relations and civic affairs. He is the last remaining child of John D. Rockefeller, Jr., who hired Ivy Lee in 1914 as the first modern-day public relations counselor.

Preface

First, thank you for buying the book. (Please don't sell it back to the bookstore. I'm begging you!)

Secondly, permit me a less-than-modest observation: The 11th edition of *The Practice of Public Relations* is really *neat*. (Do they still say that?) Okay, *tight* if you prefer. Or even *off da hook*. It's the most contemporary public relations introduction available. I mean any work of scholarship that can combine the public relations lessons learned from the likes of Barack Obama, Martha Stewart, Donald Trump, Michael Vick, and Dog the Bounty Hunter can't be all bad!

What's new in the 11th edition of *The Practice of Public Relations:*

- Eleven new cases featuring the most current and relevant topics in the industry, including:
  - Don Imus
  - Walmart
  - Hewlett Packard
  - Senator Larry Craig
  - Circuit City
  - Former Harvard President, Larry Summers
  - President Barak Obama
  - The auto industry bailout
  - Michael Vick
  - Whole Foods
  - Jet Blue
- Expanded emphasis on ethics with 18 brand-new Ethics cases including:
  - Dog the Bounty Hunter
  - Pope Benedict XVI
  - Apple iPod
  - General David Petraeus
  - Hillary Clinton's former Chief Advisor, Mark Penn
  - Former White House Press Secretary, Scott McClellan
  - Cablevision CEO, James Dolan
  - Rudy Giuliani
  - Domino's Pizza employees' YouTube video
  - Tribune CEO, Sam Zell
  - Former winner of the Nobel Prize for Biology, Holmes Sherlock
  - FEMA's phony press conference

- American Apparel
- Myanmar cyclone disaster relief efforts
- Illinois Governor, Rod Blagojevich
- Cartoon Network's Boston bomb scare
- Online Girl Scout cookie sales
- Ailing Apple CEO, Steve Jobs

- **Eight new "From the Top" interviews with today's top authorities in the worlds of management, media and academia, including:**
  - MasterCard's Harvey Greisman
  - Celebrity Attorney, Robert Shapiro
  - *USA Today* founder, Al Neuharth
  - White House Press Secretary, Robert Gibbs
  - Johnson & Johnson's Ray Jordan
  - Web Communications Specialist, Hoa Loranger
  - Public Relations executive, Richard Edelman
  - Dean of public relations recruiters, Bill Heyman

- **Expanded emphasis on writing in Chapter 16, "Writing for the Eye and Ear."**

- **New comprehensive social media content in Chapter 18, "Public Relations and Social Media."**

- **Updated "Public Relations Library" features the most current literature in the field of public relations.**

In addition, this book has a heavy emphasis on social media. Every chapter begins with a social media introduction relating to the particular subject matter discussed. Social media applications run throughout the chapters. And the chapter devoted to *"Public Relations and Social Media"* offers the most comprehensive discussion of any introductory public relations text.

As important as social media has become to public relations work, it is still but one extended *"implement"* in the public relations toolkit. The field still depends on technical skill, experience, and judgment, all grounded in solid relationships with colleagues, constituents, and media.

Above all, public relations responses and relationships must be based on the single concept of *"doing the right thing."* Indeed, acting *ethically* lies at the heart of the solutions for the more than three-dozen case studies that this edition presents.

In a day of economic and political uncertainty around the world, the practice of public relations has never been a more potent force in society or a more valuable factor in an organization's reputation. In the 21st century, public relations crises and opportunities are front-page news on a daily basis.

The field remains, at heart, a personal, relationship-oriented practice, demanding experienced judgment and finely honed interpersonal communications skills. And so, this 11th edition of *The Practice of Public Relations* places its emphasis on the principles, processes, and practices that lead to building positive relationships in a 24/7 communications environment.

Among the highlights of the 11th edition:

Comprehensive Social Media Content

As in so many other lines of work, mastering social media has become a key tool for public relations practitioners, to engage in "*direct conversations*" with public relations publics. Public relations professionals must understand the communications opportunities and limitations of blogs and wikis and podcasts and Twitter and Flickr and YouTube and MySpace and Facebook, and all the rest.

No public relations textbook offers a more comprehensive discussion of social media than the 11th edition of *The Practice of Public Relations*.

Each chapter begins with a social media application related to the chapter's particular subject matter. Chapter 18 provides a full discussion of "*Public Relations and Social Media*," from more fundamental public relations uses for e-mail and Web sites to more exotic uses for CEO blogging and Second Life sales pitches. The chapter also discusses the "*downside*" of the Internet, in terms of rogue Web sites and urban legends, and the importance of Web monitoring.

Expanded Emphasis on Ethics

Proper public relations practice must be underpinned by a strong sense of ethics. The principle of *doing the right thing* is what should distinguish the practice of public relations.

This edition focuses on the ethical base that provides the theoretical foundation of effective communications and public relations.

The book's introductory chapters place significant attention on how an understanding of and facility with communications research, theory, and public opinion can be applied to strategic public relations planning and creation of believable and persuasive messages.

New to this 11th edition is a "*PR Ethics Mini-Case*" in each chapter. These cases bring to life the daily ethical dilemmas that confront professional public relations practitioners.

New Contemporary Cases

Public relations practice confronts an ever-changing landscape of problems and opportunities. It is imperative, therefore, that a textbook in the field keep current with the most contemporary examples of the good, the bad, and the ugly in public relations work.

This 11th edition does so by chronicling the most important contemporary public relations cases—from Barack Obama's historic use of public relations and social media to become President to Martha Stewart's disastrous handling of insider trading charges to ethical dilemmas that cast doubt on great companies, from Hewlett-Packard to Whole Foods to Apple Computer. These contemporary cases are complemented by the field's most historic conundrums—from Tylenol's poisoned pills to Exxon's Gulf of Valdez disaster—as well as hypothetical student cases, from composing a complex news release to creating a speech for the CEO.

Every case is designed to test student application of the theories discussed in solving real-world challenges.

Expanded Writing Emphasis

By definition, public relations professionals must be the best "communicators" in their organizations.

That means they have to know how to write. So in this edition, we have added a chapter, beyond the introductory writing section, on "Public Relations Writing for the Eye and Ear." This chapter includes expanded "how to" counsel on two areas of increased importance in public relations practice: 1) writing techniques and vehicles that lead to publicity, from pitch letters and case histories to round up stories and op-eds and 2) speechwriting, including the preparatory elements, organizational components, and stylistic devices that comprise an effective presentation.

Additional New Elements

The strength of this book rests in its application of theory to real-life practice.

In addition to the new, contemporary cases and the expanded Social Media discussion, unique elements added in the 11th edition include:

- **NEW! From the Top** interviews with distinguished communicators from the worlds of management, media, and academe, including Presidential Press Secretary Robert Gibbs; illustrious *USA Today* publisher Al Neuharth; legendary public relations counselors, Harold Burson, Howard Rubenstein, and Richard Edelman; Johnson and Johnson communications director Ray Jordan and MasterCard communications director Harvey Greisman; Internet writing expert Hoa Loranger; and even the public relations industry's most notorious critic, John Stauber.

- **NEW! PR Ethics Mini-Cases**, which highlight the ethical challenges that public relations professionals, face on a daily basis—from Pope Benedict's historic New York City pilgrimage to American Apparel's controversial marketing program to Apple Computer's reluctance to discuss the health of its CEO.

- **NEW! Talking Points** features that expose off-line curiosities that make the practice of public relations such a fascinating art form.

- **NEW! Public Relations Library,** encompassing the most comprehensive current bibliography in public relations literature.

- **NEW! Newscom photos,** taken straight from the news wire, add a real-life feel to this edition that isn't found in any other textbook.

All of these elements add to the excitement of this book. So, too, does the full-color format that underscores the liveliness, vitality, and relevance of the field.

Unique Perspective

Clearly, *The Practice of Public Relations,* 11th Edition, isn't your mother's PR textbook.

This book is a lot different from other introductory texts in the field. Its premise is that public relations is a thoroughly engaging and constantly changing field. The extensive explanation of Social Media and its application to public relations practice is unique in public relations textbooks.

Although other texts may steer clear of the contemporary major cases, perplexing ethical mini-cases, thought leader interviews, "how to" counsel, and the public relations conundrums that force students to think, this book confronts them all.

It is, if you'll forgive the vernacular, an *in-your-face* textbook for an *in-your-face* profession.

Most important, *The Practice of Public Relations,* 11th Edition, is built around the technical knowledge of theory, history, process and practice, judgmental skills, and personal relationships that underlie public relations practice and will be so essential in building the trust and respect of diverse communities in the 21st century.

Happy reading, and thanks again for buying the book.

Student Resources

Companion Website

This text's Companion Website at **www.pearsonhighered.com/seitel** offers free access to self-assessment quizzes and applicable links.

CourseSmart eTextbooks Online

CourseSmart is an exciting new choice for students looking to save money. As an alternative to purchasing the print textbook, students can purchase an electronic version of the same content and save up to 50% off the suggested list price of the print text. With a CourseSmart eTextbook, students can search the text, make notes online, print out reading assignments that incorporate lecture notes, and bookmark important passages for later review. For more information or to purchase access to the CourseSmart eTextbook, visit www.coursesmart.com.

ACKNOWLEDGMENTS

The 11th edition of *The Practice of Public Relations* owes much to a multitude of professors and others who have helped immeasurably in the evolution of this work.

First and foremost, my friend and client **David Rockefeller** was most kind to agree to update the Foreword. David Rockefeller is a legendary world business statesman and a unique figure in modern history, not to mention one of the kindest people on the planet. It is an honor to include his words in these pages.

I am also most grateful to the busy people who agreed to be newly interviewed for this text. Public relations leaders **Richard Edelman, Harvey Greisman, Ray Jordan,** and **Hoa Loranger** are all top industry professionals who were kind enough to take time out to contribute. It was also an honor to interview legendary *USA Today* publisher **Al Neuharth** for this edition.

As an added bonus, the most powerful public relations man in the world, **Robert Gibbs,** Barack Obama's talented White House Press Secretary, was even kind enough to take time out for an insightful interview. These interviewees join an already stellar group of repeat interviewees, making the communications roster here as good as it gets.

Thank you, all.

The distinguished citizens at Pearson-Prentice Hall, recognizing the author's ineptitude in a multitude of areas, assigned the first team to this effort, led by the talented triumvirate of Product Development Manager Ashley Santora, Editorial Project Manager Kierra Kashickey, and Production Project Manager Becca Richter. These lovely ladies were supported at each step by, among others, Editorial Director Sally Yagan, Marketing Manager Anne Fahlgren, Acquisitions Editor Melissa Sabella, Senior Managing Editor Judy Leale, Art Director Steve Frim, Designer Mike Fruhbeis, Editor-in-Chief Eric Svendsen, and, of course, outstanding Production Coordinator Jen Welsch. It took the concerted wisdom of all of 'em to keep your author on course.

I am also most grateful to the very kind professors whose critiques were invaluable in preparation for this edition: Johnny Mac Allen, Oral Roberts University; Thomas Boyle, Millersville University; Christopher J. Fenner, Florida Southern College; Jan W. Kelly, University of Scranton; Bruce L. Smith, Texas State University—San Marcos; Erin E. Wilgenbusch, Iowa State University; and Beth Wood, Indiana University.

Other professors who have reviewed past editions include: Carolina Acosta-Alzuru at the University of Georgia; Bill Brewer at Miami University; Meta G. Carstarphen at University of North Texas; Jerry M. Engel at Ithaca College; Lisa Ferree at Eastern Kentucky University; Susan Gonders at Southeast Missouri State University; Carole Gorney at Lehigh University; Kirk Hallahan at Colorado State University; Christine R. Helsel at Eastern Illinois University; Liese L. Hutchison at Saint Louis University; Ken McMillen at University of Oklahoma; Robert J. O'Gara at Point Park College; E. Jerald Ogg at the University of Tennessee at Martin; Michael G. Parkinson at Texas Tech University; Betty J. Pritchard at Grand Valley State University; Robert S. Pritchard at Ball State University; William E. Sledzik at Kent State University; and Don W. Stacks at the University of Miami.

Also, Thomas Bivins at the University of Oregon, Charles Lubbers at Kansas State University, and Nancy Wolfe at Elon College all were quite helpful. They join in the Hall of Thanks those other distinguished professors who have reviewed past editions: Nickieann Fleener, Department of Communication, University of Utah; Mort Kaplan, Department of Marketing Communication, Columbia College (Chicago); Jack Mauch, Department of Communication, University of Idaho; Donnalyn Pompper, Department of Communication, Cabrini College; Cornelius B. Pratt, Department of Communications, Michigan State University; J. D. Rayburn II, Department of Communication, Florida State University; Nancy Roth, Department of Communication, Rutgers, The State University (New Jersey); William C. Adams, School of Journalism and Mass Communications, Florida International University; John Q. Butler; Rachel L. Holloway, Department of Communications Studies, Virginia Tech; Diana Harney, Department of Communication and Theater, Pacific Lutheran University; Cornelius Pratt, Department of Advertising, Communications, and Public Relations, Michigan State University; Robert Cole, Pace University; Janice Sherline Jenny, College of Business, Herkimer County Community College; Craig Kelly, School of Business, California State University, Sacramento; Lyle J. Barker, Ohio State University; William G. Briggs, San Jose State University; E. Brody, Memphis State University; John S. Detweiler, University of Florida; Jim Eiseman, University of Louisville; Sandy Grossbart, University of Nebraska; Marjorie Nadler, Miami University; Sharon Smith, Middle Tennessee State University; Robert Wilson, Franklin University; Jack Mandel, Nassau Community College; Carol L. Hills, Boston University; George Laposky, Miami-Dade Community College; Mack Palmer, University of Oklahoma; Judy VanSlyke Turk, Louisiana State University; Roger B. Wadsworth, Miami-Dade Community College; James E. Grunig, University of Maryland; Robert T. Reilly, University of Nebraska at Omaha; Kenneth Rowe, Arizona State University; Dennis L. Wilcox, San Jose State University; Albert

Walker, Northern Illinois University; Stanley E. Smith, Arizona State University; Jan Quarles, University of Georgia; Pamela J. Creedon, Ohio State University; Joel P. Bowman, Western Michigan University; Thomas H. Bivins, University of Oregon; Joseph T. Nolan, University of North Florida; Frankie A. Hammond, University of Florida; Bruce Joffe, George Mason University; Larissa Grunig, University of Maryland; Maria P. Russell, Syracuse University; and Melvin L. Sharpe, Ball State University.

Thank you, all.

Good friends and family, as ever, were there to inspire and cajole a slothful author so that the assignment could be completed in proper form and fashion. On the friends side, the ever-lovely Peter Johnson, Prof. Jay Rayburn, Marissa Hopkins, Reid Cherlin, Susan Bootze, Sandra Eisert, Dan Hansen, Jack O'Dwyer, Steve Rivkin, and Andrew Edson were, as always, invaluable. And the same was true on the family side, where Rosemary Seitel; Raina, Adam, and Theo Gittlin; and Himalayan correspondent David Seitel held forth. Finally, young Hunter Gittlin made a stirring debut in his first appearance in the driver's seat.

Finally, I should acknowledge the public relations-despising *Washington Post* columnist Gene Weingarten who, although he lacked the courtesy to answer numerous emails and overnight mailers requesting an interview, still provided your author with the inspiration to frame a most unique book dedication.

Thank you, Gene, and thank you one and all.

—Fraser P. Seitel,
November 2009

About the Author

Fraser P. Seitel is a veteran of four decades in the practice of public relations. (Although he is still extraordinarily young!) In 2000, *PR Week* magazine named Mr. Seitel one of the *100 Most Distinguished Public Relations Professionals of the 20th Century.*

In 1992, after serving for a decade as senior vice president and director of public affairs for The Chase Manhattan Bank, Mr. Seitel formed Emerald Partners, a management and communications consultancy, and also became senior counselor at the world's largest public affairs firm, Burson-Marsteller.

Mr. Seitel is a regular guest on television and radio. In addition to his appearances on a variety of programs on the Fox News Network, he has appeared on ABC's *Good Morning America*, CNBC's *Power Lunch*, CNN's *Larry King Live*, as well as on MSNBC, Fox Business Network, the Fox Radio Network and National Public Radio.

Mr. Seitel has counseled hundreds of corporations, nonprofits, associations, and individuals in the area for which he had responsibility at Chase—media relations, speech writing, consumer relations, employee communications, financial communications, philanthropic activities, and strategic management consulting.

Mr. Seitel is an Internet columnist at odwyerpr.com and a frequent lecturer and seminar leader on communications topics. Over the course of his career, Mr. Seitel has taught thousands of public relations professionals and students.

After studying and examining many texts in public relations, he concluded that not one of them "*was exactly right.*" Therefore, in 1980, he wrote the first edition of *The Practice of Public Relations* "*to give students a feel for how exciting this field really is.*" In three decades of use at hundreds of colleges and universities, Mr. Seitel's book has introduced generations of students to the excitement, challenge, and uniqueness of the practice of public relations.

Chapter **1**

What Is Public
Relations, Anyway?

FIGURE 1-1 Social media idol. Sanjaya Malakar, 21st century offspring of the marriage of social media and public relations. (Photo: Newscom)

The face of the practice of public relations in the final years of the first decade of the 21st century could be found beneath the faux-blue and yellow Mohawk hairdo, lovingly displayed here (Figure 1-1).

In 2007, Sanjaya Malakar, a 17-year-old aspiring, ahem, "singer" from Seattle burst onto the national spotlight as a semifinalist on season six of the nation's hottest TV show, *American Idol*. According to the judges, Sanjaya's singing was, well, "*horrible.*" But that didn't stop the ever-upbeat performer from moving steadily up the *Idol* charts.[1]

Sanjaya's ascent was largely due to the confluence of emerging social media with traditional public relations techniques. Specifically, his underdog cause was championed by radio commentators, cable TV pundits, and newspaper reporters, generating a tidal wave of publicity. This was followed by perpetual Internet chatter and ultimately, enough Net-recorded public votes to enable him to advance to seventh place, despite being pilloried by the on-air judges, particularly the repugnant Simon Cowell.

Sanjaya's unlikely national celebrity was a crystal clear illustration of the potential power of marrying social media with public relations.

In the 21st century, few societal forces are more powerful than either social media—the agglomeration of instant messages, email, cell phone photos, blogs, wikis, Web casting, RSS feeds, and all the other emerging technologies of the World Wide Web—or the practice of public relations.

Together, the combination of the two—social media and public relations—has revolutionized the way organizations and individuals communicate to their key constituent publics around the world.

Not convinced?

Well, how about asking Osama bin Laden (Figure 1-2)?

In the fall of 2007, after a public absence of three years (during which many thought he was dead!), the world's most wanted felon reemerged on the Internet in a public relations video.

Abandoning his trademark Kalashnikov rifle and camouflage military jacket and dyeing his beard from grey to black, the leader of al-Qaeda presented a new image to the world.

In a half-hour address released four days before the sixth anniversary of the September 11 attacks on the United States, bin Laden lurched between history lesson and sermon, urging Americans to ditch capitalist democracy and embrace Islam if they wanted to end the war in Iraq.[2]

Bin Laden's address was memorable not only because of the terrorist's bizarre appearance, but also because he chose to "stage his comeback" through a public relations video on the Internet.

The speech itself sounded like more of a political treatise than a call for annihilation of the infidels.

Bin Laden rambled across religion, history, domestic U.S. politics, and the wars in Iraq and Afghanistan, throwing in climate change and even referring to the current crisis over bad mortgage loans in the United States.

How bizarre.

The terrorist leader's attempt to restyle himself as a civilian leader and ideologist, rather than a zealous mass murderer, served as a prime example of using public relations methods and techniques to recast an image. Indeed, al-Qaeda at the time was evolving from a centrally controlled terrorist organization to a more loosely configured body of local operatives. So the al-Qaeda chief's look and demeanor were meant to express this evolution.

The point is that in the 21st century, even terrorists understood the impact of public relations messages and the reach of the World Wide Web to deliver them.

But what is *public relations*, anyway?

That is the question asked even by many of the 200,000 plus people in the United States and the thousands of others overseas who practice public relations.

In a society overwhelmed by communications—from traditional newspapers and magazines, to 24/7 talk radio and television, to nontraditional instant messages, blogs, podcasts, wikis, and assorted other Internet exotica—the public is bombarded with nonstop messages of every variety. The challenge for a communicator is to cut through this clutter to deliver an argument that is persuasive, believable, and actionable.

The answer, more often than not today, lies in public relations. Stated another way, in the 21st century, the power, value, and influence of the practice of public relations have never been greater.

FIGURE 1-2 **Social media madman.** Osama bin Laden took to the Internet on the anniversary of the terrorist attacks of September 11 to reach his followers around the world, six years after the awful strikes on America. (Photo: Newscom)

Prominence of Public Relations

In the initial decade of the 21st century, public relations as a field has grown immeasurably both in numbers and in respect. Today, the practice of public relations is clearly a growth industry.

- In the United States alone, public relations is a multibillion-dollar business practiced by 158,000 professionals, according to the U.S. Bureau of Labor Statistics. Furthermore, the Bureau says that "employment of public relations specialists is expected to increase faster than the average for all occupations through 2012. The need for good public relations in an increasingly competitive business environment should spur demand for public relations specialists in organizations of all types and sizes."[3]

- Around the world, the practice of public relations has grown enormously. The International Public Relations Association boasts a strong membership, and the practice flourishes from Latin America to Africa and from Europe to Russia to China.

- In a 2005 study by the Council of the Public Relations Society of America and Harris Interactive to assess the views of *Fortune* 1000 company executives on public relations, 84 percent felt the practice helped "raise awareness about important issues that the public might not know about," and 81 percent felt public relations helped "get the media to address issues that would otherwise fail to receive the attention they deserve."[4]

- Approximately 250 colleges and universities in the United States and many more overseas offer a public relations sequence or degree program. Many more offer public relations courses. Undergraduate enrollments in public relations programs at U.S. four-year colleges and universities are conservatively estimated to be well in excess of 20,000 majors.[5] In the vast majority of college journalism programs, public relations sequences rank first or second in enrollment.

- The U.S. government has thousands of communications professionals— although none, as we will learn, are labeled *public relations specialists*—who keep the public informed about the activities of government agencies and officials. The Department of Defense alone has 7,000 professional communicators spread out among the Army, Navy, and Air Force.

- The world's largest public relations firms are all owned by media conglomerates— among them Omnicom, The Interpublic Group, and WPP Group—which refuse to divulge public relations revenues. The field is dominated by smaller, privately held firms, many of them entrepreneurial operations. A typical public relations agency has annual revenue of less than $1 million with less than 10 employees. Nonetheless, the 7,000 U.S. public relations agencies record annual revenue of more than $6 billion.[6]

- The field's primary trade associations have strong membership, with the Public Relations Society of America encompassing nearly 20,000 members in 116 chapters and the International Association of Business Communicators including 13,000 members in more than 60 countries.

In the 21st century, as all elements of society—companies, nonprofits, governments, religious institutions, sports teams and leagues, arts organizations, and all others—wrestle with constant shifts in economic conditions and competition, security concerns, and popular opinion, the public relations profession is expected to thrive because increasing numbers of organizations are interested in communicating their stories.

Indeed, public relations people have already attained positions of prominence in every aspect of society. Robert Gibbs, President Barack Obama's Press Secretary (see "From the Top," Chapter 12), is quoted daily from his televised White House press briefings. Karen Hughes, a public relations advisor to George W. Bush since his earliest days in politics, moved from a Special Assistant to the President in the White House to become, in 2005, Undersecretary of State for Public Diplomacy (see Case Study Chapter 14), responsible primarily for changing attitudes internationally about the United States (although she didn't do very well!). That same year, the UPS Company appointed communications professional Christine Owens to its management committee. Said CEO Mike Eskew, "*Communications is just too important not to be represented on the management committee of this company.*"[7]

Perhaps the most flattering aspect of the field's heightened stature is that competition from other fields has become more intense. Today the profession finds itself vulnerable to encroachment by people with non–public relations backgrounds, such as lawyers, marketers, and general managers of every type, all eager to gain the management access and persuasive clout of the public relations professional.

The field's strength stems from its roots: "a democratic society where people have freedom to debate and to make decisions—in the community, the marketplace, the home, the workplace, and the voting booth. Private and public organizations depend on good relations with groups and individuals whose opinions, decisions, and actions affect their vitality and survival."[8]

What Is Public Relations?

Public relations is a *planned process to influence public opinion, through sound character and proper performance, based on mutually satisfactory two-way communication.*

At least that's what your author believes it is.

The fact is that there are many different definitions of public relations. American historian Robert Heilbroner once described the field as "*a brotherhood of some 100,000, whose common bond is its profession and whose common woe is that no two of them can ever quite agree on what that profession is.*"[9]

In 1923, the late Edward Bernays described the function of his fledgling public relations counseling business as one of providing

> *information given to the public, persuasion directed at the public to modify attitudes and actions, and efforts to integrate attitudes and actions of an institution with its publics and of publics with those of that institution.*[10]

Today, although a generally accepted definition of public relations still eludes practitioners, there is a clearer understanding of the field. One of the most ambitious searches for a universal definition was commissioned in 1975 by the Foundation for Public Relations Research and Education. Sixty-five public relations leaders participated in the study, which analyzed 472 different definitions and offered the following 88-word sentence:

> *Public relations is a distinctive management function which helps establish and maintain mutual lines of communications, understanding, acceptance, and cooperation between an organization and its publics; involves the management*

of problems or issues; helps management to keep informed on and responsive to public opinion; defines and emphasizes the responsibility of management to serve the public interest; helps management keep abreast of and effectively utilize change, serving as an early warning system to help anticipate trends; and uses research and sound and ethical communication techniques as its principal tools.[11]

In 1988, the Public Relations Society of America formally adopted the following definition of public relations:

Public relations helps an organization and its publics adapt mutually to each other.

The Public Relations Society noted that its definition implied the functions of research, planning, communications dialogue, and evaluation, all essential in the practice of public relations.[12]

No matter which formal definition one settles on to describe the practice, in order to be successful, public relations professionals must always engage in a planned process to influence the attitudes and actions of their targets.

Planned Process to Influence Public Opinion

What is the process through which public relations might influence public opinion? Communications professor John Marston suggested a four-step model based on specific functions: (1) research, (2) action, (3) communication, and (4) evaluation.[13] Whenever a public relations professional is faced with an assignment—whether promoting a client's product or defending a client's reputation—he or she should apply Marston's *R-A-C-E* approach:

1. **Research.** Research attitudes about the issue at hand.
2. **Action.** Identify action of the client in the public interest.
3. **Communication.** Communicate that action to gain understanding, acceptance, and support.
4. **Evaluation.** Evaluate the communication to see if opinion has been influenced.

The key to the process is the second step—action. You can't have effective communication or positive publicity without proper action. Stated another way, performance must precede publicity. Act first and communicate later. Indeed, some might say that public relations—PR—really should stand for *performance recognition*. In other words, positive action communicated straightforwardly will yield positive results.

This is the essence of the R-A-C-E process of public relations.

Public relations professor Sheila Clough Crifasi has proposed extending the R-A-C-E formula into the five-part R-O-S-I-E to encompass a more managerial approach to the field. R-O-S-I-E prescribes sandwiching the functions of objectives, strategies, and implementation between research and evaluation. Indeed, setting clear objectives, working from set strategies, and implementing a predetermined plan is a key to sound public relations practice.

Still others suggest a process called R-P-I-E for research, planning, implementation, and evaluation, which emphasizes the element of planning as a necessary step preceding the activation of a communications initiative.

All three approaches, R-A-C-E, R-O-S-I-E, and R-P-I-E, echo one of the most widely repeated definitions of public relations, developed by the late Denny Griswold, who founded a public relations newsletter.

Public relations is the management function which evaluates public attitudes, identifies the policies and procedures of an individual or an organization with the public interest, and plans and executes a program of action to earn public understanding and acceptance.[14]

The key words in this definition are *management* and *action*. Public relations, if it is to serve the organization properly, must report to top management. Public relations must serve as an honest broker to management, unimpeded by any other group. For public relations to work, its advice to management must be unfiltered, uncensored, and unexpurgated. This is often easier said than done because many public relations departments report through marketing, advertising, or even legal departments.

Nor can public relations take place without appropriate action. As noted, no amount of communications—regardless of its persuasive content—can save an organization whose performance is substandard. In other words, if the action is flawed or the performance rotten, no amount of communicating or backtracking or post facto posturing will change the reality. (Don't believe me? Check out the Don Imus Case Study at the end of this chapter!) Stated another way, it is axiomatic in public relations that *"You can't pour perfume on a skunk."*

The process of public relations, then, as Professor Melvin Sharpe has put it, *"harmonizes long-term relationships among individuals and organizations in society."*[15] To "harmonize," Professor Sharpe applies five principles to the public relations process:

- Honest communication for credibility
- Openness and consistency of actions for confidence
- Fairness of actions for reciprocity and goodwill
- Continuous two-way communication to prevent alienation and to build relationships
- Environmental research and evaluation to determine the actions or adjustments needed for social harmony

And if that doesn't yet give you a feel for what precisely the practice of public relations is, then consider public relations Professor Janice Sherline Jenny's description as *"the management of communications between an organization and all entities that have a direct or indirect relationship with the organization, i.e., its publics."*

No matter what definition one may choose to explain the practice, few would argue that the goal of effective public relations is to harmonize internal and external relationships so that an organization can enjoy not only the goodwill of all of its publics but also stability and long life.

Public Relations as Management Interpreter

The late Leon Hess, who ran one of the nation's largest oil companies and the New York Jets football team, used to pride himself on *not* having a public relations department. Mr. Hess, a very private individual, abhorred the limelight for himself and for his company.

But times have changed.

Today, the CEO who thunders, *"I don't need public relations!"* is a fool. He or she doesn't have a choice. Every organization *has* public relations whether it wants it or not. The trick is to establish *good* public relations. That's what this book is all about—professional public relations, the kind you must work at.

Public relations affects almost everyone who has contact with other human beings. All of us, in one way or another, practice public relations daily. For an organization, every phone call, every letter, every face-to-face encounter, is a public relations event.

Public relations professionals, then, are really the organization's interpreters.

■ On the one hand, they must interpret the philosophies, policies, programs, and practices of their management to the public.

■ On the other hand, they must convey the attitudes of the public to their management.

Let's consider management first.

Before public relations professionals can gain attention, understanding, acceptance, and ultimately action from target publics, they have to know what management is thinking.

Good public relations can't be practiced in a vacuum. No matter what the size of the organization, a public relations department is only as good as its access to management. For example, it's useless for a senator's press secretary to explain the reasoning behind an important decision without first knowing what the senator had in mind. So, too, an organization's public relations staff is impotent without firsthand knowledge of the reasons for management's decisions and the rationale for organizational policy.

The public relations department in any organization can counsel management. It can advise management. It can even exhort management to take action. But it is management who must call the shots on organizational policy.

It is the role of the public relations practitioner, once policy is established by management, to communicate these ideas accurately and candidly to the public. Anything less can lead to major problems.

Public Relations as Public Interpreter

Now let's consider the flip side of the coin—the public.

Interpreting the public to management means finding out what the public really thinks about the firm and letting management know. Regrettably, history is filled with examples of powerful institutions—and their public relations departments—failing to anticipate the true sentiments of the public.

■ In the 1960s, General Motors paid little attention to an unknown consumer activist named Ralph Nader, who spread the message that General Motors' Corvair was "*unsafe at any speed.*" When Nader's assault began to be believed, the automaker assigned professional detectives to trail him. In short order, General Motors was forced to acknowledge its act of paranoia, and the Corvair was eventually sacked at great expense to the company.

■ In the 1970s, as both gasoline prices and oil company profits rose rapidly, the oil companies were besieged by an irate gas-consuming public. When, at the height of the criticism, Mobil Oil spent millions in excess cash to purchase the parent of the Montgomery Ward department store chain, the company was publicly battered for failing to cut its prices.

■ In the 1980s, President Ronald Reagan rode to power on the strength of his ability to interpret what was on the minds of the electorate. But his successor in the early 1990s, George H. W. Bush, a lesser communicator than Reagan, failed to "read" the nation's economic concerns. After leading America to a victory over Iraq in the Gulf War, President Bush failed to heed the admonition, "*It's the economy, stupid*," and lost the election to upstart Arkansas Governor Bill Clinton.

■ As the 20th century ended, President Clinton forgot the candid communication skills that earned him the White House and lied to the American public about his affair with an intern. The subsequent scandal, ending in impeachment hearings before the U.S. Congress, tarnished Clinton's administration, and ruined his legacy.

■ In the first decade of the 21st century, Clinton's successor, George W. Bush, earned great credit for strong actions and communications following the September 11, 2001, attacks on the nation. The Bush administration's public relations then suffered when the ostensible reason for attacking Iraq—weapons of mass destruction—failed to materialize. Bush's failure to act promptly and communicate frankly in subsequent crises, such as Hurricane Katrina, hurt his personal credibility and irreparably tarnished his administration.

■ At the same time, CEOs of some of the nation's mightiest corporations—among them Enron, Arthur Andersen, Tyco, Sotheby's, and WorldCom—were dragged into court, and many imprisoned, for a variety of ethical violations that misled the public and in many cases ruined their companies. As a consequence, tough new laws were passed to deal with corporate criminals.[16]

■ In the spring and summer of 2008, Senators Hillary Clinton and Barack Obama waged a fierce and perpetual battle across the nation to win the Democratic nomination for president. That battle was largely based on the power of public relations (Figure 1-3). Obama emerged as the winner, and the new President promptly named his chief rival, Secretary of State.

FIGURE 1-3 Sharing the bench. In the spring and summer of 2008, Senators Hillary Clinton and Barack Obama staged a ferocious—but mostly civil—public relations battle for the Democrat Party presidential nomination. The latter wound up as President, and the former as Secretary of State. (White House Photo by Pete Souza)

■ The Obama Administration was met by a pervasive economic crisis, marked by another round of CEOs from the nation's largest companies—Citigroup, AIG, Washington Mutual, Bear Stearns, Lehman Brothers, Countrywide Financial, and others—exposed before the American public as inept stewards of the public trust.

In the first decade of the 21st century then, the savviest individuals and institutions—be they government, corporate, or nonprofit—understand the importance of effectively interpreting their philosophies, policies, and practices to the public and, even more important, interpreting back to management how the public views them and their organization.

PR Ethics

Mini-Case Shut Up, Dawg!

Duane "Dog" Chapman, a bounty hunting ex-convict known for his long gold locks and brash behavior, was an instant cable sensation on the A&E network (Figure 1-4).

Dog's televised exploits, tracking down bail jumpers and law violators of every stripe, attracted 1.2 million viewers—most of them, young. His *Dog The Bounty Hunter* program brought in $17.7 million in advertising revenue in the first half of 2007 alone.

But then Dog's off-screen language got him into hot water.

In November 2007, Mr. Chapman was recorded repeatedly using a racial slur in an obscenity-laced telephone tirade with his son, Tucker. Dog urged Tucker, one of his 12 children, to break up with his African American girlfriend, who Mr. Chapman feared might tell others about his frequent use of racist terms.

He needn't have worried. The recording of the conversation popped up on the National Enquirer Web site, leaked evidently by Tucker. And advertisers began heading for the exits.

First, Yum Brands, Inc., owner of Taco Bell, KFC, and Pizza Hut, pulled its ads, deploring Mr. Chapman's "despicable" language. Other advertisers, among them such stalwarts as Johnson & Johnson and Alltel, threatened to act similarly in light of the perception of Dog as racist.

A&E didn't have to be told what to do. Two days after the phone call went public, the network released the following statement:

"In evaluating the circumstances of the last few days, A&E has decided to take *Dog The Bounty Hunter* off the network's schedule for the foreseeable future. We hope that Mr. Chapman continues the healing process that he has begun."

A&E stopped short of canceling outright the money-making program, shown in 10 countries. A&E hoped that, with time, its advertisers would forgive and forget Dog's ethical lapse. Sure enough, with the power of Americans "to forgive and forget," A&E brought back *Dog The Bounty Hunter* to bark another day.*

FIGURE 1-4 Shut up, Dawg! Dog the Bounty Hunter and his lovely wife, Mrs. Dog. (Photo: Newscom)

Questions

1. What other options did A&E have beyond suspending Chapman?

2. Should the network have taken him back? If so, under what "conditions"?

*For further information, see Sam Schechner, "Bounty Hunter's Slurs Halt A&E Show," *The Wall Street Journal*, November 2, 2007, B4, and Jaymes Song, "A&E Pulls Bounty Hunter from Schedule Because of Dog's Tirade," Associated Press, November 2, 2007.

The Publics of Public Relations

The term *public relations* is really a misnomer. *Publics* relations, or relations with the publics, would be more to the point. Practitioners must communicate with many different publics—not just the general public—each having its own special needs and requiring different types of communication. Often the lines that divide these publics are thin, and the potential overlap is significant. Therefore, priorities, according to organizational needs, must always be reconciled (Figure 1-5).

Technological change—particularly the Internet, cell phones, blogs, satellite links for television, and the computer in general—has brought greater interdependence to people and organizations, and there is growing concern in organizations today about managing extensive webs of interrelationships. Indeed, managers have become interrelationship conscious.

Internally, managers must deal directly with various levels of subordinates as well as with cross-relationships that arise when subordinates interact with one another.

Externally, managers must deal with a system that includes government regulatory agencies, labor unions, subcontractors, consumer groups, and many other

FIGURE 1-5 **Key publics.** Twenty of the most important publics of a typical multinational corporation.

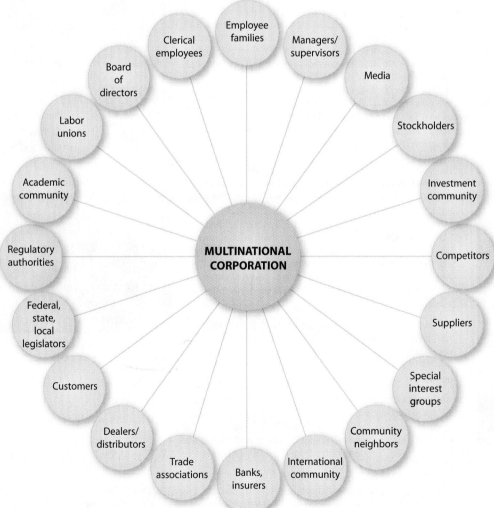

independent—but often related—organizations. The public relations challenge in all of this is to manage effectively the communications between managers and the various publics, which often pull organizations in different directions. Stated another way, public relations professionals are very much mediators between client (management) and public (all those key constituent groups on whom an organization depends).

Definitions differ on precisely what constitutes a public. One time-honored definition states that a public arises when a group of people (1) faces a similar indeterminate situation, (2) recognizes what is indeterminate and problematic in that situation, and (3) organizes to do something about the problem.[17] In public relations, more specifically, a public is a group of people with a stake in an issue, organization, or idea.

Publics can also be classified into several overlapping categories:

- **Internal and external.** Internal publics are inside the organization: supervisors, clerks, managers, stockholders, and the board of directors. External publics are those not directly connected with the organization: the press, government, educators, customers, suppliers, and the community.

- **Primary, secondary, and marginal.** Primary publics can most help—or hinder—the organization's efforts. Secondary publics are less important, and marginal publics are the least important of all. For example, members of the Federal Reserve Board of Governors, who regulate banks, would be the primary public for a bank awaiting a regulatory ruling, whereas legislators and the general public would be secondary. On the other hand, to the investing public, interest rate pronouncements of the same Federal Reserve Board are of primary importance.

- **Traditional and future.** Employees and current customers are traditional publics; students and potential customers are future ones. No organization can afford to become complacent in dealing with its changing publics. Today, a firm's publics range from women to minorities to senior citizens to homosexuals. Each might be important to the future success of the organization.

- **Proponents, opponents, and the uncommitted.** An institution must deal differently with those who support it and those who oppose it. For supporters, communications that reinforce beliefs may be in order. But changing the opinions of skeptics calls for strong, persuasive communications. Often, particularly in politics, the uncommitted public is crucial. Many a campaign has been decided because the swing vote was won over by one of the candidates.

Another way of segmenting publics is on the basis of values and lifestyles. Such segmentation is used regularly by marketers to focus product and service appeals on particular socioeconomic levels. Segmentation separates consumers into eight distinct categories:

1. Actualizers are those with the most wealth and power.
2. Fulfilleds have high resources and are principle-oriented professionals or retirees.
3. Believers are Fulfilleds without the resources.
4. Achievers have high resources and are status oriented.
5. Strivers lack the resources of Achievers but are equally status oriented.
6. Experiencers have high resources, are action oriented, and are disposed toward taking risks.
7. Makers also are action oriented but have low resources.
8. Strugglers have the lowest resources.[18]

Applying such lifestyle characterizations to publics can help companies make marketing and public relations decisions to effectively target key audiences.

The typical organization is faced with a myriad of critical publics with which it must communicate on a frequent and direct basis. It must be sensitive to the self-interests, desires, and concerns of each public. It must understand that self-interest groups today are themselves more complex. Therefore, the harmonizing actions necessary to win and maintain support among such groups should be arrived at in terms of public relations consequences.[19]

Whereas management must always speak with one voice, its communications inflection, delivery, and emphasis should be sensitive to all constituent publics.

The Functions of Public Relations

There is a fundamental difference between the functions of public relations and the functions of marketing and advertising. Marketing and advertising promote a product or a service. Public relations promotes an entire organization.

The functions associated with public relations work are numerous. Among them are the following:

- **Writing**—*the* fundamental public relations skill, with written vehicles from news releases to speeches and from brochures to advertisements falling within the field's purview.
- **Media relations**—dealing with the press is another frontline public relations function.
- **Planning**—of special events, media events, management functions, and the like.
- **Counseling**—in dealing with management and its interactions with key publics.
- **Researching**—of attitudes and opinions that influence behavior and beliefs.
- **Publicity**—the marketing-related function, most commonly misunderstood as the "only" function of public relations, generating positive publicity for a client or employer.
- **Marketing communications**—other marketing-related functions, such as creating brochures, sales literature, meeting displays, and promotions.
- **Community relations**—positively putting forth the organization's messages and image within the community.
- **Consumer relations**—interfacing with consumers through written and verbal communications.
- **Employee relations**—communicating with the all-important internal publics of the organization, those managers and employees who work for the firm.
- **Government affairs**—dealing with legislators, regulators, and local, state, and federal officials—all of those who have governmental interface with the organization.
- **Investor relations**—for public companies, communicating with stockholders and those who advise them.
- **Special publics relations**—dealing with those publics uniquely critical to particular organizations, from African Americans to women to Asians to senior citizens.
- **Public affairs and issues**—dealing with public policy and its impact on the organization, as well as identifying and addressing issues of consequence that affect the firm.

■ **Social media interface**—creating what often is the organization's principle interface with the public: its Web site, as well as creating links with social media options. Also important is monitoring the World Wide Web and responding, when appropriate, to organizational challenge.

This is but a partial list of what public relations practitioners do. In sum, the public relations practitioner is manager/orchestrator/producer/director/writer/arranger and all-around general communications counsel to management. It is for this reason, then, that the process works best when the public relations director reports directly to the CEO.

The Curse of "Spin"

So pervasive has the influence of public relations become in our society that some even fear it as a pernicious force; they worry about the power of public relations to exercise a kind of thought control over the American public.

Which brings us to *spin*.

In its most benign form, spin signifies the distinctive interpretation of an issue or action to sway public opinion, as in putting a positive slant on a negative story. In its most virulent form, spin means confusing an issue or distorting or obfuscating it or even lying.

The propensity in recent years for presumably respected public figures to lie in an attempt to deceive the public has led to the notion that "spinning the facts" is synonymous with public relations practice.

It isn't.

Spinning an answer to hide what really happened—that is, lying, confusing, distorting, obfuscating, whatever you call it—is antithetical to the proper practice of public relations. In public relations, if you lie once, you will never be trusted again—particularly by the media.

Nonetheless, public relations spin has come to mean the twisting of messages and statements of half-truths to create the appearance of performance, which may or may not be true.

This association with spin has hurt the field. *The New York Times* headlined a critical article on public relations practice, "Spinning Frenzy: P.R.'s Bad Press."[20] Other critics admonish the field as "a huge, powerful, hidden medium available only to wealthy individuals, big corporations, governments, and government agencies because of its high cost."[21]

In recent years, the most high-profile government public relations operatives have often fallen guilty to blatant spin techniques. In the Clinton administration, communications counselors, such as James Carville, Paul Begala, and Lanny Davis, eagerly spun the tale that intern Monica Lewinsky was, in effect, delusional about an Oval Office affair with the President. *(She wasn't!)* In the Bush administration, high-level advisors Karl Rove and Lewis Libby were implicated in a spinning campaign against former Ambassador Joseph Wilson, who questioned the motives of the war in Iraq. In 2005, Libby, Vice President Dick Cheney's top aide, was convicted for *"obstruction of justice, false statement, and perjury"* in the Wilson case.[22]

Faced with this era of spin and unrelenting questioning by the media and the public about the ethics of public relations, practitioners must always be sensitive to and considerate of how their actions and their words will influence the public.

Above all—in defiance of charges of spinning—public relations practitioners must consider as their cardinal rule: to never, ever lie.

What Manner of Man or Woman?

What kind of individual does it take to become a competent public relations professional?

A 2004 study of agency, corporate, and nonprofit public relations leaders, sponsored by search firm Heyman Associates, reported seven areas in particular that characterize a successful public relations career:

1. Diversity of experience
2. Performance
3. Communications skills
4. Relationship building
5. Proactivity and passion
6. Teamliness
7. Intangibles, such as personality, likeability, and chemistry[23]

Beyond these success-building areas, in order to make it, a public relations professional ought to possess a set of specific technical skills as well as an appreciation of the proper attitudinal approach to the job. On the technical side, the following six skills are important:

1. **Knowledge of the field.** The underpinnings of public relations—what it is, what it does, and what it ought to stand for.
2. **Communications knowledge.** The media and the ways in which they work; communications research; and, most important, how to write.
3. **Technological knowledge.** Familiarity with computers and associated technologies, as well as with the World Wide Web, are imperative.
4. **Current events knowledge.** Knowledge of what's going on around you—daily factors that influence society: history, literature, language, politics, economics, and all the rest—from the Ming Dynasty to Yao Ming; from Ben Stein to bin Laden; from Dr. Phil to Dr. Dre; from Three Penny Opera to 50 Cent; from Fat Joe to J Lo to Ozomatli. A public relations professional must be, in the truest sense, a Renaissance man or woman.
5. **Business knowledge.** How business works, a bottom-line orientation, and a knowledge of your company and industry.
6. **Management knowledge.** How senior managers make decisions, how public policy is shaped, and what pressures and responsibilities fall on managers.

In terms of the "attitude" that effective public relations practitioners must possess, the following six requisites are imperative:

1. **Pro communications.** A bias toward disclosing rather than withholding information. Public relations professionals should want to communicate with the public, not shy away from communicating. They should practice the belief that the public has a right to know.
2. **Advocacy.** Public relations people must *believe in* their employers. They must be advocates for their employers. They must stand up for what their employers represent. Although they should never ever lie (Never, ever!) or distort or hide facts, occasionally it may be in an organization's best interest to avoid comment on certain issues. If practitioners don't believe in the integrity and credibility of their employers, their most honorable course is to go to "Plan B"—find work elsewhere.

3. **Counseling orientation.** A compelling desire to advise senior managers. Top executives are used to dealing in tangibles, such as balance sheets, costs per thousand, and cash flows. Public relations practitioners deal in intangibles, such as public opinion, media influence, and communications messages. Practitioners must be willing to support their beliefs—often in opposition to lawyers or human resources executives. They must even be willing to disagree with management at times. Far from being compliant, public relations practitioners must have the gumption to say *no*.

4. **Ethics.** The counsel that public relations professionals deliver must always be ethical. The mantra of the public relations practitioner must be to *do the right thing*.

5. **Willingness to take risks.** Most of the people you work for in public relations have no idea what you do. Sad but true. Consequently, it's easy to be overlooked as a public relations staff member. You therefore must be willing to stick your neck out . . . stand up for what you believe in . . . take risks. Public relations professionals must have the courage of their convictions and the personal confidence to proudly represent their curious—yet critical—role in any organization.

6. **Positive outlook.** Public relations work occasionally is frustrating work. Management doesn't always listen to your good counsel, preferring instead to follow attorneys and others into safer positions. No matter. A public relations professional, if he or she is to perform at optimum effectiveness, must be positive. You can't afford to be a "sad sack." You win some. You lose some. But in public relations, at least, the most important thing is to keep on swinging and smiling.

Last Word

Spin, cover-up, distortion, and subterfuge are the antitheses of good public relations.

Ethics, truth, credibility—these values are what good public relations is all about.

To be sure, public relations is not yet a profession like law, accounting, or medicine, in which all practitioners are trained, licensed, and supervised. Nothing prevents someone with little or no formal training from hanging out a shingle as a public relations specialist. Such frauds embarrass professionals in the field and, thankfully, are becoming harder to find.

Indeed, both the Public Relations Society of America and the International Association of Business Communicators have strong codes of ethics that serve as the basis of their membership philosophies (Appendix A).

Meanwhile, the importance of the practice of public relations in a less certain, more chaotic, overcommunicated, and competitive world cannot be denied.

Despite its considerable problems—in attaining leadership status, finding its proper role in society, disavowing spin, and earning enduring respect—the practice of public relations has never been more prominent. In its first 100 years as a formal, integrated, strategic-thinking process, public relations has become part of the fabric of modern society.

Here's why.

As much as they need customers for their products, managers today also desperately need constituents for their beliefs and values. In the 21st century, the role of public relations is vital in helping guide management in framing its ideas and making its commitments. The counsel that management needs must come from advisers who understand public attitudes, moods, needs, and aspirations.

Contrary to what misinformed critics may charge, "More often than not, public relations strategies and tactics are the most effective and valuable arrows in the quiver of the disaffected and the powerless."[24] Civil rights leaders, labor leaders, public advocates, and grassroots movements of every stripe have been boosted by proven communications techniques to win attention and build support and goodwill.

Winning this elusive goodwill takes time and effort. Credibility can't be won overnight, nor can it be bought. If management policies aren't in the public's best interest, no amount of public relations effort can obscure that reality. Public relations is not effective as a temporary defensive measure to compensate for management misjudgment. If management errs seriously, the best—and only—public relations advice must be to get the truthful story out immediately. Indeed, working properly, the public relations department of an organization often serves as the firm's "conscience."

This is why the relationship between public relations and other parts of the organization—

advertising and marketing, for example—is occasionally a strained one. The function of the public relations department is distinctive from that of any other internal area. Few others share the access to management that public relations enjoys. Few others share the potential for power that public relations may exercise.

No less an authority than Abraham Lincoln once said: "*Public sentiment is everything . . . with public sentiment, nothing can fail. Without it, nothing can succeed. He who molds public sentiment goes deeper than he who executes statutes or pronounces decisions. He makes statutes or decisions possible or impossible to execute.*"[25]

Stated another way, no matter how you define it, the practice of public relations has become an essential element in the conduct of relationships for a vast variety of organizations in the 21st century.

Discussion Starters

1. How prominent is the practice of public relations around the world in the 21st century?
2. How would you define the practice of public relations?
3. Why is the practice of public relations generally misunderstood by the public?
4. How would you describe the significance of the planning aspect in public relations?
5. Within the R-A-C-E process of public relations, what would you say is the most critical element?
6. In what ways does public relations differ from advertising or marketing?
7. If you were the public relations director of the local United Way, whom would you consider your most important "publics" to be?
8. What are seven functions of public relations practice?
9. How do professional public relations people regard the aspect of "spin" as part of what they do?
10. What are the technical and attitudinal requisites most important for public relations success?

Top of the Shelf   The New PR: An Insider's Guide to Changing the Face of Public Relations / Phil Hall, North Potomac, MD: Larstan Publishing, 2007

This overview, which features real-life examples and interviews with real-life practitioners, was written by a former editor of the newsletter *PR News*.

The author describes public relations practice in a positive, but realistic, manner. He talks about what public relations can and can't do, quoting numerous professionals about "unrealistic expectations" of clients. The author also

takes the public relations industry to task for doing a poor job in defining its own "strengths and opportunities with the general public."

Through examples and interviews, the book presents a valid portrait of the state of the public relations business in the first decade of the 21st century.

Case Study   Ho Ho Ho – Out Goes the I-Man

In the spring of 2007, few radio personalities were more powerful than Don Imus.

The I-Man, as his many influential guests called him, held forth each drive-time morning on New York's WFAN radio and was simulcast nationally on MSNBC.

Imus was well known for mixing political commentary and interviews—all the leading politicians regularly paid homage to his program—with an irreverent, often close-to-the-edge style of humor. Indeed, Imus and his studio cohorts regularly trashed any interest group, regardless of age, sex, body type, political affiliation, religion, and, until one fateful day in 2007, race.

One reason Imus got away with it was because he was charitable to a fault. Imus leavened his on-air insults by contributing significantly to worthwhile causes, including his own cattle ranch for children with cancer.

Imus, in fact, was an equal-opportunity offender. His combination of clout, cynicism, and charity made him seem impervious to the criticisms that dogged lesser men.

Until the day the roof fell in April 2007.

Gone in 20 Seconds

That was the day that Imus and a radio sidekick described the inspirational Rutgers University women's basketball team as "nappy-headed hoes."

It was a throw-away discussion, typical of the politically incorrect rants that made Imus, Imus. The colloquy with his colleague lasted no more than 20 seconds. But it was the most fateful 20 seconds of the I-Man's 30-year radio career.

While few paid attention at the time, a liberal, Washington, D.C.–based monitoring group, Media Matters, posted the video and transcript on its Web site and sent an email blast to several hundred reporters.

And Imus was toast.

Almost immediately, African American leaders interpreted the unfortunate description as "racist."

- The Rev. Al Sharpton led a campaign to rid the airwaves of Imus.

- Rutgers Coach Vivian Stringer and her players held a press conference to "show the world their true identity."

- And long-term sponsors, from General Motors to Staples, started having second thoughts about their affiliation with the suddenly-radioactive broadcaster.

Most hurtful—and probably most surprising at least to Imus—was that virtually every one of his regular guests, from late broadcaster Tim Russert to journalists Howard Fineman and Frank Rich, from Senators Joe Biden and Chris Dodd to African American political leader former Congressman Harold Ford, headed for the exits, rather than support their "media friend."

A Final Futile Attempt

Abandoned by those whose books and programs and personal appearances he had flogged for years, Imus made a desperate attempt at "damage control."

- First, Imus apologized profusely on the air, painfully explaining that he meant no harm, wasn't a racist, and deserved a second chance.

- Next, he traveled to New Jersey to meet with the Rutgers team. The deal was brokered by New Jersey Governor John Corzine, who, in an ominous omen for Imus, was seriously injured in a car accident, while speeding to the meeting at the Governor's Mansion.

- Finally, in one last desperate maneuver, Imus made a pilgrimage to the radio home of the man leading the charge against him. His appearance on the *Rev. Al Sharpton Show* was an unmitigated disaster. The "ever-gracious" Rev. Sharpton let Imus have it with both barrels. The Sharpton on-air pummeling of the wounded Imus closed the lid on any chance of resurrection (Figure 1-6).

FIGURE 1-6 **Sharpton shakedown.** Don Imus made a fatal public relations blunder when he visited the Rev. Al Sharpton's radio show, looking for vindication for his stupid remarks. He was promptly immolated by the Rev. Al. (Photo: Newscom)

Shortly thereafter, their sponsors having spoken, both WFAN and MSNBC removed Imus from the airwaves. The besmirched broadcaster returned to his New Mexico ranch to lick his wounds and ponder his future.

A "Second Act" for the I-Man

In America in the 21st century, not even comments attributed as racist can put one under for good.

There is increasingly room for "second acts" in the most forgiving, celebrity-crazed nation on earth. And Imus, an experienced broadcaster with an affluent audience, found himself the subject of great attention from radio networks looking for star attractions. With the radio industry reeling from consolidation, true "stars" were few and far between. And a proven star—even one as tarnished as Imus—became a coveted commodity.

And so, eight months after his on-air self-immolation, a chastened Don Imus was hired by Citadel Broadcasting to return to the airwaves at rival WABC radio, once again drive-time host for a cumulative weekly audience of nearly one million listeners. He also was to be simulcast, not by the powerful peacock network's MSNBC, but rather by something called RFD (rural free delivery) TV. (Later, Imus switched to the Fox Business Network.)

Many of his advertisers, having forsaken him for an "acceptable" period of time, returned to the Imus fold. And while The National Association of Black Journalists objected to Imus' return, the Rev. Sharpton—content to have made his headlines and gone on to other "crusades"—said only that he would "reserve the right to agitate with advertisers."

The I-Man, himself, returned to the air a less-edgy, less-gutsy, more politically correct commentator, who had become decidedly more knowledgeable about the perception of "standards" in American broadcasting. In addition to his loyal cast, Imus had added two new regular comic commentators—one male, one female, and both black. And, oh yes, he also returned with a $5 million annual contract (Figure 1-7).

Nonetheless, even a watered-down Imus was not immune to new brushes against political correctness. In the summer of 2008, a throwaway remark about perpetually troubled NFL defensive back Adam "Pac Man" Jones landed Mr. Imus right back in the soup, as Net watchdogs pounced immediately. Mr. Jones, it seemed, would not be the only one playing "defense" for the foreseeable future.

FIGURE 1-7 Return of the I-Man. In December 2007, a chastened Don Imus returned to the airwaves, surrounded, in part, by two new African American sidekicks.
(Photo: Newscom)

Questions

1. Had you been advising Imus, what would you have counseled him to say/do after making his racial slur?

2. Had you been advising his employers, WFAN and MSNBC, what would you have counseled them to do?

3. How would you have counseled Imus with respect to Al Sharpton? Would you have gone on Sharpton's radio show?

4. How do you explain Imus' "radio friends" failing to stick up for him in his hour of need?

5. How must Imus comport himself now on the air?

For further information, see Brooks Barnes, Emily Steel and Sarah McBride, "Behind the Fall of Imus, A Digital Brush Fire," *The Wall Street Journal*, April 13, 2007, A1; Sarah McBride, "Imus Signs Deal with Citadel to Return to Radio," *The Wall Street Journal*, November 2, 2007, B4; Fraser P. Seitel, "Requiem for Imus," odwyerpr.com, April 13, 2007; Jacques Steinberg, "All Forgiven, WIMUS-AM Is on a Roll," *New York Times,* February 3, 2008; and Jacques Steinberg, "Football Talk Soon Turns to Race on Imus's Show," *New York Times*, June 24, 2008, A19.

From the Top   An Interview with Harold Burson

Harold Burson is the world's most influential and gentlemanly public relations practitioner. He has spent more than a half century serving as counselor to and confidante of corporate CEOs, government leaders, and heads of public sector institutions. As founder and chairman of Burson-Marsteller, he was the architect of the largest public relations agency in the world. Mr. Burson, widely cited as the standard bearer of public relations ethics, has received virtually every major honor awarded by the profession, including the Harold Burson Chair in Public Relations at Boston University's College of Communication, established in 2003.

How would you define public relations?
One of the shortest—and most precise—definitions of public relations I know is "doing good and getting credit for it." I like this definition because it makes clear that public relations embodies two principal elements. One is behavior, which includes policy and attitude; the other is communications—the dissemination of information. The first tends to be strategic, the second tactical—although strategy plays a major role in many, if not most, media relations programs.

How has the business of public relations changed over time?
Public relations has, over time, become more relevant as a management function for all manner of institutions—public and private sector, profit and not-for-profit. CEOs increasingly recognize the need to communicate to achieve their organizational objectives. Similarly, they have come to recognize public relations as a necessary component in the decision-making process. This has enhanced the role of public relations both internally and for independent consultants.

How do ethics apply to the public relations function?
In a single word, pervasively. Ethical behavior is at the root of what we do as public relations professionals. We approach our calling with a commitment to serve the public interest, knowing full well that the public interest lacks a universal definition and knowing that one person's view of the public interest differs markedly from that of another. We must therefore be consistent in our personal definition of the public interest and be prepared to speak up for those actions we take.

At the same time, we must recognize our roles as advocates for our clients or employers. It is our job to reconcile client and employer objectives with the public interest. And we must remember that while clients and employers are entitled to have access to professional public relations counsel, you and I individually are in no way obligated to provide such counsel when we feel that doing so would compromise us in any way.

What are the qualities that make up the ideal public relations man or woman?
It is difficult to establish a set of specifications for all the kinds of people wearing the public relations mantle. Generally, I feel five primary characteristics apply to just about every successful public relations person I know.

- They're smart—bright, intelligent people; quick studies. They ask the right questions. They have that unique ability to establish credibility almost on sight.

- They know how to get along with people. They work well with their bosses, their peers, their subordinates. They work well with their clients and with third parties like the press and suppliers.

- They are emotionally stable—even (especially) under pressure. They use the pronoun "we" more than "I."

- They are motivated, and part of that motivation involves an ability to develop creative solutions. No one needs to tell them what to do next; instinctively, they know.

- They don't fear starting with a blank sheet of paper. To them, the blank sheet of paper equates with challenge and opportunity. They can write; they can articulate their thoughts in a persuasive manner.

What is the future of public relations?
More so than ever before, those responsible for large institutions whose existence depends on public acceptance and support recognize the need for sound public relations input. At all levels of society, public opinion has been brought to bear in the conduct of affairs both in the public and private sectors. Numerous CEOs of major corporations have been deposed following initiatives undertaken by the media, by public interest groups, by institutional stockholders—all representing failures that stemmed from a lack of sensitivity to public opinion. Accordingly, my view is that public relations is playing and will continue to play a more pivotal role in the decision-making process than ever before. The sources of public relations counsel may well become less structured and more diverse, simply because of the growing pervasive understanding that public tolerance has become so important in the achievement of any goals that have a recognizable impact on society.

Public Relations Library

Cutlip, Scott M., Allen H. Center, and Glen M. Broom, *Effective Public Relations*, 9th ed. Upper Saddle River, NJ: Prentice Hall, 2006. Still the most comprehensive textbook in the field, including this one. (But don't tell my publisher!)

Ewen, Stuart, *PR! A Social History of Spin*. New York: Basic Books, 1996.

Heath, Robert L., *Handbook of Public Relations*. Thousand Oaks, CA: Sage Publications, 2004.

Heath, Robert L., and W. Timothy Coombs, *Today's Public Relations An Introduction*. Thousand Oaks, CA: Sage Publications, 2006. Two eminent professors suggest that relationship building is "more than just a buzzword," and, rather, constitutes the essence of public relations.

Henslowe, Philip, *Public Relations: A Practical Guide to the Basics*. Sterling, VA: Kogan Page, 2003. A British approach to the practice, endorsed by the London-based Institute of Public Relations.

Lattimore, Dan (Ed.), *Public Relations: The Practice and the Profession*. New York: McGraw-Hill College, 2003.

Marconi, Joe, *Public Relations: The Complete Guide*. Mason, OH: Thomson South-Western, 2004. This comprehensive book traces public relations from its earliest antecedents—the time of Edward Bernays (see Chapter 2) in the 1930s to the present day. It covers, in depth, most aspects of the field, including the role of the public relations practitioner today.

Newsom, Doug, Judy Vanslyke Turk, and Dean Kruckeberg, *This Is PR: The Realities of Public Relations*, 9th ed. Belmont, CA: Wadsworth Publishing Company, 2007.

Pohl, Gayle M., *No Mulligans Allowed: Strategically Plotting Your Public Relations Course*. Dubuque, IA: Kendall Hunt Publishers, 2005. A fresh, creative, and useful perspective on charting a public relations career, authored by one of the nation's foremost public relations educators.

Rampton, Sheldon, and John Stauber, *Trust Us, We're Experts: How Industry Manipulates Science and Gambles with Your Future*. New York: J.P. Tarcher/Putnam, 2002. A super-cynical look at what public relations people do for a living, authored by two of the industry's most ardent—yet lovable—critics.

Ries, Al, and Laura Ries, *The Fall of Advertising and the Rise of PR*. New York: Harperbusiness, 2004. An old ad hand and his daughter blow the lid off the advertising profession.

Slater, Robert, *No Such Thing as Over-Exposure: Inside the Life and Celebrity of Donald Trump*. Upper Saddle River, NJ: Financial Times/Prentice-Hall, 2005. The story, if you can bear it, of Donald Trump, in which the promotion-craving megalomaniac sat for 100 hours of private conversations.

Wilcox, Dennis (Ed.), *Public Relations: Strategies and Tactics*, 8th ed. Boston: Allyn & Bacon, 2007.

Yaverbaum, Eric, *Public Relations Kit for Dummies 2nd Edition*. Foster City, CA: IDG Books Worldwide, 2006. A tongue-in-cheek, but useful, primer.

Chapter 2

The History and Growth
of Public Relations

The Christmas Broadcast, 2007

FIGURE 2-1 Hip Majesty. Queen Elizabeth II joined the public relations/social media revolution in 2007, when she broadcast her annual Christmas message on YouTube. (Photo: Newscom)

In the annals of the practice of public relations, no day was probably more historic than December 22, 2007.

That was the day that Queen Elizabeth II launched her own YouTube video site (see Figure 2-1).

The 81-year-old British monarch included news reel footage and film snippets of daily life to keep the public informed about the ways of the Buckingham Palace royals. Palace officials said the official Royal Channel on YouTube would be the place to go to keep up with the activities of the royal family.

Said the official royal news release, "The queen always keeps abreast with new ways of communicating with people. She has always been aware of reaching more people and adapting the communication to suit."[1]

Good for Her Majesty, and not bad for a field that's been around, as a formal practice, for just about one century.

Unlike accounting, economics, medicine, and law, public relations is still a young field, approximately 100 years old.

Modern-day public relations is clearly a 20th-century phenomenon. The impetus for its growth might, in fact, be traced back to one man.

John D. Rockefeller Jr. (Figure 2-2) was widely attacked in 1914 when the coal company he owned in Ludlow, Colorado, was the scene of a bloody massacre staged by Colorado militiamen and company guards against evicted miners and their families. When a dozen women and small children were killed at the Ludlow massacre, one of those Rockefeller called in to help him deal with the crisis was a journalist named Ivy Ledbetter Lee.

Lee, whom we discuss later in this chapter, would go on to become "the father of public relations." His employer, John D. Rockefeller Jr., whose own legendary father had always adhered to a strict policy of silence, would bear responsibility for the birth of a profession built on open communications.

The relative youthfulness of the practice of public relations means that the field is still evolving. It is also getting *stronger* and gaining more *respect* every day. The professionals entering the practice today are by and large superior in intellect, training, and even experience to their counterparts of decades ago (when nobody studied "public relations").

The strength of the practice of public relations today is based on the enduring commitment of the public to participate in a free and open democratic

FIGURE 2-2 Pondering a crisis. John D. Rockefeller (center) needed public relations help in 1914, when the Colorado coal company he owned was the scene of a massacre of women and children. (Rockefeller Archive Center)

society. Several trends abroad in society have influenced the evolution of public relations theory and practice:

1. **Growth of big institutions.** The days of small government, local media, mom-and-pop grocery stores, tiny community colleges, and small local banks have largely disappeared. In their place have emerged massive political organizations, worldwide media networks, Walmarts, Home Depots, statewide community college systems, and nationwide banking networks. The public relations profession has evolved to interpret these large institutions to the publics they serve.

2. **Heightened public awareness and media sophistication.** First came the invention of the printing press. Then came mass communications: the print media, radio, and television. Later it was the development of cable, satellite, videotape, videodisks, video typewriters, portable cameras, word processors, fax machines, and cell phones. Then came the Internet, blogs, podcasts, wikis, FaceBook, MySpace, YouTube, Twitter, and all the other communications technologies that have helped fragment audiences. Fifty years ago, McGill University Professor Marshall McLuhan predicted the world would become a *"global village,"* where people everywhere could witness events—no matter where they occurred—in real time. In the 21st century, McLuhan's prophesy has become a reality.

3. **Increasing incidence of societal change, conflict, and confrontation.** Minority rights, women's rights, senior citizens' rights, gay rights, animal rights, consumerism, environmental awareness, downsizings, layoffs, and resultant unhappiness with large institutions all have become part of day-to-day

society. With the growth of the Web, activists have become increasingly more daring, visible, and effective. Today, anyone who owns a computer can be a publisher, a broadcaster, a motivator of others.

4. **Globalization and the growing power of global media, public opinion, and democratic capitalism.** While institutions have grown in size and clout in the 21st century, at the same time the world has gotten increasingly smaller and more interrelated. Today, news of a cyclone that ravages Myanmar or an earthquake that imperils China is broadcast within moments to every corner of the globe. The outbreak of democracy and capitalism in China, Latin America, Eastern Europe, the former Soviet Union, South Africa, and even, in recent years, in nations like Afghanistan, Iraq, and Kosovo, has heightened the power of public opinion in the world. The process has been energized by media that span the globe, especially social media that instantaneously connect like-minded individuals. In China alone, there are 75 million blogs, often carrying criticisms of the government. Public opinion is a powerful force not only in democracies like the United States but also for oppressed peoples around the world. Accordingly, the practice of public relations as a facilitator for understanding has increased in prominence.

5. **Dominance of the Internet and growth of social media.** Nearly 1.4 billion of the world's people today use the Internet.[2] The extraordinary growth of the Internet and the World Wide Web has made hundreds of millions of people around the world not only "instant consumers" of communication but also, with the advent of social media, "instant generators" of communication as well. The profound change this continues to bring to society—and the importance it places on communications—is monumental.

Ancient Beginnings

Although modern public relations is a 20th-century phenomenon, its roots are ancient. Leaders in virtually every great society throughout history understood the importance of influencing public opinion through persuasion. For example, archeologists have found bulletins in Iraq, dating from as early as 1800 B.C., that told farmers of the latest techniques of harvesting, sowing, and irrigating.[3] The more food the farmers grew, the better the citizenry ate and the wealthier the country became—a good example of planned persuasion to reach a specific public for a particular purpose—in other words, public relations.

The ancient Greeks also put a high premium on communication skills. The best speakers, in fact, were generally elected to leadership positions. Occasionally, aspiring Greek politicians enlisted the aid of sophists (individuals renowned for both their reasoning and their rhetoric) to help fight verbal battles. Sophists gathered in the amphitheaters of the day to extol the virtues of particular political candidates. Thus, the sophists set the stage for today's lobbyists, who attempt to influence legislation through effective communications techniques. From the time of the sophists, the practice of public relations has been a battleground for questions of ethics. Should a sophist or a lobbyist—or a public relations professional, for that matter—"sell" his or her talents to the highest bidder, regardless of personal beliefs, values, and ideologies? When modern-day public relations professionals agree to represent repressive governments, such as Iran or Zimbabwe or North Korea, or to defend the questionable actions of troubled celebrities, from Britney Spears and Barry Bonds to Amy Winehouse and O. J. Simpson, these ethical questions remain very much a focus of modern public relations.

The Romans, particularly Julius Caesar, were also masters of persuasive techniques. When faced with an upcoming battle, Caesar would rally public support through published pamphlets and staged events. Similarly, during World War I, a special U.S. public information committee, the Creel Committee, was formed to channel the patriotic sentiments of Americans in support of the U.S. role in the war. Stealing a page from Caesar, the committee's massive verbal and written communications effort was successful in marshaling national pride behind the war effort. According to a young member of the Creel Committee, Edward L. Bernays (later considered by many to be the "father of public relations"), *This was the first time in U.S. history that information was used as a weapon of war.*[4]

Even the Catholic Church had a hand in the creation of public relations. In the 1600s, under the leadership of Pope Gregory XV, the church established a College of Propaganda to "help propagate the faith." In those days, the term *propaganda* did not have a negative connotation; the church simply wanted to inform the public about the advantages of Catholicism. Today, the pope and other religious leaders maintain communications staffs to assist in relations with the public. Indeed, the chief communications official in the Vatican maintains the rank of Archbishop of the Church. It was largely his role to deal with perhaps the most horrific scandal ever to face the Catholic Church—the priest pedophile issue of 2002[5] (see PR Ethics Mini-Case).

Mini-Case   The Pope's Persuasive Public Relations Pilgrimage

In the spring of 2008, Pope Benedict XVI arrived in the United States, a little-known figure.

Indeed, if a pope could be considered *"shadowy,"* the former Joseph Ratzinger might well have qualified. As a former member of the Hitlerjugend—Hitler Youth—the new pope had some explaining to do.

Moreover, following one of history's most beloved pontiffs, Pope John Paul II—the charismatic, personable, athletic *"Pope on a Slope"*—Benedict, by comparison, seemed formal, reclusive, and aloof.

In addition, the Catholic Church had recently experienced its most damaging historic scandal involving pedophile priests, and Pope Benedict had been largely silent on the matter.

All-in-all, the new pope's trip to America was fraught with peril.

But in one whirlwind week, Pope Benedict proved himself a master of public relations strategy, winning the admiration of even the church's staunchest critics (see Figure 2-3).

Here's how he did it:

■ Even before he touched down in Washington, Pope Benedict summoned reporters on his plane to address and condemn the sex-abuse scandal.

By confronting the issue immediately and having it reported even before his plane arrived, Benedict had seized the agenda for the trip from anyone else, for example, Church critics and the media, who might have wished to use the visit for their own ends.

■ On the second day of his stay in D.C., Pope Benedict held an unscheduled meeting with sex-abuse victims from Boston.

Only a handful of bishops before him had ventured to meet with victims. Indeed, the general feeling among Church hierarchy was that it was "beneath" the station of the princes of the church to descend to the level of the victim.

Pope Benedict would have none of it.

His mantra, correctly, was that the underlying principle of effective public relations was *"Do the right thing."*

And in meeting with the victims and repudiating the baser instincts of his associates, Pope Benedict did exactly that.

■ When Pope Benedict flew off to New York, people wondered if this final leg of the trip might prove anticlimactic. Specifically, how could he ever top his stirring performance in Washington?

FIGURE 2-3 Out of the bullpen. Pope Benedict XVI arrives at Yankee Stadium for an historic mass, not to mention a public relations victory, in the spring of 2008. (Photo: Newscom)

The answer came in his first day in the Big Apple, when Pope Benedict XVI became the first pope to visit an American synagogue—right in time for Passover. He even got some gift matzo to munch on the flight back to Rome.

The net impact of the surprise synagogue stop, on top of the public relations coup registered the day before in Washington, convinced the headline writers that Pope Benedict was the real deal. To wit:

- *"Pope Benedict and the Lasting Impact of His U.S. Trip."*

- *"Benedict Hits All the Right Notes."*

- *"Mazel Tov Pope B."*

*For further information, see Fraser P. Seitel, "The Pope and the Polygamists," odwyerpr.com, April 28, 2008.

In between all this, of course, Pope Benedict addressed the United Nations, conducted a mass at Yankee Stadium, and toured the Big Apple.

The public relations impression left by the new pope as he left for home, matzo in hand, was one of complete victory.

Questions

1. What other public relations options did Pope Benedict have on his first American trip?

2. What was the downside of using the trip to highlight the Church's pedophile scandal?

Early American Experience

The American public relations experience dates back to the founding of the republic. Influencing public opinion, managing communications, and persuading individuals at the highest levels were at the core of the American Revolution. The colonists tried to persuade King George III that they should be accorded the same rights as Englishmen. *Taxation without representation is tyranny* became their public relations slogan to galvanize fellow countrymen.

When King George refused to accede to the colonists' demands, they combined the weaponry of sword and pen. Samuel Adams, for one, organized Committees of

Correspondence as a kind of revolutionary Associated Press to disseminate anti-British information throughout the colonies. He also staged events to build up revolutionary fervor, such as the Boston Tea Party, in which colonists, masquerading as Indians, boarded British ships in Boston Harbor and pitched chests of imported tea overboard—as impressive a media event as has ever been recorded sans television.

Thomas Paine, another early practitioner of public relations, wrote periodic pamphlets and essays that urged the colonists to band together. In one essay contained in his *Crisis* papers, Paine wrote poetically: *"These are the times that try men's souls. The summer soldier and the sunshine patriot will, in this crisis, shrink from the service of their country."* The people listened, were persuaded, and took action—testifying to the power of early American communicators.

Later American Experience

The creation of the most important document in America's history, the Constitution, also owed much to public relations. Federalists, who supported the Constitution, fought tooth and nail with anti-Federalists, who opposed it. Their battle was waged in newspaper articles, pamphlets, and other organs of persuasion in an attempt to influence public opinion. To advocate ratification of the Constitution, political leaders such as Alexander Hamilton, James Madison, and John Jay banded together, under the pseudonym Publius, to write letters to leading newspapers. Today those letters are bound in a document called *The Federalist Papers* and are still used in the interpretation of the Constitution.

After its ratification, the constitutional debate continued, particularly over the document's apparent failure to protect individual liberties against government encroachment. Hailed as the father of the Constitution, Madison framed the Bill of Rights in 1791, which ultimately became the first 10 amendments to the Constitution. Fittingly, the first of those amendments safeguarded, among other things, the practice of public relations:

> *Congress shall make no law respecting an establishment of religion, or prohibiting the free exercise thereof; or abridging the freedom of speech, or of the press, or the rights of the people peaceably to assemble, and to petition the government for a redress of grievances.*

In other words, people were given the right to speak up for what they believed in and the freedom to try to influence the opinions of others. Thus was the practice of public relations ratified.[6]

Into the 1800s

The practice of public relations continued to percolate in the 19th century. Among the more prominent, yet negative, antecedents of modern public relations that took hold in the 1800s was press agentry. Two of the better-known—some would say notorious—practitioners of this art were Amos Kendall and Phineas T. Barnum.

In 1829, President Andrew Jackson selected Kendall, a Kentucky writer and editor, to serve in his administration. Within weeks, Kendall became a member of Old Hickory's "kitchen cabinet" and eventually became one of Jackson's most influential assistants.

Kendall performed just about every White House public relations task. He wrote speeches, state papers, and messages, and turned out press releases. He even conducted basic opinion polls and is considered one of the earliest users of the "news leak." Although Kendall is generally credited with being the first authentic presidential press secretary, his functions and role went far beyond that position.

Among Kendall's most successful ventures in Jackson's behalf was the development of the administration's own newspaper, the *Globe*. Although it was not uncommon for the governing administration to publish its own national house organ, Kendall's deft editorial touch refined the process to increase its effectiveness. Kendall would pen a Jackson news release, distribute it for publication to a local newspaper, and then reprint the press clipping in the *Globe* to underscore Jackson's nationwide popularity. Indeed, that popularity continued unabated throughout Jackson's years in office, with much of the credit going to the president's public relations adviser.*

Most public relations professionals would rather not talk about P. T. Barnum as an industry pioneer. Barnum, some say, was a huckster whose motto might well have been *"The public be fooled."* Barnum's defenders suggest that although the impresario may have had his faults, he nonetheless was respected in his time as a user of written and verbal public relations techniques to further his museum and circus.

Like him or not, Barnum was a master publicist. In the 1800s, as owner of a major circus, Barnum generated article after article for his traveling show. He purposely gave his star performers short names—for instance, Tom Thumb, the midget, and Jenny Lind, the singer—so that they could easily fit into the headlines of narrow newspaper columns. Barnum also staged bizarre events, such as the legal marriage of the fat lady to the thin man, to drum up free newspaper exposure. And although today's practitioners scoff at Barnum's methods, in this day of Paris Hilton, Lindsay Lohan, Star Jones, Donald Trump, Al Sharpton, and on and on, there are still many press agents practicing the ringmaster's techniques. Indeed, when today's public relations professionals bemoan the specter of shysters and hucksters that still overhangs their field, they inevitably place the blame squarely on the fertile mind and silver tongue of P. T. Barnum.

Emergence of the Robber Barons

The American Industrial Revolution ushered in many things at the turn of the century, not the least of which was the growth of public relations. The 20th century began with small mills and shops, which served as the hub of the frontier economy, eventually giving way to massive factories. Country hamlets, which had been the centers of commerce and trade, were replaced by sprawling cities. Limited transportation and communications facilities became nationwide railroad lines and communications wires. Big business took over, and the businessman was king.

The men who ran America's industries seemed more concerned with making a profit than with improving the lot of their fellow citizens. Railroad owners led by William Vanderbilt, bankers led by J. P. Morgan, oil magnates led by John D. Rockefeller, and steel impresarios led by Henry Clay Frick ruled the fortunes of thousands of others. Typical of the reputation acquired by this group of industrialists was the famous—and

---

*Kendall was decidedly not cut from the same cloth as today's neat, trim, buttoned-down press secretaries. On the contrary, Jackson's man was described as "a puny, sickly looking man with a weak voice, a wheezing cough, narrow and stooping shoulders, a sallow complexion, silvery hair in his prime, slovenly dress, and a seedy appearance." (Fred F. Endres, "Public Relations in the Jackson White House," *Public Relations Review* 2, no. 3 [Fall 1976]: 5–12.)

perhaps apocryphal—response of Vanderbilt when questioned about the public's reaction to his closing of the New York Central Railroad: *"The public be damned!"*

Little wonder that Americans cursed Vanderbilt and his ilk as "robber barons" who cared little for the rest of society. Although most who depended on these industrialists for their livelihood felt powerless to rebel, the seeds of discontent were being sown liberally throughout society.

Enter the Muckrakers

When the axe fell on the robber barons, it came in the form of criticism from a feisty group of journalists dubbed *muckrakers*. The "muck" that these reporters and editors "raked" was dredged from the supposedly scandalous operations of America's business

Points P. T. Barnum Lives

Self-respecting public relations professionals despise the legacy of P. T. Barnum, who created publicity through questionable methods. They lament, as noted in Chapter 1, that public relations communication should always reflect "performance" and "truth."

Ah, were it so.

Alas, Barnum's bogus methods are just as effective with 21st-century media as they were with 19th-century media.

Doubt it?

Then consider two 21st-century public relations creations, the Reverend Al Sharpton and the real estate mogul/TV reality show star Donald Trump (Figure 2-4).

Sharpton, a minor aide in the days of Martin Luther King, first gained notoriety in the 1980s by vigorously defending a Newburgh, New York, woman who claimed she had been abducted and raped in a racially motivated crime. The woman's story turned out to be a lie, and Sharpton lost a lawsuit for his role in the ruse.

No matter. Despite a series of ethical lapses, the loquacious Reverend Al was "good copy." And when the Reverend called, the media listened. By 2004, Al Sharpton was a bona fide candidate for the Democratic presidential nomination.

Similarly, Trump, son of a wealthy New York real estate landlord, was a master wheeler-dealer, more heralded for his bravado and arrogance than for his acumen. Indeed, in the 1980s, Trump, despite outrageous claims to the contrary, narrowly escaped real estate bankruptcy and was forced to trade part of his empire to restructure debts. In 2004 and again in 2009, Trump's Atlantic City casino went bankrupt, despite The Donald's continuous claims that "*things are going great.*" And then in 2005, *The New York Times* had the audacity to question Trump's claims that he was "a billionaire."* (The Donald later sued the author.)

No matter. Trump continued to thrive with his television show, *The Apprentice,* and endorsement deals for a variety of products from Trump Perfume to Trump University. The

FIGURE 2-4 P. T. Barnum's legacy. The Reverend Al and The Donald, latter-day publicity hounds. (Photo: Newscom)

media, meanwhile, continued to quote his every word. Some even called him "*the P. T. Barnum of Finance.*"

Amen.

* Timothy L. O'Brien, "What's He Really Worth?" *New York Times* (October 23, 2005): Section 3, 1.

enterprises. Upton Sinclair's novel *The Jungle* attacked the deplorable conditions of the meatpacking industry. Ida Tarbell's *History of the Standard Oil Company* stripped away the public facade of the nation's leading petroleum firm. Her accusations against Standard Oil Chairman Rockefeller, many of which were unproven, nonetheless stirred up public attention.

Magazines such as *McClure's* struck out systematically at one industry after another. The captains of industry, used to getting their own way and having to answer to no one, were wrenched from their peaceful passivity and rolled out on the public carpet to answer for their sins. Journalistic shock stories soon led to a wave of sentiment for legislative reform.

As journalists and the public became more anxious, the government got more involved. Congress began passing laws telling business leaders what they could and couldn't do. Trust-busting became the order of the day. Conflicts between employers and employees began to break out, and newly organized labor unions came to the fore. The Socialist and Communist movements began to take off. Ironically, it was *"a period when free enterprise reached a peak in American history, and yet at that very climax, the tide of public opinion was swelling up against business freedom, primarily because of the breakdown in communications between the businessman and the public."*[7]

For a time, these men of inordinate wealth and power found themselves limited in their ability to defend themselves and their activities against the tidal wave of public condemnation. They simply did not know how to get through to the public. To tell their side of the story, the business barons first tried using the lure of advertising to silence journalistic critics; they tried to buy off critics by paying for ads in their papers. It didn't work. Next, they paid publicity people, or press agents, to present their companies' positions. Often these hired guns painted over the real problems of their client companies. The public saw through this approach.

Clearly, another method had to be discovered to get the public to at least consider the business point of view. Business leaders were discovering that a corporation might have capital, labor, and natural resources, yet be doomed to fail if it couldn't influence public opinion. The best way to influence public opinion, as it turned out, was through honesty and candor. This simple truth—the truth that lies at the heart of modern-day, effective public relations practice—was the key to the accomplishments of American history's first great public relations counselor.

Ivy Lee: The Real Father of Modern Public Relations

Ivy Ledbetter Lee was a former Wall Street reporter, the son of a Methodist minister, who plunged into publicity work in 1903 (Figure 2-5). Lee believed neither in Barnum's public-be-fooled approach nor Vanderbilt's public-be-damned philosophy. For Lee, the key to business acceptance and understanding was that the public be informed.

Lee disdained the press agents of the time, who used any influence or trick to get a story on their clients printed, regardless of the truth or merits. By contrast, Lee firmly believed that the only way business could answer its critics convincingly was to present its side honestly, accurately, and forcefully. Instead of merely appeasing the public, Lee thought a company should strive to earn public confidence and goodwill.

In 1914, John D. Rockefeller Jr., son of one of the nation's most maligned and misunderstood men, hired Lee to assist with the fallout from the Ludlow massacre,

FIGURE 2-5 Father of public relations. Ivy Lee. (Courtesy of Seely G. Mudd Manuscript Library, Princeton University Library, Ivy Lee Papers, Public Policy Papers, Department of Rare Books and Special Collections)

which was affecting his Colorado Fuel and Iron Company. Lee's advice to Rockefeller was simple:

> *Tell the truth, because sooner or later the public will find it out anyway. And if the public doesn't like what you are doing, change your policies and bring them into line with what the people want.*[8]

Despite the tragedy of Ludlow, Lee encouraged Rockefeller to create a joint labor–management board to mediate all workers' grievances on wages, hours, and working conditions. It was a great success. The mine workers—and the public—began to see John D. Rockefeller Jr. in a different light. Most important, he began to see them in a new light as well. As Rockefeller's youngest son, David, recalled nearly a century later, *"My father was changed profoundly by his meetings with the workers. It was a lesson that stayed with him throughout the rest of his life and one of the most important things that ever happened to our family."*[9]

In working for the Rockefellers, Lee tried to "humanize" them, to feature them in real-life situations such as playing golf, attending church, and celebrating birthdays. Simply, Lee's goal was to present the Rockefellers in terms that every individual could understand and appreciate.

Ironically, even Ivy Lee could not escape the glare of public criticism. In the late 1920s, Lee was asked to serve as adviser to the parent company of the German Dye Trust, which, as it turned out, was an agent for the policies of Adolf Hitler. For his involvement with the Dye Trust, Lee was branded a traitor and dubbed "Poison Ivy" by members of Congress investigating un-American activities. Ironically, the smears against him in the press rivaled the most vicious ones against any of the robber barons.[10]

Ivy Lee's critics cite his unfortunate involvement with the Dye Trust and even his association as spokesman for John D. Rockefeller, Jr., as proof that his contributions weren't particularly profound. They argue that Lee "was not someone who was particularly effective at getting business to change its behavior."[11]

Ivy Lee's proponents, on the other hand (and your author is one of them), argue that Lee was among the first to counsel his clients that "positive public relations starts with action, with performance" and that positive publicity must follow positive performance.[12] This is why Ivy Lee is recognized as the individual who began to distinguish "publicity" and "press agentry" from "public relations" based on honesty and candor. For his seminal contributions to the field, Ivy Lee deserves recognition as the real father of public relations.

The Growth of Modern Public Relations

Ivy Lee helped to open the gates for modern public relations. After he helped establish the idea that high-powered companies and individuals have a responsibility to inform their publics, the practice began to grow in every sector of American society.

Government

During World War I, President Woodrow Wilson established the Creel Committee under the leadership of journalist George Creel. Creel's group, composed of the nation's leading journalists, scholars, and public relations leaders, mounted an impressive effort to mobilize public opinion in support of the war effort and to stimulate the sale of war bonds through Liberty Loan publicity drives. Not only did the war effort get a boost, but so did the field of public relations. The nation was mightily impressed with the potential power of publicity as a weapon to encourage national sentiment and support.

During World War II, the public relations field received an even bigger boost. The Office of War Information (OWI) was established to convey the message of the United States at home and abroad. Under the directorship of Elmer Davis, a veteran journalist, the OWI laid the foundations for the U.S. Information Agency as America's voice around the world.

World War II also saw a flurry of activity to sell war bonds, boost the morale of those at home, spur production in the nation's factories and offices, and, in general, support America's war effort as intensively as possible. By virtually every measure, this full-court public relations offensive was an unquestioned success.

The proliferation of public relations officers in World War II led to a growth in the number of practitioners during the peace that followed. One reason companies saw the need to have public relations professionals to "speak up" for them was the more combative attitude of President Harry Truman toward many of the country's largest institutions. For example, Truman's seizure of the steel mills touched off a massive public relations campaign, the likes of which had rarely been seen outside the government.

Later in the century, the communications problems of President Richard Nixon, surrounding the "cover-up" of the Watergate political scandal, brought new criticism of public relations. It didn't matter that Nixon was surrounded by alumni of the advertising industry, rather than public relations professionals. The damage to the field's reputation was done. But the subsequent administration of the "great communicator" Ronald Reagan reaffirmed the value of public relations. And later, the communications skills of President Bill Clinton—before a nasty scandal in the Oval Office submerged him in scandal—added to the importance of the practice in government. In the 21st century, the extraordinary communications ability of President Barack Obama reinforced the power of communication in the White House.

Counseling

The nation's first public relations firm, the Publicity Bureau, was founded in Boston in 1900 and specialized in general press agentry. The first Washington, D.C., agency was begun in 1902 by William Wolff Smith, a former correspondent for the *New York Sun* and the *Cincinnati Enquirer*. Two years later, Ivy Lee joined with a partner to begin his own counseling firm.

The most significant counselor this side of Ivy Lee was Edward L. Bernays, who began as a publicist in 1913 and was instrumental in the war bonds effort. He was the nephew of Sigmund Freud and author of the landmark book *Crystallizing Public Opinion* (see interview at the end of this chapter).

Bernays was a giant in the public relations field for nearly the entire century. In addition to contributing as much to the field as any other professional in its history, Bernays was a true public relations scholar. He taught the first course in public relations in 1923 and was also responsible for "recruiting" the field's first distinguished female practitioner, his wife Doris E. Fleischman.

Fleischman, former editor of the *New York Tribune*, was a skilled writer, and her husband was a skilled strategist and promoter. Together they built Edward L. Bernays, Counsel on Public Relations into a top agency. In many ways, Fleischman was the "mother" of public relations, paving the way for a field that is today dominated by talented women (Figure 2-6).

Bernays's seminal writings in the field underscored the importance of strategic communications advice for clients. For example, Bernays wrote:

> *At first we called our activity "publicity direction." We intended to give advice to clients on how to direct their actions to get public visibility for them. But within a*

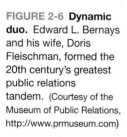

FIGURE 2-6 Dynamic duo. Edward L. Bernays and his wife, Doris Fleischman, formed the 20th century's greatest public relations tandem. (Courtesy of the Museum of Public Relations, http://www.prmuseum.com)

year we changed the service and its name to "counsel on public relations." We recognized that all actions of a client that impinged on the public needed counsel. Public visibility of a client for one action might be vitiated by another action not in the public interest.[13]

Due to his background, Bernays was fascinated by a wide range of psychological theories and practices beginning to emerge in society. One of his major contributions to the practice of public relations was transforming the practice from a purely journalistic-based approach to one underpinned by psychology, sociology, and social-psychology to reach individuals in terms of their unconscious desires, fears, and needs.[14]

After Bernays's pioneering counseling efforts, a number of public relations firms, most headquartered in New York, began to take root, most notably among them Hill & Knowlton, Carl Byoir & Associates, Newsom & Company, and Burson-Marsteller. One of the earliest African American counselors was D. Parke Gibson, who authored two books on African American consumerism and advised companies on multicultural relations.

For many years, Hill & Knowlton and Burson-Marsteller jockeyed for leadership in the counseling industry. One early counselor, Harold Burson (see From the Top in Chapter 1), emphasized marketing-oriented public relations *"to help clients sell their goods and services, maintain a favorable market for their stock, and foster harmonious relations with employees."* In 2000, Burson was named the most influential PR person of the 20th century.[15]

In the 1990s, the counseling business saw the emergence of international super-agencies, many of which were merged into advertising agencies. Indeed, both Hill & Knowlton and Burson-Marsteller were eventually merged under one corporation, WPP, which also included the J. Walter Thompson and Young & Rubicam advertising agencies. Another mega-communications firm, Omnicom Group, owned seven major public relations firms, including Fleishman-Hillard, Porter Novelli, and Ketchum. Despite these communications conglomerates, most public relations agencies still operate as independent entities. And local agencies, staffed by one or several practitioners, dominate the industry.

In the 21st century then, the public relations counseling business boasts a diverse mix of huge national agencies, medium-sized regional firms, and one-person local operations. Public relations agencies may be general in nature or specialists in everything from consumer products to entertainment to health care to technology.

Corporations

As the 20th century rolled on, the perceptual problems of corporations and their leaders diminished. Opinion polls after World War II ranked business as high in public esteem. People were back at work, and business was back in style.

Smart companies—General Electric, General Motors, and American Telephone & Telegraph (AT&T), for example—worked hard to preserve their good names through both words and actions. Arthur W. Page became AT&T's first public relations vice president in 1927. Page was a legendary public relations figure, helping to maintain AT&T's reputation as a prudent and proper corporate citizen. Page also was one of the few public relations executives to serve on prestigious corporate boards of directors, including Chase Manhattan Bank, Kennecott Copper, Prudential Insurance, and Westinghouse Electric.[16]

Page's five principles of successful corporate public relations are as relevant now as they were in the 1930s:

1. To make sure management thoughtfully analyzes its overall relation to the public
2. To create a system for informing all employees about the firm's general policies and practices
3. To create a system giving contact employees (those having direct dealings with the public) the knowledge needed to be reasonable and polite to the public
4. To create a system drawing employee and public questions and criticism back up through the organization to management
5. To ensure frankness in telling the public about the company's actions.[17]

Another early corporate public relations luminary was Paul Garrett. A former news reporter, he became the first director of public relations for mighty General Motors in 1931, working directly for GM's legendary CEO Alfred Sloan. Garrett once reportedly explained that the essence of his job was to convince the public that the powerful auto company deserved trust, that is, *to make a billion-dollar company seem small.* Ironically, as good as Garrett was, he nevertheless reflected the universal public relations complaint, still common today, of "never feeling like an insider" within his organization.[18]

One would think that companies today all recognize the importance of proper public relations in the conduct of their business. Most do. But, as the corporate scandals of the last years of the 20th century—from Enron to WorldCom to Tyco to Adelphia—and the equally embarrassing overpayment of CEOs at failing companies like Citigroup, Merrill Lynch, and Countrywide in the first decade of the 21st century indicate, CEOs don't know everything. Smart corporate leaders still need to seek out the counsel of trained public relations professionals in dealing with their key constituent publics.

Public Relations Comes of Age

As noted, public relations came of age largely as a result of the confluence of five general factors in our society:

1. The growth of large institutions
2. Heightened public awareness and media sophistication
3. Increasing incidence of societal change, conflict, and confrontation
4. Growing power of globalization
5. Dominance of the Internet and growth of social media.

Growth of Large Institutions

Ironically, the public relations profession received perhaps its most important thrust when business confidence suffered its most severe setback. The economic and social upheaval caused by the Great Depression of the 1930s provided the impetus for corporations to seek public support by telling their stories. Public relations departments sprang up in scores of major companies, among them Bendix, Borden, Eastman Kodak, Eli Lilly, Ford, General Motors, Standard Oil, and U.S. Steel. The role that public relations played in regaining post-Depression public trust in big business helped project the field into the relatively strong position it has enjoyed since World War II.

Today, businesses of every size recognize that aggressively communicating corporate products and positions can help win public receptivity and support and ward off government intrusion. The best companies in the 21st century are those that have learned, as Ivy Lee preached, that proper action results in the best public relations.

Heightened Public Awareness and Media Sophistication

In the 1970s and 1980s, companies were obligated to consider minority rights, consumer rights, environmental implications, and myriad other social issues. Business began to contribute to charities. Managers began to consider community relations a first-line responsibility. The general policy of corporations confronting their adversaries was abandoned. In its place, most large companies adopted a policy of conciliation and compromise.

This new policy of social responsibility continued into the 1990s. Corporations came to realize that their reputations are a valuable asset to be protected, conserved, defended, nurtured, and enhanced at all times. In truth, institutions in the 1990s had little choice but to get along with their publics. The general prosperity of the 1990s, fueled by enormous stock market gains, helped convey goodwill between organizations and their publics.

By 2008, most American homes had television. More than 50 percent of Americans subscribed to basic cable television and another 238 million—or 71 percent of the U.S. population—had access to the Internet.[19] Where once three television networks dominated, now a plethora of channels and cable networks, catering to every persuasion, enable media consumers to choose what they want to view. Meanwhile talk radio stations proliferate, and Internet use dominates.

As a result of all this communication, publics have become much more segmented, specialized, and sophisticated.

Societal Change, Conflict, and Confrontation

Disenchantment with big institutions peaked in the 1960s, coincident with an unpopular war.

The social and political upheavals of the 1960s dramatically affected many areas, including the practice of public relations. The Vietnam War fractured society. Movements were formed by various interest groups. An obscure consumer advocate named Ralph Nader began to look pointedly at the inadequacies of the automobile industry. Women, long denied equal rights in the workplace and elsewhere, began to mobilize into activist groups such as the National Organization for Women (NOW). Environmentalists, worried about threats to the land and water by business expansion, began to support groups such as the Sierra Club. Minorities, particularly African Americans and Hispanics, began to petition and protest for their rights. Homosexuals, AIDS activists, senior citizens, birth control advocates, and social activists of every kind began to challenge the legitimacy of large institutions. Not since the days of the robber barons had large institutions so desperately needed professional communications help.

By the 21st century, such movements had morphed into established, well-organized, and powerful interest groups. By the presidential election of 2008, public disapproval of the Iraq War, concerns about energy supplies and prices, climate change and global warming, and a host of other issues, as well as renewed disenchantment with those in charge of government and business, generated a new round of activism. Women rallied around the candidacy of Sen. Hillary Clinton. The enthusiasm, among young people, generated by Sen. Barack Obama and his call for "change and hope" was illustrative of the mood. Even old Ralph Nader announced his interest in running for president in 2008. When Sen. Obama was elected president and Sen. Clinton was named his Secretary of State in 2009, it was clear that traditional times in America had, indeed, *"changed."*

Globalization and Growth of Global Media, Public Opinion, and Capitalism

In the 21st century, democracy and capitalism, as someone once said, have "broken out everywhere." At the end of 2002, there were 121 democracies governing more than 60 percent of the world's population.[20]

In recent years, significant events to spur democracy—all conveyed in real time by pervasive global media—have been breathtaking.

- By the year 2000, the defeat and imprisonment of Slobodan Milosevic in the Balkans allowed the people of Yugoslavia to experience freedom.
- In 2002, the vanquishing in Afghanistan of the repressive Taliban regime, supported by the terrorist al-Qaeda network, allowed that country, too, to begin to experience democratic institutions.
- In 2005, after the defeat of Saddam Hussein signaled the potential for a democratic Iraq, an astounding 10 million citizens—70 percent of eligible voters— went to the polls to elect new leaders.
- Also in 2005, democratic forces in Lebanon rose up to drive out Syrian troops.
- In 2008, Kosovo declared its independence from Serbia in a stunning signal of freedom. Also, democratic revolutions in Georgia and Ukraine challenged Russian dominance.

While the world remains a troubled place, the growth of democracy remains an inexorable force that can't be denied. Even in nations that aren't democracies, like China, the spirit of capitalism, of individuals free to earn a living based on their own industriousness and entrepreneurship, pervades. Moreover, with the world near-completely "wired," the power of communications and public relations to bring down tyrants and build up democracy is profound (Figure 2-7).

Dominance of the Internet and Growth of Social Media

In the 21st century, true two-way communication has arrived largely as a result of the growth of online access. Cable, satellite, mobile phones, instant messaging, pagers, bar code scanners, voice mail systems, videodisk technologies, and a multitude of other developments revolutionized the information transmission and receiving process. The emergence of the Internet and the World Wide Web radically intensified the spread of communications even further. More recently, the advent of Web 2.0—where users are the generators of information—has taken the Internet to the next level.[21]

The Internet began during the cold war in 1969 as a U.S. Department of Defense system (and not, as Nobel Prize winner but failed U.S. presidential candidate Al Gore may have intimated was his invention!). In 2000, 22 percent of Americans had bought

FIGURE 2-7 **Televised war.** In 2003, as U.S. soldiers in Baghdad draped a statue of Saddam Hussein with Old Glory, the world watched in real time. (Photo: Newscom)

a product online. The rate grew to 49 percent in 2007. Revenues from Internet purchases grew from $7.4 billion in the third quarter of 2000 to $34.7 billion in the third quarter of 2007.[22]

The impact of the Internet on public relations practice has been phenomenal. Email dominates internal communications. Journalists, like many other Americans, regard the Internet as their primary choice of most organizational communications. In the 21st century, knowledge of and facility with the Internet—from MySpace to FaceBook, from Flickr to Twitter to Pownce to omnipresent text messaging—has become a front-burner necessity for public relations practitioners.

Public Relations Education

As the practice of public relations has developed, so too has the growth of public relations education. In 1951, 12 schools offered major programs in public relations. Today, well in excess of 200 journalism or communication programs offer concentrated study in public relations, with nearly 300 others offering at least one course dealing with the profession.

The last major study of public relations education was done in 1999 by the Commission on Public Relations Education, chartered by the Public Relations Society of America. This commission recommended a public relations curriculum imparting knowledge in such nontraditional but pivotal areas as relationship building, societal trends, and multicultural and global issues.[23]

While public relations education isn't incorporated into most business schools, it should be. As noted, the practice has become an integral part in the daily workings and ongoing relationships of most organizations—from companies to churches, from governments to schools. Therefore, business students should be exposed to the discipline's underpinnings and practical aspects before they enter the corporate world.

Likewise, in journalism, with more than 70 percent of daily newspaper copy emanating from public relations–generated releases, journalists, too, should know what public relations is all about before they graduate. As the debate continues about where public relations education should appropriately be housed—either in business or journalism schools—the best answer is that both should offer public relations courses. Increasingly, journalists and businesspeople must understand what exactly those public relations people with whom they constantly interact are up to.

Wherever the function is located on the university level, it is clear that the field's enhanced educational dimension has contributed to the respect and acceptance accorded public relations in modern society.

Last Word

From humble beginnings less than 100 years ago, the practice of public relations today is big business around the world.

- The U.S. Bureau of Labor Statistics reports that close to 250,000 individuals practice public relations across the country.[24]
- The Public Relations Society of America, organized in 1947, boasts a growing membership of 22,000 in 100 chapters nationwide.
- The Public Relations Student Society of America, formed in 1968 to facilitate communications between students interested in the field and public relations professionals, has more than 8,000 student members at close to 300 college chapters.
- The International Association of Business Communicators boasts 14,000 members in more than 70 countries.
- More than 5,000 U.S. companies, 2,100 trade associations, 189 foreign embassies, and 350 federal government departments, bureaus, agencies, and commissions have public relations departments.[25]
- More than 3,000 public relations agencies exist in the United States, with more than 700 public relations firms residing in 80 foreign countries.[26]
- Top communications executives at major companies and agencies draw six-figure salaries.

The scope of modern public relations practice is vast. Media relations, government relations, Web relations, employee communications, public relations counseling and research, local community relations, audiovisual communications, contributions, interactive public relations, and numerous other diverse activities fall under the public relations umbrella. This may be one reason public relations is variously labeled *external affairs, corporate communications, public affairs, corporate relations,* and a variety of other confusing euphemisms.

Just as the name of the field generates confusion, so too does its purpose. Specifically, public relations professionals lament that the practice is still often accused of being a haven for snake oil salesmen peddling cosmetics, subterfuge, and spin. When *The New York Times* lamented disgraced and deceased Enron CEO Ken Lay, it blamed him most for practicing what it termed "public relations." To wit:

> *Mr. Lay's belief in the power of public relations is the reason he gave a news conference the day after he was indicted. And it's the reason he made that speech in Houston this week. He seems to believe that if he says something often enough and loudly enough, it will become true.*[27]

What the *Times* and many others still fail to understand is that proper public relations—the kind that builds credibility—must begin and end with one important commodity: *truth.*

Indeed, there is no more important characteristic for public relations people to emulate than the candor that comes from high ethical character. The field's finest ethical moment, in fact, occurred when the Johnson & Johnson Company, in the wake of unspeakable tragedy brought about by its lead product Tylenol, didn't hesitate to choose the ethical course. As the case study at the conclusion of this chapter suggests, the handling of the Tylenol tragedy was public relations' most shining hour.

Despite the stereotypes that still overhang the field, the fact remains that with hundreds of thousands of men and women in its practice in the United States and thousands more overseas, public relations has become solidly entrenched as an important, influential, and professional component of 21st-century society.

Discussion Starters

1. What societal factors have influenced the spread of public relations?
2. Why do public relations professionals think of P. T. Barnum as a mixed blessing?
3. What is the significance to the practice of public relations of American revolutionary hero Samuel Adams?
4. What did the robber barons and muckrakers have to do with the development of public relations?
5. Why are Ivy Lee and Edward Bernays considered two of the fathers of public relations?

6. What impact did the Creel Committee and the Office of War Information have on the development of public relations?
7. What was the significance of Arthur Page to the development of corporate public relations?
8. What did the legacy of Watergate mean to the practice of public relations?
9. What are some of the yardsticks that indicated that public relations had "arrived" in the latter part of the 20th century?
10. What are some of the issues that confront public relations in the 21st century?

Top of the Shelf E Pluribus Unum: The Making of Burson-Marsteller /
Harold Burson, New York: Burson-Marsteller, 2004.

This 166-page memoir traces Harold Burson's beginnings as a newspaperman in Memphis and chronicles his 35 years at the formation and helm of his legendary public relations firm.

The title *"e pluribus unum,"* derived from the Latin phrase "out of many, one," conveys the author's belief that the success of Burson-Marsteller, with some 2,000 employees and 50 offices in more than 30 countries, was the result of the

efforts of hundreds of individuals, men and women of many nationalities and talents.

Harold Burson's modesty, knowledge, grace, and profound understanding of what should distinguish the practice of public relations from other fields of endeavor is reason enough to secure this book.

Case Study The Tylenol Murders

Arguably, the two most important cases in the history of the practice of public relations occurred within four years of each other to the same product and company.

For close to 100 years, Johnson & Johnson Company of New Brunswick, New Jersey, was the epitome of a well-managed, highly profitable, and tight-lipped consumer products manufacturer.

Round I

That image changed on the morning of September 30, 1982, when Johnson & Johnson faced as devastating a public relations problem as had confronted any company in history.

That morning, Johnson & Johnson's management learned that its premier product, extra-strength Tylenol, had been used as a murder weapon to kill three people. In the days that followed, another three people died from swallowing Tylenol capsules loaded with cyanide. Although all the cyanide deaths occurred in Chicago, reports from other parts of the country also implicated extra-strength Tylenol capsules in illnesses of various sorts. These latter reports were later proved to be unfounded, but Johnson & Johnson and its Tylenol-producing subsidiary, McNeil Consumer Products Company, found themselves at the center of a public relations trauma the likes of which few companies had ever experienced.

Tylenol had been an astoundingly profitable product for Johnson & Johnson. At the time of the Tylenol murders, the product held 35% of the $1 billion analgesic market. Throughout the years, Johnson & Johnson had not been—and hadn't needed to be—a particularly high-profile company. Its chairman, James E. Burke, who had been with the company for almost 30 years, had never appeared on television and had rarely participated in print interviews.

Caught by Surprise

Johnson & Johnson's management was caught totally by surprise when the news hit. The company recognized that it needed the media to get out as much information to the public as quickly as possible to prevent a panic. Therefore, almost immediately, Johnson & Johnson made a key decision: to open its doors to the media.

On the second day of the crisis, Johnson & Johnson discovered that an earlier statement that no cyanide was used on its premises was wrong. The company didn't hesitate. Its public relations department quickly announced that the earlier information had been false. Even though the reversal embarrassed the company briefly, Johnson & Johnson's openness was hailed and made up for any damage to its credibility.

Early on in the crisis, the company was largely convinced that the poisonings had not occurred at any of its plants. Nonetheless, Johnson & Johnson recalled an entire lot of 93,000 bottles of extra-strength Tylenol associated with the reported Chicago murders. In the process, it telegrammed warnings to doctors, hospitals, and distributors and suspended all Tylenol advertising.

But what about all those millions of dollars worth of Tylenol capsules on the nation's shelves?

The company was convinced such a massive recall wasn't warranted by the facts. It was convinced that the tampering had taken place during the product's Chicago distribution and not in the manufacturing process. Further, the FBI was worried that a precipitous recall would encourage copycat poisoning attempts. Nonetheless, five days later, when a copycat strychnine poisoning occurred in California, Johnson & Johnson did recall all extra-strength Tylenol capsules—31 million bottles—at a cost of more than $100 million.

Although the company believed it had done nothing wrong, Johnson & Johnson acted to assuage public concerns. It also posted a $100,000 reward for the killer or killers. Through advertisements promising to exchange capsules for tablets, through thousands of letters to the trade, and through statements to the media, the company hoped to put the incident into proper perspective.

Loyal Users but. . . . .

At the same time, Johnson & Johnson commissioned a nationwide opinion survey to assess the consumer implications of the Tylenol poisonings. The good news was that 87 percent of Tylenol users surveyed said they realized that the maker of Tylenol was "not responsible" for the deaths. The bad news was that 61 percent still said they were "not likely to buy" extra-strength Tylenol capsules in the future. In other words, even though most consumers knew the deaths weren't Tylenol's fault, they still feared using the product.

But Chairman Burke and Johnson & Johnson weren't about to knuckle under to the deranged saboteur or saboteurs who had poisoned their product. Despite predictions of the imminent demise of extra-strength Tylenol, Johnson & Johnson decided to relaunch the product in a new triple-safety-sealed, tamper-resistant package (Figure 2-8). Many on Wall Street and in the marketing community were stunned by Johnson & Johnson's bold decision.

So confident was Johnson & Johnson's management that it launched an all-out media blitz to make sure that people understood its commitment. Chairman Burke appeared on television shows and in newspaper interviews.

Welcoming *60 Minutes*

The company even invited the investigative news program *60 Minutes*—the scourge of corporate America—to film its executive strategy sessions to prepare for the new launch. When the program was aired, reporter Mike Wallace concluded that although Wall Street had been ready at first to write off the company, it was now *"hedging its bets because of Johnson & Johnson's stunning campaign of facts, money, the media, and truth."*

Finally, on November 11, 1982, less than two months after the murders, Johnson & Johnson's management held an elaborate video news conference in New York City, beamed to additional locations around the country, to introduce the new extra-strength Tylenol package.

In the months that followed Burke's news conference, it became clear that Tylenol would not become a scapegoat. In fact, by the beginning of 1983, despite its critics, Tylenol had recaptured an astounding 95 percent of its prior market share. Morale at the company, according to its chairman, was "higher than in years." It had acted true to the "Credo," which spelled

FIGURE 2-8 New packaging. The triple-safety-sealed, tamper-resistant package for Tylenol capsules had (1) glued flaps on the outer box, (2) a tight plastic neck seal, and (3) a strong inner foil seal over the mouth of the bottle. A bright yellow label on the bottle was imprinted with a red warning: "Do not use if safety seals are broken." As it turned out, all these precautions didn't work. (Courtesy of Johnson & Johnson)

out the company's beliefs (Figure 2-9). The euphoria lasted until February 1986 when, unbelievably, tragedy struck again.

Round II

Late in the evening of February 10, 1986, news reports began to circulate that a woman had died in Yonkers, New York, after taking poisoned capsules of extra-strength Tylenol.

Unbelievably, the nightmare for Johnson & Johnson was about to begin again.

And once again, the company sprang into action. Chairman Burke addressed reporters at a news conference a day after the incident. A phone survey found that the public didn't blame the company. However, with the discovery of other poisoned Tylenol capsules two days later, the nightmare intensified. The company recorded 15,000 toll-free calls at its Tylenol hot line. Once again, production of Tylenol capsules was halted. "I'm heartsick," Burke told the press. "We didn't believe it could happen again, and nobody else did either."

FIGURE 2-9 **The Johnson & Johnson credo.** (Courtesy of Johnson & Johnson)

OUR CREDO

We believe our first responsibility is to the doctors, nurses and patients,
to mothers and fathers and all others who use our products and services.
In meeting their needs everything we do must be of high quality.
We must constantly strive to reduce our costs
in order to maintain reasonable prices.
Customers' orders must be serviced promptly and accurately.
Our suppliers and distributors must have an opportunity
to make a fair profit.

We are responsible to our employees,
the men and women who work with us throughout the world.
Everyone must be considered as an individual.
We must respect their dignity and recognize their merit.
They must have a sense of security in their jobs.
Compensation must be fair and adequate,
and working conditions clean, orderly and safe.
We must be mindful of ways to help our employees fulfill
their family responsibilities.
Employees must feel free to make suggestions and complaints.
There must be equal opportunity for employment, development
and advancement for those qualified.
We must provide competent management,
and their actions must be just and ethical.

We are responsible to the communities in which we live and work
and to the world community as well.
We must be good citizens — support good works and charities
and bear our fair share of taxes.
We must encourage civic improvements and better health and education.
We must maintain in good order
the property we are privileged to use,
protecting the environment and natural resources.

Our final responsibility is to our stockholders.
Business must make a sound profit.
We must experiment with new ideas.
Research must be carried on, innovative programs developed
and mistakes paid for.
New equipment must be purchased, new facilities provided
and new products launched.
Reserves must be created to provide for adverse times.
When we operate according to these principles,
the stockholders should realize a fair return.

Johnson & Johnson

This time, the firm decided once and for all to cease production of its over-the-counter medications in capsule form. It offered to replace all unused Tylenol capsules with new Tylenol caplets, a solid form of medication that was less tamper-prone (Figure 2-10). The withdrawal of its capsules cost Johnson & Johnson more than $150 million after taxes.

Once again, in the face of tragedy, the company and its CEO received high marks. As President Reagan said at a White House reception two weeks after the crisis hit, *"Jim Burke of Johnson & Johnson, you have our deepest appreciation for living up to the highest ideals of corporate responsibility and grace under pressure."*

Today, nearly 30 years after the first customers were murdered after ingesting Tylenol capsules, in virtually every independent study of corporate reputation, the firm that is more highly regarded than any other is Johnson & Johnson.

FIGURE 2-10 A special message. (Courtesy of Johnson & Johnson)

A special message from the makers of TYLENOL products.

If you have TYLENOL capsules, we'll replace them with TYLENOL caplets.

And we'll do it at our expense.

As you know, there has been a tragic event. A small number of Extra-Strength TYLENOL Capsules in one isolated area in New York have been criminally tampered with.

This was an outrageous act which damages all of us.

Both federal and local authorities have established that it was only capsules that were tampered with.

In order to prevent any further capsule tampering, we have removed all our capsules from your retailers' shelves. This includes Regular and Extra-Strength TYLENOL capsules, CO-TYLENOL capsules, Maximum-Strength TYLENOL Sinus Medication capsules, Extra-Strength SINE-AID capsules, and DIMENSYN Menstrual Relief capsules.

And Johnson & Johnson's McNeil Consumer Products Company has decided to cease the manufacture, sale, and distribution of <u>all</u> capsule forms of over-the-counter medicines.

If you're a regular capsule user, you may be wondering what to use instead. That's why we'd like you to try TYLENOL caplets.

The caplet is a solid form of TYLENOL pain reliever, which research has proven is the form most preferred by consumers. Unlike tablets, it is specially shaped and coated for easy, comfortable swallowing.

And the caplet delivers a full extra-strength dose quickly and effectively.

So, if you have any TYLENOL Capsules in your home, do one of the following:

1. Return the bottles with the unused portion to us, together with your name and address on the form below. And we'll replace your TYLENOL capsules with TYLENOL Caplets (or tablets, if you prefer). We'll also refund your postage. Or...

2. If you prefer, you can receive a cash refund for the unused capsules by sending the bottle to us along with a letter requesting the refund.

We are taking this step because, for the past 25 years, over 100 million Americans have made TYLENOL products a trusted part of their health care.

We're continuing to do everything we can to keep your trust.

Send to:
TYLENOL Capsule Exchange
P.O. Box 2000
Maple Plain, MN 55348

Please send my coupon for free replacement caplets or tablets to:

Please print

Name _____
Address _____
City _____
State _____ Zip _____
Offer expires May 1, 1986

(Courtesy of Johnson & Johnson)

Questions

1. What might have been the consequences if Johnson & Johnson had decided to "tough out" the first reports of Tylenol-related deaths and not recall the product?

2. What other public relations options did Johnson & Johnson have in responding to the first round of Tylenol murders?

3. Do you think the company made a wise decision by reintroducing extra-strength Tylenol?

4. In light of the response of other companies not to move precipitously when faced with a crisis, do you think Johnson & Johnson should have acted so quickly to remove the Tylenol product when the second round of Tylenol murders occurred in 1986?

5. What specific lessons can be derived from the way in which Johnson & Johnson handled the public relations aspects of these tragedies?

6. What was the media environment when the Tylenol crises occurred? How might the results have differed if the crises occurred today?

7. See what information Johnson & Johnson offers for its customers on the Tylenol Web site (www.tylenol.com). Follow the links to the Care Cards, House Calls, and FAQ sections. How do these sections demonstrate Johnson & Johnson's concern for customers? How do you think Johnson & Johnson would use this Web site to communicate with the public if new health scares surfaced?

For further information on the first round of Tylenol murders, see Jerry Knight, "Tylenol's Maker Shows How to Respond to Crisis," *Washington Post* (October 11, 1982): 1; Thomas Moore, "The Fight to Save Tylenol," *Fortune* (November 29, 1982): 48; Michael Waldholz, "Tylenol Regains Most of No. 1 Market Share, Amazing Doomsayers," *The Wall Street Journal* (December 24, 1982): 1, 19; and *60 Minutes,* CBS-TV (December 19, 1982).

For further information on the second round of Tylenol murders, see Irvin Molotsky, "Tylenol Maker Hopeful on Solving Poisoning Case," *New York Times* (February 20, 1986); Steven Prokesch, "A Leader in a Crisis," *New York Times* (February 19, 1986): B4; Michael Waldholz, "For Tylenol's Manufacturer, the Dilemma Is to Be Aggressive—But Not Appear Pushy," *The Wall Street Journal* (February 20, 1986): 27; and "Tylenol II: How a Company Responds to a Calamity," *U.S. News & World Report* (February 24, 1986): 49.

For an overall view of Johnson & Johnson and Tylenol, see Lawrence G. Foster, *Robert Wood Johnson: The Gentleman Rebel.* State College, PA: Lillian Press, 1999.

From the Top   An Interview with Edward L. Bernays

Edward L. Bernays, who died in 1995 at the age of 103, was a public relations patriarch. A nephew of Sigmund Freud, Bernays pioneered the application of the social sciences to public relations. In partnership with his late wife, he advised presidents of the United States, industrial leaders, and legendary figures from Enrico Caruso to Eleanor Roosevelt. This interview was conducted with the legendary counselor in his 98th year.

When you taught the first public relations class, did you ever envision the field growing to its present stature?
I gave the first course in public relations after *Crystallizing Public Opinion* was published in 1923. I decided that one way to give the term "counsel on public relations" status was to lecture at a university on the principles, practices, and ethics of the new vocation. New York University was willing to accept my offer to do so. But I never envisioned at that time that the vocation would spread throughout the United States and then throughout the free world.

What were the objectives of that first public relations course?
The objectives were to give status to the new vocation. Many people still believed the term "counsel on public relations" was a euphemism for publicity man, press agent, flack. Even H. L. Mencken, in his book on the American language, ranked it as such. But in his *Supplement to the American Language*, published some years later, he changed his viewpoint and used my definition of the term.

What are the most significant factors that have led to the rise in public relations practice?
The most significant factor is the rise in people power and its recognition by leaders. Theodore Roosevelt helped bring this about with his Square Deal. Woodrow Wilson helped with his

New Freedom, and so did Franklin Delano Roosevelt with his New Deal. And this tradition was continued as time went on.

Do you have any gripes with the way public relations is practiced today?
I certainly do. The meanings of words in the United States have the stability of soap bubbles. Unless words are defined as to their meaning by law, as in the case of professions—for instance, law, medicine, architecture—they are in the public domain. Anyone can use them. Today, any plumber or car salesman or unethical character can call himself or herself a public relations practitioner. Many who call themselves public relations practitioners have no education, training, or knowledge of what the field is. And the public equally has little understanding of the meaning of the two words. Until licensing and registration are introduced, this will continue to be the situation.

What pleases you most about current public relations practice?
What pleases me most is that there are, indeed, practitioners who regard their activity as a profession, an art applied to a science, in which the public interest, and not pecuniary motivation, is the primary consideration; and also that outstanding leaders in society are grasping the meaning and significance of the activity.

How would you compare the caliber of today's public relations practitioner with that of the practitioner of the past?
The practitioner today has more education in his subject. But, unfortunately, education for public relations varies with the institution where it is being conducted. This is due to the lack of a standard definition. Public relations activity is applied social science to the social attitudes or actions of employers or clients.

Where do you think public relations will be 20 years from now?
It is difficult to appraise where public relations will be 20 years from now. I don't like the tendency of advertising agencies gobbling up large public relations organizations. That is like surgical instrument manufacturers gobbling up surgical medical colleges or law book publishers gobbling up law colleges. However, if licensing and registration take place, then the vocation is assured a long lifetime, as long as democracy's.

Public Relations Library

Bernays, Edward L. *Crystallizing Public Opinion.* New York: Liveright, 1961. The original 1923 version was the first significant book in the field. It deserves to be read for its historical value as well as for the amazingly progressive ideas that its author forwarded about the modern practice for which he was so responsible.

Bernays, Edward L. *Public Relations.* Norman: University of Oklahoma Press, 1963. This book offers an informative history of public relations, from Ancient Sumeria through the 1940s, and includes Bernays's view of what public relations ought to stand for.

Bernays, Edward L. *The Later Years: Public Relations Insights, 1956–1986.* Rhinebeck, NY: H & M, 1987. Essentially, this is a series of columns that Edward Bernays authored for the late *Public Relations Quarterly.*

Boorstin, Daniel J. *The Image: A Guide to Pseudo Events in America.* New York: Harper & Row, 1964. A not-very-flattering account of America's emphasis on image over reality, written 40 years ago by one of the nation's most eminent 20th-century thinkers.

Burson, Harold. "A Decent Respect to the Opinion of Mankind." Speech delivered at the Raymond Simon Institute for Public Relations (Burson-Marsteller, 866 Third Avenue, New York, NY 10022), March 5, 1987. This speech highlights public relations activities that have influenced the United States from colonial times to the present day.

Chomsky, Noam. *Necessary Illusions: Thought Control in Democratic Societies.* Boston: South End Press, 1989. A contrary view to Bernays's concept of public relations, this book, written by a well-known social critic, expresses all "that is wrong" about the media and attempts to persuade the public.

Cutlip, Scott M. *Public Relations History from the 17th to the 20th Century.* Hillsdale, NJ: Lawrence Erlbaum Associates, 1995.

Cutlip, Scott M. *The Unseen Power—Public Relations, A History.* Hillsdale, NJ: Lawrence Erlbaum Associates, 1994. This 800-page book is perhaps the definitive history of public relations in the 20th century. And it's not always "positive," either.

Marchand, Roland. *Creating the Corporate Soul: The Rise of Public Relations and Corporate Imagery in American Big Business.* Berkeley and Los Angeles: University of California Press, 2001.

Mitroff, Ian I., and Warren Bennis. *The Unreality Industry: The Deliberate Manufacturing of Falsehood and What It Is Doing to Our Lives.* London, England: Oxford University Press, 1993.

Nevins, Allan. "The Constitution Makers and the Public, 1785–1790." An address before the Conference of the Public Relations Society of America, November 13, 1962. Reprinted as "At the Beginning . . . A Series of Lecture-Essays." Gainesville, FL: The Institute for Public Relations Research and Education, 1997.

Olasky, Marvin N. "Roots of Modern Public Relations: The Bernays Doctrine." *Public Relations Quarterly,* Winter 1984. Olasky wages a spirited defense of Bernays as a more pragmatic and effective public relations representative than Ivy Lee.

Slater, Robert. *No Such Thing as Over-Exposure: Inside the Life and Celebrity of Donald Trump.* Upper Saddle River, NJ: Prentice-Hall, Inc., 2005. If you've ever wondered about the term, "*a legend in his own mind,*" read this book and find out what it means.

Tedlow, Richard S. *Keeping the Corporate Image: Public Relations and Business, 1900–1950.* Greenwich, CT: JAI Press, 1979. An analytical and comprehensive history of corporate public relations in the first half of the 20th century.

Tye, Larry. *The Father of Spin: Edward L. Bernays and the Birth of Public Relations.* The author's background as a *Boston Globe* journalist, not a public relations practitioner or professor, both limits the depth of this biography and offers the refreshing viewpoint of an "outsider."

Chapter **3**

Communication

FIGURE 3-1 Father of the communications satellite. Sir Arthur C. Clarke, science fiction novelist, in 1945 invented the concept that today beams images around the world in real time. (Photo by Rohan De Silva, Courtesy Arthur C. Clarke Foundation)

Social media so dominates communications practice today that the most venerable of communication staples, the Encyclopedia Britannica, has been uprooted by an upstart online reference source called Wikipedia.

In today's online world, Wikipedia is the first source that most people—683 million visitors annually—consult. Its name is a blend of the words "wiki," a technology for creating collaborative Web sites, and "encyclopedia." Launched in 2001 by Jimmy Wales and Larry Sanger, it is the largest, fastest-growing, and most popular general reference work on the Internet.[1]

And sometimes, that's not such a good thing.

In the spring of 2007, Wikipedia's founders were shocked when one of the service's most influential contributors and administrators, a chap who billed himself as "Essjay," was found not to be the tenured professor in Catholic Law he had claimed but rather a 24-year-old community college dropout. That revelation—along with the knowledge that every day, scores of anonymous, self-styled "correctors" of questionable knowledge are anonymously editing Wikipedia copy—made people wonder about the accuracy of all those millions of articles in 250 languages on Wikipedia.[2]

Such were the problems with communication in the age of social media.

In the 21st century, the whole world is truly "wired." The power of communication, through the oral and written word and the images that flash around the world to millions of people in real time, is more awesome than any individual or group or even nation.

What happens at a market in Baghdad is witnessed in a manner of seconds in Berlin and Bangkok and Boise. The world has truly become a "global village."

And perhaps no individual is more responsible for this global phenomenon than a British science fiction novelist, who died in 2008 (Figure 3-1). Sir Arthur Clarke wrote a short article in 1945 that talked about combining the technologies of rocketry, wireless communications, and radar to envision an extraterrestrial system that relied on orbiting space stations to relay radio signals around the world.

Today, more than a half century later, Sir Arthur's vision has morphed into the global system of two dozen geo-synchronous satellites that orbit 22,300 miles above the earth, transmitting words and images around the world at the speed of light.[3] Thanks to the "Clarke Orbit" and the uplink technology that continues to be developed, events from coronations to courtroom trials to courageous efforts in the face of overwhelming tragedy are now broadcast globally at 186,000 miles per second (Figure 3-2).

FIGURE 3-2 **Real-time tragedy.** When the worst earthquake in 58 years jolted China in the spring of 2008, people around the world—including the survivors themselves—were watching as it happened. (Photo: Newscom)

As a consequence, *communication* has never been a more potent tool, and *communications* must be handled with great care.

Which brings us back to public relations.

First and foremost, the public relations practitioner is a professional communicator. More than anyone else in an organization, the practitioner must know how to communicate.

Fundamentally, communication is a process of exchanging information, imparting ideas, and making oneself understood by others. It also includes understanding others in return. Indeed, *understanding* is critical to the communications process. If one person sends a message to another, who disregards or misunderstands it, then communication hasn't taken place. But if the idea received is the one intended, then communication has occurred. Thus, a boss who sends subordinates dozens of emails isn't necessarily communicating with them. If the idea received is not the one intended, then the sender has done little more than convert personal thoughts to words—and there they lie.

Although all of us are endowed with some capacity for communicating, the public relations practitioner must be better at it than most. Before public relations practitioners can earn the respect of management and become trusted advisers, they must demonstrate a mastery of many communications skills—writing, speaking, listening, promoting, and counseling. Just as the comptroller is expected to be an adept accountant, and the legal counsel is expected to be an accomplished lawyer, the public relations professional must be the best communicator in the organization. Period.

Goals of Communication

When communication is planned, as it should be in public relations, every communication must have a goal, an objective, and a purpose. If not, why communicate in the first place?

What are typical communications goals?

1. **To inform.** Often the communications goal of an organization is to inform or educate a particular public. For example, before holidays, the Automobile Association of America (AAA) will release information providing advice on safe driving habits for long trips. In so doing, AAA is performing a valuable information service to the public.

2. **To persuade.** A regular goal of public relations communicators is to persuade people to take certain actions. Such persuasion needn't be overly aggressive; it can be subtle. For example, a mutual fund annual report that talks about the fund's long history of financial strength and security may provide a subtle persuasive appeal for potential investors.

3. **To motivate.** Motivation of employees to "pull for the team" is a regular organizational communications goal. For example, the hospital CEO who outlines to her managers the institution's overriding objectives in the year ahead is communicating to motivate these key employees to action.

4. **To build mutual understanding.** Often communicators have as their goal the mere attainment of understanding of a group in opposition. For example, a community group that meets with a local plant manager to express its concern about potential pollution of the neighborhood is seeking understanding of the group's rationale and concern.

The point is that whether written release, annual report, speech, or meeting—all are valid public relations communications vehicles designed to achieve communications goals with key constituent publics. Again, the best way to achieve one's goals is through an integrated and strategically planned approach.

Traditional Theories of Communication

Books have been written on the subject of communications theory. This book is *not* one of them. Consequently, we won't attempt to provide an all-encompassing discussion on how people ensure that their messages get through to others. But in its most basic sense, communication commences with a source, who sends a message through a medium to reach a receiver who, we hope, responds in the manner we intended.

Many theories exist—from the traditional to the contemporary—about the most effective ways for a source to send a message through a medium to elicit a positive response. Here are but a few.

- One early theory of communication, the *two-step flow theory,* stated that an organization would beam a message first to the mass media, which would then deliver that message to the great mass of readers, listeners, and viewers for their response. This theory may have given the mass media too much credit. Indeed, when media is less "mass" than it is "targeted"—through Web sites, blogs, cable TV, talk radio, etc.—people today are influenced by a great many factors, of which the mass media may be one but is not necessarily the dominant one.

■ Another theory, the *concentric-circle theory*, developed by pollster Elmo Roper, assumed that ideas evolve gradually to the public at large, moving in concentric circles from great thinkers to great disciples to great disseminators to lesser disseminators to the politically active to the politically inert. This theory suggests that people pick up and accept ideas from leaders, whose impact on public opinion may be greater than that of the mass media. The overall study of how communication is used for direction and control is called *cybernetics*.

■ The communications theories of the late Pat Jackson have earned considerable respect in the public relations field. Jackson's public relations communications models, too, emphasized "systematic investigation—setting clear strategic goals and identifying key stakeholders."[4] One communications approach to stimulate behavioral change encompassed a five-step process:

1. **Building awareness.** Build awareness through all the standard communications mechanisms that we discuss in this book, from publicity to advertising to public speaking to word of mouth.

2. **Developing a latent readiness.** This is the stage at which people begin to form an opinion based on such factors as knowledge, emotion, intuition, memory, and relationships.

3. **Triggering event.** A triggering event is something—either natural or planned—that makes you want to change your behavior. Slimming down in time for beach season is an example of a natural triggering event. Staged functions, rallies, campaigns, and appearances are examples of planned triggering events.

4. **Intermediate behavior.** This is what Jackson called the "investigative" period, when an individual is determining how best to apply a desired behavior. In this stage, information about process and substance is sought.

5. **Behavioral change.** The final step is the adoption of new behavior.

■ Another traditional public relations theory of communications is the basic *S-E-M-D-R communications process*. This model suggests that the communication process begins with the source (S), who issues a message (M) to a receiver (R), who then decides what action to take, if any, relative to the communication. Two additional steps, an encoding stage (E), in which the source's original message is translated and conveyed to the receiver, and a decoding stage (D), in which the receiver interprets the encoded message and takes action, complete the model. It is in these latter two stages, encoding and decoding, that the public relations function most comes into play.

■ There are even those who focus on the growing import of the "silent" theories of communication. The most well known of these, Elisabeth Noelle-Neumann's *spiral of silence*, suggests that communications that work well depend on the silence and nonparticipation of a huge majority. This so-called "silent majority" fears becoming isolated from and therefore ostracized by most of their colleagues. Thus, they invariably choose to "vote with the majority."[5]

All of these theories and many others have great bearing on how public relations professionals perform their key role as organizational communicators.

Contemporary Theories of Communication

Many other communications theories abound today as Internet communication changes the ways and speed at which many of us receive our messages. Professor Everett Rogers talks about the unprecedented "diffusion" of the Internet as a communications vehicle that spans cultures and geographies. Others point to the new reality of "convergence" of video, data and voice, mobile and fixed, traditional and new age communications mechanisms with which public relations professionals must be familiar.

The complexity of communications in contemporary society—particularly in terms of understanding one's audience—has led scholars to author additional "audiencecentric" theories of how best to communicate.

- *Constructivism* suggests that knowledge is *constructed*, not transmitted. Constructivism, therefore, is concerned with the cognitive process that precedes the actual communication within a given situation rather than with the communication itself.

  This theory suggests that in communicating, it is important to have some knowledge of the receiver and his or her beliefs, predilections, and background. Simply dispensing information and expecting receivers to believe in or act on it, according to this theory, is a fool's errand. The task of the communicator, rather, is to understand and identify how receivers think about the issues in question and then work to challenge these preconceived notions and, hopefully, convert audience members into altering their views.[6]

- *Coordinated management of meaning* is a theory of communications based on social interaction. Basically, this theory posits that when we communicate—primarily through conversation—we construct our own social realities of what is going on and what kind of action is appropriate. We each have our own "stories" of life experience, which we share with others in conversation. When we interact, say the creators of this theory, we attempt to "coordinate" our own beliefs, morals, and ideas of "good" and "bad" with those of others so that a mutual outcome might occur.

  The point, again, is that communication, rather than being the simple "transmission" of ideas, is rather a complex, interconnected series of events, with each participant affected by the other.[7]

- Other widely discussed theoretical models of public relations communications are the *Grunig-Hunt public relations models*, formulated by Professors James E. Grunig and Todd Hunt. Grunig and Hunt proposed four models that define public relations communications.

  1. **Press agentry/publicity.** This early form of communication, say the authors, is essentially one-way communication that beams messages from a source to a receiver with the express intention of winning favorable media attention.

  2. **Public information.** This is another early form of one-way communication designed not necessarily to persuade but rather to inform. Both this and the press agentry model have been linked to the common notion of "public relations as propaganda."

  3. **Two-way asymmetric.** This is a more sophisticated two-way communication approach that allows an organization to put out its information and to receive feedback from its publics about that information. Under this model, an organization wouldn't necessarily change decisions as a result of

feedback but rather would alter its responses to more effectively persuade publics to accept its position.

4. **Two-way symmetric.** This preferred way of communicating advocates free and equal information flow between an organization and its publics, based on mutual understanding. This approach is more "balanced"— *symmetrical*—with the public relations communicator serving as a mediator between the organization and the publics.[8]

These are but a few of the prominent theories of communications—all revolving around "feedback"—of which public relations practitioners must be aware. In Chapter 4, we review relevant theories in forming public opinion.

The Word

Communication begins with words. Words are among our most personal and potent weapons. Words can soothe us, bother us, or infuriate us. They can bring us together or drive us apart. They can even cause us to kill or be killed. Words mean different things to different people, depending on their backgrounds, occupations, education, and geographic locations. As anyone who has ever walked into a Starbuck's and ordered a "small" caramel mocha macchiato only to be handed a "tall" caramel mocha macchiato knows, what one word means to you might be dramatically different from what that same word means to someone else. For example, when Hillary Clinton, in the heat of the 2008 Democrat presidential nomination process, labeled opponent Barack Obama as "elitist," her rival lashed back in anger, the implication being that he couldn't relate to blue-collar voters. The study of what words really mean is called *semantics,* and the science of semantics is a peculiar one indeed.

Words are perpetually changing in our language. What a word denotes according to the dictionary may be thoroughly dissimilar to what it connotes in its more emotional or visceral sense. Even the simplest words—*liberal, conservative, profits, consumer activists*—can spark semantic skyrockets. For example, in 2007 McDonald's launched a petition to get the Oxford English Dictionary to alter its definition of *McJob* as "an unstimulating low-paid job with few prospects."[9]

Particularly sensitive today is so-called "discriminatory language"—words that connote offensive meanings—in areas such as gender, race, ethnicity, and physical impairment. Words such as *firemen, manpower, housewife, cripple, midget,* and *Negro* may be considered offensive. While "political correctness" can go too far, it is nonetheless incumbent on public relations communicators to carefully assess words before using them.

Many times, without knowledge of the territory, the semantics of words may make no sense. Take the word *fat*. In our American culture and vernacular, a person who is fat is generally not associated with the apex of attractiveness. A person who is thin, on the other hand, may indeed be considered highly attractive. But along came 50 Cent and Kanye West and Jay-Z and hip-hop, and pretty soon *phat*—albeit with a new spelling—became the baddest of the bad, the coolest of the cool, the height of fetching pulchritudinousness (if you smell what I'm cookin').

Words have a significant influence on the message conveyed to the ultimate receiver. Thus the responsibility of a public relations professional, entrusted with *encoding* a client's message, is significant. Public relations encoders must understand, for example, that in today's technologically changing world, words and phrases change meaning and drop out of favor with blinding speed (see Talking Points). During the past century, the English language has added an average of 900 new words every year.[10]

For an intended message to get through, then, a public relations "interpreter" must accurately understand and effectively translate the true meaning—with all its semantic complications—to the receiver.

The Message

The real importance of words, in a public relations sense, is using them to build the messages that move publics to action. Framing "key messages" lies at the top of every public relations to-do list.

Messages may be transmitted in a myriad of communications media: speeches, newspapers, radio, television, news releases, press conferences, broadcast reports, and face-to-face meetings. Communications theorists differ on what exactly constitutes the message, but here are three of the more popular explanations.

1. **The content is the message.** According to this theory, which is far and away the most popular, the content of a communication—what it says—constitutes its message. According to this view, the real importance of a communication—the

---

Talking Points Profizzle of Lexicizzle

The 21st-century lexicon of current words and phrases is ever-changing. What's *in* today is *out* tomorrow.

Doubt it?

Then translate the following phrases that your parents considered colloquial.

- *I'll be a monkey's uncle*
- *This is a fine kettle of fish*
- *Knee high to a grasshopper*
- *Going like 60*
- *Iron Curtain*
- *Domino theory*

Or explain what they meant by the following items.

- *Boob tube*
- *L.D.*
- *Segregation*
- *Mailman*
- *Stewardess*

Or reconcile what you mean with what they mean by the following terms.

- *Gay*
- *Menu*
- *Virus*
- *Crack*, *smack*, *snow*, and, of course, *blow*

Words change so quickly these days that we even have new instant languages being created before our eyes.

FIGURE 3-3 Rapper Snoop Dogg. The Profizzle of Lexicizzle himself. (Photo: Newscom)

Among them, the *gangsta* lexicon of one, Snoop Dogg (Figure 3-3), affectionately known as *izzle speak*, is designed primarily to confuse anyone who isn't an urban Black rapper. To wit:

- *Valentizzle*
- *Tonizzle*
- *Televizzle*
- *Secretary of State Condoleezza Rizzle*

All of which means that for public relations professionals in the 21st century, properly interpreting messages to key publics has become a complicated proposition.

Fo shizzle.

message—lies in the meaning of an article or in the intent of a speech. Neither the medium through which the message is being communicated nor the individual doing the communicating is as important as the content. This is why professional public relations people insist on accurate and truthful content in the messages they prepare.

2. **The medium is the message.** Other communications theorists argue that the content of a communication may be less important than the medium in which the message is carried. This theory was originally proffered by the late Canadian communications professor Marshall McLuhan. This theory is relevant in today's hyper-media society, where the reputation and integrity of a particular media source may vary wildly. For example, a story carried on an Internet blog would generally carry considerably less weight than one reported in *The New York Times*. That is not to say that for some receivers, a particular blog's credibility might surpass that of the *Times*. Personal bias, as we will discuss, is always brought to bear in assessing the power and believability of communications messages. In other words, to some, conservative Fox News is the "last word" in credibility; to others, it's the liberal MSNBC.

3. **The man—or, to avoid political incorrectness, the person—is the message.** Still other theorists argue that it is neither the content nor the medium that is the message, but rather the speaker. For example, Adolf Hitler was a master of persuasion. His minister of propaganda, Josef Goebbels, used to say, *"Any man who thinks he can persuade, can persuade."* Hitler practiced this self-fulfilling communications prophecy to the hilt. Feeding on the perceived desires of the German people, Hitler was concerned much less with the content of his remarks than with their delivery. His maniacal rantings and frantic gestures seized public sentiment and sent friendly crowds into a frenzy. In every way, Hitler himself was the primary message of his communications.

Today, in a similar vein, we often refer to a leader's charisma. Frequently, the charismatic appeal of a political leader may be more important than what that individual says. Such was the historic appeal of Fidel Castro, for example. Political orators in particular, such as former Presidents Bill Clinton and Ronald Reagan and the Reverend Jesse Jackson, for example, could move an audience by the very inflection of their words. The smooth and confident speaking style of Barack Obama was a major plus in his winning the presidency in 2008. Experienced speakers, from James Carville on the left to Rush Limbaugh on the right, to retired military leaders like Colin Powell and Norman Schwarzkopf, to sports coaches like Bill Cowher and Mike Krzyzewski, can also rally listeners with their personal charismatic demeanor.

The point is that a speaker's words, face, body, eyes, attitude, timing, wit, presence—all form a composite that, as a whole, influences the listener. In such cases, the source of the communication becomes every bit as important as the message itself.

Receiver's Bias

Communicating a message is futile unless it helps achieve the desired goal of the communicator. As the bulk of the communications theories cited in this chapter suggest, the element of feedback is critical. This is why Web 2.0 technology—interactive wikis, blogs, and the like—are important and pervasive. Key to feedback is understanding the precognitions and predilections that receivers bring to a particular message.

Stated another way, how a receiver decodes a message depends greatly on that person's own perception. How an individual comprehends a message is a key to effective communications. The fact is, everyone is biased; no two people perceive a message identically. Personal biases are nurtured by many factors, including stereotypes, symbols, semantics, peer group pressures, and—especially in today's culture—the media.

Stereotypes

Everyone lives in a world of stereotypical figures. Gen Xers, policy wonks, feminists, bankers, blue-collar workers, PR types, and thousands of other characterizations cause people to think of specific images. Public figures, for example, are typecast regularly. The dumb blond, the bigoted right-winger, the bleeding-heart liberal, the computer geek, and the snake oil used car salesperson are the kinds of stereotypes perpetuated by our society.

Like it or not, most of us are victims of such stereotypes. For example, research indicates that a lecture delivered by a person wearing glasses will be perceived as significantly more believable than the same lecture delivered before the same audience by the same lecturer without glasses. The stereotyped impression of people with glasses is that they are more trustworthy and more believable. (Or at least that's the way it was before Lasik surgery!)

Also, like it or not, such stereotypes influence communication.

Symbols

The clenched-fist salute, the swastika, and the thumbs-up sign all leave distinct impressions on most people. Marshaled properly, symbols can be used as effective persuasive elements (Figure 3-4). The Statue of Liberty, the Red Cross, the Star of David, and many other symbols have been used traditionally for positive persuasion. On the other hand, the symbols chosen by the terrorists of September 11, 2001—the World Trade Center, the Pentagon, and most likely the U.S. Capitol and the White House—were clearly chosen because of their symbolic value as American icons.

Semantics

Public relations professionals make their living largely by knowing how to use words effectively to communicate desired meanings. Occasionally, this is tricky because the same words may hold contrasting meanings for different people. Today's contentious debate about abortion is a case in point, with the debate buttressed by confusing semantic terms—*pro-life* to signify those against abortion and *pro-choice* to signify those in favor of allowing abortions.

Controversy also surrounds the semantics associated with certain forms of rap and hip-hop music. To critics, some artists preach a philosophy of violence and hate and prejudice against women. But gangsta rappers claim that they are merely "telling it like it is" or "reporting what we see in the streets." When reporters and record company executives give credence to such misguided rhetoric, they become just as responsible as the artists for the often unfortunate outcomes that result—for example, the child pornography charges against and subsequent trial in 2008 of singer R. Kelly.

FIGURE 3-4 What's in a symbol? Located on Mount Lee in Griffith Park, the Hollywood sign is the most famous sign in the world. Originally built in 1923 for $21,000 as an advertising gimmick to promote home sales, the 45-foot high, 450-foot long, 480,000-pound sign was restored in 1978—Tinseltown's most enduring and instantly identifiable symbol. (Photo: Newscom)

Because language and the meanings of words change constantly, semantics must be handled with extreme care. Good communicators always consider the consequences of the words they plan to use before using them. On the other hand, less good communicators don't always consider the downside in the words they use (see Talking Points).

Peer Groups

In one famous study, students were asked to point out, in progression, the shortest of the following three lines.

A _____

B _____

C _____

Although line B is obviously the shortest, each student in the class except one was told in advance to answer that line C was the shortest. The object of the test was to see whether the one student would agree with his peers. Results generally indicated that, to a statistically significant degree, all students, including the uncoached one, chose C.

Such an experiment is an example of how peer pressure prevails in terms of influencing personal bias. Public relations professionals, intent on framing persuasive communications messages, must understand the importance of peer group influences on attitudes and actions.

Media

The power of the media—particularly as an agenda setter—is substantial. Agenda-setting is the creation of public awareness by the media—the ability to tell us what issues are important. As early as 1922, the legendary newspaper columnist Walter Lippman was

Talking

Points   Putting the Lolita Bed to Sleep

What's in a word?

Plenty and sometimes, plenty of trouble.

At least that's what Woolworths stores in Britain found out in 2008, when they were forced to halt the sales of their new beds designed for children. The name of the new slumber chamber?

Lolita.

Days after the new Lolita beds appeared on the retail chain's Web site, parents' organizations in Britain protested that the name was synonymous with sexually active pre-teenagers. Specifically, Lolita was the name of author Vladimir Nabokov's 1955 novel that told the tale of a middle-aged man's obsession with a sexually active 12-year-old girl.

The book, *Lolita,* sent shock waves through the world when it was published and later made into a movie, starring provocative Sue Lyon in the title role (Figure 3-5). But evidently, nobody at Woolworths was paying attention.

Said a Woolworths spokesperson, *"There aren't many people in the company, in the whole world, who know about the Lolita book or films. There might be a few people in the country who have a problem with it, but it's just a name."*

A "bad name" as it turned out.

FIGURE 3-5 **Ready for bed?** London's Woolworths quickly deep-sixed its child Lolita bed in 2008, after parents cited the decidedly nonchildlike movie of the same name a decade earlier, starring Sue Lyon. (Photo: Newscom)

Two days after the spokesperson's comment, Woolworth stopped selling the bed.*

* For further information, see Thomas Wagner, "'Lolita' Children's Beds Cause a Stir in UK," BBC.com (February 3, 2008).

concerned that the media had the power to present biased images to the public. Indeed, two basic assumptions underlie most research on agenda-setting: (1) the press and the media do not reflect reality; they filter and shape it; (2) media concentration on a few issues and subjects leads the public to perceive those issues as more important than other issues.[11]

In the 2008 Democratic presidential primary, for example, the media seized on the revelation that candidate Barack Obama's longtime preacher, Jeremiah Wright, had made racist and anti-Semitic statements. For several uncomfortable weeks (particularly for Sen. Obama), the media "agenda" was focused on Rev. Wright. Finally, after Obama denounced his former pastor's incendiary speech, the media backed off and turned to the equally inflammatory rhetoric of a clergy supporter of Republican presidential candidate, John McCain. Such are the 21st-century vagaries of agenda-setting by the media.

By the same token, in interesting the media to pursue client-oriented stories, public relations professionals also have a direct role in setting the agenda for others. The point is that people base perceptions on what they read or hear, often without bothering to dig further to elicit the facts. This is a two-edged sword: Although appearances are sometimes revealing, they are also often deceiving.

Feedback

A communicator must get feedback from a receiver to know what messages are or are not getting through and how to structure future communications.

You really aren't communicating unless someone is at the other end to hear and understand what you're saying and then react to it. This situation is analogous to the old

Mini-Case Steve Jobs' iPology

Leave it to Apple Founder and CEO Steve Jobs to introduce an entirely new public relations innovation, the iPology, that turns customer complaints into free publicity (Figure 3-6).

That's what the technology icon did in the fall of 2007, when he reduced the price of the company's hot-selling iPhone by $200. Problem was that the Apple eight-gigabyte phone was only introduced two months before. So the Apple loyalists who snapped up the new phone at inception were plenty steamed at the price cut. They screamed bloody murder that Apple had snookered them—the most devoted of the company's fan base—to buy the new product first, giving Apple enough time to lower the price for follow-on customers.

The Apple early purchasers had a point. And Apple had a huge public relations problem. But it was only a momentary one.

It took the Apple CEO just one day before realizing the error of his ways. In a letter to all those who had purchased the phone at the earlier price, Jobs apologized but noted, "*There is always someone who bought a product before a particular cutoff date and misses the new price or the new operating system or the new whatever. This is life in the technology lane.*"

Nonetheless, Jobs said the company would give all early purchasers $100 to spend on another Apple product.

Media reaction to the Jobs' "iPology" was immediate and pervasive. The Apple story dominated the Net, newspapers, and broadcast media. Rather than being criticized for better-dealing early Apple enthusiasts, Jobs and Apple were hailed for quickly acknowledging their mistake and communicating an admirable solution for customers.

Its public image once again intact, Apple resumed record-breaking sales of the iPhone, and its stock resumed its upward course.*

Questions

1. How would you assess, in public relations terms, Apple's original decision to lower the price of the IPhone?

2. What do you think of Apple's "solution" to its IPhone problem, and how do you assess Steve Jobs' communication about it?

FIGURE 3-6 "I iPologize." When Apple CEO Steve Jobs introduced the blockbuster iPhone in the fall of 2007, he had little idea he'd be communicating an "iPology" a couple of months later. (Photo: Newscom)

*For further information, see Rex Crum, "Apples' Jobs Apologizes over iPhone Cut," *MarketWatch* (September 6, 2007); "Apple Introduces the iPology," *Market Watch* (September 7, 2007); and David Lazarus, "Apple Flexes its Buzz Power," *Los Angeles Times* (September 7, 2007).

mystery of the falling tree in the forest: Does it make a noise when it hits the ground if there's no one there to hear it? Regardless of the answer, effective communication doesn't take place if a message doesn't reach the intended receivers and exert the desired effect on those receivers.

Even if a communication is understood clearly, there is no guarantee that the motivated action will be the desired one. In fact, a message may trigger several different effects.

1. **It may change attitudes.** This result, however, is very difficult to achieve and rarely happens.

2. **It may crystallize attitudes.** This outcome is much more common. Often a message will influence receivers to take actions they might already have been

thinking about taking but needed an extra push to accomplish. For example, a receiver might want to contribute to a certain charity, but seeing a child's photo on a contribution canister might crystallize his or her attitude sufficiently to trigger action.

3. **It may create a wedge of doubt.** Communication can sometimes force receivers to modify their points of view. A persuasive message on cable TV can cause viewers to question their original thinking on an issue.

4. **It may do nothing.** At times, the best laid communication plans result in no action at all. For years, the expensive communications campaigns to reduce cigarette sales, waged by government and fueled by a $246 billion industry settlement, yielded less than stellar results. More recently, the campaign has started to pay off, with the number of smokers among U.S. adults numbering 21 percent by 2008, down from 29 percent in the early 1980s.[12] This indicates another communication truism—changing attitudes and motivating action takes time.

Whether the objectives of a communication have been met can often be assessed by such things as the amount of sales, number of letters, or number of votes obtained. If individuals take no action after receiving a communication, feedback must still be sought. In certain cases, although receivers have taken no discernible action, they may have understood and even passed on the message to other individuals. This person-to-person relay of received messages creates a two-step flow of communications: (1) vertically from a particular source and (2) horizontally from interpersonal contact. The targeting of opinion leaders as primary receivers, for example, is based on the hope that they will distribute received messages horizontally within their own communities. Consequently, it is the sponsor's hope that the feedback of these influential members of the community will forward the sponsor's own key messages.

Last Word

Knowledge of how and when and to whom to communicate is the primary skill of the public relations practitioner. Above all else, public relations professionals are professional communicators. That means they must not only be knowledgeable about the various Web-based techniques and tactics available to communicators in the 21st century but also understand the theoretical underpinnings of what constitutes a credible message and how to deliver it.

The early years of the 21st century indicate that effective communication has never been more important. With the emergence of worldwide terrorism; anti-American sentiments in the Middle East and elsewhere; the deepening cultural chasm between West and East, rich and poor, and haves and have nots; along with economic challenges from the soaring cost of energy to the threat of global recession, to the emergence of China and India as economic super powers—the need for honest, straightforward, and credible communication is critical.

There is no trick to effective communication. In addition to mastery of techniques, it is knowledge, experience, hard work, and common sense that are the basic guiding principles. Naturally, communication must follow action; organizations must back up what they say with what they do. Omnipresent advertising, a winning Web site, slick brochures, engaging speeches, intelligent articles, and good press may help capture the public's attention, but in the final analysis the only way to obtain continued public support is through proper performance.

Discussion Starters

1. Why is it important that public relations professionals understand communication?
2. What are some principal goals of communication, and what are some contemporary examples?
3. Why do words such as *liberal, conservative, profits,* and *consumer activist* spark semantic skyrockets?
4. What is the role of a public relations professional in the S-E-M-D-R communications process?
5. What is the difference between the symmetric and asymmetric models of communication?
6. What is meant by constructivism and coordinated management of meaning?
7. What is meant by the media as *agenda setter?*
8. Why is feedback critical to the communications process?
9. What common mistakes do people make when they communicate?
10. What are some contemporary examples of the changing meanings of words over time?

Top of the Shelf   PowerLines: Words that Sell Brands, Grip Fans, and Sometimes Change History / Steve Cone, New York, NY: Bloomberg Press. 2008.

"Powerlines," the author says, are those memorable words and phrases that are indelibly etched in the mind, are everywhere in business, politics, the media, commercials, films, and advertisements.

Cone, marketing officer for a technology firm, focuses naturally on tag lines in commercials or movies—from *Gone with the Wind's* "Frankly my dear, I don't give a damn," to *Dr. No's* "Bond, James Bond," from Virginia's "Virginia is for Lovers," to New Hampshire's "Live Free or Die."

On a broader level, the book offers sound communications wisdom for professional communicators, particularly in emphasizing that a great communications program or a great line must "have an attitude" and "say something about you that is unique."

Case Study   Walmart Shares the "Love"

By most accounts, the world's most beleaguered corporate giant is the world's largest public company.

Walmart Stores, Inc., based in bucolic Bentonville, Arkansas, is the world's largest private employer, serving an astounding 138 million customers per week worldwide. It makes $379 billion in annual revenue—or about $32 billion a month—and controls about 20 percent of the retail grocery and consumables business in the United States (Figure 3-7).

Walmart is also the world's largest private employer, with 2.1 million worldwide employees, or, as the company puts it, "associates." In December 2006, Walmart reduced its headcount by one, firing a high-profile marketing executive whose departure set off a public relations firestorm that left even the world's "most beleaguered company" scratching its head.

The Fall of Roehm

At the end of 2006, Walmart severed its ties with Marketing Director Julie Roehm, who had been hired with great fanfare just 10 months earlier from the DaimlerChrysler Corporation, where she was director of marketing communications for several leading brands (Figure 3-8).

One reason the Walmart hiring turned heads was that Roehm was well known in advertising circles for "pushing the envelope." Her most famous marketing gambit was Dodge brand's sponsorship of the pay-per-view "Lingerie Bowl," featuring scantily clad models, at halftime of the 2003 Super Bowl. That sponsorship was aborted when Chrysler dealers and family values groups objected to the company's participation.

For staid Walmart, then, the Roehm hiring was a bit of a stretch. But Walmart was committed to reenergizing its tired brand, and the Roehm hiring, therefore, seemed appropriate. Or at least it did for about 10 months.

At the time of her dismissal in 2006, Walmart questioned Roehm about accepting gifts from an ad agency, Draftfcb, that was awarded the lucrative Walmart $580 million advertising account. Walmart's Corporate Ethics Policy expressly prohibits employees from accepting gifts.

And there the matter would presumably have been left—another unfortunate corporate hiring mismatch—had Roehm, herself, not chosen to raise the ante.

War Is Declared

Within days of her firing, Roehm sued Walmart for breach of contract, fraud, and misrepresentation.

The former marketing director sought payment of more than $1.5 million to cover severance, stock options, restricted stock, and bonus.

While Roehm acknowledged that she might have "made mistakes" in her short tenure as marketing communications officer—like painting her office chartreuse with chocolate-brown trim—she also claimed that Walmart wouldn't honor its commitment to change.

"I wanted to hit the ground running. Go. Go. Go," she said. Instead, she saw her role being minimized, as one of "handing off market research to ad agencies." In the end, Walmart's reliance on low prices trumped Roehm's desire to "upscale" the stores.

So Roehm sued and made herself available for national interviews to lay out why she felt wronged by the heirs to Sam Walton's empire. She was outspoken to a fault, publicly making fun of the retailer, and vowing to "write a book" about her Walmart experience.

And that's when the "fun" started.

Fighting Back with "Love"

Where traditional corporate wisdom would suggest that lawsuits should be handled in court and public ugliness avoided, Walmart's response to the Roehm suit was as breathtaking as it was unprecedented.

Walmart countersued with a public document so steamy that it probably would have embarrassed the Lingerie Bowl models!

In pot-boiling detail, Walmart's counterclaim described an "inappropriate romantic relationship" between Roehm and a subordinate, Sean Womack, a Walmart marketing vice president, who was fired along with his boss.

The filing was so salacious that it even included titillating email correspondence between the two and quotes from a "friend" of Womack's, who said he caught the two of them in a Fayetteville bar, where *"Womack had Roehm 'pinned' against the wall in an intimate pose."* All of which probably didn't sit well with Roehm's husband or Womack's wife.

FIGURE 3-7 Standing tall. The world's largest retailer hardly anticipated the full-scale attack that a disgruntled former marketing communications director would launch in the winter of 2006. (Courtesy of Walmart)

FIGURE 3-8 Happier times. Things were decidedly more upbeat when Julie Roehm ruled the marketing communications roost at DaimlerChrysler. (Photo: Newscom)

It also was a stunning response from a private—and in this case, very "private"—company. Said one attorney familiar with sexual misbehavior cases, *"Usually these matters are quietly resolved."*

The Long Goodbye

Close to two years after they parted company, Walmart and its former marketing communications director were finally set to battle it out in a courtroom in Michigan. For her part, Roehm vowed to call leading advertising and Walmart executives, including CEO Lee Scott, to testify.

Meanwhile, in addition to the Roehm matter, Walmart was faced with dozens of other wage-related and discrimination lawsuits. Earlier, juries in Pennsylvania and California awarded Walmart workers a total of $251 million in pay and damages over claims the company broke wage laws. Such was the territory for a company that seemed a target for critics of every stripe and passion. Or, as one observer summarized it, *"The company is in a fishbowl."*

While most expected Walmart to settle with its disgruntled former marketing executive, in order to avoid yet further ugly publicity, nobody was taking bets.

Said one law professor, *"Both sides are playing hardball."* [*]

Questions

1. What public relations options did Walmart have in response to the Roehm suit?

2. How would you assess Walmart's response to the suit of its former employee?

3. What is the downside to the Walmart response? What is the upside?

4. Critics suggest that Walmart's action will "poison" the atmosphere for hiring future executives. Do you agree? Why or why not?

5. What would you recommend Walmart do now, relative to the Roehm court case?

*For further information, see Robert Berner, "My Year at Walmart," *BusinessWeek* (February 12, 2007); Margaret Cronin Fisk and Lauren Coleman-Lochner, "Walmart Facing Another Legal Battle," *International Herald Tribune* (May 30, 2007); and Devin Leonard, "How Walmart Got the Love E-Mail," *Fortune* (April 30, 2007): 52.

Earlier assistance in compiling Walmart information was kindly provided by Professor Bonnie Grossman's public relations class at the College of Charleston in South Carolina, for which the author is most grateful.

From the Top   An Interview with Mona Williams

Mona Williams is vice president of corporate communications for Walmart Stores, Inc., the world's largest and most visible company. Williams assumed this role in 2002 and is responsible for all national and field communications. Since then, she has helped lead Walmart's aggressive public relations outreach in a variety of challenges. She has made numerous television appearances on cable and broadcast programs and is frequently quoted in *The New York Times* and *Wall Street Journal*. Williams has been profiled in both *PR Strategist* and *Fast Company* magazines, and *PR Week* continues to rank her role as one of the *"10 Most Daunting PR Jobs."*

What is Walmart's general attitude toward the media?
Sam Walton did not see the need to spend much time with the news media. His view was that as long as we took care of our customers and associates, the outside world would leave us alone. While that might have worked at the time, we are living in a different world today.

Almost 2,000 stories a day are written about Walmart. We know the media can play a huge role in shaping how others see us and that we need to be very engaged in building these relationships and sharing our side of the story. Experience has taught us that if we don't take every opportunity to define ourselves, others will step into the gap and do it for us—and maybe not in a positive way.

How would you characterize Walmart's approach to public relations?
First, as business counselors, we first try to drive improvement in how the business operates, especially in areas that can impact reputation. This helps ensure we have a good story to

tell. Part of this is acting as an "early warning system" for the company. Where are our vulnerabilities? Are we connected with people who will shoot straight with us, such as NGOs, elected officials, and industry analysts?

Second, we put a lot of energy behind developing external relationships so that audiences are receptive to our story. We have embedded field media and public affairs teams in local communities and have established a diversity communication team. We have also engaged an outside firm and centralized our initiatives in a "PR room"—called *Action Alley*—to identify and engage third parties to speak on our behalf, such as Walmart suppliers, community leaders, think tank members, and consumers.

Third, developing our story is an ongoing effort to determine the facts and then decide which ones matter. We conduct both fact-based and opinion research. How do our wages and benefits compare to our competitors'? How much money do we save consumers each year? How many American jobs do we create? Once we have our facts, we focus on shaping them into compelling messages that resonate with the audiences we

are trying to reach. Whenever possible, we try to shape these facts into an emotional story.

Fourth, we rely on a broad range of initiatives to reach our target audiences. Key audiences include customers, community leaders, elected officials, financial analysts, suppliers, and our most important audience—Walmart associates. Mass campaigns fall flat if our associates aren't telling a positive story about their own experience.

How would you characterize the communication department's relationship with Walmart's CEO?
We are fortunate that our CEO, Lee Scott, considers corporate communications one of the most important teams in the company. We work closely with him. He has a natural feel for which messages resonate with our audiences and is a valuable asset when it comes to telling the Walmart story. His primary challenge to us is to make sure any interviews or speeches we recommend are part of an overall strategic plan to advance business objectives. Within that framework, he almost always says, *"Yes."*

Public Relations Library

Argenti, Paul A. *Corporate Communication*. Burr Ridge, IL: Irwin Professional Publishing, 2005.

Brown, Paul B., and Alison Davis. *Your Attention, Please. How to Appeal to Today's Distracted, Disinterested, Disengaged, Disenchanted, and Busy Audiences*. Avon, MA: Adams Media, 2006. Excellent treatise on how to deal with the information overload with which all of us are afflicted. The trick to getting through, according to the authors: Be fast and write punchy.

Caproni, Paula J. *Management Skills for Everyday Life: The Practical Coach*. Upper Saddle River, NJ: Prentice Hall, 2004. Communication skills are stressed as priorities.

D'Vario, Marisa. *Building Buzz: How to Reach and Impress Your Target Audience*. Franklin Lakes, NJ: Career Press, 2006. This is a combination pop psychology/communication primer on how to get you and your company and its products noticed.

Demers, David. *Mass Communication and Media Research*. Spokane, WA: Marquette Books, 2005. Up-to-date dictionary of communication and media history and terms.

Green, Andy. *Effective Communication Skills for Public Relations*. London, England: Kogan Page Ltd., 2005.

Laermer, Richard. *Full Frontal PR: Getting People Talking about You, Your Business, or Your Product*. New York: Bloomberg Press, 2004.

McPhail, Thomas L. *Global Communications: Theories, Stakeholders, and Trends*, 2nd ed. Malden, MA: Blackwell Publishing, 2006. Contemporary view of global communications innovations and challenges.

Pacelli, Lonnie. *The Truth About Getting Your Point Across . . . and Nothing But the Truth*. Upper Saddle River, NJ: Prentice-Hall, Inc., 2006. This book is a terrific primer on how to get your message across convincingly whether writing or speaking, texting or tweeting.

Ragan Report. Lawrence Ragan Communications, Inc., 316 N. Michigan Ave., Chicago, IL 60601. Weekly pointed commentary on current communications issues.

Shepherd, G. J., J. St. John, and T. Striphas (Eds.). *Communications as . . . Perspectives on Theory*. Thousand Oaks, CA: Sage Publications, Inc., 2006. Communications, the authors say, is a "process of relating," and this book explains how relationships are built.

Chapter 4

Public Opinion

FIGURE 4-1 Separated at birth? You betcha'!
At least according to right-wing blogger Michelle
Malkin. (Photo: Newscom)

Public opinion is an elusive and fragile commodity. It can take an organization or individual many years to build the credibility and nurture the trust that goes into winning favorable public opinion. But it can take only a matter of minutes to destroy all that has been developed.

That's why in the summer of 2008, Dunkin' Donuts wasn't laughing when right-wing blogger and occasional talking head Michelle Malkin made a run at the coffee chain's spokesperson, perky celebrity chef Rachael Ray. An outraged Ms. Malkin blogged to her followers that the fringed black and white scarf Ms. Ray wore in a Dunkin' Donuts Internet ad looked suspiciously like the keffiyeh, "the traditional scarf of Arab men that has come to symbolize murderous Palestinian jihad."[1] Ms. Malkin's angst was triggered by first reports of the suspect scarf on the pro-Israel blog *Atlas Shrugs,* brainchild of citizen journalist Pam Geller.

While even the most ardent bloggee following either Ms. Geller or Ms. Malkin would be hard pressed to confuse Ms. Ray for the keffiyeh-adorned, dead terrorist Yasser Arafat (Figure 4-1), nonetheless Dunkin' Donuts immediately pulled the ad in question after the criticism hit the Net. Said the chain, *"The possibility of misperception detracted from its original intention to promote our iced coffee."*

Literal translation: Even though the charge was absurd on its face, taking a hit in public opinion via a potentially endless campaign on the Internet just ain't worth it.

Suffering a loss in public opinion isn't a trivial matter. Individuals and companies in the public eye can't afford to tarnish their reputations. Often, this translates into a loss of prestige and business. And that's why most public relations agencies bill themselves as experts in the field of "reputation management."

Society is littered with the reputational carcasses of once respected organizations and individuals who tested the goodwill of the public once too often. For example:

- In 2007, beloved pitcher Roger Clemens, seemingly on his way to baseball's Hall of Fame at Cooperstown, became the latest baseball great accused of prolonging his career through the injection of illegal steroids. While Clemens vehemently denied the accusations, his reputation disintegrated.[2]

- That same year, one of pro football's most talented quarterbacks, Michael Vick of the Atlanta Falcons, admitted his involvement in illegal dogfighting and was sent to jail, torpedoing his reputation (see PR Ethics Mini-Case, Chapter 17).[3]

■ Also in 2007, the president of the American Red Cross, Mark Everson, was forced to resign when it was revealed that he had engaged in a "personal relationship" with one of his subordinates. Everson had served only six months in the job.[4]

■ In 2008, the nation witnessed a parade of several of its richest business leaders, from Citigroup CEO Chuck Prince to Merrill Lynch CEO Stanley O'Neal to Bear Stearns CEO Alan Schwartz to Lehman Brothers CEO Richard Fuld, being pilloried by media and Congress for squandering shareholder trust and resources in the disastrous subprime mortgage lending fiasco. The CEO trouble was reminiscent of the start of the decade when unscrupulous executives were led to court in handcuffs, on their way to prison, for defrauding their own shareholders. Most notable was the sad saga of domestic doyenne Martha Stewart (see Case Study at end of chapter).

■ In 2004, New Jersey Governor James McGreevey abruptly announced his resignation after dropping the bombshell that he was gay, and had allegedly used taxpayer money to create a job for his lover.[5] McGreevey's was just one of many government scandals that brought down well-known politicians, including, in 2005, powerful House of Representatives Majority Leader Tom Delay, who was caught in a contributions scandal. (Four years later, a reinvented Delay returned as a contestant on TV's *Dancing with the Stars*.)

The point is that these individuals and the organizations they represented, like many others in all areas of society, suffered serious setbacks in terms of their standing with the public as a result of their actions.

The related point is, as we put it in Chapter 1, *You can't pour perfume on a skunk*.

The best public relations campaign in the world can't build trust when reality is destroying it. If your product doesn't work, if your service stinks, if you are a liar—then no amount of "public relations" will change that. You must change the "action" before credibility or trust can be built.

Such are the vulnerabilities of public opinion in a culture driven by media, fueled by the Internet, and dominated by celebrity. Public opinion in the 21st century is a combustible and changing commodity.

As a general rule, it's difficult to move people toward a strong opinion on anything. It's even harder to move them away from an opinion once they reach it. Nonetheless, the heart of public relations work lies in attempting to affect the public opinion process. Most public relations programs are designed to (1) persuade people to change their opinion on an issue, product, or organization; (2) crystallize uninformed or undeveloped opinions; or (3) reinforce existing opinions.

Public relations professionals therefore must understand what public opinion is, how it is formed, how it evolves from people's attitudes, and how it is influenced by communication. This chapter discusses attitude formation and change and public opinion creation and persuasion.

What Is Public Opinion?

Public opinion, like public relations, is not easily explained. Newspaper columnist Joseph Kraft called public opinion *"the unknown god to which moderns burn incense."* Edward Bernays called it *"a term describing an ill-defined, mercurial, and changeable group of individual judgments."*[6]

Princeton Professor Harwood Childs, after coming up with no fewer than 40 different yet viable definitions, concluded with a definition by Herman C. Boyle: *"Public opinion is not the name of something, but the classification of a number of somethings."*[7]

Splitting public opinion into its two components, *public* and *opinion*, is perhaps the best way to understand the concept. Simply defined, *public* signifies a group of people who share a common interest in a specific subject—stockholders, for example, or employees or community residents. Each group is concerned with a common issue: the price of the stock, the wages of the company, or the building of a new plant.

An *opinion* is the expression of an attitude on a particular topic. When attitudes become strong enough, they surface in the form of opinions. When opinions become strong enough, they lead to verbal or behavioral actions.

A forest products company executive and an environmentalist from the Sierra Club might differ dramatically in their attitudes toward the relative importance of global warming and continued industrial production. Their respective opinions on a piece of environmental legislation might also differ radically. In turn, how their organizations respond to that legislation—by picketing, petitioning, or lobbying—might also differ.

Public opinion, then, is the aggregate of many individual opinions on a particular issue that affects a group of people. Stated another way, public opinion represents a consensus. That consensus, deriving as it does from many individual opinions, begins with people's attitudes toward the issue in question. Trying to influence an individual's attitude—how he or she thinks on a given topic—is a primary focus of the practice of public relations.

What Are Attitudes?

If an opinion is an expression of an attitude on a particular topic, what then is an *attitude?*

Unfortunately, that also is not an easy question to answer. It was once generally assumed that attitudes are predispositions to think in a certain way about a certain topic. But research indicates that attitudes may more likely be evaluations people make about specific problems or issues. These conclusions are not necessarily connected to any broad attitude.[8] For example, an individual might favor a company's response to one issue but disagree vehemently with its response to another. Thus, that individual's attitude may differ from issue to issue.

Attitudes are based on a number of characteristics.

1. **Personal**—the physical and emotional ingredients of an individual, including size, age, and social status.

2. **Cultural**—the environment and lifestyle of a particular country or geographic area. The cultures of Saudi Arabia and the United States, for example, differ greatly; on a less global scale, cultural differences between rural and urban America are vast. Republican John McCain and Democrat Barack Obama tailored messages to appeal to the particular cultural complexions of specific regions as they crisscrossed the country looking for votes in the presidential election of 2008.

3. **Educational**—the level and quality of a person's education. To appeal to the increased number of college graduates in the United States today, public communication has become more sophisticated.

4. **Familial**—people's roots. Children acquire their parents' tastes, biases, political partisanships, and a host of other characteristics. Some pediatricians insist that children pick up most of their knowledge in the first years of their life, and few would deny the family's strong role in helping to mold attitudes.

5. **Religious**—a system of beliefs about God or a higher power. Religion is making a comeback. After a period of people turning away from religion, in the 21st century, even after several evangelical scandals, religious fervor has reemerged.

6. **Social class**—position within society. As people's social status changes, so do their attitudes. For example, college students, unconcerned with making a living, may dramatically change their attitudes about such concepts as big government, big business, wealth, prosperity, and politics after entering the job market. Indeed, arguments playing to different "social class" stood at the center of the McCain–Obama contest in 2008.

7. **Race**—ethnic origin, which today increasingly helps shape people's attitudes. Minorities in our society, as a group, continue to improve their standard of living and their relative position. African Americans head major corporations, hold cabinet positions, sit on the Supreme Court, and run for president. Latinos and Asian Americans have become coveted interest groups. And women, in many sectors—among them, college students and public relations professionals—are no longer considered a minority.

As their lot improves, African Americans, Latinos, Asians, and others have retained pride in and allegiance to their cultural heritage. These characteristics help influence the formation of attitudes. So, too, do other factors, such as experience, economic class, and political and organizational memberships. Again, research indicates that attitudes and behaviors are situational—influenced by specific issues in specific situations. Nonetheless, when others with similar attitudes reach similar opinions, a consensus, or public opinion, is born.

How Are Attitudes Influenced?

Strictly speaking, attitudes are positive, negative, or nonexistent. A person is for something, against it, or neutral. Studies show that for any one issue, most people don't care much one way or the other. A small percentage expresses strong support, and another small percentage expresses strong opposition. The vast majority is smack in the so-called "muddled middle"—passive, neutral, indifferent. Many years ago, former U.S. Vice President Spiro T. Agnew called this group "the silent majority." Years later, in many instances—political campaigns being a prime example—this silent majority, or "swing vote," still holds the key to success because they are the group most readily influenced by a communicator's message.

It's hard to change the mind of a person who is staunchly opposed to a particular issue or individual. Likewise, it's easy to reinforce the support of a person who is wholeheartedly in favor of an issue or individual.

Social scientist Leon Festinger discussed this concept when he talked about the *theory of cognitive dissonance.* He believed that individuals tend to avoid information that is dissonant or opposed to their own points of view and tend to seek out information that is consonant with, or in support of, their own attitudes.[9]

Similarly, *social judgment theory* suggests that people may have a range of opinions on a certain subject, anchored by a clear attitude.[10] Again, while it is seldom possible to change this anchor position, communicators can work within this range, called a person's "latitude of acceptance," to modify a person's opinion.

For example, while most people might not discriminate against eating Canadian seafood products, they might object to the clubbing of baby seals. Therefore, in trying to pressure Canada to stop the seal hunt, the Humane Society of the United States attempts to link the hunt with Canada's seafood industry. In so doing, it attempts to sway the undecided to take action and also to influence others within an acceptable range (Figure 4-2).

Understanding the potential for influencing the silent majority is extremely important for the public relations practitioner, whose objective is to win support through clear, thoughtful, and persuasive communication. Moving a person from a latent state of attitude formation to a more aware state and finally to an active one becomes a matter of motivation.

FIGURE 4-2 **Save the seals.** The Humane Society's campaign to stop Canada's commercial seal hunt used graphic mailings, Web video, and photos to influence public opinion. (Courtesy of the Humane Society of the United States)

Motivating Attitude Change

People are motivated by different factors, and no two people respond in exactly the same way to the same set of circumstances. Each of us is motivated by different drives and needs.

The most famous delineator of what motivates people was Abraham Maslow. Maslow's *hierarchy of needs theory* helps define the origins of motivation, which in turn helps explain attitude change. Maslow postulated a five-level hierarchy:

1. The lowest order is physiological needs: a person's biological demands—food and water, sleep, health, bodily needs, exercise and rest, and sex.
2. The second level is safety needs: security, protection, comfort and peace, and orderly surroundings.
3. The third level is love needs: acceptance, belonging, love and affection, and membership in a group.
4. The fourth level is esteem: recognition and prestige, confidence and leadership opportunities, competence and strength, intelligence and success.
5. The highest order is self-actualization, or simply becoming what one is capable of becoming; self-actualization involves self-fulfillment and achieving a goal for the purposes of challenge and accomplishment.[11]

According to Maslow, the needs of all five levels compose the fundamental motivating factors for any individual or public.

Another popular approach to motivating attitude change is the *elaboration likelihood model*, which posits that there are essentially two ways that people are persuaded:

1. When we are interested and focused enough on a message to take a direct "central route" to decision making, and
2. When we are not particularly engaged on a message and need to take a more "peripheral" route.

Translating this theory into action means that the best way to motivate interested people is with arguments that are strong, logical, and personally relevant. On the other hand, the way to motivate people who are less interested might be through putting them in a better mood—with a joke, for example, or demonstrating, through speech or clothes or mannerism, that you are very much "like" them. Such techniques, according to this theory, might help encourage listeners to accept your arguments.[12]

Power of Persuasion

Perhaps the most essential element in influencing public opinion is the principle of persuasion. Persuading is the goal of the vast majority of public relations programs.

Persuasion theory has myriad explanations and interpretations. Basically, persuasion means getting another person to do something through advice, reasoning, or just plain arm-twisting. Books have been written on the enormous power of advertising and public relations as persuasive tools.

According to classic persuasion theory, people may be of two minds in order to be persuaded to believe in a particular position or take a specific action.

First is the "systematic" mode, referring to a person who has carefully considered an argument—actively, creatively, and alertly.

Second is the "heuristic" mode, referring to a person who is skimming the surface and not really focusing on the intricacies of a particular position to catch flaws, inconsistencies, or errors.[13]

That is not to say that all systematic thinkers or all heuristic thinkers think alike. They don't. Things are more complicated than that. Let's say your little brother wants a pair of basketball shoes and your dad accompanies him to the store to buy them. Both are systematic thinkers. But they have different questions.

Your dad asks:

1. How much do they cost?
2. How long will they last?
3. Is the store nearby so I can get back to watch the ball game?
4. Will they take a personal check?

Your brother asks:

1. Does LeBron James endorse them?
2. Do all my homeboys wear them?
3. Will Wanda Sue go out with me if I buy them?

The point is that all of us are persuaded by different things, which makes the challenge of public relations persuading much more a complex art form than a science. No matter how one characterizes persuasion, the goal of most communications programs is, in fact, to influence a receiver to take a desired action.

How are people persuaded? Saul Alinsky, a legendary radical organizer, had a simple theory of persuasion: *"People only understand things in terms of their own experience. . . . If you try to get your ideas across to others without paying attention to what they have to say to you, you can forget about the whole thing."*[14] In other words, if you wish to persuade people, you must cite evidence that coincides with their own beliefs, emotions, and expectations.

What kinds of "evidence" will persuade?

1. **Facts.** Facts are indisputable. Although it is true, as they say, that "liars figure and figures lie," empirical data are a persuasive device in hammering home a point of view. This is why any good public relations program always starts with research—the facts.

2. **Emotions.** Maslow was right. People do respond to emotional appeals—love, peace, family, patriotism. Arguably, the most riveting moment in George W. Bush's presidency came in the Oval Office on September 13, 2001, when a reporter asked about Bush's personal concerns.

   Reporter: *About the prayer day tomorrow, Mr. President. Could you give us a sense as to what kind of prayers you are thinking and where your heart is for yourself?*

   The President: *Well, I don't think about myself right now. I think about the families, the children. I am a loving guy, and I am also someone, however,* *who has got a job to do—and I intend to do it. And this is a terrible moment. But this country will not relent until we have saved ourselves and others from the terrible tragedy that came upon America.*[15]

In less than 50 words, a visibly shaken Bush had made an emotional connection with the American public that proved elusive through much of his presidency. Alas, to many of his fellow Americans, this sad, shining moment was the pinnacle of the Bush administration.

3. **Personalizing.** People respond to personal experience.

   - When poet Maya Angelou talks about poverty, people listen and respect a woman who emerged from the dirt-poor environs of the Deep South in a day of segregation.
   - When *America's Most Wanted* TV host John Walsh crusades against criminals who prey on children, people understand that his son was abducted and killed by a crazed individual.
   - When former baseball pitcher Jim Abbott talks about dealing with adversity, people marvel at a star athlete born with only one arm.

     Again, few can refute knowledge gained from personal experience.

4. **Appealing to "you."** The one word that people never tire of hearing is *you. What is in this for me?* is the question that everyone asks. One secret to persuading, therefore, is to constantly think in terms of what will appeal most to the audience.

As simple as these four precepts are, they are often difficult for some to grasp. Emotion, for example, is a particular challenge for business leaders, who presume, incorrectly, that showing it is a sign of weakness. This, of course, is wrong. The power to persuade—to influence public opinion—is the measure not only of a charismatic but also of an effective leader.[16]

Influencing Public Opinion

Public opinion is a lot easier to measure than it is to influence. However, a thoughtful public relations program can crystallize attitudes, reinforce beliefs, and occasionally change public opinion. First, the opinions to be changed or modified must be identified and understood. Second, target publics must be clear. Third, the public relations professional must have in sharp focus the "laws" that govern public opinion—as amorphous as they may be.

In that context, the "Laws of Public Opinion," developed many years ago by social psychologist Hadley Cantril, remain pertinent. Few recent events more strongly underscored the relevance of Cantril's laws than the unprecedented attacks on America of September 11, 2001.[17]

1. **Opinion is highly sensitive to important events.** Events of unusual magnitude are likely to swing public opinion temporarily from one extreme to another. Opinion doesn't become stabilized until the implications of events are seen in some perspective. For example, after the terrorist attacks, President Bush's popularity rose to unprecedented heights as Americans of every age group and background rallied behind the war against terrorism.

2. **Opinion is generally determined more by events than by words—unless those words are themselves interpreted as an event.** In a speech to a joint

Mini-Case General *Betray Us* and the Great Gray Lady

FIGURE 4-3 General outrage. Republican presidential standard bearer John McCain was just one of those incensed when a moveon.org ad challenged Gen. David Petraeus's honesty. (Photo: Newscom)

No issue was more contentious in the final months of the George W. Bush administration than the war in Iraq. The vast majority of Americans grew to loathe the war, and no group was more anti-Bush than the liberal Web site moveon.org.

Moveon.org, which received the vast majority of its funding from billionaire George Soros, was a powerful, unabashedly left-wing force in the Democratic Party. And the individual MoveOn "bashed" the most was George W. Bush. As public opinion against the war grew, MoveOn's contentious views appeared to become more mainstream.

But then the group went over the edge.

In the fall of 2007, on the day when respected Iraq commander Gen. David Petraeus was to testify before Congress, MoveOn questioned the general's ethics. It ran a full-page ad in *The New York Times* with the damning headline, "General Petraeus or General Betray Us?" The ad questioned whether the general was telling the whole truth about Iraq or, in fact, *"cooking the books."*

The political fallout from the MoveOn ad was instantaneous. Public opinion stood staunchly behind the brave general and the brave soldiers he commanded in Iraq, whether or not people agreed with the war. To make matters worse, it was revealed that the *Times* had awarded MoveOn a $70,000 discount for the ad. Overnight, the chorus of condemnation was deafening across the land (Figure 4-3).

The *Times*—already suspected by conservatives of being a liberally-biased newspaper—had egg on its face and immediately announced that its salesperson had erred in giving MoveOn a discount. The paper, sensitive to public opinion, said it would adjust the bill and charge MoveOn the standard $142,083 for the ad.

Moveon.org paid the difference without additional fanfare.

Questions

1. What are the implications in terms of its credibility of *The New York Times* discounting the MoveOn ad?

2. How would you assess the *Times'* reaction to the controversy?

*For further information, see Katharine Q. Seelye, "Group Pays Higher Price for an Ad In The Times," *New York Times* (September 26, 2007): A25.

session of Congress nine days after the terrorist attacks, the President vowed to "lift the dark threat of violence from our people and our future. We will rally the world to this cause by our efforts, by our courage. We will not tire, we will not falter, and we will not fail." Bush's words became a rallying cry for the nation and, temporarily at least, transformed his presidency.[18]

3. **At critical times, people become more sensitive to the adequacy of their leadership. If they have confidence in it, they are willing to assign more than usual responsibility to it; if they lack confidence in it, they are less tolerant than usual.** Relatively few voices rose in protest when the Bush administration, in the cause of fighting terrorism, imposed sweeping changes in privacy rights, regarding such traditional areas as library use and securing court orders before wiretapping suspected American evildoers.

4. **Once self-interest is involved, opinions are slow to change.** Even after the United States invaded Iraq to oust Saddam Hussein in March 2003, American support continued for the war effort. That support began to wane when the 2,000th American soldier was killed in October 2005.[19] By the end of the Bush administration, the public seemed to have had it with the war, and public support of the Bush program plummeted.

5. **People have more opinions and are able to form opinions more easily on goals than on methods to reach those goals.** For example, few questioned the need for a new U.S. Department of Homeland Security to protect the land within our borders from terrorism. However, the organization, components, and functions of that department were the subject of continued debate and criticism, reaching its apex in the wake of Hurricane Katrina in 2005.

6. **By and large, if people in a democracy are provided with educational opportunities and ready access to information, public opinion reveals a hardheaded common sense.** In the weeks and months following the attacks of September 11, as Americans became more enlightened about the implications and threats of terrorism within the United States, the administration's strategy of continuous communication helped solidify public opinion.[20] In 2006, with opposition to the war mounting, President Bush launched a renewed campaign to inform the American public about what was happening in Iraq.[21] But again, as progress waxed and waned and American troops were made to serve extended tours in a long, drawn-out conflict, public opinion in 2008 as the Bush years ended had grown decidedly negative relative to Iraq.

Polishing the Corporate Image

Most organizations today and the people who manage them are extremely sensitive to the way they are perceived by their critical publics. This represents a dramatic change in corporate attitude from years past. Less than two decades ago, only the most enlightened companies dared to maintain anything but a low profile. Management, frankly, was reluctant to step out publicly *to stand up for what it stood for.*

Today, however, organizations—particularly large ones—have little choice but to go public. The accounting and corporate scandals that continued into 2006 threatened the confidence of the American capitalistic system. The credit crisis of 2008, which triggered rampant rumors that, in turn, triggered the demise of venerable companies like Bear Stearns, Washington Mutual and Lehman Brothers, was yet another reminder that smart companies and their leaders simply couldn't "hide" any longer from public scrutiny.

- In the winter of 2005, when oil costs and higher gas prices infuriated Americans, oil companies like Chevron got out in front by discussing conservation in public relations programs and ads.

- In 2008, with the price of oil skyrocketing, ExxonMobil faced criticism from shareholders, including heirs of Standard Oil Company founder, John D. Rockefeller.[22] Exxon responded with a far-reaching program, addressing the controversial area of climate change (Figure 4-4).

- In 2005, when Hank Greenberg, the powerful chairman of the world's largest insurance company, American International Group, was ousted amid probes of improper accounting, he publicly went after his accuser, politically ambitious New York Attorney General Eliot Spitzer, and enlisted other opinion leaders in a full-court public relations blitz to win public opinion.[23] Alas for Mr. Greenberg, Attorney General Spitzer won out, and the former AIG CEO lost the public opinion battle, until . . .

- Three years later, now New York State Governor Spitzer was forced to resign after it was revealed that he had paid for prostitutes (which is illegal), and may have even transported them across state lines (which is also illegal). Mr. Spitzer was forced to resign as governor, and Hank Greenberg shed no tears.

The point is that most organizations and individuals in the spotlight today understand, first, that credibility is a fragile commodity, and second, to maintain and

FIGURE 4-4 Setting the public opinion agenda. In 2008, Exxon Mobil answered its critics with a comprehensive public issues advertising campaign that talked about a more energy efficient future. (Courtesy of ExxonMobil)

improve public support they must operate with the "implicit trust" of the public. That means that for a corporation in the 21st century, winning favorable public opinion isn't an option—it's a necessity, essential for continued long-term success.

Managing Reputation

For an organization or an individual concerned about public opinion, what it comes down to is managing reputation. Reputation is gained by what one *does,* not by what one *says.* Reputation is present throughout our lives. It's how we choose business partners, which dentist or mechanic to visit, the stores we frequent, the neighborhood we live in, and the friends we keep. In recent years, *reputation management* has become a buzzword in public relations and in the broader society. At the start of the century, the term was little known. Today, a Google search on "reputation management" produces nearly four million results.

Many public relations firms have introduced reputation management divisions, and some have even billed themselves as being in the business of "relationship management." Generally defined, relationship management aligns communications with an organization's character and action. It creates recognition, credibility, and trust among key constituents. It stays sensitive to its conduct in public with customers and in private with employees. It understands its responsibilities to the broader society and is empathetic to society's needs.

While reputation itself may be difficult to measure, its value to an organization or an individual is indisputable.[24] And it's also indisputable that "managing" reputation is a front-line responsibility of public relations.

Talking Points   Winning Reputation . . .

How do you measure reputation?

Each year, survey firm Harris Interactive polls consumers on what companies they feel have the highest reputation.

Harris asks respondents to rank organizations on six primary measures of reputation: (1) emotional appeal, (2) financial performance, (3) products and services, (4) vision and leadership, (5) workplace environment, and (6) social responsibility.

Other characteristics, such as ethics and sincerity of corporate communications, were also probed. Not surprisingly, the companies known for candor and communications ranked best and those embroiled in scandal ranked worst.

Here are the top and bottom 10 companies for 2007. (Note the lagging auto, cable, and oil companies, some of which may no longer be around as you read this book.)

Top 10

1. Google
2. Johnson & Johnson
3. Intel Corporation
4. General Mills
5. Kraft Foods Inc.
6. Berkshire Hathaway Inc.
7. 3M Company
8. The Coca-Cola Company
9. Honda Motor Co.
10. Microsoft Corporation

Bottom 10

51. Daimler Chrysler
52. General Motors Corporation
53. ChevronTexaco Corporation
54. Ford Motor Company
55. Sprint Corporation
56. Comcast Corporation
57. ExxonMobil Corporation
58. Northwest Airlines
59. Citgo Oil
60. Halliburton Company

For further information, see "Seventy-One Percent of Consumers Say the Reputation of Corporate America Is 'Poor', But Consumers Will Buy, Recommend and Invest in Companies that Concentrate on Building Their Corporate Reputation," Harris Interactive (June 23, 2008).

Talking Points ... Losing Reputation

On the other hand, there was edgy teenage retailer Abercrombie & Fitch.

A&F, famous for its provocative Christmas Calendar (Figure 4-5) and sexy ads, in the spring of 2008 donated $10 million to a Columbus, Ohio children's hospital for a new emergency department.

Nothing wrong with that.

But when the company asked for the new department to be named in its honor, the hospital was challenged by a Boston-based advocacy group, objecting to the sponsor's *"highly sexualized images and clothing which objectifies and demeans teens and preteens."* The Campaign for a Commercial-Free Childhood exhorted the hospital not to name the emergency room for Abercrombie & Fitch. (But they didn't say, *"Give the money back!"*)

The hospital, obviously uncomfortable with the public opinion uproar, smartly said it wouldn't decide on the name until the department opened in 2012. (Hoping, one assumes, that the issue might evaporate by then.)

FIGURE 4-5 Emergency treatment. When edgy teen retailer Abercrombie & Fitch donated $10 million for a new emergency department at a children's hospital, an advocacy group charged it would be indecent to name the new facility in the sponsor's honor. (Photo: Newscom)

*For further information, see Stuart Elliott, "When a Corporate Donation Raises Protests," *New York Times* (March 12, 2008).

Last Word

Influencing public opinion remains at the heart of professional public relations work. Public opinion is a powerful force that can impact the earnings of corporations through such actions as product boycotts, union strikes, and the misdeeds of key executives; influence government legislation through campaign support, product recalls, and letters and emails from constituents; and even unify a nation through calls to action by strong and committed leaders.

In order to influence public opinion, public relations professionals must anticipate trends in our society. At the start of the 21st century, one self-styled prognosticator, John Naisbitt, predicted the new directions that would influence American lives in the near future. Among them were the following:

- Inflation and interest rates will be held in check.
- There will be a shift from welfare to workfare.
- There will be a shift from public housing to home ownership.
- There will be a shift from sports to the arts as the primary leisure preference.
- Consumers will demand more customized products.
- The media will amplify bad economic news.
- The rise of the Pacific Rim will be seen in terms of economic dominance.

- Asia will add 80 million more people.
- CEOs in a global economy will become more important and better known than political figures.[25]

With the first decade of the century nearly over, a number of Nesbitt's "megatrends" appear to be coming to pass. Public relations professionals need to take note of these and other trends in gauging how public opinion will impact their organizations. They also should consider what the late public relations counselor Philip Lesly once pointed out: "The real problems faced by business today are in the outside world of intangibles and public attitudes."[26]

To keep ahead of these intangibles, public attitudes, and kernels of future public opinion, managements will turn increasingly for guidance to professional public relations practitioners.

Discussion Starters

1. What is the relationship between public relations and public opinion?
2. What are attitudes, and on what characteristics are they based?
3. How are attitudes influenced?
4. What is Maslow's hierarchy of needs?
5. What is the theory of cognitive dissonance?
6. How difficult is it to change a person's behavior?
7. What are several key public opinion laws, according to Cantril?
8. What kinds of evidence persuade people?
9. What are the elements involved in managing reputation?
10. In assessing the list of best and worst companies in terms of reputation, what specific characteristics influence these rankings?

Top of the Shelf   The Wall Street Journal, wsj.com / The New York Times, nytimes.com

Public relations can be practiced only by understanding public opinion, and two of the most prominent daily forums in which to study it are *The New York Times* and *The Wall Street Journal*.

Despite the 21st-century problems of newspapers, these two most venerable news organizations reveal the diverse views of pundits, politicians, and plain people. The *Times* is arguably the primary source of printed news in the world. The *Journal,* likewise, is the primary printed source of the world's business and investment news—an area of increasingly dominant importance.

Both papers, through their opinion pages and in-depth stories, express the attitudes of leaders in politics, business, science, education, journalism, and the arts, on topics ranging from abortion rights to genetic engineering to race relations. Occasionally, the *Times* and the *Journal* supplement their usual coverage with public opinion polls to gauge attitudes and beliefs on particularly hot issues.

It may, indeed, be the Internet age, but if you really want to know what's going on in the world and be a lot more knowledgeable than most of those with whom you work, read *The New York Times* and *The Wall Street Journal* every day. You can even do it online. Sure, the news is often infuriating, but it's also a joy to know more about what's going on than virtually anyone else with whom you work.

The *Times* and the *Journal* are clearly the most important reference works any public relations professional can read (even including this book!).

Case Study   The Rise and Fall and Rise of Queen Martha

In the winter of 2001, few Americans could dispute that Martha Stewart was "Queen of the Kitchen." Few Americans enjoyed more robust acclaim in terms of public opinion.

The tough-willed, hot-tempered, blunt-speaking perfectionist had morphed from a modest upbringing to become the undisputed, multimillionaire-closing-in-on-billionaire, domestic doyenne—the homemaker's homemaker, arbiter of all things tasteful in the home, numero uno in all matters of domesticity.

Her parents, Martha and Edward Kostyra, were Polish Americans, her mother a school teacher and her father a pharmaceutical salesman, who raised their five children in Nutley, New Jersey. Her mother taught young Martha cooking and baking and sewing, and her father taught her how to garden. That was just the start the serious-minded model student needed. After a brief fling in the stock brokerage business and a failed marriage, Stewart began to build an empire that would become the stuff of legends.

- She co-authored a book called *Entertaining,* which became an instant best seller.
- She followed that with lucrative publishing ventures, producing videotapes, dinner-music CDs, television specials, and dozens of books on matters of domesticity—from hors d'oeuvres to pies, from weddings to Christmas, from gardening to restoring old houses.
- She appeared regularly on NBC's *Today Show,* becoming a household name.
- She became a board member of the New York Stock Exchange.
- She delivered lectures for $10,000 a pop and charged eager attendees $900 a head to attend seminars at her farm.
- She signed an advertising/consulting contract with department chain Kmart for $5 million.
- She presided over a long-running syndicated television show, *Martha Stewart Living.*
- She parlayed the program into the creation of multimillion-dollar company Martha Stewart Living Omnimedia (MSO), with branches in publishing, merchandising, and Internet/direct commerce, selling products in eight discrete categories.

Without exaggeration, Stewart was Queen of the Kitchen, until one day when it all came tumbling down.

Selling in the Nick of Time

In December 2001, Stewart sold nearly 4,000 shares of biotech company ImClone Systems stock under mysterious circumstances. The company was run by Stewart's pal Samuel Waksal, who had presided over a rapid stock price ascension, due principally to the company's promising cancer-fighting drug, Erbitux, which had been submitted for approval to the Food and Drug Administration (FDA).

So with everything looking good for the company, it was surprising on December 27 that Stewart decided suddenly to unload all her shares at a $60 price. The next day, the case got even curiouser: On December 28, the FDA rejected ImClone's application for Erbitux. The stock cratered. But Stewart, having presciently decided to sell the day before, avoided a $51,000 loss.

Serendipity perhaps?

The government didn't think so.

Charges of Insider Trading

Stewart may have been smart, but according to the U.S. attorney for the Southern District of New York, she was not smart enough to know about the FDA's timing in rejecting Erbitux. Rather, argued the government, Stewart had learned about the FDA's intention from her stockbroker. The stockbroker had received an urgent call from Waksal, then relayed the information to Stewart, who immediately decided to sell.

If true, Stewart had acted on classic insider information, a federal crime, which gives privileged investors an unfair advantage over all other shareholders. Indeed, prosecutors argued that this was precisely what had happened and that Stewart and her stockbroker were both guilty of illegally acting on insider information. Accordingly, in June 2003, the U.S. Attorney formally indicted both of them.

Stewart's attorneys argued that this was not the case at all. Stewart, they said, had always had a "plan" to sell her stock when it reached the $60 level.

After Waksal was sentenced to seven years in prison and family members he had tipped off were fined, attention turned to Stewart. The question was: Would she come forward and acknowledge "mistakes," or would she hold firm and deny any impropriety?

Silence of the Diva

The answer, painfully revealed over the next excruciating two years, was that Stewart became the "silent diva." She said little to elaborate on the case, preferring instead to allow her attorneys to speak for her. In one celebrated appearance on the *CBS Morning Show,* Stewart defiantly cut cabbage while an exasperated host tried to get her to react to the charges against her.

Soon thereafter, Stewart's guest appearances on television became fewer and fewer. She stopped lecturing. Her ubiquitous Kmart ads ceased to appear. She resigned as chairwoman and CEO of MSO. Indeed, the woman who had seemed to be everywhere was now virtually out of sight.

In her place, a battery of lawyers negotiated with the Feds and argued with the judge to have her charges reduced. U.S. District Judge Miriam Cedarbaum, taking a page from the domestic doyenne herself, adamantly refused to throw out the charges.

Those who expected the typically feisty Stewart to come out fighting were sadly disappointed. In June 2003, Stewart unveiled a personal Web site on which she proclaimed her innocence and insisted she would fight to clear her name. But beyond those Web site notations, she remained tight-lipped. Meanwhile, in the vacuum of Stewart's silence, the Internet, cable television, and the public press were flooded with "experts" surmising on just what poor Martha Stewart had done to herself.

An Excruciating Trial

Stewart's trial began January 27, 2004, two full years after the alleged insider trading violation.

The trial was excruciating for Martha. For two months, she was forced to endure a phalanx of cameras greeting her in the morning for her arrival at the lower Manhattan courthouse and waiting for her each evening when the day's session was over (Figure 4-6). She said nothing, again relying on attorneys to

FIGURE 4-6 **Fall of a diva.** Grim-faced Martha Stewart is flanked by lawyers and court security after she was sentenced to five months in prison in July 2004. (Photo: Newscom)

explain to the media exactly what went on that day in court. As her lawyers spoke each night, a stone-faced Stewart would stare straight ahead. Meanwhile, the share price of her company's stock plummeted, and her reputation wasn't far behind.

On March 5, 2004, with the world waiting breathlessly for the verdict, Stewart was found guilty on all four counts of obstructing justice and lying to federal investigators. Her broker was also found guilty, and both faced prison time.

About an hour after the verdict was read, Stewart—radiant as ever with a fur around her neck, a black overcoat, and a tasteful, brown leather bag at her side—strode poker-faced down the stairs of the courthouse, accompanied by her lawyers. She did not respond to questions shouted at her by reporters. Instead, the following statement was posted on her Web site:

Dear Friends,
I am obviously distressed by the jury's verdict but I take comfort in knowing that I have done nothing wrong and that I have the enduring support of my family and friends.

Her lawyers vowed to appeal.

Four months later, after losing her job, her company, close to $500,000 in stock market wealth, and her reputation, Martha Stewart lost her freedom. She was sentenced to five months in prison and two years' probation.

Still, Stewart was defiant, telling a television interviewer that "many, many good people have gone to prison" and comparing herself to Nelson Mandela, South Africa's persecuted anti-apartheid hero. And outside the courthouse, after her sentencing, an unrepentant Stewart vowed, "I'll be back."

Winter at Camp Cupcake

Stewart's attorneys, taking the lead from their defiant client, appealed her conviction and vowed to spare her hard time. But suddenly, in mid-September 2004, Stewart had a change of heart.

Shocking her supporters, the domestic doyenne announced that she would not wait for the verdict on her appeal and rather wished to begin serving her five-month prison sentence early "to put this nightmare behind me, both personally and professionally."

And so on October 8, 2004, Stewart, 63 and a multimillionaire, slipped into the women's federal prison in Alderson, West Virginia,

to join petty thieves and embezzlers and drug offenders, all performing day labor at rates between 12 and 40 cents an hour.

And wonder of wonder, Stewart was an ideal prisoner. Reports from "Camp Cupcake," as it was labeled, were glowing in their praise of Stewart.

- She praised her guards, the warden, and fellow prisoners.
- She wrote passionately about the unfairness of federal sentencing guidelines, which shackled many of those whom she met behind the walls.
- She even participated in prison events—failing to win the "prison bakeoff."

On Thursday, March 3, 2005, when Stewart was sprung from the slammer to return to her 153-acre Westchester Estate, she was met with cameras, microphones, and a hero's welcome (Figure 4-7).

Comeback Kid

It was a new Martha Stewart who emerged from prison. She was more relaxed, more open, and more available to questioners. She also was very much back in business.

- She signed deals to begin two new television shows—one a daytime lifestyles show, the other a spinoff of Donald Trump's *The Apprentice.*
- She signed a $30 million deal for a Sirius satellite radio program.
- She signed a lucrative book deal to produce a Martha memoir, discussing her time in prison.

By the winter of 2005, Stewart was back with a vengeance. She still hadn't acknowledged—even after her conviction and subsequent jail time—that she had done anything "wrong." But there would be ample opportunity for an admission, as Martha momentum—"Martha Mo"—began to build and the "queen" set out to retake her throne.

On January 6, 2006, the United States Court of Appeals for the Second Circuit rejected the arguments of Stewart's lawyers and upheld her conviction.

By the summer of 2008, Martha Stewart was back on television and prominent once again. But the layoff in prison had clearly taken its toll. While Martha was gone, a number of other homemaking

heroines—led by Dunkin' Donuts own terrorist-scarf-wearing Rachel Ray—had moved eagerly to supplant her.

And while it was clear that Martha Stewart would never again want for money, fame, or power, it was also safe to assume that in terms of public opinion, she would never get back to where she had been prior to taking her fatal fall.

Questions

1. How would you characterize Martha Stewart's initial public relations response to the charges against her?

2. What key public relations principle did Martha Stewart violate?

3. Had you been advising her, what public relations strategy and tactics would you have recommended? How "vocal" should she have been?

4. How important, from a public relations perspective, was her decision to go to jail early?

5. What public relations strategy should Stewart adopt now?

6. Should she acknowledge that she made mistakes?

FIGURE 4-7 **Lemonade out of lemons.** A relieved Martha Stewart, back at her New York estate after being released from prison in March 2005, shows reporters the lemons grown in her hothouse as she commences her comeback.
(Photo: Getty Images, Inc.–Getty News)

For further information, see Michael Barbaro, "Court Rejects Appeal by Martha Stewart," *New York Times* (January 7, 2006): C3; Krysten Crawford, "Martha: I Cheated No One," *CNN Money* (July 20, 2004); Krysten Crawford, "Martha, Out and About," (March 4, 2005); Gene Healy, "Lessons of Martha Stewart Case," *Cato Institute* (July 16, 2004); "Martha Stewart Wants to Enter Prison Early," *CBC News* (September 16, 2004); Brooke A. Masters, "Stewart Begins Prison Term," *Washington Post* (October 9, 2004): EO1; Fraser P. Seitel, "Martha's Final PR Hurdle," http://www.odwyerpr.com (March 6, 2005); Fraser P. Seitel, "Martha Finally Gets PR Religion," (August 26, 2005); "Stewart Convicted on All Charges," *CNN Money* (March 5, 2004); "Timeline of Martha Stewart Scandal," *Associated Press,* Copyright 2005.

From the Top   An Interview with Harvey Greisman

Harvey W. Greisman is senior vice president and group executive, worldwide communications, for MasterCard Worldwide, responsible for communications consulting support for customers, reputation and issues management, media and influencer relations, executive and employee transformational communications, public policy support and knowledge leadership, and corporate philanthropy. A former executive at IBM and GTE Corporation, Mr. Greisman co-authored "Beyond Vietnam: Public Opinion and Foreign Policy" with Justice Arthur J. Goldberg et al., which had significant impact on public policy.

How important is "reputation" for a company today?
If reputation isn't everything, it's the closest thing to it. How a company is perceived—such as trustworthy or not, easy to do business or not, well managed or not, a good investment or not, a good corporate citizen or not—can affect your business success with all the key stakeholders. After all, so many

products and services are commodity-like, it's the reputation factors that make a difference in the buying decision.

How can a communications department help build reputation?
Reputation is how you are perceived by others. The best thing to do is assess how a cross-section of senior management and the board want the company to be perceived, and then do a professional survey assessment of how your critical stakeholders actually do perceive you. Then, the communications department can note where the gaps are and work with various parts of the company to close the gaps. PR alone cannot close perception gaps! The company must take the appropriate business actions first. Sometimes that means quality improvement, stepped up customer service, etc., Then the PR department can tell that story of improved service . . . and also make sure that areas of the company that are capable of meeting perceptions are better known and understood.

The 21st-century PR team will employ both traditional and social media, and reach out to a wide variety of influencers and stakeholders with that messaging.

What is the optimal organization for a communications department today?
As lean and as technologically competent and as holistic in skill sets and worldviews as possible. Just focusing on the latter two, I believe the day of the niche PR person is over. The department should be composed of people who can manage a variety of disciplines including internal and external communications, financial and product communications, etc. In a transparent world and corporate environment, what's internal becomes external very quickly, and vice versa. I also believe that we should be looking for much broader general skills, such as staff members with studies in psychology, cultural geography, and economics. And they need a global mindset, if not experience.

How should a communications group accommodate social media?
Social media isn't an end to itself, it is a means for accomplishing communications objectives that lend themselves to social media platforms. This will vary depending on the stakeholders that need to be reached. It is worth noting that more and more key stakeholder groups rely on this New Media for information and interaction. Therefore, social media are more and more staples of a 21st century communications department.

How important is the CEO in building positive public opinion for a company?
Very important. The CEO represents the company to its most important stakeholders. But the CEO can't do it alone. As a representative of the company, it is the company's values, products, quality standards, etc., that he/she represents. The CEO and the company are inextricably intertwined.

How important is it for the communications department to report to the CEO?
The most important factor is "access" to the CEO, C-suite, and other centers of power in the corporation, especially in decision-making forums. Reporting directly into the centers of power is usually a big plus, but it does not have to be a fatal flaw if that's not the case.

Why use a public relations agency?
Strategically outsourcing some degree of work to an agency can be more productive, efficient, and less costly than doing everything in-house. These are assets that can be employed at will, fill special talent, and extend the reach of one's own staff when necessary. The most important reason why I hire agency resources is to give me alternative opinions and to keep me current with all the trends I can't stay on top of.

Public Relations Library

Alsop, Ron J., *The 18 Immutable Laws of Corporate Reputation: Creating, Protecting, and Repairing Your Most Valuable Asset*. New York: Free Press, 2004. A *Wall Street Journal* veteran's step-by-step guide to winning a positive reputation and communicating it.

Bloomgarden, Kathy. *Trust: The Secret Weapon of Effective Business Leaders*. New York, NY: St. Martins Press, 2007. Ruder Finn's co-CEO traces a road map for corporations to build support among their most important publics.

Kotler, Philip, and Nancy Lee. *Corporate Social Responsibility: Doing the Most Good for Your Company and Your Cause*. Hoboken, NJ: John Wiley & Sons, 2005.

Manheim, Jarol B. *Biz-War and the Out-of-Power Elites: The Progressive-Left Attack on the Corporation*. Mahwah, NJ: Lawrence Erlbaum Associates, 2004. What certain critics in society would like public opinion to resemble.

Murray, Allan. *Revolt in the Boardroom*. New York, NY: Harpercollins, 2007. A *Wall Street Journal* editor traces reasons why the "reputations" of corporations are prone to suffering in a post-Enron world.

Shapiro, Cynthia. *Corporate Confidential: 50 Secrets Your Company Doesn't Want You to Know—and What to Do About Them*. New York: St. Martin's Press, 2005. A human resources executive opens the curtain on the real truth about such issues as free corporate speech, age discrimination, and being too smart in a corporation.

www.mediainfo.com. *Editor & Publisher* magazine's database offers access to more than 11,000 news Web sites.

www.prnewswire.com. Public Relations Newswire. Features corporate press releases and backgrounders, with a link to Expert Contacts.

www.publicagenda.org. Public Agenda Online. "The inside source for public opinion and policy analysis."

Chapter 5

Management

General Electric is a worldwide colossus, one of the globe's great companies.

But boy did it have problems in the spring of 2008.

Even though the company continued to perform well, its stock price floundered. CEO Jeffrey R. Immelt tried everything—stock buybacks, dividend increases, audio and video messages on the GE Web site—but nothing worked.

So in March 2008, Mr. Immelt decided to reach out and touch his two million individual shareholders through the inherent interactivity of the Internet (see Figure 5-1). GE solicited shareholder questions through the Internet, and CEO Immelt answered some of the 6,000 submitted in a Web cast, moderated by two financial journalists.[1]

If nothing else (alas, the stock didn't move), the GE Web cast indicated that management had, indeed, discovered the benefits of using social media for public relations purposes.

It has been said that the only difference between the public relations director and the CEO is that the latter gets paid more.

In many ways, that's quite true. The CEO, after all, is the firm's top manager, responsible for, in addition to setting strategy and framing policy, serving as the organization's chief spokesperson, corporate booster, and reputation defender—not at all unlike the responsibilities assigned the public relations professional.

To be effective—and respected—in his or her job, the public relations professional in the 21st century must understand management. That means that public relations people must master knowledge of such management functions as planning, budgeting,

FIGURE 5-1 Global reach. General Electric CEO Jeff Immelt tried a Web cast in 2008 to try to convince shareholders around the world to buy more GE stock. (Photo: Newscom)

objective setting, and how top management thinks and operates. That's what this chapter discusses.

It also deals with the differences between working as a staff public relations practitioner inside a corporation, nonprofit, or other organization, where the job is to support management in achieving its objectives, and working as a professional in a public relations agency, where the job is to contribute to the revenue generation of the company. Finally, it provides some feel of what to expect in terms of income in public relations.

Management Process of Public Relations

Like other management processes, professional public relations work emanates from clear strategies and bottom-line objectives that flow into specific tactics, each with its own budget, timetable, and allocation of resources. Stated another way, public relations today is much more a planned, persuasive social managerial science than a knee-jerk, damage-control reaction to sudden flare-ups.

Don't get me wrong. As we will learn later, the public relations professionals who have the most organizational clout and get paid the most are those who demonstrate the ability to perform in a crisis. Thinking "on your feet" is very much a coveted ability in the practice of public relations. But so, too, is the ability to think strategically and plan methodically to help change attitudes, crystallize opinions, and accomplish the organization's overall goals.

Managers insist on *results,* so the best public relations programs can be measured in terms of achieving results in building the key relationships on which the organization depends. The relevance of public relations people in the eyes of top management depends largely on the contribution they make to the management process of the organization.

With nearly a century under its belt, the practice of public relations has developed its own theoretical framework as a management system. According to communications professors James Grunig and Todd Hunt, public relations managers perform what organizational theorists call a *boundary* role: They function at the edge of an organization as a liaison between the organization and its external and internal publics. In other words, public relations managers have one foot inside the organization and one outside. Often this unique position is not only lonely but also precarious.

As boundary managers, public relations people support their colleagues by helping them communicate across organizational lines both within and outside the organization. In this way, public relations professionals also become systems managers, knowledgeable about and able to deal with the complex relationships inherent in the organization.[2]

Top managers are forced to think strategically about reaching their goals. So, too, should public relations professionals think in terms of the strategic process element of their own roles. Specifically, they must constantly ask, in relation to their departments, functions, and assignments:

- What are we attempting to achieve, and where are we going in that pursuit?
- What is the nature of the environment in which we must operate?
- Who are the key audiences we must convince in the process?
- How will we get to where we want to be?

It is this procedural mind-set—directed at communicating key messages to realize desired objectives to priority publics—that makes the public relations professional a key adviser to top management.

Reporting to Top Management

The public relations function, by definition, must report to top management.

If public relations, as noted in Chapter 1, is truly to be the "interpreter" for management philosophy, policy, and programs, then the public relations director should report to the CEO.

In many organizations, this reporting relationship is not the case. Public relations is often subordinated to advertising, marketing, legal, or human resources. Whereas marketing and advertising promote the product, public relations promotes the entire organization. Therefore, if the public relations chief reports to the director of marketing or advertising, the job mistakenly becomes one of promoting specific products rather than one of promoting the entire organization.

For the public relations function to be valuable to management, it must remain independent, credible, and objective. This also mandates that public relations professionals have not only communication competence but also an intimate knowledge of the organization's business. Without the latter, according to research, public relations professionals are much less effective as top-management advisers.[3]

Public relations should be the *corporate conscience*. An organization's public relations professionals should enjoy enough autonomy to deal openly and honestly with management. If an idea doesn't make sense, if a product is flawed, if the general institutional wisdom is wrong, it is the duty of the public relations professional to challenge the consensus. As Warren Buffet, the legendary CEO of Berkshire Hathaway, put it, "We can afford to lose money—even a lot of money. But we cannot afford to lose reputation—even a shred of reputation."[4]

This is not to say that advertising, marketing, and all other disciplines shouldn't enjoy a close partnership with public relations. Clearly, they must. All disciplines must work to maintain their own independence while building long-term, mutually beneficial relationships for the good of the organization. However, public relations should never shirk its overriding responsibility to enhance the organization's credibility by ensuring that corporate actions are in the public interest.

To perform that function effectively, it needs to report directly to top management, and ultimately to the CEO.

Conceptualizing the Public Relations Plan

Strategic planning for public relations is an essential part of management. Planning is critical not only to know where a particular campaign is headed but also to win the support of top management. Indeed, one of the most frequent complaints about public relations is that it is too much a "seat-of-the-pants" activity, impossible to plan and difficult to measure. Management's perspective is, "How do we know the public relations group will deliver and fully leverage the resources they're asking for?" They must see a plan.[5] With proper planning, public relations professionals can indeed defend and account for their actions.

Before organizing for public relations work, practitioners must consider objectives and strategies, planning and budgets, and research and evaluation. The broad environment in which the organization operates must dictate the overall business objectives. These, in turn, dictate specific public relations objectives and strategies. Once these have been defined, the task of organizing for a public relations program should flow naturally.

Environment
└──▶ Business objectives
     └──▶ Public relations objectives and strategies
          └──▶ Public relations programs

Setting objectives, formulating strategies, and planning are essential if the public relations function is to be considered equal in stature to other management processes. Traditionally, the public relations management process involves four steps:

1. **Defining the problem or opportunity.** This requires researching current attitudes and opinions about the issue, product, candidate, or company in question and determining the essence of the problem.
2. **Programming.** This is the formal planning stage, which addresses key constituent publics, strategies, tactics, and goals.

3. **Action.** This is the communications phase, when the program is implemented.

4. **Evaluation.** The final step in the process is the assessment of what worked, what didn't, and how to improve in the future.[6]

Each of these four process steps is important. Most essential is starting with a firm base of research and a solid foundation of planning.

All planning requires thinking. Planning a short-term public relations program to promote a new service may require less thought and time than planning a long-term campaign to win support for a public policy issue. However, in each case, the public relations plan must include clear-cut objectives to achieve organizational goals, targeted strategies to reach those objectives, specific tactics to implement the strategies, and measurement methods to determine whether the tactics worked.

PR Ethics

Mini-Case   Perils of an Out-of-the-Shadows PR CEO

Traditionally, public relations advisors have been "the power behind the throne."

Their role is to stay in the shadows, counseling the client on the best public course. Conversely, when the public relations advisor becomes the focus of attention, bad things are sure to happen.

That's precisely what occurred in the spring of 2008, when Democratic presidential primary candidate Hillary Clinton's chief advisor, Mark Penn, became a lightning rod for controversy. Penn, who headed Clinton's counselors even while he maintained his "day job" as CEO of the Burson-Marsteller public relations counseling firm, suddenly found himself in the media soup when his two roles came into conflict.

Specifically, as the primary campaign reached a particularly difficult juncture, *The Wall Street Journal* reported that Penn, as Burson CEO, had met with officials of the Colombian government, which had hired the firm to help it pass a proposed free-trade pact. This free-trade pact was vehemently opposed by candidate Clinton.

That's all Penn's enemies in the Clinton camp needed to hear (Every political campaign is filled with back-biting snakes!). Penn was put on the defensive, forced to face the press (see Figure 5-2) to explain his ethical

FIGURE 5-2 One more thing before I go. Burson-Marsteller CEO Mark Penn was forced to face the media and step down as an advisor to Hillary Clinton in 2008, when he was accused of conflict of interest in serving both Burson and the candidate. (Photo: Newscom)

lapse, and defended by WPP Group CEO Martin Sorrell, whose holding company owned Burson (and not unimportant, profited handsomely from the Penn affiliation with Clinton).

Ultimately, Mark Penn was demoted from his lofty campaign position—proving that in public relations, one head is better than two.*

Questions

1. What could Mark Penn have done to avoid conflict-of-interest contentions in serving Hillary Clinton?

2. What is the potential danger of heading a public relations firm and representing a particular political candidate at the same time?

*For further information, see Michael Bush, "Mark Penn Gets Run Over on the Way to the White House," *Advertising Age* (April 7, 2008): 1; Burt Helm, "A Spinmeister in Need of Spin, " *Business Week* (April 21, 2008): 24; Fraser P. Seitel, "PR Lessons from the Perils of Penn," *O'Dwyer's PR Report* (May 2008): 43; and "Sorrell Sticks with Penn," *Jack O'Dwyer's Newsletter* (April 16, 2008).

Creating the Public Relations Plan

The public relations plan must be spelled out in writing. Its organization must answer management's concerns and questions about the campaign being recommended. Here's one way it might be organized and what it should answer.

1. **Executive summary**—an overview of the plan.
2. **Communication process**—how it works, for understanding and training purposes.
3. **Background**—mission statement, vision, values, events that led to the need for the plan.
4. **Situation analysis**—major issues and related facts the plan will deal with.
5. **Message statement**—the plan's major ideas and emerging themes, all of which look to the expected outcome.
6. **Audiences**—strategic constituencies related to the issues, listed in order of importance, with whom you wish to develop and maintain relationships.
7. **Key audience messages**—one- or two-sentence messages that you want to be understood by each key audience.
8. **Implementation**—issues, audiences, messages, media, timing, cost, expected outcomes, and method of evaluation—all neatly spelled out.
9. **Budget**—the plan's overall budget presented in the organization's accepted style.
10. **Monitoring and evaluation**—how the plan's results will be measured and evaluated against a previously set benchmark or desired outcome.[7]

A simpler, hypothetical five-part public relations plan for the fictional Fribbert's Frosty Frappacino might break down like this:

I. Situation

Our world is moving faster than ever before. Blackberries and cell phones have overtaken our every minute. Even leisure time activities have morphed into intensity—from power yoga to power lunch to the 20-minute workout. The coffee break has become passé. In short, the world desperately needs "to chill." And what better beverage to chill with than Fribbert's Frosty Frapp?

II. **Business Objectives**
- To increase Fribbert's Frosty Frapp market share nationally by 20 percent.
- To increase Fribbert's Frosty Frapp market share among young adults by 30 percent.
- To increase product recall of Fribbert's among all cold beverages by 25 percent.

III. **Public Relations Objectives**
- Tie coffee break time with the need to "chill" with Fribbert's Frosty Frapp.
- Generate buzz among younger workers to chill not with coffee but with Fribbert's Frosty Frapp.
- Instill the importance of "chillin'."

IV. **Strategies**
- Leverage a familiar concept—the coffee break—with a new approach—the Frapp chill.
- Spread the word about the Frosty Frapp chill.
- Commission original research to underscore the importance of chillin'.
- Recruit topic-specific experts to discuss chillin' and Frosty Frapp.

V. **Public Relations Program Elements**
- Fribbert's commissions survey of human resources professionals on the importance of short breaks during the day and associated increases in productivity. The survey will determine how a selection of leading companies handle the need for chillin' time among employees.
- Fribbert's launches national "Need to Chill" (NTC) program to introduce the ritual of "chillin' breaks" in workplaces across America. The NTC program will be led by a board composed of professionals in pertinent areas, such as a psychiatrist, a life coach, a relaxation expert, and a food expert.
- Fribbert's launches a viral email campaign across the nation to encourage recipients to sign a "petition" to appeal to Congress to make the Chillin' Break a federally mandated activity.
- Fribbert's announces a nationwide Chillin' Day, designating a moment in time when employees around the nation will be asked to "stop and chill."
- Advertising support is leveraged with Chillin' Day promotions, particularly on local radio.
- A Chillin' Day spokesperson is appointed, representative of what it means to be "cool and chillin'." Such "cool" personalities as LeBron James, Tiger Woods, Usher, and George Clooney will be considered.
- Local news hooks in key market areas are investigated to promote Fribbert's and chillin'.

The beauty of creating a plan like this is that it clearly specifies tactics against which objectives can be measured and evaluated. In devising the public relations plan along these lines, an organization is assured that its public relations programs will reinforce and complement its overall business goals.

Activating the Public Relations Campaign

Any public relations campaign puts all of the aspects of public relations planning—objectives, strategies, research, budgeting, tactics, and evaluation—into one cohesive framework. The plan specifies a series of *what's* to be done and *how* to get them done—whatever is necessary to reach the objectives.

Every aspect of the public relations plan should be designed to be meaningful and valuable to the organization. The four-part skeleton of a typical public relations campaign plan resembles the following:

1. **Backgrounding the problem.** This is the so-called situation analysis, background, or case statement that specifies the major aims of the campaign. It can be a general statement that refers to audiences, known research, the organization's positions, history, and the obstacles faced in reaching the desired goal. A public relations planner should divide the overriding goal into several subordinate objectives, which are the *what's* to be accomplished.

2. **Preparing the proposal.** The second stage of the campaign plan sketches broad approaches to solve the problem at hand. As in the Fribbert's hypothetical, it outlines the strategies—the *hows*—and the public relations tools to be used to fulfill the objectives. The elements of the public relations proposal may vary, depending on the subject matter, but generally include the following:

   ■ Situational analysis—description of the challenge as it currently exists, including background on how the situation reached its present state.

   ■ Scope of assignment—description of the nature of the assignment: what the public relations program will attempt to do.

   ■ Target audiences—specific targets identified and divided into manageable groups.

   ■ Research methods—specific research approach to be used.

   ■ Key messages—specific selected appeals: What do we want to tell our audiences? How do we want them to feel about us? What do we want them to do?

   ■ Communications vehicles—tactical communications devices to be used.

   ■ Project team—key players who will participate in the program.

   ■ Timing and fees—a timetable with proposed costs identified.

   The specific elements of any proposal depend on the unique nature of the program itself. When an outside supplier submits a proposal, additional elements—such as cancellation clauses, confidentiality of work, and references—should also be included.

3. **Implementing the plan.** The third stage of a campaign plan details operating tactics. It may also contain a time chart specifying when each action will take place. Specific activities are defined, people are assigned to them, and deadlines are established. This stage forms the guts of the campaign plan.

4. **Evaluating the campaign.** To find out whether the plan worked, evaluation methods should be spelled out here.

   ■ Did we implement the activities we proposed?

   ■ Did we receive appropriate public recognition for our efforts?

   ■ Did attitudes change—among the community, customers, management—as a result of our programs?

   Pretesting and posttesting of audience attitudes, quantitative analysis of event attendance, content analysis of media success, surveys, sales figures, staff reports, letters to management, and feedback from others—the specific method of evaluative testing is up to the practitioner. But the inclusion of a mechanism for evaluation is imperative in terms of verifying results based on shifts in public opinion or actions taken to benefit an organization and its goals.[8]

Finally, although planning the public relations campaign is important, planning must never become an end in itself. The fact is that no matter how important planning may be, public relations is still assessed principally in terms of its action, performance, and practice.

Setting Public Relations Objectives

An organization's goals must define what its public relations goals will be, and the only good goals are ones that can be measured. Public relations objectives and the strategies that flow from them must achieve results. As the baseball pitcher Johnny Sain used to say, "Nobody wants to hear about the labor pains, but everyone wants to see the baby."

So, too, must public relations people think strategically. Strategies are the most crucial decisions of a public relations campaign. They answer the general question *How will we manage our resources to achieve our goals?* The specific answers then become the public relations tactics used to implement the strategies. Ideally, strategies and tactics should profit from pretesting.

As for objectives, good ones stand up to the following questions:

- Do they clearly describe the end result expected?
- Are they understandable to everyone in the organization?
- Do they list a firm completion date?
- Are they realistic, attainable, and measurable?
- Are they consistent with management's objectives?

Increasingly, public relations professionals are managing by objectives (MBO) and by results (MBR) to help quantify the value of public relations in an organization. The two questions most frequently asked by general managers of public relations practitioners are *How can we measure public relations results?* and *How do we know whether the public relations program is making progress?* MBO can provide public relations professionals with a powerful source of feedback. MBO and MBR tie public relations results to management's predetermined objectives in terms of audiences, messages, and media. Even though procedures for implementing MBO programs differ, most programs share four points:

1. Specification of the organization's goals, with objective measures of the organization's performance
2. Conferences between the superior and the subordinate to agree on achievable goals
3. Agreement between the superior and the subordinate on objectives consistent with the organization's goals
4. Periodic reviews by the superior and the subordinate to assess progress toward achieving the goals

Again, the key is to tie public relations goals to the goals of the organization and then to manage progress toward achieving those goals. The goals themselves should be clearly defined and specific, practical and attainable, and measurable.

The key to using MBO effectively in public relations work can be broken down into seven critical steps:

1. Defining the nature and mission of the work
2. Determining key result areas in terms of time, effort, and personnel
3. Identifying measurable factors on which objectives can be set
4. Setting objectives or determining results to be achieved
5. Preparing tactical plans to achieve specific objectives, including:
   - Programming to establish a sequence of actions to follow
   - Scheduling to set time requirements for each step
   - Budgeting to assign the resources required to reach the goals
   - Fixing individual accountability for the accomplishment of the objectives
   - Reviewing and reconciling through a testing procedure to track progress
6. Establishing rules and regulations to follow
7. Establishing procedures to handle the work[9]

Budgeting for Public Relations

Like any other business activity, public relations programs must be based on sound budgeting. After identifying objectives and strategies, the public relations professional must detail the particular tactics that will help achieve those objectives. No organization can spend indiscriminately. Without a realistic budget, no organization can succeed. Likewise, public relations activities must be disciplined by budgetary realities.

In public relations agencies responsible for producing revenue, *functional budgeting* is the rule; that is, dollars for staff, resources, activities, and so on are linked to specific revenue-generating activities. Employees are required to turn in time sheets detailing hours worked in behalf of specific clients. In organizations where public relations is a "staff" activity and not responsible for revenue generation, *administrative budgeting* is the rule; that is, budget dollars are assigned generally against the department's allocation for staff and expenses.

The key to budgeting may lie in performing two steps: (1) estimating the extent of the resources—both personnel and purchases—needed to accomplish each activity, and (2) estimating the cost and availability of those resources. With this information in hand, the development of a budget and monthly cash flow for a public relations program becomes easier. Such data also provide the milestones necessary to audit program costs on a routine basis and to make adjustments well in advance of budget crises.

In recent years, as media outlets have expanded exponentially, public relations budgets have increased. National campaigns for national companies—including public relations writing and media placement, media monitoring, tool kits for localized grassroots programs, and special events—often exceed $1 million per year. The Defense Department's public relations work to influence attitudes in the Middle East ran into the tens of millions of dollars. In perhaps the largest public relations budget ever awarded, the American Legacy Foundation—established as a result of the Master Settlement Agreement between 46 states and the tobacco industry in 1999—named Arnold Communications of Boston and its partnering agencies to lead an antismoking public education campaign. The fee? The contract was valued at 50 to 85 percent of the $300 million received annually by the foundation.[10]

Whew!

Such whopping budgets are still the exception. Most public relations programs operate on limited budgets. In a growing number of instances, "pay-for-performance" public relations has emerged. The premise of this arrangement is that the buyer pays only for what he or she gets, meaning that fees are based on the depth of coverage and the circulation or audience rating of the venue in which coverage appears. If no coverage is achieved, no fee is paid. Most public relations agencies, however, make "no guarantees" that their efforts will be successful and therefore frown on pay-for-performance contracts.[11]

Most public relations agencies treat client costs in a manner similar to that used by legal, accounting, and management consulting firms: The client pays for services rendered, either on a monthly or yearly retainer basis or on minimum charges based on staff time. Time records are kept by every employee—from chairperson to mail clerk—on a daily basis to be sure that agency clients know exactly what they are paying for. Hourly charges for public relations agency employees can range from low double figures per hour to upwards of $500-an-hour and beyond for agency superstars.

Because agency relationships are based on trust, it is important that clients understand the derivation of costs. In recent years, debate has raged over markups on expenses paid on behalf of clients by public relations firms. Out-of-pocket expenses—for meals, hotels, transportation, and the like—are generally charged back to clients at cost. But when an agency pays in advance for larger expense items—printing, photography, graphics, design—it is standard industry practice to mark up such expenses by a factor approximating 17.65 percent. This figure, which the vast majority of agencies use, was borrowed from the advertising profession and represents the multiplicative inverse of the standard 15 percent commission that ad agencies collect on advertising placement.

Talking Points Fudging the Fleishman Budget

Public relations budgeting is an art, not a science. And public relations counselors make their living defending clients who find themselves thrashing about in the midst of scandal. Such representation demands that public relations advisors themselves command pristine reputations.

But in 2005, one of the world's foremost public relations agencies found itself on the wrong end of a media onslaught because of one of the ugliest budgetary snarls in the history of public relations practice. Fleishman-Hillard, founded in St. Louis in 1946, has offices stretching from Australia to Tokyo, from Frankfurt to Atlanta. Fleishman represents some of the world's largest companies.

Late in 2004, one of those clients, the City of Los Angeles, hired a private investigator to assist in a lawsuit that charged Fleishman-Hillard with massively overbilling the city as much as $30,000 a month under a $3 million-a-year contract with several city agencies, including the Department of Water and Power, the Department of Airports, and the Convention and Visitors Bureau.

After a three-month investigation, the city claimed Fleishman overbilled it by a whopping $4.2 million over six years. Fleishman management was livid, blasting the audit as representing "erroneous assertions to arrive at an inflated overall estimate of questioned costs."

Or at least that's what the company said initially.

Five months later, a more sheepish Fleishman agreed to settle the overbilling lawsuit by paying $4.5 million and waiving an additional $1.3 million in unpaid invoices for public relations services. Fleishman's Los Angeles office manager was one of two senior managers indicted on 15 counts of wire fraud and a single charge of conspiracy. Another Fleishman senior officer pleaded guilty to three counts of fraud for his role in padding the bills.

The overbilling budget scandal was a stunning embarrassment to Fleishman. Summarized the Los Angles controller, "Fleishman-Hillard not only violated the public trust, they broke the time-honored principles of the public relations profession."

For further information, see "F-H Hits Audit Report, Admits Mistakes," *Jack O'Dwyer's Newsletter 37*, No. 46 (November 24, 2004): 1; "F-H Settles L.A. Legal Squabble," *Jack O'Dwyer's Newsletter 38*, No. 17 (April 27, 2005): 1; Greg Hazley, "Political Winds Blow as F-H Takes Stand in L.A.," *O'Dwyer's PR Services Report* (January 2005): 1–13; Rick Orlov, "City Hires Private Eye in P.R. Case," *Los Angeles Daily News* (August 13, 2004).

The guiding rule in agency budgeting is to ensure that the client is aware of how charges are being applied so that nasty surprises might be avoided when bills are received.

Implementing Public Relations Programs

The duties and responsibilities of public relations practitioners are as diverse as the publics with whom different institutions deal. Specific public relations tasks are as varied as the organizations served. Here is a partial list of public relations duties:

- **Media relations:** Coordinating relationships with the online, print, and electronic media, which includes arranging and monitoring press interviews, writing news releases and related press materials, organizing press conferences, and answering media inquiries and requests. A good deal of media relations work consists of attempting to gain favorable news coverage for the firm.

- **Social network marketing:** The digital revolution has introduced a whole new component to public relations skills sets. Web 2.0 has transformed the publication of information into a legitimate two-way street. Marketing via social networking sites, from MySpace to Facebook to Friendster to all the rest has become a frontline responsibility of public relations agencies. So, too, has been counsel on when and how to use blogs, wikis, podcasts, RSS feeds, and all the other Internet-based communications tools that help organizations communicate and market.

- **Internal communications:** Informing employees and principals through a variety of means, including intranet, newsletters, television, and meetings. Traditionally, this role has emphasized news-oriented communications rather than benefits-oriented ones, which are usually the province of personnel departments.

- **Government relations and public affairs:** Coordinating activities with legislators on local, state, and federal levels. This includes legislative research activities and public policy formation.

- **Community relations:** Orchestrating interaction with the community, perhaps including open houses, tours, and employee volunteer efforts designed to reflect the supportive nature of the organization to the community.

- **Investor relations:** Managing relations with the investment community, including the firm's present and potential stockholders. This task emphasizes personal contact with securities analysts, institutional investors, and private investors.

- **Consumer relations:** Supporting activities with customers and potential customers, with activities ranging from hard-sell product promotion activities to "soft" consumer advisory services.

- **Public relations research:** Conducting opinion research, which involves assisting in the public policy formation process through the coordination and interpretation of attitudinal studies of key publics.

- **Public relations writing:** Coordinating the institution's printed voice with its public through reprints of speeches, annual reports, quarterly statements, and product and company brochures.

- **Special publics relations:** Coordinating relationships with outside specialty groups, such as suppliers, educators, students, nonprofit organizations, and competitors.

- ■ **Institutional advertising:** Managing the institutional—or nonproduct—advertising image as well as being called on increasingly to assist in the management of more traditional product advertising.

- ■ **Graphics:** Coordinating the graphic and photographic services of the organization. To do this task well requires knowledge of desktop publishing, typography, layout, and art.

- ■ **Web site management:** Coordinating the organization's online "face," including Web site design and ongoing counsel, updating, and even management of the site.

- ■ **Philanthropy:** Managing the gift-giving apparatus, which ordinarily consists of screening and evaluating philanthropic proposals and allocating the organization's available resources.

- ■ **Special events:** Coordinating special events, including travel for company management, corporate celebrations and exhibits, dinners, groundbreakings, and grand openings.

- ■ **Management counseling:** Advising managers on alternative options and recommended choices in light of public responsibilities.

Again, this is but a partial list of the tasks ordinarily assigned to public relations professionals.

Public relations managers frequently use the visualization tools of Gantt and PERT charts to control and administer these project tasks. The Gantt chart, developed by Charles Gantt in 1917, focuses on the sequence of tasks necessary for completion of the project at hand. Each task on a Gantt chart is represented as a single horizontal bar. The length of each bar corresponds to the time necessary for completion. Arrows connecting independent tasks reflect the relationships between the tasks. PERT (program evaluation and review technique) charts were first developed in the 1950s by the Navy to help manage complex projects with a high degree of intertask dependency. The PERT chart shows the relationship between each activity. These relationships create pathways through the process. The "critical path" is a series of tasks that must be completed in a certain time period for the project to be completed on schedule (see Figure 5-3).

The Public Relations Department

Public relations professionals generally work in one of two organizational structures: (1) as a staff professional in a public relations department of a corporation, university, hospital, sports franchise, political campaign, religious institution, and so on, whose task is to support the primary business of the organization, or (2) as a line professional in a public relations agency, whose primary task is to help the organization earn revenue.

Consider the public relations department. Once an organization has analyzed its environment, established its objectives, set up measurement standards, and thought about appropriate plans, programs, and budgets, it is ready to organize a public relations department. Departments range from one-person operations to far-flung networks of hundreds of people, such as at the U.S. Department of Defense, Johnson & Johnson, or ExxonMobil, with staff around the world, responsible for relations with the press, investors, civic groups, employees, and many different governments.

Today, appropriately, about half of all corporate communications departments report to the chairman, president, and/or CEO. This is an improvement from the past and indicative of the higher stature that the function enjoys. About one-sixth

Prototype Gantt Chart
Packaged Goods Product
Target Start of Ship at Start of Year, Retail Availability in March, Marketing Support in April

Category	Activity	Jan	Feb	Mar	Apr	May	Jun	Jul	Aug
Product	Exploratory Research	XXX							
	Concept Development		XXX						
	Quantitative Research			XXX					
Package	Product Development			XXX	XXX				
	Structural Package Dev			XXX	XXX	XXX	XXX	XXX	
	Graphics Development				XXX	XXX	XXX	XXX	
Financial	Pricing & Profit	XXX							
	Volume Projections	XXX							
	Budget Development					XXX			
Marketing Plan	Sales Promotion				XXX	XXX	XXX	XXX	
	Advertising				XXX	XXX	XXX	XXX	
	Publicity								
	Produce Ads/Collateral Material								XXX
Purchasing	Long Lead Supplies				XXX	XXX	XXX	XXX	
	Shorter Lead Supplies						XXX	XXX	
Begin Production	Inventory Build								XXX
	Ship To Field Warehouses								XXX
Sales Meetings	Present To Sales Force								
	Present To Trade								
Start Shipping	Begin Delivery To Trade								XXX

FIGURE 5-3 **Critical path chart.** Daniel Jay Morrison & Associates (www.djmconsult.com) created this prototypical chart to trace the critical path of a product coming to market. (Courtesy of Daniel Jay Morrison & Associates, Inc.)

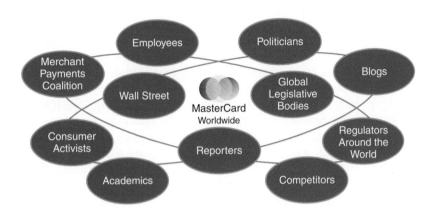

FIGURE 5-4 Organizing for public relations. These diverse publics are some of those who make up the evolving ecosphere of influencers of MasterCard World-wide. (See "From the Top" in Chapter 4.) (Courtesy MasterCard Worldwide)

of public relations departments report to advertising or marketing, and another one-sixth report to a vice president of administration.[12] Clearly, reporting to the CEO is eminently preferable to reporting to a legal, financial, or administrative executive, who may tend to "filter" top-management messages.

In government, public relations professionals (although, as we will see in Chapter 12, they're not called *"public relations"* professionals) typically report directly to department heads. In universities, the public relations function is frequently coupled with fund-raising and development activities. In hospitals, public relations is typically tied to the marketing function.

In terms of structure, corporate public relations departments today are faced with stakeholders who are more "empowered" than ever. It's not just the media who publish about the company—it's everybody—activists, employees, consumers, bloggers of every stripe and attitude. For the first time in history, corporate communicators no longer control the conversation.[13] This group of diverse influencers means that companies must organize communications departments to reflect a new diverse group of influencers (see Figure 5-4). This new reality suggests that corporate communications departments must focus more on "engaging" their constituent publics in two-way dialogue, to keep informed about their views and to keep them informed as to the company's motives and actions.

As for the names of the departments in which public relations is housed, organizations use a wide variety of names for the function. Ironically, the trend today seems to be away from use of the traditional term *public relations* and toward *corporate communications*.

Whatever the department is called and to whomever it reports, the pressing need today for chief communications officers and their colleagues is to demonstrate a high level of skills—from writing to counseling to understanding the critical importance of information in the wired world in which we live.

The Public Relations Agency

Now consider the public relations agency. The biggest difference between an external agency and an internal department is perspective. The former is outside looking in; the latter is inside looking out (sometimes literally for itself!). Sometimes the use of an agency is necessary to escape the tunnel-vision syndrome that afflicts some firms, in which a detached viewpoint is desperately needed. An agency, unfettered by internal corporate politics, might be better trusted to present management with an objective reading of the concerns of its publics.

An agency has the added advantage of not being taken for granted by a firm's management. Unfortunately, management sometimes has a greater regard for an outside specialist than for an inside one. This attitude frequently defies logic but is nonetheless often true. Generally, if management is paying (sometimes quite handsomely) for outside counsel, it tends to listen carefully to the advice.

Agencies generally organize according to industry groupings, with specialization in industry functions—media relations, government relations, social media, investor relations, etc. Larger agencies are divided into such areas as health care, sports, fashion, technology, finance, and so on. Account teams are assigned specific clients. Team members bill clients on an hourly basis, with most firms intending to retain two-thirds of each individual's hourly billing rate as income. In other words, if an account executive bills at a rate of $300 per hour—and many senior counselors do—the firm expects to retain $200 of that rate toward its profit. As to billing rates, one survey indicated that agency CEOs average an hourly rate of $322, with the hourly rate of an account executive averaging $140.[14]

In recent years, as clients have begun to manage resources more rigorously, agencies have gotten much more systematic in measuring success and in keeping customers from migrating to a competitor. Indeed, the most difficult part of agency work is not *attracting* clients but *retaining* them.

Public relations agencies today, as noted, are huge businesses. In its last compilation of public relations revenues, The Council of Public Relations Firms estimated the revenue of the worldwide public relations industry at approximately $5.4 billion.[15] In the United States, spending on public relations has grown strongly, approaching $4 billion.[16]

Over the past two decades, most of the top public relations firms have been subsumed by communications holding companies, the most prominent of which, along with the agencies they own, are the following:

- **Omnicom:** Fleishman-Hillard, Ketchum, Porter-Novelli, Brodeur Worldwide, Clark & Weinstock, Gavin Anderson & Company, and Cone
- **Interpublic Group:** Access Communications; Carmichael, Lynch, Spong; DeVries Public Relations; Golin-Harris; MWW; Tierney Public Relations; and Weber-Shandwick Worldwide
- **WPP Group:** Burson-Marsteller, Cohn & Wolfe, Hill & Knowlton, and Ogilvy Public Relations Worldwide
- **Havas:** Euro RSCG Middleberg, Magnet Communications, and Noonan Russon Presence Euro RSCG West
- **Grey:** APCO Worldwide and GCI Group
- **Publicis:** Manning, Selvage & Lee, Publicis Dialog, Rowland Worldwide, and, in 2008, Kekst and Company.

Public relations purists bemoan the incursion of these mammoth companies because many are dominated by advertising agencies. Defenders point to the potential synergy between the two disciplines. One casualty of the takeover of the world's leading public relations firms by these holding companies is that the largest agencies no longer make public their annual revenues and earnings. Nonetheless, a compilation of the net fees of the largest independent public relations firms still shows robust annual revenues (Table 5-1). What is indisputable is the tremendous growth of the profession.

Table 5-1

O'Dwyer's Rankings: Top 25 Independent PR Firms with Major U.S. Operations

Beyond the largest public relations firms, most owned by advertising-oriented multinational holding companies, are thousands of independent public relations firms—many entrepreneurial in nature. Others, like the family-owned Edelman Company—begun by father Dan and now run by son Richard—are large organizations.

Many of these independent shops are thriving. In 2007, more than half of the top 50 independent public relations firms enjoyed double-digit gains in fee income, testifying to the strength of the public relations counseling business.

Firm	2008 Net Fees	Emp	% Change from 2007
1. Edelman, NY	$449,231,000	2,997	+13%
2. Waggener Edstrom, WA	119,670,000	843	+12
3. APCO Worldwide, DC	112,400,000	569	+15
4. Ruder Finn Group, NY	96,112,000	599	+15
5. Text 100 International, CA	63,000,000	540	+5
6. Qorvis Comms, DC	30,497.000	86	+28
7. Schwartz Comms, MA	34,919,000	96	+15
8. ICR, CT	31,050,000	199	+2
9. Dan Klores Comms, NY	22,400,000	120	+3
10. Taylor Comms, NY	20,205,000	105	flat
11. Gibbs & Soell, NY	19,259,000	101	flat
12. WeissComm Partners, CA	18,981,000	86	+46
13. Padilla Speer Beardsley, MN	15,952,000	102	+8
14. Peppercorn, NY	13,548,000	75	+15
15. Allison & Partners, CA	13,082,000	81	+13
16. Capstrat, NC	12,500,000	77	+3
17. French/West/Vaughan, NC	12,497,000	83	+2
18. Shift Communications, MA	12,234,000	100	+15
19. RF/Binder Partners, NY	12,220,000	74	+3
20. CRT/Tanaka, VA	12,100,000	64	+7
21. 5W Public Relations, NY	11,920,000	79	+3
22. Coyne PR, NJ	11,654,000	86	+35
23. M Booth & Assocs, NY	11,368,000	55	flat
24. Zeno Group, NY	11,216,000	62	- (2)
25. Makovsky & Co., NY	11,100,000	50	+19

Courtesy of Jack O'Dwyer Company, www.odwyerpr.com.

While an outsider's fresh point of view can be helpful in focusing a client on particular problems and opportunities and on how best to capitalize on them, outside agencies are still just that—"outside." As a consequence, they are often unfamiliar with details affecting the situation of particular companies and with the idiosyncrasies of company management. The good external counselor must constantly work to overcome this barrier. The best client–agency relationships are those with free-flowing communications between internal and external public relations groups so that both resources are kept informed about corporate policies, strategies, and tactics. A well-oiled, complementary department–agency relationship can result in a more positive communications approach for an organization.

Reputation Management

Many public relations agencies in recent years, particularly those purchased by the large advertising agency conglomerates, have declared special emphasis on *reputation management*.

What is reputation management? Public relations purists argue that this is precisely what they have been doing all along—helping to "manage" an organization's "reputation," that is, its brand, position, goodwill, or image.

Essentially, an organization's reputation is composed of two elements: (1) the more "rational" products and performance, and (2) more "emotional" behavioral factors, such as customer service, CEO performance, personal experience with the company, and the like. Stated another way, reputation is gained by what one *does*, not by what one *says*.[17]

Reputations matter because a company with a good reputation can charge premium prices, have greater access to new markets and products, have greater access to capital, profit from greater word-of-mouth endorsement, and possess an unduplicated identity. Such distinctive organizations as Tiffany, Google, Dreamworks, and the New York Yankees are all examples of entities with unique and positive reputations that translate into hard-nosed advantages. One quantitative study of reputation concluded that more than one-quarter of a company's stock market value was attributable to intangibles, like its reputation.[18]

Reputation management, then, is *the ability to link reputation to business goals to increase support and advocacy and increase organizational success through profits, contributions, attendance, and so on.*

What do reputation managers do? The behaviors they attempt to influence include (1) persuading consumers to recommend and buy their products, (2) persuading investors to invest in their organization, (3) persuading competent job seekers to enlist as employees, (4) persuading other strong organizations to joint venture with them, and (5) persuading people to support the organization when it is attacked.

Stated another way, the requisite of reputation managers is to help build, defend, and maintain an organization's reputation. Public relations purists would argue that these reputation management functions have always been the province of two individuals within an organization—its CEO and its public relations professional.

As the extraordinarily successful commissioner of the National Basketball Association, David Stern, puts it, "I am the protector of the brand and its integrity. That's a job that every CEO has, and I consider it my job to be out there to be protective and to respond so that I can be the spokesperson."[19]

Assisting the CEO in "managing" the reputation of the organization is the public relations professional. Indeed, for the public relations person, reputation management reflects the function's fundamental mandate to promote, maintain, defend, enhance, and sustain the organization's credibility, as the economists put it, *"in perpetuity;"* in other words, forever.

Where Are the Jobs?

Like other support functions, public relations suffered when the high-tech stock market bubble burst at the beginning of the 21st century. In recent years, however, the field has made a substantial comeback.

As recessionary clouds hovered over the U.S. and world economies in 2008, the remarkable public relations hiring boom of the early years of the 21st century began to wane.

Nonetheless, the long-term future of the practice of public relations, like the future of the U.S. and world economy, promises to be steady and strong.

■ In terms of industry specialization, public relations positions in health care–related fields have been particularly strong in recent years, and the area of consumer/ retail has also rebounded nicely.[20]

■ Meanwhile, the high-tech industry, which fell farther and faster than most others after its unprecedented buildup in the 1990s, has begun to build back its cadre of skilled public relations managers to help it regain a position of prominence, trust, and respect among investors and others.

■ In a related sense, the great growth of social media, as a mechanism through which Generation X and Yers communicate, has introduced new opportunities for public relations professionals.

■ In terms of other functional areas of specialization, the function of managing a company's reputation ranks high on the public relations job scale. So, too, do the areas of investor relations and crisis management. The increase in demand for specialists in these three high-level areas probably explains why the number of public relations people earning between $100,000 and $249,000 has grown markedly in recent years.[21]

■ Worldwide corporations, faced with increased scrutiny from the media, government, and the general public to act ethically and behave responsibly, have recognized the need for talented, top communications managers. And the practice has grown exponentially beyond the United States.

■ Public relations agencies, wiser and more experienced after the boom-bust phenomenon of the early years of the 21st century, will continue to expand. Just as a plethora of high-tech public relations agencies emerged in the 1990s, so, too, is it likely that the move toward agency specialization in areas such as social media will continue in the 21st century.

■ In the nonprofit realm, public relations positions in hospitals, in particular, are likely to grow as managed care becomes the reality and health care organizations become more competitive in attracting patients and winning community approval. Other nonprofits—charities, schools, museums, associations—all faced with fewer resources and more competition for community funding—will also require increased public relations help to attract development and membership funds.

■ Finally, one other public relations skill that will be in increased demand, certainly for the remainder of this decade, is employee communications. Employees in the 21st century, empowered by the Internet and burned by layoffs, pension fund losses and restructurings, and failures of management to be credible, must be convinced that their organizations deserve their allegiance. This will be a job largely for public relations practitioners—to win back employee trust.[22]

What Does It Pay?

Without question, the communications function has increased in importance and clout in the new century. Top communications professionals in many large corporations today draw compensation packages well into six figures. According to one survey, the average senior vice president of corporate communications earned almost $190,000 annually, with executive vice presidents earning close to $230,000.[23]

The same survey indicated that the median annual salary base for corporate public relations employees was $97,500, while respondents in public relations agencies reported a median base salary of $75,400 annually. The median annual salary base for all public relations respondents was $82,400.

According to a 2007 report of the U.S. Bureau of Labor Statistics, annual mean wages in major categories of public relations work break down as follows:

- Public relations agencies $118,350
- Companies and other enterprises $107,480
- Professional organizations $100,720
- Local colleges and universities $ 87,900
- Local governments $ 74,710[24]

Yet another study, by *PR Week* magazine and Korn/Ferry International, of 1,864 public relations people indicated that the average salary of public relations professionals—with an average of 12 years in the business—was once again on the upswing, rising 7 percent year-to-year to $87,461. As one executive recruiter summarized the renewed demand for public relations workers, "There is a real sense of optimism. Companies are willing to spend. There is a huge increase in demand for corporate communications."[25]

In terms of geography, the top-paying areas for public relations practitioners were the following:

- Northwest $93,700
- Northeast $92,700
- West $86,200
- Mid-Atlantic $85,500
- Plain States $82,800
- Midwest $80,100

As to the difference in public relations skills, the 2008 *PR Week* survey revealed that investor relations specialists still earned the highest salaries in the field. As in the past, these financial specialists were followed by experts in reputation management and crisis management. Financial services firms paid far-and-away the most for public relations talent.

Women and Minorities

Two decades ago, the practice of public relations was overwhelmingly a bastion of white males. Today, it is women who predominate in public relations work. And minorities—African Americans, Asians, and Hispanics—while still small in total numbers in the field, have nonetheless increased their participation in public relations.

The issue of increased feminization of public relations—the establishment of a so-called "velvet ghetto"—is a particularly thorny one for the practice. One area of constant consternation is the traditional discrepancy between men's and women's salaries and upper-management positions—the glass ceiling for women in public relations.

Recent experience suggests that times are changing, albeit more slowly than some would prefer. University public relations programs across the country report a preponderance of female students, outnumbering males by as much as 80 percent. Moreover, the number of women executives in public relations has also increased in recent years. While the number of male public relations executives still exceeds the number of female public relations executives, the existence of a glass ceiling seems to be a relic of the past.[26]

That's the good news.

The not-so-good news is that women and minorities are still paid less than their male counterparts. One 2008 survey reported that the median income for men with five or more years' experience in the field was $143,700, while the equivalent for women with the same experience was $91,800. At less than five years' experience, the gap narrows. But the field still has a ways to go on the gender front.[27]

Last Word

In the 21st century, the practice of public relations is firmly accepted as part of the management process of any well-run organization.

Public relations objectives and goals, strategies, and tactics must flow directly from the organization's overall goals. Public relations strategies must reflect organizational strategies, and tactics must be designed to realize the organization's business objectives. Stated another way, public relations programs are worth little if they fail to further management's and the organization's goals.

As media communications have proliferated and an organization's reputation has become more essential, the practice of public relations enjoys a significant management role and challenge in this new century. Coming out of the corporate and accounting scandals of the early 2000s and the loss of confidence in business and CEOs, management must depend on the able assistance of proper public relations practice to help reestablish trust in society's major institutions.

That may be one reason why *Fortune* listed PR specialists as one of the fastest-growing professional jobs between now and 2012, predicted to increase by more than 20 percent.[28] Or, in the words of one public relations recruiter, "There has never been a better time to be in the business. And that will continue for the next 10 to 20 years."[29]

Discussion Starters

1. What is the management process of public relations?
2. Why is it imperative that public relations report to top management?
3. What are the elements that make up a public relations plan?
4. What questions must be answered in establishing valid public relations objectives?
5. What elements go into framing a public relations budget?
6. What were the "conflict of interest" consequences that Burson CEO Mark Penn should have considered before accepting a high-profile role with a presidential candidate?
7. What are the fundamental differences between working in a corporation and working in an agency as a public relations professional?
8. What are several of the primary tactical tasks assigned to the public relations function?
9. What may be the primary areas of opportunity for public relations professionals in the years ahead?
10. Why has the field of public relations been accused of being a "velvet ghetto"?

Top of

the Shelf   Reputation Management: The Key to Successful PR and Corporate Communication / John Doorley and Helio Fred Garcia, New York, NY: Taylor and Francis Group, 2006

Two eminent public relations professors (full disclosure: I work with 'em, but they're still "eminent!") prescribe a best-case formula for achieving positive recognition for any organization.

Both authors bring a wealth of corporate and consulting experience to this seminal work that transcends any other in the area of "reputation management." For one thing, the authors contend that reputation management can be measured, and they present methods to help quantify the elusive, but essential, commodity.

The authors dissect the various elements of managing one's reputation, from community relations to crisis. In terms of the latter, they detail, as definitively as anyone ever has, how an organization can respond effectively in the midst of crisis, by assessing specific measures that trigger strategic action. And they also offer five guest chapters, written by experienced practitioners, who have helped build reputations at leading corporations. Clearly, Doorley and Garcia have written the number one text on "reputation management" in the practice of public relations.

Case Study   Exxon Corporation's Bad Good Friday

In the summer of 2008—nearly 20 years after the worst oil spill in history—the U.S. Supreme Court slashed the $2.5 billion punitive damages awarded in the 1989 Exxon Valdez disaster to $500 million. The court ruled that the approximately 33,000 victims of the disaster at Prince William Sound, Alaska—many of them Alaskan fishermen and 8,000 of whom had died in the two decades of litigation—may collect punitive damages from Exxon Mobil Corp., but not as much as a federal appeals court had earlier determined.

Thus ended the saga that constituted a seminal case in the annals of public relations management

In the history of public relations practice, few communications issues have been handled as questionably, received as much global notoriety, and had such far-reaching implications on the profession as those involving the Exxon Corporation in 1989.

A "Tanked" Tanker Captain

At 8:30 a.m. on March 24, 1989—Good Friday, no less—Lawrence G. Rawl, chairman and chief executive of the Exxon Corporation, one of the world's largest companies, was in his kitchen sipping coffee when the phone rang.

"What happened? Did it lose an engine? Break a rudder?" Rawl asked the caller.

What happened was that an Exxon tanker had run aground and was dumping gummy crude oil into the frigid waters of Prince William Sound, just outside the harbor of Valdez, Alaska.

What was about to happen to Mr. Rawl and his company—and to the environment—was arguably the worst environmental disaster in the history of the United States.

The facts, painfully portrayed in media across the country, were these: The Exxon Valdez, a 987-foot tanker (see Figure 5-5),

FIGURE 5-5 **The Exxon Valdez.** (Courtesy of O'Dwyerpr.com)

piloted by a captain who was later revealed to have been legally drunk, ran aground on a reef 25 miles southwest of the port of Valdez. The resulting rupture caused a spill of 260,000 barrels, the largest spill ever in North America, affecting 1,300 square miles of water, damaging some 600 miles of coastline, and killing as many as 4,000 Alaskan sea otters.

The communications disaster also enshrined the name Exxon in the all-time Public Relations Hall of Shame.

To Go or Not to Go

The first problem that confronted Exxon and its top management after news of the Good Friday spill had broken was whether Chairman Rawl should fly to Prince William Sound to demonstrate the company's concern. This was what Union Carbide Chairman Warren Anderson did when his company suffered a devastating industrial explosion in Bhopal, India.

If Rawl went to Alaska, the reasoning went, he might be able to reassure the public that the people who run Exxon acknowledged their misdeed and would make amends. What could be a better show of concern than the chairman flying to the local scene of the tragedy?

On the other hand, a consensus of executives around Rawl argued that he should remain in New York. "What are you going to do?" they asked. "We've already said we've done it, we're going to pay for it, and we're responsible for it." Rawl's more effective role, said these advisers, was right there at Exxon headquarters in Manhattan.

In the end, the latter view triumphed. Rawl did not go to Alaska. He left the cleanup in "capable hands" and sent a succession of lower-ranking executives to Alaska to deal with the spill. As he summarized in an interview one year after the Prince William Sound nightmare, "We had concluded that there was simply too much for me to coordinate from New York. It wouldn't have made any difference if I showed up and made a speech in the town forum. I wasn't going to spend the summer there; I had other things to do."

Rawl's failure to fly immediately to Valdez struck some as shortsighted. Said one media consultant about Rawl's communications decision, "The chairman should have been up there walking in the oil and picking up dead birds."

Where to Establish Media Central

The second dilemma that confronted Exxon was where to establish its media center. This decision started, correctly enough, with Exxon senior managers concluding that the impact of the spill was so great that news organizations should be kept informed as events unfolded. Exxon wanted to take charge of the news flow and give the public, through the news media, a credible, concerned, and wholly committed corporate response.

It decided that the best place to do this would be in Valdez, Alaska, itself. "Just about every news organization worth its salt had representatives in Valdez," said Exxon's publicity chief. "But in retrospect, we should have sent live broadcasts of news conferences to several points around the country."

The problem was that Valdez was a remote Alaskan town with limited communications operations. This complicated the ability of Exxon to disseminate information quickly. As *Oil & Gas Journal* stated later: "Exxon did not update its media relations people elsewhere in the world. It told reporters it was Valdez or nothing."

Additionally, there was a four-hour time difference between Valdez and New York. The phone lines to Valdez quickly became jammed, and even Rawl couldn't find a knowledgeable official to brief him. That left news organizations responsible for keeping the public informed cut off from Exxon information during the early part of the crisis. Because news conferences took place at unsuitable viewing hours for television networks and too late for many morning newspapers, predictable accusations of an Exxon cover-up resulted. Said one Exxon official about the decision to put the communications center in Valdez, "It didn't work."

Rapidity of Response

A cardinal rule in any crisis is: Keep ahead of the information flow—try not to let events get ahead of you. Here Exxon had a third problem.

First, it took Chairman Rawl a full week to make any public comment on the spill. When he did, it was to blame others: The U.S. Coast Guard and Alaskan officials were "holding up" his company's efforts to clean up the spill. But Rawl's words were too little, too late. The impression persisted that, in light of the delay in admitting responsibility, Exxon was not responding vigorously enough.

A full 10 days after the crisis, Exxon placed an apologetic advertisement in 166 newspapers. To some readers, the ad seemed self-serving and failed to address the many pointed questions raised about Exxon's conduct.

"It seems the company was a bit too relaxed in its capabilities," offered the president of the Public Relations Society of America. Meanwhile, one group that wasn't relaxed was the Alaska state legislature, which enacted a tax increase on oil from the North Slope fields within weeks of the Exxon spill. Congressional committees in Washington moved just as quickly to increase liability limits and potential compensation for oil-spill damage and to increase the money available through the industry-financed Offshore Oil Pollution Compensation Fund. When Exxon hesitated, its opponents seized the initiative. Concluded another public relations executive, "They lost the battle in the first 48 hours."

How High the Profile

Exxon's communications response in the face of this most challenging crisis in its history was, to put it mildly, muted.

From an operations and logistics viewpoint, Exxon did a good job. The company immediately set up animal rescue projects, launched a major cleanup effort, and agreed to pick up a substantial percentage of the cost. But it made the mistake of downplaying the crisis in public.

Exxon's public statements sometimes contradicted information from other sources. At one point, an Exxon spokesperson said that damage from the oil spill would be minimal. Others watching the industry said the damage was likely to be substantial.

Chairman Rawl, an otherwise blunt and outspoken CEO, seemed defensive and argumentative in his public comments. In one particularly disastrous personal appearance on *CBS Morning News,* Rawl glared at interviewer Kathleen Sullivan and snapped: "I can't give you details of our cleanup plan. It's thick and complicated. And I haven't had a chance to read it yet. The CEO of a major company doesn't have time to read every plan."

Exxon's attempts to calm the public also were criticized. Its ad drew fire for not expressing enough concern. It hired an outside firm to do a series of video news releases to show how the company was cleaning up the spill. At an estimated cost of more than $3 million, a 13-minute tape was shown at the corporation's annual meeting. The video, called *Progress in Alaska,* attracted intense criticism from those attending the conference as well as from the press. *USA Today* called the tape "Exxon's worst move of the day." When the consultant who devised the video wrote an article in the *New York Times* defending Exxon's approach in Alaska, the Alaskan representative to the National Wildlife Federation responded with a blistering letter to the editor, noting that the consultant omitted in his article that the spill had resulted in the death of more than 15,000 sea birds and numerous otters and eagles.

Exxon then added an environmental expert to its board of directors, but only after pension funds, which control a large chunk of its stock, demanded such a response.

Dealing with the Aftermath

Finally, Exxon was forced to deal with all the implications of what its tanker had wrought in Valdez. The company became embroiled in controversy when it sent a $30,000 contribution to the Alaska Public Radio Network, which covered the crisis on a daily basis. The network, sniffing "conflict of interest," flatly turned down Exxon's attempted largesse. Subsequently, a special appropriations bill was introduced in the Alaskan legislature to forward an identical amount to Alaska Public Radio.

The accident and the company's reaction to it also had consequences for the oil industry. Plans to expand drilling into the Alaskan National Wildlife Refuge were shelved by Congress, and members called for new laws increasing federal involvement in oil spills.

The company's employees, too, felt confused, embarrassed, and betrayed. Summarizing the prevailing mood at the company, one Exxon worker said, "Whenever I travel now, I feel like I have a target painted on my chest."

In 1996, seven years after the *Exxon Valdez* ran aground, a weary Exxon announced to the world that it was closing the books on its unforgettable disaster.

Total cost to Exxon: $2.5 billion.

But that wasn't all. In 1999, a full decade after the *Exxon Valdez* dumped 11 million gallons of oil into Prince William Sound, the Exxon Corporation—rechristened ExxonMobil—went to court in Alaska to get the courts to overturn an unusual federal restriction. The unique law barred one ship, the *Exxon Valdez,* from ever again sailing into Prince William Sound. Exxon alleged that the ship, renamed the *SeaRiver Mediterranean,* was being unfairly singled out. Specifically, the legislation barred "vessels that have spilled more than 1 million gallons of oil into the marine environment after March 22, 1989" from entering Prince William Sound.

Coincidentally, only one sailing vessel fit that description.

The Lessons

Two decades after the Exxon Valdez washed its oil ashore at Prince William Sound, the reverberations of the management crisis still affect the successor ExxonMobil company. In 2008, a shareholder revolt, led by descendants of the company's founder, John D. Rockefeller, exhorted the now ExxonMobil to do more in the area of alternative energy sources. Exxon's 21st century management listened and responded.

The lessons of the *Exxon Valdez*'s Good Friday oil spill would not soon be forgotten by corporate managers. The episode, predicted one, "*will become a textbook example of what not to do when an unexpected crisis thrusts a company into the limelight.*"

Questions

1. What would you have recommended Chairman Rawl do upon learning of the Prince William Sound oil spill?

2. How would you have handled the media in this case?

3. What would have been your timing in terms of public relations responses in this case?

4. What would be your overall public relations strategy—aggressive, low key, or middle-of-the-road—if you were Exxon's public relations director?

5. Do you think this case will ever qualify as a "textbook example" of what not to do in a crisis?

6. Now that Exxon has merged with Mobil, what is the corporation doing about environmental issues? Visit the news release homepage (www.exxon.com/em_newsrelease/index.html) and follow the link to browse the oil giant's recent news releases. What is ExxonMobil doing about environmental issues? Why would the company continue to issue news releases about environmental activities so many years after the *Exxon Valdez* incident?

For further information about the *Exxon Valdez* case, see Richard Behar, "Exxon Strikes Back," *Time* (March 26, 1990): 62–63; Claudia H. Deutsch, "The Giant with a Black Eye," *New York Times* (April 2, 1989): B1–4; E. Bruce Harrison, with Tom Prugh, "Assessing the Damage," *Public Relations Journal* (October 1989): 40–45; John Holusha, "Exxon's Public-Relations Problem," *New York Times* (April 21, 1989): D1–4; Peter Nulty, "Exxon's Problem: Not What You Think," *Fortune* (April 23, 1990): 202–204; James Lukaszewski, "How Vulnerable Are You? The Lessons from Valdez," *Public Relations Quarterly* (Fall 1989): 5–6; Phillip M. Perry, "Exxon Falters in PR Effort Following Alaskan Oil Spill," *O'Dwyer's PR Services Report* (July 1989): 1, 16–22; Bill Richards, "Exxon Is Battling a Ban on an Infamous Tanker," *Wall Street Journal* (July 29, 1998): C1; Allanna Sullivan, "Rawl Wishes He'd Visited Valdez Sooner," *Wall Street Journal* (June 30, 1989): B7; Joseph B. Treaster, "With Insurers' Payment, Exxon Says *Valdez* Case Is Ended," *New York Times* (November 1, 1996): B2; Paul Wiseman, "Firm Finds *Valdez* Oil Fowls Image," *USA Today* (April 26, 1990): B1; and Pete Yost, "Court Slashes Judgment in Exxon Valdez Disaster," *Associated Press*, June 25, 2008.

From the Top   An Interview with Peter Drucker

Peter Drucker, who died in 2005 at the age of 95, was called the "greatest thinker management theory has produced" by the *London Economist.* His work influenced Winston Churchill, Bill Gates, Jack Welch, and the Japanese business establishment. His more than three dozen books, written over 66 years and translated into 30 languages, also delivered his philosophy to newly promoted managers just out of the office cubicle. Dr. Drucker counseled presidents, bishops, baseball managers, CEOs, and symphony conductors on the finer points of management success. In his 88th year, Dr. Drucker sat with the author for this interview.

What would you say have been your greatest contributions to business and society?
One, I made management visible. People say I've discovered management—that's nonsense. I made it into a discipline.

Second, I was also the first one who said that people are a resource and not just a cost, and they have to be placed where they can make a contribution. The only ones who took me up on it were the Japanese for a long time.

The third one is knowledge—that knowledge work would be preeminent.

Four, I was the first to say that the purpose of business is to create the customer and to innovate. That I think is a major contribution. That took a long time to sink in—that management is not this mad dog of internal rules and regulations, that it's a discipline that can be learned and taught and practiced.

I think those four. The rest are secondary.

What is your view of today's public relations practice?
There is no public relations. There's publicity, promotion, advertising; but "relations" by definition is a two-way street. And the more important job and the more difficult is not to bring business and the executives to the outside but to bring the outside to these terribly insulated people. And this will be far more important in the next 20 years, when the outside is going to change beyond all recognition. I'm not only talking business CEOs but also university presidents and even bishops—several of my charity patients are bishops—all need to know what's going on outside.

Can you elaborate?
With an example. Have you ever heard of Paul Garrett?

Paul Garrett came out of journalism. He wanted to build a proper public relations department, to bring to General Motors what the outside was like. He would have been very effective. But GM didn't let him. Alfred Sloan (GM's CEO) brought Garrett in 1930 to keep GM out of *Fortune. Fortune* was founded as a muckraking magazine with investigative journalism.

Why didn't Sloan, supposedly one of the greatest managers of all time, want to listen to Garrett?
Neither Sloan nor anybody else in top management of General Motors wanted to hear what Garrett would have told them. And this was still the case much later.

Paul Garrett was a professional who would have told them things they didn't want to hear and wouldn't believe. Killing the messenger is never the right policy.

And in GM's case, the employee relations people totally failed to warn the company of the horrible sit-down strike they would suffer. And then when investor relations became important, it wasn't assigned to the public relations people.

And to this day, most institutions still look upon public relations as their "trumpet" and not as their "hearing aid." It's got to be both.

What do you see as the future of the practice of public relations?
I think there is a need. It is a very complicated and complex function. The media are no longer homogenous and are much more critical. But there is a need for an intermediary to tell the truth to management. Public relations people today don't do that because they're scared, because the people they work for don't like to hear what they don't want to hear.

Let's face it. There's an old saying, "If I have you for a friend, I don't need an enemy."

Public Relations Library

Aylward, Scott, and Pattye Moore. *Confessions from the Corner Office.* New York: John Wiley & Sons, 2007. Two communications executives, who rose through the ranks, credit their mastery of "the art of survival and behavior."

Bloom, Robert H., and Dave Conti. *The Inside Advantage: The Strategy that Unlocks the Hidden Growth in Your Business.* New York: McGraw-Hill, 2007. Words of wisdom from an experienced business CEO, who suggests that every company has "hidden strengths," which it must find, unleash, and communicate.

Croft, A. C. *Managing a PR Firm for Growth and Profit.* New York: Haworth Press, 2006. A public relations agency executive offers advice on attracting, winning, and keeping clients.

Davies, G., R. Chun, and S. Roper. *Corporate Reputation and Competitiveness.* New York: Rutledge, 2003.

Dilenschneider, Robert. *A Time for Heroes.* Bell Gardens, CA: Phoenix Press, 2005. A public relations veteran interviews business leaders and others on who they consider to be "heroes" and why.

Fombrun, D. J., and R. VanRiel. *Fame and Fortune: How Successful Companies Build Winning Reputations.* Upper Saddle River, NJ: Financial Times Prentice Hall, 2004.

Ind, N. (Ed.). *Beyond Branding: How the New Values of Transparency and Integrity Are Changing the World of Brands.* London, England: Kogan Page Ltd., 2004.

Lordan, Edward J. *Essentials of Public Relations Management.* Chicago: Branham, 2003. Introduction to organizing and managing a public relations function within an organization.

Lukaszewski, James E. *Why Should the Boss Listen to You? The 7 Disciplines of the Trusted Strategic Advisor.* New York: Jossey Bass/Wiley, 2008. An experienced management counselor offers advice on landing a seat at the management table, based on trustworthiness, thinking strategically, and developing a management perspective.

Pagano, B., E. Pagano, and S. Lundin. *The Transparency Edge: How Credibility Can Make or Break You in Business.* New York: McGraw-Hill, 2003.

Rayner, J. *Managing Reputational Risk: Curbing Threats, Leveraging Opportunities.* New York: John Wiley & Sons, 2003.

Rivkin, Steve, and Fraser P. Seitel. *Idealwise: How to Transform Today's Ideas into Tomorrow's Innovations.* New York: John Wiley & Sons, 2002. Two communications veterans (one of whom is exceedingly good looking) provide commonsense rules on sparking creativity and "finding the muse."

Trout, Jack. *Jack Trout on Strategy.* New York: McGraw-Hill, 2004. An advertising veteran discusses the strategic courses that successful companies have chosen.

Chapter 6

Ethics

In the spring of 2008, Bob Satchwell, the executive director of the Society of Editors in Great Britain, was worried.

Every morning for 10 weeks he typed the words, *"Prince Harry"* and *"Afghanistan"* into Google, and every morning the top result was the same: *"Prince Harry Is Forbidden to Fight Alongside Soldiers in Afghanistan."*

This relieved Mr. Satchwell, since weeks before, he had brokered a top-secret agreement with the British government to keep the fact out of the media that Prince Harry was, in fact, a ground soldier in the Afghanistan war zone (see Figure 6-1). The agreement of silence stemmed from the concern that Prince Harry's Afghanistan outing would put him and his comrades in special jeopardy.

But one morning, when U.S. Internet columnist Matt Drudge plastered the secret in an oversize banner headline on his Web site, The Drudge Report, Mr. Satchwell's and the British government's secret was out and flying at warp speed around the world.

Within minutes of the Drudge bulletin, the British press blackout was over, and so was Prince Harry's tenure in Afghanistan. What was left were questions about the "ethics," not only of Mr. Drudge for breaking the story but also of Mr. Satchwell and the British government for withholding it.[1]

The practice of public relations is all about earning *credibility*. Credibility, in turn, begins with telling the truth. Public relations, then, must be based on "doing the right thing"—in other words, acting ethically.

FIGURE 6-1 Outed in Afghanistan. The secret was out when Britain's Prince Harry was exposed on The Drudge Report as serving in Afghanistan. (Photo: Newscom)

In the 21st century, with scandals popping up periodically in every sector of society—from politics to religion, from business to sports—the subject of ethics is a pervasive one.

What precisely are *ethics*?

A sociologist posed that question to businesspeople and got these answers:

- "Ethics has to do with what my feelings tell me is right or wrong."
- "Ethics has to do with my religious beliefs."
- "Being ethical is doing what the law requires."
- "Ethics consists of the standards of behavior our society accepts."
- "I don't know what the word means."

Classical ethics means different things to different people. Ethics theories range from utilitarianism (i.e., the greatest good for the greatest number) to deontology (i.e., do what is right, though the world should perish).

While the meaning of ethics may be hard to pin down, there's no secret to what constitutes unethical behavior. Unfortunately, it's all around us. Consider the following:

- In **government**, ethical lapses know no party affiliation. Washington was rocked in 2006 by the revelations of multimillionaire lobbyist Jack Abramoff, who pleaded guilty to fraud, tax evasion, and conspiracy to bribe public officials. Abramoff dispensed most favors to Republicans, including former Speaker of the House Tom Delay, but he also trapped Democrats in his web of corruption.[2] In 2008, when former George W. Bush Presidential Press Secretary Scott McClellan wrote a tell-all memoir in 2008, critics decried his ethical impropriety (see "PR Ethics Mini-Case" at the end of this chapter).

- In **business**, the corporate trial of the century kicked off in Houston at the start of 2006, when the two highest-ranking officials of once high-flying energy trading firm Enron Corporation, former Chairman Ken Lay and former CEO Jeffrey Skilling, were charged with lying about the financial health of the company, so they could dump company stock before Enron went bankrupt.[3] Mr. Lay died before the proceedings, and Mr. Skilling headed for the slammer, along with many other former titans of other equally unethical companies.

  Then in 2008, the financial world was rocked by mega-scam artists like Bernard Madoff and Robert Stanford and mega-incompetent CEOs of venerable banks and investment companies, from Bank of America to Citigroup to Merrill Lynch.

- In **sports**, several of history's most legendary baseball players, from slugging Mark McGwire to fire-balling Roger Clemens to slammin' Sammy Sosa to all-everything Alex "A-Rod" Rodriguez, were all tarnished in the wake of a 21st century steroids scandal. Doping problems also plagued other sports, from track and field to cycling.

- In **education,** the president of American University was drummed out in 2005 after it was revealed that he spent more than $100,000 for such expenses as French wine, expensive foreign restaurants, and chauffeurs who ran personal errands.[4]

- Even venerable **non-profits** weren't immune from ethical transgression. The Red Cross was rocked by ethical scandal in 2007, when its president was forced to resign after only six months on the job, because of a secret "personal relationship" he had maintained with a staff member.[5]

- Then, of course, there was the ethical scandal involving the Catholic Church, the ostensible symbol of morality and decency in society, which was rocked in the spring of 2002 by a priest pedophilia scandal in the United States. In July, Pope John Paul II called the crimes and misdeeds of some priests "a source of shame."[6] And the aftermath of the scandal continued to plague the Church under his successor, Pope Benedict XVI (see "PR Ethics Mini-Case" in Chapter 2).

- Not even the practice of **public relations** could escape serious ethical lapses. In 2005, one of public relations' most respected firms, Ketchum, was embroiled in a "pay for publicity" scandal involving its client, the U.S. Department of Education.

The Ketchum calamity was particularly troubling, because the heart of public relations counsel is, as noted, to *do the right thing*. The cardinal rule of public relations is to *never lie*.

Nonetheless, in one startling survey of 1,700 public relations executives, it was revealed that 25 percent of those interviewed admitted they had "lied on the job," 39 percent said they had exaggerated the truth, and another 44 percent said they had felt "uncertain" about the ethics of what they did.[7]

That was reason enough to propel the Public Relations Society of America (PRSA) to invest $100,000 in revamping its code of ethics. The code (Appendix A), underscored by six fundamental values that the PRSA believes vital to the integrity of the profession (see Figure 6-2), demonstrates the significance of ethics to the practice of public relations.

Are We Doing the Right Thing?

What exactly are ethics? The answer isn't an easy one.

The Josephson Institute, which studies ethics, defines ethics as *standards of conduct that indicate how one should behave based on moral duties and virtues.*

In general, ethics are the values that guide a person, organization, or society—concepts such as right and wrong, fairness and unfairness, honesty and dishonesty. An individual's conduct is measured not only against his or her conscience but also against some norm of acceptability that society or an organization has determined.

Roughly translated, an individual's or organization's ethics comes down to the standards that are followed in relationships with others—the real integrity of the individual or organization. Obviously, a person's ethical construct and approach depend on numerous factors—cultural, religious, and educational, among others. Complicating the issue is that what might seem right to one person might not matter to someone else. No issue is solely black or white but is rather a shade of gray—particularly in making public relations decisions.

That is not to say that classical ethical distinctions don't exist. They do. Philosophers throughout the ages have debated the essence of ethics.

- *Utilitarianism* suggests considering the "greater good" rather than what may be best for the individual.
- To Aristotle, the *golden mean of moral virtue* could be found between two extreme points of view.
- Kant's *categorical imperative* recommended acting "on that maxim which you will to become a universal law."
- Mill's *principle of utility* recommended "seeking the greatest happiness for the greatest number."
- The traditional *Judeo-Christian ethic* prescribes "loving your neighbor as yourself." Indeed, this golden rule makes good sense as well in the practice of public relations.

Because the practice of public relations is misunderstood by so many—even including some of those for whom public relations people work—public relations people, in particular, must be ethical. They can't assume that ethics are strictly personal choices without relevance or related methodology for resolving moral quandaries. Public relations people

PRSA Member Code of Ethics 2000

PRSA Member Statement of Professional Values

This statement presents the core values of PRSA members and, more broadly, of the public relations profession. These values provide the foundation for the Member Code of Ethics and set the industry standard for the professional practice of public relations. These values are the fundamental beliefs that guide our behaviors and decision-making process. We believe our professional values are vital to the integrity of the profession as a whole.

ADVOCACY

We serve the public interest by acting as responsible advocates for those we represent. We provide a voice in the marketplace of ideas, facts, and viewpoints to aid informed public debate.

HONESTY

We adhere to the highest standards of accuracy and truth in advancing the interests of those we represent and in communicating with the public.

EXPERTISE

We acquire and responsibly use specialized knowledge and experience. We advance the profession through continued professional development, research, and education. We build mutual understanding, credibility, and relationships among a wide array of institutions and audiences.

INDEPENDENCE

We provide objective counsel to those we represent. We are accountable for our actions.

LOYALTY

We are faithful to those we represent, while honoring our obligation to serve the public interest.

FAIRNESS

We deal fairly with clients, employers, competitors, peers, vendors, the media, and the general public. We respect all opinions and support the right of free expression.

The Public Relations Society of America, 33 Irving Place, New York, NY 10003-2376

must adhere to a high standard of professional ethics, with truth as the key determinant of their conduct.

Indeed, ethics must be the great differentiator between public relations practice and other functions. Public relations people must always tell the truth. That doesn't mean they divulge "everything" about those for whom they work. But it does mean that they should never, ever lie. All one has in public relations is his or her reputation. When you lie, you lose it. So a high sense of ethical conduct must distinguish those who practice public relations.

Professional ethics, often called *applied ethics*, suggests a commonly accepted sense of professional conduct that is translated into formal codes of ethics.

The essence of the codes of conduct of both the Public Relations Society of America and the International Association of Business Communicators is that honesty and fairness lie at the heart of public relations practice. Indeed, if the ultimate goal of the public relations professional is to enhance public trust of an organization, then only the highest ethical conduct is acceptable.

Inherent in these standards of the profession is the understanding that ethics have changed and continue to change as society changes. Over time, views have changed on such issues as discrimination, the treatment of women and minorities, pollution of the environment, concern for human rights, acceptable standards of language and dress, and so on. Again, honesty and fairness are two critical components that will continue to determine the ethical behavior of public relations professionals.

Boiled down to its essence, the ethical heart of the practice of public relations lies, again, in posing only one simple question to management: *Are we doing the right thing?* In posing that critical question, the public relations officer becomes the "conscience" of the organization.

Often the public relations professional will be the only member of management with the nerve to pose such a question. Sometimes this means saying no to what the boss wants to do. Public relations professionals must be driven by one purpose—to preserve, defend, sustain, and enhance the health and vitality of the organization. Simply translated, the bottom line for public relations professionals must always be to counsel and to do what is in the best long-term interests of the organization.

Ethics in Business

For many people today, regrettably, the term *business ethics* is an oxymoron. Its mere mention stimulates images of disgraced CEOs being led away in handcuffs after bilking their shareholders and employees out of millions of dollars. In one period alone, the 2002 "summer of shame," a dizzying array of corporate executives was charged with ethical violations.

- The summer began with executives of Enron being charged with massive accounting fraud, which effectively destroyed the life savings of shareholders— many of them longtime Enron employees. Even before Lay and Skilling were put on trial in 2006, other Enron executives were serving hard time.

- In Enron's wake, the bedrock accounting firm of Arthur Andersen was decimated for aiding and abetting in the Enron accounting duplicity.

- WorldCom, Global Crossing, and Qwest Communications executives, accused of massive accounting fraud, were charged soon thereafter, and several were later taken into custody by the FBI.

■ The executives of Adelphia Communications, a leading cable TV company, were charged with using the corporation as their own private "piggy bank."[8] Even worse, the three chief culprits were members of the founding Rigas family.

■ Even Martha Stewart, celebrity homemaking idol, was charged with insider trading violations (see Case Study in Chapter 4).

Since those corporate scandals, people have become outraged at executive compensation packages, such as Philip Purcell's $113 million payout to resign as Morgan Stanley's CEO, James M. Kilts's $165 million payoff for selling Gillette to Procter & Gamble, and the compensation packages of three failed CEOs, Stanley O'Neal of Merrill Lynch, Charles Prince of Citigroup, and Angelo Mozilo of Countrywide, all of whom were forced to resign in 2007 after the subprime lending fiasco rocked the economy (see Figure 6-3). Each, for his efforts, received well in excess of $100 million in parting compensation.

No wonder confidence in business has deteriorated. One 2007 survey by the Ethics Resource Center found rates of business misconduct increasing, management awareness declining, and momentum behind corporate ethics and compliance programs deteriorating. Another 2007 survey, conducted by Junior Achievement and Deloitte, found that 41 percent of teenagers believe one must act unethically in order to get ahead. In a similar survey two years earlier, only 22 percent expressed that view.[9]

Indeed, many believed the term "crooked CEO" was redundant. One book, written by former management consultants, described CEOs thusly:

Among the more than 14,000 publicly registered companies in the U.S. and the even larger number of privately held companies there is a class of people who will lie to the public, the regulators, their employees and anyone else in order to increase personal wealth and power.[10]

To stem the feeling that chief executives and their companies weren't acting ethically, a number of firms increased their efforts to make their activities more transparent to the public. Companies from Coca-Cola to Amazon.com to General Electric

FIGURE 6-3 **Facing the music.** A 2008 Capitol Hill hearing on CEO compensation featured three of corporate America's most disgraced dimwits, Citigroup's Charles Prince (left), Merrill Lynch's Stanley O'Neal (third from left), and Countrywide's Angelo Mozilo (right). (Photo: Newscom)

announced plans to make accounting procedures more understandable. One CEO, Henry Paulson of investment banking giant Goldman Sachs, who would later become Secretary of the Treasury, called on his fellow CEOs to reform before regulation forced them to do so. *"In my lifetime, American business has never been under such scrutiny. To be blunt, much of it is deserved,"* said Paulson.[11]

Corporate Codes of Conduct

By 2007, most organizations devoted an increasing amount of time and attention to corporate ethics.

The vast majority of companies conducted periodic risk assessments, with more than half doing so annually. Three-quarters of all companies conducted training in such areas as sexual/workplace harassment, conflicts of interest, and protecting confidential information. Many firms devoted upwards of $500,000 a year, exclusive of personnel costs, for ethics and compliance programs.[12]

Most organizations also adopted formal codes of conduct to guide their activities. Indeed, the New York Stock Exchange mandated such codes after the corporate scandals of 2002. A code of conduct is a formal statement of the values and business practices of a corporation. A code may be a short mission statement, or it may be a sophisticated document that requires compliance with articulated standards and that has a complicated enforcement mechanism. Whatever its length and complexity, the corporate code of conduct dictates the behavioral expectations that an organization holds for its employees and agents.

Formal codes of conduct can help accomplish a number of public relations purposes.

- **To increase public confidence.** Scandals, credit crises, oil shocks, etc., have all shaken investor confidence and have led to a decline of public trust and confidence in business. Many firms have responded with written codes of ethics.

- **To stem the tide of regulation.** As public confidence has declined, government regulation of business has increased. Some estimated the cost to society of compliance with regulations at $100 billion per year. Corporate codes of conduct, it was hoped, would help serve as a self-regulation mechanism.

- **To improve internal operations.** As companies became larger and more decentralized, management needed consistent standards of conduct to ensure that employees were meeting the business objectives of the company in a legal and ethical manner.

- **To respond to transgressions.** Frequently, when a company itself is caught in the web of unethical behavior, it responds with its own code of ethics.

Ralph Waldo Emerson once wrote, "An organization is the lengthened shadow of a man." Today, many corporate executives realize that just as an individual has certain responsibilities as a citizen, so, too, does a corporate citizen have responsibilities to the society in which it is privileged to operate.

As business becomes globalized, companies are being encouraged by interest groups, governments, educational institutions, industry associations, and others to adopt codes of conduct. Accordingly, formal ethical codes, addressing such topics as executive compensation, accounting procedures, confidentiality of corporate information, misappropriation of corporate assets, bribes and kickbacks, and political contributions, have become a corporate fact of life for every company executive, up to and including the members of the board of directors (see Figure 6-4).

Code of Conduct for the Board of Directors of McDonald's Corporation

The members of the Board of Directors of McDonald's Corporation acknowledge and accept the scope and extent of our duties as directors. We have a responsibility to carry out our duties in an honest and businesslike manner and within the scope of our authority, as set forth in the General Corporation Laws of the State of Delaware and in the Certificate of Incorporation and By-Laws of McDonald's Corporation. We are entrusted with and responsible for the oversight of the assets and business affairs of McDonald's Corporation in an honest, fair, diligent and ethical manner. As Directors we must act within the bounds of the authority conferred upon us and with the duty to make and enact informed decisions and policies in the best interests of McDonald's and its shareholders. The Board of Directors has adopted the following Code of Conduct and our Directors are expected to adhere to the standards of loyalty, good faith, and the avoidance of conflict of interest that follow:

Board Members will:

- Act in the best interests of, and fulfill their fiduciary obligations to, McDonald's shareholders;
- Act honestly, fairly, ethically and with integrity;
- Conduct themselves in a professional, courteous and respectful manner;
- Comply with all applicable laws, rules and regulations;
- Act in good faith, responsibly, with due care, competence and diligence, without allowing their independent judgment to be subordinated;
- Act in a manner to enhance and maintain the reputation of McDonald's;
- Disclose potential conflicts of interest that they may have regarding any matters that may come before the Board, and abstain from discussion and voting on any matter in which the Director has or may have a conflict of interest;
- Make available to and share with fellow Directors information as may be appropriate to ensure proper conduct and sound operation of McDonald's and its Board of Directors;
- Respect the confidentiality of information relating to the affairs of the Company acquired in the course of their service as Directors, except when authorized or legally required to disclose such information; and
- Not use confidential information acquired in the course of their service as Directors for their personal advantage.

A Director who has concerns regarding compliance with this Code should raise those concerns with the Chairman of the Board and the Chair of the Governance Committee, who will determine what action shall be taken to deal with the concern. In the extremely unlikely event that a waiver of this Code for a Director would be in the best interest of the Company, it must be approved by the Governance Committee.

Directors will annually sign a confirmation that they have read and will comply with this Code.

Adopted by the Board of Directors
as of May 22, 2003

FIGURE 6-4 **Conduct of the Board.** Many companies, such as McDonald's, ensure that even the members of the board of directors live by a code of conduct. (Used with permission from McDonald's Corporation)

Corporate Social Responsibility

Closely related to the ethical conduct of an organization is its social responsibility. Simply stated, corporate social responsibility is about how companies manage the business processes to produce an overall positive impact on society. This implies that any social institution, from the smallest family unit to the largest corporation, is responsible for the behavior of its members and may be held accountable for their misdeeds.

In the late 1960s, when this idea was just emerging, initial responses were of the knee-jerk variety. A firm that was threatened by increasing legal or activist pressures and harassment would ordinarily change its policies in a hurry. Today, however, organizations and their social responsibility programs are much more sophisticated. Social responsibility is treated just like any other management discipline: Analyze the issues, evaluate performance, set priorities, allocate resources to those priorities, and implement programs that deal with issues within the constraints of the organization's resources. Many companies have created special committees to set the agenda and target the objectives.

Social responsibility touches practically every level of organizational activity, from marketing to hiring, from training to work standards. A partial list of social responsibility categories might include the following:

- **Product lines**—dangerous products, product performance and standards, packaging, and environmental impact
- **Marketing practices**—sales practices, consumer complaint policies, advertising content, and fair pricing
- **Corporate philanthropy**—contribution performance, encouragement of employee participation in social projects, and community development activities
- **Environmental activities**—pollution-control and climate change projects, adherence to federal standards, and evaluation procedures for new packages and products
- **External relations**—support of minority enterprises, investment practices, and government relations
- **Employment diversity in retaining and promoting minorities and women**—current hiring policies, advancement policies, specialized career counseling, and opportunities for special minorities such as the physically handicapped
- **Employee safety and health**—work environment policies, accident safeguards, and food and medical facilities

More often than not, organizations have incorporated social responsibility into the mainstream of their practices. Most firms recognize that social responsibility, far from being an add-on program, must be a corporate way of life. They recognize that in a skeptical world, business must be responsible to act ethically and improve the quality of life of their workforce, their families, and the broader society.

Ethics in Government

Politics has never enjoyed an unblemished reputation when it comes to ethics. In the first decade of the 21st century, politicians seemed to be losing further ground in terms of trustworthiness and ethical values.

Both the legislative and executive branches of the federal government took a beating in the public eye. Congress, according to Zogby Interactive polling, continued its downward slide with 76 percent of Americans expressing "low trust" in Congress and only 3 percent reporting "high trust." The president didn't fare much better, with 69 percent expressing "low trust" but 24 percent expressing "high trust."[13]

The advent of 24-hour cable news and the 24/7 Internet blogosphere cast a perpetual 21st-century spotlight on the activities of the president and his allies. No administration could escape the harsh glare of prying eyes noting ethical failures. Both President George Bush and Vice President Dick Cheney were criticized harshly for everything from the disposition of and reasons for war in Iraq to their past corporate energy affiliations. President Bill Clinton, of course, suffered the ultimate ethical ignominy: being impeached by the House of Representatives for his inexplicable and embarrassing behavior with a young intern in the White House.

The "sleaze factor" in government continued to poison politics.

- Republican House majority leader Tom Delay, one of the nation's most powerful politicians, was forced to step down from the leadership in 2005 and ultimately left office after being implicated in a corruption scandal and later linked to renegade lobbyist Abramoff.

- That same year, decorated Republican war hero Randy "Duke" Cunningham tearfully resigned his congressional seat after pleading guilty to taking more than $2 million in bribes.

- In 2006, another congressman, Democrat William Jefferson, was linked to a bribery scandal promoting a business deal in Africa. The fact that a raid on the congressman's house found $90,000 worth of bills in his freezer didn't help his claim of innocence.

- In 2007, Republican Senator Larry Craig was arrested for lewd conduct in a Minneapolis International Airport men's room. The senator's immediate "guilty" plea and subsequent attempts to plead innocent didn't help his claim (see PR Ethics Mini-Case, Chapter 7).

- In 2008, New York's crusading Democratic Governor Elliott Spitzer was forced from office when he was found to have been a client of a high-priced prostitution ring. And in 2009, Republican Mark Sanford refused to resign as South Carolina governor, after his extra-marital affair was exposed.

After all the white-collar crime and political scandals that have marked the first decade of the 21st century, the public is less willing to tolerate such ethical violations from their elected officials. It is likely that ethics in government will become an even more important issue as voters insist on representatives who are honest, trustworthy, and ethical.

PR Ethics

Mini-Case   The Sad Memoir of Scott McClellan

By 2006, when he was "relieved" of his duties as President George W. Bush's press secretary, Scott McClellan was a dazed and bitter man.

Arguably one of the weakest presidential press secretaries in history, McClellan was labeled "*the human piñata*" because of the way he was battered at White House press conferences.

Forced to deal with several embarrassing White House problems, not the least of which was the accusation against Vice President Dick Cheney and his deputy, Lewis Libby, in leaking the name of a CIA operative, McClellan was forced to endure constant battering at the hands of an empowered White House press corps. If nothing else, he served the Bush Administration as a "*good soldier*" (see Figure 6-5).

FIGURE 6-5 Et tu, Brute? In happier times, President George W. Bush and "loyal" Presidential Press Secretary Scott McClellan. (Photo: Newscom)

In the spring of 2006, McClellan was mercifully replaced by Fox News broadcaster Tony Snow, who quickly brought order and credibility back to the press secretary job with a confident, open approach.

A year later, inexplicably, Scott McClellan turned on the hand that had fed him for his entire career as a government employee. Indeed, George W. Bush had loyally taken McClellan with him from the State House in Texas to the White House in Washington for the better part of two decades.

But when McClellan left the White House, he let his former patron have it with both barrels blazing.

In his memoir, segments of which were leaked less than a year after his White House departure, McClellan ripped into Bush, claiming his former mentor, among other things:

- Relied on "propaganda" to sell the Iraq war,
- Veered "terribly off course" in war policy,
- Refused to be "open and forthright on Iraq," and
- Took a "permanent campaign approach" to governing.

The McClellan memoir sent shockwaves through Washington and was an instant best-seller. Democratic opponents of President Bush hailed it as a "smoking gun," revealing all the improprieties of the Bush White House.

But others wondered about the "ethics" of a former press secretary choosing to attack the only former client he ever had; a man whom the press secretary had publicly praised just months before the tell-all book.

Moreover, if the essence of public relations counsel is to advise an employer on "how to act," some wondered why McClellan hadn't offered the advice to the president when he served next to him, rather than criticizing him, for money, well after the fact.*

Questions

1. How would you assess Scott McClellan's ethical responsibility to be loyal to his boss vs. his ethical responsibility to reveal what happened at the White House?

2. What are the public relations ethical considerations revealed by the McClellan case?

*For further information, see Mike Allen, "McClellan Rips Bush, White House," Politco.com (May 27, 2008); Elisabeth Bumiller, "In Ex-Spokesman's Book, Harsh Words for Bush," *New York Times* (May 28, 2008); and Fraser P. Seitel, "The Sad Memoir of Scott McClellan," odwyerpr.com (November 26, 2007).

Ethics in Journalism

The Society of Professional Journalists is quite explicit on the subject of ethics (see Figure 6-6).

Journalists at all times will show respect for the dignity, privacy, rights, and well-being of people encountered in the course of gathering and presenting the news.

1. The news media should not communicate unofficial charges affecting reputation or moral character without giving the accused a chance to reply.

FIGURE 6-6
Journalists' code. The Society of Professional Journalists has elaborated in some detail on the ethical guidelines that should govern all journalists. (Copyright © 1996–2007. Reprinted by permission of the Society of Professional Journalists, www.spj.org)

THE SOCIETY OF PROFESSIONAL JOURNALISTS, SIGMA DELTA CHI

THE SOCIETY of Professional Journalists, Sigma Delta Chi believes the duty of journalists is to serve the truth.

WE BELIEVE the agencies of mass communication are carriers of public discussion and information, acting on their Constitutional mandate and freedom to learn and report the facts.

WE BELIEVE in public enlightenment as the forerunner of justice, and in our Constitutional role to seek the truth as part of the public's right to know the truth.

WE BELIEVE those responsibilities carry obligations that require journalists to perform with intelligence, objectivity, accuracy and fairness.

To these ends, we declare acceptance of the standards of practice here set forth:

RESPONSIBILITY:
The public's right to know of events of public importance and interest is the overriding mission of the mass media. The purpose of distributing news and enlightened opinion is to serve the general welfare. Journalists who use their professional status as representatives of the public for selfish or other unworthy motives violate a high trust.

FREEDOM OF THE PRESS:
Freedom of the press is to be guarded as an inalienable right of people in a free society. It carries with it the freedom and the responsibility to discuss, question and challenge actions and utterances of our government and of our public and private institutions. Journalists uphold the right to speak unpopular opinions and the privilege to agree with the majority.

ETHICS:
Journalists must be free of obligation to any interest other than the public's right to know the truth.
1. Gifts, favors, free travel, special treatment or privileges can compromise the integrity of journalists and their employers. Nothing of value should be accepted.
2. Secondary employment, political involvement, holding public office and service in community organizations should be avoided if it compromises the integrity of journalists and their employers. Journalists and their employers should conduct their personal lives in a manner which protects them from conflict of interest, real or apparent. Their responsibilities to the public are paramount. That is the nature of their profession.

3. So-called news communications from private sources should not be published or broadcast without substantiation of their claims to news value.
4. Journalists will seek news that serves the public interest, despite the obstacles. They will make constant efforts to assure that the public's business is conducted in public and that public records are open to public inspection.
5. Journalists acknowledge the newsman's ethic of protecting confidential sources of information.

ACCURACY AND OBJECTIVITY:
Good faith with the public is the foundation of all worthy journalism.
1. Truth is our ultimate goal.
2. Objectivity in reporting the news is another goal, which serves as the mark of an experienced professional. It is a standard of performance toward which we strive. We honor those who achieve it.
3. There is no excuse for inaccuracies or lack of thoroughness.
4. Newspaper headlines should be fully warranted by the contents of the articles they accompany. Photographs and telecasts should give an accurate picture of an event and not highlight a minor incident out of context.
5. Sound practice makes clear distinction between news reports and expressions of opinion. News reports should be free of opinion or bias and represent all sides of an issue.
6. Partisanship in editorial comment which knowingly departs from the truth violates the spirit of American journalism.
7. Journalists recognize their responsibility for offering informed analysis, comment and editorial opinion on public events and issues. They accept the obligation to present such material by individuals whose competence, experience and judgment qualify them for it.
8. Special articles or presentations devoted to advocacy or the writer's own conclusions and interpretations should be labeled as such.

FAIR PLAY:
Journalists at all times will show respect for the dignity, privacy, rights and well-being of people encountered in the course of gathering and presenting the news.
1. The news media should not communicate unofficial charges affecting reputation or moral character without giving the accused a chance to reply.
2. The news media must guard against invading a person's right to privacy.
3. The media should not pander to morbid curiosity about details of vice and crime.
4. It is the duty of news media to make prompt and complete correction of their errors.
5. Journalists should be accountable to the public for their reports and the public should be encouraged to voice its grievances against the media. Open dialogue with our readers, viewers and listeners should be fostered.

PLEDGE:
Journalists should actively censure and try to prevent violations of these standards, and they should encourage their observance by all newspeople. Adherence to this code of ethics is intended to preserve the bond of mutual trust and respect between American journalists and the American people.

2. The news media must guard against invading a person's right to privacy.

3. The media should not pander to morbid curiosity about details of vice and crime.

And so on.

Unfortunately, what is in the code often doesn't reflect what appears in print or on the air. More often than not, journalistic judgments run smack into ethical principles.

- Plagiarism scandals at three of the nation's leading newspapers—*The New York Times, Washington Post,* and *Boston Globe*—resulted in the firings of high-profile journalists. The *Times* fell victim to the new century's most embarrassing instance of suspect journalistic ethics. In 2003, the "Great Gray Lady" was stunned when one of its promising young reporters, Jayson Blair, was discovered to have fabricated numerous dispatches for the paper over an extended period. The *Times* found out about Blair's fraud only when a reporter from another paper tipped it off. Blair was immediately fired, and the *Times* took a major reputation hit.

- In 2005, the *Times* was shocked again after one of its star reporters, Judith Miller, served 85 days in prison for refusing to reveal confidential administration sources related to stories involving the leak of the name of a CIA operative married to a Bush administration critic. Upon her release, the *Times* criticized her for being too cozy with the White House. Miller hastily resigned after 28 years at the *Times.*

- In 2009, the *Times* was faced with a different kind of ethical dilemma, when Editor Bill Keller decided to keep quiet the kidnapping by the Taliban in Afghanistan of investigative reporter David Rohde. After seven months in captivity, Rohde escaped to freedom, and his story was communicated around the world. In the midst of the celebration, the *Times* was criticized by some for suppressing the news.

- In the new millennium, the proliferation of blogs—expanding at the rate of 70,000 sites a day—and other online media, publishing round the clock, as well as the exponential increase in TV news, cable stations, and programming on the Internet, increased the pressure on news outlets to report as scrupulously as possible lest they be caught in an inextricable ethical crisis.[14] Such was the case late in 2004, when venerable CBS anchor Dan Rather cited "exclusive documents" alleging that President George W. Bush had shirked his duties while in the Texas Air National Guard. When the documents turned out to be forgeries, CBS launched its own investigation, which resulted in the firing of several long-time staff members. Less than a year later, after 43 years with CBS, Dan Rather was gone. In 2007, Rather sued his former employer for violating his contract.

- Television news itself, particularly cable TV, was rocked by the phenomenon in the 21st century of "nonstop screaming," where adversaries on either side spent most of their air time declaring a "my way or the highway" point of view. Partisanship was the order of the day. Such popular programs as Fox News Channel's *The O'Reilly Factor with Bill O'Reilly,* MSNBC's *Countdown with Keith Olbermann,* and *CNN Headline News' Headline Prime with Nancy Grace,* all distinguished by their voluble hosts, added plenty of heat but little light to the national dialogue. And many times, it was non-journalist late-night comedians who landed the top name guests—or "gets" as they say in the news biz (see Figure 6-7).

Such was the state of journalistic ethics in the last half of the first decade of the 21st century.

FIGURE 6-7 The new "journalists." Late-night comics, like Jay Leno, out-muscled journalists in the 21st century to interview the really big "gets." (White House Photo by Pete Souza)

Ethics in Public Relations

As noted, ethics is—or at least, should be—the great differentiator between public relations and other professions. In light of numerous misconceptions about the practice of public relations, it is imperative that practitioners emulate the highest standards of personal and professional ethics (see Appendix B). Within an organization, public relations practitioners must be the standard bearers of corporate ethical initiatives. By the same token, public relations consultants must always counsel their clients in an ethical direction—toward accuracy and candor and away from lying and hiding the truth.

The public relations department should be the seat of corporate ethics. At least four ethical theories are relevant to the practice of public relations.

- The *attorney/adversary model,* developed by Jay Barney and Ralph Black, compares the legal profession to that of public relations in that (1) both are advocates in an adversarial climate and (2) both assume counterbalancing messages will be provided by adversaries. In this model, Barney and Black suggest practitioners have no obligation to consider the public interest or any other outside view beyond that of their client.

- The *two-way communication model,* developed by Jim Grunig, is based on collaboration, working jointly with different people, and allowing for both listening and give-and-take. In this model, Grunig suggests that the practitioner balance his or her role as a client advocate with one as social conscience for the larger public.

- The *enlightened self-interest model,* developed by Sherry Baker, is based on the principle that businesses do well by doing good. In this model, Baker suggests that companies gain a competitive edge and are more respected in the marketplace if they behave ethically.

■ The *responsible advocacy model,* developed by Kathy Fitzpatrick and Candace Gauthier, is based on the ideal of professional responsibility. It postulates that practitioners' first loyalty is to their clients, but they also have a responsibility to voice the opinions of organizational stakeholders. In this model, Fitzpatrick and Gauthier suggest that the practitioner's greatest need for ethical guidance is in the reconciliation of being both a professional advocate and a social conscience.

The PRSA has been a leader in the effort to foster a strong sense of professionalism among its membership, particularly in its new code of ethics. Its six core values underpin the desired behavior of any public relations professional.

■ **Advocacy.** The PRSA Code endorses the Fitzpatrick and Gauthier model in stating: "We serve the public interest by acting as responsible advocates for those we represent." For example, public relations professionals must never reveal confidential or private client information, even if a journalist demands it. The only way such information might be revealed is after a thorough discussion with the client.

■ **Honesty.** For example, a client asking a public relations representative to "embellish" the performance the company expects to achieve should be told diplomatically, but firmly, no. Public relations people don't lie.

■ **Expertise.** For example, a client in need of guidance as to whether to accept a sensitive interview invitation for a cable TV talk show must be carefully guided through the pros and cons by a skilled public relations practitioner.

■ **Independence.** For example, when everyone in the room—lawyer, human resources, treasurer, and president—all agree with the CEO's rock-headed scheme to disguise bad news, it is the public relations professional's duty to strike an independent tone.

■ **Loyalty.** For example, if a competing client offers a practitioner more money to abandon his or her original employer, the public relations professional should understand his or her loyalties must remain constant.

■ **Fairness.** For example, when a rude and obnoxious journalist demands information, a practitioner's responsibility is to treat even the most obnoxious reporter with fairness.

What these tenets indicate is that proper public relations practice is just the opposite of what many accuse public relations people of being—deceivers, obfuscators, con artists, spinners, or even liars. Rather, public relations people and practice ought to be "transparent."[15]

Sadly, the practice hasn't always lived up to these ethical principles. As a consequence, the field, even more sadly, regularly ranks toward the bottom on credibility surveys.[16] Changing this view to one of a more ethical and honest practice is a great challenge for public relations leaders in the 21st century.

Talking Points Test Your Workplace Ethics

So you want to enter the workplace? The question of ethics looms larger today than at any previous time, especially with the advent of technology and the potential abuses it brings.

To test how you might measure up as an ethical worker, answer the following questions. And don't cheat!

Questions

1. Is it wrong to use company email for personal reasons?

2. Is it wrong to use office equipment to help your family and friends with homework?

3. Is it wrong to play computer games on office equipment during the workday?

4. Is it wrong to use office equipment to do Internet shopping?

5. Is it unethical to visit pornographic Web sites using office equipment?

6. What's the value at which a gift from a supplier or client becomes troubling?

7. Is a $50 gift to a boss unacceptable?

8. Is it okay to take a pair of $200 football tickets as a gift from a supplier?

9. Is it okay to take a $120 pair of theater tickets?

10. Is it okay to take a $100 holiday fruit basket?

11. Is it okay to take a $25 gift certificate?

12. Is it okay to accept a $75 prize won at a raffle at a supplier's conference?

Answers

From a cross-section of workers at nationwide companies, the answers to these questions were compiled by the Ethics Officer Association, Belmont, Massachusetts, and the Ethical Leadership Group, Wilmette, Illinois.

1. 34% said personal email on company computers is wrong.

2. 37% said using office equipment for schoolwork is wrong.

3. 49% said playing computer games at work is wrong.

4. 44% said Internet shopping at work is wrong.

5. 87% said it is unethical to visit pornographic sites at work.

6. 33% said $25 is the amount at which a gift from a supplier or client becomes troubling. Another 33% said $50. Another 33% said $100.

7. 35% said a $50 gift to the boss is unacceptable.

8. 70% said it is unacceptable to take $200 football tickets.

9. 70% said it is unacceptable to take $120 theater tickets.

10. 35% said it is unacceptable to take a $100 fruit basket.

11. 45% said it is unacceptable to take a $25 gift certificate.

12. 40% said it is unacceptable to take the $75 raffle prize.

Last Word

The scandals in government and business in the first decade of the 21st century have placed a premium in every sector of society on acting ethically. More than half of the 3,000 workers who took part in a National Business Ethics Survey said they witnessed at least one type of ethical misconduct on their job.[17] That's disgraceful. As the CEO of Eaton Corporation, the manufacturing giant, put it, "There is no truer window into a corporation's soul than its approach to ethics."[18]

The same can be said for the practice of public relations.

The success of public relations in the 21st century will depend largely on how the field responds to the issue of ethical conduct. Public relations professionals must have credibility in order to practice. They must be respected by the various publics with which they interact. This is as true overseas as it is in the United States. To be credible and to achieve respect, public relations professionals must be ethical. It is that simple.

Stated another way, for public relations practice in general and individual public relations professionals in particular, credibility in the next few years will depend on how scrupulously they observe and apply the principles and practice of ethics in everything they do.

Discussion Starters

1. How would you define ethics?

2. How would you describe the state of ethics in business, government, and journalism?

3. How important is the ethical component of the practice of public relations?

4. Why have corporations adopted corporate codes of conduct?

5. What is corporate social responsibility?

6. What were the ethical implications of Scott McClellan's memoirs?

7. What are the pros and cons of the attorney/adversary public relations model compared to the enlightened self-interest model?

8. Is the public more tolerant or less tolerant of ethical violators today? Why?

9. What is the significance of the six ethical values that underscore the Public Relations Society of America Code of Ethics?

10. What are the ethical responsibilities of a public relations professional?

the Shelf   What Happened: Inside the Bush White House and Washington's Culture of Deception / Scott McClellan,

New York: Public Affairs, 2008

Read it for yourself and make your own determination.

The memoir by the former Bush Administration White House press secretary is a tell-all—some would say "get-even"—account of seven years within the inner circle. McClellan recounts his views of the events that he claims took the Bush administration "disastrously and irretrievably off course."

To his credit, the author makes no attempt to hide his disdain for Bush luminaries like Vice President Dick Cheney,

Chief of Staff Karl Rove, and Secretary of State Condoleezza Rice. What is more questionable is precisely how much "access" to the chief McClellan enjoyed as press secretary. Indeed, a cynic might suggest the book is retribution for being frozen out of the consultatory loop.

But don't take my word for it. Read it, and you be the judge.

Case Study   Hewlett-Packard Spies on Itself

For decades, the Hewlett-Packard Company—or HP, as it was known—was one of Silicon Valley's most respected technology companies. Its founders, Stanford classmates David Packard and William Hewlett, created their partnership in 1939 and built a worldwide computer colossus.

Both Hewlett and Packard, after they retired, became well known as philanthropists, each of them the epitome of high ethics and propriety.

Well after the founders departed, the company appointed its first woman CEO, Carly Fiorina, in 1999. The former AT&T executive, who seemed more interested in personal publicity than aiding HP—she was ordained by *Forbes* as *"the most powerful woman in business"*—presided over a controversial merger with Compaq in 2002 and left the company ignominiously in 2005. (Later, she turned up as a financial advisor to the John McCain 2008 presidential campaign.)

As inauspicious as Carly Fiorina's tenure at HP, the Fiorina era was a walk in the park compared to what was to come next for venerable Hewlett-Packard.

Snoops on Board

In September 2006, *Newsweek* published a story revealing that the chair of HP, Patricia Dunn, had hired a team of independent electronic-security experts to spy on fellow HP board members, staff members, and journalists who covered the company (see Figure 6-8).

Chair Dunn was concerned about "persistent disclosure of confidential information from within the ranks." The primary target of the investigation was the company's longest-serving board member, George A. Keyworth II, a notoriously loose-lipped physicist and former presidential science advisor, who had earlier been asked to resign but refused. Others targeted included Dunn's chief antagonist on the board, Thomas J. Perkins, a venture capitalist and author of the novel "*Sex and the Single Zillionaire.*"

To "get the goods" on its board members, the HP electronic security experts used a technique known as "pretexting" to

FIGURE 6-8 Dunn and done. *Newsweek* blew the lid off Hewlett-Packard's internal spying scandal in September 2006. (Photo: Newscom)

obtain call records of board members and nine journalists, including reporters for CNET, *The New York Times*, and *The Wall Street Journal*.

The investigators misrepresented themselves as the board members and journalists to their phone companies, in order to obtain their phone records. A reeling Chair Dunn claimed that she hadn't known beforehand the methods the investigators used to try and determine the source of the leaks.

By the end of the ordeal, the chair and millions of observers had a pretty good understanding of what exactly led to Hewlett-Packard's ethical tribulation.

Plugging the Leaks

The leak that sent Dunn and others over the edge was a CNET article that quoted plans reached at a board retreat. The article used quotes about long-term HP plans from a "source," who turned out to be director Keyworth.

While the leak really didn't tell anybody anything of consequence, it may have been enough to subject blabbermouth Keyworth to a lawsuit for breach of fiduciary duty. Was that enough to cause famously ethical HP to go after its director with an identity theft scam to invade his privacy? Not hardly.

But that's exactly what Chair Dunn apparently authorized. She hired a Boston-area investigative firm that used "pretexting," which used Social Security and other information, to impersonate Keyworth and others to obtain calling records from the phone company.

The ethically questionable practice proceeded with full support from HP's senior counsel, Kevin Hunsaker, who also—ironically—held the title of "director of ethics." Mr. Hunsaker worked in concert with the company's Boston-based manager of global investigations, Anthony Gentilucci.

Ms. Dunn was regularly briefed on the findings of the investigation, including the source of leaks and the techniques used to get information.

Ferreting Out Nosey Reporters

After the HP spy plan was exposed, reporters began to reveal that the effort was an ongoing one and involved great planning on the part of several HP executives. Indeed, the internal investigation commenced early in 2005 and consisted of two phases, code named Kona I and Kona II (Ms. Dunn owned a vacation home in Kona, Hawaii).

One intriguing part of HP's grand design for its leak detection operation was to plant spies in the news bureaus of two primary recipients of leaks—CNET and *The Wall Street Journal*. While nine journalists were targeted by the company, CNET and the *Journal* drew special attention from the HP snoops.

The idea, which was distributed in a confidential report to Hunsaker and Gentilucci, called for placing undercover HP confederates as clerical personnel inside the subject newsrooms.

While HP stopped short of placing undercover operatives within the news organizations, the company fought back its suspicions that its pretexting technique might not be especially kosher.

Mr. Hunsaker, the chief ethics officer, questioned in an email how the company was able to collect personal cell and home phone records. *"Is it all above board?"* he asked Mr. Gentilucci.

Mr. Gentilucci responded, *"I think it is on the edge but above board. We use pretext interviews on a number of investigations to extract information and/or make covert purchases of stolen property, in a sense, all undercover operations."*

Mr. Hunsaker emailed the response, *"I shouldn't have asked . . ."*

Dunn, Done

The revelations of ethical impropriety from one of the nation's historically most ethical companies sent reverberations throughout the business community.

The California Attorney General charged Dunn with four felonies for her role in the HP investigation into the unauthorized disclosure of company information.

The Securities and Exchange Commission launched a full scale investigation. Lawsuits were filed. HP's stock price tumbled. Congress leaped into the fray with hearings. And journalists exposed new elements of HP spying on a daily basis.

Just weeks after the first stories appeared, Hewlett-Packard's CEO, Mark Hurd (who managed to duck for cover through most of the ordeal) announced that Ms. Dunn had resigned, and that Messrs. Hunsaker and Gentilucci would join her in departing.

In a quivering voice, Mr. Hurd apologized profusely for running roughshod over the privacy of directors and even company employees. One such employee, as it turned out, was HP's public relations spokesman, Michael Moeller, a former *Business Week* reporter.

In the end, the California Superior Court dropped criminal charges against Dunn in the "interest of justice." And things gradually returned to normal for Hewlett-Packard, although the company would never again enjoy the ethical stature it maintained for so many decades.

Summarized *The New York Times*, *"It was Ms. Dunn's responsibility to ensure that the company's standards were met in any investigation, no matter who was tasked with the job. We hope that Hewlett-Packard's mistakes provide an instructive example to the ethically impaired."*

Somewhere, Carly Fiorina was laughing.*

Questions

1. Were you the public relations director of HP, what would you have advised Chair Dunn in terms of "plugging leaks"?

2. Had you not been consulted in advance but found out about the leak investigation after-the-fact, what would you have done?

3. What steps would you recommend Hewlett-Packard take to avoid such ethical problems in the future?

*For further information, see Damon Darlin and Matt Richtel, "H.P. Studied Infiltrating Newsrooms, "*New York Times* (September 20, 2006): C1; Damon Darlin and Matt Richtel, "Chairwoman Leaves Hewlett in Spying Furor," *New York Times* (September 23, 2006): 1; Jim Hopkins and Jon Swartz, "Plot Thickens in HP's News Leak Probe," *USA Today* (September 22, 2006): 3B; "H-P Spokesman Targeted During Media Leak Probe," *Associated Press* (September 16, 2006); Justin Fox, "Board Games," *Fortune* (October 2, 2006): 23; and "Outsourcing Ethics," *New York Times* (September 20, 2006): A26.

From the Top An Interview with Howard J. Rubenstein

Howard J. Rubenstein, president of Rubenstein Associates since founding the firm in 1954, is one of the world's most well-known and respected public relations counselors, advising some of the world's most influential corporations, organizations, and opinion leaders. In addition to managing the day-to-day activities of his firm, Rubenstein is involved in numerous civic and philanthropic organizations. A Phi Beta Kappa graduate of the University of Pennsylvania, he finished first in his class in the night school division of St. John's University School of Law, which subsequently awarded him an honorary Doctor of Law degree. As an attorney, he served as assistant counsel to the House of Representatives Judiciary Committee.

How would you define the practice of public relations?
Public relations is the art of conveying an idea or message to a wide variety of publics utilizing multiple forms of communications. It can be broadly applied and used to advance the interests of businesses, governments, and society in general. It can achieve objectives as narrow as promoting a product or as broad as creating a movement. The communications themselves can be targeted to the general public or to very select groups of individuals, conveyed via media or person-to-person. The tools employed encompass a wide array, from press releases, news conferences, special events, speaking engagements, webinars, blogs, and grass-roots organizations down to a single conversation with one influential person.

How important is communications for organizations in today's society?
Communications in its many forms creates and projects messages with the power to affect great change and achieve tremendous success, while a breakdown in communications can lead to dismal failure. Clearly, communications is critical for organizations as they seek public acceptance, support, and understanding of their activities. Communication today is a major focus for presidents, prime ministers, and legislators, as well as religious leaders, as they try to shape the directions of entire societies and world events.

What are the key attributes that distinguish the best public relations professionals?
Ethics, intelligence, and willingness to put in the time and hard work are core characteristics. Good PR professionals should have the ability to write well and speak effectively. The final attribute is creativity and imagination, combined with an understanding of reality and practicality. Professionals in the field should be able to stretch the envelope as far as technique and methodology go, without forgetting what they are trying to achieve.

What is the key to interesting a journalist in a client's story?
There are many keys to piquing media interest. First, however, you must know the media outlet and understand what a news story is and what a reporter wants to see as the components of a story. You must target and reach out selectively, rather than just send out releases. Then, once you know where to go, find the human-interest angle, keep the pitch succinct, and offer what the reporter needs to cover the story. Forget the term *spinmeister*. Offer a story that is accurate, do it in an honorable and forthright way, and help the reporter do his or her job well. Above all, don't waste reporters' time with something that isn't right for the publication or the beat the reporter covers. And don't be nasty if your idea is rejected. You'll likely want to approach that reporter again some day. Instead take that rejection as a sign that you need to refine the pitch or find a better fit for it.

What inspired you, personally, to go into public relations?
I was inspired to enter public relations by my father, who was a crime reporter with the *New York Herald Tribune*. From his perspective as a journalist, he believed that PR had the untapped potential to be a great career. Not only did he get me my first account, he explained to me the importance of ethics, honesty, and integrity in dealing with the press, conducting business, and communicating with the public. He taught me the importance of good writing, finding the news value in a story, and working hard to achieve coverage in the media. He was very supportive when I began my company with that single account at my new office, which was also known as *my mother's kitchen table!* He encouraged me and always believed that public relations had a bright future. I remember him saying that public relations as a field was malleable, like clay, and could be formed to fit any idea that I had. As a result, I started out believing that if I was honest, thoughtful, and hard working, I could be successful, earn a living, and establish a good reputation in what was then a barely recognized field. That's what happened, so I guess my father was right.

What are the greatest challenges facing the practice of public relations?

In every aspect of society, leaders seek public relations counsel. Because media scrutiny is so intense today, it takes a professional to understand and advise society's leaders as to how best to respond and engage. As a result, PR people today are professionals with as much credibility and weight as lawyers, accountants, bankers, architects, or engineers. We alone offer the ability to design communications programs, judge their potential, and execute them to achieve results. That guarantees for PR professionals tremendous opportunity and a seat at the table at the highest levels.

Yet for all that progress in the evolution of the profession, there are still too many people, especially in the general public, who hold public relations in low esteem. PR professionals are still viewed in many quarters as snake-oil salesmen, ready to stoop to conquer or employ deceptive tactics. The great challenge today is changing that perception and winning for the profession the respect that it deserves. The way to meet that challenge as an industry is through superb professional performance and continued adherence to the highest ethical and business standards.

Public Relations Library

Badaracco, Jr., Joseph L. *Leading Quietly: An Unorthodox Guide to Doing the Right Thing.* Cambridge, MA: Harvard Business School Press, 2002. A Harvard professor focuses on how leadership can be both effective and ethical at the same time.

Barney, Ralph, and Jay Black. *Ethics and New Media Technology.* Mahwah, NJ: Lawrence Erlbaum Associates, 2002.

Boatright, John R., and John Raymond. *Ethics and the Conduct of Business,* 4th ed. Upper Saddle River, NJ: Prentice Hall, 2002.

Business Ethics, "Corporate Social Responsibility Report," Marjorie Kelly, editor. Bimonthly magazine, Mavis Publications, Minneapolis, MN.

Day, Louis A. *Ethics in Media Communications: Cases and Controversies,* 4th ed. Belmont, CA: Wadsworth, 2002.

Hartley, Robert F. *Business Ethics: Mistakes and Successes.* New York: John Wiley & Sons, 2005. This book discusses all the killer ethical cases of our time, from Ford's Explorer and Firestone tires to WorldCom's accounting fraud to "Chainsaw" Al Dunlap's duplicity at Sunbeam.

Seymann, Marilyn, and Michael Rosenbaum. *The Governance Game: Restoring Boardroom Excellence and Credibility in Corporate America.* Mahwah, NJ: Aspatore, 2003. This book explores one of corporate America's most prominent ethical vulnerabilities, the board of directors. The authors suggest what corporate boards can do to improve their performance in terms of management of the board and the ethical behavior of directors. They stress that corporate boards must go beyond making sure their companies are simply complying with existing laws and regulations.

Snoeyenboes, Milton, Robert Almeder, and James Humber (Eds.). *Business Ethics,* 3rd ed. Amherst, NY: Prometheus Book, 2001. A classic, comprehensive view of the ethical issues that confront business, from drug testing to Internet privacy to conflicts of interest.

Stauber, John, and Sheldon Rampton. *Trust Us, We're Experts.* New York: Penguin Putnam, 2001. The anti–public relations authors of *Toxic Sludge Is Good for You* are at it again. This time they explain—from their unique perspective—how "corporations and public relations firms have seized upon remarkable new ways of exploiting your trust to get you to buy what they have to sell." Strap yourself in.

Trevino, Linda K., and Katherine A. Nelson. *Managing Business Ethics: Straight Talk About How to Do It Right,* 3rd ed. New York: John Wiley & Sons, 2004. Discusses not only what business ethics are but also why business should care.

FIGURE 7-1 Where are my lawyers?!? Among the most innovative and persuasive—and public relations conscious—non-profit organizations is People for the Ethical Treatment of Animals, which has featured celebrities like Charlize Theron and Pink to get across messages that gave their adversaries and the attorneys of their adversaries fits. (Courtesy of PETA)

Chapter 7

The Law

In the summer of 2008, Scott Sidell had plenty of reason to be incensed with his former employer.

In a lawsuit filed against the finance company he used to run, Structured Settlement Investments, Mr. Sidell claimed that his former employer not only fired him but read his personal Yahoo! email messages—weeks after he left the company. Not only that, but the intercepted emails concerned discussions on strategy that Mr. Sidell was having with his attorneys.

At issue in the case is whether the company had invaded Mr. Sidell's privacy by monitoring email communications on company computers.[1] In other words, where does the right to privacy end and the law begin?

As the practice of public relations has gained stature, a natural tension has developed between public relations practitioners and lawyers.

Ideally, public relations counselors and lawyers should work together to achieve a client's desired outcomes. Indeed, this is often the case. But there is also a fundamental difference in legal versus public relations advice.

- ■ Lawyers correctly advise clients on what they *must* do, within the letter of legal requirements, to defend themselves in a court of law.

- ■ Public relations advisers counsel clients on not what they *must* do but what they *should* do to defend themselves in a different court—the court of public opinion.

There is a vast difference between the two.

In recent years, however, lawyers have moved increasingly to invade the publicity turf traditionally manned by public relations professionals. Some lawyers have become ubiquitous—on radio and television and in the middle of press conferences—in using public relations techniques to further their clients' and their own ends.

In many ways, it makes sense that lawyers and public relations people should work in concert. Public relations and the law both begin with the First Amendment to the Constitution that guarantees freedom of speech in our society.

But in the 21st century, ensuring freedom of speech is not as easy as it sounds. One question is, *Where does one's freedom start and another's end* (see Figure 7-1)? Another question is, *How much freedom of speech is appropriate—or advisable—in any given situation?* And yet another question is, *How does the freedom of the Internet impact on communications rights and responsibilities?*

Such are the dilemmas in the relationship between public relations principles and the law.

Public Relations and the Law: An Uneasy Alliance

The legal and public relations professions have historically shared an uneasy alliance. Public relations practitioners must always understand the legal implications of any issue with which they become involved, and a firm's legal position must always be the first consideration.

From a legal point of view, normally the less an organization says prior to its day in court, the better. That way, the opposition can't gain any new ammunition that will become part of the public record. A lawyer, the saying goes, tells you to say two things: "Say nothing, and say it slowly!"

From a public relations standpoint, though, it may often make sense to go public early on, especially if the organization's integrity or credibility is being called into public question. In the summer of 2003, for example, when NBA star Kobe Bryant was accused of raping a woman at a Colorado hotel, on the advice of his lawyers and public relations counsel, Bryant immediately held a press conference, with his wife at his side, to acknowledge he had erred but denied the charges. A year later, the sexual assault charge was dismissed, and by 2009, Kobe Bryant, his credibility restored, had led his Los Angeles Lakers to the NBA championship.

The point is that legal advice and public relations advice may indeed be different. In an organization, a smart manager will carefully weigh both legal and public relations counsel before making a decision.

It also should be noted that law and ethics are interrelated. The Public Relations Society of America's Code of Professional Standards (see Appendix A) notes that many activities that are unethical are also illegal. However, there are instances in which something is perfectly legal but unethical and other instances in which things might be illegal but otherwise ethical. Thus, when a public relations professional reflects on what course to take in a particular situation, he or she must analyze not only the legal ramifications but also the ethical considerations.[2]

This chapter examines the relationship between the law and public relations and the more prominent role the law plays in public relations practice and vice versa. The discussion introduces the legal concerns of public relations professionals today: First Amendment considerations, insider trading, disclosure law, ethics law, privacy law, copyright law, and the laws concerning censorship of the Internet—issues that have become primary concerns for public relations practitioners in the 21st century.

Public Relations and the First Amendment

Any discussion of law and public relations should start with the First Amendment, which states: *"Congress shall make no law . . . abridging the freedom of speech or the press."* The First Amendment is the cornerstone of free speech in our society: This is what distinguishes democratic nations from many others.

Recent years have seen a blizzard of problems and challenges regarding the First Amendment.

■ In 2005, *New York Times* reporter Judith Miller was jailed for failing to disclose her sources in the outing of CIA agent Valerie Plame, wife of a former ambassador and enemy of the Bush administration. Miller pleaded that under the First Amendment, she had a right to protect her sources. But the court disagreed.[3]

- In 2006, when an obscure Danish newspaper published cartoons depicting the prophet Muhammad in a tasteless way, Muslims protested around the world, resulting in destruction, injuries, and deaths. While the Western world considered the cartoons—as offensive as they were—examples of "freedom of expression," much of the Muslim world was outraged. Two years later, a Danish anti-Koran film triggered a renewal of Muslim outrage (see Figure 7-2).

- In 2008, a former *USA Today* reporter faced fines and imprisonment, in a suit by former Army scientist Steven Hatfill, when she was ordered her to reveal her sources about the anthrax attacks on America, which killed five people in 2001. Hatfill had been labeled a "person of interest" in the attacks but was never charged. Ultimately, the government wound up paying him $4.6 million for accusing him undeservedly. And the threats against the reporter were dropped.[4]

- Later in 2008, San Francisco Circuit Court Chief Judge Alex Kozinski declared that the *"First Amendment is dead."* The judge made his declaration after the obscenity case at which he was scheduled to preside was interrupted when the *Los Angeles Times* revealed that Judge Kozinski *"maintained a publicly accessible Web site featuring sexually explicit photos and videos 'at alex.kozinski.com.'"*After the humiliating revelation, the judge fumed, "Anyone can share valuable information about government conduct, celebrity news, or private misconduct at very little risk. And any attempt to suppress that information will only guarantee its exponential multiplication. . . . As such the First Amendment jurisprudence that we cherish so clearly is now obsolete."[5]

As these skirmishes suggest, interpreting the First Amendment, especially in the Internet age, is no simple matter. One person's definition of obscenity or divulging state secrets may be someone else's definition of art or freedom of expression. Because the First Amendment lies at the heart of the communications business, defending it is a front-line responsibility of the public relations profession.

FIGURE 7-2 Freedom of speech? In 2008, 5,000 people gathered in Kabul, Afghanistan, to burn a Dutch flag and protest a Danish movie, critical of the Koran. (Photo: Newscom)

Public Relations and Defamation Law

The laws that govern a person's privacy have significant implications for journalists and other communicators, such as public relations professionals, particularly laws that touch on libel and slander—commonly known as defamation laws—by the media.

Defamation is the umbrella term used to describe libel—a printed falsehood—and slander—an oral falsehood. For defamation to be proved, a plaintiff must convince the court that certain requirements have been met, including.

1. The falsehood was communicated through print, broadcast, or other electronic means.

2. The person who is the subject of the falsehood was identified or easily identifiable.

3. The identified person has suffered injury—in the form of monetary losses, reputational loss, or mental suffering.[6]

Generally, the privacy of an ordinary citizen is protected under the law. A citizen in the limelight, however, has a more difficult problem, especially in proving defamation of character through libel or slander.

To prove such a charge, a public figure must show that the media acted with actual malice in their reporting. *Actual malice* in a public figure slander case means that statements have been published with the knowledge that they were false or with reckless disregard for whether the statements were false. In a landmark case in 1964, *New York Times* v. *Sullivan,* the Supreme Court nullified a libel award of $500,000 to an Alabama police official, holding that no damages could be awarded "in actions brought by public officials against critics of their official conduct" unless there was proof of actual malice. And proving actual malice is a difficult task.

Several historic libel cases have helped pave the case law precedent.

- In 1992, *The Wall Street Journal* and its award-winning reporter Bryan Burrough were served with a $50 million libel suit by Harry L. Freeman, a former communications executive of American Express. The suit stemmed from the way Freeman was characterized in Burrough's book, *Vendetta: American Express and the Smearing of Edmund Safra.*[7]

- A decade earlier, in a landmark case, the *Washington Post* initially lost a $2 million suit after a federal jury decided that the newspaper had libeled William P. Tavoulareas when it alleged that he had used his position as president of Mobil Oil to further his son's career in a shipping business. The next year, a federal judge overturned the verdict against the *Post* because the article in question didn't contain "knowing lies or statements made in reckless disregard of the truth." The Supreme Court later corroborated the ruling in favor of the *Post.*

- In another celebrated case, Israeli General Ariel Sharon brought a $50 million libel suit against *Time* magazine. Once again, the jury criticized *Time* for negligent journalism in reporting Sharon's role in a massacre in a Palestinian refugee camp. However, this case, too, ended without a libel verdict.

- In 1996, Atlanta security guard Richard A. Jewell sued both *NBC News* and the *Atlanta Journal-Constitution* for reporting that he was the lead suspect in the Atlanta Olympic bombing, which led to two deaths. The reports caused a media feeding frenzy, which disrupted Jewell's life and tarnished his name. A decade later, Jewell was cleared of any involvement in the bombing and reached a settlement with his media accusers, averting a libel lawsuit.

The 21st-century proliferation of blogs, wikis, podcasts, and cable and radio talk shows, where hosts and guests say what they want regardless of factual accuracy or

to 90 days in prison and fined $30,000 for violating the Federal Ethics in Government Act, which forbids lobbying former contacts within one year of leaving the government. A related fate was meted out to former White House Deputy Chief of Staff Michael K. Deaver, another well-known public relations professional, who was found guilty of perjury over his lobbying activities. He also faced a jail sentence and a serious fine. And in 2005, political public relations professional Michael Scanlon, an associate of crooked lobbyist Jack Abramoff, also was sentenced to hard time as a result of conspiracy to bribe public officials.

The activities of lobbyists, in particular, have been closely watched by Congress since the imposition of the Federal Regulation of Lobbying Act of 1946. In recent years, however, the practice of lobbying has expanded greatly.

In recent years, campaign finance reform to limit—if not eradicate—the acceptance by legislators of favors and money from wealthy interest groups has intensified. With the reputation and public approval of politicians, particularly on the national level, at an all-time low, Congress had to focus on restoring ethics to government and winning back the public trust.[17]

PR Ethics

Mini-Case   Tap-Tap-Tappin' on the Stall Room Door

The elements of ethics, politicians, and the law all converged in August 2007, when it was revealed in *Roll Call*, the Capitol Hill newspaper read by anyone who's anyone in Washington, that Idaho Republican Senator Larry Craig had been arrested two months earlier by police in Minneapolis (see Figure 7-5).

That was the less bad part.

The *real* bad part was that Sen. Craig had been collared by an undercover agent in the men's room at the Minneapolis-St. Paul International Airport, in a sting targeting bathroom sex. The police officer who arrested him said Craig peered through a crack in a restroom stall door for two minutes and made tapping gestures suggesting to the officer he wanted to engage in "lewd conduct." The senator was charged with disorderly conduct, to which he signed a guilty plea.

A few days after the *Roll Call* bombshell, Sen. Craig, his wife by his side, announced plans to resign by the end of September and not finish his third term in the Senate. Republican Senate colleagues breathed a sigh of relief; that is, until Sen. Craig changed his mind and filed a motion seeking to withdraw his guilty plea. "I did nothing inappropriate," said Craig, adding that, "I am not gay and never have been."

When the judge in the case said it might take some time to sort things out, Sen. Craig reversed his position and vowed to stick around the Senate to serve out his term. In October, when the judge ruled against him, Sen. Craig filed an appeal with the Minnesota Court of Appeals, attempting once again to reverse his guilty plea.

In February 2008, with Craig still refusing to desist, the Senate Ethics Committee wrote him a letter, suggesting that he acted improperly in connection with the men's room sex sting and had brought discredit on the Senate. The ethics panel said Craig's attempt to withdraw his guilty plea after his

FIGURE 7-5 Meet the press. With his wife by his side, Sen. Larry Craig announces that he won't be finishing his term. Later, he recanted that announcement. (Photo: Newscom)

arrest was an effort to evade legal consequences of his own actions. In an emailed statement, Craig said he disagreed with the ethics panel's action.

Mercifully, the senator also announced he wouldn't run for reelection in the fall of 2008.

Questions

1. Had you been Sen. Craig's public relations advisor, what would you have advised him after his guilty plea in Minneapolis?

2. What were the public relations vs. legal arguments in considering appealing the guilty plea?

Public Relations and Copyright Law

One body of law that is particularly relevant to public relations professionals is copyright law and the protections it offers writers. Copyright law provides basic, automatic protection for writers, whether a manuscript is registered with the Copyright Office or even published. Under the Copyright Act of 1976, an "original work of authorship" has copyright protection from the moment the work is in the following fixed form:

- literary works
- musical works
- dramatic works
- pantomimes and choreographic works
- pictorial, graphic, or sculptural works
- motion pictures
- sound recordings

The word *fixed* means that the work is sufficiently permanent to permit it to be perceived, reproduced, or otherwise communicated.[18]

Copyright law gives the owner of the copyright the exclusive right to reproduce and authorize others to reproduce the work, prepare derivative works based on the copyrighted material, and perform and/or display the work publicly. That's why the late Michael Jackson had to pay $47.5 million for the rights to the Beatles' compositions to the duly sworn representatives and heirs of John, Paul, George, and Ringo.

Copyright law is different from trademark law, which refers to a word, symbol, or slogan, used alone or in combination, that identifies a product or its sponsor—for example, the Nike swoosh.

What courts have stated again and again is that for the purposes of criticism, news reporting, teaching, scholarship, or research, use of copyrighted material is not an infringement but rather constitutes *fair use*. Although precise definitions of fair use—like everything else in the law—is subject to interpretation, such factors as "the effect on the future market" of the copyrighted work in question or the "volume of quotation used" or even whether the "heart" of the material was ripped off are often considered.[19]

That's why the Associated Press (AP), one of the nation's largest news organizations, announced in 2008 that it had had it with bloggers copying its works word-for-word and would impose strict guidelines on the blogosphere, as to how much quoting and copying of AP stories would be tolerated. The AP dictum was aimed squarely at the vague doctrine of *fair use*.[20]

Over time, the Supreme Court has strengthened the copyright status of freelance artists and writers—many of whom are independent public relations practitioners—ruling that such professionals retain the right to copyright what they create "as long as they were not in a conventional employment relationship with the organization that commissioned their work." As a result of this ruling, public relations professionals must carefully document the authorization that has been secured for using freelance material. In other words, when engaging a freelance professional, public relations people must know the law.

Public Relations and Internet Law

The Internet has introduced a new dimension to the law affecting free speech. The premise in American law is that "not all speech is created equal."[21] Rather, there is a hierarchy of speech, under Supreme Court precedents dating back many decades, that calibrates the degree of First Amendment protection with, among other tests, the particular medium of expression. For example, speech that would be perfectly acceptable if uttered in a public park could constitutionally be banned when broadcast from a sound truck.

Dealing with the Internet has introduced new ramifications to this legal principal. Indeed, cyberlaw has brought into question many of the most revered communications law principles.

Censorship

In 1996, Congress passed the Communications Decency Act (CDA) as an amendment to a far-reaching telecommunications bill. The CDA introduced criminal penalties, including fines of as much as $250,000 and prison terms up to two years, for making "indecent" speech available to "a person under 18 years of age." A Philadelphia court a few months later struck down the law, contending that such censorship would chill all discourse on the Internet.[22]

Then, in the summer of 1997, the Supreme Court, in a sweeping endorsement of free speech, declared the CDA unconstitutional. The decision, unanimous in most respects, marked the highest court's first effort to extend the principles of the First Amendment into cyberspace and to confront the nature and the law of this new, powerful medium. In summarizing the Court's finding, Justice John Paul Stevens said the Court considered the "goal of protecting children from indecent material as legitimate and important" but concluded that "the wholly unprecedented breadth of the law threatened to suppress far too much speech among adults and even between parents and children."[23]

In 1998, Congress passed the Child Online Protection Act (COPA), which made it a federal crime to "knowingly communicate for commercial purposes material considered harmful to minors." In 2002 and again in 2004, the high court once again repelled legislation to censor child pornography on the Internet, ruling that it would be unconstitutional to criminalize protected free speech on the Internet.

In 2006, federal prosecutors preparing to defend the 1998 Act asked Google, Microsoft, Yahoo!, and America Online to hand over millions of search records. Google alone refused, claiming such a disclosure would violate the privacy of its users.[24] On the other hand, in the same year, Google agreed to censor its results in China, adhering to the country's free-speech restrictions, in return for better access in the Internet's fastest-growing market.[25]

In 2008, COPA continued to be challenged, by the American Civil Liberties Union in particular, which led the charge to keep the Internet free of censorship, even of material deemed "harmful to minors."

Intellectual Property

Few cyberlaw cases have drawn more headlines than the 2001 case against Napster, the popular application that allowed users to exchange music files. Because Napster ran the file-swapping through a central server, it was an easy target for legislation.

In the end—for Napster—the protest, led by those heavy-metal defenders of the First Amendment, Metallica, and backed by the large music companies, convinced the Court that the company was infringing on copyright protections of intellectual property.[26]

Two years later, the recording industry waged all-out war on those who downloaded intellectual property without paying. On a larger level, intellectual piracy of everything from video games to music to software has become rampant, with estimates that 90 percent of virtually every form of intellectual property in China is pirated.[27]

Cybersquatting

Another complex issue is that of cybersquatting—grabbing domain names in bad faith, expressly for the purpose of tormenting or "shaking down" a rightful registrant. It costs an infiltrator about $35 to register a variation of a domain name.

Companies from Wendy's to General Motors to Walmart have been beset by cybersquatters. Kmart Corporation successfully mounted a legal challenge to fight a rogue Web site, Kmartsucks.com. Ultimately, the site was forced to change its name to Themartsucks.com.

Current trademark law prohibits a company from registering a name that exactly duplicates a registered trademark, but cybersquatters frequently register names that differ only slightly. They know that Web surfers will type in a variation of a company's name when searching for its site. They then either attempt to sell the names or use the sites to disrupt the company's commerce.[28]

E-Fraud

Fraud is fraud, no matter where it is domiciled. And on the World Wide Web, where anyone who wants to can choose anonymity, strip in a logo, and pretend to be someone he or she is not—fraud runs rampant. (Just check your inbox for "inheritance gift" emails from Nigeria!)

The problem is that e-crooks are not only difficult to stop, but also difficult to define, at least in legal terms. Often it depends on companies policing the Internet themselves, frequently to go after former employees.

For example:

■ Varian Medical Systems of Palo Alto won a $775,000 verdict against two former employees who posted 14,000 messages on 100 message boards, accusing the firm of being homophobic and of discriminating against pregnant women.

■ A California court ruled against a fired Intel employee who sent emails to about 35,000 staffers, criticizing the company.

■ St. Paul–based insurer Travelers accused one former vice president of trying to sabotage the company with anonymous blog postings, charging, among other things, that one executive was little more than a "glorified secretary" and another "would stab his own mother in the back to make money." Travelers took the case all the way to federal court.[29]

And then there's "click fraud," which threatens to disrupt the largest search engines. Search engines rank listings by the number of clicks they receive: the more clicks, the higher the ranking. Click fraud occurs when a concerted effort is initiated to register multiple clicks to drive specific listings higher in a search-ranking algorithm.

Such fraudulent activity affects marketers, who advertise on a site and pay rates based on usage.[30]

These are but a few of the burgeoning legal issues that surround the World Wide Web.

Litigation Public Relations

In court cases, plaintiffs and defendants are often scrupulously warned by judges not to influence the ultimate verdict outside the courtroom.

Forget it.

In the 21st century, with the Internet, CNN, MSNBC, Fox News Channel, CNBC, Headline News, Court TV, and talk radio incessantly jabbering about possible trials, upcoming trials, and current trials, there is little guarantee that any jury can be objective about any high-profile legal case.

That's why litigation public relations has become so important.

Litigation public relations can best be defined as managing the media process during the course of any legal dispute so as to affect the outcome or its impact on the client's overall reputation.

Although court proceedings have certain rules and protocols, dealing in the public arena with a matter of litigation has no such strictures. The Sixth Amendment to the Constitution guarantees accused persons "a speedy and public trial, by an impartial jury," but television commentary by knowledgeable—and in many cases, unknowledgeable—"experts" can help influence a potential jury for or against a defendant (see Figure 7-6).

As a consequence, communications has become central to the management of modern litigation.[31] Smart lawyers understand that with cable TV, in particular, being so pervasive, they have little choice but to engage in litigation public relations to provide their clients with every advantage.

FIGURE 7-6 **Fighting Murphy's Law.** The Institute for Justice epitomized the best of litigation public relations when it went after Pittsburgh's mayor, who sought to impose eminent domain by tearing down small businesses to build a shopping mall. (Courtesy of Institute for Justice)

According to one counselor who works exclusively with litigation, there are seven keys to litigation visibility.

1. **Learn the process.** All involved should be aware of the roadmap for the case and the milestones ahead, which may lend themselves to publicity.

2. **Develop a message strategy.** Think about what should be said at each stage of a trial to keep the press and public focused on the key messages of the client.

3. **Settle fast.** Settlement is probably the most potent litigation visibility management tool. The faster the settlement, the less litigation visibility there is likely to be. This is often a positive development.

4. **Anticipate high-profile variables.** Often in public cases everybody gets into the act—judges, commentators, jury selection experts, psychologists, and so on. Always anticipate all that could be said, conjectured, and argued about the case. Always try to be prepared for every inevitability.

5. **Keep the focus positive.** Ultimately, it's a positive, productive attitude that leads to effective negotiations with the other side. So the less combative you can be—especially near settlement—the better.

6. **Try settling again.** Again, this ought to be the primary litigation visibility strategy—to end the agony and get it out of the papers.

7. **Fight nicely.** Wars are messy, expensive, and prone to producing casualties. It is much better to be positive. This will give both sides a greater chance of eventually settling.[32]

Last Word

As our society becomes more contentious, fractious, and litigious, public relations must become more concerned with the law. On the one hand, because management must rely so heavily on legal advice and legal judgments, it is imperative that public relations people understand the laws that govern their organizations and industries. Public relations people must understand that their views may differ from those of an attorney. As a defense lawyer once described his role, *"You should do what a client wants, period. That's what you're paid for."* By contrast, public relations people are paid to advise their clients what is *"the right thing to do."* And they should never shrink from that obligation.

On the other hand, public relations advisers must depend on "buy-in" from others in management. Lawyers are among the most influential of these associates. Therefore, forming an alliance with legal counselors must be a front-line objective for public relations professionals.

Beyond the working relationship between public relations people and lawyers, the practice of public relations has, itself, wrestled with legal questions in recent years. Increasingly, public relations practice is based on legal contracts: between agencies and clients, employers and employees, purchasers and vendors. All contracts—both written and oral—must be binding and enforceable.

In recent years, controversy in the field has erupted over noncompete clauses, in which former employees are prohibited, within certain time parameters, from working for a competitor or pitching a former account. Time and again the courts have ruled in favor of public relations agencies and against former clients in noncompete cases.

Likewise, legal challenges have been made relative to the markup of expenses that public relations agencies charge clients. Standard practice in the industry is to mark up by 15 to 20 percent of legitimate printing and advertising bills submitted to clients.

Add to these the blurring of the lines between public relations advice on the one hand and legal advice on the other, and it becomes clear that the connection between public relations and the law will intensify dramatically in the 21st century.

Discussion Starters

1. What is the difference between a public relations professional's responsibility and a lawyer's responsibility?
2. What have been recent challenges to the First Amendment?
3. How can someone prove that he or she has been libeled or slandered?
4. What is meant by the term *insider trading*?
5. What is the SEC's overriding concern when considering disclosure?
6. How have Regulation FD and Sarbanes-Oxley changed the disclosure environment?
7. Whom does copyright law protect?
8. What are some of the dominant issues in laws affecting the Internet?
9. What are several general principles with respect to litigation public relations?
10. What general advice should a public relations professional consider in working with lawyers?

Top of the Shelf   Stop the Presses: The Crisis and Litigation PR Desk Reference (Second Edition) / Richard Levick and Larry Smith, Ann Arbor, MI: Watershed Press, 2008

This book, written by two public relations agency veterans, focuses on litigation public relations in crisis situations. Indeed, the book offers 15 pages of fictional crisis scenarios, where readers can role-play solutions.

The book is particularly strong in discussing the new media, which the authors say, "doesn't need to buy ink by the barrel every week. They pay Internet fees instead and enlist (without qualifying degrees) in the army of opinion-shapers and world movers universally known as bloggers."

There is also a litigation planning guide and crisis management primer included in the book.

Case Study   Black Shirt, Black Shoes, Black Hat, Cadillac: The CEO's a Time Bomb

Madison Square Garden (MSG) is the world's most famous arena. Its owner, Cablevision Corporation, also owns the storied franchises of the New York Knicks basketball team and the New York Rangers hockey team.

In 2007, the CEO of Cablevision was a 52-year-old executive named James J. Dolan. Mr. Dolan was CEO of Cablevision for one reason in particular—his father founded the company!

Indeed, as his performance as CEO would suggest, the fact that young Mr. Dolan's father, Charles, was founder of the company was arguably the *only* reason that young James had been elevated to CEO.

And in the summer of 2007, as the Knicks labored through a very public sexual harassment suit, James Dolan's tribulations as Cablevision CEO became painfully apparent.

"Money, Lots of Money"

In the winter of 2005, a female Knicks marketing senior vice president and former college basketball star, Anucha Browne Sanders, complained to management about sexual harassment in the workplace. Her attorney met with Garden attorneys, who learned that Browne Sanders was particularly resentful of Knicks' Coach Isaiah Thomas, who, she claimed, occasionally used profanity, raised his voice, and, on one occasion, greeted Browne Sanders with a hug and a kiss (see Figure 7-7).

The attorneys attempted to "expedite a negotiated, good faith resolution" of Browne Sanders' claims.

The Garden investigated the complaint and MSG's general counsel recommended that Thomas receive sensitivity training. Garden investigators also concluded that most of Browne Sanders' allegations weren't confirmed, especially since she had exhibited "a poor relationship and difficulty interacting with members of Madison Square Garden management."

At one point, Browne Sanders offered to settle her claim for $6 million—equivalent to 20 years of compensation. According to court documents released later, she also threatened to go public with a lawsuit to "teach Madison Square Garden a lesson" if she didn't receive "money, lots of money."

In January 2006, after the MSG internal investigation was completed, Browne Sanders was fired.

She responded by filing a $10 million suit against Madison Square Garden, Thomas, other executives, and CEO Dolan, claiming she was discriminated against and forced to work in a sexually hostile environment, and then was fired in retaliation for making a complaint.

FIGURE 7-7 **The victor.** Anucha Browne Sanders was awarded even more money than she asked for in her 2007 sexual harassment case against Madison Square Garden. (Photo: Newscom)

Charges, Countercharges, and a Public Relations Disaster

Depositions in the upcoming sexual harassment case continued through the summer of 2007, with damaging leaks aplenty.

Among the most juicy:

- Browne Sanders alleged that Thomas encouraged Knicks' cheerleaders to flirt with referees before games.
- Browne Sanders alleged that Thomas admitted he was "very attracted" to her and "in love" with her.
- Browne Sanders alleged that Knicks' point guard Stephon Marbury called her a derogatory name, after she complained about Marbury's cousin (also employed by the Knicks), who made graphic sexual comments to her staff.
- The Garden alleged that Browne Sanders never worked for Thomas and that, in effect, she had created the sexual harassment claim out of whole cloth simply to collect money she didn't deserve.

No mater who was telling the truth, it was clear from the negative publicity alone that neither the Garden nor the Knicks (who were suffering through another losing year) would gain anything in public relations terms from a public trial.

That's why, in September 2007 when the case headed for court, most observers thought the Garden would settle the suit. Most were shocked when the case actually went to trial.

Dumb Fans, Skimpy Dance Costumes, Point Guard Sex

Fears of a nasty show trial proved to be well-founded. For Madison Square Garden, the jury trial that ensued was a public relations disaster.

Thomas, who sat at the defense bench flanked by two female attorneys, testified, as did Marbury, Sanders, and, ultimately, Dolan.

Among the public relations knives thrust into the heart of the Knicks were the following:

- Marbury acknowledged that he had seduced an intern on a late-night jaunt through Manhattan night clubs. Front-page headlines, *"Lured Into My Limo,"* accompanied by Marbury flashing a goofy grin, didn't help the Knicks' case.
- Sanders testified that CEO Dolan was more concerned about offering "feedback on what the Knicks City Dancers were wearing" than he was on sexual harassment charges in his organization.
- Most damning, Sanders testified that Thomas repeatedly used slurs to refer to her and once rebuffed her attempts to get involved in fan promotions by intoning, "I don't give a (expletive) about these white people."

Garden lawyers—and there were lots of them—labeled Brown Sanders' allegations as "outrageous." But the daily diet of devastating headlines proved disastrous for the Garden.

As a final attempt to convince the jury, Garden attorneys called the company's CEO, James Dolan, himself, to testify.

As it turned out, this was not one of the most brilliant strategic gambits in the history of American jurisprudence.

CEO Testimony in Schlep-avision

Rather than testifying directly in front of the jury, CEO Dolan—perhaps because he was "otherwise occupied"—chose to testify via videotape.

The Dolan videotape testimony was projected in the courtroom on a larger-than-life screen for the jury to see. And they saw plenty!

Dolan appeared slumped in a chair, speaking in an off-handed way, and dressed in a collarless, black shirt—looking, frankly, like a schlep (see Figure 7-8).

One commentator described the Cablevision chairman as appearing *"more like the high school sophomore sitting in the principal's office than a CEO testifying in an important lawsuit."*

His trial testimony also seemed dismissive; he testified he hadn't read Browne Sanders' performance evaluations nor did he require Thomas to attend sensitivity training. Dolan testified, *"When the lawsuit came, that's about as much sensitivity training as he'd ever want."* (Cute.)

The Dolan testimony probably didn't qualify as one of the proudest moments of Madison Square Garden's 128-year history.

At least not with the jury, who, after viewing the CEO and listening to his associates, came back with a verdict, awarding Anucha Browne Sanders $11.6 million—nearly $2 million *more* than she had asked for in her complaint!

Postscript 1: Shortly after the verdict in the MSG case, NBA Commissioner David Stern declared about the team running the New York Knicks, *"It demonstrates that they're not a model of intelligent management. There were many checkpoints along the way where more decisive action would have eliminated the issue."*

Postscript 2: Three months after the humiliating Knicks' suit, Madison Square Garden quietly settled out of court with a former New York Rangers cheerleader, who had accused executives of making unwanted advances. At least somebody was paying attention!*

FIGURE 7-8 **The schlepper.** Madison Square Garden CEO James Dolan wore his best collarless black shirt (sans jacket), when he presented video testimony in the losing harassment case. (Photo: Newscom)

Further, Dolan testified that he, alone, without consultation with others, decided to have Browne Sanders' employment terminated. He said he didn't talk to Browne Sanders' supervisor or read the report of the in-house investigation.

Questions

1. After Browne Sanders went public with her charges, what public relations options did MSG have? What public relations strategy should MSG have followed?

2. What were the public relations considerations for MSG, and how did they differ from the legal considerations?

3. If you were advising James Dolan on his video testimony, what would you have advised him to wear? How would you have advised him to act?

4. In terms of post mortem actions after the verdict, what would you advise CEO Dolan?

*For further information, see Anthony M. Destafno, "Isaiah Thomas Harassment Case Begins," newsday.com (September 11, 2007); Alan L. Rupe, "The Knicks Mess," workforce.com (November 2007); "Former Knicks Exec: Thomas Urged Cheerleader to Flirt with Refs," *Associated Press* (June 30, 2007); "Sex Harassment Trial Turns into PR Disaster, *Associated Press* (September 14, 2007).

the Top   An Interview with Robert Shapiro

From

Robert Shapiro (right) and a former client. (Photo: Newscom)

Celebrity attorney Robert Shapiro has represented many of Hollywood's most famous and notorious defendants, from his tenure as a member of football great and accused murderer O.J. Simpson's "dream team" to his defense of legendary record producer and convicted murderer Phil Spector. After the Simpson trial, Shapiro offered the following insights into how a modern-day lawyer views public relations.

How do you view a lawyer's public relations responsibilities?
When we are retained for those high-profile cases, we are instantly thrust into the role of a public relations person—a role for which the majority of us have no education, experience, or training. The lawyer's role as spokesperson may be [as] equally important to the outcome of a case as the skills of an advocate in the courtroom.

How important is the media to a trial?

The importance and power of the media cannot be overemphasized. The first impression the public gets is usually the one that is most important. The wire services depend on immediate updates. Therefore, all calls should be returned as quickly as possible.

"No comment" is the least appropriate and least productive response. Coming at the end of a lengthy story, it adds absolutely nothing and leaves the public with a negative impression.

How important are relationships with the media in a trial setting?

Initial relationships with legitimate members of the press are very important. Many times a lawyer will feel it is an intrusion to be constantly beset by seemingly meaningless questions that take up a tremendous amount of time. But the initial headlines of the arrest often make the sacred presumption of innocence a myth. In reality, we have the presumption of guilt. This is why dealing with the media is so important.

How carefully should lawyers construct answers to reporters' questions?

Just as you would do in trial, anticipate the questions a reporter will pose. Think out your answers carefully. . . . Use great care in choosing your words. Keep your statements simple and concise. Pick and choose the questions you want to answer. You do not have to be concerned with whether the answer precisely addresses the question, since only the answer will be aired.

What about dealing with the tabloids?

My experience is that cooperating with tabloid reporters only gives them a legitimate source of information which can be misquoted or taken out of context and does little good for your client. My personal approach is not to cooperate with tabloid reporters.

What about dealing with television?

The television media, either consciously or unconsciously, create an atmosphere of chaos. Immediately upon arriving at the courthouse, you are surrounded by television crews. We have all seen people coming to court and trying to rush through the press with their heads down or covering them with newspapers or coats. Nothing looks worse. I always instruct my clients upon arrival at the courthouse to get out in a normal manner, to walk next to me in a slow and deliberate way, to have a look of confidence and acknowledge with a nod those who are familiar and supportive.*

*Excerpted from Robert Shapiro, "Secrets of a Celebrity Lawyer," *Columbia Journalism Review* (September/October 1994): 25–29. Copyright © 1994 Columbia Journalism Review. Reprinted by permission.

Public Relations Library

Brinson, J. Dianne, and Mark F. Radcliffe. *Internet Law and Business Handbook*. Port Huron, MI: Ladera Press, 2004.

Bybee, Keith. *Bench Press: The Collision of Courts, Politics and the Media*. Stanford, CA: Stanford University Press, 2007.

Collins, Matthew. *The Law of Defamation and the Internet*. New York: Oxford University Press, 2005. Useful overview of evolving Internet law.

Fishman, Stephen. *The Copyright Handbook*. Berkeley, CA: Nolo, 2004. A comprehensive guide on what one needs to know to protect authored works.

Goldsmith, Jack, and Tim Wu. *Who Controls the Internet? Illusions of a Borderless World*. New York: Oxford University Press, 2008. Two legal scholars examine the reality of the laws that attempt to govern the Net.

Mitchell, Paul. *The Making of the Modern Law of Defamation*. Oxford, England: Hart Publishing 2005. Libel, slander, and hate speech share center stage in this useful compendium.

Moore, Roy L., and Michael D. Murray. *Media, Law and Ethics* (3rd Ed.) New York: Taylor and Francis Group, 2008. An updated compendium of the laws that govern the media.

Sell, Susan K. *Private Power, Public Law: The Globalization of Intellectual Property Rights*. Cambridge, UK: Cambridge University Press, 2003. This book examines the role of private enterprise in shaping government policy.

Zittrain, Jonathan. *The Future of the Internet and How to Stop It*. Harrisonburg, VA: R.R. Donnelly, 2008. Especially interesting is the chapter on "cybersecurity."

Chapter **8**

Research

FIGURE 8-1 The real winner . . . . . . in the U.S. presidential election of 2008 was the **Internet,** which both candidates utilized to the fullest, especially to research the electorate. (Photo: Shutterstock)

Campaign managers for presidential candidates McCain and Obama had no question where to direct their news resources in 2008.

You Tube. MySpace. Facebook. The Internet (see Figure 8-1).

Nearly a quarter of Americans regularly learned something about the campaign from the Internet, almost double the percentage during the 2004 campaign. Moreover, the Internet has become the leading source of campaign news for young people, and the role of social networking sites, such as MySpace and Facebook, have increased materially in importance.[1]

How could the campaigns be so certain of the growing news dominance of the Internet?

One word: Research.

Research is the natural starting point for any public relations assignment—from plotting a political campaign to promoting a product to designing a program to confronting a crisis. The first step in solving any public relations challenge is to conduct research.

At the same time, it should be recognized that research, particularly in an art form as intuitive as public relations, is no panacea. Research is but a foundation upon which a sensible programmatic initiative must be based. Research must always be complemented by analysis and judgment.

Nonetheless, in public relations it is obligatory to begin with research.

Why?

Frankly, the answer stems from the fact that few managers understand what public relations is and how it works. Managers—particularly those guided by quantitative, empirical measurement—want "proof" that what we advise is based on logic and clear thinking.

In other words, most clients are less interested in what their public relations advisers *think* than in what they *know*. The only real way to know your advice is on the right track is by ensuring that it is grounded in hard data whenever possible. So before recommending a course of action, public relations professionals must analyze audiences, assess alternatives, and generally do their homework.

In other words, do research.

Essential First Step

Every public relations program or solution should begin with research. Most don't, which is a shame.

The various approaches to public relations problem solving, discussed in Chapter 1, all start with research.

Instinct, intuition, and gut feelings all remain important in the conduct of public relations work, but management today demands more—measurement, analysis, and evaluation at every stage of the public relations process. In an era of scarce resources, management wants facts and statistics from public relations professionals to show that their efforts contribute not only to overall organizational effectiveness but also to the bottom line. For example:

- **Outputs**—Did we get the coverage we wanted?
- **Outtakes**—Did our target audience see and/or believe our messages?
- **Outcomes**—Did audience behavior or relationships change, and did sales increase?[2]

Questions such as these must be answered through research.

In a day when organizational resources are precious and companies don't want to spend money unless it enhances results, public relations programs must contribute to meeting business objectives.[3] That means that research must be applied to help segment market targets, analyze audience preferences and dislikes, and determine which messages might be most effective with various audiences. Research then becomes essential in helping realize management's goals.

Research should be applied in public relations work both at the initial stage, prior to planning a campaign, and at the final stage to evaluate a program's effectiveness. Early research helps to determine the current situation, prevalent attitudes, and difficulties that the program faces. Later research examines the program's success, along with what else still needs to be done. Research at both points in the process is critical.

What Is Research?

Research is the systematic collection and interpretation of information to increase understanding (Figure 8-2). Most people associate public relations with conveying information; although that association is accurate, research must be the obligatory first step in any project. A firm must acquire enough accurate, relevant data about its publics, products, and programs to answer these questions:

- How can we identify and define our constituent groups?
- How does this knowledge relate to the design of our messages?

FIGURE 8-2 **Early research.** An early research effort, albeit a futile one, was the return of the biblical scouts sent by Moses to reconnoiter the land of Canaan. They disagreed in their reports, and the Israelites believed the gloomier versions. This failure to interpret the data correctly caused them to wander another 40 years in the wilderness. (An even earlier research effort was Noah's sending the dove to search for dry ground.) (Courtesy of Trout & Partners)

- How does it relate to the design of our programs?
- How does it relate to the media we use to convey our messages?
- How does it relate to the schedule we adopt in using our media?
- How does it relate to the ultimate implementation tactics of our program?

It is difficult to delve into the minds of others, whose backgrounds and points of view may be quite different from our own, with the purpose of understanding why they think as they do. Research skills are partly intuitive, partly an outgrowth of individual temperament, and partly a function of acquired knowledge. There is nothing mystifying about them. Although we tend to think of research in terms of impersonal test scores, interviews, or questionnaires, these methods are only a small part of the process. The real challenge lies in using research—knowing when to do what, with whom, and for what purpose.

Principles of Public Relations Research

For years, public relations professionals have debated the standards of measuring public relations' effectiveness. The Institute for Public Relations Research and Education offered several guiding principles in setting standards for public relations research.

- Establish clear program objectives and desired outcomes tied directly to business goals.
- Differentiate between measuring public relations "outputs," generally short-term and surface (e.g., amount of press coverage received or exposure of a particular message), and measuring public relations "outcomes," usually more far-reaching and carrying greater impact (e.g., changing awareness, attitudes, and even behavior).
- Measure media content as a first step in the public relations evaluation process. Such a measure is limited in that it can't discern whether a target audience actually saw a message or responded to it.
- Understand that no one technique can be expected to evaluate public relations effectiveness. Rather, this requires a combination of techniques, from media analysis to cyberspace analysis, from focus groups to polls and surveys.
- Be wary of attempts to compare public relations effectiveness with advertising effectiveness. One particularly important consideration is that while advertising placement and messages can be controlled, their equivalent on the public relations side cannot be.
- The most trustworthy measurement of public relations effectiveness is that which stems from an organization with clearly identified key messages, target audiences, and desired channels of communication. The converse of this is that the more confused an organization is about its targets, the less reliable its public relations measurement will be.

Public relations evaluation cannot be accomplished in isolation. It must be linked to overall business goals, strategies, and tactics.[4]

Types of Public Relations Research

In general, research is conducted to do three things: (1) describe a process, situation, or phenomenon; (2) explain why something is happening, what its causes are, and what effect it will have; and (3) predict what probably will happen if we do or don't take action. Primary, or original, research in public relations is either theoretical or applied. Applied research solves practical problems; theoretical research aids understanding of a public relations process.

Most public relations analysis, however, takes the more informal form called secondary research. This relies on existing material—books, articles, Internet databases, and the like—to form the research backing for public relations recommendations and programs.

Applied Research

In public relations work, applied research can be either strategic or evaluative. Both applications are designed to answer specific practical questions.

- Strategic research is used primarily in program development to determine program objectives, develop message strategies, or establish benchmarks. It often examines the tools and techniques of public relations. For example, a firm that wants to know how employees rate its candor in internal publications would first conduct strategic research to find out where it stands.

- Evaluative research, sometimes called summative research, is conducted primarily to determine whether a public relations program has accomplished its goals and objectives. For example, if changes are made in the internal communications program to increase candor, evaluative research can determine whether the goals have been met. A variant of evaluation can be applied during a program to monitor progress and indicate where modifications might make sense.

Theoretical Research

Theoretical research is more abstract and conceptual than applied research. It helps build theories in public relations work about why people communicate, how public opinion is formed, and how a public is created.

Knowledge of theoretical research is important as a framework for persuasion and as a base for understanding why people do what they do.

Some knowledge of theoretical research in public relations and mass communications is essential for enabling practitioners to understand the limitations of communication as a persuasive tool. Attitude and behavior change has been the traditional goal in public relations programs, yet theoretical research indicates that such a goal may be difficult or impossible to achieve through persuasive efforts. According to such research, other factors are always getting in the way.

Researchers have found that communication is most persuasive when it comes from multiple sources of high credibility. Credibility itself is a multidimensional concept that includes trustworthiness, expertise, and power. Others have found that a message generally is more effective when it is simple, because it is easier to understand, localize, and make personally relevant. According to still other research, the persuasiveness of a message can be increased when it arouses or is accompanied by a high level of personal involvement in the issue at hand.

The point here is that knowledge of theoretical research can help practitioners not only understand the basis of applied research findings but also temper management's expectations of attitude and behavioral change resulting from public relations programs.

Secondary Research

Secondary research is research on the cheap. Basically, secondary research allows you to examine or read about and learn from someone else's primary research, such as in a library.

Also called "desk research," secondary research uses data that have been collected for other purposes than your own. Among the typical sources of secondary research are the following:

- Online database mining, for example, Google searches
- Industry trade journals
- Government
- Informal contacts
- Published company accounts
- Business libraries
- Professional institutes and organizations
- Omnibus surveys
- Census data
- Public records

Database monitoring is particularly important for public relations researchers. Such online resources as Claritas, which supplies marketing analysis and demographic tools; SurveyMonkey.com, which provides the resources to create tailored online surveys (Figure 8-3); and the omnipresent Google search engine are popular outlets to aid public relations researchers.

Because public relations budgets are limited, it always makes sense first to consider secondary sources in launching a research effort.

Methods of Public Relations Research

Observation is the foundation of modern social science. Scientists, social psychologists, and anthropologists make observations, develop theories, and, hopefully, increase understanding of human behavior. Public relations research, too, is founded on observation. Indeed, examining human behavior was pivotal to the early public relations work of Edward Bernays. Three primary forms of public relations research dominate the field.

- *Surveys* are designed to reveal attitudes and opinions—what people think about certain subjects.
- *Communications audits* often reveal disparities between real and perceived communications between management and target audiences. Management may

FIGURE 8-3 **Survey monkey.** Services, such as SurveyMonkey.com, allow you to design your own online survey, such as the hypothetical one shown here.

| Volunteer Input Requested | Exit this survey >> |

1. Survey Regarding Financial Issues

1. Should we be permitted to incur an annual operating deficit?

Yes

No, Never

No, Except in an urgent situation

Other (please specify)

2. Should members be kept informed of projected operating deficits and other material financial issues and the steps being taken to address those issues?

Yes

No

Other (please specify)

3. Should we take steps to reduce or eliminate the projected operating deficit for the current year?

Yes, the deficit should be completely eliminated this year and each following year

Yes, the deficit should be reduced as much as possible this year and fully eliminated starting next year

No

Other (please specify)

4. Would you support an increase in annual membership dues?

No

Yes, up to $25

Yes, up to $50

Yes, up to $75

Yes, up to $100

Yes, more than $100

Other (please specify)

5. Should we take steps to reduce or eliminate the projected operating deficit for the current year?

Yes, the deficit should be completely eliminated this year and each following year

Yes, the deficit should be reduced as much as possible this year and fully eliminated starting next year

No

Other (please specify)

6. Should Board members be required to make a minimum annual contribution?

No,

Yes, $1,000

Yes, $2,000

Yes, $3,500

Yes, $5,000
Yes, more than $5000

Other (please specify)

make certain assumptions about its methods, media, materials, and messages, whereas its targets may confirm or refute those assumptions.

■ *Unobtrusive measures*—such as fact-finding, content analysis, and readability studies—enable the study of a subject or object without involving the researcher or the research as an intruder.

Each method of public relations research offers specific benefits and should be understood and used by the modern practitioner.

Surveys

Survey research is one of the most frequently used research methods in public relations. Surveys can be applied to broad societal issues, such as determining public opinion about a political candidate, or to more focused issues, such as satisfaction of hospital patients or hotel guests or reporting relationships of public relations people (Figure 8-4). Most survey research is now done online.

Surveys come in two types.

1. *Descriptive surveys* offer a snapshot of a current situation or condition. They are the research equivalent of a balance sheet, capturing reality at a specific point in time. A typical public opinion poll is a prime example.

2. *Explanatory surveys* are concerned with cause and effect. Their purpose is to help explain why a current situation or condition exists and to offer explanations for opinions and attitudes. Frequently, such explanatory or analytical surveys are designed to answer the question "why?" Why are our philanthropic dollars not being appreciated in the community? Why don't employees believe management's messages? Why is our credibility being questioned?

Surveys generally consist of four elements: (1) sample, (2) questionnaire, (3) interview, and (4) analysis of results. (Direct-mail surveys, of course, eliminate the interview step.) Because survey research is so critical in public relations, we examine each survey element in some detail.

The Sample

The sample, or selected target group, must be representative of the total public whose views are sought. Once a survey population has been determined, a researcher must select the appropriate sample or group of respondents from which to collect information. Sampling is tricky. A researcher must be aware of the hidden pitfalls in choosing a representative sample, not the least of which is the perishable nature of most data. Survey findings are rapidly outdated because of population mobility and changes in the political and socioeconomic environment. Consequently, sampling should be completed quickly.

Two cross-sectional approaches are used in obtaining a sample: random sampling and nonrandom sampling. The former is more scientific, the latter more informal.

Random Sampling

In random sampling, two properties are essential—equality and independence. *Equality* means that no element has any greater or lesser chance of being selected.

FIGURE 8-4 **Reaching the corporate summit survey.** This survey, co-sponsored by *PR News* and the International Association of Business Communicators, polled reporting relationships among public relations professionals. (Reprinted with permission from the International Association of Business Communicators)

PR News/IABC Joint Survey: Getting a Taste of the C-Suite

Please take a few minutes to fill out the following survey by April 25th. Coverage of the study's results will appear in the May 4th issue of PR News as well as the May 2005 edition of IABC's CW Bulletin. We're hopeful that the results will enable senior PR pros to devise strategies that will help them reach the corporate summit—and stay there.

1. I report directly to the CEO   [Please Choose ▼]

2. I am a member of the top management team   [Please Choose ▼]

3. I regularly attend meetings of the top management team (whether or not I am a member)   [Please Choose ▼]

4. How many employees are there in your corporate affairs/PR department?   [Please Choose ▼]

5. What country are you in?   [Please Select ▼]

	Strongly Agree	Agree	Neither Agree nor Disagree	Disagree	Strongly Disagree
6. My CEO:					
a . . . understands the importance of communication, not just when there is an issue or crisis	○	○	○	○	○
b. . . . sees PR as an investment in the future not just a cost	○	○	○	○	○
c. . . . asks my opinion about PR implications of future directions of the business	○	○	○	○	○
d. . . . usually accepts my recommendations	○	○	○	○	○
e. . . . would say I understand the business	○	○	○	○	○
7. My CEO values corporate affairs / PR advice at least as much as that from:					
a. . . . Advertising	○	○	○	○	○
b. . . . Sales	○	○	○	○	○
c. . . . Marketing	○	○	○	○	○
d. . . . Legal	○	○	○	○	○
e. . . . Human Resources	○	○	○	○	○
8. My CEO makes an effort (e.g. willingly puts in time) to maintain good relations with the following stakeholders:					
a. . . . employees	○	○	○	○	○
b. . . . stockholders	○	○	○	○	○
c. . . . analysts	○	○	○	○	○
d. . . . customers/clients	○	○	○	○	○
e. . . . business or alliance partners	○	○	○	○	○
f. . . . media	○	○	○	○	○

9.

a. What do you mostly discuss at your meetings with the CEO? (e.g. high-level strategy, business reputation, communication tactics, your career path, media relations, CEO presentations, analyst relationships, publications?)

b. Has the CEO redefined your role or mandate at any stage (e.g. upgraded it, expanded it, downgraded it, etc.)? Please explain what and why.

10.

a. To what extent does your CEO expect PR results to be measured? Does he/she take PR less seriously because measurement is not easy to do? To what extent is your CEO skeptical of anything without numbers attached?

b. What demands does the CEO have of the PR function that are not currently being met?

c. What three things would you like to see improved in regard to the CEO and PR/coms function or your relationship with him/her?

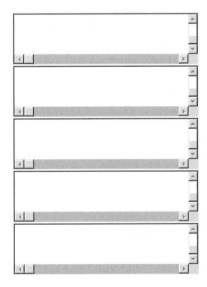

Independence means that selecting any one element in no way influences the selection of any other element. Random sampling is based on a mathematical criterion that allows generalizations from the sample to be made to the total population. There are four types of random or probability samples.

1. **Simple random sampling** gives all members of the population an equal chance of being selected. First, all members of the population are identified, and then as many subjects as are needed are randomly selected—usually with the help of a computer. Election polling uses a random approach; although millions of Americans vote, only a few thousand are ever polled on their election preferences. The Nielsen national television sample, for example, consists of only 10,000 homes, encompassing 25,000 people; this, despite the fact there are 112 million TV households in the U.S.[5] Despite the relatively small sample size, TV networks live and die on the basis of Nielsen data.

    How large should a random sample be? The answer depends on a number of factors, one of which is the size of the population. In addition, the more similar the population elements are in regard to the characteristics being studied, the smaller the sample required. In most random samples, the following population-to-sample ratios apply, with a 5 percent margin of error:

Population	Sample
1,000	278
2,000	322
3,000	341
5,000	355
10,000	370
50,000	381
100,000	383
500,000	383
Infinity	384

    Random sampling owes its accuracy to the laws of probability, which are best explained by the example of a barrel filled with 10,000 marbles—5,000 green ones and 5,000 red ones. If a blindfolded person selects a certain number of marbles from the barrel—say, 400—the laws of probability suggest that the most frequently drawn combination will be 200 red and 200 green. These laws further suggest that with certain margins of error, a very few marbles can represent the whole barrel, which can correspond to any size—for example, that of a city, state, or nation.

2. **Systematic random sampling** is closely related to simple random sampling, but it uses a random starting point in the sample list. From then on, the researcher selects every *n*th person in the list. As long as every person has an equal and independent chance to be selected on the first draw, then the sample qualifies as random and is equally reliable to simple random sampling. Random telephone dialing, for example, which solves the problem of failing to consider unlisted numbers, may use this technique.

3. **Stratified random sampling** is a procedure used to survey different segments or strata of the population. For example, if an organization wants to determine the relationship between years of service and attitudes toward the company, it may stratify the sample to ensure that the breakdown of respondents accurately reflects the makeup of the population. In other words, if more than half of the employees have been with the company more than 10 years, more

than half of those polled should also reflect that level of service. By stratifying the sample, the organization's objective can be achieved.

4. **Cluster sampling** involves first breaking the population down into small heterogeneous subsets, or clusters, and then selecting the potential sample from the individual clusters or groups. A cluster may often be defined as a geographic area, such as an election district.

Nonrandom Sampling

Nonrandom samples come in three types: convenience, quota, and volunteer.

1. **Convenience samples,** also known as accidental, chunk, or opportunity samples, are relatively unstructured, rather unsystematic, and designed to elicit ideas and points of view. Journalists use convenience samples when they conduct person-on-the-street interviews. The most common type of convenience sample in public relations research is the focus group. Focus groups generally consist of several people, with a moderator encouraging in-depth discussion of a specific topic. Focus groups generate concepts and ideas rather than validate hypotheses.

2. **Quota samples** permit a researcher to choose subjects on the basis of certain characteristics. For example, the attitudes of a certain number of women, men, blacks, whites, rich, or poor may be needed. Quotas are imposed in proportion to each group's percentage of the population. The advantage of quota sampling is that it increases the homogeneity of a sample population, thus enhancing the validity of a study. However, it is hard to classify interviewees by one or two discrete demographic characteristics. For example, a particular interviewee may be black, Catholic, female, under 25, and a member of a labor union all at the same time, making the lines of demographic demarcation pretty blurry. (A derivative of quota sampling is called purposive sampling.)

3. **Volunteer samples** use willing participants who agree voluntarily to respond to concepts and hypotheses for research purposes.

The Questionnaire

Before creating a questionnaire, whether to be mailed or emailed, a researcher must consider his or her objective in doing the study. What you seek to find out should influence the specific publics you ask, the questions you raise, and the research method you choose. After determining what you're after, consider the particular questionnaire design. Specifically, researchers should observe the following in designing their questionnaire:

1. **Keep it short.** Make a concerted attempt to limit questions. It's terrific if the questionnaire can be answered in five minutes.

2. **Use structured rather than open-ended questions.** People would rather check a box or circle a number than write an essay. But leave room at the bottom for general comments or "Other." Also, start with simple, nonthreatening questions before getting to the more difficult, sensitive ones. This approach will build respondent trust as well as commitment to finishing the questionnaire.

3. **Measure intensity of feelings.** Let respondents check "very satisfied," "satisfied," "dissatisfied," or "very dissatisfied" rather than "yes" or "no." One popular approach is the semantic differential technique shown in Figure 8-5.

Bauman
Research & Consulting, LLC

Dear Susan,

A few months ago you contacted XYZ company about your health condition. We'd like some feedback on how we did – and how you're doing.

Please take 5 minutes to tell us about your experiences and help us do better.

This survey is being conducted for XYZ company by an independent research firm, Bauman Research & Consulting. Your responses are completely confidential and will <u>not</u> be used for any marketing or selling purposes.

As a token of our appreciation for your participation, we have enclosed $5.

If you have any questions about this survey, please contact Sandra Bauman at sandra@baumanresearch.com or 201-444-6894.

Q1.   In general, how would you describe your own health?

EXCELLENT	VERY GOOD	GOOD	FAIR	POOR
$\square_1$	$\square_2$	$\square_3$	$\square_4$	$\square_5$

Q2.   What is your current general level of activity?

Not at all Active ← → Extremely Active

1   2   3   4   5   6   7   8   9   10

Q3.   Which joint is causing you pain? [Choose one.]

HIP	KNEE	SHOULDER	ELBOW	OTHER
$\square_1$	$\square_2$	$\square_3$	$\square_4$	$\square_5$

Q4.   How effective was XYZ company at communicating information in each of these areas?

	EXTREMELY EFFECTIVE	VERY EFFECTIVE	SOMEWHAT EFFECTIVE	NOT TOO EFFECTIVE	NOT AT ALL EFFECTIVE
a. Information about possible prescription treatment options for your joint pain	$\square_1$	$\square_2$	$\square_3$	$\square_4$	$\square_5$
b. Information about possible physical therapy options for your joint pain	$\square_1$	$\square_2$	$\square_3$	$\square_4$	$\square_5$
c. Information about possible surgical options for your joint pain	$\square_1$	$\square_2$	$\square_3$	$\square_4$	$\square_5$

➔ *CONTINUED*

 44 Abbington Terrace, Glen Rock, NJ 07452 • Phone: 201.444.6894 • Fax: 201.701.0271 • www.baumanresearch.com

FIGURE 8-5 Measuring intensity, rewarding respondents. One common device to measure intensity of feelings is the semantic differential technique, which gives respondents a scale of choices from the worst to the best. Respondents will comply more gladly if a "crisp new bill" is included— and even more gladly to two "crisp new bills." (Courtesy of Bauman Research & Consulting LLC)

4. **Don't use fancy words or words that have more than one meaning.** If you must use big words, make the context clear.

5. **Don't ask loaded questions.** "Is management doing all it can to communicate with you?" is a terrible question. The answer is always no.

6. **Don't ask double-barreled questions.** "Would you like management meetings once a month, or are bimonthly meetings enough?" is another terrible question.

7. **Pretest.** Send your questionnaire to a few colleagues and listen to their suggestions.

8. **Attach a letter explaining how important the respondents' answers are, and let recipients know that they will remain anonymous.** Respondents will feel better if they think the study is significant and their identities are protected. Also, specify how and where the data will be used.

9. **When mailing, hand-stamp the envelopes, preferably with unique commemorative stamps.** Metering an envelope indicates assembly-line research, and researchers have found that the more expensive the postage, the higher the response rate. People like to feel special.

10. **Follow up your first mailing.** Send a reminder postcard three days after the original questionnaire. Then wait a few weeks and send a second questionnaire, just in case recipients have lost the first.

11. **Send out more questionnaires than you think necessary.** The major weakness of most mail surveys is the immeasurable error introduced by nonresponders. You're shooting for a 50 percent response rate; anything less tends to be suspect.

12. **Enclose a reward.** (One reason to mail and not email.) There's nothing like a token gift of merchandise or, better yet, money to make a recipient feel guilty for not returning a questionnaire.

Interviews

Interviews can provide a more personal, firsthand feel for public opinion. Interview panels can range from focus groups of randomly selected average people to Delphi panels of so-called opinion leaders. Interviews can be conducted in a number of ways, including face-to-face, telephone, mail, and through the Internet.

Focus Groups

This approach is used with increasing frequency in public relations today. A traditional focus group consists of a 90- to 120-minute discussion among 8 to 10 individuals who have been selected based upon having predetermined common characteristics, such as buying behavior, age, income, family composition, and so on.[6]

With the focus group technique, a well-drilled moderator leads a group through a discussion of opinions on a particular product, organization, or idea. Participants represent the socioeconomic level desired by the research sponsor—from college students to office workers to millionaires. Almost always, focus group participants are paid for their efforts. Sessions are frequently videotaped and then analyzed, often in preparation for more formal and specific research questionnaires.

Focus groups should be organized with the following guidelines in mind:

1. **Define your objectives and audience.** The more tightly you define your goals and your target audience, the more likely you are to gather relevant information. In other words, don't conduct a focus group with friends and family members, hoping to get a quick and inexpensive read. Nothing of value will result.

2. **Recruit your groups.** Recruiting participants takes several weeks, depending on the difficulty of contacting the target audience. Contact is usually made by phone with a series of questions to weed out employees of competitors, members of the news media (to keep the focus group from becoming a news story), and those who don't fit target group specifications.

3. **Choose the right moderator.** Staff people who may be excellent conversationalists are not necessarily the best focus group moderators. The gift of gab is not enough. Professional moderators know how to establish rapport quickly, how and when to probe beyond the obvious, how to draw comments from reluctant participants, how to keep a group on task, and how to interpret results validly.

4. **Conduct enough focus groups.** One or two focus groups usually are not enough. Four to six are better to uncover the full range of relevant ideas and opinions. Regardless of the number of groups, however, you must resist the temptation to add up responses. That practice gives the focus group more analytical worth than it deserves.

5. **Use a discussion guide.** This is a basic outline of what you want to investigate. It will lead the moderator through the discussion and keep the group on track.

6. **Choose proper facilities.** The discussion room should be comfortable, with participants sitting around a table that gives them a good view of each other. Observers can use closed-circuit TV and one-way mirrors, but participants should always be told when they are being observed.

7. **Keep a tight rein on observers.** Observers should rarely be in the same room with participants; the two groups ordinarily should be separated. Observers should view the proceedings seriously; this is not "dinner and a show."

8. **Consider using outside help.** Setting up focus groups can be time-consuming and complicated. Often the best advice is to hire a professional firm to conduct the research.

Telephone Interviews

In contrast to personal interviews, telephone interviews suffer from a high refusal rate. Many people just don't want to be bothered. Such interviews may also introduce an upper-income bias because lower-income earners may lack telephones. However, the increasing use of unlisted numbers by upper-income people and the proliferation of "caller I.D." to screen unwanted calls may severely mitigate this bias. Telephone interviews must be carefully scripted so that interviewers know precisely what to ask, regardless of a respondent's answer. Calls should be made at less busy times of the day, such as early morning or late afternoon.

With both telephone and face-to-face interviews, it is important to establish rapport with the interview subject. It makes good sense to begin the interview with nonthreatening questions, saving the tougher, more controversial ones—on income level or race, for example—until last.

Email Interviews

This is the least expensive approach, but it often suffers from a low response rate. Frequently, people who return email or even snail mail questionnaires are those with strong biases either in favor of or (more commonly) in opposition to the subject at hand. As noted, one way to generate a higher response from mail interviews is through the use of self-addressed, stamped envelopes or enclosed incentives such as dollar bills or free gifts.

Drop-off Interviews

This approach combines face-to-face and mail interview techniques. An interviewer personally drops off a questionnaire at a household, usually after conducting a face-to-face interview. Because the interviewer has already established some rapport with the interviewee, the rate of return with this technique is considerably higher than it is for straight mail interviews.

Intercept Interviews

This approach is popular in consumer surveys, where researchers "intercept" respondents on the street, in shopping malls, or in retail outlets. Trained interviewers typically deliver a short (5- to 20-minute) questionnaire concerning attitudes, perceptions, preferences, and behavior.

Delphi Panels

The Delphi technique is a qualitative research tool that uses opinion leaders—local influential persons as well as national experts—often to help tailor the design of a general public research survey. Designed by the Rand Corporation in the 1950s, the Delphi technique is a consensus-building approach that relies on repeated waves of questionnaires sent to the same select panel of experts. Delphi findings generate a wide range of responses and help set the agenda for more meaningful future research. Stated another way, Delphi panels offer a "research reality check."

Internet Interviews

Web-based surveying is becoming more widely used. In its ubiquitous availability, the Web offers significant advantages over more traditional survey techniques. However, Internet interviews also introduce problems, among them that significant numbers of people either don't have access to or choose not to use the Internet. Several studies have found Internet surveys have significantly lower response rates than comparable mailed surveys. Several factors have been found to increase response rates, including personalized email cover letters, follow-up reminders, pre-notification of the intent to survey, and simpler formats. While there is a need for caution, the use of Web-based surveying is clearly growing.[7]

Results Analysis

After selecting the sample, drawing up the questionnaire, and interviewing the respondents, the researcher must analyze the findings. Often a great deal of analysis is required to produce meaningful recommendations.

The objective of every sample is to come up with results that are valid and reliable. A margin of error explains how far off the prediction may be. A sample may be large enough to represent fairly the larger universe; yet, depending on the margin of sampling error, the results of the research may not be statistically significant. That is, the differences or distinctions detected by the survey may not be sizable enough to offset the margin of error. Thus, the margin of error must always be determined.

Popular political polls, in particular, are fraught with problems. They cannot predict outcomes scientifically. Rather, they provide a snapshot, freezing attitudes at a certain point in time—like a balance sheet for a corporation. Obviously, people's attitudes change with the passage of time, and pollsters, despite what they claim, can't categorically predict the outcome of an election. In the 2008 Democratic presidential primary, Hillary Clinton won a startling victory in New Hampshire, after most polls showed her losing soundly to Barack Obama. The polls simply couldn't measure her last-minute upsurge in popularity.[8] The most notorious example of this problem was the political poll sponsored by the *Literary Digest* in 1936, which used a telephone polling technique to predict that Alf Landon would be the nation's next president. Landon thereupon suffered one of the worst drubbings in American electoral history at the hands of Franklin Roosevelt. It was probably of little solace to the *Literary Digest* that most of its telephone respondents, many of whom were Republicans wealthy enough to afford phones, did vote for Landon.

The point is that in analyzing results, problems of validity, reliability, and levels of statistical significance associated with margins of error must be considered before concrete recommendations are volunteered.

Talking Points Figures and Faces—Lie

If you don't believe the old maxim that "figures lie and liars figure," consider the following: In often repeated research, randomly selected participants are shown the two faces in Figure 8-6 and asked, *"Which woman is lovelier?"* Invariably, the answer is split 50–50.

However, when each woman is named, one "Jennifer" and the other "Gertrude," respondents overwhelmingly—more than 80 percent—vote for Jennifer as the more beautiful woman.

Why? "Jennifer" is more hip, more happening, more, uh, "phat." (Sorry, all you Gertrudes out there!)

The point is that people can't help but introduce their own biases, including even in presumably "objective" research experiments. This factor always should be taken into account in evaluating public relations research.

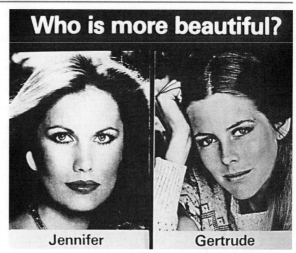

FIGURE 8-6 Jennifer/Gertrude. (Courtesy of Fraser P. Seitel)

Communications Audits

Communications audits are an increasingly important method of research in public relations work. Such audits are used frequently by corporations, schools, hospitals, and other organizations to determine whether a communications group and the products it produces are realizing objectives and also how the institution is perceived by its core constituents. Communications audits help public relations professionals understand more clearly the relationships between management actions and objectives on the one hand, and communications methods to promote those objectives on the other.

Communications audits are typically used to analyze the standing of a company with its employees or community neighbors; to assess the readership of routine communication vehicles, such as annual reports and news releases; or to examine an organization's performance as a corporate citizen. Communications audits often provide benchmarks against which future public relations programs can be applied and measured. The data uncovered are frequently used by management to make informed decisions about future communications needs and goals.

Audit Scope

The scope of an audit may be as broad or as narrow as the size and complexity of the organization's demands. The audit can measure the effectiveness of communications programs across the organization or the programs of a single division. It can also hone in on a specific subject—readability of written materials, understanding of an issue, or use of an internal intranet, for example. An audit can also uncover misunderstandings and information barriers and bottlenecks, as well as opportunities.

Audit Subjects

Typically, communications audits are used to provide information on whether communications have met predetermined objectives and goals. This is most critical. Other subjects that audits typically dissect include:

- Existing communications programs—methods and media
- Existing communications vehicles—publications, manuals, bulletin boards, closed-circuit TV, videotape, slides, teleconferencing, memos, meetings, Internet, reports, correspondence, and so on
- Uneven communications workloads
- Employees working at cross-purposes
- Hidden information within an organization that, to the detriment of the institution, is not being used
- Bottlenecked information flows
- Conflicting notions about what the organization is and does

Audit Methodology

A communications audit is a straightforward analysis.

1. It begins with a researcher studying all pertinent literature about the organization.
2. Competitive literature is then reviewed for purposes of comparison and contrast.

3. Interviews with top management and the rank and file are then conducted to detect areas of commonality and discontinuity. In other words, what do people agree on and where do they disagree? Interviews with key outsiders, such as the board and customers, also may be included.

4. Recommendations are then presented from the audit knowledge gleaned.

A communications audit, of course, is not an end in itself. Rather it must be part of a process of measurement and performance improvement.[9] In that context, an extensive audit should be conducted every couple of years to keep an organization's communications fresh and relevant and consistent with 21st-century methods and techniques.

PR Ethics

Mini-Case   Rudy's Recounting Reveals Rocky Research

Rudy Giuliani, former New York City mayor and hero of 9/11, began the 2007 Republican presidential primary as the odds-on front runner (see Figure 8-7).

In virtually every appearance, "America's mayor" cited a fusillade of research statistics and facts to make his arguments about his successes in running New York City and why that made him the best choice to win the nomination.

The data Rudy cited included:

- The only major U.S. city to reduce crime every year since 1994 when he became mayor;

- Under his lead, the murder rate in New York City had declined from an average of 1,800 murders a year recorded steadily over a 30-year period; and

- Under his lead, New York City spending declined 7 percent.

As mayor, Giuliani regularly referred to research statistics as the centerpiece of his record. His anticrime strategy as

FIGURE 8-7 Victim of faulty research. Republican 2008 presidential primary hopeful Rudy Giuliani was questioned on the research he cited and ultimately dropped out of the running. (Photo: Newscom)

mayor was built around a system known as Compstat that closely tracked crimes to focus law enforcement efforts.

Similarly on the campaign trail, the former mayor wielded research data as weapons to authenticate his hard-nosed leadership style and achievement. Indeed, Rudy was known to cite facts and figures and statistics far more often than any other candidate.

And the strategy worked well—until people started checking the research. And not just any "people," but "Internet people."

Specifically, the former mayor began getting hounded by Factcheck.org, a project of the Annenberg Public Policy Center of the University of Pennsylvania, whose mission was to check candidate claims.

What the Web site revealed was that contrary to Giuliani's claims on the campaign stump, the following was true:

- New York was *not* the only city to reduce crime since 1994. Chicago did too.

- Homicides in New York City didn't reach 1,800 until 1980—far more recent than the "30-year period" cited by Giuliani.

- Under Giuliani's lead, New York City spending actually grew an average of 3.7 percent.

While these research gaffes weren't fatal, publicity about them in *The New York Times* and around the country helped to tarnish the Giuliani star. By January 2008, the former front-runner's star had dimmed so much that Giuliani pulled out of the presidential primary race.*

Questions

1. Had you been advising Giuliani, what would you have counseled him relative to citing research?

2. What does the Giuliani experience indicate about citing research as a high profile candidate or organization?

*For further information, see Michael Cooper, "Citing Statistics, Giuliani Misses Time and Again," *New York Times* (November 30, 2007): 1.

Unobtrusive Methods

Of the various unobtrusive methods of data collection available to public relations researchers, probably the most widely used is simple fact-finding. Facts are the bricks and mortar of public relations work; no action can be taken unless the facts are known, and the fact-finding process is continuous.

Each organization must keep a fact file of the most essential data with which it is involved. For example, such items as key organization statistics, publications, management biographies and photos, press clippings, media lists, competitive literature, pending legislation, organizational charters, and bylaws should be stored electronically and updated.

Another unobtrusive method is simple content analysis, the primary purpose of which is to describe a message or set of messages. For example, an organization with news releases that are used frequently by local newspapers can't be certain, without research, whether the image conveyed by its releases is what the organization seeks. By analyzing the news coverage, the firm can get a much clearer idea of the effectiveness of its communications. Such content analysis might be organized according to the following specific criteria:

- ■ **Frequency of coverage.** How many releases were used?
- ■ **Placement within the paper.** Did releases appear more frequently on page 1 or page 71?
- ■ **People reached.** What was the circulation of the publications or approximate Web hits where the releases appeared?
- ■ **Messages conveyed.** Did the releases used express the goals of the organization, or were they simply informational in content?
- ■ **Editing of releases.** How much did news organizations or news sites edit the submitted copy? Were desired meanings materially changed?
- ■ **Attitude conveyed.** Was the reference to the organization positive, negative, or neutral?

Copy testing, in which public targets are exposed to public relations campaign messages to be used in brochures, memos, online, and so on, in advance of their publication, is another viable method that ensures campaign messages are understandable and effective.

Finally, case study research that analyzes how other organizations handled similar challenges is a constructive, unobtrusive research method.

Clearly, there is nothing particularly mysterious or difficult about unobtrusive methods of research. Such methods are relatively simple to apply—and also inexpensive—yet they are essential for arriving at appropriate refinements for an ongoing public relations program.

Evaluation

No matter what type of public relations research is used, results of the research and the research project itself should always be analyzed for meaning and action. Evaluation is designed to determine what happened and why by measuring results against established objectives. As public relations Prof. James Grunig has said, "The main reason to measure objectives is not so much to reward or punish individual communications managers for success or failure, as it is to learn from the research whether a program should be continued as is, revised, or dropped in favor of another approach."[10]

The key word in organizations today is *accountability,* which means taking responsibility for achieving the performance promised. With resources limited and competition fierce, managers at every level demand accountability for every activity on which they spend money. That's what evaluation is all about. Public relations professionals are obligated today to assess what they've done to determine whether the expense was worth it.

Evaluation of public relations programs depends on several things:

- **Setting measurable public relations program objectives.** Goals should specify who the target publics are, what impact the program seeks to have on those publics, and when the results are expected.

- **Securing management commitment.** Public relations people and management should always agree in advance on the program's objectives so that the results can be clearly evaluated. Without management buy-in that the program is objective and well targeted, management may not believe the results.

- **Determining the best way to gather data.** Again, raw program records and observation are a rudimentary but acceptable method of evaluative measurement. Better would be attitude pretesting and posttesting to determine if a particular program helped facilitate a shift in attitudes toward a program, company, or issue. Surveys may or may not be called for.

- **Reporting back to management.** Evaluation findings should be shared with management. This reinforces the notion that public relations is contributing to management goals for the organization.

- **Selecting the most appropriate outcomes.** Although public relations outputs are important, public relations *outcomes* are more important. Outcome evaluation may be a measurement of the press clippings a program received— that is, the number of column inches or airtime devoted to the program. A more sophisticated evaluation of program effectiveness is a content analysis of the messages conveyed as a result of the program.

Outcome evaluation measures whether targets actually *received* the messages directed to them, *paid attention* to them, *understood* the messages, *retained* those messages, and even *acted* on them.[11]

In many respects, a measurement of public relations outcomes is the most important barometer in assessing success or failure of a program.

Measuring Public Relations Outcomes

What kinds of tools are used to measure public relations outcomes? Here are four of the most common.

Awareness and Comprehension Measurement

This measurement probes whether targets received the messages directed at them, paid attention to them, and understood them. Measuring awareness and comprehension levels requires "benchmarking," or determining preliminary knowledge about a target's understanding so that the furthering of that knowledge can be tracked. Stated another way, both "before" and "after" research should be conducted. To do this, both quantitative (e.g., surveys and polls) and qualitative (e.g., focus groups and interviews) methods should be applied.

Recall and Retention Measurement

This is a commonly used technique in advertising in which sponsors want to know if their commercials have lasting impact. Such measurement analysis may be equally important in public relations. It is one thing for a target to have seen and understood a message but quite another for someone to remember what was said. In applying such follow-up research, it is also instructive to see if targets can differentiate between public relations and advertising media. In other words, did the target audience retain the knowledge through media stories, speeches, presentations, or ads?

Attitude and Preference Measurement

Even more important than how much someone retained from a message is a measure of how the message moved an individual's attitudes, opinions, and preferences. This involves the areas of opinion research and attitude research. The former is easier because it can be realized simply by asking a few preference questions. The latter, however, is derived from more complex variables, such as predispositions, feelings, and motivational tendencies regarding the issue in question. Preference measurement is often derived by listing alternative choices and asking respondents to make decisions about their relative worth.

Behavior Measurements

This is the ultimate test of effectiveness. Did the message get people to vote for our candidate, buy our product, or agree with our ideas?

Measuring behavior in public relations is difficult, especially in "proving" that a certain program "caused" the desired outcome to occur. In other words, how do we know that it was our input in particular that caused people to contribute more to our charity, or legislators to vote for our issue, or an editor to report favorably on our organization? So although it's difficult to measure causation in public relations behavioral research, it's less difficult to show correlations of outcomes with public relations activity.[12]

Regardless of the evaluative technique, by evaluating after the fact, researchers can learn how to improve future efforts. Were the right target audiences surveyed? Were the correct research assumptions applied to those audiences? Were questions from research tools left unanswered?

Again, research results can be evaluated in a number of ways. Unfortunately, the most common method in public relations may be "seat-of-the-pants" evaluation, in which anecdotal observation and practitioner judgment are used to estimate the effectiveness of the public relations program. Such evaluation might be based on feedback from members of a key public, personal media contacts, or colleagues, but the practitioner alone evaluates the success of the program with subjective observation.

In the fiercely competitive, resource-dear 21st century, the practice of public relations will increasingly be called on to justify its activities and evaluate the results of its programs with formal research.

Research and the Web

Research techniques in evaluating the effectiveness of programs and products and messages on the Web are constantly being perfected.

What can today's Web analytics measure in terms of consumer-generated media (CGR, as it's known in the trade)? Lots of things. Among them:

- Unique visitors
- Returning visitors
- Costs per click through
- Total time spent on a site
- Downloads
- Costs per contact
- Links from other sites
- Google page rank
- Content popularity
- Sales

Evaluating Web Sites

In assessing the impact of the Web, the two most frequent research terms discussed are *hits* and *eyeballs*. The former refers to the number of times a Web site is visited by an individual. The latter refers to the orbital lobes affixed to that hit. Obviously, these are but the most rudimentary of measurement tools in that they don't assess the visitors' interest in the product or service or information conveyed, the duration of their stay at the site, or whether they were driven to act on the information—that is, buy the product, subscribe to the service, or vote for the candidate. Indeed, the first 5,000 hits to a new Web site may mean nothing more than the firm's employees checking out the latest communications tool.

In light of this inherent problem in extracting value from Web site measurement data, the best advice is to begin by identifying the key questions the Web site sponsor wants answered. For example:

- How much traffic is coming to the site?
- What pages are people looking at?
- How often do they go beyond the homepage?
- What is it they find most useful and interesting?
- What parts never get looked at?
- Where do visitors come from?
- Is the site functioning as expected—for advertisers, sales leads, requests, and so on?[13]

Value of Web Research

Like everything else associated with the Internet, measurement techniques will continue to develop rapidly. Consider the additional contributions Web research offers:

- **Intimacy.** Site-based research can bring organizations closer to their constituents.
- **Precision.** Web-based research can provide more detailed answers about consumers than traditional research methods.
- **Timeliness.** Web-based research is eminently more timely than traditional methods.
- **Cost.** Web-based research will reduce costs considerably compared to traditional surveying methods.

Web Research Considerations

The value of Web-oriented research is indisputable. In preparing for such Internet evaluation—just as in preparing for any public relations research—an organization should take several factors into consideration:

1. **Establish objectives.** Again, implicit in any meaningful measurement is the setting of objectives. Why are we on the Web? What is our site designed to do? What are we attempting to communicate?
2. **Determine criteria.** Define success with tangible data—for example, percentage of people likely to purchase from the site and positive interactive publication mentions that the site will receive.
3. **Determine benchmarks.** Project the hits the site will receive. Base this on competitive data to see how this site stacks up against the competition or other forms of communication.
4. **Select the right measurement tool.** Numerous software packages exist to track site traffic and provide other measurements, among them:

   - Web traffic: Clicktrax, Web trends, WebSide Story
   - Awareness/preference: SurveyMonkey, Zoomerang
   - Marketplace engagement: Type pad, Technorati
   - Messages: Dashboards, Vizu

5. **Compare results to objectives.** Success of online marketing and communications cannot be concluded in a vacuum. Numbers of visitors, hits, and eyeballs must be correlated with original objectives. For example, if the objective is to strengthen investor relations, then determine how many visitors made their way to the annual report and how long they stayed reading it. Combine that information with the cost to print the annual report, and this will help determine how much money the Web might save the company.
6. **Draw actionable conclusions.** Research indicates you've received 100,000 visitors to the site. So what? Interpret the significance of the numbers and do something with the data to make progress.[14]

Finally, in terms of researching the Web, there is the aspect of monitoring what is being said about the organization. With the proliferation of rogue sites, anti-business blogs, and chain letter email campaigns, monitoring the Web has become a frontline public relations responsibility. Web 2.0 has been called the "great equalizer," which means that all individuals can have their say—mean, nasty, belligerent—and organizations must constantly keep track of what is being said about them by consumer-generated media.

Using Outside Research Help

Despite its occasional rough spots, public relations research has made substantial gains in quantifying the results of public relations activities. Counseling firms have organized separate departments to conduct attitude and opinion surveys as well as other types of research projects.

Interactive public relations specialists have emerged to help monitor organizational references on the Web. Some outside agencies even volunteer to launch "whisper" campaigns on blogs to neutralize negative or inaccurate messages about clients.

Beyond these services, there are research tools, such as Statistical Package for the Social Sciences (SPSS) technology, which mines and analyzes social sciences data. Such systematic approaches are beneficial in analyzing the results of public relations research.

Often, before turning to outside consultants, the best first step—particularly with the wealth of data available on the Internet—is to determine whether research has already been done on what you are trying to find out. Because research assistance is expensive, it makes little sense to reinvent the wheel. It is much wiser to piggyback on existing research.

Last Word

Research is a means of both defining problems and evaluating solutions. Even though intuitive judgment remains a coveted and important public relations asset, management must see measurable results.

Nonetheless, informed managements recognize that public relations may never reach a point at which its results can be fully quantified. Management confidence is still a prerequisite for active and unencumbered programs. Indeed, the best measurement of public relations value is a strong and unequivocal endorsement from management that it supports the public relations effort. However, such confidence can only be enhanced as practitioners become more adept in using research.

Whether it's as basic as researching through the *"thud factor,"* that is, dumping a pile of publications

on a client's desk to assessing the AVE (advertising value equivalent of publicity)—to the more sophisticated techniques of measuring outputs and evaluating outcomes—research must be part of any 21st-century public relations enterprise.[15]

Frankly, practitioners don't have a choice. With efficiency driving today's bottom line and with communications about organizations percolating at a 24/7 clip around the world through a variety of media, organizations must always know where they stand. It is the job of public relations to keep track of, record, and research changing attitudes and opinions about the organizations for which they work.

According to Stuart Z. Goldstein, well-respected communications director of the Depository Trust & Clearing Corporation, strategic public relations research is best achieved through two obligatory databases that form the core of strategy development:

1. An integrated relational database that allows a practitioner to leverage internal information across all public relations disciplines.
2. A diagnostic database that tracks and helps analyze opinion data on a wide range of issues across key segments of an organization's primary constituencies.[16]

The need for greater analytical backup for public relations activities will make it increasingly incumbent on public relations people to reinforce the value of what they do and what they stand for through constantly measuring their contribution to their organization's goals.[17]

Discussion Starters

1. Why is research important in public relations work?
2. What are the differences between primary and secondary research?
3. What are the four elements of a survey?
4. What is the difference between random and stratified sampling?
5. What are the keys to designing an effective questionnaire?
6. What is a communication audit?
7. What kinds of tools are used to measure public relations outcomes?
8. Why is evaluation important in public relations research?
9. What kinds of questions are pertinent in evaluating a Web site?
10. What are the characteristics that can be measured in Web-based research?

Top of the Shelf Measuring Public Relationships, The Data-Driven Communicator's Guide to Success / Katie Paine, Berlin, NH: KDPaine & Partners, 2007

Katie Paine is one of the foremost researchers in the public relations business. She lives, breathes, and sleeps research.

That zeal is translated into this easily understandable, step-by-step guide to measuring public relations outputs and outcomes in a social media era. The book takes a "cookbook" approach, providing specific steps to measure all forms of public relationships, from social media measurement to tracking relationships with local communities, industry analysts, and social networks.

This is an important reference to truly understand what public relations measurement is all about.

Case Study Researching a Position for Alan Louis General

The administrator at Alan Louis General Hospital confronted a problem that he hoped research could help solve. Alan Louis General, although a good hospital, was smaller and less well-known than most other hospitals in Laredo, Texas. In its area alone, it competed with 10 other medical facilities. Alan Louis needed a "position" that it could call unique to attract patients to fill its beds.

For a long time, the Alan Louis administrator, Sven Rapcorn, had believed in the principle that truth will win out. Build a better mousetrap, and the world will beat a path to your door. Erect a better hospital, and your beds will always be 98 percent filled. Unfortunately, Rapcorn learned, the real world seldom recognizes truth at first blush.

In the real world, more often than not, perception will triumph. Because people act on perceptions, those perceptions become reality. Successful positioning, Rapcorn learned, is based on recognizing and dealing with people's perceptions. And so, Rapcorn set out with research to build on existing perceptions about Alan Louis General.

He decided to conduct a communications audit to help form a differentiable "position" for Alan Louis General.

Interview Process

As a first step, Rapcorn talked to his own doctors and trustees to gather data about their perceptions not only of Alan Louis General but also of other hospitals in the community. He did this to get a clear and informed picture of where competing hospitals ranked in the minds of knowledgeable people.

For example, the University Health Center had something for everybody—exotic care, specialized care, and basic bread-and-butter care. Laredo General was a huge, well-respected hospital whose reputation was so good that only a major tragedy could shake its standing in the community. Mercy Hospital was known for its trauma center. And so on.

As for Alan Louis itself, doctors and trustees said that it was a great place to work, that excellent care was provided, and that the nursing staff was particularly friendly and good. The one problem, everyone agreed, was that "nobody knows about us."

Attribute Testing

The second step in Rapcorn's research project was to test attributes important in health care. He did this to learn what factors community members felt were most important in assessing hospital care.

Respondents were asked to rank eight factors in order of importance and to tell Rapcorn and his staff how each of the surveyed hospitals rated on those factors. The research instrument used a semantic differential scale of 1 to 10, with 1 the worst and 10 the best possible score. Questionnaires were sent to two groups: 1,000 area residents and 500 former Alan Louis patients.

Results Tabulation

The third step in the research was to tabulate the results in order to determine community priorities.

Among area residents who responded, the eight attributes were ranked accordingly:

1. Surgical care—9.23
2. Medical equipment—9.20
3. Cardiac care—9.16
4. Emergency services—8.96
5. Range of medical services—8.63
6. Friendly nurses—8.62
7. Moderate costs—8.59
8. Location—7.94

After the attributes were ranked, the hospitals in the survey were ranked for each attribute. On advanced surgical care, the most important feature to area residents, Laredo General ranked first, with University Health Center a close second. Alan Louis was far down on the list. The same was true of virtually every other attribute. Indeed, on nursing care, an area in which its staff thought Alan Louis excelled, the hospital came in last in the minds of area residents. Rapcorn was not surprised. The largest hospitals in town scored well on most attributes; Alan Louis trailed the pack.

However, the ranking of hospital scores according to former Alan Louis patients revealed an entirely different story. On surgical care, for example, although Laredo General still ranked first, Alan Louis came in a close second. Its scores improved similarly on all other attributes. In fact, in nursing care, where Alan Louis came in last on the survey of area residents, among former patients its score was higher than that of any other hospital. It also ranked first in terms of convenient location and second in terms of costs, range of services, and emergency care.

Conclusions and Recommendations

The fourth step in Rapcorn's research project was to draw some conclusions to determine what the data had revealed.

He reached three conclusions:

1. Laredo General was still number one in terms of area hospitals.
2. Alan Louis ranked at or near the top on most attributes, according to those who actually experienced care there.
3. Former Alan Louis patients rated the hospital significantly better than did the general public.

In other words, thought Rapcorn, most of those who try Alan Louis like it. The great need was to convince more people to try the hospital.

But how could this be accomplished with a hospital? Other marketers generate trial by sending free samples in the mail, offering cents-off coupons, holding free demonstrations, and the like. Hospitals are more limited in this area. Rapcorn's challenge was to launch a communications campaign to convince prospects to see other area hospitals in a different, less favorable light or to give people a specific reason to think about trying Alan Louis. In other words, he needed to come up with a communications strategy that clearly differentiated Alan Louis—admittedly, among the smallest of area hospitals—from the bigger, less personal hospitals. Rapcorn was confident that the data he had gathered from the research project were all he needed to come up with a winning idea.

He then set out to propose his recommendations.

Questions

1. What kind of communications program would you launch to accomplish Rapcorn's objectives?

2. What would be the cornerstone—the theme—of your communications program?

3. What would be the specific elements of your program?

4. In launching the program, what specific steps would you follow—both inside and outside the hospital—to build support?

5. How could you use the Internet to conduct more research about area hospitals and residents' perceptions of the care at these hospitals? How could you use the Internet to research the effectiveness of the communications program you implement?

the Top   An Interview with John James Fahey

In a communications and public relations career spanning 28 years with the IBM Corporation, Jim Fahey has had managerial responsibilities in all areas of public relations, from employee communications and community relations to government relations and graphic arts. Mr. Fahey is in his second decade as Associate Professor of Communications at Marist College, Poughkeepsie, NY, teaching communications and public relations courses.

How important is research in public relations?
Research is vital to the professional PR practitioner today.
   It should be the "alpha and the omega," the beginning and the end of any public relations project.

What is the state of research among most public relations professionals?
Research in public relations today is not as good as it should be. Today's management demand facts, statistics, and results. Good research can provide these things.

Is it possible to measure public relations success?
Absolutely—by establishing methods to measure *outputs* and *outcomes* against a given time frame. No PR program is complete until it has been measured against given objectives.

How do you respond to those who say public relations is based purely on intuition?
Intuition in many ways is based on experience and knowledge and can be extremely useful in PR. However, there is no substitute for sound legitimate research to solve public relations problems. The best situation is a combination of the two.

What kinds of research are valuable for public relations professionals?
Two kinds come to mind: (1) Preliminary Research, to get the best understanding of the current problem or situation and (2) Evaluative Research, which is used to determine the success or failure of a program, project, or event. I'm reminded of the quote by the British physicist Lord Calvin. "When you can measure what you are talking about and express it in numbers, you know something about it. But, when you cannot measure it, when you cannot express it in numbers, your knowledge is meager and unsatisfactory."

How important is reading the daily newspaper as part of public relations "research"?
Very important. PR professionals are the eyes and the ears of the organization and should be consistently aware of what's going on in both the local and national media as well as the Internet.

How important is the Internet as a public relations research tool?
The Internet and the computer make up the new frontier in information and communications research. As a result, PR professionals *must* be proficient in the use of the computer, both as a research and a communication tool, and they *must* stay abreast of the new techniques and applications in the use of computers.

What weight should public relations students place on research?
Students must learn to have a great appreciation for the value of research. The quality of the research is of vital importance. First, management expects it. Second, it will determine the success or failure of their PR programs. Third, the ability to provide quality research directly affects their careers.

Public Relations Library

Barzun, Jacques, and Henry F. Graff. *The Modern Researcher,* 6th ed. Ft. Worth, TX: HBJ College Publications, 2002.

Erikson, Robert, and Kent L. Tedin. *American Public Opinion, Its Origin, Contents and Impact,* 6th ed. New York: Longman, 2000.

Fowler, Floyd J., Jr. *Survey Research Methods,* 2nd ed. Newbury Park, CA: Sage Publications, 2002.

Gregory, James R. *The Best of Branding.* New York: McGraw-Hill, 2004. Gregory's allegiance to quantifying brand management and relying on measurement and quantitative analysis for corporate imaging makes this a worthwhile reference.

Hoover's Handbooks of American Business, Major U.S. Companies, World Business, Emerging Companies, and Private Companies. Austin, TX: Hoover's Inc. The Web site www.hoovers.com features Hoover's Online: The Business Network and profiles of more than 12,000 public and private companies.

Kennedy, Dan. *No B.S.: Marketing to the Affluent.* Irvine, CA: Entrepreneur Media, 2008. Interesting research on the affluent in America, what makes them tick, what intrigues them, and what they buy.

Pavlik, John V. *Public Relations: What Research Tells Us.* Newbury Park, CA: Sage Publications, 1987. Old, but a classic in the field.

Stacks, Don W. *Primer of Public Relations Research.* New York: Guilford Press, 2002. An authoritative and comprehensive guide to public relations research motives and methods, authored by one of the field's foremost research experts.

Tourangeau, Roger, Lance Rips, and Kenneth Rasinski. *The Psychology of Survey Response.* Cambridge University Press, 2000.

www.odwyerpr.com. *Jack O'Dwyer's Newsletter* offers online logos, agency statements, and complete listings of 550 PR firms. The best choice on the Web for accessing any part of the Web site, including news from the newsletter and other publications, hyperlinks to articles on PR, job listings, and more than 1,000 PR services in 58 categories.

Watson, Tom, and Paul Noble. *Evaluating Public Relations* (2nd ed.). London, England: Kogan Page Ltd., 2007. A respected treatise on public relations measurement and research, complete with online environment commentary and case studies.

Chapter 9

Media Relations/
Print & Broadcast

The Internet has changed forever the public relations practice of dealing with the media.

■ In 2008 in the midst of researching a story on Microsoft, *Wired* magazine reporter Fred Vogelstein received an email from Microsoft's public relations firm, Waggener Edstrom Worldwide, with a 13-page, 5,500-word internal memo attachment, meant to prepare company executives for specific media interviews—including an upcoming one with one, Fred Vogelstein. One sentence read *"Fred's stories tend to be a bit sensational, though he would consider them to be balanced and fair."* Some public relations person at Waggener Edstrom evidently pushed the wrong button. Oops![1]

■ That same year, after Target Corp. launched a provocative woman's clothing ad to which some observers took offense, the ShapingYouth.org. blog contacted the company for an explanation. What it got was the following response:

> *"Thank you for contacting Target; unfortunately we are unable to respond to your inquiry because Target doesn't participate with nontraditional media outlets. This practice is in place to allow us to focus on publications that reach our core guest."*

The ensuing uproar in the blogosphere caused Target immediately to revise its policy relative to Web-based media.[2]

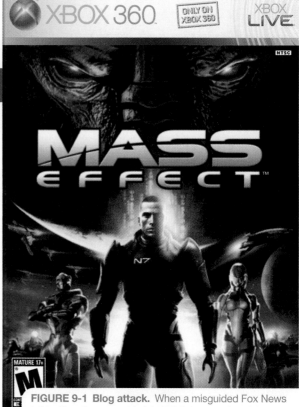

FIGURE 9-1 Blog attack. When a misguided Fox News talking head erroneously labeled the gun-toting desperadoes of the *Mass Effect* video game as "sexist," the attack of the blogosphere made her recant. (Photo: Newscom)

■ Finally in 2008, there was the case of the *Mass Effect* video game vs. Fox News. When a guest talking head psychologist on Fox described *Mass Effect* as a game that shows women only as *"objects of desire, as these, you know, hot bodies,"* the network suffered an avalanche of criticism on global message boards, blogs, and chat rooms, all claiming the Fox commentator didn't have a clue what she was talking about. As it turned out, they were right. Within hours of the attack of the game, the embarrassed psychologist admitted she had never actually seen the game, had relied on an associate's view, and acknowledged she had been wrong (see Figure 9-1).[3]

The point is that in the 21st century, thanks largely to the consumer-generated media of the Net, it's no longer your mama's media.

Where once the media were dominated by a handful of powerful, truth-minded reporters and editors at a handful of newspapers and three national TV networks, today the media are fragmented, omnipresent, busy 24 hours a day/seven days a week, and populated by a breed of reporter—in print, on the air, and, now more than ever, online—who is aggressive, opinionated, sharp-elbowed, and more than willing to throw himself or herself personally into the story being covered.

This latter point presents a particular difference with the reporting style of the past century. Today, more often than not, with competition from thousands of daily newspapers, talk radio stations, cable TV channels, and bloggers as far as the eye can see, reporters have few qualms about using anonymous sources, losing their historic anonymity, and becoming part of the story.

And this poses a particular challenge to those who practice public relations.

As we have noted, modern public relations practice got its start as an adjunct to journalism, with former reporters, such as Ivy Lee, hired to refine the image of well-to-do clients. In the old days (before 2000), most of the professionals who entered the practice of public relations were former journalists.

Today, of course, with public relations professionals emanating from many different fields of study and directly from college, the field is no longer dominated by former journalists. Nonetheless, the importance of the media to the practice of public relations cannot be denied.

Put simply, if you're in public relations, you must know how to deal with the press.

Therein lies the problem, because in the 21st century, the "press" has changed, often for the worst. As President Bush's first press secretary, Ari Fleischer, said:

> We've reached a point where the press, in pursuit of its devil's advocate role, would do well to ask itself, are they "informing" the public or are they being so negative about the institutions they cover, that they're not covering all the news, but only the "bad news"?[4]

This "devil's advocate" role is the key to why many people don't like the press. As the circulation of daily newspapers continues to decline, polls suggest that Americans are growing increasingly disenchanted with the media. One study indicated that 40 percent of Americans felt that *The New York Times* had a liberal bias, while 30 percent felt similarly about *The Washington Post*. Meanwhile, 40 percent of Americans felt all three major networks displayed a liberal bias, 33 percent felt CNN, MSNBC, CNBC, and National Public Radio had a liberal bias, and 30 percent felt the Fox News Network had a conservative bias. Perhaps most disheartening, even the Associated Press is seen by 30 percent of the public to have a liberal bias.[5] Traditionally, of course, the media have represented themselves as beacons of "objectivity," which assess the stories covered with fairness and impartiality. Opinion polls in the 21st century would appear to dispute this notion.

Freedom of the press, of course, is a hallmark of American democracy. It is a right guaranteed by the First Amendment to the U.S. Constitution. Written in 1789, the 45 words contained in the First Amendment protect the freedom of speech, press, religion, and assembly.

Over the years, in pursuing that freedom, the media have regularly challenged authority with pointed, nasty, even hostile questions. Their proper role in a democracy, as embodied in the First Amendment, is to independently ferret out the truth. Often this means "breaking eggs" in the process. Whether it means hounding a public figure, invading the privacy of a private figure, or just plain being obnoxious, that is what journalists have become known to do.

What this means to public relations professionals is that dealing with the media has never been more challenging. When one adds the growing impact of Internet journalism, where 70 percent accuracy is considered "acceptable," dealing with the media has become a high-risk business.

This is the business of the public relations professional, who serves as the first line of defense and explanation with respect to the media. It is the public relations practitioner who meets the reporter head on. In the 21st century, media relations is not a job for the squeamish.

Objectivity in the Media

Whether the mass media have lost relative influence to the Internet and its various vehicles, the fact remains that securing positive publicity through the media still lies at the heart of public relations practice.

Why attract publicity?

The answer, as we will see, is that publicity is regarded as more credible than advertising. To attract positive publicity requires establishing a good working relationship with the media. This is, of course, easier said than done. In the 21st century, faced with intense competition from on-air and online journalists, print reporters are by and large more aggressive.

They are also decidedly less "objective."

The presumed goal of a journalist is objectivity—fairness with the intention of remaining neutral in reporting a story. But total objectivity is impossible. All of us have biases and preconceived notions about many things. Likewise, in reporting, pure objectivity is unattainable; it would require complete neutrality and near-total detachment in reporting a story. Reporting, then, despite what some journalists might suggest, is subjective. Nevertheless, scholars of journalism believe that reporters and editors should strive for maximum objectivity (Figure 9-2).

By virtue of their role, the media view officials, particularly business and government spokespersons, with a degree of skepticism. Reporters shouldn't be expected to accept on faith the party line. By the same token, once a business or government official effectively substantiates the official view and demonstrates its merit, the media should be willing to report this accurately without editorial distortion.

Stated another way, the relationship between the media and the establishment— that is, public relations people—should be one of *friendly adversaries* rather than of bitter enemies. Unfortunately, this is not always the case. According to one *Washington Post* columnist, the fault may lie with the American public:

> *We are only incidentally bringing truth to the world—although don't get me wrong, from time to time we manage to do just that. But most journalists most of the time are just trying to give the public what it wants—and much of the time, the public wants trash.*[6]

THE JOURNALIST'S Creed

$\mathcal{I}$ believe IN THE PROFESSION OF

JOURNALISM.

I BELIEVE THAT THE PUBLIC JOURNAL IS A PUBLIC TRUST; THAT ALL CONNECTED WITH IT ARE, TO THE FULL MEASURE OF THEIR RESPONSIBILITY, TRUSTEES FOR THE PUBLIC; THAT ACCEPTANCE OF A LESSER SERVICE THAN THE PUBLIC SERVICE IS BETRAYAL OF THIS TRUST.

I BELIEVE THAT CLEAR THINKING AND CLEAR STATEMENT, AC-CURACY, AND FAIRNESS ARE FUNDAMENTAL TO GOOD JOUR-NALISM.

I BELIEVE THAT A JOURNALIST SHOULD WRITE ONLY WHAT HE HOLDS IN HIS HEART TO BE TRUE.

I BELIEVE THAT SUPPRESSION OF THE NEWS, FOR ANY CONSIDER-ATION OTHER THAN THE WELFARE OF SOCIETY, IS INDEFENSIBLE.

I BELIEVE THAT NO ONE SHOULD WRITE AS A JOURNALIST WHAT HE WOULD NOT SAY AS A GENTLEMAN; THAT BRIBERY BY ONE'S OWN POCKETBOOK IS AS MUCH TO BE AVOIDED AS BRIBERY BY THE POCKETBOOK OF ANOTHER; THAT INDIVIDUAL RESPONSIBIL-ITY MAY NOT BE ESCAPED BY PLEADING ANOTHER'S INSTRUC-TIONS OR ANOTHER'S DIVIDENDS.

I BELIEVE THAT ADVERTISING, NEWS AND EDITORIAL COLUMNS SHOULD ALIKE SERVE THE BEST INTERESTS OF READERS; THAT A SINGLE STANDARD OF HELPFUL TRUTH AND CLEANNESS SHOULD PREVAIL FOR ALL; THAT THE SUPREME TEST OF GOOD JOURNAL-ISM IS THE MEASURE OF ITS PUBLIC SERVICE.

I BELIEVE THAT THE JOURNALISM WHICH SUCCEEDS BEST—AND BEST DESERVES SUCCESS—FEARS GOD AND HONORS MAN; IS STOUTLY INDEPENDENT, UNMOVED BY PRIDE OF OPINION OR GREED OF POWER, CONSTRUCTIVE, TOLERANT BUT NEVER CARE-LESS, SELF-CONTROLLED, PATIENT, ALWAYS RESPECTFUL OF ITS READERS BUT ALWAYS UNAFRAID, IS QUICKLY INDIGNANT AT IN-JUSTICE; IS UNSWAYED BY THE APPEAL OF PRIVILEGE OR THE CLAMOR OF THE MOB; SEEKS TO GIVE EVERY MAN A CHANCE, AND, AS FAR AS LAW AND HONEST WAGE AND RECOGNITION OF HUMAN BROTHERHOOD CAN MAKE IT SO AN EQUAL CHANCE; IS PROFOUNDLY PATRIOTIC WHILE SINCERELY PROMOTING IN-TERNATIONAL GOOD WILL AND CEMENTING WORLD-COMRADE-SHIP; IS A JOURNALISM OF HUMANITY, OF AND FOR TODAY'S WORLD.

Walter Williams

DEAN SCHOOL OF JOURNALISM, UNIVERSITY OF MISSOURI, 1908-1935

FIGURE 9-2 **Code of objectivity.** "The Journalist's Creed" was written after World War I by Dr. Walter Williams, dean of the School of Journalism at the University of Missouri. (Courtesy of Luce Press Clippings)

That is not to say that the vast majority of journalists don't try to be fair. They do. Despite the preconceived biases that all of us have, most reporters want to get the facts from all sides. An increasing number of journalists acknowledge and respect the public relations practitioner's role in the process. (Some don't, but there are rotten apples in any profession!) If reporters are dealt with fairly, most will reciprocate in kind.

However, some executives fail to understand the essential difference between the media and their own organizations. That is:

1. The reporter wants the "story" whether bad or good.
2. Organizations, on the other hand, want things to be presented in the best light.

Because of this difference, some executives consider journalists to be the enemy, dead set on revealing all the bad news they can about their organization. These people fear and distrust the media. As a consequence, the practice of public relations—intermediary between the executive and the journalist—gets knocked as a profession of *"stonewallers"* intent on keeping journalists out.[7]

Print: Number One Medium

Recent years have not been kind to the print medium, particularly newspapers.

As the recession deepened, once-powerful newspapers, hit by rising costs and declining readership, struggled to survive. After a century of daily publishing, the *Rocky Mountain News* in Denver closed. Another mainstay, the *Philadelphia Inquirer*, declared bankruptcy. And in 2009 in Seattle, the daily *Post-Intelligencer* became exclusively a Web-based newspaper. Indeed, by the spring of 2009, print circulation at the nation's newspapers had dropped by more than 7 percent from the previous year.

On the other hand, despite the growth of the Internet and electronic media, print still stands as an important medium among public relations professionals.

Why?

The answer probably lies in the fact that many departments at newspapers and magazines use news releases and other publicity vehicles compared to the limited opportunities on network and cable TV. In addition, online databases, blogs, and other Web-based media regularly use wire service material destined for print usage, so the Internet—while originating an increasing amount of original copy—still often serves as a residual target for print publicity.

Thomas Jefferson one famously said, *"Were it left to me to decide whether we should have a government without newspapers or newspapers without a government, I should not hesitate a moment to prefer the latter."*

While it is true that newspaper circulation in recent years has continued to tumble, the nation's largest newspapers are still powerful. (More than 104 million adults still read a print newspaper every day, more than 115 million on Sundays.) There is no question that the growth of alternative sources of information has hurt newspaper readership. *The Los Angeles Times* and *Chicago Tribune,* both purchased in 2007 by Chicago real estate magnate Sam Zell, have been hard hit, losing 20 percent of their readership in four years. Even the revered *New York Times* has suffered circulation falloff in recent years. Indeed, only *The Wall Street Journal* and *USA Today,* among major papers, have seen circulations rise slightly[8] (see Table 9-1).

Despite their circulation problems, newspapers still dominate the nation's news schedule. Stated another way, what appears on the front page of the nation's leading dailies sets the news agenda for the nation. Specifically, electronic news directors and bloggers regularly check the national dailies to determine the news of the day. Moreover, newspaper readership on the Web has increased exponentially, even while print circulation has declined. Newspaper Web sites attract more than 66 million unique visitors every quarter; 40 percent of all Internet users visit a newspaper site.[9] While economic downturn today affects online advertising just as similar setbacks affected print advertising yesterday, overall online advertising remains strong. And the technology of new, newspaper Web devices—such as creating Web sites for cell phones—continues to proliferate. The conclusion, then, stated simply, is that even in the wired 21st century, print media still dominate the nation's news diet.

Table 9-1

Top 100 U.S. Newspapers

This list, provided by Burrelles/Luce and compiled by the Audit Bureau of Circulation, shows newspaper circulation through March 31, 2008.

Rank	Newspaper	Daily	Sunday	Rank	Newspaper	Daily	Sunday
1	USA Today	2,284,219	N/A	51	The Boston Herald	182,350	105,629
2	The Wall Street Journal	2,069,463	N/A	52	Arkansas Democrat-Gazette-Little Rock, AR	182,212	274,494
3	The New York Times	1,077,256	1,476,400	53	New Orleans Times-Picayune	179,834	199,970
4	Los Angeles Times	773,884	1,101,981	54	Omaha World-Herald	178,545	219,795
5	The Daily News-New York, NY	703,137	704,157	55	The Buffalo News	178,365	260,445
6	The New York Post	702,488	401,315	56	The News & Observer-Raleigh, NC	176,083	211,245
7	Washington Post	673,180	890,163	57	Richmond Times-Dispatch	175,265	205,895
8	Chicago Tribune	541,663	898,703	58	The Virginian Pilot	175,005	200,012
9	Houston Chronicle	494,131	632,797	59	Las Vegas Review-Journal	174,341	199,602
10	Arizona Republic-Phoenix, AZ	413,332	515,523	60	Austin American-Statesman	170,309	206,505
11	Newsday-Melville, NY	379,613	441,728	61	The Hartford Courant	168,158	237,933
12	San Francisco Chronicle	370,345	424,603	62	The Palm Beach Post	164,474	195,608
13	Dallas Morning News	368,313	520,215	63	The Press-Enterprise-Riverside, CA	164,189	172,730
14	The Boston Globe	350,605	525,959	64	The Record-Hackensack, NJ	163,329	195,525
15	The Star-Ledger-Newark, NJ	345,130	500,382	65	Investor's Business Daily-Los Angeles, CA	161,421	N/A
16	Philadelphia Inquirer	334,150	630,665	66	The Tennessean-Nashville, TN	161,131	219,044
17	The Plain Dealer-Cleveland, OH	330,280	428,090	67	Tribune-Review-Greensburg, PA	150,911	192,423
18	The Atlanta Journal-Constitution	326,907	497,149	68	The Fresno Bee	150,334	171,039
19	Star-Tribune-Minneapolis, MN	322,362	534,750	69	The Commercial Appeal	146,961	188,040
20	St. Petersburg Times	316,007	432,779	70	Democrat & Chronicle-Rochester, NY	145,913	199,533
21	The Chicago Sun-Times*	312,274	247,469	71	The Florida Times-Union	144,391	201,352
22	Detroit Free Press	308,944	606,374	72	Daily Herald-Arlington Heights, IL	143,152	141,091
23	The Oregonian-Portland, OR	304,399	361,988	73	Asbury Park Press-Neptune, NJ	140,882	184,095
24	The San Diego Union Tribune	288,669	355,537	74	The Birmingham News	140,438	170,151
25	The Sacramento Bee	268,755	307,480	75	The Honolulu Advertiser	140,331	150,276
26	The Indianapolis Star	255,303	324,349	76	The Providence Journal	139,055	192,849
27	St. Louis Post-Dispatch	255,057	414,564	77	The Des Moines Register	138,519	222,122
28	The Kansas City Star	252,785	345,332	78	The Los Angeles Daily News-Woodland Hills, CA	137,344	145,164
29	The Orange County (CA) Register	250,724	311,982	79	Seattle Post-Intelligencer*	129,563	N/A
30	The Miami Herald	240,223	311,245	80	The Grand Rapids Press	128,930	177,026
31	San Jose Mercury News	234,772	251,851	81	The Salt Lake Tribune	121,699	143,296
32	The Sun-Baltimore, MD	232,360	372,970	82	The Akron Beacon Journal	119,929	155,436
33	The Orlando Sentinel	227,593	332,030	83	The Blade-Toledo, OH	119,901	147,141
34	San Antonio Express-News	225,447	315,959	84	The Knoxville News-Sentinel	117,262	147,939
35	The Rocky Mountain News*	225,226	*N/A	85	Dayton Daily News	116,690	157,833
36	The Denver Post*	225,193	*N/A	86	Sarasota Herald-Tribune	114,904	125,644
37	The Seattle Times*	220,863	*N/A	87	La Opinion-Los Angeles, CA	114,892	56,027
38	Tampa Tribune*	220,522	*N/A	88	Arizona Daily Star-Tucson	113,373	164,033
39	South Florida Sun-Sentinel-Ft. Lauderdale, FL	218,286	303,399	89	Tulsa World	112,968	160,052
				90	The News Tribune-Tacoma	111,778	125,955
40	Milwaukee Journal Sentinel	217,755	384,539	91	The News Journal-New Castle, DE	110,171	125,244
41	The Courier-Journal-Louisville, KY	215,328	258,778	92	Post-Standard, Syracuse, NY	110,061	158,529
42	Pittsburgh Post-Gazette	214,374	331,053	93	Lexington (KY) Herald-Leader	109,624	135,250
43	The Cincinnati Enquirer	212,369	279,825	94	Morning Call-Allentown, PA	108,797	140,789
44	The Charlotte Observer	210,616	264,170	95	Journal News-Rockland County	108,092	125,829
45	Fort Worth Star-Telegram	207,045	289,974	96	Philadelphia Daily News	107,269	N/A
46	The Oklahoman-Oklahoma City, OK	201,771	262,150	97	Albuquerque Journal	102,902	137,623
47	The Columbus Dispatch	199,524	334,422	98	The State-Columbia, SC	101,010	128,564
48	St. Paul Pioneer-Press	191,768	252,055	99	The Post and Courier-Charleston, SC	100,400	110,289
49	The Detroit News*	188,171	*N/A	100	The Daytona Beach News-Journal	99,627	116,700
50	Contra Costa (CA) Times	183,086	194,203				

(Courtesy of Burrelles/Luce)

Table 9-2

Top U.S. Magazines

This list, provided by Burrelles/Luce and compiled by the Audit Bureau of Circulation, shows magazine circulation—from senior citizens news magazines to *People* to *O* (Oprah's magazine)—through March 31, 2008.

Rank	Magazine	Total Paid & Verified Circulation	Rank	Magazine	Total Paid & Verified Circulation
1	AARP The Magazine	24,444,293	14	TV Guide (U.S.)	3,288,740
2	AARP Bulletin	23,815,128	15	Sports Illustrated	3,213,025
3	Reader's Digest	9,322,833	16	Taste Of Home	3,163,669
4	Better Homes And Gardens	7,638,912	17	Newsweek	3,109,228
5	National Geographic	5,042,672	18	Cosmopolitan	2,902,797
6	Good Housekeeping	4,632,531	19	VIA	2,829,413
7	Family Circle	4,011,530	20	Southern Living	2,802,258
8	Woman's Day	3,930,566	21	Playboy	2,700,262
9	Ladies' Home Journal	3,911,188	22	AAA Going Places	2,557,486
10	AAA Westways	3,775,228	23	Maxim	2,548,610
11	People	3,618,718	24	American Legion Magazine	2,542,176
12	Prevention	3,383,408	25	O-The Oprah Magazine	2,405,177
13	Time	3,351,872			

(Courtesy of Burrelles/Luce)

In the United States today, despite declining news staffs, advertising revenues, and circulation, some 1,400 daily newspapers are published. Every day, about 50 million newspapers are sold, and more than 100 million people read one.[10] There are upwards of 19,000 consumer and business magazines published in the United States today, according to the National Directory of Magazines. After a rough stretch at the end of the 20th century, magazine readership is on the increase again with specialty publications leading the way. Like their newspaper brethren, magazine publishers and editors also have stepped up their Web presence as readership habits migrate increasingly to online sources (see Table 9-2).

For the public relations professional, then, with so many print outlets—newspapers, magazines, and online publications—the area of public relations publicity remains broad and deep.

Electronic Media: A New Dominance

The first decade of the 21st century saw a dramatic increase in the number of Americans turning to cable television—CNN, MSNBC, Fox, CNBC, and even the Comedy Channel—for their daily news.

By 2009, while the three major broadcast network newscasts still drew eight million total viewers each evening, just under two million viewers a night tuned into cable television for their news. One cable news channel, Fox News, ranked third in overall viewership, behind entertainment channels, USA and TNT. And while the audience for the networks continued an inexorable decline, as older viewers dropped out of the mix, cable viewership held steady and even, especially in periods of hot news, increased markedly.[11]

The pervasive power of the electronic media was seen in a variety of quarters:

- Faced with daily challenges from cable news, broadcast networks worked to find the personalities and formulas that would continue to attract an even younger audience. In one famous experiment in 2006, CBS moved longtime *Today Show* host Katie Couric into the anchor spot on its historic nightly news broadcast, where Walter Cronkite once reigned. Ratings dipped, and the experiment failed.[12] Broadcast news magazines, however, led by CBS' *60 Minutes,* still maintained huge audiences for their extended features.

▪ Meanwhile, the impact of 24/7 cable news meant that Americans were barraged with a continuous loop of unrelated events that seemed to all run together in perpetual images, from Angelina Jolie and Brad Pitt to terrorism and kidnapped children to insider trading scandals and pending murder verdicts. While broadcast news tried to retain at least some vestige of "impartial" journalism, cable news made no such attempt. Fox News, with lead hosts Bill O'Reilly and Sean Hannity, was clearly conservative, while MSNBC, with anchors Keith Olbermann and Rachel Maddow, was unabashedly liberal. In such an environment, it was difficult to discern the truly newsworthy from the inconsequential and the hopelessly biased.

▪ Specialized cable networks, offering everything from sports and food and fashion to weather and history, beam nonstop across the land. In the financial area, for example, CNBC, Fox Business Channel, Bloomberg Television, PBS Nightly Business Report, and other similar efforts have become enormously popular barometers of the nation's stock market appetite. The most outrageous cable phenomenon was the popularity—particularly with younger viewers—of "fake news," served up nightly by the likes of John Stewart and Stephen Colbert (see Figure 9-3). Stewart's *The Daily Show* drew nearly two million viewers a night, and Stewart showed up fourth on a national poll of "most admired journalists"—even though he wasn't (a "journalist" that is!).[13]

▪ Meanwhile, talk radio has become an enormous political and social force. Each week, mostly conservative talk show hosts lead call-in discussions of the issues of the day. The undisputed dean of this ilk, Rush Limbaugh, reaches a gargantuan 14 million listeners (known as "ditto heads" because they *always* agree with the host!). In 2008, Limbaugh signed a new eight-year contract that pays $40 million annually—more than the three TV network anchors combined.[14] Following Limbaugh in the national rankings were a host of equally "right-minded" conservatives, including, in order, Sean Hannity, Dr. Michael Savage, Dr. Laura Schlesinger, Glenn Beck, Laura Ingraham, and Mark Levin.[15] In 2004, frustrated liberals attempted to counteract *El Rushbo* and his conservative armada with a radio network of their own, Air America, which promptly went bankrupt.

FIGURE 9-3 **Truth vs. truthiness.** In the 21st century, pseudo-newscasters, like Stephen Colbert, ranked high enough to be invited as guests even on respected news programs, like *Meet the Press* with the late Tim Russert (and, in this case, Bert from *Sesame Street*). (Photo: Newscom)

■ A more recent upstart in the media wars is satellite radio—basically a digital radio signal broadcast by a communications satellite—which began with a commercial-free flourish early in the decade with two primary networks, Sirius and XM. When radio icon Howard Stern departed terrestrial (land-based) radio for Sirius in 2006—for a budget reported at $500 million—many thought satellite radio was on its way. It wasn't. Interest in the new format waned. Stern's popularity waned. And in 2008, their stocks battered, Sirius and XM merged, with the bloom most decidedly off the satellite radio rose.

What makes the electronic media's news dominance so disconcerting—some would say scary—is that the average 30-minute television newscast would fill, in terms of words, only one-half of one page of the average daily newspaper! That means that if you're getting most of your news from television, you're *missing* most of the news.

Despite the evolving strength of the Internet as a communications medium, the electronic media undoubtedly will remain a force in the new millennium. Given the extent to which the electronic media dominate society, public relations people must become more resourceful in understanding how to deal with television and radio.

The Internet Factor

Further complicating the relationship between journalists and executives is the Internet. To some, the Internet has ushered in a new age of journalistic reporting: immediate, freewheeling, unbridled. Indeed, when Iranians rebelled against a rigged presidential election in 2009, it was Twitter that broadcast the news and images from the rioting Tehran streets. To others, the Internet is responsible for the collapse of journalistic standards and the ascendancy of rumormongering.

As noted, while many bemoan "the end of newspapers as we know them," the fact is that newspaper Web sites have been growing in popularity. And smart publishers are incorporating print and online more seamlessly. Indeed when the *Washington Post* chose a new editor in 2008, it picked an outsider charged with "converting heavy Web traffic to its site into enough dollars to outweigh the loss of print advertising and circulation revenue."[16] The point is that while print staffs and editions shrink, the online wing of many newspapers continues to expand.

So the irony is that while the Internet may kill the daily newspaper as we know it, it's allowed some papers to increase their readership by quantum leaps.[17]

As to the indigenous news-oriented inhabitants of the Web, "new-age news sources" abound, offering increased targets for public relations practitioners (see Figure 9-4). The granddaddy of these Internet news denizens was Matt Drudge, whose drudgereport.com regularly ranked as the top online global news destination. Drudge, a fedora-wearing, tough-talking, "new-age journalist," leaped to prominence when he became the first to report that White House intern Monica Lewinsky had retained an incriminating blue dress from her liaisons with President Bill Clinton. The story quickly turned out to be the smoking gun leading to President Clinton's 1994 impeachment. Today, Drudge's Web site, *Drudge Report,* remains "must reading" for many in the national media.

Close behind the three million visitors that Drudge attracts each month are the Fox News site on the right and the Huffington Post site on the left, as well as AOL News, CNN Digital Network, Yahoo! News, Politico.com and many others in between.[18]

Finally, there are the blogs—all 115 million of them and counting.

FIGURE 9-4 **This is a "journalist?"** You betcha'. This unlikely specimen is 21st-century Internet journalist Matt Drudge, whose drudgereport.com broke enough blockbusting national stories to qualify as "must reading" for reporters everywhere. He is pictured here in his *"office."* (Only kidding.) (Photo: Newscom)

Blogs, of course, come in all shapes, sizes, pedigrees. Many are of passing interest, many more are worthless, and several—a precious few, really—have become important sources of news and commentary. Measuring agency Tehnorati ranks blogs by their links to Web sites. The higher the number of links, the greater the ranking by Technorati. Leading blogs (see Table 9-3) are all over the lot, ranging from liberal news-oriented Huffington Post to Web 2.0–oriented TechCrunch to Boing Boing, a blog that discusses everything from science fiction and politics to "useful" gadgets like Soviet gas masks and zombie lawn sculpture.

The point is that Internet reporters and bloggers from every political bias and ulterior motive remain busy 24 hours a day, seven days a week, churning out continuous stories—some true, others not—about companies, government agencies, nonprofits, and prominent individuals.

The challenge for public relations professionals in dealing with print, electronic, or online commentators is to foster a closer relationship between their organizations and those who present the news. The key, once again, is fairness, with each side accepting—and respecting—the other's role and responsibility.

Dealing with the Media

It falls on public relations professionals to orchestrate the relationship between their organizations and the media, whether print, electronic, or Internet-based. To be sure, the media can't ordinarily be manipulated (and they *hate* it if you try!). They can, however,

Table 9-3

Most Popular Blogs

This list, provided by Burrelles/Luce and compiled by Technorati, shows the most popular English language blogs through April, 28, 2008.

Rank	Blog	Blog Address	Technorati's Authority Figures as of 4/28/08
1	Huffington Post	huffingtonpost.com	24,166
2	TechCrunch	techcrunch.com	23,264
3	Engadget	engadget.com	22,365
4	Gizmodo	gizmodo.com	22,073
5	Boing Boing	boingboing.net	16,974
6	LifeHacker	lifehacker.com	15,446
7	Ars-Technica (CA)	arstechnica.com	14,725
8	I Can Has Cheezburger?	icanhascheezburger.com	11,770
9	Mashable! The Social Network Blog	mashable.com	11,739
10	Daily Kos	dailykos.com	10,192
11	ReadWriteWeb	readwriteweb.com	10,175
12	Smashing Magazine	smashingmagazine.com	9,452
13	Official Google Blog	googleblog.blogspot.com	8,867
14	Seth's Blog	sethgodin.typepad.com	8,785
15	Blog Tips To Help You Make Money Blogging	problogger.net	8,566
16	Dosh Dosh	doshdosh.com	8,448
17	Perez Hilton	perezhilton.com	8,440
18	Gawker	gawker.com	7,993
19	PostSecret	postsecret.blogspot.com	7,773
20	TreeHugger	treehugger.com	7,599
21	Copyblogger	copyblogger.com	6,627
22	Valleywag	valleywag.com	6,329
23	Think Progress	thinkprogress.org	6,251
24	Shoemoney	shoemoney.com	6,071
25	The Consumerist	consumerist.com	6,047

(Courtesy of Burrelles/Luce)

be engaged in an honest and interactive way to convey the organization's point of view in a manner that may merit being reported. First, an organization must establish a formal media relations policy (Figure 9-5). Second, an organization must establish a philosophy for dealing with the media, keeping in mind the following dozen principles:

1. **A reporter is a reporter.** A reporter is never "off duty." Anything you say to a journalist is fair game to be reported. Remember that, and never let down your guard, no matter how friendly you are.

2. **You are the organization.** In the old days, reporters disdained talking to public relations representatives, who they derisively labeled "flacks" (as in "catching flak," or bad news). Public relations people, therefore, were rarely quoted and remained anonymous. Today the opposite is true. The public relations person represents the policy of an organization. He or she is quoted by name and interviewed on camera, so every word out of the public relations professional's mouth must be carefully weighed in advance.

3. **There is no standard issue reporter.** The sad fact is that many business managers want nothing to do with the press. They believe them to be villains. But that isn't necessarily true. As noted, most are simply trying to do their jobs, like anyone else, so each should be treated as an individual, until, cynics might say, "proven guilty."

4. **Treat journalists professionally.** As long as they understand that your job is different than theirs and treat you with deference, you should do likewise. A journalist's job is to get a story, whether good or bad. A public relations person's job is to present the organization in the best light. That difference understood, the relationship should be a professional one.

5. **Don't sweat the skepticism.** Journalists aren't paid to ask nice questions. They are paid to be skeptical. "Bad news" is *news*, while "good news" isn't usually *news*. Some interviewees resent this. Smart interviewees realize it comes with the territory.

Organization and Policy Guide

Unit with Primary Responsibility for Review Corporate Communications

It is frequently in Chase's best interest to take advantage of interest from the media to further the reputation and services of the bank. In dealing with the media, Chase officers must be careful to protect the best interests of the bank, particularly with regard to the area of customer confidence.

The following policies will serve as a guideline for media relationships. Specific questions regarding the media should be addressed to the Public Relations Division.

Inquiries from the Media

Most journalists call the Public Relations Division when they need information about the bank or wish to arrange an interview with a bank officer. Many times, public relations officers are able to handle inquiries directly. Occasionally, however, more complex questions require input from appropriate bank officers. In these cases, inasmuch as journalists are often under deadline pressures, it is important that bank officers cooperate as fully and respond as promptly as possible. Such cooperation enhances Chase's reputation for integrity with the news media.

Less frequently, reporter inquiries will go directly to line officers. In this case, either one of two responses may be appropriate:

1. If a journalist seeks simple, factual information such as Chase's current rate on a particular savings instrument or the factual details of a new bank service, officers may provide it directly.

2. If a reporter seeks Chase policy or official opinion on such subjects as trends in interest rates, legislation, etc., responses should be reviewed with the Public Relations Division. If an officer is unfamiliar with a particular policy or requires clarification of it, he or she should always check first with the Public Relations Division before committing the bank in print.

In talking with a reporter, it is normally assumed that whatever a bank officer says may be quoted and attributed directly to him or her by name as a spokesperson for the bank. An officer not wishing to be quoted must specify that desire to the journalist.

(continued)

FIGURE 9-5 Media relations policy. Every organization should have a formal policy such as the one shown here to guide its activities with the press. Public relations should have the primary responsibility of liaison with the media.

FIGURE 9-5 *(continued)*

Most reporters with whom the bank deals with respect an officer's wishes to maintain anonymity. Most journalists recognize that it is as important for them to honor the wishes of their sources at the bank as it is for the bank to disseminate its comments and information to the public through the news media. Chase's policy toward the media should be one of mutual trust, understanding, and benefit.

Interviews with the Media

In order to monitor the bank's relationships with journalists, all requests for interviews with bank officers by journalists must be routed through the Public Relations Division.

As a rule, public relations officers check the credentials of the journalist and determine the specific areas of inquiry to be examined. The public relations officer will then decide whether the interview is appropriate for the bank. When the decision is affirmative, the public relations officer will discuss subject matter with the recommended interviewee and together they will decided on a course of action and Chase objectives for the interview.

A member of the public relations staff is normally present during any face-to-face interview with an officer of the bank. The purpose of the public relations staffer's attendance is to provide assistance in handling the interview situation as well as to aid the reporter with follow-up material.

When a reporter calls an officer directly to request an interview, the officer should check with the Public Relations Division before making a commitment.

Authorized Spokespersons

Vice presidents and above are normally authorized to speak for the bank on matters in their own area of responsibility.

Normally, officers below the level of vice president are not authorized to speak for attribution on behalf of the bank except where they are specialists in a particular field, such as technical directors, economists, etc.

Exceptions may be made in special situations and in concert with the Public Relations Division.

Written Material for the Media

Chase articles bylined by officers may either be written by the officer approached or by a member of the public relations staff. If an officer decides to author his or her own article, the public relations division must be consulted for editing, photographic support and policy proofing.

Occasionally, customers or suppliers may wish to include Chase in an article or advertisement they are preparing. This material too must be routed through the Public Relations Division for review.

6. **Don't try to "buy" a journalist.** Never try to threaten or coerce a journalist with advertising. The line between news and advertising should be a clear one. No self-respecting journalist will tolerate someone trying to "bribe" him or her for a positive story.

7. **Become a trusted source.** Journalists can't be "bought," but they can be persuaded by your becoming a source of information for them. A reporter's job is to report on what's going on. By definition, a public relations person knows more about the company and the industry than does a reporter. So become a source and a positive relationship will follow.

8. **Talk when not "selling."** Becoming a source means sharing information with journalists, even when it has nothing to do with your company. Reporters need leads and story ideas. If you supply them, once again a positive relationship will follow.

9. **Don't expect "news" agreement.** A reporter's view of "news" and an organization's view of "news" will differ. If so, the journalist wins. (It's the reporter's paper/Web site/TV station, after all!) Don't complain if a story doesn't make it into publication. Sometimes there is no logical reason, so never promise an executive that a story will "definitely make the paper."

10. **Don't cop a 'tude.** Don't have an attitude with reporters. They need the information that you possess. If you're coy or standoffish or reluctant to share, they will pay you back. Although reporters vary in look and type, they all share one trait: They remember.

11. **Never lie.** This is the cardinal rule. As one *Wall Street Journal* reporter put it, "Never lie to a reporter or that reporter will never trust you again."[19]

12. **Read the paper.** The number one criticism of public relations people by journalists is that they often don't have any idea what the journalist writes, comments, or blogs about. This is infuriating, especially when a journalist is approached on a story pitch. Lesson: Read the paper!

Although some may deny it, reporters are human beings, so there is no guarantee that even if these principles are followed, all reporters will be fair or objective. Most of the time, however, following these dozen rules of the road will lead to a better relationship between the journalist and the public relations professional.

Attracting Publicity

Publicity, through news releases—mostly via email—and other methods, is eminently more powerful than advertising. Publicity is most often gained by dealing directly with the media, either by initiating the communication or by reacting to inquiries. Although most people—especially CEOs!—confuse the two, *publicity* differs dramatically from *advertising*.

First and most important, advertising costs money—lots of it. A full-page, one-time, nonrecurring ad in the national edition of *The Wall Street Journal,* for example, costs upwards of $180,000—for one ad!

On the other hand, the benefits of paid advertising include the following communications areas that can be "guaranteed":

- **Content:** What is said and how it is portrayed and illustrated.
- **Size:** How large a space is devoted to the organization.
- **Location:** Where in the paper the ad will appear.
- **Reach:** The audience exposed to the ad—that is, the number of papers in which the ad appears.
- **Frequency:** How many times the ad is run.

Frequency is extremely important. Today, with 500 cable and broadcast television channels, thousands of newspapers and magazines, and millions more Internet sites, people often skip over or surf by the ads or commercials. The only way to get through is to repeat the ad over and over again. In that manner, the largest advertisers—McDonald's, Microsoft, Coca-Cola, and so on—blast their way into public consciousness.

Publicity, on the other hand, offers no such guarantees or controls. Typically, publicity is subject to review by news editors who may decide to use all of a story, some of it, or none of it. Many news releases, in fact, never see the light of print.

When the story will run, who will see it, and how often it will be used are all subject to the whims of a news editor. However, even though attracting publicity is by no means a sure thing, it does offer two overriding benefits that enhance its appeal far beyond that of advertising:

- First, although not free, publicity costs only the time and effort expended by public relations personnel and management in conceiving, creating, and attempting to place the publicity effort in the media. Therefore, relatively speaking, its cost is minimal compared to advertising; the rough rule of thumb is 10 percent of equivalent advertising expenditures.

- Second and more important, publicity, which appears in news rather than in advertising columns, carries the implicit *third-party* endorsement of the news source that reports it. In other words, publicity is perceived not as the sponsoring organization's self-serving view but as the view of the objective, unbiased, neutral, impartial news source. For years, for example, when surveys asked people to name their most trusted American, respondents invariably answered not the president or first lady but rather Walter Cronkite, the late former news anchor at CBS. NBC's Tom Brokaw and the late Tim Russert became equally trusted over the years.

That is the credibility that a news reporter or publication enjoys. When an organization's publicity is reported by such a source, it instantly becomes more credible, believable, and, therefore, valuable *news*.

That, in essence, is why publicity is more powerful than advertising.

Value of Publicity

For any organization, then, publicity makes great sense in the following areas:

- **Announcing a new product or service.** Because publicity can be regarded as news, it should be used before advertising commences. A new product or service is news only once. Once advertising appears, the product is no longer news. Therefore, one inflexible rule—that most organizations, unfortunately, don't follow—is that publicity should always precede advertising.

- **Reenergizing an old product.** When a product has been around for a while, it's difficult to make people pay attention to advertising. Therefore, publicity techniques—staged events, sponsorships, and so on—may pay off to rejuvenate a mature product (see Figure 9-6).

- **Explaining a complicated product.** Often there isn't enough room in an advertisement to explain a complex product or service. Insurance companies, banks, and mutual funds, which offer products that demand thoughtful explanation, may find advertising space too limiting. Publicity, on the other hand, allows enough room to tell the story.

- **Little or no budget.** To make an impact, advertising requires frequency—the constant repetition of ads so that readers eventually see them and acknowledge the product. In the case of Samuel Adams Lager Beer, for example, the company lacked an advertising budget to promote its unique brew, so it used public relations techniques to spread the word about this different-tasting beer. Over time, primarily through publicity about its victories at beer-tasting competitions,

FIGURE 9-6 Papa Spidey. When Papa John's pizza needed a publicity boost, it teamed with the world's most famous arachnid. (Courtesy of Odwyerpr.com)

Samuel Adams grew in popularity. Today its advertising budget is robust, but the company's faith in publicity endures.

- **Enhancing the organization's reputation.** Advertising is, at its base, self-serving. When a company gives to charity or does a good deed in the community, taking out an ad is the wrong way to communicate its efforts. It is much better for the recipient organization to commend its benefactor in the daily news columns.

- **Crisis response.** In a crisis, publicity techniques are the fastest and most credible means of response. Indeed, in the 21st century, it has become a cliché for celebrities to "apologize" for transgressions by seeking out a high-profile TV interviewer for instant publicity.

These are just a few of the advantages of publicity over advertising. A smart organization, therefore, will always consider publicity a vital component in its overall marketing plan.

PR Ethics

Mini-Case Domino's President Confronts the YouTube Idiots

With the Internet loaded with 200 million Web sites and 70 million blogs, it's difficult to know when to strike back at a social media attack.

In the case of Domino's Pizza in the spring of 2009, the company couldn't answer fast enough when it was made the target of a gross YouTube video—produced, directed, and starred in by two soon-to-be-former Domino's Pizza employees at a store in Conover, N.C. (Figure 9-7). The two thought it

"cute" to film themselves doing all manner of disgusting things with Domino's ingredients and then narrating the video.

A day later, the video had been viewed more than a million times on YouTube. The company initially chose to handle the emerging crisis by answering one-on-one to blog sites where the issue was raised. Said Domino's Communications Vice President Tim McIntyre, *"Domino's doesn't want to put the candle out with a fire hose."*

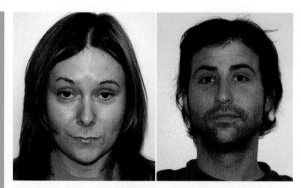

FIGURE 9-7 The idiots . . . (Photo: Newscom)

FIGURE 9-8 . . . and the President. (Courtesy Domino's Pizza)

Some social media activists criticized Domino's one-on-one strategy, arguing that the pizza chain should have been more proactive in engaging in social media discussions. In short order, Domino's was faced with an escalating, full-scale, front-page crisis.

Although it monitored Web sites and blogs, Domino's public relations department failed to monitor Twitter, where the issue spread like wild fire. It took the company two days to post its own YouTube commentary from Domino's USA President Patrick Doyle. (Figure 9-8)

President Doyle started the video by *"sincerely apologizing"* and acknowledged the *"hurt"* his company had suffered, stipulated the new policies it had adopted to screen employees, and even thanked *"members of the online community,"* who alerted the company to the offensive video. President Doyle also announced that felony warrants had been issued for the arrest of its former employees.

At the same time, Dominos inundated its own Web site with customer care messages responding to the incident, went public in the national media about the situation, and engaged (admittedly belatedly) the Twitter community in response by establishing its own Twitter account to address the issue. It tweeted links to articles about the crisis and responded to concerned customers.

Summarized Domino's spokesman after the week-long crisis had died down, *"We got blindsided by two idiots with a video camera and an awful idea."*

Questions

1. How do you think Domino's handled the public relations fallout from the unethical video?

2. What do you think the long-term impacts of this incident will be for the Domino's brand?

*For further information, see Stephanie Clifford, "Video Prank at Domino's Taints Brand," *New York Times* (April 16, 2009); Jessica Levco, "The Domino's Effect: The Potential Danger of Ignoring Social Media," ragan.com (April 16, 2009); Richard E. Nicolazzo, "Message to Domino's: Contingency Planning Still Rules the Roost," odwyerpr.com (April 16, 2009); and Fraser P. Seitel, "Domino's Did the Right Thing," odwyerpr.com (April 20, 2009).

Pitching Publicity

The activity of trying to place positive publicity in a periodical, on a news site, or in the electronic media—of converting publicity to news—is called *pitching*. The following hints may help achieve placement of a written release:

1. **Know deadlines.** Time governs every newspaper. Even with the flexibility of the computer, newspapers have different deadlines for different sections of the paper. For example, *The New York Times* business section essentially closes down between 6 and 7 p.m. News events should be scheduled, whenever possible, to accommodate deadlines. An old and despised practice (at least by journalists) is to announce bad news on Friday afternoon, the premise being that newspaper

journalists won't have time to follow up on the story and that few people will read Saturday's paper anyway. What happens today, with newspaper Web sites increasingly popular, the paper "scoops" itself on the Web and occasionally takes out its wrath on the Friday evening issuer.

2. **Generally write first, then call.** Reporters are barraged with deadlines. They are busiest close to deadline time, which is late afternoon for morning newspapers and early afternoon for local television news. Thus, it's preferable to email news releases first, rather than try to explain them over the telephone. Follow-up calls to reporters to "make sure you got our release" also should be avoided. If reporters are unclear on a certain point, they'll call to check.

3. **Direct the release to a specific person or editor.** Newspapers are divided into departments: business, sports, style, entertainment, and so on. Assignment editors are generally in charge of television news. The release directed to a specific person or editor has a greater chance of being read. At smaller papers, a few people may handle all news. Public relations people should know who covers their beat and target releases accordingly.

4. **Determine how the reporter wants to be contacted.** Methods include email, mail, fax, paper, and so on. Treat the reporter as the client. How he or she prefers to get the news should guide how you deliver it.

5. **Don't badger.** Journalists are generally fiercely independent about the copy they use. Even a major advertiser will usually fail to get a piece of puffery published. Badgering an editor about a certain story is bad form, as is complaining excessively about the treatment given a certain story. Worst of all, little is achieved by acting outraged when an editor chooses not to run a story.

6. **Use exclusives, but be careful.** Reporters get credited for getting *"scoops"* and citing *"trends."* So public relations people might promise exclusive stories to particular publications. The exclusive promises one publication or other news source a scoop over its competitors. Although the chances of securing a story are heightened by the promise of an exclusive, the risk of alienating the other papers exists. Thus, the exclusive should be used sparingly.

7. **When you call, do your own calling.** Reporters and editors generally don't have assistants. Most resent being kept waiting by a secretary calling for the boss. Public relations professionals should make their own initial and follow-up calls. Letting a secretary handle a journalist can alienate a good news contact. Above all, be pleasant and courteous.

8. **Don't send clips of other stories about your client.** Rather than interesting a journalist in your story, this will just suggest that others have been there already and make the story potential less attractive.

9. **Develop a relationship.** Relationships are the name of the game. The better you know a reporter, the more understanding and accommodating to your organization he or she will be.

10. **Never lie.** This is *the* cardinal rule.

Although cynics continue to predict "the end of reading as we know it," newspapers and magazines continue to endure. Magazines, particularly special interest magazines, are proliferating. Publications range from the mainstream *Time* and *Newsweek* to the trendy, not to mention just a tad egotistical, *O,* the *Oprah Winfrey* magazine, and *Martha Stewart Living;* from the gossipy *People* and *Vanity Fair;* to one publication so exclusive it has no name. To get a subscription you have to hold a Centurion card, which is offered by American Express by invitation only to those who spend at least $200,000 a year on their credit card. In fact, "controlled circulation" magazines that "pick you" now number more than 300 in the United States.[20]

The fact remains that dealing with the print media is among the most essential technical skills of the public relations professional. Anyone who practices public relations must know how to deal with the press. Period.

Online Publicity

With online outlets increasing in numbers and use, it is important to consider how to secure online publicity. While those who predicted that the Internet would change public relations thinking forever are wrong, it's still a "relationship business"—seeking Internet outlets for publicity is an important complement to publicity in more traditional media.

Knowledge of Web hosting and Web casting and blogs and chat rooms and discussion groups and investor "threads" and search engine optimization are critical for modern public relations people. At the top of this list of Internet public relations tools is knowledge of online publicity.

Here, in summary, are the several vehicles that form the nucleus of online publicity.

- **News releases.** What else? The news release forms the backbone of all publicity, and that applies as well to online efforts. The release is the document that lets the media know what might merit coverage.

  On the Internet, news releases are delivered by email and should be shorter than their offline counterparts. Often the Internet "release" is more an *editorial advisory* to interest a journalist in a story. Most important, *key words* in releases—words likely to be searched for by readers—should be considered in order to attract Web interest.

- **Headlines.** Pay special attention to headlines. Internet readers in a hurry, that is, journalists, see a headline and instantly assess whether the subsequent story is worth reading. Google recommends headlines between 2 and 22 words for optimum visibility and search results. Google results display only the first 63 characters of each headline. So keep heads short.

- **Announcements.** An announcement is posted to online discussion groups, including Usenet newsgroups, Internet mailing lists, forums on commercial online services, and discussion threads built into Web sites.

  Like a news release, an announcement is short—a few paragraphs—and designed to encourage readers to visit a Web site or request further information. Announcements are used to promote online events, chats, or sites.

- **Links.** Links are vehicles that transport readers to Web sites. On the surface, a link is an image or a word that, once clicked, retrieves a file for the reader. When a link is activated, a new Web site appears on-screen.

  Links are important publicity vehicles in that they immediately and automatically deliver the audience to a Web site being promoted. Indeed, links are the simplest way to get potentially interested parties to visit Web sites. Links also take viewers to new pages within the current site.

Be careful, though, not to overdo links. Many links can flag a release as spam, so it's important to choose relevant links that direct traffic to the specific Web pages being promoted.

- **Newsletters.** Online newsletters are used to keep audiences updated on new products, services, issues, or events. Newsletters are easy and cheap to set up online. They also provide a continuing point of contact with key publics through automatic email delivery.

  As with any other vehicle written for the Internet, online newsletters should be more succinct than print counterparts. One-paragraph items are standard fare. Also, the graphic touches of print newsletters have little relevance on the Web.

- **Libraries.** The ability of the Web to cheaply store vast quantities of information online is a clear advantage over print. Online news releases or announcements can be "backed up" with a library of supporting data at a Web site—support files, product brochures and facilities statements, backgrounders, press kits, frequently asked questions (FAQ) files, newsletters, events calendars, interview transcripts, help files, audio sound bites, video clips, press clips, and more. A well-structured library of supporting data adds depth to online publicity efforts and makes responding to inquiries as easy and instantaneous as pushing a button.

- **Public appearances.** Online chat sessions can be the equivalent of offline press conferences or public forums. Chats allow special guests to entertain questions from online audiences in a real-time format. Also possible are "dead chats," where guests (still very "live") answer questions that have been solicited in advance and these are posted in the form of an interview. Finally, there is the cyber-media tour, which links the spokesperson with television, radio, Web site, and print journalists via satellite, the Web, and telephone simultaneously. The cyber-media tour takes advantage of streaming video and audio, both becoming commonplace in Web usage.

- **Promotions.** Internet users are notorious giveaway fanatics. Entering a sweepstakes online is so easy that such promotions often make eminent sense. Promotions—treasure hunts, trivia contests, coupons, quizzes, surveys, and the like—are often tied to other online activities, such as the launch of a new Web site or a major Web event.

- **News wires.** The most important releases are those carried on the news wires, most particularly the "free" wires of Associated Press (AP), Dow Jones, Reuters, Bloomberg, and numerous others from various countries. AP, the granddaddy of news wires founded in 1848, is a cooperative owned by contributing media outlets. It has 243 bureaus and serves 121 countries. The others are largely business-oriented. All choose their news on the basis of merit.

  Paid wires, such as PR Newswire, Business Wire (purchased in 2006 by investor Warren Buffet's Berkshire Hathaway), and Internet Wire, disseminate full text news releases to media, investors, and online databases. These are wires that guarantee use of your material (you pay them!). News rooms regularly check the paid wires for information of interest.

  All these paid wires offer services to enhance Web use, including search engine optimization and social media "tags" to encourage online sharing and a *Long Tail*, that is, a longer life for the release on the Internet.

Talking Points Confessions of a Media Maven

Dealing with the media for fun and profit, even for an experienced public relations hand, is a constant learning experience. It is also risky business. Consider the real-life case of an up-and-coming, daring, but wet-behind-the ears public relations trainee.

In the 1980s, many of the nation's largest banks were a bit jittery about negative publicity on their loans to lesser developed countries. One of the most vociferous bank bashers was Patrick J. Buchanan, a syndicated columnist who later became President Reagan's communications director and still later ran for president (Figure 9-9).

After one particularly venomous syndicated attack on the banks, the young and impetuous bank public affairs director wrote directly to Buchanan's editor asking whether he couldn't "muzzle at least for a little while" his wild-eyed columnist. The letter's language, in retrospect, was a tad harsh.

Some weeks later, in a six-column article that ran throughout the nation, Buchanan wrote in part:

> Another sign that the banks are awaking to the reality of the nightmare is a screed that lately arrived at this writer's syndicate from one Fraser P. Seitel, director of public affairs of the Chase Manhattan Bank.
>
> Terming this writer's comments "wrong," "stupid," "inflammatory," and "the nonsensical ravings of a lunatic," Seitel nevertheless suggested that the syndicate "tone down" future writings, "at least 'til the frenetic financial markets get over the current hysteria."*

Buchanan went on to describe the fallacy in bankers' arguments and ended by suggesting that banks begin immediately to cut unnecessary frills—such as "directors of public affairs!"

Moral: Never get into a shouting match with somebody who buys ink by the barrel.

Secondary moral: Just because you write a textbook doesn't mean you know everything!

FIGURE 9-9 Put 'em up. Syndicated columnist, TV commentator, and presidential contender Patrick Buchanan was ready to duke it out when challenged by one bright-eyed media relations novice. (Photo: Newscom)

*Patrick J. Buchanan, "The Banks Must Face Up to Losses on Third World Loans," *New York Post* (July 12, 1984): 35.

■ **Events.** Staging events is another way to draw reporters and other publics online. Popular events include movie sneak previews, concerts broadcast online, candidate debates, roundtable forums, Web site grand openings, conventions, and trade shows.

As the Internet has become a more commonplace communications vehicle, the bar for Web events has been raised. A new Web site is no longer cause for attention. Nor is an online news conference. So a Web event today, to attract publicity, must be really "big."[21]

Although establishing a relationship with online reporters may not be as easy as with print journalists because of the physical remoteness, the same principle still holds: The closer you are to reporters, the more fairly they will treat you.

Handling Media Interviews

A primary task of public relations people—perhaps the most essential task in the eyes of those for whom public relations people work—is to coordinate interviews for their executives with the media. Most executives are neither familiar with nor comfortable in such interview situations. For one thing, reporters ask a lot of searching questions, some of which may seem impertinent. Executives aren't used to being put on the spot. Instinctively, they may resent it, and thus the counseling of executives for interviews has become an important and strategic task of the in-house practitioner as well as a lucrative profession for media consultants.

In conducting interviews with the media, the cardinal rule to remember is that such interviews are not *"intellectual conversations."* Neither the interviewee nor the interviewer seek a lasting friendship. Rather, the interviewer wants only a good story, and the interviewee wants only to convey his or her key messages. Period.

Accordingly, the following 11 do's and don'ts are important in media interviews:

1. **Prepare.** An interviewee must be thoroughly briefed—either verbally or in writing—before the interview. Know the interviewer's point-of-view, interests, and likely questions. Preparation is key.

2. **Know your lines.** In other words, know what you will say *before* you begin the interview. This is the most important thing to remember in any interview.

   Again, an interview isn't a conversation. Nor is it the place for original thought. Walk into the interview knowing the three or four points that must make it on the air or in print. Hammer away at those points, so the interviewer uses them.

3. **Relax.** Remember that the interviewer is a person, too, and is just trying to do a good job. Building rapport will help the interview. Even though a media interview isn't a "conversation," it should like seem like one (see Figure 9-10).

4. **Speak in personal terms.** People distrust large organizations. References to "the company" and "we believe" sound ominous. Use "I" as much as possible. Personalize. Speak as an individual, as a member of the public, rather than as a mouthpiece for an impersonal bureaucracy.

5. **Welcome the naive question.** If the question sounds simple, it should be answered anyway. It may be helpful to those who don't possess much knowledge of the organization or industry.

6. **Answer questions briefly and directly.** Don't ramble. Be brief, concise, and to the point—especially on television An interviewee shouldn't get into subject areas about which he or she knows nothing. This situation can be dangerous and counterproductive when words are transcribed in print.

7. **Don't bluff.** If a reporter asks a question that you can't answer, admit it. If there are others in the organization more knowledgeable about a particular issue, the interviewee or the practitioner should point that out and get the answer from them. But play it straight. Bluffing will be obvious to the reporter and his readers/listeners/viewers.

8. **State facts and back up generalities.** Facts and examples always bolster an interview. An interviewee should come armed with specific data that support general statements. Again, the practitioner should furnish all the specifics.

FIGURE 9-10 **Just chatting.** Or at least that's the way it ought to seem in a media interview, even though the key to an interview is to walk in knowing your lines. (Courtesy of Fraser P. Seitel)

9. **There is no such thing as "off the record."** A person who doesn't want to see something in print shouldn't say it. It's that simple. Print reporters, in particular, may get confused as to what was "off the record" during the interview. Although most journalists will honor an off-the-record statement, some may not. It's not generally worthwhile to take the risk. Occasionally, reporters will agree not to attribute a statement to the interviewee but to use it as background. Mostly, though, interviewees should be willing to have whatever they say in the interview appear in print.

10. **Don't say, "No comment."** "No comment" sounds evasive and suggests to people you're hiding something or worse. If you can't answer a question for confidential or proprietary reasons, explain why. "No comment" too often sounds "guilty."

11. **Tell the truth.** It sounds like a broken record, but telling the truth is the key criterion. Journalists are generally perceptive; they can detect a fraud. So don't be evasive, don't cover up, and, most of all, don't lie. Be positive but be truthful. Occasionally, an interviewee must decline to answer specific questions but should candidly explain why. This approach always wins in the long run. Remember, in an interview, your integrity is always on the line. Once you lose your credibility, you've lost everything.[22]

Last Word

When journalists were asked at the beginning of the 21st century how much respect they had for public relations people, less than half answered in the affirmative. That's the bad news. The better news is that the scores accorded public relations professionals ranked higher in the eyes of these scribes than did the scores of lawyers, salespeople, celebrities, or politicians.[23] So there's always hope. On the other hand, it must be acknowledged that a good portion of journalists still seem to regard public relations people with suspicion and maybe even (though they won't admit it) envy.

As is true of any other specialty, in public relations work the key to productive media relations is professionalism. Because management relies principally on public relations professionals for expertise in handling the media effectively, practitioners must not only know their own organization and management but also be conversant in and respectful of the role and practice of journalists. That means knowing their deadlines, understanding their pressures, and returning their calls.

Indeed, public relations professionals must understand what a reporter goes through each day—intractable deadlines, spotty information, frequently uncooperative sources, and sometimes even mortal danger (Figure 9-11).

All that has been discussed in this chapter must be practiced: transmitting only newsworthy information to journalists; knowing how to reach reporters most expeditiously; understanding that journalists have become more pressured, by the Internet and cable, to produce material that is "immediate" and "entertaining" and therefore potentially controversial; and recognizing that a reporter has a job to do and should be treated with respect.

At the same time, all public relations practitioners should understand that their role in the news-gathering process has become more respected by journalists. As a former business/finance editor of the *New York Times,* once said:

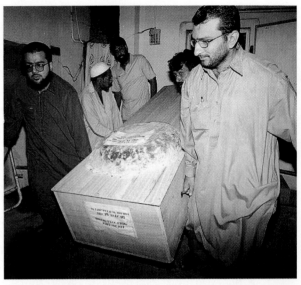

FIGURE 9-11 Perilous profession. The coffin of *Wall Street Journal* war reporter Danny Pearl, who was kidnapped and killed by al-Qaeda terrorists in Pakistan in 2002, is carried to the Karachi airport for the flight back home. (Photo: Newscom)

PR has gotten more professional. PR people can be a critical element for us. It makes a difference how efficiently they handle things, how complete the information is that they have at hand. We value that and understand all the work that goes into it.[24]

Indeed, the best public relations–journalist relationship today—the only successful one over the long term—must still be based on mutual understanding, trust, and respect.

Talking Points   Two-Minute Media Relations Drill

How well would you do if you were asked to go toe-to-toe with a reporter? Take this yes-or-no quiz and find out. Answers follow.

Questions

1. When addressing a print reporter or electronic medium moderator, should you use his or her first name?

2. Should you ever challenge a reporter in a verbal duel?

3. Are reporters correct in thinking that they can ask embarrassing questions of anyone in public office?

4. Should you answer a hypothetical question?

5. Should you ever say "No comment"?

6. When a reporter calls on the telephone, should you assume that the conversation is being taped?

7. Do audiences remember most of the content of a television interview 30 minutes after it is broadcast?

8. Should you ever admit you had professional training to handle the media?

9. If you don't know the correct answer to a reporter's question, should you try to answer it anyway?

Bonus Question

What did Henry Kissinger say at the start of his press briefings as secretary of state?

Answers

1. **Yes.** In most cases, using first names is the best strategy. It makes the discussion much more conversational and less formal than using Mr. or Ms.

2. "Never say never," but the answer most often is **No.** You can and should challenge a faulty premise. But most people should try to gain goodwill in an interview. This is rarely achieved by getting into an acrimonious debate.

3. **Yes.** Journalists are suspicious of any claim by a public person that he or she is telling not only the truth but also the whole truth. Anyone in public office must be prepared to respond to such questions.

4. **No.** Avoid hypothetical questions. Rarely can you win by dealing with them.

5. **No.** It is tantamount to taking the Fifth Amendment against self-incrimination. You appear to be hiding something.

6. **Yes.** Many state laws no longer require the "beep" that signals a taped call. Always assume that everything you say is being recorded and will be used.

7. **No.** Studies have found that audiences remember less and less as time wears on. Indeed, on television (even though self-absorbed TV hosts would never admit it) it's often more important to "look good."

8. **Yes.** By all means. You should point out that good communication with the public is a hallmark of your organization and that you're proud it has such a high priority.

9. **No.** Don't be afraid to say, "I don't know." Offer to find the answer and get back to the interviewer. Don't dig yourself into a hole you can't get out of.

Bonus answer: "Does anyone have any questions . . . for my answers?"

Discussion Starters

1. What is meant by the "devil's advocate" role of the media?
2. What is the current state of the newspaper industry?
3. What is the importance of objectivity to a reporter?
4. What are some of the key principles in dealing with the press?
5. What is the difference between advertising and publicity?
6. What is the value of publicity?
7. What are some of the keys in pitching publicity?
8. What are the several do's and don'ts of interviews?
9. What are several methods of online publicity?
10. What's the most important thing to remember in any interview?

Top of the Shelf Manage the Media (Don't Let the Media Manage You) /

William Holstein, Cambridge, MA: Harvard University Press, 2008

Former *Business Week* editor William Holstein believes that "most CEOs don't get PR."

He faults those who run companies for believing that their public relations professionals can assure them of positive media coverage.

"Forget it!" says Holstein. What results are companies that perform woefully in their relationships with the news media. To meet this challenge, Holstein suggests that board of directors should pay more attention to appointing media-savvy CEOs.

Also, he says, media training for chief executives should be compulsory.

Holstein says that CEOs should hire a communications "consigliore" to advise them on offensive media relations. The worst thing, he cautions, is falling into the "airline syndrome," responding to media only when the organization is faced with a plane crash or similar catastrophic occurrence. He also suggests that CEOs meet regularly with those who cover them.

All good ideas, but oh so hard to accomplish.

Case Study   They're Heeere!

Suppose you gave a party and *60 Minutes* showed up at the door. Would you let them in? Would you evict them? Would you commit hara-kiri?

Those were the choices that confronted the Chase Bank at the American Bankers Association convention, when *60 Minutes* (see Figure 9-12) came to Honolulu to "get the bankers."

The banking industry was taking its lumps. Profits were lagging. Loans to foreign governments weren't being repaid. Financings to bankrupt corporations were being questioned. And it was getting difficult for poor people to open bank accounts.

Understandably, few bankers at the Honolulu convention cared to share their thoughts on camera with *60 Minutes.* Some headed for cover when the cameras approached. Others barred the unwanted visitors from their receptions. In at least one case, a *60 Minutes* cameraman was physically removed from the hall. By the convention's third day, the *60 Minutes* team was decrying its treatment at the hands of the bankers as the "most vicious" it had ever been accorded.

By the third night, correspondent Morley Safer and his *60 Minutes* crew were steaming and itching for a confrontation.

That's when *60 Minutes* showed up at our party.

For 10 years, with your intrepid author as its public affairs director, Chase had sponsored a private convention reception for the media. It combined an informal cocktail party, where journalists and bankers could chat and munch hors d'oeuvres, with a more formal, 30-minute press conference with the bank's president. The press conference was on the record, no-holds-barred, and frequently generated news coverage by the wire services, newspapers, and magazines that regularly sent representatives. No television cameras were permitted.

But when we arrived at Honolulu's scenic Pacific Club, there to greet us—unannounced and uninvited—were Morley and the men from *60 Minutes,* ready to do battle.

The ball was in our court. We faced five questions that demanded immediate answers.

■ **First, should we let them in?** What they wanted, said Safer, was to interview our president about "critical banking issues." He said they had been "hassled" all week and were "entitled" to attend our media reception. But we hadn't invited them. And they hadn't had the courtesy to let us know they were coming. It was true that they were members

of the working press. It was also true that our reception was intended to generate news. So we had a dilemma.

■ **Second, should we let them film the press conference?** Chase's annual convention press conference had never before been filmed. Television cameras are bulky, noisy, and intrusive. They threatened to sabotage the normally convivial atmosphere of our party. Equally disconcerting would be the glaring camera lights that would have to be set up. The *60 Minutes* crew countered that their coverage was worthless without film. Theirs, after all, was a medium of pictures, and without pictures, there could be no story. As appetizing as this proposition sounded to us, we were worried that if we refused their cameras, what they might film instead would be us blocking the door at an otherwise open news conference. So we had another problem.

■ **Third, should we let them film the cocktail party?** Like labor leader Samuel Gompers, television people are interested in only one thing: "*More!*" In the case of our reception, we weren't eager to have CBS film the cocktails and hors d'oeuvres part of our party. We were certain the journalists on hand would agree with us. After all, who wants to see themselves getting sloshed on national television when they're supposed to be working?

■ **Fourth, should we let them film a separate interview with our president?** Because few top people at the convention were willing to speak to CBS, *60 Minutes* was eager to question our president in as extensive and uninterrupted a format as possible. Safer wanted a separate interview before the formal press conference started. So we also had to deal with the question of whether to expose our president to a lengthy, one-on-one, side-room interview with the most powerful—and potentially negative—television news program in the land.

■ **Fifth, should we change our format?** The annual media reception/press conference had always been an informal affair. Our executives joked with the journalists, shared self-deprecating asides, and generally relaxed. Thus, in light of the possible presence of *60 Minutes,* we wondered if we should alter this laid-back approach and adopt a more on-guard stance.

We had 10 minutes to make our decisions. We also had splitting headaches.

Questions

1. Would you let *60 Minutes* in?
2. Would you let them film the press conference?
3. Would you let them film the cocktail party?
4. Would you let them film a separate interview with the president?
5. Would you change the format of the party?
6. How does the American Bankers Association (ABA) deal with the media today? Visit its online press room (www.aba.com/press+room/default.html). What resources can members of the press access on this site? How does ABA make it easy for reporters to make contact?

FIGURE 9-12 For 40 years, this genial band of lovely reporters has struck abject fear into the hearts of powerful CEOs everywhere. What would you do if you woke up one morning and found Morley Safer (far left) or one of his cohorts from CBS' *60 Minutes* in your living room?   (Photo: Newscom)

From the Top   An Interview with Al Neuharth

Al Neuharth was born a poor country boy in South Dakota in 1924. He became a self-made multimillionaire who built the nation's largest newspaper company, Gannett Co. Inc., and started the nation's most widely read newspaper, *USA Today*. Since his "retirement" from Gannett in 1989 at age 65, he has been an active author, speaker, columnist, and world traveler. He "retired a second time" on June 1, 1997, as chairman of one of the nation's largest private charitable foundations, The Freedom Forum, which he founded in 1991 as the successor to the Gannett Foundation, established in 1935 by Frank E. Gannett. This interview was conducted in September of 2007, on the occasion of *USA Today's* 25th anniversary.

How did you know *USA Today* would work?
We didn't. It was a gamble. But we did an awful lot of research. We hired the pollster Lou Harris, who extensively analyzed whether a national newspaper could make it. One of Lou's conclusions was that *"The TV generation won't fight its way through dull, gray newspapers."* So we shortened stories, added color, and made an exciting product.

What do you read each day?
I read *The New York Times* and *The Wall Street Journal* every day. I travel a great deal. One of the benefits I received in retiring from Gannett is that the company agreed to provide me with the *Times, Journal, USA Today,* and a local newspaper, wherever I am.

So you don't agree with Ted Turner that newspapers are dying?
No way. Critics who predict the death of newspapers are nuts. Circulation falloffs are not nearly as excessive as critics suggest. People said newspapers were dying when television first appeared. Whenever a new medium enters the picture, critics predict the demise of newspapers. The challenge for publishers is to blend newspapers with the most popular features of the Net.
By the way, I asked Ted once if he really believed what he said, and he told me, *"You know me. I mix a lot of bull@#@$@ in to get people's attention!"*

Do you think newspapers can compete with the Internet?
I have great confidence that executives at *USA Today, the Journal,* and the *Times* will find the key to successfully marrying the Internet and print. We did it at *USA Today* with the challenge of television. Look at the *Times,* under Arthur Sulzberger, its publisher, who is doing a great job. He took a risk by adding color and other things. People criticized him for changing the look of the "great gray lady." Arthur told me, *"I know it's risky. But it's more risky if we didn't do it."* That's the kind of attitude that will return people—even young people—to print.

What has been the role of cable television on journalism?
Cable news is largely opinion. But the good thing is that what cable forced editors and reporters to do was focus on what the public was following. If the public wants O.J. and Britney Spears, then newspaper editors can't ignore that.

But are O.J. and Britney really "news"?
According to whom? I have always felt that newspapers and the media in general must keep in mind what readers want. If the public is interested in a topic, you can't ignore it. Once upon a time, newspapers editors and reporters were convinced that they knew more than their readers. Big mistake. We've learned over the past 25 years to factor in reader judgements.

How do you feel about reporters appearing on TV and giving their opinions?
It's absolutely appropriate. For too long, publishers forbade their editors from appearing on television, because it would "compromise the integrity" of the publication. Nonsense. What it does is increase the audience for the paper.

How does this impact the "quality" of journalism?
Who defines *"quality"*? Readers ought to have a voice in what we're giving them. An editor's job is to diversify and debate but not to dictate. When I was CEO of Gannett, we changed the makeup of the board of directors, because we realized that a

bunch of middle-aged white males couldn't possibly make appropriate decisions for a diversified audience.

How do you feel about public relations?
The job of a public relations person is to pedal propaganda. The good ones don't lie. They make it clear when they are providing facts and when they are providing something else. Our job in the media business is to make damn sure PR people aren't lying.

What's the future of the news business?
The future is bright. In the U.S., there's a great appetite for "hard news," particularly at night. That's why the "evening news" has survived. In the morning, the desire is more for "entertainment." Outside the U.S., there are few news vacuums left in the world thanks to the Net and the satellite. In places like China, Africa, India and the like, people want more news. I see this everywhere I travel, and I travel a lot. Well, we're in the news business. So I'm optimistic.

Public Relations Library

Beckwith, Sandra. *Complete Publicity Plans: How to Create Publicity that Will Spark Media Excitement and Exposure.* Avon, MA: Adams Media, 2003.

Bland, Michael, Alison Theaker, and David Wragg. *Effective Media Relations: How to Get Results*, Third Edition. London, UK: Kogan Page Limited, 2005.

Carney, William Wray. *In the News: The Process of Media Relations in Canada.* Alberta, Ontario: University of Alberta Press, 2008. The view of the media north of the border.

Cottle, Simon. *Media in Focus.* London, England: Sage Publications, 2004. The view of the media from across the pond.

Crilley, Jeff. *Free Publicity: A TV Reporter Shares Secrets for Getting Covered on the News.* Dallas, TX: Charisma Press, 2003. Crilley, an Emmy Award–winning journalist from Dallas with more than two decades of TV news experience, tells readers that journalists want fun, interesting, newsworthy stories with good visuals.

D'Vari, Marisa. *Building Buzz: How to Reach and Impress Your Target Audience.* Franklin Lakes, NJ: Career Press, 2006. A primer, from soup to nuts, on securing publicity, including news release and interview tips, media training, and branding advice.

Hayes, Richard, and Daniel Grossman. *A Scientist's Guide to Talking with the Media.* Cambridge, MA: Union of Concerned Scientists, 2006.

Henderson, David. *Media Relations: From a Journalist's Perspective.* Lincoln, NE: iUniverse, 2005. David Henderson was an award-winning network news correspondent for CBS News, so he knows whereof he speaks. And just to make sure, Henderson interviewed 60 other journalists for insight on how public relations people can better work with the media.

Lewis, Benjamin, *Perfecting the Pitch: Creating Publicity Through Media Rapport.* No. Potomac, MD: Larstan Publishing, 2008. A solid primer on how even a sole practitioner can solicit coverage by the media.

O'Dwyer, Jack (Ed.). *O'Dwyer's Directory of Corporation Communications.* New York: J. R. O'Dwyer, annually. This guide provides a full listing of the public relations departments of thousands of public companies and shows how the largest companies define public relations and staff and budget for it.

O'Dwyer, Jack (Ed.). *O'Dwyer's Directory of PR Firms.* New York: J. R. O'Dwyer, annually. This directory lists thousands of public relations firms. In addition to providing information on executives, accounts, types of agencies, and branch office locations, the guide provides a geographical index to firms and cross-indexes more than 8,000 clients.

Persinos, John. *Confessions of an Ink-Stained Wretch.* No. Potomac, MD: Larstan Publishing, 2006. This former journalist/editor/press secretary explains how marketing can mesh with media to attract publicity.

Rampton, Sheldon, and John Stauber. *Weapons of Mass Deception: The Uses of Propaganda in Bush's War on Iraq.* New York: Tarcher/Penguin Press, 2003. The two irrepressible anti-Bush zealots are at it again with the aggressive publicity campaign that led to the invasion of Iraq. Right-wing conservatives beware.

Salzman, Jason. *Making the News: A Guide for Activists and Nonprofits.* London, UK: Westview Press, 2003. This former official with Greenpeace provides a provocative look at manufacturing publicity when you don't have much money. Such techniques as "wheatpasting," "wildposturing," and "swimming in the cold New York harbor" are all discussed.

Schenkler, Irv, and Tony Herrling. *Guide to Media Relations.* Upper Saddle River, NJ: Prentice Hall, 2004. The book offers guidelines on all areas of media relations, including how to identify media contacts, establish relationships with reporters, prepare for media interviews, write news releases, and communicate with the financial media, among many other areas.

Stewart, Sally. *Media Training 101: A Guide to Meeting the Press.* New York: John Wiley & Sons, 2004. Written by a former *USA Today* journalist, this book gives insight into how reporters think, what appeals to them, and what doesn't.

Theater, Alison. *The Public Relations Handbook,* Second Edition. Abingdon, Oxfordshire: Routledge, 2004.

Trump, Donald, and Robert Slater. *No Such Thing as Over-Exposure.* Upper Saddle River, NJ: Pearson Prentice-Hall, 2005. And, of course, there isn't, particularly if you're a self-inflated megalomaniac who can afford to hire a competent business writer willing to sacrifice his pride to extol the virtues of a somewhat questionable man of wealth and privilege. (And that's the good part.)

Walker, T.J. *Media Training: A Complete Guide to Controlling Your Image, Message & Sound Bites.* New York: Media Training Worldwide, 2004. Media trainer Walker knows his stuff. Good advice.

Warren, Lissa. *The Savvy Author's Guide to Book Publicity.* New York: Caroll & Graf Publishers, 2004. Lots of people are authors, and precious few sell books. That's why book publicity is a special art that requires special expertise. This is as good an explanation as any.

Chapter 10

Employee Relations

FIGURE 10-1 Unhappy campers. U.S. workers, like these American Airlines pilots, generally weren't pleased with their treatment by management in the first decade of the 21st century. (Photo: Newscom)

United Airlines used to have a slogan, *"Fly the Friendly Skies."* But in 2008, a group of dissatisfied pilots, unhappy with the impact on them of CEO Glenn Tilton's policies to deal with higher oil prices and recession, carried a far less pleasant message. In the old days, they would have gone on strike. But in the 21st century, they started a Web site with the welcoming name, *"Glenn Tilton Must Go."*[1]

And airline pilots weren't the only disgruntled workers in an environment of economic uncertainty (see Figure 10-1).

Not surprisingly, as the U.S. economy sputtered at the end of the first decade of the 21st century and more people either got fired or worried that unemployment might lie around the corner, Americans workers grew increasingly unhappy with their jobs.

In 2008, companies across the board—from Starbucks and Yahoo! to General Motors and BMW—laid off thousands of workers. In the first six months of 2008, the U.S. Labor Department reported that nearly 460,000 people lost jobs in banking, pharmaceutical, airlines, and many other industries.[2]

No wonder less than half of all Americans said they were satisfied with their jobs, compared to 61 percent 20 years ago. And the least satisfied with their jobs were the newest entrants to the workforce, with less than 39 percent of workers under the age of 25 satisfied with their employment situation.[3]

So what's an organization to do, especially to reassure these younger participants in the workforce?

For an increasing number of companies, the answer was the CEO blog.

- In 2006, Sun Microsystem's Jonathan Schwartz became the first CEO to begin his own (usually) once-a-week blog, *"On Blogging as CEO,"* to keep the troops informed about what was going on around the company and who was doing what. The blog proved popular and inspired many comments from the staff, and the social media–savvy CEO kept it up (at least until Sun was merged into Oracle in 2009).

- In 2007, a not-as-tech-savvy CEO, 75-year-old Bill Marriott of Marriott Hotels, launched a periodic blog that mostly talked about his thoughts about customer service and all things Marriott. After an initial flurry of responses, the blog settled in as another internal communications tool.

- In contrast to the septuagenarian Marriott CEO was Mark Zuckerberg, the 24-year-old billionaire (gasp!) CEO of social media giant, Facebook. CEO Zuckerberg, a Generation Y "digital native," was one of 47 Facebook employees contributing to the external *Facebook Blog*. Zuckerberg was initially criticized for only participating on the blog in time of crisis.[4]

But just as with any other communications tool, CEO blogs and all other aspects of social media depend on "content" to win the day. And according to research in 2008, most corporate blogs miserably failed the "content" test. *"Many corporate blogs read like tired, warmed-over press releases,"* concluded Forrester Research. *"Good blogging style should resemble a coffee shop, not a white paper,"* the research firm said.[5]

The fact is that communications to employees must be candid, clear, and credible. If these requisites aren't attained, then all the fancy social media techniques will be for naught. Employees—arguably, the most savvy public with which management must deal—just won't buy the same old, same old, even in a fancy new package.

That's why organizing effective, believable, and persuasive internal communications—particularly in the midst of economic uncertainty and organizational change—is such a challenging and critical public relations responsibility in the 21st century.

Strong Employee Relations = Solid Organizations

In the 21st century, employee relations matters—a lot. Approximately 60 percent of corporate CEOs, according to one well-regarded survey, reported spending more of their time communicating with employees.[6]

The reason is obvious, when one considers the fortunes of employees in recent years and the growing importance of internal communications.

- First, the wave of downsizings and layoffs that dominated business and industry both in the United States and worldwide after the high-tech bubble burst in the early years of the 21st century has taken its toll on employee loyalty. Although employees once implicitly trusted their organizations and superiors, today they are more hardened to the realities of a job market dominated by technological change that reduces human labor. Today, when companies lay off workers, they are often rewarded by the stock market for becoming more productive and efficient. This phenomenon has caused employees to understand that in today's business climate, every employee is expendable and there is no such thing as "lifetime employment." Consequently, companies must work harder at honestly communicating with their workers.

- The wide gulf between the pay of senior officers and common workers is another reason organizations must be sensitive to employee communications. The *"good news"* was that in recent years, the gap between CEO pay and average worker pay seems to have declined. The *"bad news"* was that the average CEO of a large U.S. company made roughly $10.8 million in 2006, or 364 times that of U.S. full-time and part-time workers, who made an average of $29,544. That huge gap, however, was still down from 411 times in 2005 and well-below the record high of 525 times recorded in 2000.[7] Nonetheless, when the Congress debated financial industry reform in 2009, the issue of going after "CEO pay" dominated the discussion.

- The move toward globalization, including the merger of geographically dispersed organizations, was another reason for increased focus on internal communications. Technology has hastened the integration of business and markets around the world. Customers on far-away continents are today but a

mouse-click away. Alliances, affiliations, and mergers among far-flung companies have proliferated. Organizations have become much more cognizant of the
importance of communicating the opportunities and benefits that will enhance
support and loyalty among worldwide staffs.

- Finally, research indicates that companies that communicate effectively with
  their workers financially outperform those that don't. One study found that
  companies with the most effective internal communications programs returned
  57 percent more to their shareholders than companies with the least effective
  programs.[8]

These phenomena suggest that the value of "intellectual capital" has increased in
importance. In the new information economy, business managers have realized that
their most important assets are their employees. Employee communications, then, has
become a key way to nurture and sustain that intellectual capital.

This was not always the case. For years, employee communications was considered
less important than the more glamorous and presumably more "critical" functions of
media, government, and investor relations.

Today, with fewer employees expected to do more work, staff members are calling
for empowerment—for more of a voice in decision making. Just about every researcher
who keeps tabs on employee opinion finds evidence of a *"trust gap"* that exists
between management and workers. To narrow that gap demands that more effective
employee communications play a pivotal role.

Dealing with the Employee Public

Just as there is no such thing as the *"general public,"* there is also no single *"employee
public."*

The employee public is made up of numerous subgroups: senior managers, first-
line supervisors, staff and line employees, union laborers, per diem employees, contract
workers, and others. Each group has different interests and concerns. A smart organization will try to differentiate messages and communications to reach these segments.

Indeed, in a general sense, today's staff is younger, increasingly female, more
diverse, ambitious and career oriented, less complacent, and less loyal to the company
than in the past. Today's more hard-nosed employee demands candor in communications. Internal communications, like external messages, must be targeted to reach
specific subgroups of the employee public.

Grounding in effective employee communications requires management to ask
three hard questions about the way it conveys knowledge to the staff.

- Is management able to communicate effectively with employees?
- Is communication trusted, and does it relay appropriate information to
  employees?
- Has management communicated its commitment to its employees and to fostering a rewarding work environment?

In many instances, the biggest problem is that employees don't know where they
stand in the eyes of management. This is particularly true in a period of high
unemployment. In addition, they often don't understand how compensation programs
work or what they need to do to move ahead. This lack of understanding leads to

discontent, frustration, miscommunication, problems, and eventually to the feeling that the grass is greener elsewhere.[9]

Clearly, organizing effective, believable, and persuasive internal communications in the midst of organizational change is a core critical public relations responsibility in the 21st century.

Trusted Communications in Uncertain Times

An organization truly concerned about "getting through" to its employees in an era of downsizing, displacement, and dubious communications must reinforce five specific principles:

- **Respect.** Employees must be respected for their worth as individuals and their value as workers. They must be treated with respect and not as interchangeable commodities.

- **Honest feedback.** By talking to workers about their strengths and weaknesses, employers help employees know where they stand. Some managers incorrectly assume that avoiding negative feedback will be helpful. Wrong. Employees need to know where they stand at any given time. Candid communications will help them in this pursuit.

- **Recognition.** Employees feel successful when management recognizes their contributions. It is the duty of the public relations professional to suggest mechanisms by which deserving employees will be honored.

- **Voice.** In the era of blogs, talk radio, and cable talk shows, almost everyone wants their voice to be heard in decision making. This growing "activist communications" phenomenon must be considered by public relations professionals seeking to win internal goodwill for management.

- **Encouragement.** Study after study reveals that money and benefits motivate employees up to a point, but that *"something else"* is generally necessary. That something else is encouragement. Workers need to be encouraged. Communications programs that provide encouragement generally produce results. What kinds of qualities distinguish the communication effort at a "better place to work"?

According to Milton Moskowitz, coauthor of the *100 Best Companies to Work For in America,* six criteria, in particular, have stood the test of time:

1. **Willingness to express dissent.** Employees want to be able to *"feed back"* to management their opinions and even dissent. They want access to management. They want critical letters to appear in internal publications. They want management to pay attention.

2. **Visibility and proximity of upper management.** Enlightened companies try to level rank distinctions, eliminating such status reminders as executive cafeterias and executive gymnasiums. They act against hierarchical separation. Moskowitz. says that smart CEOs practice MBWA—*"management by walking around."*

3. **Priority of internal to external communication.** The worst thing to happen to any organization is for employees to learn critical information

about the company on a renegade blog or the 10 o'clock news. Smart organizations always release pertinent information to employees first and consider internal communication primary. (That's why Barack Obama in the summer of 2008 "announced" his choice for vice president "first" to supporters via email.)

4. **Attention to clarity.** How many employees regularly read benefits booklets? The answer should be "many" because of the importance of benefit programs to the entire staff, but most employees never do so. Good companies write such booklets with an emphasis on clarity as opposed to legalities—to be readable for a general audience rather than for human resources specialists. (The "downside" to this can be seen in this chapter's PR Ethics Mini-Case.)

5. **Friendly tone.** The best companies *"give a sense of family"* in all that they communicate. One high-tech company makes everyone wear a name tag with the first name in big block letters.

6. **Sense of humor.** People are worried principally about keeping their jobs. Corporate life for many is grim. Moskowitz says this is disastrous. *"It puts people in straitjackets, so they can't wait to get out at the end of the day."*[10] So employees seem to enjoy themselves more at companies like Southwest Airlines, which prides itself on keeping things in "perspective" and not taking itself too seriously (see Figure 10-2).

What internal communications comes down to—just like external communications—is, in a word, *credibility*. The task for management is to convince employees that it not only desires to communicate with them but also wishes to do so in a truthful, frank, and direct manner. That is the overriding challenge that confronts today's internal communicator.

FIGURE 10-2 Alien company. Southwest Airlines was one of the few companies in the early trying years of the 21st century to retain its sense of humor. Here the company, in conjunction with Sue Bohle Public Relations and Infogames Entertainment, decked out these passengers in out-of-this-world masks on the way to the E3 Entertainment Trade Show. (Courtesy of the Bohle Company)

PR Ethics

Mini-Case   Meet the New Boss

Positive employee relations may be at a premium in the 21st century, but evidently nobody told Sam Zell (see Figure 10-3).

Zell, a self-made Chicago real estate magnate, described by Gawker.com as the "salty billionaire," sent shockwaves through the media community in 2007 when he paid $8.2 billion for the venerable Tribune Company, owner of the *Chicago Tribune*, *Los Angeles Times*, and *Orlando Sentinel*, among other newspapers.

One of the CEO's first projects was to put his 20,000 employees on notice with a revised 3,663-word employee handbook, about a third as long as the leaden, overly legalistic one it replaced. The handbook began thusly:

Rule No. 1:   Use your best judgment.

Rule No. 2:   See Rule No. 1.

The handbook further stated "*Question authority and push back if you do not like the answer.*"

"*Good for Sam,*" you say, but . . .

In a subsequent meeting in Orlando with the Sentinel staff, a photographer asked her new boss what he thought "*the role of journalism was in the community.*"

Her new CEO shot back, "I want to make enough money so that I can afford you. You need to in effect help me by being a journalist that focuses on what our readers want that generates more revenue."

The exchange grew more testy, and as Zell left the stage, he muttered a two-word obscenity (not fit for a family textbook), all of which was captured on YouTube. One wondered whether the offending photographer was rewarded for her propensity to "*push back.*"

Perhaps the new owner grew exasperated because he sensed what was to come: Namely, in September 2008, Zell was sued by a group of current and former Los Angeles Times reporters accusing him of "recklessness."

FIGURE 10-3 New sheriff in town. New newspaper owner Sam Zell holds court at his flagship *Chicago Tribune*. (Photo: Newscom)

And in the end, alas for poor, blustery Sam, "recklessness" it was. On December 9, 2008, Zell's Tribune Company, choking under a mountain of unrepayable debt, filed for bankruptcy protection.*

Questions

1. What do you think of Zell's new handbook, and might there be legal problems with it?

2. What do you think of the CEO's response to the photographer, in terms of employee relations and the "ethic" of journalism?

*For further information, see Steve Crescenzo, "Finally . . . an Employee Handbook Someone Might Actually Read," *Ragan Report* (January 28, 2008): 1; Richard Perez-Pena, "Reporters from Paper Suing Chief of Tribune," *New York Times* (September 16, 2008); Richard Perez-Pena, "Crippled by Debt, Tribune Co. Seeks Bankruptcy Protection," *New York Times* (December 9, 2008): 1; and Molly Selvin, "Challenge Authority, If You Dare," *Los Angeles Times* (February 5, 2008).

Credibility: The Key

The employee public is a savvy one. Employees can't be conned because they live with the organization every day. They generally know what's going on and whether management is being honest with them. That's why management must be truthful.

Employees want managers to level with them. They want facts, not wishful thinking. The days when management could say, "*Trust us, this is for your own good*" are over. Employees like hearing the truth, especially in person. Indeed, survey after survey suggests that face-to-face communications—preferably between a supervisor and subordinate—is the hands-down most effective method of employee communications.

Employees also want to know, candidly, how they're doing. Research indicates that trust in organizations would increase if management (1) communicated earlier and more frequently, (2) demonstrated trust in employees by sharing bad news as well as good, and (3) involved employees in the process by asking for their ideas and opinions. Effective employee communication means that an organization's leaders have taken the time to clearly and succinctly articulate the vision of the business, show how employees can contribute to it, and demonstrate how it can be "lived" in the daily jobs.[11]

Today, smart companies realize that well-informed employees are the organization's best goodwill ambassadors. Managements have become more candid in their communications with the staff. Gone are the days when all the news coming from management is all good. In today's environment, being candid means treating people with dignity, addressing their concerns, and giving them the opportunity to understand the realities of the marketplace (Figure 10-4).

One reason that organizations such as Hewlett-Packard, which cut out its magazine for employees in 2001 after 58 years, opt out of print publications is the tremendous growth of email and intranets. These instant, direct devices provide greater opportunity today to increase the frequency and candor of communications. A major part of the challenge that confronts internal communicators is to reflect credibility in communicating that underscores the level of respect with which employees should be held by management.

Most employees desperately want to be treated as important parts of an organization; they should not be taken for granted, nor should they be shielded from the truth. Thus, the most important ingredient of any internal communications program must be credibility.

S-H-O-C the Troops

Enhancing credibility, being candid, and winning trust must be the primary employee communications objectives in the new century. Earning employee trust may result in more committed and productive employees. But scraping away the scar tissue of distrust that exists in many organizations requires a strategic approach.

The question is: How does management build trust when employee morale is so brittle?

Part of the answer lies in an approach to management communication built around the acronym S-H-O-C. That is, management should consider a four-step communications approach—built on communications that are **strategic, honest, open,** and **consistent**—to begin to rebuild employee trust.

- **First, all communications must be strategic.** What strategic communication essentially boils down to is this: Most employees want you to answer only two basic questions for them:
  1. Where is this organization going?
  2. What is my role in helping us get there?

     That's it. Once you level with the staff as to the organization's direction and goals and their role in the process, even the most ardent bellyachers will grudgingly acknowledge your attempt to "keep them in the loop."

- **Second, all communications must be honest.** The sad fact is that while most executives may pay lip service to candor and honesty, in the end, too many turn out like the managements in 2008 at Bear Stearns, Washington Mutual, Lehman Brothers, Countrywide Financial, and all the other companies caught dissembling, obfuscating, pulling their punches, and eventually fading into oblivion.

     They seem to fear, as Jack Nicholson raged in *A Few Good Men,* that the staff *"can't handle the truth."*

FIGURE 10-4 **Credible communication.** The best communication is direct communication, which is what Chenango Memorial Hospital in Norwich, New York, did when questions of layoffs pervaded the staff. The CEO answered the questions directly and in print. (Courtesy of Chenango Memorial Hospital)

AN UPDATE ON THE "BRIDGE TO EXCELLENCE" PROGRAM

THE BRIDGE REPORT

VOLUME 1 NUMBER 10
MAY 21, 2004

A number of important developments have occurred recently in our *Bridge to Excellence* initiative that I wanted to bring to your attention, before announcing to the general community.

First, we have reached agreement with Crothall Services Group to assume all environmental services, effective June 21.

Crothall, based in Wayne, Pennsylvania, has extensive experience in managing and operating environmental services for 300 healthcare institutions in the U.S. and Canada.

Our agreement calls for Crothall to provide leadership, training and capital equipment, to enhance the professionalism and improve the delivery of environmental services at Chenango Memorial Hospital.

The Crothall Chenango management team will arrive here in early June. All current CMH environmental services employees will become employees of Crothall, effective June 21.

Similarly, we have reached agreement with Morrison Healthcare Food Services to assume Chenango Memorial's food services, also effective June 21. Morrison, which has served the healthcare food and nutrition business for nearly a century, has been providing us with management and dietician services for some time.

Under this new agreement, all food services personnel will become Morrison employees, effective June 21. This will not only provide continuity of food services management at CMH but also, like the environmental services change, introduce a new level of professionalism

and quality to our food services operation.

In a related move, we have retained Canteen Corp. to replace our current vending machine supplier.

Canteen, which like Crothall and Morrison is an operating unit of the $6 billion Compass Group North America, has been charged with the task of upgrading our vending machine equipment and expanding available offerings.

All three of these moves, which affect about 10% of our workforce, will not only benefit the hospital financially but will also allow us to focus on our primary mission – delivering the highest quality patient care to the people of Chenango County.

With the encouragement and support of United Health Services we are also moving forward the business relationship with Bassett Healthcare that I announced in the last *Bridge Report.*

By July 1, we hope to have credentialed Bassett physicians in the areas of orthopedics, gastroenterology, urology and general surgery. The Bassett physicians will be utilizing our operating rooms to perform procedures on their patients. This change will make it more convenient for Bassett patients in our community, who currently travel to Oneonta and Cooperstown for treatment, and will also enable us to take advantage of underutilized CMH capacity, while increasing our volumes and improving our financial situation. The arrangement will not affect our referral patterns to United Health

United Health Services

Chenango Memorial Hospital

Executive Leadership Team

Frank W. Mirabito
President & CEO
Ext. 4113

Jay Alfirevic
Project Director/CTO
Ext. 4169

Julie Briggs, RN
VP Patient Care/CNO
Ext. 4243

Shirley Caezza, RN
Dir. of Performance Improvement
Ext. 4033

Ronald Cerow
Administrator, RHCF
Ext. 4715

Mark Kishel, MD
Interim CMO
Ext. 4239

Robert McCarthy
VP Finance/CFO
Ext. 4221

Peter Mike
Interim Materials Mgr.
Ext. 4106

Richard Park
Dir. of Human Resources
Ext. 4508

Garry Root
Director Comm. Relations
Ext. 4028

Gary Van House
Interim Clinic Admin.
Ext. 4260

Employee Hotline
Ext. 4578

Employee Hotline Drop Box Locations
Hops Yard Bistro
2nd Floor RHCF
4th Floor Ambulatory Dept.
Main Lobby

(continued)

Such trepidation is foolish. For one thing, the staff already may discount anything management tells them. For another, you can't hope to build credibility through prevaricating or sugarcoating.

■ **Third, all communications must be open.** This is another way of saying that there must be feedback. The best communications are two-way communications. That means that no matter how large the organization, employee views must be solicited, listened to, and most important, acted upon.

FIGURE 10-4 *(continued)*

THE BRIDGE REPORT   **Page 2**

Services and United Medical Associates, which will remain our clinical partners. CMH patients will continue to be referred within our system.

In terms of orthopedics, Dr. Jose Lopez will leave Chenango Memorial at the end of this month. As a result, we have accordingly downsized and restructured the Orthopedic Institute staff. Efforts are underway to establish additional relationships with Bassett and United Medical Associates (UMA) to help serve the patients of Dr. Lopez.

Finally, I am pleased to report that we have received the $500,000 grant from the New York State Healthcare Reform Act, which I mentioned in a prior *Bridge Report.* The proceeds of this will go toward completing the Wellspring consultant engagement. Most important, this grant triggers an equivalent amount in the form of a 0% interest loan from the New York State Dormitory Authority. We expect to receive the proceeds of this loan, which will be used for general hospital purposes, by the end of the month.

As you can tell, much has been happening around our hospital, as we continue to make progress in restoring our financial strength and rebuilding our reputation in the community.

We continue to receive questions and suggestions on the x4578 Hotline and in the Hotline Drop Boxes. Here are some of the most recent:

Is it true all nurses receive a bonus?
   No. We have no bonus plan in effect at this time for any Chenango Memorial employee, from the CEO on down.

How about pay increases for long term employees?
   Our general procedure with respect to pay increases is to evaluate each employee on an annual basis. Once an employee has maxed out due to length of service, he or she is awarded a $1,000 annual longevity increase. I might add that despite our current financial challenges, pay policies have remained constant.

Shouldn't we have a sign posted on the 4th Floor near the elevators, so that patients know where Dr. Converse is located?
   Yes we should. It's in the works. Thanks for the good suggestion.

I have heard various talk about PTO policy. What is the situation?
   The whole area of PTO is currently under review. Once we have clarified our intentions, I will discuss this issue in depth in a future *Bridge Report.*

As always, thank you for your questions and comments and your continuing best efforts in our *Bridge to Excellence* initiative.

    That latter aspect is most important. Often, managers stage elaborate forums and feedback sessions, listen to employee gripes and suggestions, and yet do nothing. The key must be *action*.

- **Fourth, all communications must be consistent.** Once you've begun to communicate, you must keep it up. Maintain a regular, on-time, and predictable program of internal newsletters, employee forums, leadership meetings, and reward celebrations.

On again, off again communications or programs that start with bold promises only to peter out question management's commitment to keeping the staff informed. Generally, employee information, education, and morale-boosting programs start with great pomp and promise. The CEO blusters his way through a rousing speech, literature pours out from on high, task forces plunge into quick-fix assignments, and then, over time, nada.

This obviously is wrong. Communications, if they are to work, must be steadily, sometimes painfully, consistent.[12]

Employee Communications Tactics

Once objectives are set, a variety of techniques can be adopted to reach the staff. The initial tool again is research. Before any communications program can be implemented, communicators must have a good sense of staff attitudes.

Internal Communications Audits

Both a strategy and a tactic, the internal communications audit is the most beneficial form of research on which to lay the groundwork for effective employee communications. Ideally, this starts with old-fashioned, personal, in-depth interviews with both top management and communicators. It is important to find out from top management what it "wants" from the communications team. It is also important to find out what communicators "think" management wants. Often the discontinuities are startling. The four critical audit questions to probe are:

1. How do internal communications support the mission of the organization?
2. Do internal communications have management's support?
3. Do internal communications justify the expense?
4. How responsive to employee needs and concerns are internal communications?[13]

Audits help determine staff attitudes about their jobs, the organization, and its mission, coupled with an analysis of existing communications techniques. The findings of such audits are often revealing, always informative, and never easily ignored.

Internal audits can be conducted by organizational personnel or consultants. Sometimes consultants provide a more objective analysis of the situation and what is required to improve it. (But, then, as a consultant, I'm biased!)

Once internal communications research is completed, the public relations practitioner has a clearer idea of the kinds of communications vehicles that make sense for the organization.

Online Communications

The age of online communications has ushered in a whole new set of employee communications vehicles—from instant messaging to email to voice mail to tailored organizational intranets to employee and CEO blogs. Such vehicles are more immediate than earlier print versions. They reach employees at their desks and are more likely to be read, listened to, and acted on. Indeed, employees without computer access are increasingly losing their "voice" and ability to be heard, especially the ability to submit ideas for improvement or to access a company intranet remotely.

Online communications also have the capability of reaching virtual employees at their desks in their homes, on their BlackBerrys or Palm Pilots, in their cars, or wherever they remotely may be.

As print publications become steadily fewer, tailored online newsletters have begun to replace them. In many cases, organizations are using print vehicles to push readers to new intranet portals.[14]

Many organizations, from traditional companies such as Xerox, Exxon, and Ford to more recent high-tech giants such as Google, Yahoo!, Intel, and Oracle, increasingly rely on intranets to exchange information quickly and effectively. Miller Brewing Company's intranet, "Miller Time," sponsors an interactive forum through which employees offer suggestions to and ask questions of management. Everyone who offers an idea through the Miller intranet is guaranteed a response (not a beer!). Such feedback is critical to corporate credibility.[15]

Among growing online, internal communications vehicles are the following:

- *Blogs*—or technically, Web logs—are a type of frequently updated online journal. Blogs provide an easy way for employees to post opinions and views of the company on the Internet. Blogging by senior management, a potentially useful device to reach the staff, is still not the rule among cautious CEOs but, as noted earlier, is also a slowly growing phenomenon.

- *Podcasts*, in which audio or video monologue, interview or on-location content is broadcast online to employees. At Hewlett-Packard, for example, division presidents are podcast discussing new products and organizational developments with rank-and-file employees. The HP podcasts have proven immensely popular.[16]

- *Wikis,* a dynamic Web site to which any user can add pages, modify content, and comment on existing content, is even less widespread than blogs internally. Wikis may be better suited than a blog for a smaller group, and their ability to provide instant interactive capabilities are unmatched.[17]

    Such social media innovations are still in their infancy in terms of being used as internal communications tools. So-called "employee networking" is still very much a work-in-process. Just like any other communications vehicle, for social media to be effective within an organization environment, it (1) must have a business purpose, (2) be entertaining as well as informative, and (3) be composed of riveting content.[18] Consequently, the most developed online, internal communications vehicle, bar none, is the intranet.

The Intranet

In 1997, the people at Forrester Research predicted that within the first few years of the 21st century, the vast majority of American companies would have intranet capability.[19] They were right. Today, in many organizations, the intranet has overtaken and even emulsified print communications. Intranet investments remain strong as companies continue to convert sites to portal technology and add streaming video capability. At IBM, for example, where just about everyone is computer savvy, the company has eliminated every other internal communications medium but the corporate intranet to reach IBM's 300,000 employees.[20]

At British American Tobacco, 25,000 intranet users can create their own Facebook-like profiles and networks by linking with other members. Members of the company's

Connect network can link up with others in the 40-country company through a variety of social media derivatives.[21]

Borders is already in its second generation of intranets, integrating its three main online communications tools for employees, corporate offices, and daily email newsletter into one portal called *"BookMark"* to provide one-stop online internal communicating.[22]

Unfortunately, having an intranet site doesn't mean employees will necessarily go there for information. Sites high in visual appeal but low in usefulness will likely be ignored. To prevent that, intranet creators should keep in mind several important considerations:

1. **Consider the culture.** If the organization is generally collaborative and collegial, it will have no trouble getting people to contribute information and materials to the intranet. But, if the organization is not one that ordinarily shares, a larger central staff may be necessary to ensure that the intranet works.

2. **Set clear objectives and then let it evolve.** Just as in setting up a corporate Web site, intranets must be designed with clear goals in mind: to streamline business processes, to communicate management messages, and so on. Once goals are established, however, site creators ought to allow for growth and evolution as new intranet needs become apparent.

3. **Treat it as a journalistic enterprise.** Company news gets read by company workers. That's a truism throughout all organizations. Employees must know what's going on in the company and complain bitterly if they are not given advance notice of important developments. In this way, the intranet can serve as a critical journalistic communications tool within the organization.

4. **Market, market, market.** The intranet needs to be "sold" within the company. Publicize new features or changes in content. Weekly emails can be used to highlight noteworthy additions and updates. Just as with any other internal communications vehicle, the more exposure the site gets, the more frequently it will be used.

5. **Link to outside lives.** Some CEOs may not recognize it, but employees have lives outside the corporation. An intranet site that recognizes that simple fact can become quite popular. Links to classified ads, restaurant and movie reviews, and information on local concerts are ways to reinforce both the intranet's value and the organization's concern for its staff.

6. **Senior management must commit.** Just like anything else in an organization, if the top executive is neither interested nor supportive, the idea will fail. Therefore, the perceived value of an organization's intranet will increase dramatically if management actively supports and uses it.[23]

Print Publications

The advent of online internal communications has been hard on print publications. It's happening all over corporate America: Print editors are being told to either kill their publication entirely or move it onto the company's intranet.[24]

■ At Tennessee's Eastman Chemical Company, for example, the CEO's drive to convert the firm to a Web-based organization tolled the death knell for the *Inside Eastman* newsletter after 50 years of publication.

■ At another Eastman, New York's Eastman Kodak Company, the internal publication was not used when the company announced that it would lay off 16,600 workers and save $1 billion. Supervisors were briefed by special emails and then directed to personally relay the bad news to their subordinates.

■ When Michigan's Fel-Pro Incorporated agreed to be acquired by Federal-Mogul Corporation, it "cascaded" the information down from departmental managers to supervisors to staff.

To print critics, these instances are exemplary of the trend across corporate internal communications departments to move from print to Internet-oriented employee information.

Print defenders, on the other hand, argue that print still must play a role, particularly in helping create a "climate" that bears the stamp of management (Figure 10-5).

FIGURE 10-5 Prince of print. Southwest Airlines is a one-of-a-kind company, thanks principally to its founder and former CEO Herb Kelleher. Kelleher helped build a climate of creativity, productivity, and fun at Southwest by sponsoring some of the most far-out internal print publications ever seen on this planet (and perhaps any other!). (Reprinted courtesy of Southwestern Airlines)

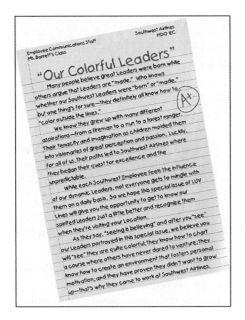

Writing and editing employee newsletters, for example, are typical entry-level public relations responsibilities. In many firms, the mandate is to integrate print and online publications, with each vehicle realizing a different communications objective.

One innovation that enhanced the role of internal editors was the advent of desktop publishing, which allows a user to control the typesetting process in-house, provides faster turnaround for clients, and saves money on outside design. The desktop operation allows scanning photos and drawings, incorporating those images into page layouts, using the computer to assign color in design elements, and producing entire color-separated pages of film from which a printer can create plates for printing.

Whether using conventional print or desktop publishing, an internal newsletter editor must consider the following steps in approaching the task:

1. **Assigning stories.** Article assignments must focus on organizational strategies and management objectives. Job information—organizational changes, mergers, reasons behind decisions, and so on—should be stressed.

2. **Enforcing deadlines.** Employees respect a newsletter that comes out at a specific time. An editor, therefore, must assign and enforce rigid copy deadlines on contributors. Deadline slippage can't be tolerated if the newsletter is to be respected.

3. **Assigning photos.** People like photographs. Because internal publications compete with glossy, high-tech newspapers and magazines and the Internet, organizational photos can't be dull (see Figure 10-6).

4. **Editing copy.** An editor must be just that: a critic of sloppy writing, a student of forceful prose, a motivator to improve copy style. This is especially true now that the computer does at least part of the job for you. However, spell check isn't foolproof, especially when it comes to context.

5. **Formatting copy.** An editor, particularly a desktop editor, must also make the final decisions on the format of the newsletter: how long articles should run, where to put photos, how to crop artwork, what headlines should say, and so on.

FIGURE 10-6 **Ya' gotta' have heart.** Publicity photos for internal and external use don't have to be mundane. At least that's the view of Schneider Associates and client, the New England Confectionary Company (NECCO), which launched its 2007 Sweethearts Conversation Hearts sayings, with the help of the Massachusetts Society for the Prevention of Cruelty to Animals. (Courtesy Jack O'Dwyer Company)

6. **Ensuring on-time publication.** In publishing, timeliness is next to godliness. It is the editor's responsibility to ensure that no last-minute glitches interfere with on-time publication.

7. **Critiquing.** After the fact, the editor's job must continue. He or she must scrupulously review copy, photos, placement, content, philosophy, and all the other elements to ensure that the next edition will be even better.

One organization devoted originally to internal communications, the International Association of Business Communicators, founded in 1970, has come to rival the older Public Relations Society of America. With more than 13,000 members throughout the United States and in 60 countries, the IABC helps set journalistic standards for internal communicators of both print and online publications.

Bulletin Boards

Bulletin boards—not necessarily *electronic* ones—may be among the most ancient of employee communications vehicles, but they have made a comeback in recent years.

For years, bulletin boards were considered second-string information channels, generally relegated to the display of federally required information and policy data for such activities as fire drills and emergency procedures. Most employees rarely consulted them. But the bulletin board has experienced a renaissance and is now being used to improve productivity, cut waste, and reduce accidents on the job. Best of all, employees are taking notice.

How come?

For one thing, yesterday's bulletin board has become today's news center. It has been repackaged into a more lively visual and graphically arresting medium. Using enlarged news pictures and texts, motivational messages, and other company announcements—all illustrated with a flair—the bulletin board has become an important source of employee communications (Figure 10-7). Hospitals, in particular, have found that a strategically situated bulletin board outside a cafeteria is a good way to promote employee understanding and cooperation.

One key to stimulating readership is to keep boards current. One person in the public relations unit should be assigned to this weekly task.

Suggestion Box and Town Hall Meetings

Two other traditional staples of employee communication are the suggestion box and the town hall meeting.

In the old days, suggestion boxes were mounted on each floor, and employees, often anonymously, deposited their thoughts on how to improve the company and its processes and products. Often rewards were awarded for the most productive or profitable suggestions.

Today, the only necessity in implementing a successful suggestion box program is to ensure that there is "feedback"—that is, management action that deals with valid suggestions.

Town hall meetings are large gatherings of employees with top management, where no subject is off limits and management–staff dialogue is the goal. That was the conclusion of one study of 200 employees, some of whom labeled these vehicles "charades, phony, management games, and a joke."[25]

ETHICS
QUESTIONS OR CONCERNS

For help...

STEP 1

Contact your supervisor. If necessary, take it up the chain of command at your location.

STEP 2

Contact your Company Ethics Officer in person, by phone, or by mail.

LMASC Ethics Director:	Tom Salvaggio
Location:	B-2, 2nd Floor, Col. 28
Phone:	Helpline Coordinator, (770) 494-3999
Mailing Address:	LMASC Ethics Office
	P O Box 1771
	Marietta, GA 30061

STEP 3

If the first two steps do not resolve the matter, contact the Corporate Office of Ethics and Business Conduct for confidential assistance:

Helpline:	800 LM ETHIC (800 563-8442)
Fax:	(818) 876-2082
Or Write:	Corporate Office of Ethics and Business Conduct
	Lockheed Martin Corporation
	P O Box 34143
	Bethesda, MD 20827-0143

STEP 4

Contact the Department of Defense Hotline to report fraud, waste and abuse, and/or security violations.

Hotline:	800 424-9098
Or Write:	Defense Hotline
	The Pentagon
	Washington, DC 20301-1900

IDENTITIES OF WRITERS AND CALLERS ARE FULLY PROTECTED.

LOCKHEED MARTIN

FIGURE 10-7 Comeback kid. Among important announcements included on organizational bulletin boards are updates on key corporate issues such as ethical questions and concerns.

Town hall meetings must encourage unfettered two-way communication. In his 2008 presidential campaign, John McCain used these almost to the exclusion of large forum speeches. The more open the format, the greater management and the organization will be trusted. Also of extreme importance is "follow-up." That is, when managers tell Town Hall meeting goers they will "*look into*" something or "*get action*" or something—they need to do it. If not, they impair their own credibility.

Internal Video

As important as Internet video, broadcast, and cable television are as communications media in society today, video has had an up-and-down history as an internal communications medium. On the one hand, internal television, including streaming video, can be demonstrably effective. A 10-minute Web video of an executive announcing a new corporate policy imparts hundreds of times more information than an audiotape of that same message, which in turn contains hundreds of times more information than a printed text of the same message.

A number of organizations work skillfully with internal video:

- Burger King produced a video in an in-house studio and soundstage to train workers in its 5,000 restaurants.
- Miller Brewing Company produced a 20-minute video magazine and distributed it to all company locations. It featured new company commercials, brand promotions, happenings at Miller plants, and employee human interest stories.
- The Ford Motor Company took the unprecedented step of stopping work on assembly lines to show videos to workers.
- The most unique internal video ever produced was the legendary "Southwest Shuffle," in which the employees of Southwest Airlines—from maintenance crews to pilots—chimed in on a rap video extolling the virtues of their innovative carrier. Deejay for the rap extravaganza was—who else?—former Southwest CEO Herb Kelleher!

On the downside, internal video is a medium that must be approached with caution. Unless video is of broadcast quality, few will tolerate it—especially an audience of employees weaned on television. So there are always risks in producing an internal video.

The keys to any internal video production are first to examine internal needs; next to plan thoughtfully before using the medium; and finally to keep it short and keep it exciting.[26] Broadcast quality is a tough standard to meet. If an organization can't afford high-quality video, it shouldn't get involved.

Face-to-Face Communications

Despite the social media revolution, the best communications vehicle to reach employees is face-to-face, preferably from a supervisor. Supervisors, in fact, are the preferred source for the vast majority of employees, making them the top choice by far. The reason is obvious. You report to your supervisor, who awards your raise, promotes you, and is your primary source of corporate information.

That's the good news.

The bad news is that despite paying attention to enhanced supervisory communications, most companies are still inconsistent when it comes to supervisors relaying important information. Thus, even though most employees vastly prefer information from their supervisor over what they learn through rumors, many still rely on the grapevine as a primary source of information.

What can public relations departments do to combat this trend?

Some departments formalize the meeting process by mixing management and staff in a variety of formats, from gripe sessions to marketing or planning meetings. Many organizations embrace the concept of skip-level meetings in which top-level managers meet periodically with employees at levels several notches below them in the organizational hierarchy. As with any other form of communication, the value of meetings lies in their substance, their regularity, and the candor managers bring to face-to-face sessions.[27]

The Grapevine

In far too many organizations, it's neither print nor the Internet that dominates communications but rather the company grapevine. The rumor mill can be treacherous. As one employee publication described the grapevine:

> *"Once they pick up steam, rumors can be devastating. Because employees tend to distort future events to conform to a rumor, an organization must work to correct rumors as soon as possible."*

Identifying the source of a rumor is often difficult, if not impossible, and it's usually not worth the time. However, dispelling the rumor quickly and frankly is another story. Often a bad-news rumor—about layoffs, closings, and so on—can be dealt with most effectively through forthright communication. Generally, an organization makes a difficult decision after a thorough review of many alternatives. The final decision is often a compromise, reflecting the needs of the firm and its various publics, including, importantly, the workforce.

In presenting a final decision to employees, management often overlooks the value of explaining how it reached its decision. By comparing alternative solutions so that employees can understand more clearly the rationale behind management decisions, an organization may make bad news more palatable.

As diabolical as the grapevine can become, it shouldn't necessarily be treated as the enemy of effective communications with employees. Management might even consider ways to use it to its advantage. A company grapevine can be as much a communications vehicle as internal publications or employee meetings. It may even be more valuable because it is believed, and everyone seems to tap into it.

Talking Points   Dear AOL Colleague,

Just over a year ago, AOL embarked on an incredibly complex and significant transformation as we fundamentally shifted our business model from a subscription-based ISP to an advertising-supported Web company.

Today, I want to give you an update on where we are in this transition, and talk about further actions we're taking and where we're headed as a company.

So began AOL CEO Randy Falco's 2007 memo to the staff, seemingly updating the employees on developments at the embattled search engine company.

But after 10 long paragraphs of repositioning and refocusing and reenergizing the operation, right down there in paragraph 11, comes the following mention:

As a part of this realignment, tomorrow we begin a reduction in force that will, over the next couple of months, affect a total of about 2,000 people out of our worldwide workforce of 10,000.

Hello.

In other words, starting tomorrow, we begin axing 20 percent of the staff!

Talk about "hidden messages!"

AOL, it seemed, was one company that didn't have to worry about the "grapevine" giving it a bad name: Management took care of that detail, themselves!*

*For further information, see Kara Swisher, "AOL Layoffs Letter from Randy Falco," karaswisher.allthingsd.com (October 15, 2007).

Last Word

The best defense against damaging grapevine rumors is a strong and candid internal communications system. Employee communications, for years the most neglected communications opportunity in corporate America, is today much more appreciated for its strategic importance. Organizations that build massive marketing plans to sell products have begun today to apply that same knowledge and energy to communicating with their own employees.

A continuing employee relations challenge for public relations communicators is to work hand in hand with human resources officials. In the 1950s, personnel departments began to change their name to "human resources" to more accurately reflect the personal focus of their responsibilities. Over the past half century, human resources functions have concentrated on such areas as organization, staffing, benefits, and recruitment rather than communications.

The responsibility for communicating to employees has largely fallen on the public relations function, which must coordinate its initiatives with human resources priorities to create a culture of professionalism, accountability, and candor.

In the 21st century, organizations have no choice but to build rapport with and morale among employees. The shattering of morale and distrust of top management prevalent in the early years of the century will take time to repair. Building back internal credibility is a long-term process that depends on several factors—among them, listening to employees, developing information exchanges to educate employees about changing technologies, empowering them with new skills and knowledge through strategic business information they require, and adapting to the new culture of job "mobility" that is replacing job "stability."

Most of all in this new century, effective employee communications requires openness and honesty on the part of senior management. Repeating legendary Berkshire Hathaway CEO Warren Buffet: "We can afford to lose money—even a lot of money. We cannot afford to lose reputation—even a shred of reputation."[28]

Public relations professionals must seize this initiative to foster the open climate that employees want and the two-way communications that organizations need.

Discussion Starters

1. What societal factors have caused internal communications to become more important today than in the past?
2. What is the general mood of the employee public today?
3. What are the key elements to effective employee relations?
4. What are some important employee communications strategies today?
5. What are the key questions of an employee communications audit?
6. What is the status of internal print communications?
7. What are the key considerations in communicating through an intranet?
8. What are the primary tasks of an employee newsletter's editor?
9. What are the primary considerations in adopting internal video?
10. What is the best way to combat the grapevine?

Top of the Shelf   Effective Internal Communications, 2nd Edition / Lyn Smith with Pamela Mounter, Philadelphia, PA: Kogan Page Ltd., 2008

Written by a veteran of all phases of public relations work, as well as time spent as a journalist, this book offers a sound and comprehensive overview of the strategic and technical necessities of internal communications.

Included in the subject matter are chapters on organizing the function, measuring results, and dealing with the lawyers. This second edition offers updated cases and examples of how effective internal communications can help an organization achieve its goals.

Case Study   Short Circuiting the Employees at Circuit City

Electronics giant Circuit City prided itself on the knowledge and service of its cadre of in-store customer service representatives, who stood at the heart of the big retail store's operations.

That's why in the spring of 2007, the company praised its sales staff effusively—right after it lowered the boom on 3,400 stalwarts—essentially for being "*overpaid!*"

Even worse, the company invited all fired employees to "reapply" for their old jobs, at dramatically reduced salaries.

In the annals of employee relations, the Circuit City firings seemed to set a new low in "how not to deliver bad news."

Bad Days for the Big Box

As the U.S. headed into the early stages of recession in 2007, times began to get tough for big-box chain establishments, such as Circuit City (Figure 10-8). The company found itself in a perpetual price war with fellow big boxers Walmart and Best Buy over items like flat-panel televisions.

With housing markets contracting, consumers began cutting back on electronics and appliance purchases. So stores like Circuit City had no choice but to retrench as well. Circuit City braced for financial losses.

Circuit City's immediate challenge was to reduce expenses, while ensuring that customer service—for which it was well known—wouldn't be materially impacted.

The company's "solution" to this conundrum had observers scratching their heads.

On March 28, Circuit City announced that it would fire 3,400 employees—9 percent of its 40,000 staff—in stores across the country. The reason for the mass layoff, the company suggested, was that the people affected were making too much money and would be replaced by new hires willing to work for less. Specifically, many of the Circuit City salespeople, according to the company, received pay that was "*well above the market-based salary range for their role.*"

"*Retail is very competitive and store operations just have to contain their costs,*" said a slightly embarrassed Circuit City spokesman. "*We deeply regret the negative impact that was had on these folks. It was no fault of theirs.*"

Fired employees were told to leave immediately, but encouraged to reapply after 10 weeks severance pay for any openings.

Predictable Backlash

The backlash from the Circuit City beheadings was blunt and immediate.

"Circuit City Firings Blow Public Fuse," was the headline in the next day's *Washington Post*. The story quoted disgruntled Circuit City customers, who said they would become "former customers" in light of the company's treatment of its employees.

"*They weren't going after the big guys,*" said one 71-year-old former customer, "*They were going after the little guys again.*"

FIGURE 10-8 Circuit City Setback. Declining customer flow in 2007 caused Circuit City to lower the boom on 3,400 employees. (Photo: Newscom)

The fired employees, themselves, were more than eager to be interviewed by the national press. Many earned around the average hourly wage for retail salespeople of $11.50. Circuit City CEO Philip J. Schoonover, meanwhile, received a salary of $716,000, along with a $705,000 bonus and long-term compensation of $3 million in stock awards and another $340,000 in underlying options.

Said one fired computer department staff member, "*I'm ticked off that they can just come at you from one day to another, no warning, and oh, you're gone. I dedicated seven years to them. Loyalty gets you nothing.*"

Even securities analysts, who normally applaud expense cutting measures, weren't so sure the Circuit City firings might not backfire. Said one, "*It's definitely going to have some cost savings, but I think the bigger impact could be seen in weaker, poor service.*"

Despite the onslaught of bad press, Circuit City did see fit to treat at least one outgoing employee a bit better than others. When Chief Financial Officer Michael Foss announced he would be leaving the company for another position, Circuit City obligingly revised the terms of his options agreement, so that the outgoing $1-million-a-year CFO could cash in an additional $250,000 in options payoffs.

Sadly, Circuit City's teetering state of affairs, both internally and externally, helped lead to the company's filing for bankruptcy protection in November 2008.*

*For further information, see Amy Joyce, "Circuit City Firings Blow Public's Fuse," *The Seattle Times* (May 6, 2007); Yian Q. Mui, "Circuit City Cuts 3,400 'Overpaid' Workers," *Washington Post* (March 29, 2007): D1; Michael Rapoport, "After Firing 3,400 Circuit City Enriches CFO," *USA Today* (2007); and Vinee Tong and Michael Felberbaum, "Circuit City Files for Chapter 11 Protection, Will Stay Open," *Associated Press* (November 10, 2008).

Questions

1. How do you feel Circuit City handled the communications of the layoffs?

2. How would you have improved on the communication?

3. How would you characterize the company's treatment of its fired employees?

4. What would you have counseled management in terms of the departure of the CFO?

From the Top An Interview with Shaunée L. Wallace

Dr. Shaunée L. Wallace is an experienced public relations teacher and practitioner. In addition to serving as an adjunct professor at Iona College, she has worked with a variety of clients, including Def Jam Recordings, *Essence* magazine, the government of Hong Kong, Kmart, Sally Hansen Beauty Products, Royal Caribbean Cruise Lines, and United States Postal Service.

How important is employee communications today?
Employee communications is extremely important. No corporation can succeed with poor communication skills among management and their employees. In order for most organizations to accomplish their internal and external goals, communication on several levels is essential. Whether it is verbal, nonverbal, via email, or through listening, employee communications is significant.

How would you assess the level of trust between management and employees?
The level of trust between managers and employees solely depends on the individual organization. Every corporation is different. Ideally, trust is an important element within the workplace that is needed to strengthen these professional relationships.

Are print publications still effective in dealing with employees?
Print publications will always be effective, because although technology has provided that many publications can be electronic, there are still those who rely on print. As a result, you must cater to all employees.

How has the Internet affected employee communications?
The Internet has affected employee communications in a major way. Technology has made great strides in our society in general. Whether it is being used as a research tool or for email, the Internet is a necessity for most corporations. Some critics say that email has cut down on face-to-face communication time between employees and management. From an organizational communication perspective, this can have negative effects. However, overall the Internet has contributed to corporations being able to communicate more effectively and efficiently.

What can management do to improve the climate of trust within an organization?

Management can reach out to employees by showing its appreciation in several ways. These include having events such as employee appreciation days, company banquets, summer barbeques, and holiday gatherings. Additionally, providing workshops for the betterment of employees, discounts on gym memberships, and summer or relaxed Fridays (where employees in the summertime can either work half days or wear casual attire on Fridays) may ensure a comfortable work environment.

What communications advice would you give any CEO?

The advice that I would give a CEO is to have an open door policy. This states that at any time he or she is willing to listen to any issues that employees may have within the organization. I would also remind him or her that making a commitment to the success of the organization also means making a commitment to the well-being of the employees.

What can students do to prepare for internal communications work?

Students' preparation for work in internal communications can start right now. While in college, students can apply for work-study positions on campus in the communications department. I also recommend joining the student division of professional organizations such as Public Relations Society of America. Additionally, they can intern at communications firms during the summer months. This will provide a foundation for the students as they begin to build their careers in communications.

Public Relations Library

Aud, Jody Buffington. "What Internal Communicators Can Learn from Enron," *Public Relations Strategist,* Spring 2002, 11–12.

Connolly, Mickey, and Richard Rianoshek. *The Communication Catalyst.* Dearborn, MI: Conversant Solutions, LLC, 2002. Communications consultants offer a parable to help integrate internal communications.

Hollinshead, Graham, Peter Nicholls, and Stephanie Tailby. *Employee Relations,* 2nd Edition. London, England: Pearson Limited, 2003. Comprehensive and up-to-date analysis of all aspects of dealing with employees, including communications.

Holtz, Shel. *Corporate Conversations: A Guide to Crafting Effective and Appropriate Internal Communications.* New York, NY: Anacom, 2004. One of the most learned Internet experts presents a guidebook to managing all aspects of internal communications.

Leat, Mike. *Exploring Employee Relations,* 2nd Edition. Burlington, MA: Butterworth-Heinemann, 2007. Used in colleges, this text is an excellent introduction to the art of dealing with employees.

MacDonald, Lynda. *Managing Email and Internet Use,* 2nd Edition. London, England: Reed Elsevier, 2004. Solid review of the boundaries and legalities of internal email and Internet usage.

Mogel, Leonard. *An Insider's Guide to Career Opportunities,* 2nd ed. Lawrence Erlbaum, 2002.

Quirke, Bill. *Making the Connections,* 2nd Edition. Hampshire, England: Gower Publishing Limited, 2008. Outstanding analysis of how businesses can use internal communications to enhance everything from productivity to differentiation.

Ragan Report. Chicago: Ragan Communications. Weekly newsletter, written in an irreverent tone, that captures the very best and worst in internal communications.

Taylor, Winnifred. *The Dragon Complex, Identifying and Conquering Workplace Abuse.* Leawood, KS: Cypress Publishing, 2002.

Chapter 11

Community Relations

In the 21st century, most organizations—companies, hospitals, schools, sports teams, etc.—understand they have an obligation to their communities, including supporting nonprofits. But in times of economic downturn and scarce corporate resources, charitable groups must go all out to attract donations.

Occasionally, due to the Internet, they go a bit too far.

- In July 2008, Virgin Mobile began testing a national Web campaign that encouraged young people to post striptease videos of themselves as a way of raising clothing donations for homeless youth. Almost immediately, Catholic Charities and other outraged groups complained about Virgin Mobile's *"Strip2Clothe"* campaign. The company backed off.[1]

- In January 2008, the founder of GiveWell, a nonprofit research organization that assesses the effectiveness of charities, was demoted by his board and stripped of his executive director title, after it was revealed that he had promoted the organization on a Web site by posing as a prospective charitable donor seeking information. The executive director-turned-"program officer" originally posted a question on a community blog, asking about "good charities." He then answered his own question a half hour later, by praising, anonymously, his own organization. As a result, GiveWell volunteered to return money to donors.[2]

FIGURE 11-1 Mighty community relations. Catan Communications created the Mighty Milk Nutritional Drink campaign in 2007, devising the *"Be Mighty, Get Active"* essay contest to raise awareness among children to learn about living a healthier lifestyle. Winners got to meet preeminent basketball ambassador Shaquille O'Neal. (Courtesy of O'Dwyer Company)

- A month earlier, charitable donors also were impacted by the Web when hackers obtained access to the email addresses and passwords of thousands of donors to 92 charities, including the huge American Red Cross, CARE, and the American Museum of Natural History.[3]

Even the most charitable among us, it seems, are not immune to the vicissitudes of social media in the 21st century.

In the old days—1960s, 1970s, and 1980s—corporations prided themselves on their *"social responsibility."* Their premise was that with the great opportunities they were afforded, companies needed to *"give back"* to society through participation in and contributions to not-for-profit organizations committed to confront society's most pressing problems—from poverty to education to cultural and health enrichment (see Figure 11-1).

Then came the go-go 1990s and the "bubble years" of the early 2000s, when Internet stocks zoomed to dizzying heights, and corporate social responsibility took a back seat to making money—as much money as possible. When the stock market bubble burst in the early part of the decade, and economic doldrums hit in the latter years, companies struggled to support charities and charities struggled to support their constituents.

Regardless of the fortunes of the economy, there is no question that serving one's community makes good business sense. The importance of being responsible to diverse, multicultural communities has, in fact, become a front-burner business mandate.

Today's society is increasingly multicultural. America has always been a melting pot, attracting freedom-seeking immigrants from countries throughout the world. Never has this been more true than today, as America's face continues to change. Consider the following:

- By 2008, slightly more than one-third of the U.S. population of more than 300 million—about 34 percent—claimed "minority" racial or ethnic heritage, a jump of 11 percent from the start of the decade.[4] Approximately 45 million Latinos live in the United States, accounting for 15 percent of the population. African-Americans comprised the second-largest minority group, with nearly 41 million people, or almost 14 percent. Asians accounted for 15 million people, or 5 percent.

- The largest numbers of immigrants flock to six U.S. states—California, New York, Texas, Florida, Illinois, and New Jersey.[5] There is an increase in the flow of immigrants to the Southeast, upper Northeast, and the Rocky Mountain States. All of this has great influence on the messages that public relations people create.

- The minority population's buying power has been increasing as its numbers have grown. Today, ethnic minorities spend upwards of $600 billion a year out of a total U.S. economy of more than $4 trillion. Minorities own nearly 20 percent of the 23 million small business firms in the United States, according to the U.S. Small Business Administration.[6]

- Thirty years ago, there were 67 Spanish-language radio stations in the United States; today that number has increased fivefold. By 2008, African Americans and Spanish-dominant Hispanics had the highest radio listening levels of all demographic groups, propelling urban and Spanish-language stations to the top in major U.S. markets, including New York, Chicago, and San Francisco.[7] At the same time, there were also 100 Spanish-language television stations and 350 Spanish-language newspapers, serving the expanding audience.

- And, of course, the Internet, a broad canvas of interactive sites uniting the world, has spawned numerous micro-community sites, such as iVillage for women, Africana.com and BlackPlanet.com for blacks, SeniorNet for senior citizens, and Myspace.com and Facebook.com for Generation Xers. While only a handful of such communities have shown staying power over the past decade, the power of the Internet as a community "uniter" is significant.[8]

Such is the multicultural diversity enjoyed today by America and the world. The implications for organizations are profound. Almost two-thirds of the new entrants into the workforce are women, with people of color making up nearly 30 percent of these new entrants.[9]

As the arbiters of communications in their organizations, public relations people must be sensitive to society's new multicultural realities. This is a particular challenge with respect to an increasingly disenfranchised Muslim community, still impacted by the events of September 11, 2001, and the war on terrorism. Dealing in an enlightened manner with multicultural diversity and being sensitive to nuances in language and differences in style are logical extensions of the social responsibility that has been an accepted part of American organizational life since the 1960s.

Community Social Responsibility

In light of the increasing diversity of U.S. society, both profit and nonprofit organizations are also becoming more diverse and learning to deal and communicate with those who differ in work background, education, age, gender, race, ethnic origin, physical abilities, religious beliefs, sexual orientation, and other perceived differences.

More and more, organizations acknowledge their responsibilities to the community: helping to maintain clean air and water, providing jobs for minorities, enforcing policies in the interests of all employees, and, in general, enhancing everyone's quality of life. This concept of corporate social responsibility (CSR) has become widely accepted among enlightened organizations.

For example, most companies today donate a percentage of their profits to nonprofit organizations—schools, hospitals, social welfare institutions, and others. Charitable giving in the United States was estimated to be more than $306 billion in 2007, the first time in history such giving exceeded $300 billion.[10] That's good. On the other hand, in the face of the global economy's economic downturn, many nonprofit organizations who depend on corporate support feel threatened. The sad fact is that as the economy goes, so goes corporate charity.

The best companies donate as much as 2 percent or more of pretax profits. In 2004, according to the Conference Board, which polled 189 companies and corporate foundations, the philanthropic numbers were striking:

- $12 billion total estimated corporate charitable contributions in the world
- $7.8 billion corporate giving in the United States and abroad
- 54 percent of U.S. companies giving to health and human services
- 22 percent rise in U.S. giving from 2003 to 2004[11]

Until recent years, corporate philanthropy and social responsibility were uniquely American concepts. U.S. firms feel an obligation to support thousands of community-based groups working to expand affordable housing, create economic opportunity, improve public schools, and protect the environment.

Increasingly, corporate leaders—long absent from the public dialogue on community issues—have begun again to take an active stance in confronting societal challenges, such as protecting the environment. General Electric CEO Jeffrey Immelt, for example, has led his company's effort to reduce its greenhouse gas emission by 1 percent by 2012, which is really a 40 percent reduction when factoring in GE's presumed growth. Ford Motor Company executives also have worked to shift the company's energy use to renewable sources, which account for 3 percent of Ford's energy use.[12] Tiger Management founder and legendary Wall Street investor Julian Robertson has devoted significant foundation money to curbing greenhouse gasses.

Again, corporate contributions like these very much depend on profits. In the case of car companies like Ford, General Motors, and Toyota, the onset of economic crisis has effectively derailed CSR initiatives. If a company earns little, it can't give much to the community. Lucent Technologies, for example, boasted a foundation that annually contributed more than $50 million to the community (Figure 11-2).When Lucent merged with Alcatel in 2006, these grants were dramatically reduced.

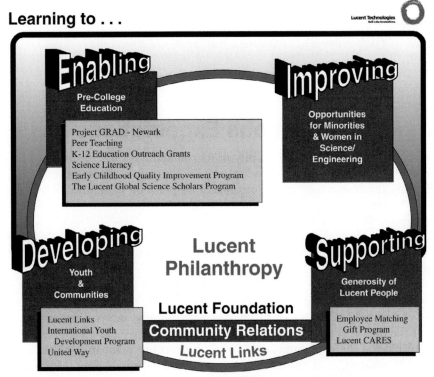

FIGURE 11-2
Enlightened self-interest. Until the fall of the telecom sector and its subsequent merger with Alcatel, Lucent Technologies was one of the most "enlightened" of corporations, annually donating more than $50 million to a wide variety of worthwhile charitable endeavors in education and youth development.

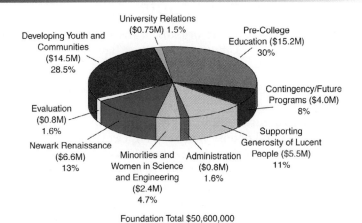

2000 Foundation Budget

Foundation Total $50,600,000

Another element of "giving back to the community" is voluntarism. A new generation of employees is coming into the business world, aware of and concerned about their firm's contribution to society.[13] Consequently, many firms, which have given generously to their communities, have become more directly involved by actively encouraging executives and employees to roll up their sleeves and volunteer to help out in their communities. At the Walt Disney Company, for example, Disney VoluntEARS spent more than 800,000 hours in volunteer services over a two-year span. At Volvo, hundreds of car dealers join forces to raise funds for pediatric cancer research at local hospitals (Figure 11-3, Figure 11-4).

Such initiatives reject the oft-quoted notion of the late University of Chicago economics professor Milton Friedman that a corporation's only responsibility is to make money and sell products so that people can be hired and paid. It is the job of the individual, not the company, Friedman argued, to serve society through philanthropy. Most companies today flatly reject the Friedman argument. They understand that in the 21st century an organization must be a *citizen* of the community in every respect and accept its role as an agent for social change in the community.

Community Relations Expectations

For an organization to coexist peacefully in its community, three skills in particular are required: (1) determining what the community knows and thinks about the organization, (2) informing the community of the organization's point of view, and (3) negotiating or mediating between the organization and the community and its constituents should there be a significant discrepancy.

Basically, every organization wants to foster positive reactions in its community. This becomes increasingly difficult in the face of protests from and disagreements with community activists. Community relations, therefore—to analyze the community, help understand its makeup and expectations, and communicate the organization's story in an understandable and uninterrupted way—are critical.

The community of an organization can vary widely, depending on the size and nature of the business. The 7-Eleven convenience store may have a community of only a few city blocks, the community of a Cadillac assembly plant may be the city where the plant is located, and the community of multinational giant McDonald's may embrace much of the world.

What the Community Expects

Communities expect from resident organizations such tangible commodities as wages, employment, and taxes. But communities have come to expect intangible contributions, too:

- **Appearance.** The community hopes that the firm will contribute positively to life in the area. It expects facilities to be attractive, with care spent on the grounds and structures. Increasingly, community neighbors object to plants that belch smoke and pollute water and air. Occasionally, neighbors organize to oppose the entrance of factories, coal mines, oil wells, drug treatment centers, and other facilities suspected of being harmful to the community's environment. NIMBY, *"not in my back yard,"* is their rallying cry.

FIGURE 11-3
From this . . .
(Courtesy of Alex's
Lemonade Stand
Foundation)

**FIGURE 11-4   . . . to
this.** In 2004, *Volvo for
Life Days* celebrated the
memory of Alexandra
Scott, a young
Philadelphia cancer
patient, who earned a
Volvo for Life award by
selling lemonade to raise
money for pediatric
cancer in 2003. A year
later Alex died, and the
car company sponsored
Alex's Lemonade Stands
throughout the country,
such as this one in
Minneapolis, to raise
funds for pediatric
cancer research.
(Courtesy of Alex's
Lemonade Stand
Foundation)

- **Participation.** As a citizen of the community, an organization is expected to participate responsibly in community affairs, such as civic functions, park and recreational activities, education, welfare, and support of religious institutions.

- **Stability.** A business that fluctuates sharply in volume of business, number of employees, and taxes paid can adversely affect the community through its impact on municipal services, school loads, public facilities, and tax revenues. Communities prefer stable organizations that will grow with the area. Conversely, they want to keep out short-term operations that could create temporary boom conditions and leave ghost towns in their wake.

- **Pride.** Any organization that can help put the community on the map simply by being there is usually a valuable addition. Communities want firms that are proud to be residents. For instance, to most Americans, Battle Creek, Michigan, means cereal; Armonk, New York, means IBM; and Hershey, Pennsylvania, *still* means chocolate (see the "Talking Points" discussion). Organizations that help build the town generally become revered symbols of pride.

What the Organization Expects

Organizations, in turn, expect to be provided with adequate municipal services, fair taxation, good living conditions for employees, a good labor supply, and a reasonable degree of support for the business and its products. When some of these requirements are missing, organizations may move to communities where such benefits are more readily available.

Talking Points A Misguided "Kiss" Goodbye

Since its founding in 1894, Hershey's was synonymous with chocolate.

Founded by Milton S. Hershey as the Hershey Chocolate Company, the firm and its legendary "Hershey's Kiss" put Hershey, Pennsylvania, on the map, as it became the largest chocolate manufacturer in North America.

Hershey, PA, was a tourist mecca, with visitors coming to partake in the 10 roller coasters at Hershey Park or line up for tours at Hershey Chocolate World or merely stroll down Chocolate Avenue and gawk at the Hershey Kiss–shaped street lights. All was blissful in Hershey (see Figure 11-5).

But then one day in 2002, it was revealed that the Hershey Trust Company, which controlled the company, was secretly trying to sell out to the William Wrigley Jr. Company of Chicago. Once the publicity hit the press, the community hit the fan!

A coalition of angry citizens formed within hours. It included former Hershey executives, union leaders, alumni of the Milton Hershey School—an educational center for orphans that Milton Hershey founded—and thousands of business owners and neighbors, all of whom feared that the sale would mean the death of their town.

In the end, the effort to "Derail the Sale" worked. The Pennsylvania Attorney General personally removed the trustees

FIGURE 11-5 Guarding the community. A statue of Milton Hershey stands guard at Hershey Park, keeping watch on the city of chocolate that he loved. (Photo: Newscom)

who voted for the sale. Other trustees were forced to resign. The sale was abandoned. The Hershey Company remained a Hershey citizen, and the value of community relations and the power of community activism triumphed.*

*For further information, see "A Wholesome Image, Jealously Guarded," ethicalcorp.com (January 23, 2006).

In the latter years of the last century, New York City experienced a substantial exodus of corporations when firms fled to neighboring Connecticut and New Jersey, as well as to the Sun Belt states of the Southeast and Southwest. New York's state and city legislators responded to the challenge by working more closely with business residents on such issues as corporate taxation. By the new century, not only had the corporate flight to the Sun Belt been arrested, but with business-oriented billionaire Michael Bloomberg as mayor, many firms reconsidered the Big Apple and returned to the now more business-friendly city and state.

The issue for most urban areas faced with steadily eroding tax bases is to find a formula that meets the concerns of business corporations while accommodating the needs of other members of the community.

Community Relations Objectives

Research into community relations indicates that winning community support for an organization is no easy matter. Studies indicate difficulty in achieving rapport with community neighbors, who expect support from the company but object to any dominance on its part in community affairs.

Organizations profit by a written community relations policy that clearly defines the philosophy of management as it views its obligation to the community. Employees, in particular, must understand and exemplify their firm's community relations policy; to many in the community, the workers are the company.

Typical community relations objectives may include the following:

1. To tell the community about the operations of the firm: its products, number of employees, size of the payroll, tax payments, employee benefits, growth, and support of community projects.

2. To correct misunderstandings, reply to criticism, and remove any disaffection that may exist among community neighbors.

3. To gain the favorable opinion of the community, particularly during strikes and periods of labor unrest, by stating the company's position on the issues involved.

4. To inform employees and their families about company activities and developments so that they can tell their friends and neighbors about the company and favorably influence opinions of the organization.

5. To inform people in local government about the firm's contributions to community welfare and to obtain support for legislation that will favorably affect the business climate of the community.

6. To find out what residents think about the organization, why they like or dislike its policies and practices, and how much they know of its policy, operations, and problems.

7. To establish a personal relationship between management and community leaders by inviting leaders to visit the plant and offices, meet management, and see employees at work.

8. To support health programs through contributions of both funds and employee services to local campaigns.

9. To contribute to culture by providing funds for art exhibits, concerts, and drama festivals and by promoting attendance at such affairs.

10. To aid youth and adult education by cooperating with administrators and teachers in providing student vocational guidance, plant tours, speakers, films, and teaching aids and by giving financial and other support to schools.

11. To encourage sports and recreational activities by providing athletic fields, swimming pools, golf courses, or tennis courts for use by community residents and by sponsoring teams and sports events.

12. To promote better local and county government by encouraging employees to run for public office or to volunteer to serve on administrative boards, by lending company executives to community agencies or to local government to give specialized advice and assistance on municipal problems, and by making company facilities and equipment available to the community in times of emergency.

13. To assist the economy of the community by purchasing operating supplies and equipment from local merchants and manufacturers whenever possible.

14. To operate a profitable business in order to provide jobs and to pay competitive wages that increase the community's purchasing power and strengthen its economy.

15. To cooperate with other local businesses in advancing economic and social welfare through joint community relations programs (Figure 11-6).

FIGURE 11-6

Community favorite. The Lowell Spinners baseball team in Lowell, Massachusetts, is an example of a beloved member of the community, not to mention of the "Red Sox Nation." The Spinners' innovative public relations director Jon Goode (left), here with 2007 World Series hero Jonathan Papelbon (and an appropriate piece of hardware), created a host of fan-sponsored events to raise money for local charities, such as cerebral palsy and cystic fibrosis. (Courtesy of Lowell Spinners)

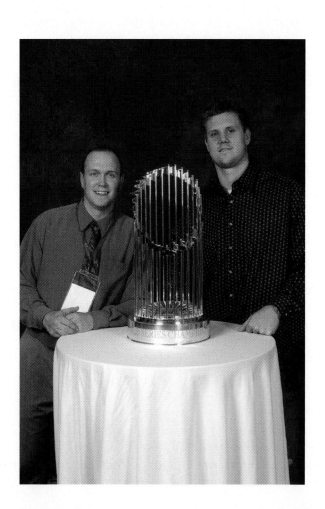

Community Relations on the Web

At the heart of the Internet is a sense of community. Indeed, the Web links people of like-minded interests in a virtual community, although "community members" may live continents away.

From this concept of community has emerged an effort to use the Internet for social good, to expand educational and commercial opportunities for minority communities as well as provide a philanthropic forum. For example:

- Black Entertainment Television created BET.com to bring "connectivity, content, and commerce" to African Americans, a community relatively underrepresented in cyberspace. Although 80 percent of non-Hispanic white children use a computer at home, only 48 percent each of African American and Hispanic children use a computer at home.[14] So, armed with $35 million, the largest online investment ever aimed at African Americans, BET.com hoped to help African Americans become more computer savvy. Although some black-oriented sites, like other so-called "vertical Web sites," among them the NetNoir.com pop culture portal and the urban youth-oriented Volume.com portal, have suffered cutbacks in recent years, established media companies have used the Web to attract minority followers. Time Warner paid $10 million for Africana.com in an effort to attract more African American users to AOL.[15] And in 2008, the Washington Post launched *The Root*, an online magazine focused on black culture and society.[16]

- In a more global community effort, AOL teamed up with the world's greatest musicians in July 2005 to present LIVE 8, a simultaneous concert in Philadelphia, London, Paris, Berlin, and Rome, designed to turn the world's attention to ending poverty. AOL streamed the broadcast, featuring artists from Alicia Keys and Linkin Park in Philadelphia to Paul McCartney and UB40 in London to Green Day and Roxy Music in Berlin. Five days after the concerts, the G8 leaders of the world's most industrialized nations met and promised to contribute $50 billion more in aid per year by 2010 and to cancel debts owed by 18 of the world's poorest countries.[17]

- Less successful have been socially responsible Web sites, wholly devoted to raising e-commerce funds for charity. One of the most ambitious, GreaterGood.com, closed in 2001, unable to sustain itself.[18] In less prosperous economic times, a more viable model seemed to be one where for-profit and nonprofit organizations alike devoted part of online purchases toward charitable causes.

Although the Web may be characterized by some as anonymous, acrimonious, and heartless, efforts such as these underscore the Internet's immense potential in furthering human relations and progress—across common communities and for the larger society.

Serving Diverse Communities

What were once referred to as minorities are rapidly becoming the majority. Today, 38 million Americans are foreign born.[19] The U.S. Census Bureau reports that more than two-thirds of current U.S. and future population growth is and will be the result of immigration.

According to the Census Bureau, Latinos have overtaken African Americans as the America's largest minority group, reaching 45.5 million in 2007, compared to about 41 million blacks and 15 million Asians.

For many years, women were considered a minority by public relations professionals. This is no longer the case; women now dominate not only the public relations field but also many service industries. Women, African Americans, Latinos, Asians, gays, seniors, persons with disabilities, and a variety of other groups have become not only important members of the labor force but also important sources of discretionary income.

Public relations professionals must be sensitive to the demands of all for equal pay, promotional opportunities, equal rights in the workplace, and so on. Communicating effectively in light of the multicultural diversity of society has become an important public relations challenge.

Women

In the 21st century, women have made great strides in leveling the playing field between their roles and compensation schedules and those of their male counterparts. The days of "mommy tracks" and "mommy wars," glass ceilings, and pink-collar ghettos are rapidly falling by the wayside.

Women today head large corporations and serve as economic advisers to presidential candidates, with John McCain's 2008 campaign boasting two such female financial experts—Meg Whitman, former CEO of eBay, and Carly Fiorina, former CEO of Hewlett-Packard—as well as vice president nominee Alaska Gov. Sarah Palin.

In public relations, women have steadily climbed into middle- and upper-management positions, both at corporations and public relations agencies. Indeed, with the Public Relations Student Society of American now reporting 90 percent women, the field is among the strongest for opportunities for women.[20]

Hispanics

There is little question that companies need to reach Latinos. Currently 45.5 million strong, Hispanics are the fastest growing minority in the nation. The Census Bureau predicts that by 2050, Latinos will comprise one-third of the population, nearly 100 million people.[21]

The U.S. Hispanic population already ranks as the fifth largest in the world, behind Mexico, Spain, Colombia, and Argentina. In the United States, 77 percent of Hispanics reside mainly in seven states—California, Texas, New York, Florida, Arizona, New Jersey, and Illinois.

New York City has the largest Latin population with 2 million residents. Los Angeles rates second with 1.7 million. The majority of U.S. Latinos—59 percent—are of Mexican origin. About 10 percent are of Puerto Rican origin, and 4 percent are of Cuban origin. In Los Angeles, Latino kindergarten enrollment is 66 percent and rising. The Anglo enrollment is 15 percent and falling.[22]

Accordingly, Latinos comprise a potent political and economic force. Between 1994 and 1998, Latino voting in nationwide midterm elections jumped 27 percent, even as overall voter turnout dropped. In terms of commerce, U.S. Latinos pump $400 billion a year into the economy.[23]

Latinos are voracious media consumers, relying heavily on television and radio to stay informed. Two large Spanish-programming networks, Univision and Telemundo, dominate the airwaves, with Univision drawing 83 percent of the country's adult, prime-time, Spanish-language viewing audience. CNN also offers a daily program in Spanish for its Latin American viewers.

Magazines also are a great source of entertainment to the Latino community, with more than 200 Hispanic publications hitting the market in the last 10 years, including *Latin CEO* for top executives to *Latina* magazine for teenage girls to *Healthy Kids en Español* for parents to the general-interest *Latina* and *People en Español*.[24]

In addition, radio stations and newspapers that communicate in Spanish, such as *El Mundo, El Tiempo, El Diario,* and *La Prensa,* are all prominent voices in reaching this increasingly important community.

Blacks

The black population has slowed its growth in recent years, increasing by just 1 percent between 2006 and 2007. New York has the largest black population, followed by Florida and Texas. In the District of Columbia, the black population comprises 56 percent of the population.[25] In addition, foreign-born blacks have increased materially in numbers. In Miami, the West Indian population makes up nearly 50 percent of the black population. In New York, nearly a third of the black population is foreign-born.

The socioeconomic status of blacks has improved in recent years primarily due to large increases in women's incomes. While black median family income has improved, black men have recently experienced a decline in income. Median family income of blacks ages 30 to 39 was only 58 percent that of white families in the same age group ($35,000 for blacks compared to $60,000 for whites).[26] As a consequence, black children grow up in families with much lower income than white children.

Black disposable income has increased markedly in recent years, now well in excess of $700 billion yearly.[27] Despite their continuing evolution in the white-dominated workplace, the nation's 41 million blacks can still be reached effectively through special media:

- Black Entertainment Television is a popular network that has done well.
- Local African American radio stations have prospered.
- Pioneering Internet sites, such as TheRoot.com, BlackFamilies.com, Blackvoices.com, NetNoir.com, and the Black World Today (www.tbwt.com), have created a culture of acceptance and desirability for Web access among African Americans.
- Magazines such as *Black Enterprise* and *Essence* are national vehicles. *Ebony*, the largest African American–oriented publication in the world and publishing since 1945, has a circulation of 1.6 million.[28]
- Newspapers, such as the *Amsterdam News* in New York City and the *Daily Defender* in Chicago, also are targeted to African Americans. Such newspapers are controlled by active owners whose personal viewpoints dominate editorial policy.

One area of frustration in improving the livelihood of African Americans is the practice of public relations. The field has failed to attract sufficient numbers of African American practitioners to its ranks. In recent years, the Public Relations Society of America has increased outreach efforts to attract and retain African Americans. It established the D. Parke Gibson Pioneer Award in 1994 to recognize a practitioner who increases awareness of public relations within multicultural communities. Parke Gibson was a pioneer in multicultural relations and author of two books on African American consumerism. In 2008, the PRSA launched a three-year "State of Multicultural Public Relations" initiative to assess the gains and needs in increasing the diversity of public relations practitioners.

The National Black Public Relations Society was created to increase the participation of and resources available to black public relations professionals. It has seven chapters and sponsors an annual conference.

Attracting African Americans to the field remains a great challenge to public relations leaders in the new century.

Other Ethnic Groups

Beyond Latinos, other ethnic groups—particularly Asians—have increased their importance in the American marketplace.

The U.S. Asian population totals 15 million, with California hosting one-third of that total. New York and Texas follow. Asians comprise the largest minority group in Hawaii and Vermont.

Japanese, Chinese, Koreans, Vietnamese, and others have gained new prominence as consumers and constituents.

The formation of the Asian American Advertising and Public Relations Alliance in California underscored the increasing prominence of Asian Americans in the public relations profession.

Finally, there is perhaps the most misunderstood and put-upon public in this post-9/11 world: Muslims. Since the attacks on America in 2001, life has become more difficult for many of the estimated 1.4 million Muslims living in the United States. In terms of U.S. media, Arabic television stations like Al Jazeera or PTV, the state-run Pakistan Television, are accessible and frequently employ American journalists. In 2004, Bridges TV, an English-language network with programming aimed at American Muslims, made its debut. The primary purpose of Bridges TV, said its founder, was to *"build bridges of understanding between American Muslims and mainstream America."*[29]

Gays, Seniors, and Others

In the 21st century, a diverse assortment of special communities has gravitated into the mainstream of American commerce. One such group is the gay market. To some, homosexuality may remain a target of opprobrium, but in the 21st century, the gay market, estimated at 12 to 20 million Americans, comprises a major target of opportunity.

Advocates for the lesbian, gay, bisexual, and transgender (LGBT) community, such as the Gay & Lesbian Alliance Against Defamation, are increasingly active and outspoken. In the 2008–2009 television season, a record 16 LGBT characters were regulars on network scripted series programs.[30] More major companies offer benefits and protections to LGBT employees. An increasing number of marketers, including IBM, United Airlines, and Anheuser-Busch, run advertisements with gay themes. Accordingly, a vibrant gay media market—from magazines *The Advocate* and *Out* to Internet portal GayWired.com to premium gay cable TV network Here—has emerged.[31]

Attitudes toward gay people, too, are changing. The number of Americans who think gays should have access to equal rights in employment and public accommodations rose from 56 percent in 1977 to 83 percent in 2000.[32] And gay marriage has become a prominent issue in state and federal elections, although the Census Bureau—to much protest in the gay community—announced early that it wouldn't recognize such unions in the 2010 Census.[33]

The clear conclusion is that the gay market—average age 36, household income six times higher than the national average and with more discretionary income than average, three times more likely to be college graduates than the national average, and 86 percent of whom saying they would purchase products specifically marketed to them—has become extremely attractive to all kinds of marketers.

Senior citizens also have become an important community for public relations professionals and the organizations they represent. The baby boomer generation has steamed past 50 years of age. Together, the over-50 crowd controls more than 50 percent of America's discretionary income. The American Association of Retired Persons, founded in 1958 for women and men over 50, has a membership of more than 35 million, about half of whom, despite the group's name, still work for a living.

As the American population grows older, the importance of senior citizens—as consumers, voters, and opinion leaders—will increase. Public relations professionals must be sensitive to that reality and to the fact that other special communities in society will increasingly demand specialized treatment and targeted communications.

PR Ethics

Mini-Case Loose-Lipped Laureate Utters a Diversity "No-No"

"Loose lips," so the saying goes, *"sink ships."*

And that, alas, turned out to be the case (all fictitious) with the eminent biologist, Holmes Sherlock, former winner of the Nobel Prize for Biology and one of the world's most knowledgeable experts in the field of DNA.*

While in Paris in October to promote his latest book on scientific research and to give a speech before the Paris Council of Scientists, the 80-year-old Dr. Sherlock agreed to an interview with the newspaper, *Le Monde.*

In discussing the relative intelligence of different groups of people, the irascible scientist was quoted in *Le Monde* as suggesting that *"People of African descent are less intelligent than people of European descent."*

The newspaper interview, which smacked of "racism," was reported around the world and immediately touched off an immediate international firestorm.

- The Paris Council of Scientists canceled the Sherlock lecture.

- The laboratory where Dr. Sherlock served as president, Warm Springs Laboratory on Staten Island, suspended him.

- Dr. Sherlock, himself, immediately apologized for his comments and canceled the remainder of his European trip. Said a shaken and chagrined Dr. Sherlock, *"I am ashamed of these comments, do not believe them, did not mean them to be interpreted this way, and don't believe at all that there is any scientific basis for them."*

Meanwhile, the president of the University of Chicago faced a dilemma. In April, the board of trustees of Chicago's prestigious Science Institute voted to award Dr. Sherlock the Distinguished Prize for Lifetime Contribution to Science. The prize consists of an award of $10,000 and a speech by the honoree before the university community.

Dr. Sherlock's speech at the university is scheduled next week.

The university president knows that whatever decision the university makes, relative to the Sherlock speech, will become big news.

On the one hand, he already has received a slew of emails from students and faculty, demanding the university revoke the award and the speech. One student blogger wrote, *"We should not be a party to racism in any dimension. The University must, under no circumstances, reward such a bigot and allow him to speak on our hallowed premises."*

Several members of the 20-person board of trustees of the Chicago Science Institute have called the president, wondering whether the university should revoke Dr. Sherlock's prize.

On the other hand, the president is well aware of the furor surrounding the 2007 speech of Iranian President Mahmoud Ahmadinejad at Columbia University and the stand that university took as a defender of *"freedom of speech."* In this regard, another student blogger wrote," *Academic freedom means we are confident enough to hear from all viewpoints, including those like Pres. Ahmadinejad and Prof. Sherlock, whose attitudes may be repugnant to civil thinking. We should allow the lecture to go on."*

Questions

1. Should the university award Dr. Sherlock the prize and allow him to speak?

2. Depending on your answer to question 1, how would you explain the university's decision?

*This case is true. The names have been changed to protect your author!

Nonprofit Public Relations

Among the most important champions of multiculturalism in any community are not-for-profit or just plain *nonprofit* organizations. Nonprofit organizations serve the social, educational, religious, and cultural needs of the community around them. So important is the role of public relations in nonprofit organizations that this sector is a primary source of employment for public relations graduates.

The nonprofit sector is characterized by panoply of institutions: hospitals, schools, trade associations, labor unions, chambers of commerce, social welfare agencies, religious institutions, cultural organizations, and the like. The general goals of nonprofit agencies are not dissimilar to those of corporations. Nonprofits seek to win public support of their mission and programs through active and open communications.

Unlike corporations, though, nonprofits also seek to broaden volunteer participation in their efforts, often through the use of controversial communications tactics to raise public awareness through *media advocacy*. Media advocacy, simply defined, is public relations without resources. Protests, marches, demonstrations, media photo opportunities, stealth Internet campaigns, and the like are all fair game in media advocacy (Figure 11-7).

Master of Many Trades

Also unlike corporations, nonprofits generally don't have much money for key activities—especially in times of economic downturn. That's why public relations professionals in nonprofits must be masters of many functions; key among them are positioning the organization, developing a marketing or promotional plan, orchestrating media relations, and supporting fund-raising.

Positioning the Organization

With thousands of competitors vying for support dollars, a nonprofit must stand out from the rest. This positioning initiative, to differentiate itself, depends largely on the

FIGURE 11-7 Grin and bear it. A "polar bear" sliced into the world's largest "Baked Alaska" during an '05 "Earth Day" demonstration against drilling in the Arctic National Wildlife Region. (Courtesy of O'Dwyer Company)

Points 13 Rules for Radicals

Want to know how to organize a winning protest on campus with no money?

No problem.

Here are the time-honored suggestions of labor leader Saul Alinsky, from his 1971 classic, *Rules for Radicals* (see "Top of the Shelf"). They are just as relevant now as they were nearly four decades ago. (*Just don't tell anybody where you learned 'em!*)

1. Power is not only what you have but what the enemy thinks you have.
2. Never go outside the experience of your people.
3. Whenever possible, go outside the experience of the enemy.
4. Make the enemy live up to its own book of rules.
5. Ridicule is a person's most potent weapon.
6. A good tactic is one that your people enjoy.
7. A tactic that drags on too long becomes a drag.
8. Keep the pressure on.
9. The threat is usually more terrifying than the thing itself.
10. The major premise for tactics is the development of operations that will maintain a constant pressure on the opposition.
11. If you push a negative hard and deep enough, it will break through to its counter side.
12. The price of a successful attack is a constructive alternative.
13. Pick the target, freeze it, personalize it, and polarize it.

public relations function. To successfully position the organization, a practitioner must ask:

1. What position do we own; that is, who are we?
2. What position do we want?
3. Who else is out there, and what is their position?
4. Do we have the funds to get us where we wish to go?
5. Can we stick it out over time?
6. Do all our communications line up with each other?

No organization, particularly a resource-challenged nonprofit, can afford to be all things to all people. The best nonprofits, like the best corporations, stand for something. And they are unafraid to "break a few eggs" in order to achieve a clear and differentiable identity (Figure 11-8).

Developing a Marketing/Promotional Plan

Often in nonprofits, the public relations director is the marketing director is the advertising director is the promotion director. The job, simply, is marketing the organization to raise its profile, respect, and levels of support. This requires planning in terms of audiences, messages, and vehicles to deliver those messages to those audiences. Crucial in framing these messages is to recognize the *cause-related* quotient—that is, what the organization stands for—around which the marketing campaign is based.

Nonprofit public relations campaigns must depend on clear and coherent messages that articulate well-formulated strategies. Therefore, the nonprofit public relations professional must (1) plan, (2) define issues, (3) build strategies, (4) frame issues, (5) develop talking points, (6) choose appropriate spokespersons, (7) develop communications materials, and (8) target messages.

Media Relations

Because most nonprofits lack sufficient resources for advertising or formal marketing, the use of "free" media is a critical public relations function. As National Public Radio

FIGURE 11-8
Communications hardball. Nonprofits must make every communications dollar count: When the American Cancer Society, American Heart Association, American Lung Association, and Campaign for Tobacco-Free Kids got together against big tobacco, they pulled no punches. (Courtesy of Tobacco Free Kids)

broadcaster Daniel Schorr once put it, *"If you don't exist in the media, for all practical purposes you don't exist."* Nonprofits desperately need media advocates who champion their cause and mission. Advocacy strategy can take the form of a variety of initiatives:

- **Talk radio.** The extensive audience of this medium is a natural way to spread the nonprofit gospel.
- **Cable television.** So, too, is the nonstop menu of nightly cable talk television programs, all hungry for outspoken, opinionated, articulate guests.
- **Op eds.** Opinion editorials drafted by nonprofit executives are another prominent—and cheap!—way of getting points of view aired to an influential audience.
- **Cable access.** Community channels are generally willing repositories for nonprofit programming and talent.
- **Web access.** The Internet has opened up a limitless vista for nonprofits to spread their messages, not only throughout the community but around the world.

Supporting Fund-Raising

Nonprofits depend on donors for support. Fund-raising, therefore, is a key nonprofit challenge that must engage the attention of the organization's key executives. Public relations professionals must be intimately involved in fund-raising communications and appeals so that messages can be targeted and consistent with the organization's general position.

Clearly, there are many other duties of the nonprofit public relations professional. Nonprofit public relations and marketing are described by some as *"performing, pleading, petitioning, and praying."*

Nonetheless, because America is a nation of joiners and belongers, nonprofit organizations in our society will most certainly continue to proliferate. And the need for competent public relations help will continue to be central to their existence and vitality.

Fund-raising—the need to raise money to support operations—lies at the heart of every nonprofit institution. Schools, hospitals, churches, and organizations—from the mighty United Way to the smallest block association—can't exist without a constant source of private funds. Frequently, the fund-raising assignment becomes the province of public relations professionals. Like other aspects of public relations work, fund-raising must be accomplished in a planned and programmatic way.

A successful fund-raising campaign should include the following basic steps:

1. **Identify campaign plans and objectives.** Broad financial targets should be set. A goal should be announced. Specific sectors of the community from which funds might be extracted should be targeted in advance.

2. **Organize fact-finding.** Relevant trends that might affect giving should be noted. Relations with various elements of the community should be defined. The national and local economies should be considered, as should current attitudes toward charitable contributions.

3. **Recruit leaders.** The best fund-raising campaigns are those with strong leadership. A hallmark of local United Way campaigns, for example, is the recruitment of strong business leaders to spearhead contribution efforts. It is the responsibility of the nonprofit itself to direct its leaders, particularly outside directors, so that their efforts can be targeted in the best interests of the organization.

4. **Plan and implement strong communications activities.** The best fund-raising campaigns are also the most visible. Publicity and promotion must be stressed. Special events should be organized, particularly featuring national and local celebrities to support the drive. Updates on fund-raising progress should be communicated, particularly to volunteers and contributors.

5. **Periodically review and evaluate.** Review the fund-raising program as it progresses. Make midcourse corrections when activities succeed or fail beyond expectations. Evaluate program achievements against program targets. Revise strategies constantly as the goal becomes nearer.[34]

Because many public relations graduates enter the nonprofit realm, knowledge of fund-raising strategies and techniques is especially important. Beginning practitioners, once hired in the public relations office of a college, hospital, religious group, charitable organization, or other nonprofit organization, are soon confronted with questions about how public relations can help raise money for the organization.

Last Word

The increasing cultural diversity of society in the 21st century has spawned a wave of "political correctness," particularly in the United States. Predictably, many have questioned whether sensitivity to women, people of color, the physically challenged, gays, seniors, and other groups has gone too far. One thing, however, is certain. The makeup of society—of consumers, employees, political constituents, and so on—has been altered inexorably. The number of discrete communities with which organizations must be concerned will continue to increase.

Intelligent organizations in our society must be responsive to the needs and desires of their communities. Positive community relations must begin with a clear understanding of community concerns, an open door for community leaders, an open and honest flow of information from the organization, and an ongoing sense of continuous involvement and interaction with community publics.

The public relations profession, responsible as it is for managing the communications of an organization, must take the lead in dealing with diversity. Indeed, in 2004, the Public Relations Society of America initiated Advancing Diversity, a national initiative uniting various elements to promote multiculturalism in both the public relations industry and the business community.[35]

Community relations is only as effective as the support it receives from top management. Once that support is clear, it becomes the responsibility of the public relations professional to ensure that the relationship between the organization and all of its multicultural communities is one of mutual trust, understanding, and support.

Discussion Starters

1. How is the atmosphere for community relations different today than it was even at the turn of the century?
2. What is meant by the term *multicultural diversity*?
3. In general terms, what does a community expect from a resident organization?
4. What are typical community relations objectives for an organization?
5. What was the philosophy of corporate responsibility espoused by economist Milton Friedman?
6. What is meant by the term *media advocacy*?
7. Why do companies need to reach the Latino community?
8. What are the primary responsibilities of a nonprofit public relations professional?
9. What is meant by the term *corporate social responsibility*?
10. What are the basic steps of a fund-raising campaign?

Top of the Shelf Rules for Radicals: A Practical Primer for Realistic Radicals / Saul D. Alinsky, New York: Vintage Books, 1989

As ancient as it is, Alinsky's *Rules for Radicals,* originally published in 1971, is still the classic handbook for those bent on organizing communities, rattling the status quo, and effecting social and political change as well as for those who wish to learn from a legendary master.

Alinsky, a veteran community activist who fought on behalf of the poor from New York to California, provides strategies for building coalitions and for using communication, conflict, and confrontation advantageously.

In "Of Means and Ends," Alinsky lists his 13 tactics of engagement (See "*Talking Points,*" this chapter) and 11 rules of ethics that define the uses of radical power.

Alinsky supports his principles with numerous examples, the most colorful of which occurred when he wanted to draw attention to a particular cause in Rochester, New York. Alinsky and his group attended a Rochester Symphony Orchestra performance—after a meal of nothing but beans. The results were predictable—and very funny.

Alinsky died in 1972, but his lessons endure in this offbeat guide to seizing power. Whether your goal is to fluster the establishment or defend it, *Rules for Radicals* is the organizer's bible.

Case Study | The Summers of Harvard's Diversity Discontent

As any self-respecting professor knows all too well, the halls of academia are loaded with sharks. And few are more vulnerable to those denizens of the deep than university presidents who choose to rock the boat. When the presidential boat-rocking concerns the issue of diversity—look out.

An Ideal President

When Lawrence Summers became the president of Harvard University in 2001, it seemed like the perfect choice. His career as a college professor and government official had culminated in his service as U.S. Secretary of the Treasury under President Clinton. A distinguished academic in his earlier days at Harvard, Summers seemed ideal to lead his alma mater, arguably the nation's most prominent institution of higher learning.

Summers, known for his candor and outspokenness, dedicated his presidency to refining Harvard's approach to enhance student learning. He called for a new emphasis on undergraduates and argued that their curriculum should focus more on actual knowledge and quantitative disciplines and less on ways of thinking. And he took bold steps to make a Harvard education more accessible to low-income families. While these objectives were all laudable, the approach Summers took to realize them was most controversial—particularly in an environment like Harvard's, where professors were used to calling their own shots.

Rapping the Rapper

Summers's first public brouhaha occurred when he called in well-known black studies professor and inspired self-promoter Cornel West for a private chat. The president was concerned that West was falling down in one particular area that Summers somehow thought important for an institution of higher learning: scholarship. Specifically, Summers wanted West to produce more scholarly articles and do more scholarly research. While West wrote prolifically, the caliber of that writing, according to some, left something to be desired. The *New Republic,* for example, labeled West's books as *"almost completely worthless."*

Not that Cornel West wasn't busy. He was a frequent talking head on cable television talk shows, an outspoken political activist, and an active entertainer, writing and performing rap music. As a teacher, West was renowned for giving out lots of A's. The students loved him.

When Summers, in West's opinion, pushed too hard, the professor loudly went public to protest. The dispute quickly took on overtones of racism, and when the dust cleared and Summers had apologized, West had flown the coop to take up residence at Harvard rival Princeton University.

Summers also stirred up the campus by belittling a campaign that urged divestment of Harvard investments in Israeli companies, suggesting that such an approach was a form of subtle anti-Semitism. This bold stance, too, angered some in the faculty.

Women and Science

Summers's diversity dilemma deteriorated further in the spring of 2001 when, at a closed-door, off-the-record conference of economists, he raised the subject of why there were so few women in the sciences and engineering profession. The leaked transcript revealed that Summers wondered about the "intrinsic aptitude" of women, the career pressures they face, and discrimination within universities.

The Harvard president went on to compare the relatively low number of women in the sciences to the numbers of Catholics in investment banking, whites in the National Basketball Association, and Jews in farming.

As soon as the remarks hit the press—in the form of a front-page story in the *New York Times*—the Harvard campus went ballistic (see Figure 11-9). Irate faculty members called for the president's scalp. Charges of sexism were added to the earlier charges of racism.

Lost in the hysteria were other remarks Summers made at the same conference, that racial and sex discrimination needed to be "absolutely, vigorously" combated. It didn't seem to matter. It was open season on the president. As one *"objective authority"* quoted by the *Times,* good old Princeton Professor Cornel West , charitably put it, *"It was good to see the faculty wake up. The chickens have come home to roost."*

Once again, faced with growing hostility, Summers went public and apologized, offering to redouble resources for women in science. But his apology wasn't in time to stop a "no confidence" vote of the faculty of Arts and Sciences.

FIGURE 11-9 "Larry must go." At least that's what the protesters who sought the Harvard president's scalp were advocating. (Photo: Newscom)

The Final Straw

The end for Larry Summers at Harvard came a year after the women in science flap, ignominiously enough, with the president away on a skiing vacation in the first months of 2006.

Summers's detractors among Harvard's faculty were circling to unseat him. While Summers was vacationing, a former Arts and Sciences dean went public with the two-word reason for his departure a year earlier: "Larry Summers."

The former dean gave the *Boston Globe,* Harvard's hometown newspaper, a searing account of Summers's autocratic management style, accusing the president of declaring that those in the field of economics (Summers's field) were *"smarter than political scientists and sociologists."* The interview ended with the former dean calling for the resignation of his former boss.

The groundswell of faculty opprobrium could not be stopped. Calls came for Summers's firing. Even supporters in the faculty expressed frustration that Summers was forever apologizing for his remarks. An emergency meeting of the Harvard Board was discussed.

And Summers, the experienced Washington political hand hunkered down in his mountaintop vacation retreat, knew the party was over.

On February 21, 2006, Larry Summers returned to Harvard, called a news conference on the quadrangle, and announced his resignation (see Figure 11-10).

In a poll of the Harvard student body, only 19 percent thought the president should resign. It was too late.*

*In America, there are always *"second acts."* True to form, two years after Larry Summers resigned ignominiously from Harvard, he was right back on top as President Barack Obama's lead White House economic advisor and architect of the President's plans to revive the American economy. (Even Cornel West was impressed!)

FIGURE 11-10 **Larry's last stand.** Surrounded by "death watch" media and students, Harvard President Larry Summers prepares to announce his resignation. (Photo: Newscom)

Questions

1. Do you think Larry Summers was too outspoken?

2. How would you characterize Summers's remarks about diversity?

3. Was it wise for the president to apologize after his public spats with the faculty?

4. If you were Larry Summers's public relations advisor, what would you have counseled him to do in presiding over such a tumultuous situation?

5. If you were the Harvard Board's public relations advisor, what would you have advised it to do about the Summers situation?

For further information, see Dean Barnett, "The End of Summers," *Weekly Standard* (February 22, 2006); Peter Beinart, "Harvard: Coup of the Selfish," *New York Post* (February 25, 2006); Sara Rimer and Patrick D. Healy, "Furor Lingers as Harvard Chief Gives Details of Talk on Women," *New York Times* (February 18, 2005): A1, 20; Thomas Sowell, "Another Victim of Academe Run Amok," *The Record* (February 26, 2006); James Traub, "Lawrence Summers, Provocateur," *New York Times* (January 23, 2005).

From the Top An Interview with Mike Paul

Mike Paul, the "Reputation Doctor," is a veteran of strategic public relations, corporate communications, and reputation management. He is president and senior counselor of MGP and Associates PR (MGP). MGP was founded by Paul in 1994 and is a leading boutique public relations and reputation management firm based in New York, providing senior counseling services to top corporate, government, nonprofit, sports, and entertainment clients. In 2004, *PRWeek Magazine* named Paul one of the top crisis communications and reputation management counselors in the world.

How important is an organization's or individual's reputation?

Reputations of all types are so important, I made it our firm's tag line: "Because Your Reputation Is Everything!"™ A reputation is the greatest asset we have, for both a public company and an individual. It must be built, maintained, and repaired to thrive for a lifetime. Sadly, many corporations, organizations, and individuals talk the talk of the importance of reputation, but don't walk the walk.

(Courtesy of Fraser P. Seitel)

How can reputation be managed?
The big "bricks" of managing an excellent reputation include truth, humility, transparency, accountability, consistency. Honesty and humility are the most important tools in a reputation management tool belt. Like any disease, a reputation in crisis is a disease that can be cured or can grow out of control and cause severe damage in other areas. Admitting mistakes, lies, and deceit is the first step in reputation management.

What is the state of community relations among organizations today?
Community relations among U.S. organizations are becoming much better, but there is still much work to be done and further commitment and accountability from senior management is necessary to achieve excellence. For example, many community organizations are not teaming up with similar organizations in their arena to achieve community goals. Many are islands among themselves and believe partnering with other community organizations is not part of their mission. One goal of any community relations campaign should be to mirror the population in which you serve.

What is the state of social responsibility among corporations?
Corporate social responsibility has become a key communications and business tool for most corporations today. However, corporations must realize social responsibility has both a community responsibility and a business obligation.

For example, a successful social responsibility campaign—local, national, or global—cannot be just a pet project of a CEO or senior management. It must include social and community responsibility interests important to many key audiences, including employees, investors, customers, and the communities in which the corporation operates.

How important is it for an organization to focus on dealing with minorities?
Minorities have become the majority in many communities across the United States and around the world. As a result, minority is not an accurate word to use any more for communities or people of color. People, employees, or executives of color are now the appropriate terms to use because of the huge demographic shift in the world. As a result, corporate America and other organizations have begun to truly embrace diversity, but there is much more work to be done. However, the executive ranks are still void of many people of color, and sadly, racism is still alive in many corporations, organizations, and communities in the United States and around the world.

What is the state of African Americans in the public relations business?
Two words: in crisis. There are still few African Americans in public relations overall and even fewer executives of color in leadership positions. Most work for community organizations and in government. There has still not been an African American CEO within any of the top 10 global PR firms and very few top global corporate communications executives. Until the CEOs of PR firms and corporate America embrace the problem with the same intensity from both the bottom and the top levels, diversity in PR will continue to be in crisis. Accountability and transparency are both necessary to develop lasting change.

What advice would you give young minority members interested in a public relations career?
First, for young people of color, there are not many executives of color in our business. As a result, seeking a career in our business is a tougher road. The numbers don't lie. Second, seek employment at a top global PR firm to best learn the business and work in as many different divisions as possible. The training programs at these firms are superior to others, and the type of clients you will work with are top notch and best for building skills and an excellent resume. Third, seek out an excellent mentor, and the mentor does not have to be an executive of color. For example, I have the best mentor in our business, Harold Burson of Burson-Marsteller. He gave me excellent advice years ago when I was at B-M, and he still gives me excellent advice today. Many young professionals of color make the mistake of only seeking executives of color. This is a big mistake.

Public Relations Library

Banks, James A., and Cherry Banks. *Multicultural Education: Characteristics and Goals*. Hoboken, NJ: John Wiley & Sons, 2005. A compilation of leading academic scholars and researchers about multiculturalism.

Burke, Edmund. *Managing a Company in an Activist World*. Westport, CT: Praeger Publishing, 2005. Outstanding explanation of corporate outreach to enhance community citizenship.

Derickson, Rossella, and Krista Henley. *Awakening Social Responsibility*. Silicon Valley, CA: Derickson and Henley, 2007. This text calls for individuals to lead their companies down the path of sustainable development, business ethics, philanthropy, and giving.

Dresser, Norine. *Multicultural Manners: Essential Rules of Etiquette for the 21st Century*. Hoboken, NJ: John Wiley & Sons, 2005. The do's and don'ts of dealing in business with people of different backgrounds.

Fineglass, Art. *The Public Relations Handbook for Nonprofits*. San Francisco: Jossey-Bass, 2005. All a nonprofit organization needs to organize and implement an effective public relations program.

Harrison, E. Bruce. *Corporate Greening 2.0: Create and Communicate Your Company's Climate Change and Sustainability Strategies*. Exeter, NH: Publishing Works, 2008. The most knowledgeable person in public relations about climate change analyzes the positions on the environment of 40 companies and business groups.

Haywood, Roger. *Corporate Reputation, The Brand and the Bottom Line*. 3rd Edition. London, England: Kogan Page, Ltd., 2005. Storehouse of case studies on institutions that have successfully managed their reputations.

John, Steve, and Stuart Thomson. *New Activism and the Corporate Response*. New York, NY: Palgrave MacMillan, 2003. Interesting discussion of Internet activism and how to deal with it.

Kotler, Philip, and Nancy Lee. *Corporate Social Responsibility: Doing the Most Good for Your Company and Your Cause*. Hoboken, NJ: John Wiley & Sons, 2005. Real-world advice from noted marketing professor Kotler and a respected colleague.

Levine, Bertram. *Resolving Racial Conflict*. Columbia, MO: University of Missouri Press, 2005. The former community relations director of the U.S. Justice Department traces the history of the civil rights movement in America.

McIntosh, Malcolm. *Raising a Ladder to the Moon*. New York, NY: Palgrave MacMillan, 2003. Comprehensive discussion of all aspects of corporate responsibility and citizenship.

Miller, Patrick. *Sport and the Color Line: Black Athletes and Race Relations in Twentieth Century America*. London, England: Routledge, 2004. A historical look at how race relations has influenced sports in America.

Rubenstein, Doris. *The Good Corporate Citizen: A Practical Guide*. Hoboken, NJ: John Wiley & Sons, 2004. A primer for CEOs, COOs, and public relations professionals on how to maintain responsible corporate citizenship.

Tench, Ralph, and Liz Yeomans. *Exploring Public Relations*. Essex, England: Pearson Education, Ltd., 2006. A general public relations text, written by British authors, with a strong section on community and society, as well as corporate social responsibility.

Visser, Wayne, Dirk Matten, Manfred Pohl, and Nick Tolhurst. *The A to Z of Corporate Social Responsibility*. Chichester, England: John Wiley & Sons, 2007. Literally soup to nuts in organizing for corporate social responsibility.

Vogel, David. *The Market for Virtue: The Potential and Limits of Corporate Social Responsibility*. Washington, DC: The Brookings Institution, 2005. A candid look at the constant business battle of "doing what's right" versus "doing what makes the most money."

Chapter 12

Government Relations

American politics, like all other sectors of society, has been overrun by social media and the Web.

Consider these instances from the 2008 race for the U.S. presidency.

- By February, with months to go before a nominee was declared, Sen. Barack Obama's fund-raising machine eclipsed all other Democratic candidates, primarily due to online contributions. The Obama $150 million war chest was propelled by an unprecedented $36 million raised in the month of January, with $28 million of it arriving over the Internet. Even more astounding, 90 percent of the online transactions came from people who donated $100 or less, and 40 percent from donors who gave $25 or less. Obama's closest rival, Sen. Hillary Clinton, raised $13.5 million in January.[1] Most astounding of all, in the last month of his candidacy, Obama announced he had raised a whopping $150 million in September alone.

- In May, Mrs. Clinton triggered a firestorm when she defended her decision to stay in the race by pointing out, "We all remember Bobby Kennedy was assassinated in June in California." The Obama campaign was outraged, after the Clinton remarks were initially reported online by *The New York Post,* quickly picked up by the online *Drudge Report,* and then whipped around the Web to become major news.[2]

- Obama suffered perhaps his only online setback on the campaign trail when, in April, a

FIGURE 12-1 Meet the new boss(es). For the first time in U.S. history, a presidential nominee introduced his vice presidential nominee via text messaging in the wee hours of the morning. (White House Photo by Pete Souza)

blogger for the *Huffington Post* reported that the candidate told a confidential San Francisco meeting of contributors that small-town voters had grown "bitter" over lost jobs, causing them to *"cling to guns or religion or antipathy toward people who aren't like them."*[3] The comments caused the Obama campaign great angst. Obama himself called the online leaked remarks, *"my biggest boneheaded move."*

- And then in August, after he had won his party's nomination, Sen. Obama decided on a novel way to name his vice presidential pick—text messaging. After days of suspense, Obama's campaign sent the following text message to supporters at 3 o'clock in the morning:

  "Barack has chosen Senator Joe Biden to be our VP nominee. Watch the first Obama-Biden rally live at 3pm ET on www.BarackObama.com. Spread the word!"[4] (See Figure 12-1.)

The Web had truly arrived as "the place to be" in 21st-century political public relations.

Don't Call It "Public Relations"

It is ironic that the practice of *"public relations"*—so defined—has been barred from the federal government since 1913. Congress at the time was worried that those who inhabited the corridors of power might be tempted to use the privileges granted and the attention paid to them by the American people for the advancement of their own agendas or, heaven forbid, the promotion of themselves.

One wonders, therefore, how the legislators of that day would think of their 21st-century publicity-seeking successors.

Every day, the Washington, D.C., seat of the federal government is a public relations free-for-all, with 435 congressmen, 100 senators, 15 cabinet secretaries, and thousands of federal employees supporting them, all jockeying to make the morning newspapers and evening talk shows. One U.S. senator, Democrat Charles Schumer of New York, was legendary for holding press conferences every Sunday—some (most?) of dubious value—simply because Sunday was a notoriously slow news day. On the state and local levels, where the situation is just slightly less blatant, politicians similarly jockey for attention in the media.

Legislators in the 21st century, it seems, have come a far distance from the days of President Dwight D. Eisenhower, a former general, who once famously remarked, *"If the Army is good, the story will be good, and the public relations will be good. If the Army is bad, the story will be bad, and the public relations will be bad."*[5]

Today, by contrast—good, bad, or indifferent; story or no story—politicians crave publicity. In many ways, the importance of constant government communications became more profound after the terrorist attacks on America on September 11, 2001.

The war on terrorism depended on candid, frank, and informative communications with the American people and the world. Said President Bush's first press secretary, Ari Fleischer, *"The American people are appreciative of the forthrightness of the government. I think the government has an obligation to be forthright."*[6]

"Why do they hate us?" the president asked rhetorically about the Muslim attackers and their sympathizers in his historic speech before Congress the week after the terrorist attacks.[7] To combat such hate and to reassure the American people about the goodness of the war effort, the government's public relations initiatives took center stage, particularly in the initial stages of the conflict. Among those initiatives were the following:

- The White House created a permanent Office of Global Communications to coordinate the administration's foreign policy message and supervise America's image abroad.[8]

- Bush mounted the "bully pulpit" of the American presidency often in the first days of the war to win public support. In a riveting speech before Congress and the nation, Bush vowed: *"I will not yield. I will not rest. I will not relent in waging this struggle. We will not tire. We will not falter, and we will not fail."*[9]

- Also early on in the war, the Bush cabinet, particularly Defense Secretary Donald Rumsfeld, Attorney General John Ashcroft, and Secretary of State Colin Powell, regularly conducted press conferences of their own to keep the country apprised of developments in their spheres and to cut off critics suspicious of secrecy. Once Ashcroft and Powell departed in Bush's second term and Rumsfeld's popularity diminished, the frequency of press conferences lessened.

■ The position of Undersecretary for Public Diplomacy and Public Affairs was created in the State Department, immediately after the 2001 attacks, to work to convince the Muslim world of the true values and ethics of America. In 2005, to spearhead this effort, President Bush named his longtime, close public relations advisor, Karen Hughes, to be Undersecretary of State for Public Diplomacy and Public Affairs (see Case Study, Chapter 14).

Ironically, while George W. Bush and his administration used public relations to build support for the early stages of the war, they dissipated most of the nation's goodwill, so that at the end of Bush's presidency, with the nation facing ferocious economic crisis, the clout of the *"bully pulpit"* had withered. In his last months as president, Bush's popularity had sunk precipitously.

Despite these missteps in cultivating public opinion and public support, the fact remains that the smartest politicians recognize the importance of the practice of public relations to their own success in getting themselves elected, their programs supported, and their policies adopted. Indeed, when he became President in 2009, Barack Obama conducted more one-on-one media interviews than any of his predecessors.

As such, the practice of public relations is represented throughout government—in each government branch, in all government agencies, on the state and local levels, and also in lobbying the government to maintain or change legislation. All of these functions are part of the multiple levels of public relations communications in and around government.

Public Relations in Government

The growth of public relations work both with and in the government has exploded in recent years. Although it is difficult to say exactly how many public relations professionals are employed at the federal level, it's safe to assume that thousands of public relations–related jobs exist in the federal government and countless others in government at the state and local levels. Thus, the field of government relations is a fertile one for public relations graduates.

Since the 1970s, more than 20 new federal regulatory agencies have sprung up—including the Office of Homeland Security, the Environmental Protection Agency, the Consumer Product Safety Commission, the Department of Energy, the Department of Education, and the Drug Enforcement Administration. Moreover, according to the Government Accounting Office (GAO), more than 120 government agencies and programs now regulate business.

It is little wonder that American business spends more time calling on, talking with, and lobbying government representatives on such subjects as trade, interest rates, taxes, budget deficits, and all the other issues that concern individual industries and companies. It is also little wonder that political interest groups of every stripe—from Wall Street bankers to Native American tribes to friends of the Earth—contribute more to political coffers than ever before. Thus, today's organizations continue to emphasize and expand their own government relations functions.

Beyond this, the nation's defense establishment offers some 7,000 public relations jobs, although, again, none are labeled *"public relations,"* in Department of Defense military and civilian positions. Indeed, with military service now purely voluntary and an increasingly difficult war on terrorism nearly a decade old, the nation's defense machine must rely on its public information, education, and recruiting efforts to maintain a sufficient military force. Thus, public relations opportunities in this realm of government work should continue to expand.

As noted, the public relations function has traditionally been something of a "poor relation" in the government. In 1913, Congress enacted the Gillette Amendment, which almost barred the practice of public relations in government. The amendment stemmed from efforts by President Theodore Roosevelt to win public support for his programs through the use of a network of publicity experts. The law was a specific response to a Civil Service Commission help wanted advertisement for a "publicity man" for the Bureau of Public Roads. Congress, worried about the potential of this unlimited presidential persuasive power, passed an amendment stating: *"Appropriated funds may not be used to pay a publicity expert unless specifically appropriated for that purpose."*

Several years later, still leery of the president's power to influence legislation through communication, Congress passed the gag law, which prohibited *"using any part of an appropriation for services, messages, or publications designed to influence any member of Congress in his attitude toward legislation or appropriations."* Even today, no government worker may be employed in the "practice of public relations." Public affairs, yes. But public relations, no. As a result, the government is flooded with "public affairs experts," "information officers," "press secretaries," and "communications specialists."

Government Practitioners

Most practitioners in government communicate the activities of the various agencies, commissions, and bureaus to the public. As consumer activist and recurring presidential candidate Ralph Nader has said, *"In this nation, where the ultimate power is said to rest with the people, it is clear that a free and prompt flow of information from government to the people is essential."*

It wasn't always as essential to form informational links between government officials and the public. In 1888, when there were 39 states in the Union and 330 members in the House of Representatives, the entire official Washington press corps consisted of 127 reporters. Today, even with the cutbacks in the ranks of newspaper reporters, there are close to 4,000 full-time journalists covering the capital.

Twenty years ago, the U.S. Office of Personnel Management reported nearly 15,000 public relations–related jobs in the federal government. Today, estimates are much higher. The National Association of Government Communicators is a national not-for-profit professional network of federal, state, and local government employees who disseminate information within and outside government. Its members are editors, writers, graphics artists, video professionals, broadcasters, photographers, information specialists, and agency spokespersons.

The closest thing to an audit of government public relations functions came in 1986 when former Senator William Proxmire, a notorious gadfly, asked the GAO to tell him "how much federal executive agencies spend on public relations."

At the time, the GAO reported that the 13 cabinet departments and 18 independent agencies spent about $337 million for public affairs activities during fiscal 1985, with almost 5,600 full-time employees assigned to public affairs duties. In addition, about $100 million was spent for congressional affairs activities, with almost 2,000 full-time employees assigned.

Now fast-forward to 2005, where a similar GAO report revealed that the Bush administration paid $1.6 billion—that's $1.6 *billion*—on advertising and public relations contracts over a two-and-a half-year period, with $88 million spent in 2004 alone. The Department of Defense spent $1.1 billion of that for recruitment campaigns and public relations efforts. A total of 54 public relations firms were contracted as part of this effort.[10]

Two Prominent Departments

Even before the war on terrorism, the most potent public relations voices in the federal government, exclusive of the president, were first, the U.S. Department of State, and second, the U.S. Department of Defense. After September 11, 2001, the communications importance of both increased, but their relative positions were reversed.

The State Department

The State Department, like other government agencies, has an extensive public affairs staff, responsible for press briefings, maintaining secretary of state homepage content, operating foreign press centers in Washington, New York, and Los Angeles, as well as managing public diplomacy operations abroad.

In October 1999, as part of the Foreign Affairs Reform and Restructuring Act of 1998, the State Department inherited the United States Information Agency (USIA), for many years the most far-reaching of the federal government's public relations arms. USIA had been an independent foreign affairs agency within the executive branch created in 1953 by President Dwight Eisenhower. Its job was to explain and support American foreign policy and promote U.S. national interests through a wide range of overseas information programs and educational and cultural activities.

The State Department consolidated USIA's 6,352 employees, of whom 904 are foreign service personnel and 2,521 are locally hired foreign service nationals overseas. There are 2,927 civil service employees based in the United States, of whom 1,822 work in international broadcasting and 1,105 are engaged in USIA's educational and informational programs.

The director of the USIA had reported directly to the president and received policy guidance from the secretary of state. Under the 1999 integration plan, an undersecretary for public diplomacy and public affairs within the State Department was chosen to head the operation. The USIA's annual appropriation has exceeded $1 billion since the late 1980s.

In the 21st century, with America's motives for the war on terrorism challenged around the world, the former USIA's mission—"to support the national interest by conveying an understanding abroad of what the United States stands for"—has been modified to include new challenges:

- Build the intellectual and institutional foundations of democracy in societies around the globe.
- Support the war on drugs in producer and consumer countries.
- Develop worldwide information programs to address environmental challenges.
- Bring the truth to any society that fails to exercise free and open communication.

In its nearly half a century, the USIA was a high-level public relations operation and not without controversy. Under the direction of such well-known media personalities as Edward R. Murrow, Carl Rowan, Frank Shakespeare, and Charles Z. Wick, the agency prospered. In 2002, the Voice of America (VOA), the State Department's leading voice overseas, named veteran *Time* magazine correspondent David Jackson as director. Jackson lasted until 2006, when his relations with the organization's powerful Broadcasting Board of Governors apparently grew frosty, over charges that the board sought to "politicize" the VOA.[11] Jackson was succeeded by Dan Austin, a 36-year veteran of Dow Jones & Company.

The communications initiatives of the State Department to spread the *"gospel of America"* are far-reaching. Among them are the following:

1. **Radio.** VOA, which first went on the air in 1942, broadcasts more than 1,000 hours of programming weekly in 45 languages, including English, to an international audience of more than 100 million listeners. In 2006, the U.S. Congress appropriated $166 million for VOA. In addition to VOA, the USIA in 1985 began Radio Marti, in honor of José Marti, father of Cuban independence. Radio Marti's purpose was to broadcast 24 hours a day to Cuba in Spanish and *"tell the truth to the Cuban people"* about ruler Fidel Castro and communism. With Raul Castro succeeding his ailing brother in 2008, it remained to be seen whether Radio Marti's mandate would change.

2. **Film and television.** The agency annually produces and acquires an extensive number of films and videocassettes for distribution in 125 countries. VOA produces more than 30 hours of television per week in 24 languages, from Albanian to Urdu. TV Marti in Cuba, for example, telecasts four-and-a-half hours daily.

3. **Internet.** VOA uses a distributed network, including more than 14,000 servers in 65 countries, to deliver Internet content. News is also available via email subscription service in English and an increasing number of broadcast languages. Electronic journals were created to communicate with audiences overseas on economic issues, political security and values, democracy and human rights, terrorism, the environment, and transnational information flow.[12]

4. **Media.** About 25,000 words a day are transmitted to 214 overseas posts for placement in the media.

5. **Publications.** Overseas regional service centers publish 16 magazines in 18 languages and distribute pamphlets, leaflets, and posters to more than 100 countries.

6. **Exhibitions.** Approximately 35 major exhibits are USIA-designed annually for worldwide display, including in Eastern European countries and the former Soviet Union.

7. **Libraries and books.** The agency maintains or supports libraries in more than 200 information centers and bi-national centers in more than 90 countries and assists publishers in distributing books overseas.

8. **Education.** The agency is also active overseas in sponsoring educational programs through 111 bi-national centers where English is taught and in 11 language centers. Classes draw about 350,000 students annually.

The Defense Department

The importance of Department of Defense (DOD) communications has been intensified in wartime. The DOD's public affairs network is massive—3,727 communicators in the Army, 1,250 in the Navy, 1,200 in the Air Force, 450 in the Marines, and 200 at headquarters. The DOD public affairs department is headed by an assistant secretary of defense for public affairs, one of six direct reports to the deputy secretary of defense (see Figure 12-2).

With the DOD consisting of more than 3 million active duty forces, reserves, and civilian employees, information is the strategic center of gravity. Communications must be organized, secure, and rapid to fulfill the department's mission.

Office of the Secretary of Defense

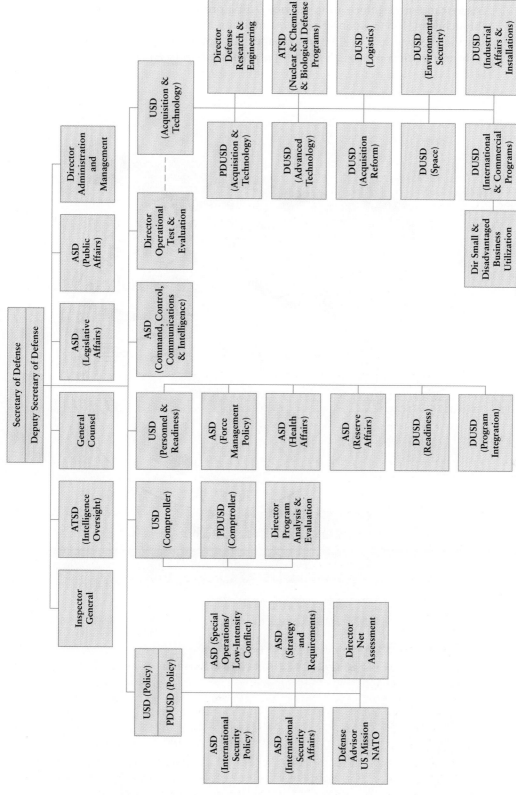

FIGURE 12-2 DOD public relations organization. The Assistant Secretary of Defense for Public Affairs was one of six who reported to the Defense Secretary's chief deputy. (Courtesy of Department of Defense)

Although each service has its own public affairs organization and mission, DOD's American Forces Information Service (AFIS) promotes cooperation among the various branches. AFIS is responsible for maintaining the Armed Forces Radio and Television Service, *Stars and Stripes* newspaper, communications training at the Defense Information School, and a variety of other functions (see Figure 12-3).

FIGURE 12-3
AFIS. The primary mission of the American Forces Information Service is to integrate the vast communications resources of the various military branches under one communications umbrella. (Courtesy of Department of Defense)

Public relations efforts of the Department of Defense in the 21st century have run the gamut from drawing universal praise to generating opprobrium. When the United States invaded Iraq in 2003, the department was lauded for "embedding" reporters with the troops in the field in order for Americans to get first-hand information about the battle.

By 2005, with the war now decidedly unpopular with the public and with much of the criticism focusing on the Guantanamo Bay detention center, a group of retired military officers took to the airwaves to defend the Bush administration. The soldiers, most of them generals, appeared frequently on talk shows as "analysts" on the war and its aftermath, frequently agreeing with the Department of Defense. The only problem was, as *The New York Times* revealed three years later, most of the retired officers had ties to military contractors and were largely directed by the Pentagon. Said one retired Green Beret and former Fox News analyst about the "guidance" he received from DOD, "It was them saying, '*We need to stick our hands up your back and move your mouth for you.*'" Clearly, the Pentagon's public relations initiative did little to endear the department with the media.[13]

Other Government Agencies

Beyond the State and Defense departments, other government departments also have stepped up their public relations efforts. The Department of Health and Human Services has a public affairs staff of 700 people. The Agriculture, State, and Treasury departments each have communications staffs in excess of 400 people, and each spends more than $20 million per year in public relations–related activities. One of the most controversial public relations operations was housed in the U.S. Department of Homeland Security, created in 2003 to combine the two dozen or so agencies that dealt with protecting the nation's homeland. In perhaps its most embarrassing episode after the calamity of Hurricane Katrina (see the Case Study), the Department's Federal Emergency Management Association staged a fake press conference in 2007 that enraged everyone up to and including Homeland Security Director Michael Chertoff (see the PR Ethics Mini-Case).[14] Even the U.S. Central Intelligence Agency has three spokespersons. Out of how many CIA public relations people, you ask? Sorry, that's classified.

The President

Despite early congressional efforts to limit the persuasive power of the nation's chief executive, the president today wields unprecedented public relations clout. The president travels with his own media entourage, controls the "*bully pulpit,*" and with it, a large part of the nation's agenda. Almost anything the president does or says makes news.

The broadcast networks, daily newspapers, and national magazines follow his every move. His press secretary provides the White House press corps (a group of national reporters assigned to cover the president) with a constant flow of announcements supplemented by daily press briefings. Unlike many organizational press releases that seldom make it into print, many White House releases achieve national exposure.

Prior to our nation's current president, Ronald Reagan and Bill Clinton were perhaps the most masterful, modern presidential communicators. Reagan gained experience in the movies and on television, and even his most ardent critics agreed that he possessed a compelling stage presence. As America's president, he was truly the *"Great Communicator."* Mr. Reagan and his communications advisers followed seven principles in helping to "manage the news":

1. Plan ahead.
2. Stay on the offensive.
3. Control the flow of information.
4. Limit reporters' access to the president.
5. Talk about the issues you want to talk about.
6. Speak in one voice.
7. Repeat the same message many times.[15]

So coordinated was Reagan's effort to *"get the right story out"* that even in his greatest public relations test—the accusation at the end of his presidency that he and his aides shipped arms to Iran and funneled the payments to support Contra rebels in Nicaragua, in defiance of the Congress—the president's "Teflon" image remained largely intact. The smears simply washed away.

George H. W. Bush was not as masterful as his predecessor in communicating with the American public. Indeed, Bush met his communications match in 1992 when Bill Clinton beat him soundly in the presidential race.

The press had a love–hate relationship with President Clinton. On the one hand, Clinton's easygoing, *"just folks"* demeanor, combined with an unquestioned intelligence and grasp of the issues, was praised by the media. On the other hand, the president's legendary "slickness," accentuated by his false statements and downright lying to the American people during the Monica Lewinsky affair, caused many journalists to treat him warily.[16]

President Clinton's accessibility to the media—except during the saga with the White House intern—and his commonsense approach to dealing with media were greatly responsible for his popularity, despite a series of embarrassing scandals afflicting his administration during both terms of his presidency. (Of course, a booming economy helped too!)

George W. Bush, like his father, wasn't particularly comfortable with the press and public speaking. After the terrorist attacks of September 11, 2001, Bush delivered an historic speech before Congress, addressed workers at the World Trade Center site through a bullhorn, and conducted frequent press conferences in Washington and at his ranch in Crawford, Texas. The terrorist challenge of Bush's first term had awakened his communications instincts (see Figure 12-4).

In his second term, however, particularly due to his premature announcement of *"Mission Accomplished"* in Iraq and disastrous handling of Hurricane Katrina in New Orleans, Bush's relationship with the media soured significantly. As his presidency limped to a close in 2008, Bush's public attempts to reassure Americans about the resilience of the falling economy were largely ignored, and his "approval rating" sunk to an unprecedented level of 27 percent, with 72 percent "disapproving."[17]

In his first months in office in 2009, President Barack Obama proved himself an adept communicator with a natural, easy-going and believable style. Faced with mounting economic crises, Obama immediately became the most telegenic president in U.S. history, with daily televised press conferences and announcements characterizing his early presidential tenure.

FIGURE 12-4 **Hail to the public relations chief.** As a wartime president, George W. Bush, here with first-term Press Secretary Ari Fleischer, met the media challenge immediately after 9/11 with strength and confidence. (Courtesy of the White House Photo Office)

The President's Press Secretary

The press secretary to the President of the United States is the most visible public relations position in the world.

Some have called the job of presidential press secretary the second-most difficult position in any administration. The press secretary is the chief public relations spokesperson for the administration. Like practitioners in private industry, the press secretary must communicate the policies and practices of the management (the president) to the public. Often it is an impossible job.

In 1974, Jerald ter Horst, President Ford's press secretary, quit after disagreeing with Ford's pardon of former President Richard Nixon. Said ter Horst, *"A spokesman should feel in his heart and mind that the chief's decision is the right one so that he can speak with a persuasiveness that stems from conviction."*[18]

A contrasting view of the press secretary's role was expressed by ter Horst's replacement in the job, former NBC reporter Ron Nessen, who said, *"A press secretary does not always have to agree with the president. His first loyalty is to the public, and he should not knowingly lie or mislead the press."*[19] A third view of the proper role of the press secretary was offered by a former public relations professional and Nixon speech-writer who became a *New York Times* political columnist, William Safire:

> *A good press secretary speaks up for the press to the president and speaks out for the president to the press. He makes his home in the pitted no-man's land of an adversary relationship and is primarily an advocate, interpreter, and amplifier. He must be more the president's man than the press's. But he can be his own man as well.*[20]

In recent years, the position of press secretary to the president has taken on increased responsibility and has attained a higher public profile. Jimmy Carter's press secretary, the late Jody Powell, for example, was among Carter's closest confidants and frequently advised the president on policy matters. He went on to found his own Washington public relations agency. James Brady, the next press secretary, who was permanently paralyzed in 1981 by a bullet aimed at President Reagan, later joined his

PR Ethics

Mini-Case PR Chief Falls from Phony FEMA Press Conference

Surprisingly, nobody had tough questions in October 2007 for the deputy administrator of the Federal Emergency Management Association (FEMA), who held a news conference to address the embattled agency's handling of California wildfires.

"Are you happy with FEMA's response so far?" someone asked.

"I am very happy with FEMA's response so far," responded Vice Admiral Harvey E. Johnson, Jr.

For an agency tarnished by its inept handling of Hurricane Katrina, it appeared that FEMA had recorded a stunning success in response to a disaster.

But the wildfires, alas, turned out to be the least potent *"disaster"* FEMA faced.

More damaging was the press conference, itself.

A day after Adm. Johnson breezed through his meeting with reporters, an embarrassed FEMA admitted that the softball questions were posed by its own employees, not journalists. In fact, no genuine journalists attended, although they were given a conference call number they could use to listen in—but not ask questions. FEMA's excuse was that the news conference was announced with only 15 minutes notice, and no reporters were able to show up. So it supplied its own "reporters."

Response from the Bush administration was immediate and unforgiving.

"It is not a practice that we would employ here at the White House," said Presidential Press Secretary Dana Perino, calling the faux press conference an "error in judgment."

As a good soldier, FEMA's external affairs director took the "hit" and was relieved of a planned promotion to take over public affairs for the Director of National Intelligence.

And as far as Homeland Security Director Michael Chertoff was concerned, the fake press conference was beyond the pale (see Figure 12-5). Summarized the man charged with the responsibility of winning back credibility after Katrina, *"I think it was one of the dumbest and most inappropriate things I've seen since I've been in government."**

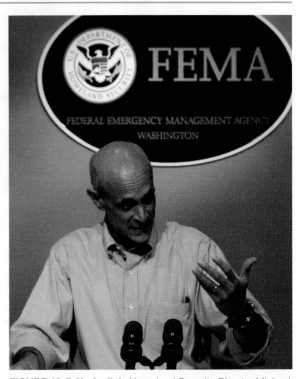

FIGURE 12-5 No foolin'. Homeland Security Director Michael Chertoff wasn't amused about FEMA's staged-question press conference. (Photo: Newscom)

Questions

1. Do you agree with the harsh response of the White House and Secretary Chertoff, relative to the fake press conference?

2. Is there anything wrong with preparing newsmakers for interviews?

3. Is there anything wrong with public relations people posing as reporters?

*For further information, see "Chertoff Rips Phony Press Event," *Associated Press* (October 27, 2007); Eric Lipton, "Fake News Briefing by FEMA Draws Official Rebukes," *New York Times* (October 27, 2007); Jack O'Dwyer, "PA Blamed for 'Fake' FEMA Conference," *O'Dwyer's PR Report* (December 2007); Joe Strupp, "FEMA Staffers Posed as Reporters at Press Briefing," *Editor & Publisher* (October 26, 2007); and Jordy Yager, "FEMA Blasted for 'News' Conference," *Los Angeles Times* (October 27, 2007).

wife, Sarah, to lobby hard for what would become known as the Brady Bill, establishing new procedures for licensing handguns.

Over time, the position of press secretary has been awarded more to career political public relations people than to career journalists. Larry Speakes, who followed Brady, was a former Hill and Knowlton executive and was universally hailed by the media for his professionalism. During Reagan's second term, Speakes apparently was purposely kept in the dark by Reagan's military advisers planning an invasion of the island of Grenada. The upset press secretary later apologized to reporters for misleading them on the Grenada invasion.

The next press secretary was a low-key, trusted, and respected lifetime government public relations professional, Marlin Fitzwater. His successor was another career political public relations professional, Dee Dee Myers, who was respected by the media and brought a refreshing perspective to her role as President Clinton's press secretary. She went on to become a cable talk show host and magazine editor.

The trend toward retaining experienced communications people continued in the second Clinton White House, with the president hiring political public relations veteran Mike McCurry. When McCurry left in 1998 to help form a new Washington public affairs agency, he was replaced by another public relations veteran, Joe Lockhart.

President George W. Bush appointed another government communications veteran, Ari Fleischer, as his press secretary. Upon taking over, Fleischer looked at the challenge optimistically, *"I may be crazy, but I like working with reporters."*[21] In his second term, Bush appointed his longtime Texas press aide Scott McClellan as press secretary.

McClellan, a member of a prominent Texas political family, had his hands full as White House reporters grew increasingly more testy when Bush's second term ran into problems.[22] McClellan's ineffectual performance as press secretary made him an easy target for the press and only added to Bush's public relations problems in his second term. In April 2006, McClellan was dumped and replaced by Fox News host Tony Snow. A year later, McClellan wrote a blistering, tell-all book (see Top of the Shelf, Chapter 6) about the Bush administration he had served.

Snow brought a renewed sense of vitality and sense of respect—both absent during the tenure of the hapless McClellan—back to the office of presidential press secretary. Snow was an iron-fisted charmer, standing up for his president, but always delivering his message with confidence, flair, and humor. Some, like former White House operative David Gergen, objected to Snow's outspoken support of Bush and his policies. Tut-tutted Gergen, *"If he is seen as wearing two hats, reporters as well as the public will inevitably wonder: Is he speaking to us now as the traditional press secretary, or is he speaking to us as a political partisan."*[23] That Snow was a lightning rod for controversy only added to the credibility he brought to his job. And when Snow resigned from the White House, to fight a battle with cancer, he received universal praise from friend and foe alike. Tony Snow died at the age of 53 in July 2008.

For his first choice as White House Press Secretary, President Barack Obama chose Robert Gibbs (see From the Top at the end of this chapter), a career political public relations strategist who gained the new president's trust over four years as a wise and trusted advisor (see Figure 12-6).

Over the years, the number of reporters hounding the presidential press secretary—dubbed by some "the imperial press corps"—has grown from fewer than 300 reporters during President Kennedy's term to around 3,000 today.

Dealing with such a host of characters is no easy task, and the role of press secretary is neither easy nor totally satisfactory. As former press secretary McCurry, who began the practice of televising the daily White House press secretary press briefing, put it, *"Having a single person standing at a podium and answering questions and trying to explain a complicated world is not a very efficient way to drive home the idea that government can make a difference."*[24] Perhaps President Johnson, the first chief executive to be labeled an "imperial president" by the Washington press corps, said it best when asked by a television reporter what force or influence he thought had done the most to shape the nature of Washington policy. *"You bastards,"* Johnson snapped.[25]

FIGURE 12-6
The press secretary's mission. White House Press Secretary Robert Gibbs reviews President Barack Obama's 2009 NCAA Final Four selections with the "handicapper in chief." (White House Photo by Pete Souza)

FIGURE 12-6
The press secretary's mission. White House Press Secretary Robert Gibbs reviews President Barack Obama's 2009 NCAA Final Four selections with the "handicapper in chief." (White House Photo by Pete Souza)

Lobbying the Government

The business community, foundations, and philanthropic organizations have a common problem: dealing with government, particularly the mammoth federal bureaucracy. Because government has become so pervasive in organizational and personal life, the number of corporations and trade associations with government relations units has grown steadily in recent years.

The occupation of lobbyist is one of the nation's greatest growth industries. The number of registered lobbyists in Washington has more than doubled since 2000 to more than 34,750—a 66 percent increase. Why? Three factors, according to experts:

1. Rapid growth in government
2. Republican control of both the White House and Congress
3. Wide acceptance among corporations that they need to hire professional lobbyists to secure their share of the federal budget[26]

In terms of spending, lobbying is such big business that approximately $2 billion a year—$6 million a day—is spent lobbying the federal government.[27] And that's just federal. State government lobbying is only slightly less active. In New Jersey alone, lobbyists spent $28.5 million in 2005, moving or stopping particular legislation.[28]

Government relations people are primarily concerned with weighing the impact of impending legislation on the company, industry group, or client organization. Generally, a head office government relations staff complements staff members who represent the organization in Washington, D.C., and state capitals. These representatives have several objectives:

1. To improve communications with government personnel and agencies
2. To monitor legislators and regulatory agencies in areas affecting constituent operations

3. To encourage constituent participation at all levels of government

4. To influence legislation affecting the economy of the constituent's area, as well as its operations

5. To advance awareness and understanding among lawmakers of the activities and operations of constituent organizations

Carrying out these objectives requires knowing your way around the federal government and acquiring connections. A full-time Washington representative is often employed for these tasks.

To the uninitiated, Washington (or almost any state capital) can seem an incomprehensible maze. Consequently, organizations with an interest in government relations usually employ a professional representative, who may or may not be a registered lobbyist, whose responsibility, among other things, is to influence legislation. Lobbyists are required to comply with the federal Lobbying Act of 1946, which imposed certain reporting requirements on individuals or organizations that spend a significant amount of time or money attempting to influence members of Congress on legislation.

In 1995, the Lobbying Disclosure Act took effect, reforming the earlier law. The new act broadened the activities that constitute lobbying and mandated government registration of lobbyists. Under the new law, a lobbyist is an individual who is paid by a third party to make more than one "lobbying contact," defined as an oral or written communication to a vast range of specific individuals in the executive and legislative branches of the federal government.

In fact, one need not register as a lobbyist in order to speak to a senator, congressional representative, or staff member about legislation. But a good lobbyist can earn the respect and trust of a legislator. Because of the need to analyze legislative proposals and to deal with members of Congress, many lobbyists are lawyers with a strong Washington background. Lobbying ranks are loaded with former administration officials and congressional members, who often turn immediately to lobbying when they move out of office. In 2006, even the former attorney general of the United States, John Ashcroft, announced that he, too, would hang up his shingle and become a lobbyist.[29]

Lobbyists, at times, have been labeled everything from influence peddlers to fixers to downright crooks. In 2005, with the admissions of convicted super-lobbyist Jack Abramoff—and his equally convicted public relations consigliore, Michael Scanlon—about luring congressmen on golf outings and in the process ripping off Native American tribe clients for millions of dollars, the practice of lobbying reached a new low.

Despite the slings and arrows, the fact is that today's lobbyist is likely to be a person who is well informed in his or her field and who furnishes Congress with facts and information necessary to make an intelligent decision on a particular issue. This task—the lobbyist's primary function—is rooted in nothing less than the First Amendment right of all citizens to petition government.

What Do Lobbyists Do?

The number of lobbyists registered with the U.S. Senate has increased from just over 3,000 in 1976 to just under 35,000 today. Lobbying has become big business.

But what exactly do lobbyists do?

The essence of a lobbyist's job is to inform and persuade. The contacts of lobbyists are important, but they must also have the right information available for the right legislator. The time to plant ideas with legislators is well before a bill is drawn up, and skillful lobbyists recognize that timing is critical in influencing legislation. The specific activities performed by individual lobbyists vary with the nature of the industry or group represented. Most take part in these activities:

1. **Fact-finding.** The government is an incredible storehouse of facts, statistics, economic data, opinions, and decisions that generally are available for the asking.

2. **Interpretation of government actions.** A key function of the lobbyist is to interpret for management the significance of government events and the potential implications of pending legislation. Often a lobbyist predicts what can be expected to happen legislatively and recommends actions to deal with the expected outcome.

3. **Interpretation of company actions.** Through almost daily contact with congressional members and staff assistants, a lobbyist conveys how a specific group feels about legislation. The lobbyist must be completely versed in the business of the client and the attitude of the organization toward governmental actions.

4. **Advocacy of a position.** Beyond the presentation of facts, a lobbyist advocates positions on behalf of clients, both pro and con. Hitting a congressional representative early with a stand on pending legislation can often mean getting a fair hearing for the client's position. Indeed, few congressional representatives have the time to study—or even read—every piece of legislation on which they are asked to vote. Therefore, they depend on lobbyists for information, especially on how the proposed legislation may affect their constituents.

5. **Publicity springboard.** More news comes out of Washington than from any other city in the world. It is the base for thousands of press, television, radio, and magazine correspondents. This multiplicity of media makes it the ideal springboard for launching organizational publicity. The same holds true, to a lesser degree, in state capitals.

6. **Support of company sales.** The government is one of the nation's largest purchasers of products. Lobbyists often serve as conduits through which sales are made. A lobbyist who is friendly with government personnel can serve as a valuable link for leads to company business.[30]

Do-It-Yourself Lobbying

Even though in recent years, the activity of lobbying has been associated with the largest corporations, individuals and smaller groups can also benefit through legislative contact. The following are the principles that any citizen can use in lobbying a legislator:

■ **Know the subject and status of the legislation.** Like any other practitioner of public relations, lobbyists must demonstrate a comprehensive knowledge of the legislation on which they seek action. That means first—before even considering calling on a legislator—you must review thoroughly the history of the bill in question, its supporters and detractors over time, and the detours it has experienced as it has meandered its way through the legislative process.

■ **Know the position of the legislator and the staff.** Just as you would never approach a journalist about a story without first reviewing how he or she has treated similar subject matter, so, too, would you never approach a legislator about a piece of legislation without first considering the person's background and biases.

■ **Represent a key constituency.** Obviously, you can't dictate the importance of your employer to the legislator. The hard reality is that regardless of the

Points   El Rushbo Repels Reverse-Lobbying

While it often makes sense to "lobby" the Congress, it may not be as sensible to "reverse the process."

At least that's what 41 Democratic U.S. senators found in 2007, when they mailed a complaint letter to none other than radio talk show host Rush Limbaugh, "self-proclaimed 'all-mighty, all-knowing MahaRushie' of conservative Republicans." The letter was critical of Limbaugh's reference to Iraqi war veterans critical of the war as "phony soldiers."

Wrote Senate Majority Leader Harry Reid:

"I normally ignore Rush Limbaugh, but his comments last Wednesday went too far for me to remain silent. It's one thing to call me 'Dingy Harry'— it's another to insult our men and women in uniform, calling those who oppose the war 'phony soldiers' as Rush did during his Sept. 26 broadcast" (see Figure 12-7).

So what did El Rushbo do in response to this direct lobbying by the Senate?

He decided to auction the letter off for charity on eBay, as a *"glittering jewel of colossal ignorance."* Limbaugh claimed he was referring only to one soldier, who was critical of the war and had served only 44 days in the Army, never seeing combat. In addition, said Limbaugh, he would, personally, match the winning eBay bid, dollar-for-dollar.

Limbaugh predicted the letter would bring in as much as $1 million.

He was wrong.

The winning bid on eBay was actually *$2 million*! The bidder, the Eugene B. Casey Foundation, pledged the money to the Marine Corps-Law Enforcement Foundation Inc., which provides scholarships and other assistance to families of marines and federal law enforcement officials who die or are wounded in the line of duty.

Rush kicked in his matching contribution and offered, "This is more fun than I've ever had in my life."

There was no comment from *"Dingy Harry"* or his 40 Senatorial co-signers.*

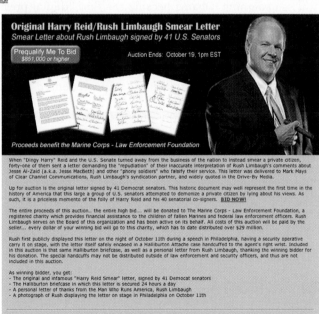

FIGURE 12-7 And the lobbying winner is . . . El Rushbo. (Photo: Newscom)

---

*For further information, see Stephanie Strom, "Letter to Limbaugh Fetches $2 Million," *New York Times* (October 20, 2007).

cogency or urgency of your arguments, legislators will be a lot more interested in your views if you represent a group that means *votes*. After all, politicians are, by definition, well, *politicians*.

■ **Be available and eager to please.** A good lobbyist must be an eager suppliant to the distinguished legislator. That means making himself or herself available whenever the legislator needs to talk. It also means delivering requested information immediately and in a form readily understandable.

■ **Have influential backup at the ready.** It is also obligatory for a lobbyist to prepare influential backup support in the legislator's home state, district, or community. Part of a lobbyist's homework—well before confronting the legislator—is to identify important local opinion leaders, speak with them, determine where they stand on the issue in question, and attempt to prevail upon them to support your view.

■ **Keep your word.** The cardinal rule in the practice of public relations is *Never lie*. That goes double for lobbyists.

■ **Know how the system functions.** Common sense: If you're a state house lobbyist, know all you can about the real-world workings of the state legislative body and its members. If you're a federal lobbyist, you simply must understand the real-world workings of the Congress and the executive branch.[31]

Just as in any other part of public relations practice, the success of a lobbyist depends largely on one thing: preparation.

Emergence of E-Lobbying

As it has in every other area of society and public relations work, the Internet has influenced the practice of lobbying as well. In terms of political campaigning and grassroots lobbying, as noted, the presidential campaign of Barack Obama cemented the role of the Web in political campaigning. Obama became the first "digital presidential candidate." He raised millions in campaign contributions via the Internet. He announced his vice presidential running mate via instant messaging. He created a blog, "Fight the Smears," to extinguish scurrilous rumors. He had more than $1\frac{1}{2}$ million "friends" on MySpace and Facebook and 45,000 followers on Twitter. His facility with the Web allowed the Obama campaign to get its word out in lightning, unprecedented speed to vast numbers of voters.[32]

The 2008 Obama campaign was the greatest indication that social media and the Internet had changed politics and lobbying forever. One Democratic Web site, in particular, MoveOn.org, financed by the billionaire George Soros, was credited as *"one of the most influential . . . organizations in U.S. politics."*[33] Founded in 1998 by Clinton sympathizers opposed to impeachment and eager for the Congress to "move on," the site has become a rallying point for liberal issues. On the other side, a host of conservative sites—from GOP Cyber Volunteers to Log Cabin Republicans to GOPAC—lead the charge from the right of the aisle.

Political Action Committees

The rise of political action committees (PACs) has been among the most controversial political developments in recent years. A political action committee is the name commonly given to a private group, regardless of size, organized to elect political candidates. In the mid-1970s, there were about 600 PACs. Today, there are approximately

4,200, with the largest—among them, EMILY's List, the Service Employees International Union, American Federation of Teachers, American Medical Association, National Rifle Association, Teamsters Union, and the like—donating millions of dollars to get candidates elected.

Each PAC can give a maximum of $5,000 to a federal candidate in a primary election and another $5,000 for the general election. The top 50 PACs contribute in excess of $60 million annually. An organization with many individual PACs can have a tremendous monetary influence on an election.

The increased influence of such groups on candidates is one reason why Senators John McCain and Russ Feingold led the Congress in 2002 to pass new strictures on campaign financing and particularly advertising for or against a candidate just prior to an election. Some would like to go further to see PACs severely curtailed or even banned. Indeed, over the years, Congress has limited what its members could accept in the form of trips and other niceties from the sponsors of PACs.

Critics of campaign finance reform argue that the First Amendment allows the freedom to speak out for or against any candidate. The tobacco industry, they note, was one of the most prominent PAC contributors to Congress, but the industry still got hammered. Although the number and size of PACs have increased, evidence of PAC-inspired indiscretions or illegalities has been minimal.

Dealing with Local Government

In 1980, Ronald Reagan rode to power on a platform of New Federalism, calling for a shift of political debate and public policy decisions from national to state and local levels. Presidents Clinton and Bush picked up the same initiative when they assumed power. By the time of the election of 2008 and with financial recession in full force—due at least in part to financial industry deregulation—sentiment shifted back to a more fortified national government role and increased regulation.

Dealing with local entities, of course, differs considerably from dealing with the federal government. For example, opinion leaders in communities (those constituents with whom an organization might want to affiliate to influence public policy decisions) might include such sectors as local labor unions, teachers, civil service workers, and the like. Building a consensus among such diverse constituents is pure grassroots public relations. The very nature of state and local issues makes it impossible to give one all-encompassing blueprint for successful government relations strategies.

Although the federal government's role in wielding power and employing public relations professionals is significant, state and local governments also are extremely important. Indeed, one viable route for entry-level public relations practitioners is through the local offices of city, county, regional, and state government officials.

Local agencies deal directly—much more so than their counterparts in Washington—with individuals. State, county, and local officials must make themselves available for local media interviews, community forums and debates, and even door-to-door campaigning. In recent years, local and state officials have found that direct contact with constituents—often through call-in radio programs—is invaluable not only in projecting an image but also in keeping in touch with the voters.

The public information function at state and local levels—to keep constituents apprised of legislative and regulatory changes, various government procedures, and notices—is a front-line public relations responsibility on the local level.

Local government officials, assigned to ensure the quality of local schools, the efficiency of local agencies, and the reliability of local fire and police departments, increasingly require smart and experienced public relations counsel. State and local information officer positions, therefore, have become valued and important posts for public relations graduates.

Last Word

The pervasive growth of government at all levels of society may not be welcome news for many people. But with the nation and the world confronting unprecedented economic challenges in the latter part of the first decade of the 21st century, an increased government role is inevitable.

Government's growth has stimulated the need for increased public relations support and counsel. Indeed, in recent years, the once overwhelming power of television advertising on political campaigns has declined, and the importance of individuals has increased.[34] The importance of communicating directly with individual voters therefore has become paramount for politicians.

The massive federal government bureaucracy, organized through individual agencies that seek to communicate with the public, is a vast repository for

public relations jobs. The most powerful position in the land—that of president of the United States—has come to rely on public relations counsel to help maintain a positive public opinion of the office and the incumbent's handling of it.

On state and local levels, public relations expertise also has become a valued commodity. Local officials, too, attempt to describe their programs in the most effective manner. In profit-making and nonprofit organizations alike, the need to communicate with various layers of government also is imperative.

Like it or not, the growth of government in our society appears unstoppable, particularly now that the United States is engaged in a long-term war on terror. As a result, the need for public relations support in government relations will clearly continue to grow in the 21st century.

Discussion Starters

1. Why is the public relations function regarded as something of a stepchild in government?
2. What is the current status of the Voice of America, and what are its responsibilities?
3. What is meant by the term *embedded reporter*?
4. Why was Ronald Reagan called the Great Communicator?
5. Contrast the performances of Scott McClellan and Tony Snow as White House press secretaries.

6. What are the objectives of government relations officers?
7. What are the primary functions of lobbyists?
8. What impact has the Internet had on lobbying?
9. What are the pros and cons of PACs?
10. What are the key considerations in individually lobbying a legislator?

Top of the Shelf Lipstick on a Pig / Torie Clarke, New York: Free Press, 2006

The individual credited with creating the concept of embedded reporters, public relations veteran Torie Clarke, served as Donald Rumsfeld's Assistant Secretary of Defense for Public Affairs.

Clarke praises her former boss. She says that Donald Rumsfeld felt strongly about the embedding program and believed that American citizens deserved to know as much about the military as possible. And Clarke states that her group did everything possible to make the military accessible to them.

Her premise is that spin is out and transparency is in. She says that corporations and governments must be open with the public because eventually their audiences will discover anything they are trying to hide.

Clarke herself is honest enough to admit that President Bush's premature declaration of "Mission Accomplished" in the Iraq War was a major public relations blunder. "You can put a lot of lipstick on a pig," she warns, "but it's still a pig."

Case Study | The Presidential PR Performance of Barack Obama

The presidential election of 2008 was historic from many aspects—the oldest presidential candidate in history, John McCain; the potential of the nation's first woman vice president, Sarah Palin; and, ultimately, the election of the nation's first black President, Barack Obama.

Sen. Obama's campaign for the presidency was hailed as one of the most astute in the nation's history. But also memorable was the near picture perfect public relations that helped propel Obama to the White House.

The juxtaposition of Sen. McCain's public relations problems versus Sen. Obama's public relations triumphs was striking. Here are the pivotal public relations decisions that helped propel the latter and sink the former.

John McCain

Sen. McCain was a bona fide war hero and, most people agreed, all-around nice guy. He was generally beloved by the media and clearly their favorite when he ran against ultimate winner George W. Bush in the Republican primary of 2004.

But McCain's 2008 presidential campaign was largely marked by public relations blunders that confused the McCain "identity" and conveyed a perception of discord and disarray. Among the McCain's camp's most egregious public relations missteps were the following:

- **The wrong third parties**
  The key to positive public relations is "third-party endorsement." You need others, by your side, to endorse your policies and support your programs.

  As the nation headed into its worst economic downturn since the Great Depression, McCain found himself surrounded by the wrong third-party endorsers.

  In the Obama corner stood an economic advisory team anchored by two former treasury secretaries, Robert Rubin and Larry Summers, and respected former Federal Reserve Chairman Paul Volcker—all recognized financial heavyweights.

  McCain, by contrast, chose financial flyweights.

  One was Carly Fiorina, failed CEO of Hewlett-Packard, who was relieved of her duties after questionable acquisitions and declining earnings. Fiorina's role in the McCain campaign was downgraded after she acknowledged that neither Obama nor her own man possessed the competence to run a corporation.

  Another of McCain's lead economic voices was the perpetually public relations–challenged former Sen. Phil Gramm, who lost his clout in the campaign when he characterized economically despairing Americans as *"whiners."*

- **Premature debate cancellation**
  Two months before the election, with Congress contemplating a $700 billion bailout bill, McCain made an abrupt decision to suspend his campaign and call for cancellation of the first debate with Obama in order to race back to Washington to "rescue" the bill.

It was a transparent public relations attempt at grandstanding that predictably reverberated to his detriment.

In point of fact, neither McCain nor Obama knew much about economics, neither was directly involved in the bailout talks, and neither, therefore, could be of much practical help to resolve the dispute. (Indeed, it was widely reported that at the emergency White House bailout meeting that McCain called for, the Republican candidate didn't say anything.)

The best—and only—solution was for the candidates to return to D.C. to try to help and then fly off to Mississippi to conduct their debate, on schedule. That's what a cooler-headed Obama proposed and that, ultimately, is what McCain wound up doing—with considerable egg on face.

- **Michigan mismanagement**
  In October, the McCain campaign announced it would "pull out" of Michigan in order to shift the $1 million a week it was spending there to a more potentially victorious venue.

  Even vice presidential candidate Sarah Palin was stunned. *"I want to get back to Michigan, and I want to try,"* she said when informed of the McCain retreat.

  The signal of giving up on any state with a full month left in the fight was indefensible. Talk about sending out a sign of defeat!

  And while some in the McCain camp attempted to backtrack from the original announcement, the public relations axiom that *"You never get a second chance to make a first impression,"* rang loud and clear.

- **The "Hail Sarah"**
  Finally, there was the out-of-the-blue decision to name Alaska Gov. Palin as McCain's running mate.

  While the Palin decision kick-started a moribund campaign, it backfired almost immediately when the candidate conducted dreadful national media interviews, in which she sounded ill-prepared for the enormous burden of national office.

  In the end, while voters seemed to give less weight to the Palin place on the ticket, her inexperience clearly caused some to wonder whether an untested, less-than-one-term, Alaska governor was really the best person available to backstop—and more important, suddenly have to succeed—a 72-year-old president (see Figure 12-8).

Barack Obama

In April during the Democratic primary, a *Huffington Post* blogger reported that Sen. Obama had told a small gathering at a closed San Francisco cocktail party that white working-class voters in Pennsylvania were *"bitter . . . so they cling to guns or religion or antipathy to people who aren't like them."*

Dumb.

And Obama paid the price for the inelegant remarks with a week's worth of negative publicity.

FIGURE 12-8 **The vanquished.** Sen. John McCain and Gov. Sarah Palin. (Photo: Newscom)

It was the last public relations mistake his campaign made.

With that one exception, Obama's public relations performance was as good as any presidential candidate in history.

Among Obama's primary public relations victories on the road to the White House were these:

- **Discarding Rev. Wright**

  Rev. Jeremiah Wright was Obama's spiritual mentor for 20 years in Chicago. But Rev. Wright was widely quoted for anti-American statements that embarrassed Obama and gave the Republicans fresh meat.

  It took about a month, during which the candidate tried to dismiss his preacher as nothing more dangerous than a *"wacky uncle,"* but ultimately, Obama did the right thing and threw Rev. Wright under the bus.

  Some criticized the candidate for lack of loyalty. But had Obama remained loyal to the rebellious reverend, it would have cost him dearly.

  So in March, Obama cut his ties to his longtime mentor. For good measure, as the candidate lowered the boom on his former pastor, he labeled Wright's speech as *"inflammatory and appalling."*

  Obama, coolly assessing the bigger picture with his eye clearly on the prize, made the right public relations call. And Rev. Wright, despite the right wing's repeated attempts to resurrect him, never again became a campaign factor.

- **Disdaining the gas holiday pandering**

  In May, voters got a glimpse of the difference between Obama and his primary rival, Sen. Hillary Clinton.

  With the price of gas spiraling out of control, Clinton called for a *"holiday"* on gasoline taxes, so that hurting middle-class families could enjoy the summer with affordable gas.

  Never mind that such a relaxation would have driven up consumption, thus digging the nation into a deeper dependence on foreign oil; the Clinton camp was interested in making Obama look like an *"elitist, out of touch with the common man."*

  John McCain, on the Republican side, agreed with the Clinton plan.

  But Obama refused to take the bait.

  Labeling the proposal as *"a pure political stunt,"* Obama, alone among the candidates, did the right thing and denounced the idea, which died immediately thereafter.

- **Backing off the Brandenburg Gate**

  Obama's advisors hinted in July that his big pre-election trip to Europe would be punctuated by a speech before hundreds of thousands of Berliners at the Brandenburg Gate, where Presidents Kennedy and Reagan delivered famous addresses.

  German Chancellor Andrea Merkel voiced unease at the prospects of a mere U.S. candidate using such an historic venue for a campaign speech. For weeks, the Obama camp stayed mum about plans for the speech, thus "milking" the anticipation. Meanwhile, conservative commentators played into the suspense by condemning Obama for going forward.

  They needn't have worried. Obama never had any intention of defying the German chancellor.

  When his Berlin moment arrived, the candidate addressed an adoring crowd in front of the Victory Column in Tiergarten, a far less controversial venue.

FIGURE 12-9
The victor. President Barack Obama.
(White House Photo by Pete Souza)

The theatrical buildup and ultimate delivery of his *"citizen of the world"* address proved the public relations highlight of what would be Obama's only foreign trip during the campaign.

■ **Ignoring Ayers**

Bill Ayers was a former Weatherman Underground domestic terrorist turned Chicago college professor. Obama had served on a board with him and been to his home. Ayers' wife, Bernardine Dohrn, was another former Underground bomber.

Most said that Ayers and Dohrn had renounced their past antisocial activities and were now productive citizens. Whatever the case, the Ayers connection, when it surfaced as early as April, could have been toxic for Obama.

That it never proved to be was yet additional testimony to the savvy public relations strategy of the Obama camp to be prepared with "standby" rebuttal, but essentially to ignore the Ayers connection as a "non-starter."

Sure enough, try as they might to make the Ayers link stick, right-wing attack dogs were ultimately frustrated as Obama sailed above the battle, dismissing his relationship with Ayers as a casual one that began 20 years after the former terrorist committed his crimes against humanity.

Consequently, the Ayers factor never proved to be much of an issue.

■ **Empathy for a grandmother**

Both candidates *"suspended"* their campaigns once during the battle:

- McCain in his ill-advised and ultimately aborted September grandstand play to fly back to Washington to "rescue" the bailout package.

- Obama in an October "final visit" to see his terminally ill grandmother in Hawaii.

Obama's white grandmother, Madelyn Dunham, had helped raise young Barack and teach him values. The candidate noted that when his mother died in Hawaii, he had failed to get there in time, and that he wouldn't make the same mistake with his grandmother.

And while a few adversaries criticized Obama for spending campaign money to fly to Hawaii to visit his dying grandmother, most Americans were sympathetic to the candidate's obvious sadness and impressed by the sensitive yet tactful way he handled his grief.

As it turned out, it was another wise public relations move for Obama to suspend campaign activity to visit his grandmother. Mrs. Dunham died Monday, November 3, 2008—one day before her grandson was elected the 44th President of the United States (see Figure 12-9).

Questions

1. Had you been John McCain's public relations advisor, what would you have counseled him relative to (1) third-party supporters, (2) debate cancellation, (3) Michigan pullout, and (4) the choice for vice president?

2. Had you been Barack Obama's public relations advisor, how would you have handled the San Francisco flap?

3. In terms of lessons learned—from both the campaign and the experience of his predecessor—were you President Obama's communications advisor, what public relations principles would you counsel him to follow in the White House?

From the Top   An Interview with Robert Gibbs

(White House Photo by Joyce N. Boghosian)

Robert Gibbs, President Barack Obama's Press Secretary, was named the nation's 28th White House Press Secretary in January 2009. An experienced political public relations counselor, Mr. Gibbs was communications director for Senator Obama, for whom he had worked since 2004, and for Sen. Obama's 2008 presidential campaign. Prior to that, Mr. Gibbs served as press secretary of Sen. John Kerry's 2004 presidential campaign. He also served as communications director for the Democratic Senatorial Campaign Committee and for four individual Senate campaigns, including those of Mr. Obama in 2004 and Fritz Hollings in 1998. Mr. Gibbs was also press secretary for Congressman Bob Etheridge. (This interview was conducted after Mr. Gibbs' first 100 days in the White House.)

How would you describe your job?
This is the most fun I've ever had in a job in my life. It is the best job that you could have.

What do you consider your primary mission as press secretary?
I am the primary representative for the President with the White House press corps. I help them get access to the information and facts they need to cover what the President does each day.

What is a typical day for the White House Press Secretary?
I try to be on the job about 6 o'clock in the morning, and sometimes I get home to read to my son at 8:30. But most nights, I'm not able to do that. And so far, we've worked every day of every weekend. The President, of course, lives above the "company store," which has its advantages!

How much access do you have to the President?
I see him every day in several meetings in the Oval Office. Most important, if I need anything at any point during the day, I can walk in and ask him a question. A press secretary has to have the ability to do that, or it's very tough to do your job.

How does President Obama feel about the press?
He understands very much the role they play in a representative democracy. He understands that that democracy is as strong as the people who cover the President and help the public understand what government is doing and holding it accountable.

How would you characterize the White House press corps?
They do a remarkable job under difficult circumstances. It's a grueling pace in terms of time and what you give up in terms of your personal life.

Is the press "fair" in its coverage of the President?
Absolutely. They ask the right questions. They're tough, but they're fair.

What should be the proper relationship between the press secretary and the press?
I think it's important to have good relationships. We can disagree, but we can do it in a way that is respectful and personable. I've been told this by my predecessors—that the Press Secretary occupies a unique position in the physical structure of the White House. Your office is equidistant from the Oval Office and the Briefing Room. So your role is one of spokesperson to and advocate for the President, but you are also the representative of the press inside the White House, in order for them to get the facts, information, and access they need. So there's a dual role you must play to serve both of the people you are tasked to work for.

Do you consider yourself a "counselor" to the President?
The role that I play in parts of my day would typically be reserved for more of a behind-the-scenes advisor. While that does take some of my day away from dealing with reporters, I believe it helps the press get a better sense for who the President is and the reasons for his decisions. It allows me to speak more authoritatively for his viewpoint.

How does being the President's press secretary differ from other public relations jobs?
This job has evolved into one where you play the traditional role of working with reporters but with the added responsibility of hosting your own cable TV show. I literally spend half of my day getting ready for the one hour that I spend in front of the press corps on camera. This requires a great deal of preparation and study.

How does someone become the President's Press Secretary?
You have to get good work experience in government, in press, and public relations. Also, because of the daily on-camera responsibilities, you have to be someone who is intellectually curious and can understand the rigors of the job. You have to also be *"lucky"* because you have to pick the right guy or woman. I wouldn't disavow anybody of the luck that's involved.

Public Relations Library

Bacevitch, Andrew J. *The Limits of Power.* New York, NY: Henry Holt and Company, 2008. A university international relations professor analyzes what's behind America's international relations problems.

Beck, Glenn. *An Inconvenient Book: Real Solutions to the World's Biggest Problems.* New York, NY: Simon & Schuster, 2007. The conservative commentator takes 'em all on—from poverty and marriage to liberalism and radical Islam.

Chemerinsky, Erwin. *Enhancing Government: Federalism for the 21st Century.* Stanford, CA: Stanford University Press, 2008. A political science professor explores the evolution of government in U.S. society.

Fleischer, Ari. *Taking Heat: The President, the Press and My Years in the White House.* New York: HarperCollins, 2005. First-hand account from President Bush's first press secretary, who answered the media mob during wartime.

Hughes, Karen. *Ten Minutes from Normal.* New York: Penguin Books, 2004. A personal account of tumultuous days in the White House and a return to civilian life by the closest public relations advisor to the president.

Klein, Joe. *The Natural: The Misunderstood Presidency of Bill Clinton.* New York: Random House, 2002. A critical view of the man "born to be president" from a journalist who got in trouble for writing a thinly disguised novel about Clinton and then wouldn't admit he wrote it.

Morris, Dick, and Eileen McGann. *Fleeced.* New York, NY: HarperCollins, 2008. A reborn, former Bill Clinton advisor rants about what's wrong with liberals.

Phillips, Kevin. *Bad Money.* New York, NY: Penguin Group, 2008. A sobering look at American foreign policy from a former White House strategist.

Smith, Kevin R. (ed.). *State and Local Government 2007–2008 Edition.* Washington, DC: CQ Press, 2008. Practitioners discuss various aspects of government on the state and municipal levels.

Smith, Sally Bedell. *For Love of Politics.* New York, NY: Random House, 2007. The unadulterated story of America's funniest political couple, Bill and Hillary.

Woodward, Bob. *The War Within: A Secret White House History 2006–2008.* New York, NY: Simon & Schuster, 2008. *Washington Post* reporter convinced Bush administration people to speak with him about this inside story. They learned to regret it.

Chapter 13

Consumer Relations

FIGURE 13-1 Fiji fiasco. A misprinted $51 Fiji airfare inundated Travelocity call centers, cost the firm $2 million, and served as a reminder of the public relations dangers of e-commerce. (Photo: Newscom)

By 2009, according to Nielsen Research, more than 875 million consumers had shopped online, with the number of worldwide Internet shoppers—from South Korea to Germany, from Great Britain to Japan—up 40 percent in two years. The most popular Internet-purchased items were books, clothing, videos, and airline tickets.[1]

And in the case of Travelocity.com, it was the Web sale of airline tickets that almost sunk the online travel agency.

The nightmare began in April 2005 when an incorrect airfare from Los Angeles to Fiji was mistakenly loaded into Travelocity's reservations system. Before long, travel sites across the Internet were buzzing with the Travelocity's "all in $51 from L.A. to Fiji." Yikes! The posts were blood in the water for the Web community of "mileage runners," who comb online travel sites for cheap fares.

Before Travelocity CEO Michelle Peluso could retrieve the e-commerce error from the site, Travelocity call centers were deluged for Fiji flights (see Figure 13-1). CEO Peluso valiantly decided to "eat" the $2 million in costs in order to protect her company's reputation. She also installed new software to guard against a recurrence.

But the pitfalls to a company of the brave, new area of Internet consumer shopping were clear.[2]

Worldwide Consumer Class

Notwithstanding the recession that gripped the globe at the end of the first decade of the 21st century, nearly two billion people worldwide now belong to the "consumer class"—the group of people characterized by diets of highly processed food, the desire for bigger houses and more and bigger cars, higher levels of debt, and lifestyles devoted to the accumulation of nonessential goods.[3] Rising consumption has helped meet basic needs and create jobs around the world. Today nearly half of global consumers reside in developing countries, including 240 million in China and 120 million in India—markets that, even with recession, still command the highest potential for expansion.

Companies like McDonald's, the world's largest restaurant chain, work constantly to hone their iconic status and improve their image with consumers around the world. McDonald's serves nearly 60 million customers a day and makes a point of affiliating with the world's brightest stars (see Figure 13-2).

Globalization and the spread of the Internet introduce new pressures on such companies to walk a fine line between behaving "responsibly" and promoting their products. More often than not,

FIGURE 13-2 **Clowning glory.** McDonald's is one global consumer giant that has associated itself with high-wattage celebrities, including tennis star Serena Williams; the late, legendary actor Paul Newman; and the ubiquitous Ronald McDonald. (Photo: Newscom)

meeting this challenge means differentiating one's product from all the rest. Often it is public relations techniques and societal sensitivities that help distinguish a company and its products from the competition.

- In 2006, the Walt Disney company, addressing the concerns of parents over child nutrition, decided to curtail the use of its name and popular characters like Buzz Lightyear and Lightning McQueen with food items that didn't meet acceptable nutritional standards. The new guidelines affected Disney licensing agreements with a variety of snacks and foods that were too rich in sugar, calories, and fat.[4]

- In 2007, the Mattel Company battled ferociously to protect the reputation of its toys. A lead paint scandal emanating from China, where many of the company's toys were made, caused Mattel to revamp safety measures at Chinese manufacturing plants and caused the firm's CEO to film an online video apology to parents.[5]

- That same year, Burger King, the world's second largest hamburger chain behind McDonald's, announced it would begin buying eggs and pork only from suppliers that did not confine their animals in cages and crates. The decision was hailed by animal rights activists as a "historic advance."[6]

- In 2008, as its subsidiary, NBC, broadcast the Olympics from Beijing, the General Electric Company launched its "EcoMagination" campaign on the Olympic grounds, to showcase the company's environmentally friendly products from wind turbines to LED lighting to eco-friendly nanofiltration and recycling water systems. Three years earlier, GE CEO Jeff Immelt announced the global company would bet its future on environmentally hospitable products.[7]

Such were the socially responsible public relations initiatives companies used to enhance consumer relations.

As Bruce Springsteen once put it, with "57 channels and nuthin' on" (or today, more like 557!) all offering commercial after commercial, and with Internet banner ads, "pop up ads" and "pop under ads," and streaming video infomercials and all the rest, it has become increasingly difficult for consumers to penetrate the advertising clutter to identify winning products and services.

In an era overwrought with advertising "noise"—tens of thousands of blaring messages beamed in the direction of a single consumer—public relations solutions can help cut through the clutter and distinguish one company from the next, enhancing the sale of a firm's products. This chapter examines how public relations helps attract, win, and keep consumers.

Consumer Relations Objectives

Building sales is the primary consumer relations objective. A satisfied customer may return; an unhappy customer may not. Here are some typical goals:

■ **Keeping old customers.** Most sales are made to established customers. Consumer relations efforts should be made to keep these customers happy. Pains should be taken to respond to customers' concerns, particularly in times of hardship—bereavement airline travel, for example, or phone calls to loved ones during natural disasters.

■ **Attracting new customers.** Every business must work constantly to develop new customers. In many industries, the prices and quality of competing products are similar. In choosing among brands, customers may base decisions on how they have been treated.

■ **Marketing new items or services.** Customer relations techniques can influence the sale of new products. Thousands of new products flood the market each year, and the vast array of information about these products can confuse the consumer. When General Electric's research revealed that consumers want personalized service and more information on new products, it established the GE Answer Center, a national toll-free, 24-hour service that informs consumers about new GE products and services. Building such company and product loyalty lies at the heart of a solid consumer relations effort.

■ **Expediting complaint handling.** Few companies are free of complaints. Customers protest when appliances don't work, errors are made in billing, or deliveries aren't made on time. Many large firms have established response procedures, often outsourcing call centers to places like Lakeland, Florida; Johnson City, Tennessee; or Bangalore, India, where personnel are trained to answer questions and direct responses. Such call centers have replaced company ombudspersons, who used to draw the assignment of handling customer complaints.

■ **Reducing costs.** For three decades, the Sym's clothing company used to advertise that *"An educated customer is our best customer."* Indeed, to most companies, an educated consumer is the best consumer. Uninformed buyers cost a company time and money—when goods are returned, service calls are made, and instructions are misunderstood. Many firms have adopted programs to educate customers about use of their products.

Consumer-Generated Media

For decades, publicity to consumers about products and services revolved around the mass media. While the traditional media are still important avenues through which to promote organizational offerings, the new lead voice in town is the Internet. It has given consumers a voice, a publishing platform, and a forum where their collective voices on products and services can be heard, shared, and researched.

Consumer-generated media (CGM) encompasses the millions of consumer-generated comments, opinions, and personal experiences posted in publicly available online sources on a wide range of issues, topics, products, and brands. CGM is also referred to as "online consumer word-of-mouth," originated from a variety of sources:

- blogs
- message boards and forums
- public discussions (Usenet newsgroups)
- discussions and forums on large email portals (Yahoo!, AOL, MSN)
- online opinion/review sites and services
- online feedback/complaint sites

Consumers seem to place trust in their fellow consumers. For any marketer trying to be heard or to break through the clutter, understanding and managing CGM may be critical. Then too, CGM is increasingly easy and inexpensive to create. Online discussion forms, membership groups, boards, blogs, and Usenet newsgroups are all easy to access.[8]

One ethical consideration for companies is how aggressive—and visible—they should be in directly accessing CGM. The best policy, always, is to disclose one's identity in Internet locales to avoid subsequent criticism.

Handling Consumer Complaints

Research indicates that only a handful of dissatisfied customers—4 percent—will ever complain. But that means that there are many others with the same complaint who never say anything. And the vast majority of dissatisfied customers won't repurchase from the offending company.

In the old days, a frequent response to complaint letters was to dust off the so-called "bedbug letter"—a term that stemmed from occasional letters to the railroads complaining about bedbugs in the sleeper cars. To save time, railroad consumer relations personnel simply dispatched a prewritten bedbug letter in response. Today, with the volume of mail, email, and faxes at a mountainous level, 21st-century versions of the bedbug letter still appear from time to time.

To respond quickly to complaints, companies established ombudsperson offices. The term *ombudsman* originally described a government official—in Sweden and New Zealand, for example—appointed to investigate complaints about abuses committed by public officials. Today, more often than not, the ombudsperson function is outsourced to a central (often overseas) location that customers can call to seek redress of grievances.

Typically, call center personnel monitor the difficulties customers are having with products. Often they can anticipate product or performance deficiencies. Corporate complaint handlers are in business to inspire customer confidence and to influence an organization's behavior toward improved service. They accomplish this by responding, hopefully more often than not, in the following manner:

- *"We'll take care of that for you."*
- *"We'll take full responsibility for that defect."*
- *"We want your business."*
- *"Thank you for thinking of us."*
- *"Consider it done."*

Alas, in these days of voice mail, email, and recorded voice recognition systems, such personalized "magic words" seem to be in short supply. Pity. The companies that express such understanding and courtesy will be the ones that keep the business.

PR Ethics

Mini-Case It's Good to Be the King

Consumers are fickle. What's "in" one day is "out" the next. Staying "trendy" is one of the 21st century's most mystifying consumer challenges—particularly in the area of retail clothing.

One chain that seemed to master the challenge was American Apparel (AA), an edgy, progressive clothes emporium known for its snug-fitting, logo-free T-shirts, underwear, and casual clothes, all on sale at AA outlets around the world. AA is the store where you are most likely to see the stars of sports and stage—from Lindsay Lohan to Seth Rogan to Anna Kournikova—hanging out.

AA is also the chain where you were likely to find ethical controversy, due to one man.

American Apparel founder Dov Charney (see Figure 13-3), a self-described "Jewish hustler" from Montreal, built the business into a 230-store, 19-country, 10,000-employee colossus while, at the same time, repeatedly embarrassing everyone associated with AA by performing in a most peculiar manner. For example:

- In 2008, a former employee sued Charney, charging that he sexually harassed her. Specifically, the former AA employee charged that Charney barged into her office shouting obscenities and physical threats and simulating sexual acts. This was the fifth such Charney-related case in four years. In one 2005 suit, another former employee claimed that Charney once greeted her wearing only an AA sock draped over his genitals. (Not exactly normal CEO-like behavior.)

- Video footage posted on the company's Web site showed the founder touring AA factories, dressed only in AA briefs.

- AA ads and in-store signage feature un-airbrushed young women and men in various voyeuristic stages. Charney, himself, shot some of the photos.

FIGURE 13-3 The king . . . (Photo: Newscom)

Balancing this "unorthodox" approach to business, Charney insisted on manufacturing in America, often bringing much-needed employment to marginal neighborhoods. While competitors headed overseas or closed in the face of economic downturn, Charney kept opening new stores and kept hiring—3,500 new employees in the dismal 2008 economy alone.

And while competitors struggled, AA's sales continued to soar, and products like the Tuna Safe Thong—designed "*to keep your underwear smelling fresh*"—continued to push the envelope (sometimes over a cliff!). (See Figure 13-4.)

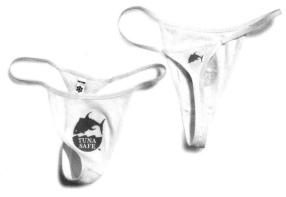

FIGURE 13-4 ... and his thongs. (Photo: Newscom)

While some marketing experts wondered if Charney's boorish behavior would one day sink his brand, the American Apparel founder suggested that people "get over it." In fact, perhaps in honor of its founder's proclivities, AA employees had to sign a document acknowledging that, given the sexualized nature of the company's garments and promotional materials, they should expect to encounter "sexually charged language and visual images" on the job.*

Questions

1. Do you think the founder's questionable behavior will ultimately hurt his product?

2. If you were American Apparel's public relations director, what would you recommend in terms of refining Charney's approach?

*For further information, see Justin Ravitz, "The Emperor's Clothes," *Worth* (December/January 2009).

The Consumer Movement

Although consumerism is considered to be a late 20th-century concept, legislation to protect consumers first emerged in the United States in 1872, when Congress enacted the Criminal Fraud Statute to protect consumers against corporate abuses. In 1887, Congress established the Interstate Commerce Commission to curb freewheeling railroad tycoons.

However, the first real consumer movement came right after the turn of the century when journalistic muckrakers encouraged legislation to protect the consumer. Upton Sinclair's novel *The Jungle* revealed scandalous conditions in the meatpacking industry and helped usher in federal meat inspection standards as Congress passed the Food and Drug Act and the Trade Commission Act. In the second wave of the movement, from 1927 to 1938, consumers were safeguarded from the abuses of manufacturers, advertisers, and retailers of well-known brands of commercial products. During this time, Congress passed the Food, Drug, and Cosmetic Act.

Later, the movement was boosted by the activities of a lone consumer crusader, Ralph Nader, who brought the world's most powerful auto company, General Motors, to its knees. Nader's thin 1965 book, *Unsafe at Any Speed,* pointed out how the GM Corvair was literally a "death trap." After trying to stop Nader at every turn—including assigning private detectives to trail his every move—GM relented and stopped production of the Corvair. Consumerism had won its most significant battle.

By the early 1960s, the movement had become stronger and more unified. President John F. Kennedy, in fact, proposed that consumers have their own bill of rights, containing four basic principles:

1. **The right to safety:** to be protected against the marketing of goods hazardous to health or life.

2. **The right to be informed:** to be protected against fraudulent, deceitful, or grossly misleading information, advertising, labeling, or other practices and to be given the facts needed to make an informed choice.

3. **The right to choose:** to be assured access, whenever possible, to a variety of products and services at competitive prices.

4. **The right to be heard:** to be assured that consumer interests will receive full and sympathetic consideration in the formulation of government policy.

Subsequent American presidents have continued to emphasize consumer rights and protection. Labeling, packaging, product safety, and a variety of other issues continue to concern government overseers of consumer interests.

Federal Consumer Agencies

Today a massive government bureaucracy attempts to protect the consumer against abuse: There are more than 900 different programs administered by more than 400 federal entities. Key agencies include the Justice Department, Federal Trade Commission, Food and Drug Administration, and Consumer Product Safety Commission.

- **Justice Department.** The Justice Department has had a consumer affairs section in its antitrust division since 1970. Its responsibilities include the enforcement of such consumer protection measures as the Truth in Lending Act and the Product Safety Act. The Justice Department is particularly concerned with antitrust and monopolistic activities. This was the root of the initiative against the world's largest computer company, Microsoft, in the early years of the George W. Bush administration. Subsequent to the Microsoft case, the Bush administration didn't aggressively pursue antitrust.

- **Federal Trade Commission.** The FTC, perhaps more than any other agency, has vigorously enforced consumer protection. Its national advertising division covers television and radio advertising, with special emphasis on foods, drugs, and cosmetics. Its general litigation division covers areas not included in national advertising, such as magazine subscription agencies, door-to-door sales, and income tax services. Its consumer credit and special programs division deals with such areas as fair credit reporting and truth in packaging.

- **Securities and Exchange Commission.** The SEC is the government agency that supervises disclosure among public companies. This is the province of investor relations, which was born in the mid-1930s, shortly after the passage of the Securities Act of 1933 and the Securities Exchange Act of 1934, which attempted to protect the public from abuses in the issuance and sale of securities. With the recession of 2008, spurred by proliferating investments in risky subprime mortgages, the SEC was taken to task for being "asleep at the switch" while Wall Street got rich at the expense of the rest of the country. The agency took the hit for allowing once regal firms—from Lehman Brothers to Washington Mutual to Bear Stearns to Countrywide Mortgage to AIG Insurance—to implode and take hapless investors with them. In late 2008, focus on the SEC intensified when one single fund manager, Bernard Madoff (pronounced "Made off"), literally "made off" with $60 billion—that's *billion* with a *"b"*—of investors' money, the largest investor fraud in history. Madoff had been the subject of complaints to the SEC over two decades, but the Commission failed to act. In 2009, Madoff was sentenced to 150 years in prison, the maximum allowable by law. (So chances are, he won't be defrauding any other investors!) The Madoff scandal, in particular, put great pressure on the Obama administration to straighten out the battered Securities and Exchange Commission. Sure enough, in October 2009, billionaire Raj Rajaratnam was hauled off by the SEC for "the biggest insider trading scheme ever involving a hedge fund."

- **Food and Drug Administration.** The FDA is responsible for protecting consumers from hazardous items: foods, drugs, cosmetics, therapeutic and radiological devices, food additives, and serums and vaccines. Under Dr. David Kessler, during the Clinton administration, the FDA waged an all-out war against cigarette advertising, especially to children. In 1997, the nation's four largest tobacco companies reached an agreement with 46 states, which included a payment by the firms of $366 million. As part of the overall tobacco promotion retrenchment, the industry removed its teenager-targeted Joe Camel symbol from its ads (see Figure 13-5).

- **Consumer Product Safety Commission.** This bureau is responsible for overseeing product safety and standards and has been particularly aggressive in recent years in the area of seat belt restraints, strollers, blankets, and other products for small children.

- In the late 1990s, the Clinton administration closed down the White House **Office of Consumer Affairs,** the agency that strongly advised Presidents Johnson and Carter, in particular, on matters of consumer interest. In 2009, after scandals regarding everything from lead in children's toys to tainted meat to killer spinach, the Obama administration was urged to appoint a strong White House advocate for consumers.[9]

In the 21st century, clearly the best policy for any public company is to communicate directly and frequently with regulators in Washington, ultimately to win their understanding and support.

Consumer Activists on the Internet

In the 21st century, with the Internet as stimulus, organic consumer movements—directed at individual companies, industries, or even multinational agencies like the World Trade Organization—have spread like wildfire around the globe. As one harassed executive put it, "In the old days, if you had an unlisted number, it was hard to find you. Now you do a Google search and find out the most intimate details."[10]

Although private testing organizations that evaluate products and inform consumers about potential dangers have proliferated, the most significant activity to keep companies honest has occurred on the Internet.

Perhaps the best-known testing group, Consumers Union was formed in 1936 to test products across a wide spectrum of industries. It publishes the results in a monthly magazine, *Consumer Reports,* which reaches about 3.5 million readers. Often an evaluation in *Consumer Reports,* either pro or con, greatly affects how customers view particular products. Occasionally *Consumer Reports* flubs its reviews, such as

FIGURE 13-5 **Good-bye, Joe.** For years, Joe Camel was the too-cool symbol that helped lure teenage smokers. Ultimately, the industry, at the government's insistence, killed old Joe. (Courtesy of Tobacco Free Kids)

Does RJR Nabisco Lie About Marketing To Kids?

In public they say:

"I do not want to sell tobacco to children. I'd fire anyone on the spot if I found they were doing it." (Steven Goldstone, CEO, RJR Nabisco Holdings Corp., 12/6/96).

But a 1976 RJR internal memo stated:

"Evidence is now available to indicate that the 14-to-18-year-old group is an increasing segment of the smoking population. RJR-T must soon establish a successful new brand in this market if our position in the industry is to be maintained over the long term."

You Decide.

In 1988, RJR introduced Joe Camel. Subsequently, Camel's share of the kids' market quadrupled. Camel is now the second most popular cigarette among children, and kids were found to be as familiar with Joe Camel as Mickey Mouse.

Tell your elected officials to support restrictions on tobacco marketing to children, including the Food and Drug Administration rule.

**Tobacco vs. Kids.
Where America draws the line.**

CAMPAIGN for TOBACCO-FREE Kids

To learn more, call 1-800-284-KIDS.

This ad supported by: American Cancer Society; American Lung Association; American Heart Association; Center for Women Policy Studies; National Federation of State High School Associations; Committee for Children; Intercultural Cancer Council; Interreligious Coalition on Smoking OR Health; Youth Service America; American College of Preventive Medicine; Girl Scouts USA; Child Welfare League of America; National Association of Secondary School Principals; National Association of Elementary School Principals; American Federation of Teachers; Women's Legal Defense Fund; Association of State and Territorial Health Officials.

The National Center for Tobacco-Free Kids, 1707 L Street NW, Suite 800, Washington, DC 20036

the famous case in 2007 when the magazine embarrassingly backed off its negative report on infant car seats, when manufacturers complained that test crashes were conducted at speeds higher than the publication claimed.[11] Consumers Union also produces books, a travel newsletter, a column for 450 newspapers, and monthly features for network television. It has an annual budget of $70 million.

The Consumer Federation of America was formed in 1968 to unify lobbying efforts for pro-consumer legislation. Today the federation consists of 200 national, state, and local consumer groups, labor unions, electric cooperatives, and other organizations with consumer interests.

With more than 200 million Americans accessing the Internet annually, Internet consumer activism has become much more prominent.[12] Internet activism uses Internet communications technologies to enable faster communications and coordination by citizen movements. From the Yahoo! Boycott Board, which lists actions being taken against organizations, to so-called rogue Web sites, which air the gripes of dissatisfied consumers, to wildfire email campaigns and discussion groups directed at product abuse—the Internet has become a prime source of consumer activism.

The most stirring example of anticorporate Internet activism took place in 1999, when opponents of corporate-led globalization used the Internet effectively to coordinate protests against the World Trade Organization (WTO), an effort that came to be known as the Battle in Seattle. Thus began an annual battle between activists and WTO attendees.

Internet activism has been criticized on grounds that it gives disproportionate access to affluent activists because poor people, minorities, and elderly citizens either lack access or are inexperienced in the new technologies.

Nonetheless, smart companies take Internet challenges seriously and act on them immediately. They have found that word-of-mouth criticism, aided and abetted by the Internet, must be dealt with—quickly.

Although companies often find such activists' criticism annoying, the emergence of the consumer watchdog movement has generally been a positive development for consumers. Ralph Nader, still going strong into the 21st century, and others have forced organizations to consider, even more than usual, the downside of the products and services they offer. Smart companies have come to take seriously the pronouncements of consumer activists.

Business Gets the Message

Obviously, few organizations can afford to shirk their responsibilities to consumers. Consumer relations divisions have sprung up, either as separate entities or as part of public relations departments.

In many companies, consumer relations began strictly as a way to handle complaints, an area to which all unanswerable complaints were sent. Such units have frequently provided an alert to management. More recently, companies have broadened the consumer relations function to encompass such activities as developing guidelines to evaluate services and products for management, developing consumer programs that meet consumer needs and increase sales, developing field-training programs, evaluating service approaches, and evaluating company effectiveness in demonstrating concern for customers.

The investment in consumer service apparently pays off. Marketers of consumer products say that most customer criticism can be mollified with a prompt, personalized reply. Throw in a couple of free samples and consumers feel even better. In any case, consumers are impressed when a company takes the time to drop them a line for whatever reason.

On the other hand, failing to answer a question, satisfy a complaint, or solve a problem can result in a blitz of bad word-of-mouth advertising.

In adopting a more activist consumerist philosophy, firms have found that consumer relations need not take a defensive posture. Consumer relations professionals must themselves be activists to make certain that consumers understand the benefits and realities of using their products.

The consumer philosophy of Jet Blue Airways, embodied in the company's "Customer Bill of Rights," is typical of the more enlightened attitude of most companies today.[13]

> JetBlue issued its *Customer Bill of Rights* in 2007, a week after a disastrous Valentine's Day ice storm stranded thousands of customers and saddled the formerly beloved airline with oppressive national opprobrium. Said embattled CEO David Neeleman (who was replaced shortly thereafter), *"We had a weakness in our system. We were completely overwhelmed. I don't blame our customers for being upset with this. This was a big wakeup call for JetBlue"*[14] (see Case Study, Chapter 19).

No question that in the 21st century, business was starting to understand that with heightened competition and more immediate and public ways to complain, the consumer most certainly was "king."

Talking Points   Promoting an Unapologetic Monster . . .

Even in the days of consumer activism and food company nutrition-mindedness, one has to admire an organization committed to the blissful piling on of calories.

So it was, with the help of Weber Shandwick public relations, that in the spring of 2005 Hardee's announced, with great fanfare, the Monster Thickburger, a mammoth 1,420-calorie hamburger with 104 grams of fat (see Figure 13-6).

Launch of the Monster Thickburger generated publicity across the globe, including a skit about a new "Killer Kamikaze Burger" on *The Tonight Show* with Jay Leno. The publicity took on an "anti-political correctness" tone, with critics citing the dangers of obesity and fad diets in the United States. The *London Telegraph* quipped, *"America's appetite for junk food has taken on terrifying new proportions."*

Hardee's not only took it in stride but, as sales went up, ran with the criticism. Said Hardee's marketing director, *"We're unapologetic about the product and getting out the word that the Thickburger may not be for everyone."*

Besides, you could always wash it down with a Diet Coke.*

FIGURE 13-6 The monster. Hardee's hit the publicity jackpot with its very un-politically correct new offering. (Courtesy of O'Dwyer.com)

*For further information, see Kevin McCauley, "Monster Thickburger Gives Hardee's PR Lift," *O'Dwyer's PR Services Report* (March 2005): 8.

Points . . . But Withdrawing an Apologetic Drugster

One beverage with which you won't be washing down your Monster Thickburger is Cocaine, the energy drink (see Figure 13-7).

That catchy concoction was withdrawn from the shelves in 2007, when the FDA warned manufacturer Redux Beverages that the company was illegally marketing the drink as a street drug alternative and dietary supplement.

The FDA cited as proof the drink's labeling and Web site, which included the statements "Speed in a Can," "Liquid Cocaine," and "Cocaine—Instant Rush."

In withdrawing the product and agreeing to change its name, the company said its drink contained no drugs. Said a Redux partner, "*We like to think we have a great sense of humor. And our market, primarily folks from ages 20 to 30, they love the ideas, they love the name, they love the whole campaign. These are not drug users.*"

Evidently, the FDA didn't get the joke.*

FIGURE 13-7 Flying high. Cocaine, the energy drink, had a short flight in 2007, when the product was withdrawn after the FDA protested. (Photo: Newscom)

*For further information, see "Energy Drink Is Withdrawn over Concerns About Name," *New York Times* (May 8, 2007): C3.

Last Word

Without consumers, there would be no companies. Increased concerns about climate change, increased environmental concerns about packaging and pollution, rising outrage about trans fats and secondhand smoke, and numerous other causes indicate that the push for product safety and quality will likely increase in the years ahead.

Indeed, the smartest companies are those that tie their products and services to larger societal causes, thus establishing a link in the minds of consumers that represents "loftier" goals than merely making money (see Figure 13-8).

That is not to say there is anything wrong with making money. Companies depend on their profits

FIGURE 13-8 Flood relief. New Orleans Mayor Ray Nagin praised Shell Oil for being part of his city's renaissance, after flood waters ravaged the city. (Courtesy of Jack O'Dwyer's Newsletter)

to exist. Without profitability, corporations can't contribute to bettering society.

Safeguarding the relationship with consumers of products and services is fundamental to continuing to earn profits. That's why the efforts of public relations professionals, assigned to maintaining, sustaining, and enhancing a company's standing with its customers, is a core communications challenge in the 21st century.

Discussion Starters

1. Why is dealing with consumers so important for public relations?
2. What are typical consumer relations objectives?
3. What is the office of the ombudsperson?
4. What is consumer-generated marketing?
5. What key federal agencies are involved in consumerism?
6. What is the purpose of the SEC?
7. What is a consumer bill of rights?
8. What is the impact of the Internet on a company's consumer relations?
9. Who is Ralph Nader, and what is his significance to consumerism?
10. What constitutes a quality consumer-oriented company?

Top of the Shelf Waiting for Your Cat to Bark? / Bryan and Jeffrey Eisenberg, Nashville, TN: Thomas Nelson Publishers, 2006

The Eisenberg brothers are best-selling authors who have made their living examining the communication gap between marketers and the buying public, and what marketers can do to redress the problem. They begin by declaring "mass marketing" deader than Saddam Hussein.

A growing sense of consumer cynicism, coupled with a deluge of information and the Internet's ability to offer an egalitarian marketplace at the fingertips of millions, has given buyers more control now than ever before. What marketers need, the Eisenbergs say, is greater "personalization," approaching the consumer on a one-to-one basis. The book goes on to suggest ways—some traditional, others ingenious—to accomplish this minimized but Herculean feat.

Case Study Flying to the Auto Bailout on a Private Jet

The greatest corporate public relations blunder of the 21st century (so far) took place on November 19, 2008, when the CEOs of the nation's three largest automobile manufacturing companies each flew a private jet to Washington in order to secure billions of dollars in taxpayer funds to keep their firms afloat.

"There is a delicious irony in seeing private luxury jets flying into Washington, D.C., and people coming off of them with tin cups in their hand, saying that they're going to be trimming down and streamlining their businesses," Rep. Gary Ackerman, D-New York, told the chief executive officers of Ford, Chrysler, and General Motors (GM) at a hearing of the House Financial Services Committee.

And even though congressmen are perpetually guilty of hyperbole to get their names in the papers, in this case, Rep. Ackerman had it cold.

Students of public relations could only shake their heads ruefully at the amazing display of ignorance displayed by the once-powerful heads of once-dominant companies.

Traditionally Lousy Public Relations

Auto executives, traditionally, were among the most insulated and isolated business *men* (and until recently, all were 'men'!) in the nation. Just as an earlier General Motors CEO, Ralph Wilson, famously told Congress, *"What's good for GM is good for America"*—so did the auto industry imagine that it could do no wrong.

And while GM, Ford, and Chrysler regularly recruited public relations heavyweights to direct their communications departments, company management and their industry remained relatively tone-deaf to such public relations concepts as disclosure and openness and accessibility.

It was only when Chrysler nearly went bust in the 1980s that the industry produced a true public relations leader, Lee Iacocca, willing to step up to make the case that his company deserved saving. Iacocca, an auto industry sales and marketing legend, mounted a fearsome public relations campaign to reassure the nation that Chrysler was a solid company that made worthwhile cars. His efforts helped turn around the company, and all monies borrowed from the government were returned—with interest.

Since Iacocca, the U.S. auto industry produced little more than steadily declining companies producing costly and underappreciated products. Meanwhile, competitors from Germany, Japan, Korea, and elsewhere surged ahead of the domestic automakers, by manufacturing attractive and fuel-efficient vehicles.

By the fall of 2008, with the American economy in deep meltdown, workers being fired, and credit being squeezed, the auto companies found themselves unable to move product and running out of cash. Bankruptcy for GM and Chrysler loomed on the horizon, unless a government bailout could be achieved.

Disaster in D.C.

The Big Three CEOs headed to the nation's capitol in November 2008 to make their case, before a Congress willing to fork over $25 billion of taxpayer money, in order to save the livelihood of such a pivotal domestic industry and the jobs of millions of Americans.

Within a mere 24 hours in the nation's capital, the Big Three's CEOs persuaded the initially sympathetic Democratic Congress that first, they lacked the intelligence to come up with a coherent plan to rescue their own industry from the abyss, and second, they lacked the common sense to take public transport to a hearing seeking handouts.

The arrival in Washington of the Ford, Chrysler, and GM private jets made CEOs Alan Mulally, Robert Nardelli, and Rick Waggoner look like Moe, Larry, and Curley and effectively ruined any chance of returning to Detroit with taxpayer booty. Headline writers and TV anchors had a field day with the irony of *"speeding the bailout by taking the private jet."* And predictably, the Congress was unmerciful (see Figure 13-9).

Beyond the rock-headedness of showing up in luxury, the CEOs seemed unprepared with "reasons" as to why the taxpayers should subsidize their corporate failures. The Congress sent them back to Detroit to come up with more concrete plans.

As one longtime auto industry observer described the amazing rejection, *"The automakers never miss an opportunity to miss an opportunity."*

Adopting a New Public Relations Strategy

Two weeks later, the auto executives were back in D.C., this time better prepared for the likely reception, with a public relations strategy that basically broke down thusly:

- **Leave the driving to us.**
  This time around there were no private jets.

  Instead, the industry executives drove to D.C. from Detroit in their most fuel-efficient automobiles. At the same time, the companies announced they would jettison their private jets, as part of an austerity program.

  While critics scoffed that driving, instead of flying, to Washington was a bit "hokey" (because it was!), nonetheless the cosmetic gesture showed that even auto CEOs can learn from prior mistakes.

FIGURE 13-9 Hat in hand. Auto industry executives received a rude awakening in November 2008, when they arrived before Congress to seek a government bailout of their industry. (Photo: Newscom)

■ **Emphasize the plan—and the cars.**

The three CEOs each sketched a well-developed plan to combine expense cuts with product innovation to attempt to resurrect the fallen industry.

At the heart of each plan was an emphasis on the cars.

In point of fact, U.S.-manufactured cars had gotten a bad deal in recent years. They really had become much more competitive, efficient, and stylish than most people thought. The industry had worked hard in recent years to produce cars that people want. For example:

• Fords and Lincolns were rated highly in safety.
• Cadillacs continued to be respected.
• The Pontiac Solstice and the Dodge Viper were as hot as any foreign product.

The problem was the U.S. auto industry hadn't promoted its product well. In the old days, "Buy American" was the watchword to rally round domestic producers. Why not champion this refrain again with the auto industry?

Sure, the cars cost too much relative to the competition. And absolutely, the industry needed to respond by cutting redundant employees, excessive health care costs and labor benefits, and bloated executive salaries (Iacocca made $1 a year during the Chrysler bailout).

But the cars, themselves had to be given more credit and emphasis in the spotlight.

■ **Think not UAW but rather, "IWS."**

It's the workers stupid.

The best weapons the auto companies had were the six million line auto workers and countless millions of parts suppliers, dealership employees, materials workers, service industry staffers, and even race car drivers, etc., all dependent on the auto industry.

The workers.

These were the people who should have been front-and-center in interviews, ads, and even testimony. CEOs were non-starters. Nobody believed 'em. But workers—common men and women—carried the ability to persuade the populace that their families deserved support.

In fact, the most believable auto executive seemed to be Ron Gettelfinger, the president of the United Auto Workers (UAW), the only one in charge to place the country's focus on all the millions of workers who would be left on the beach, should Armageddon strike the industry.

Eventually, the companies themselves began to focus on their workers to win public support. UAW members began appearing prominently in auto industry ads and speaking out as to the value of their industry to the country that they loved.

■ **Visibility and transparency.**

Despite the criticism of their desired mode of transport to Washington, the three auto CEOs, Nardelli, Mulally, and Waggoner, were all strong and credible spokesman for the industry.

Nardelli, who famously got thrown out of Home Depot after censoring shareholders at an annual meeting, was articulate and tough. Mulally was personable and smart. And Waggoner was direct and sincere. They were all good communicators.

Their initial problem was they weren't willing enough to go directly to the American public to plead their case. Rather, they relied on ham-handed public relations stunts—lugubrious YouTube videos and insipid Web site messages—to carry the flag.

In the weeks subsequent to their second successful Washington foray, the auto CEOs seemed to have gotten the message. First, they all accepted—a la Lee Iacocca before them—$1 in salary for the next year. They also promised full transparency as to how the bailout money was to be used.

But was it too little, too late? In March 2009, Rick Waggoner stepped down as CEO of General Motors. In May 2009, Chrysler filed for bankruptcy protection and, in effect, subordinated itself to Italian automaker Fiat. Two months later, GM filed for bankruptcy protection. Only Ford, among the "Big Three," avoided bankruptcy and becoming a "ward" of the U.S. government.

As to its ultimate survival, the U.S. auto industry finally recognized that almost as critical for their survival as adopting a realistic plan for reemergence was their pursuit of a sound and thoughtful strategy for public relations.

Questions

1. What would you have counseled the auto executives in terms of their first trip to Washington for bailout funds?

2. What public relations posture would you recommend the executives adopt with respect to the UAW?

3. How visible would you suggest the auto CEOs be as they continue to work out of their problems? What kind of public relations initiative would you design for them?

For further information, see Michael Bush, "Detroit's Big Bungle in D.C. and the PR Lessons Learned," *Advertising Age* (December 8, 2008): 3; Jerry Flint, "Everybody's an Expert," *Forbes* (December 22, 2008): 40; David M. Herszenhorn, "Detroit's Bid for Aid Fails for Now," *New York Times* (November 20, 2008); David M. Herszenhorn and Bill Vlasic, "Auto Executives Still Find Skeptics," *New York Times* (December 4, 2008); Herszenhorn and Vlasic, "Democrats Set to Offer Loans for Carmakers," *New York Times* (December 5, 2008); Herszenhorn, "Deal to Rescue American Automakers Is Moving Ahead," *New York Times* (December 8, 2008); and David E. Sanger, David M. Herszenhorn, and Bill Vlasic, "Bush Aids Detroit but Hard Choices Wait for Obama," *New York Times* (December 19, 2008).

From the Top   An Interview with Amy Binder

Amy Binder is CEO of the New York City–based RFI Binder Partners, Inc., one of the companies of the Ruder Finn Group. In addition to overseeing the business direction and growth of the agency, Binder is focused on ensuring that every client receives consistent, high-quality service and has continual access to the agency's best creative and strategic thinking. She is a veteran of two-and-a half decades in public relations, developing corporate reputations and branding programs for some of the world's largest organizations. For the five years leading to the formation of RFIBinder Partners, she was president/Ruder Finn Americas.

Did you study public relations in college?
No, I went to Brown University and majored in history. While at Brown, I also studied photography, which had been a passion of mine since I was a teenager. I actually combined both interests in my thesis, which was about using photographs taken by 19th-century British photographers to gain a better and different understanding of society in Victorian England. Photographers at that time, in many ways, were photojournalists documenting their time. Through my thesis, I began to be interested in how outside third parties could shape public opinion.

Did your family influence you to seek a career in public relations?
When I grew up, very few people understood what public relations was. In the 1960s, it was still a relatively young field. As a child, people would ask me what my father did and when I said public relations, they would stare at me blankly. Saying your father was a doctor, lawyer, banker, or businessman would have been much easier. It finally got to a point where I would say, one, do you know what the public is; two, do you understand what relationships are all about; three, public relations is about building relationships among different publics. That they got. Given how people reacted, public relations was not a career that came to mind first.

What qualities are most important for a client's benefit?
The following five qualities are the most important:

- **Learning how to listen:** All consultants need to understand the problem and the challenge that a client is facing. We need to listen to our clients to better understand their culture as well as their specific business challenges.

- **Being strategic:** Public relations is perceived to be a soft discipline, and many ideas for programs come out of creative sessions. An idea needs to emerge from logical thinking and research that can demonstrate the rationale for choosing a specific creative platform. One needs the discipline to be able to demonstrate the framework for why an idea is right for addressing a specific business challenge. And one needs the research or data, which will help you understand the dynamics in the marketplace.

- **Being creative:** We live in a world where there is a lot of clutter. Consumers and businesspeople are being bombarded with messages from a variety of brands, businesses, institutions, et cetera. Creativity enables you to find a new way of looking at something or enabling other people to hear the message that you want to convey. That is more important than ever.

- **Being interested in how opinion is shaped:** While it is still critical for someone going into this profession to read, listen, and watch the media, that is no longer enough. With the fragmentation of the media, there are so many ways that consumers and customers get information and are influenced. There are think tanks which issue reports, individuals who write blogs on the Internet, seminars held every day both offline and online through Webcasts. It is important that a consultant is very aware and interested in learning about the new ways that are emerging to influence opinions.

- **Being curious:** You have to be interested in learning about a lot of different industries and business issues. One day you might find yourself dealing with skincare issues and the next day a crisis with an oil company. As a consultant, you need to be curious about learning new areas.

What is most compelling about the public relations consulting business?
There are pros and cons. On the one hand, we can never truly understand our clients' business because we are outsiders. Until you sit inside a corporation, you cannot understand as fully the culture and challenges that the company faces every day. On the other hand, being an outsider can be a real advantage. We are willing to take risks that insiders might be more hesitant to take. We also bring the objectivity of an outsider. One of the most compelling aspects of the consulting business is bringing new points of view and different types of insights to solving a problem. The task of changing opinions and closing communications gaps is not easy. Sometimes you need to do something bold to accomplish this task.

Why should an organization seek outside public relations counsel?

There are four important reasons to bring in an outside agency.

1. The most important is to support the launch of a new strategic, proactive initiative. An internal public relations group, unless it is very large, most often is driven by addressing the reactive needs of a company and servicing their internal business partners. An outside agency can be very helpful in taking an objective point of view about an issue and investing the time to develop a program which addresses all of the challenges facing either the brand or the company. The outside agency can also devote staff that will not be distracted by another internal issue or crisis of the day, ensuring that the program is well executed.

2. A second important role is when there is a crisis. The outside agency can offer an objective or outsider's point of view, which is critical because during a crisis, one can become mired in the details and the pressures of the moment. In addition, there is always a need for seasoned professionals who have been through a crisis before.

3. Third, an agency can bring relationships with key opinion leaders and the media that are important. The agency may have developed programs for clients who have faced similar challenges and will bring knowledge about what will work and what won't.

4. And finally, more often than not, consultants can bring a different—if not broader—perspective on an issue because of the range of his or her experiences. This perspective is useful in helping a company take a fresh view on an issue.

How would you assess the state of the public relations business today?

This may be one of the strongest times in the history of this profession. The media from *The Economist* to *The Wall Street Journal* have written articles recently about the growing recognition for the field and what it can offer. The public relations field is all about building credibility. In a time when so many organizations have had their reputations called into question, there is an important opportunity for the field.

Public Relations Library

Bloom, Robert H., and Dave Conti. *The Inside Advantage: The Strategy that Unlocks the Hidden Growth in Your Business*. New York, NY: McGraw-Hill, 2007. The premise here is that in order to grow your consumer base, a firm must tap its "inner strength" by looking internally for that which differentiates you.

Careers in Advertising and Public Relations: The WetFeet Insider Guide. San Francisco: WetFeet, Inc., 2004. Soup-to-nuts primer on getting a job in one of these creative fields.

Cone, Steve. *Powerlines: Words that Sell Brands, Grip Fans & Sometimes Change History*. New York, NY: Bloomberg Press, 2008. These are the lines that moved marketing, according to the author, from "Only You Can Prevent Forest Fires" to "Virginia is for Lovers."

Hawkins, Del I., and Kenneth A. Coney. *Consumer Behavior: Building Marketing Strategy*. New York: McGraw-Hill Irwin, 2004. This book tells you everything you need to know about consumer behavior—what it is and why it's worthy of study.

Johnson, Lisa, and Cheri Hanson. *Mind Your X's & Y's: Satisfying the 10 Cravings of a New Generation of Consumers*. New York, NY: Free Press, 2006. There are 62 million Americans aged 27–41 and 74 million aged just below. This book tells how to reach these Gen X and Yers, who grew up on the Internet.

Kush, Christopher. *The One Hour Activist*. San Francisco: Jossey-Bass, 2004. Packed with advice on getting your message across.

Martin, Dick. *Rebuilding Brand America*. New York, NY: Amacom, 2007. Dick Martin is a longtime public relations professional and a smart fellah. His prescription to build back the American brand makes great good sense.

Ries, Laura, and Al Ries. *The Fall of Advertising and the Rise of PR*. New York: Harper Business, 2002. Legendary positioning guru and his talented daughter declare that their former business has had it. Long live public relations!

Schiffman, Stephan. *E-Mail Selling Techniques: That Really Work*. Avon, MA: Adams Media, 2007. This book is all about creating targeted emails to reach potential customers and earn coveted face time with them.

Schneider, Joan, with Jeanne Yocum. *New Product Launch: 10 Proven Strategies*. Deerfield, IL: Stagnito Communications, 2004. A roadmap for companies ready to launch a new product. According to the authors, of the 33,000 products introduced each year, 75 percent fail.

Spizman, Robyn, and Rick Frishman. *Where's Your WOW? 16 Ways to Make Your Competitors Wish They Were You*. New York, NY: McGraw-Hill, 2008. All about growing creatively by seeking and winning new business.

Stevens, Howard, and Theodore Kinni. *Achieving Sales Excellence: The 7 Customer Rules for Becoming the New Sales Professional*. Avon, MA: Platinum Press, 2007. The result of 14 years of research into how people can become better salesmen. (And all of us in public relations are—"salespeople.")

Chapter 14

International Relations

FIGURE 14-1 Terror monger and her computer. Malika El Aroud spread jihadist messages of hate to female Islamists, via the Internet, from her Brussels home. (Photo: Newscom)

In 2008, Brussels police, not to mention law enforcement authorities around the world, were on the lookout for a 48-year-old woman regularly dressed in a T-shirt and pants, a pair of powder-blue slippers monogrammed in gold with the letters "SEXY," and draped in an Islamic black veil, covering all but her eyes.

This seemingly harmless, middle-aged lady, Malika El Aroud, or "Oum Obeyda," as she was better known on the Internet, filled her days as a self-described female holy warrior for al-Qaeda, spreading anti-Western messages of Internet jihad to Muslim women far and wide (see Figure 14-1).

Through her Web site and daily blogging, Ms. El Aroud became "a role model" for women suicide bombers and was assessed by international authorities as "very clever—and extremely dangerous."[1]

Countering the terror-mongering Brussels resident was another middle-aged lady from New Jersey, whose blog on affairs in Yemen was banned in that nation. The blogger, Jane Novak, had never been to Yemen but became interested in the plight of a Yemeni journalist, who incurred his government's wrath by writing about a bloody rebellion in the country. When the journalist was tried and threatened with the death penalty, Ms. Novak took Internet action and became a "public enemy" to the government of Yemen.[2]

Such was the public relations/communications power of the Internet on the international stage.

A half century ago, the late Canadian communications professor Marshall McLuhan wrote that "*the world is a global village.*" Today, of course, there is no

question but that that is the case. As a consequence, the practice of public relations is very much an international phenomenon.

And the Internet has greatly expedited the process—as companies, nonprofits, governments, and even terrorists participate in a global challenge to win the battle of ideas by persuading the world's citizens to support their point of view.

The fact is that information now travels at 15,000 miles an instant. We are, according to some, transitioning from an age of "globalization" to one of "cognitive understanding," where citizens are compelled to become better at absorbing, processing, and combining the information that is readily available all around them.[3]

As the world has become a smaller place and the power of communications has expanded exponentially, the public relations challenge for organizations, nations, and governments—some used to operating in secrecy—has also increased. As proof, in 2008 Prime Minister Wen Jiabao of China—a nation not exactly known for its openness—jumped into the social networking world with a page on Facebook. (Mr. Wen's site became an overnight success, attracting 13,000 "supporters" in its first day!)[4]

As trade and information flows have become borderless, so, too, has public relations. Indeed, the International Public Relations Association, founded in 1955, has members in 95 countries.

Although the reality of peoples and nations of the world becoming more closely connected is largely positive for society, there is also a dark side. The images beamed by satellite signals and the Internet have, in some quarters, fomented misunderstandings and jealousies, as the chasm between rich and poor, haves and have-nots, comes more sharply into focus.

The attacks on America of September 11, 2001, followed by the War in Iraq, exacerbated these problems, particularly with respect to understanding the practice of Islam and relations with people of Middle Eastern descent. Repairing these rifts will take time as well as thoughtful action and communication from all sectors of society. This is a key international public relations challenge for the Obama administration and the world in the 21st century (see the Case Study at the conclusion of this chapter).

In this chapter, we briefly explore the state of public relations practice around the world and the opportunities available for international public relations practice.

Operating Around the Globe

The actions of individuals and organizations in one part of the world are felt instantly and irrevocably by people around the globe. As a consequence, multinational corporations, in particular, must be sensitive to how their actions might affect people of different cultures in different geographies.

Companies, in fact, have become the most prominent standard bearers of their countries. American companies, with eight of the 10 most powerful brands in the world, are the most prominent of the prominent.

Consider the challenges multinational companies face.

- In 2006, when French students rioted to protest proposed changes in France's employment policies, one of the most prominent targets was McDonald's. Why? Because it was American, it represented "evil capitalism," and it was there. Earlier in Paris, demonstrators protested working conditions at McDonald's restaurants.[5]

- In 2007, when *The New York Times* published a report that manhole covers made for utility Con Edison were being produced by "barefoot, shirtless, whip-thin men" in oven-like temperatures in India, the utility said it was unaware of the foundry conditions in New Delhi and immediately imposed new safety standards on its manufacturer.[6]

- Around the world, other symbols of American capitalism, from Nike to Pepsi to Microsoft, remain on guard to local conflagration.

All foreign companies operating internationally must constantly reinforce the notion that they are responsible and concerned residents of local communities. Most resort to the public relations philosophy of leading with proper action and then communicating it. KFC, for example, has 158 franchises in Indonesia, most of which are locally owned and operated. McDonald's has a poster in the window of the Jakarta McDonald's that reads:

In the name of Allah, the merciful and the gracious, McDonald's Indonesia is owned by an indigenous Muslim Indonesian.

Smart multinationals also support local causes and incorporate international audiences and celebrities in their philanthropic efforts. Stated another way, the most well-known companies and best brands in the world observe a mantra of "thinking global, acting local" in order to win lasting friendship and support in other countries (see Figure 14-2).

2008 Rank	2007 Rank	Brand	Country of Origin	Sector	2008 Brand Value ($m)	Change in Brand Value
1	1	Coca-Cola	US	Beverages	66,667	2%
2	3	IBM	US	Computer Services	59,031	3%
3	2	Microsoft	US	Computer Software	59,007	1%
4	4	GE	US	Diversified	53,086	3%
5	5	Nokia	Finland	Consumer Electronics	35,942	7%
6	6	Toyota	Japan	Automotive	34,050	6%
7	7	Intel	US	Computer Hardware	31,261	1%
8	8	McDonald's	US	Restaurants	31,049	6%
9	9	Disney	US	Media	29,251	0%
10	20	Google	US	Internet Services	25,590	43%
11	10	Mercedes	Germany	Automotive	25,577	9%
12	12	HP	US	Computer Hardware	23,509	6%
13	13	BMW	Germany	Automotive	23,298	8%
14	16	Gillette	US	Personal Care	22,069	8%
15	15	American Express	US	Financial Services	21,940	5%
16	17	Louis Vuitton	France	Luxury	21,602	6%
17	18	Cisco	US	Computer Services	21,306	12%
18	14	Marlboro	US	Tobacco	21,300	0%
19	11	Citi	US	Financial Services	20,174	-14%
20	19	Honda	Japan	Automotive	19,079	6%
21	21	Samsung	South Korea	Consumer Electronics	17,689	5%
22	-	H&M	Sweden	Apparel	13,840	NEW
23	27	Oracle	US	Computer Software	13,831	11%
24	33	Apple	US	Consumer Electronics	13,724	24%
25	25	Sony	Japan	Consumer Electronics	13,583	5%
26	26	Pepsi	US	Beverages	13,249	3%
27	23	HSBC	UK	Financial Services	13,143	-3%
28	24	Nescafe	Switzerland	Beverages	13,055	1%
29	29	Nike	US	Sporting Goods	12,672	6%
30	28	UPS	US	Transportation	12,621	5%
31	34	SAP	Germany	Computer Software	12,228	12%
32	31	Dell	US	Computer Hardware	11,695	1%
33	30	Budweiser	US	Alcohol	11,438	-2%
34	22	Merrill Lynch	US	Financial Services	11,399	-22%
35	38	IKEA	Sweden	Home Furnishings	10,913	8%
36	36	Canon	Japan	Computer Hardware	10,876	3%
37	32	JPMorgan	US	Financial Services	10,771	-6%
38	35	Goldman Sachs	US	Financial Services	10,331	-3%
39	40	Kellogg's	US	Food	9,710	4%
40	44	Nintendo	Japan	Consumer Electronics	8,772	13%
41	39	UBS	Switzerland	Financial Services	8,740	-11%
42	37	Morgan Stanley	US	Financial Services	8,696	-16%
43	42	Philips	Netherlands	Diversified	8,325	8%
44	-	Thomson Reuters	Canada	Media	8,313	NEW
45	46	Gucci	Italy	Luxury	8,254	7%
46	48	eBay	US	Internet Services	7,991	7%
47	50	Accenture	US	Computer Services	7,948	9%
48	43	Siemens	Germany	Diversified	7,943	3%
49	41	Ford	US	Automotive	7,896	-12%
50	45	Harley-Davidson	US	Automotive	7,608	-2%
51	51	L'Oreal	France	Personal Care	7,508	7%
52	52	MTV	US	Media	7,193	4%
53	54	VW	Germany	Automotive	7,047	8%
54	47	AIG	US	Financial Services	7,022	-6%
55	49	Axa	France	Financial Services	7,001	-4%
56	53	Heinz	US	Food	6,646	2%
57	57	Colgate	US	Personal Care	6,437	7%
58	62	amazon.com	US	Internet Services	6,434	19%
59	56	Xerox	US	Computer Hardware	6,393	6%
60	58	Chanel	France	Luxury	6,355	9%
61	59	Wrigley	US	Food	6,105	6%
62	64	Zara	Spain	Apparel	5,955	15%
63	63	Nestle	Switzerland	Food	5,592	5%
64	60	KFC	US	Restaurants	5,582	-2%
65	55	Yahoo!	US	Internet Services	5,496	-9%
66	67	Danone	France	Food	5,408	8%
67	68	Audi	Germany	Automotive	5,407	11%
68	66	Caterpillar	US	Diversified	5,288	5%
69	65	Avon	US	Personal Care	5,264	3%
70	69	Adidas	Germany	Sporting Goods	5,072	6%
71	71	Rolex	Switzerland	Luxury	4,956	8%
72	72	Hyundai	South Korea	Automotive	4,846	9%
73	-	BlackBerry	Canada	Consumer Electronics	4,802	NEW
74	70	Kleenex	US	Personal Care	4,636	1%
75	75	Porsche	Germany	Automotive	4,601	0%
76	73	Hermes	France	Luxury	4,575	8%
77	61	Gap	US	Apparel	4,357	-20%
78	78	Panasonic	Japan	Consumer Electronics	4,281	4%
79	83	Cartier	Switzerland	Luxury	4,236	10%
80	79	Tiffany & Co	US	Luxury	4,208	5%
81	74	Pizza Hut	US	Restaurants	4,067	-4%
82	80	Allianz	Germany	Financial Services	4,033	2%
83	85	Moet & Chandon	France	Alcohol	3,951	6%
84	84	BP	UK	Energy	3,911	3%
85	88	Starbucks	US	Restaurants	3,879	7%
86	81	ING	Netherlands	Financial Services	3,768	-3%
87	77	Motorola	US	Consumer Electronics	3,721	-10%
88	89	Duracell	US	Consumer Electronics	3,682	2%
89	91	Smirnoff	UK	Alcohol	3,590	6%
90	92	Lexus	Japan	Automotive	3,588	7%
91	94	Prada	Italy	Luxury	3,585	9%
92	90	Johnson & Johnson	US	Personal Care	3,582	4%
93	-	Ferrari	Italy	Automotive	3,527	NEW
94	-	Armani	Italy	Luxury	3,526	NEW
95	87	Hennessy	France	Alcohol	3,513	-7%
96	-	Marriott	US	Hospitality	3,502	NEW
97	93	Shell	Netherlands	Energy	3,471	4%
98	96	Nivea	Germany	Personal Care	3,401	9%
99	-	FedEx	US	Transportation	3,359	NEW
100	-	Visa	US	Financial Services	3,338	NEW

FIGURE 14-2 **Global brand leaders.** And the Top 10 winners are . . . Coca-Cola, IBM, Microsoft, General Electric, Nokia, Toyota, Intel, McDonald's, Disney, and Google. (Courtesy of Interbrand)

Hopscotching the World for Public Relations

In the 21st century, public relations has become a global phenomenon. Major political shifts toward democracy throughout the world, coupled with the rapidity of worldwide communications and the move to form trading alliances of regional nations, have focused new attention on public relations. The collapse of communism, the coming together of European economies, wars against totalitarianism in Afghanistan and Iraq, the explosion of commerce in China and India, and the growth of democracy everywhere from Eastern Europe to South Africa have brought the global role of public relations into a new spotlight.

In 2000, the Global Alliance for Public Relations and Communications Management was formally established at a meeting in Bled, Slovenia, linking 63 member countries and representing more than 75,000 practitioners around the world. The purpose of the alliance was to provide a forum to share ideas and best public relations practices, seek common standards, and provide a better understanding of each culture in which practitioners operate.[7]

Here, in globe-trotting summary, are developments depicting the state of public relations beyond the borders of the United States.

Canada

Canadian public relations is the rival of American practice in terms of its level of acceptance, respect, sophistication, and maturity. The Canadian Public Relations Society (CPRS), formed in 1948, is extremely active, representing more than 1,600 public relations professionals in 16 member societies throughout the country.

Like its American counterparts, the CPRS maintains a code of professional standards that revolves around *"dealing fairly and honestly with the communications media and the public."* A professional accreditation program, job registry, and affiliations with Canadian university public relations programs are included in CPRS offerings.

Canadian public relations professionals must be conversant not only in the English-speaking parts of their country but also in the French-speaking markets, such as Quebec. Also, Canada in recent years, like America, has become a nation of nations, with great multicultural diversity. Dealing with diverse ethnicity also becomes a public relations challenge. Beyond Canada, America's other neighbors to the north also have become active in public relations efforts (see Figure 14-3).

Europe

The formation of the European Community (EC) in 1992 had major implications on the practice of public relations in Europe. As in Canada, public relations developed more or less simultaneously in Europe and the United States during the 20th century. The term "public relations" isn't used in many European countries, where terms like "communication management" and "corporate communications" are more the rule.

Whatever it's called, privatization and the synthesis of the European Community into a more unified bloc have spurred increased public relations action in many European countries. Among the factors that have enhanced public relations growth in Europe are:

- Importance of reputation management in an increasingly-globalized world,
- Favorable tax reforms in countries like the Czech Republic,
- Political stability, and
- Relatively strong and democratic economies.

FIGURE 14-3 **Natural public relations.** The Icelandic Tourist Board called on Salo Productions to introduce the country's many wonders to its southern neighbors. (Reprinted by permission of Salo Productions)

Public relations has experienced tremendous growth in Great Britain, employing 30,000 practitioners and growing at a rate of 20 percent annually. The United Kingdom remains the second largest market for public relations in the world.[8]

The Chartered Institute of Public Relations, headquartered in London and in its fifth decade, is the largest professional organization in Europe, with 8,000 public relations practitioner members. It encompasses 13 regional groups, has a Web site at www.cipr.org.uk, and produces a monthly magazine. It also issues a CIPR Diploma for practitioners who demonstrate the requisite knowledge of theory and practice of public relations.

The stature of the field in Europe was underscored in 2006, when British Prime Minister Tony Blair's oldest son, Euan, interned at a leading financial public relations firm. Said the *Financial Times, "Skillful, well-judged PR advice can make or break a situation."*[9] Such journalistic praise for public relations was unheard of even a decade earlier.

Europe is the domicile of some of the world's mightiest companies, from BMW and Volkswagen in Germany to HSBC and British Petroleum in Britain to Nestlé and Rolex in Switzerland. As European organizations pay increased attention to their reputations and how they are perceived, public relations is certain to be at the forefront of European commercial concern in the years ahead.

Latin America

Latin America is expanding at a faster rate than virtually any other region in the world. In terms of public relations development in Latin America, the scene is more chaotic than in the United States, Canada, or Europe.

The field is most highly developed in Mexico, where public relations practice began in the 1930s. Mexican corporations all have communications and public relations departments, and many employ local or U.S. public relations agencies. Mexican schools of higher learning also teach public relations. The passage of NAFTA under President Clinton and the reinforcement of generally solid relations with Mexico under Presidents Bush and Obama signal increasing opportunities for U.S–Mexican trade and therefore for public relations growth.

In the other countries of Latin America, public relations is an important growing phenomenon. Argentina, Brazil, and Chile all have developed practices. Chile, with its robust economy and approach to capitalism, is a particularly prominent candidate for increased public relations activity. In 2004, one of Chile's most prominent public relations educational institutions, Universidad De Vina Del Mar, staged an international public relations summit, Congreso Internacional de Relaciones Publicas, attracting prominent professionals from across the country and the world. The most prominent socialist voice in Latin America, President Hugo Chavez in Venezuela, also is a zealous proponent of spreading his message far and wide through media channels.

Further indication of potential Latin American public relations expansion is the fact that *The Wall Street Journal Americas* edition, nestled amidst the pages of 20 Latin American newspapers, reaches more than 2.5 million readers.

Japan

The technological communications prowess of Japan is like nowhere else on earth. Japan is composed of 127 million inhabitants, with 120 million cell phones! Indeed, most packed commuter trains in Japan are silent, except for the sound of thumbs attacking cell phone keyboards, so prominent is the cell phone as the primary communications tool in the country.

In Japan, the practice of public relations, by definition, is contrary to the nation's cultural heritage. Japanese culture values modesty and promotes silence over eloquence (although the worldwide recession of 2009 stimulated an unprecedented, increasingly vocal protest movement among Japanese youth in particular). Public relations, mistakenly equated with self-publicity, has therefore not traditionally been valued in Japanese society.

The public relations profession in Japan was established after World War II. Although the Japanese take a low-key approach to public relations work—especially self-advocacy—the field is growing, particularly as the six major national newspapers and four national networks become more aggressive in investigating a proliferation of national scandals. By far the most important aspect of Japanese public relations is dealing with the media.

The mass media in Japan are extremely powerful—much more so than their equivalents in the United States. Newspapers like the *Yomiuri Shimbun* and the *Asahi Shimbun* are among the world's most dominant. The *Yomiuri* alone sells 14 million copies a day—compared to *The New York Times,* which sells one million copies. The combined circulation of Japan's 120 newspapers is a mind-boggling 70 million copies. Moreover, more than 58 million people—about one-half the Japanese population—can access Web-delivered media sources via their mobile phones. In recent years, television in general and talk shows in particular have become increasingly popular in Japan. The average Japanese person watches just under four hours of television each day.

As a consequence of the nation's media and communications literacy, the practice of hiring a public relations agency to assist in navigating journalistic waters has grown. The three largest Japanese indigenous firms, Dentsu, Kyoto, and Prap Japan, employ about 200 people each and share the business with several American and European firms with Japanese offices.

Unlike in the West, where organizations arrange their own press coverage, in Japan there are thousands of individual "reporters' clubs"—known as *kisha clubs*—attached to everything from government agencies to corporations. Institutions with a kisha club limit their press conferences to the journalist members of that club, and membership rules for kisha clubs are restrictive. This limits access by domestic magazines and the foreign media, as well as freelance reporters to press events. Such a practice, critics allege, gives source organizations enormous influence over what is covered and how it is covered and fosters a "too cozy" relationship between journalist and source. Obviously, such clubs would be antithetical to U.S. journalists.[10]

In light of Japan's unique system of press relations, Japanese public relations differs markedly from that of the West. For example, the need for maintaining an outward display of harmony that influences much of Japanese business has ramifications for public relations. The majority of Japanese companies shun the kind of aggressive public relations favored by American companies. They prefer, instead, to disseminate only the most positive news, taking care not to boast or appear to triumph through the failures of others.[11]

Despite the differences with Western practice, the need for effective public relations in Japan is indisputable.

China

After a number of false starts, China holds great potential for public relations expansion. By 2020, some predict, 70 percent of the world will speak Mandarin as their principal language. China is the world's fastest-growing economy, second only to the United States, which it should pass soon. As the nation with the largest consumer population, China ranks fifth in world trade and is climbing.

Western-style public relations is a recent phenomenon in China, having been introduced only in 1980 by way of a foreign joint venture. Today there are 1,500 public relations firms in China, employing more than 30,000 people, including more than 15,000 professionals. China's public relations industry accounts for upwards of $400 million in annual revenue.

With media competition in China consisting of 8,000 magazines, 2,000 newspapers, and 3,000 television stations, the number of public relations professionals are certain to skyrocket.[12]

In 2004, the Shanghai International Public Relations Summit, co-sponsored by the Shanghai Public Relations Association, the China International Public Relations Association, and the Institute of Public Relations of Singapore, attracted more than 200 practitioners from the region. Public relations courses are offered at leading universities, such as China's Institute of International Relations in Beijing, Nankai University in Tianjin, and Zhongshan University in Guangzhou.

As China modernizes its way into the 21st century, one of the greatest challenges for indigenous business enterprises will be increased foreign and domestic competition in everything from soap products to household appliances and from cars to banking to telecommunications.[13] Public relations will be called on to help differentiate these enterprises from the competition, and accordingly, many foreign public relations agencies have moved to China to take advantage of the presumed activity.

China's new commercial openness occasionally clashes with its traditional statist government, yielding conflicting communications messages. For example, China has repeatedly criticized and acted to censor search engines like Google and Baidu in an effort to limit pornography on the Internet.[14] In 2008 in the run-up to the Olympics in Beijing, for example, China ham-handedly handled its relations with peace-loving Tibet, thus evoking the ire of the world, when the passing of the Olympic torch was disrupted by protesters around the world. On the other hand, months later when the Olympics were held, the government acquitted itself well and the games proceeded with nary a hitch. Thus, in one event, China demonstrated how its reputation could sag one day and soar the next.[15]

In any event, one thing is clear: The public relations business in China has only just begun and will enjoy a bright future in the 21st century.

PR Ethics

Mini-Case Two Steps Forward, One Step Back

Despite the great strides the world has made in becoming more open and transparent in its communications, all is not perfect.

When the Communist nation of Myanmar suffered a devastating cyclone in May 2008, the world responded immediately to the country's pressing need for food and water for 220,000 cyclone victims. The International Red Cross sent tons of relief goods, from pumps to generators to all variety of shelter supplies.

The United States immediately dispatched four Navy ships carrying supplies to deliver to areas hit by the storm.

The problem was that Myanmar's military regime was suspicious of the West and feared that the humanitarian supplies were a ruse to attack the country. While the U.S. Navy ships circled Myanmar for days, the military leaders refused to allow the goods to enter the country. U.S. Defense Secretary Robert Gates accused the regime of "criminal neglect" for blocking the international aid and causing more people to die. Ultimately, the four U.S. ships gave up and departed without delivering their needed cargo.

Finally, when supplies were ultimately distributed, the ruling Myanmar junta plastered the boxes with the names of top generals, attempting to turn the relief effort into an exercise in propaganda. Sadly, little relief reached the most stricken parts of the country (see Figure 14-4).

The world watched in horror as more than 23,000 people died and 37,000 went missing as a result of the Myanmar cyclone.

That same month, two months prior to the Olympics in China, the nation's Sichuan Province experienced the 19th

FIGURE 14-4 As the generals dithered . . . Sick and starving Myanmar children queued up for limited food supplies in the country's Ayeyawady Delta one month after the cyclone that killed 23,000. (Photo: Newscom)

deadliest earthquake of all time, accounting for 69,000 deaths. But this time, China's socialist leaders seemed to have learned from the Myanmar experience.

Government leaders responded quickly. Just 90 minutes after the earthquake, Premier Wen Jiabao flew to the earthquake area to oversee the rescue work. Soon afterward, China's Health Ministry sent 10 emergency medical teams to Wenchuan County in southwest China's Sichuan Province.

That same day, China's Chengdu Military Area Command dispatched 50,000 troops and armed police to help with disaster relief work in Wenchuan County.

As the death toll rose, China departed from past diplomatic practice and openly accepted disaster relief experts and heavy equipment from other nations, including longtime rivals Japan and Taiwan.

While the response to the Myanmar junta stonewalling was one of global approbation, the open and accommodative Chinese response grew worldwide acclaim.*

*For further information, see Howard French and Edward Wong, "In Departure, China Invites Outside Help," *New York Times* (May 16, 2008); Howard French, "U.N. Leader Praises China's Quake Response," *New York Times* (May 25, 2008); and Eric Schmitt, "Gates Accuses Myanmar of 'Criminal Neglect,'" *New York Times* (June 2, 2008).

Questions

1. How would you characterize the Myanmar generals' attempt to influence public opinion?

2. How much do you think the upcoming Olympics had to do with China's public relations response in dealing with its earthquake?

3. How might its response have impacted world opinion, vis-à-vis the Olympics?

Asia

Elsewhere in Asia, public relations also has begun to take root. It is important to remember that every Asian country is different, and public relations practice differs considerably from that in the United States. For example, in certain Asian nations, news releases are printed verbatim—a practice not followed in the United States.

In India, the antecedents of modern public relations practice have been traced to around 300 B.C., when the Indian Emperor Asoka used rock and pillar edicts as effective communications tools. Modern-day Indian public relations emerged during World War II, as public opinion became more important and mass-circulation newspapers proliferated. It was at this time that the powerful Tata industrial conglomerate formed the first public relations department in India.[16]

In 1958, eight years after India became a republic, the Public Relations Society of India was formed. Today, public relations practice in India is largely a subordinate of the marketing function. This is not uncommon throughout Asia and around the world.

In recent years, American firms have continued their march through Asia and into India. In 2005, Burson-Marsteller acquired Genesis, India's leading public relations company, with close to 200 employees in five cities. Genesis was one of the founding members of the Public Relations Consultants Association of India, modeled after a similar association in Britain, to establish benchmark standards for the profession. As India continues to take its place in the world as a high-tech nation and a fertile source of knowledge workers, its public relations industry will expand greatly.

In Malaysia, with more than 50 colleges and universities offering public relations as a professional course and degree program, the nation has created a pool of talent, vying to become a hub in the field.[17] The Institute of Public Relations Malaysia (IPRM) was formed in the early 1960s and trains 2,000 professionals annually. Like its counterpart in the United States, IPRM has launched an accreditation program and received government funds to increase its role and leadership in the practice of public relations.

In Singapore, a bastion of private enterprise, public relations was boosted in the late 1990s by new companies raising funds through a booming stock market and active economy. Technology, financial services, and real estate development also are burgeoning areas of public relations growth. The Institute for Public Relations Singapore, begun in 1970, today boasts 500 members and offers training courses in the field.

In the other Asian capitals, Korea has an active public relations community, as do Indonesia and Taiwan. In Vietnam, too, opportunities for public relations work promise to emerge as the country increases its financial might and entrepreneurial class.

Perhaps the truest test of the public relations boom in Asia was seen in the Philippines in 2006, when President Gloria Arroyo faced increasing disenchantment at home. In a speech before the Third Public Relations Summit in the country, the president's press secretary appealed to the Philippines public relations community to balance a negative media and use their offices *"to support and assist the president instead of wishing her downfall."*[18] Yes, in Asia, the practice of public relations had most certainly taken hold.

Eastern Europe

In the new democracies of Eastern Europe, there are 370 million consumers, and so the prospects for public relations expansion are enticing.

- More than 80 percent of all Eastern Europeans watch television daily. Nearly all watch several times a week.
- In Hungary, about 20 percent of the population have television sets connected to satellite dishes.
- In Poland, 13 percent of the population report owning VCRs.
- In Hungary, Serbia, and Croatia, about two-thirds of the population read newspapers daily.

Since public relations practice follows the development of a strong business sector, the nations of Eastern Europe, which claimed their first PRSA-accredited practitioner in 2001, are certain to see quantum leaps in the indigenous public relations business in the years immediately ahead.

Russia

Although "newly-capitalist Russia" (how strange that sounds!) has suffered fits and starts—not to mention scandals and bloody internal conflicts during its initial capitalistic years—the practice of public relations has been steadily developing.

AT&T, Intel, Pepsi-Cola, and many other companies are already ensconced in Russia. Large American public relations firms have also set up bases. PR Newswire, in combination with the news agency TASS, distributes news releases from U.S. companies to locations in the Commonwealth of Independent States. Releases are translated into Russian and reach 40 newspapers in Moscow alone. In 2005, *Russia Today*, the first 24/7 English-language TV news channel, was launched in Moscow.

Even Russian Prime Minister Vladimir Putin has gotten into the public relations act. When Putin's image tumbled in 2006—as a result of government crackdowns, violations of press freedoms and human rights, attempts to cut gas supplies, strong-arm tactics with enemies, and a host of other similar "imperfections"—the then-president enlisted media advisors to embark on an emergency propaganda campaign to bolster Russia's image among its citizens.

Based on the comments of Putin's media advisor, the practice of public relations still has a ways to go in Russia. Summarized the less-than-diplomatic Kremlin adviser: *"The Russians have become the Jews of the 21st century. They are regarded as the pariahs of Europe."*[19] Ivy Lee, he wasn't.

Australia and New Zealand

Public relations in the land down under is also alive and thriving. The Public Relations Institute of Australia is an extremely active organization, and the practice is widespread, particularly in the country's two commercial centers, Melbourne and Sydney. Australian public relations practice, like Australians themselves, is more low key and less flashy than American practice but no less competent and sophisticated (see Appendix B).

In New Zealand, too, public relations is practiced through local and international public relations agencies and communications practitioners at major companies and nonprofits. In fact, one New Zealand nonprofit, Queensland Health, was accused in 2006 of being *"more interested in public relations than in health care."* The organization caused a furor when it was reported that it had increased its public relations staff by 45 percent while increasing its medical workforce by just 14 percent. The public affairs director's salary? One hundred thousand dollars. Not bad for New Zealand or anywhere for that matter.[20]

Africa

In Africa, too, the practice of public relations is growing. In 1990, the largest public relations meeting in the history of the continent was held in Abuja, Nigeria, with 1,000 attendees from 25 countries. In 1994, as a result of an extensive worldwide communications and public relations campaign, Nelson Mandela became the first democratically elected president of the nation of South Africa.

As the most developed country in sub-Saharan Africa, South Africa led the continent in sophisticated public relations. It boasted more than 30 public relations–related companies and a professional association, the Institute for Public Relations and Communication Management. As in the United States, the public relations counseling industry in South Africa is dominated by alumni from larger agencies setting out on their own to launch independent consultancies.

In several African countries, public relations practitioners are not allowed to practice their craft unless they are registered members of designated national public relations associations, which adhere to strict standards and ethics.

Middle East

Despite the misunderstandings, hostilities, and frayed feelings that seem often to exist between the Middle East and the West, the practice of public relations—in parts of the Middle East at least—has grown nicely. The practice itself is far different than that practiced in the United States.

In Egypt, according to one native consultant, *"Public relations is an old-fashioned thing. It's the guy who goes to the airport; it's the flower arrangement in a hotel; it's things like this."*[21] That may be the case for some. However, it is also true that in Egypt's intense business environment, where rumors spread like wildfire, public relations is essential to giving the public a clearer image of the truth.

In the United Arab Emirates, another burgeoning capital of trade and commerce, one positive sign of the last decade was the admission of women students into the public relations major program at the United Arab Emirates University in Al-Ain.

Other Middle Eastern nations, from Saudi Arabia to Libya, have spent millions of dollars in recent years on public relations support to help improve their image.

What is indisputable in the Middle East is that even terrorists have adapted the techniques of public relations. Even public enemy #1 Osama bin Laden, the orchestrator of the attacks on America, is a savvy student of public relations. Al-Qaeda terrorist leaders regularly use the Internet and Arab-language television to spew out their messages of fear and hate.

The most significant media player in the Middle East was Al Jazeera, the Arab news channel that began in 1996. Critics call it "radical and biased"; its admirers lionized it. Al Jazeera had news channels in Arabic and English, a pan-Arab newspaper, Web sites and blogs, sports and children's outlets, and even a channel modeled after C-SPAN. It broadcast from network hubs in Qatar, London,

Talking Points   Think Multilingual—or Else

Steve Rivkin is America's foremost "nameologist," having written extensively on what organizations and products must consider before they choose a name (see Figure 14-5). When it comes to organizations dealing overseas, the nameologist warns, you'd better think multilingual—or else.

Or else what? Or else this:

■ A food company named its giant burrito a *Burrada.* Big mistake. The colloquial meaning of that word in Spanish is "big mistake."

■ Estée Lauder was set to export its Country Mist makeup when German managers pointed out that *mist* is German slang for, uh, well, to put it gently, "manure." (The name became Country Moist in Germany.)

■ Colgate introduced a toothpaste in France called Cue, the name of a notorious French porno magazine.

■ The name Coca-Cola in China was first rendered as *ke-kou-ke-la.* Unfortunately, Coke did not discover until after thousands of signs had been printed that the phrase means "bite the wax tadpole." Coke then researched 40,000 Chinese characters and found a close phonetic equivalent, *ko-kou-ko-le,* which loosely translates as "happiness in the mouth." Much better.

■ A leading brand of car de-icer in Finland will never make it to America. The brand's name: *Super Piss.*

FIGURE 14-5 Namemeister extraordinaire, Steve Rivkin. (Courtesy of Rivkin & Associates, Inc.)

■ Ditto for Japan's leading brand of coffee creamer. Its name: *Creap.*

Points   Straighten Out Your English—or Else

On the other hand, it might be equally beneficial for our friends in foreign lands to make sure of their own English.

Consider these actual signs posted in various establishments around the world.

- In a Copenhagen airline ticket office: *"We take your bags and send them in all directions."*

- In a Norwegian cocktail lounge: *"Ladies are requested not to have children in the bar."*

- At a Budapest zoo: *"Please do not feed the animals. If you have any suitable food, give it to the guard on duty."*

- In a doctor's office in Italy: *"Specialist in women and other diseases."*

- In a Paris hotel elevator: *"Please leave your values at the front desk."*

- From the brochure of a Tokyo car rental firm: *"When passenger of foot heave in sight, tootle the horn. Trumpet him melodiously at first, but if he still obstacles your passage then tootle him with vigor."*

- In an advertisement by a Hong Kong dentist: *"Teeth extracted by the latest Methodists."*

- In an Acapulco hotel: *"The manager has personally passed all the water served here."*

- In a Bucharest hotel lobby: *"The lift is being fixed for the next day. During that time we regret that you will be unbearable."*

Washington, and Kuala Lumpur. Its executives called Al Jazeera "a channel that covers untold stories." But its detractors insisted the channel prefers to cover terrorists—positively.[22]

Communicating to the Global Village

Communications media around the world have truly converted the globe into one large "village" united by satellite and Internet technology. What happens in one corner of the globe is instantly transmitted to another.

The world relearned this lesson in brutal fashion in the spring of 2006, when a Danish newspaper published cartoons that depicted the prophet Muhammad in an unflattering light. The cartoons, instantly transmitted around the globe, set off a firestorm in the Arab world. It triggered demonstrations, boycotts of Danish goods, and a wave of violence resulting in at least 50 deaths.[23] Such is the danger of communications in an increasingly interconnected—not to mention, sensitive—world.

One of the most active global communications factors—especially on the Internet—are the tens of thousands of nongovernmental organizations (NGOs), from Greenpeace to Friends of the Earth, from Africa Action to the World Rainforest Movement. For minimal expense, such organizations can spread their views—often criticisms of multinationals—across the globe (see Figure 14-6).

As globalization and international trade impact societies, such NGOs have become increasingly influential in world affairs. They are consulted by governments as well as international organizations, such as the United Nations, which have created associative status for them. These organizations are not directly affiliated with any national government but often have a significant impact on the social, economic, and political activity of the country or region involved.

In the 21st century, as the world continues to get "smaller" in a communications sense, public relations professionals, knowledgeable about foreign customs and cultures and skilled in the practice of communication, will be in great demand.

FIGURE 14-6
Worldview. NGOs, such as True Majority, started by the founders of Ben & Jerry's Ice Cream, are united in generally seeking "a better world." (Courtesy of True Majority)

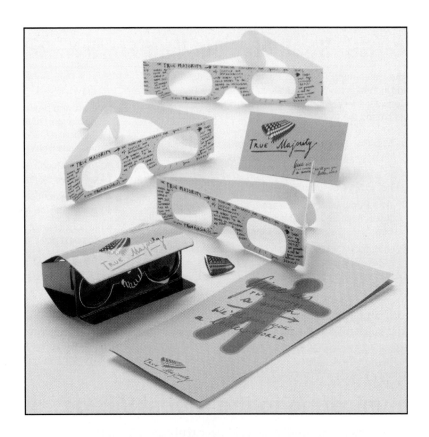

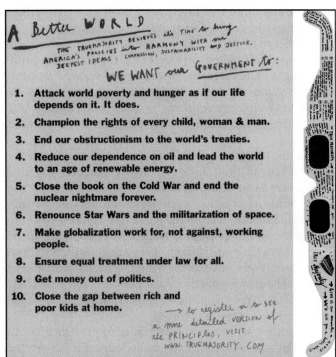

Last Word

The "brave new world" that emerged after September 11, 2001, promises to remain the reality well into the 21st century. The more standoffish and isolationist America that emerged after 9/11 has given way to the more internationally-accommodative, Nobel Prize-winning President Barack Obama and Secretary of State Hillary Clinton. At the same time, the world is getting "smaller," with phenomena such as MTV, CNN, basketball, baseball, hip-hop, and Britney Spears knowing no geographic boundaries.

The conflicts around the globe—between democracy and totalitarianism, peace and terrorism, Arabs and Israelis in the Middle East, Catholics and Protestants in Ireland, warring factions in Africa, and discontent in various other geographies—make it even more imperative that companies, governments, and individuals reach out to communicate with each other.

Stated another way, organizations desperately need professional communicators to navigate through this brave new world of instantaneous communication. As the world's companies continue to expand across borders, they must be sensitive to local customs and people. As global competition intensifies, so will global communications, making it easier to communicate around the world but much more difficult to be heard.

Faced with such a formidable global reality, smart organizations will deal honestly, forthrightly, and frequently with world media and work diligently to build harmonious relationships with others around the world.

Discussion Starters

1. What evidence can you point to that indicates the increased stature of public relations practice around the world?
2. What factors have necessitated the need for increased international public relations?
3. What is meant by the term *global village?*
4. What kinds of public relations practices should be observed by multinationals operating in a foreign country?
5. What is the state of public relations in the Western hemisphere?
6. What is the state of public relations in Europe?
7. What is the state of public relations in Asia?
8. What is the state of public relations in Latin America?
9. What is the significance of Al Jazeera?
10. What has been the recent public relations history of the totalitarian government of China?

Top of the Shelf International Public Relations / Patricia A. Curtin

and T. Kenn Gaither, Thousand Oaks, CA: Sage Publications, Inc., 2007

This text contains an inclusive compendium of the state of public relations around the world. After defining the field generally, the authors tour the world's public relations sophistication, from South Korea to Swaziland, from multinationals to international NGOs, from travel and tourism to sports and international goodwill.

The authors point out that the growth of public relations throughout the world has been explosive, with Ireland, Rumania, Russia, and Italy among 20 European nations with their own public relations associations. This is an outstanding primer on global public relations.

Case Study | Karen Hughes Stumbles Selling Uncle Sam

Karen Hughes came out of retirement for this? President Bush's closest public relations advisor, who counseled him throughout his first two years in the White House, didn't exactly find her new job a bed of roses. Thorns, maybe, but roses—no way.

Hughes, who left the Bush White House to return to her family in Texas, was wooed back by the president and Secretary of State Condoleezza Rice in the spring of 2005 to become Undersecretary of State for Public Diplomacy and Public Affairs. Hughes's assignment, simply stated, was convert *the negative image of America around the world.*

Too Much Gas

Almost immediately, Hughes realized that the task of aiding America's global image was as tough as any in government. She immediately set out to visit the Muslim world to reach out to the people to demonstrate the best intentions of America (see Figure 14-7).

On a trip to Indonesia a little more than six months into her tenure, Hughes defended the U.S. invasion of Iraq to a group of animated students by incorrectly claiming that Saddam Hussein had "gassed hundreds of thousands of his own people."

"The consensus of the world intelligence community was that Saddam was a very dangerous threat," she said. *"After all, he used weapons of mass destruction against his own people. He had murdered hundreds of thousands of his own people using poison gas."*

While it was true that at least 300,000 Iraqis were reported to have died during Saddam's bloody 24-year reign, his government's use of chemical weapons against Iraqi Kurds during a 1988 military campaign cost the lives of an estimated 5,000 people.

Hours later, Hughes was asked twice for the basis of her numbers during a meeting with journalists from foreign news organizations.

"It's something that our U.S. government has said a number of times in the past. It's information that was used very widely after his attack on the Kurds. I believe it was close to 300,000," Hughes said when questioned the first time. When asked again several minutes later, she said: *"I think it was almost 300,000. It's my recollection. They were put in mass graves."*

At the end of the day, the State Department acknowledged that the numbers cited by its Undersecretary were incorrect.

It was a flabbergasting faux pas for the formerly invincible presidential counselor. Thus was an experienced government public relations professional introduced to the treacherous fishbowl of international public diplomacy.

FIGURE 14-7 Best intentions. Public relations veteran Karen Hughes, shown here in Banda Aceh, Indonesia, found some elements of her new job more pleasant than others. (Photo: Newscom)

Advertising Approach

With two billion Muslims in the world, and the religion the globe's fastest growing, the backlash among Muslims to tougher post-9/11 U.S. policies and attitudes was a source of great concern to the United States.

Hughes's predecessors in the job failed to make much impact. Both Margaret Tutweiler, a long-time Republican bureaucrat, and Charlotte Beers, a veteran of the advertising industry, were only marginally effective in countering America's image as "the Great Satan" in the Muslim world.

Beers, for example, took a traditional advertising approach to the problem, creating first a 24-page booklet, in print and on the Internet, in 14 languages, which featured graphic pictures of the September 11 attacks. The booklet used bin Laden's own words to accuse him of masterminding the murderous attacks.

A poster was also created and plastered around the Arab world, offering $25 million for information leading to the arrest of the Most Wanted Terrorists, including bin Laden and his key aides.

Public Relations Approach

Notwithstanding her difficult baptism of fire in Indonesia, Hughes's approach was much more a traditional public relations initiative. Hughes adopted a "four E" strategy of public relations—engagement, exchanges, education, and empowerment. As she described it, *"One of my goals is to put a human face on America and American policy. I want to challenge the notion that public diplomacy is somehow about public relations or polls. It's about policy."*

To add teeth to the effort, the Bush administration devoted $670 million to change worldviews. Hughes set about immediately to engage in face-to-face dialogue, personally traveling around the world as a listener first and a doer second. She made a point of emphasizing that her visits were "listening tours," designed to hear, in a sincere and friendly way, the views and concerns of the people.

Hers was a noble effort but not an easy one. Opinion polls across the Muslim world suggested that U.S. favorability ratings had dropped into the single digits after the Iraq war, even in friendly countries like Egypt and Jordan, where the United States spends millions in aid.

Making Hughes's job even tougher were the often conflicting messages sent out from the home front. In 2006, for example, the country—both liberals and conservatives—rebelled when it was reported that a company, owned by U.S. friend and supporter the United Arab Emirates, would have a hand in running U.S. ports. The deal was scuttled, much to the chagrin of the administration. And Karen Hughes's job just got that much tougher.

Said the president of the Arab American Institute of Washington, D.C., *"We're stepping on ourselves every day. The domestic message ends up trumping the public diplomacy message every time."*

Questions

1. What would you have advised relative to Karen Hughes's unfortunate statements in Indonesia?

2. How would you compare Hughes's approach to public diplomacy with that of her predecessor?

3. If you were public relations advisor to the Undersecretary for Public Diplomacy, what other programmatic elements would you recommend be instituted?

4. If you were the Undersecretary herself, how would you go about changing the image of the United States overseas?

For further information, see Chris Brummitt, "U.S. Diplomat Defends Iraq War," Associated Press (October 21, 2005); Stephen Johnson, "Public Diplomacy Needs a Commander, Not a Spokesman," The Heritage Foundation (September 30, 2005); Glen Kessler and Robin Wright, "Report: U.S. Image in Bad Shape," *Washington Post* (September 24, 2005): A16; "Karen Hughes: Under Secretary for Public Diplomacy," *Newsweek* (October 24, 2005); Alan Sipress, "U.S. Envoy Makes Big Iraq Blunder," *Washington Post* (October 22, 2005); Robin Wright, "Hughes Launches 9/11 Anniversary Image Campaign," *Washington Post* (September 1, 2005).

From the Top   An Interview with Ray Jordan

Ray Jordan is Corporate Vice President, Public Affairs and Corporate Communication for Johnson & Johnson, and is responsible for public relations and corporate communication for the broadly based, diversified global health care company. He oversees the public affairs responsibilities and activities of the company's more than 250 operating companies in 57 countries around the world.

What is your primary mission as Johnson & Johnson's chief communications officer?

Our function has a clear vision and strategy, broad enough to be relevant and applicable to all our businesses, and my principal role is to drive that throughout the organization. Our mission involves three primary components: (1) maintaining and enhancing the reputation of the company and our businesses, (2) ensuring our core values, and (3) improving the environment for growth.

How do you manage the worldwide J&J communications network, across international borders?

We manage more than 200 people around the world, including those who report up through various solid and dotted lines. We don't have communications people in all of our countries. Our corporate team is about 20 professionals. We operate through a council of senior communications officers, who are responsible for each of our four primary groups: (1) consumer, (2) pharmaceuticals, (3) surgical care, and (4) comprehensive care.

How do you influence perceptions in different geographies?
At Johnson & Johnson, our *Credo* is the galvanizing element across all geographies and businesses. That's at the core of driving our reputation externally and our behavior inside the company. In other words, across the world, we focus on who we are and what we stand for and then on acting consistent with that definition. And then we work on letting those actions become visible within the marketplace.

Has the Tylenol case influenced the way J&J conducts itself around the world?
Yes. It's a powerful story and representation of how we think as a company. Those stories, like Tylenol, and the people who have lived and carry them are powerful influencers in our culture.

How important is it for communications officers to interact constructively with corporate lawyers?
To be effective in my job, this is essential. Our lawyers are "facilitators," not "roadblocks." One obligation we have as communicators is to help ensure that our company's actions are consistent with who we are. That means we need to reflect on how other constituencies might react to a particular corporate action—before we take it. Lawyers are always engaged around potential actions. So a good relationship with lawyers means they will bring us into an assessment of whether an impending action may have consequences for other stakeholders. We are fortunate that at the corporate level of Johnson & Johnson, the communications group is always invited into discussions of this sort. And I lobby our communications staff around the world to build strong working relationships with their senior lawyer—and also their senior finance officer. It's curious that many communications people tend to wither in terms of dealing with legal or finance groups. But they are both critically important for a communicator to get to know and work with.

How do you measure your success in your job?
Measurement in our business has always been a conundrum. My CEO gave me good guidance early on. He suggested focusing on a five-year mission at any given time. You need that much time to make meaningful "change" in terms of realizing a particular mission. So we manage our group in terms of "priorities" over the next five years. We assess progress against these larger objectives that are clearly embraced by management. We meet each fourth quarter with our senior executives to review what, if anything, we must change in our framework, what environmental factors will weigh on our priorities, and what commitments we plan to make for the year ahead. We use these updates to strike the theme for all subsequent communications—annual report, internal town hall meetings, analyst meetings, etc. In this way, our communications messages are consistent across geographies and businesses. And we can track progress in conveying these messages.

What qualities do you value most in a communications professional?
I look for three things:
1. *Business acumen is vital.* You must be able to relate to business leaders on the basis of what the business is and how to think about it.
2. *Excellent writing or editing capacity.* This is still vitally important in what we do.
3. *Tenacity to help the business operate in "the right way" is third.* You've got to possess a passion for this.

Public Relations Library

Epstein, Charlotte. *The Power of Words in International Relations.* Boston, MA: Massachusetts Institute of Technology, 2008. This is a fascinating analysis of how the whaling industry evolved from an attitude of widespread acceptance to one of worldwide opprobrium.

Franks, Tommy. *American Soldier.* New York: HarperCollins, 2004. The American general in charge of the first stages of the war on terrorism offers, among other things, a fascinating perspective on the use of embedded reporters.

Grosse, Robert (ed.). *International Business and Government Relations in the 21st Century.* New York, NY: Cambridge University Press, 2005. With chapters by prominent international researchers, this offers a comprehensive look at government relations in the international arena.

Hughes, Karen. *Ten Minutes from Normal.* New York: Viking Penguin, 2004. A post-9/11 memoir about returning to private life before venturing back onto a bigger, more global, more difficult stage.

Jackson, Robert, and George Sorenson. *Introduction to International Relations: Theories and Approaches.* New York, NY: Oxford University Press, 2007. An excellent introductory text to international relations.

McPhail, Thomas L. *Global Communication: Theories, Stakeholders and Trends, Second Edition.* Malden, MA: Blackwell Publishing, 2006. In addition to tracking the elements that impact global communication, the author also provides a primer on the latest global theories of communication, from electronic colonialism theory to world-system theory.

Weiner, Mark. *Unleashing the Power of PR: A Contrarian's Guide to Marketing and Communication.* San Francisco, CA: Jossey-Bass, 2006. The author's strong research orientation dominates this compendium of case studies and measurement techniques, chartered by the International Association of Business Communicators.

Chapter 15

Public Relations
Writing

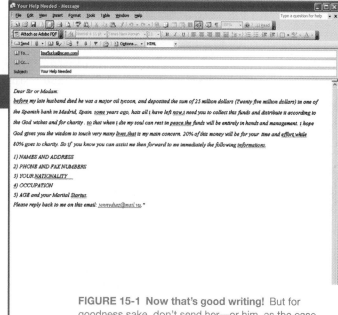

FIGURE 15-1 Now that's good writing! But for goodness sake, don't send her—or him, as the case may be—any money!

"*. . . before my late husband died he was a major oil tycoon, and deposited the sum of 25 million dollars (Twenty five million dollars) in one of the Spanish bank in Madrid, Spain. some years ago, hats all i have left now,i need you to collect this funds and distribute it according to the God wishes and for charity . so that when i die my soul can rest in peace.the funds will be entirely in hands and management. i hope God gives you the wisdom to touch very many lives,that is my main concern. 20% of this money will be for your time and effort,while 80% goes to charity. So if you know you can assist me then forward to me immediately the following informations.*

1. NAMES AND ADDRESS

2. PHONE AND FAX NUMBERS

3. YOUR NATIONALITY

4. OCCUPATION

5. AGE and your Marital Startus.

Please reply back to me on this email: jennydiaz@ mail.vu."

The "Nigerian bank scam"—or the "419 Letter," named for the Nigerian penal code that addresses crime schemes—in which the sender promises to send you a large sum in exchange for your personal financial information, has become an Internet staple. (And, alas, some poor fools even fall prey to it!) The point is that in the era of the Internet, criminals around the world have learned that it pays to be a writer.

Even in the age of the Internet, writing remains the key to public relations: Public relations practitioners are professional communicators. And communications means writing.

All of us know how to write and speak—even Nigerian bank scammers! But public relations professionals should write and speak better than their colleagues. Communication—that is, effective writing and speaking—is the essence of the practice of public relations.

There is no substitute for clear and precise language in informing, motivating, and persuading. The ability to write and speak with clarity is a valuable and coveted skill in any organization. Stated another way, the pen is, indeed, mightier than the sword.

The ability to write easily, coherently, and quickly distinguishes the public relations professional from others in an organization. It's not that the skills of counseling and marketing and judgment aren't just as important; some experts argue that these skills are often *more* important than knowing how to write. Perhaps. But not knowing how to write—how to express ideas on paper—may reduce the opportunities to ascend the public relations success ladder.

Senior managers usually have finance, legal, engineering, or sales backgrounds, where writing is not stressed. But when they reach the top, they are expected to write articles, speeches, memos, and testimony. They then need advisers, who are often their trusted public relations professionals. That's why it's imperative that public relations students know how to write—even before they apply public relations techniques to marketing or cyberspace.

Stated bluntly, beginning public relations professionals are expected to have mastery over the written word. So this chapter and the next will explore the fundamentals of writing: (1) discussing public relations writing in general and the staple of that writing, news releases, in particular, (2) reviewing writing for reading, and (3) discussing writing for listening.

Writing for the Eye and the Ear

The sad fact is that public relations people, by and large, are horrible writers. This is the unfortunate conclusion of public relations teachers, supervisors, and executive recruiters assigned to find jobs for public relations applicants.[1] That, of course, is unacceptable in a field in which the fundamental skill must be the ability to write.

What does it take to be a public relations writer?

For one thing, it takes a good knowledge of the basics. Although practitioners probably write for a wider range of purposes and use a greater number of communications methods than do other writers, the principles remain the same whether writing for the Internet, an annual report or a case history, an employee newsletter, or a public speech.

Writing for a reader differs dramatically from writing for a listener. A reader has certain luxuries a listener does not have. For example, a reader can scan material, study printed words, dart ahead, and then review certain passages for better understanding. A reader can check up on a writer; if the facts are wrong, for instance, a reader can find out pretty easily. To be effective, writing for the eye must be able to withstand the most rigorous scrutiny.

On the other hand, a listener gets only one opportunity to hear and comprehend a message. If the message is missed the first time, there's usually no second chance. This situation poses a special challenge for the writer—to grab the listener quickly. A listener who tunes out early in a speech or a broadcast is difficult to draw back into the listening fold.

Public relations practitioners—and public relations students—should understand the differences between writing for the eye and the ear. Although it's unlikely that any beginning public relations professional would start by writing speeches, it's important to understand what constitutes a speech and how it's prepared and then be ready for the assignment when opportunity strikes. Because writing lies at the heart of the public relations equation, the more beginners know about writing, the better they will do.

Any practitioner who doesn't know the basics of writing and doesn't know how to write—even in the age of the Internet—is vulnerable and expendable.

Fundamentals of Writing

Few people are born writers. Like any other discipline, writing takes patience and hard work. The more you write, the better you should become, provided you have mastered the basics. Writing fundamentals do not change significantly from one form to another.

What are the basics? Here is a foolproof, four-part formula for writers, from the novice to the novelist:

1. **The idea must precede the expression.** Think before writing. Few people can observe an event, immediately grasp its meaning, and sit down to compose several pages of sharp, incisive prose. Writing requires ideas, and ideas require thought. Ideas must satisfy four criteria:
   - They must relate to the reader.
   - They must engage the reader's attention.
   - They must concern the reader.
   - They must be in the reader's interest.

   Sometimes ideas come quickly. Other times, they don't come at all. But each new writing situation doesn't require a new idea. The trick in coming up with clever ideas lies more in borrowing old ones than in creating new ones. What's that, you say? Is your author encouraging "theft"? You bet! The old cliché "Don't reinvent the wheel" is absolutely true when it comes to good writing. Never underestimate the importance of maintaining good files.

2. **Don't be afraid of the draft.** After deciding on an idea and establishing the purpose of a communication, the writer should prepare a rough draft. This is a necessary and foolproof method for avoiding a mediocre, half-baked product. Writing, no matter how good, can usually be improved with a second look. The draft helps you organize ideas and plot their development before you commit them to a written test. Writing clarity is often enhanced if you know where you will stop before you start. Organization should be logical; it should lead a reader in a systematic way through the body of the text. Sometimes, especially on longer pieces, an outline should precede the draft.

3. **Simplify, clarify.** In writing, the simpler the better. Today, with more and more consumers reading from computer screens, simplicity is imperative. The more people who understand what you're trying to say, the better your chances for stimulating action. Shop talk, jargon, and "in" words should be avoided. Standard English is all that's required to get an idea across. In practically every case, what makes sense is the simple rather than the complex, the familiar rather than the unconventional, and the concrete rather than the abstract. Clarity is another essential in writing. The key to clarity is tightness; that is, each word, each passage, each paragraph must belong. If a word is unnecessary, a passage redundant, a paragraph vague—get rid of it. Writing requires judicious editing; copy must always be reviewed with an eye toward cutting.

4. **Finally, writing must be aimed at a particular audience.** The writer must have the target group in mind and tailor the message to reach that audience. To win the minds and hearts of a specific audience, one must be willing to sacrifice the understanding of certain others. Writers, like companies, can't expect to be all things to all people. Television journalist Bill Moyers offered this advice for good writing:

   > *Strike in the active voice. Aim straight for the enemy: imprecision, ambiguity, and those high words that bear semblance of worth, not substance. Offer no quarter to the tired phrase or overworn idiom. Empty your knapsack of all adjectives, adverbs, and clauses that slow your stride and weaken your pace. Travel light. Remember the most memorable sentences in the English language are also the shortest: "The King is dead" and "Jesus wept."[2]*

Flesch Readability Formula

Through a variety of writings, the late Rudolf Flesch staged a one-man battle against pomposity and murkiness in writing. According to Flesch, anyone can become a writer. He suggested that people who write the way they talk will be able to write better. In other words, if people were less inclined to obfuscate their writing with 25-cent words and more inclined to substitute simple words, then not only would communicators communicate better but receivers would receive more clearly.

In responding to a letter, Flesch's approach in action works as follows: *"Thanks for your suggestion, Tom. I'll mull it over and get back to you as soon as I can."* The opposite of the Flesch approach would read like this: *"Your suggestion has been received; and after careful consideration, we shall report our findings to you."* See the difference? In writing for the Internet, such straightforward writing is the only approach.

There are countless examples of how Flesch's simple dictum works.

- Few would remember William Shakespeare if he had written sentences such as *"Should I act upon the urgings that I feel or remain passive and thus cease to exist?"* Shakespeare's writing has stood the test of centuries because of sentences such as *"To be or not to be?"*

- A scientist, prone to scientific jargon, might be tempted to write, *"The biota exhibited a 100 percent mortality response."* But how much easier and infinitely more understandable to write, *"All the fish died."*

- One of President Franklin D. Roosevelt's speechwriters once wrote, *"We are endeavoring to construct a more inclusive society."* FDR changed it to *"We're going to make a country in which no one is left out."*

- Even the most famous book of all, the Bible, opens with a simple sentence that could have been written by a 12-year-old: *"In the beginning, God created the heaven and the earth."* Simple but brilliant!

Flesch gave seven suggestions for making writing more readable.

1. Use contractions such as *it's* and *doesn't*.
2. Leave out the word *that* whenever possible.
3. Use pronouns such as *I, we, they,* and *you*.
4. When referring back to a noun, repeat the noun or use a pronoun. Don't create eloquent substitutions.
5. Use brief, clear sentences.
6. Cover only one item per paragraph.
7. Use language the reader understands.

Ylisela Cornerstones of Corporate Writing

To Flesch and others, the secret to good writing is getting to the point.

To Flesch's latter-day alter ego, Jim Ylisela, a journalist and organizational writing instructor without equal, the reason most corporate writing is mostly dull, uninspired, and convoluted is that writers, themselves, are "fearful" to express themselves forcefully (see Figure 15-2). That's a tragedy, says Ylisela, because *"What value is the corporate mission if people don't understand it?"*

FIGURE 15-2 Latter-day Flesch. Even in the age of the laptop, writing instructor Jim Ylisela preaches the same scintillating simplicity that Rudolf Flesch said made "good writers." (Courtesy of Ragan Communications)

The secret, he says, is to make the words count. Here's how, according to Prof. Ylisela:

1. **Be specific.** Corporate writing is too vague. Evoke E.B. White's *Rules of Style*: *"Prefer the specific to the general, the definite to the vague, the concrete to the abstract."* Demand writing that is about something we can grasp.

2. **Use more words.** English gives us anywhere from 250,000 to one million words. So why are companies limited to the same handful—like "strategic," "key," and "quality"? It's time to stretch your vocabulary.

3. **Find better verbs.** This is where corporate language really sags. We're "leveraging" and "facilitating" everything under the sun. Action-oriented verbs drive sentences. So use 'em.

4. **Pursue the active voice.** There's no reason if you're in public relations to write like a lawyer. Public relations writers should write "subject/verb/object" sentences and not use passive construction.

5. **Omit needless words.** Give your sentences a haircut. Count the number of words in any document, print it, and then cut it by 10 percent. You'll be amazed at the improvement.

6. **Embrace simplicity and clarity.** Avoid big words and convoluted phraseology. The best way to communicate, from the Bible to the blogosphere, is through clear, simple language, rid of hype and corporate-speak.

7. **Tell a good story.** This is another way of saying "Use examples, illustrations, anecdotes, and personal experience to make points." It's a good way to get rid of generalities.

8. **Find interesting voices.** Everybody in the corporate worlds sounds the same. So quote people who are interesting and say interesting things.

9. **Take chances.** You only go around once, so stick your neck out with writing that defies the conventional.

10. **Rewrite.** Everything can be improved. So rewrite.[3]

Talking Points Speaking Like the Suits

Worried about fitting in a corporate environment? Concerned that the suits speak and write a different language than do you—more convoluted, hyperextended, and obtuse?

Relax. You can rely on the following "Jargon Master Matrix," developed by a former bank communicator, a chart consisting of three columns of jargon words that can be mixed and matched for any occasion.

Just select any three words from the three columns, such as *value-based process model* or *overarching support centralization*, and you will fit right in. (Just don't tell Jim Ylisela!)

1. overarching	visionary	objectives
2. strategic	support	alternatives
3. special	customer-oriented	expectations
4. specific	stretch	excellence
5. core	planning	assessment
6. long-term	marketing	update
7. quality	service	model
8. technology-based	process	product
9. formal	fundamental	centralization
10. exceptional	sales	incentive
11. value-based	budget	initiatives
12. executive	operating	feedback
13. immediate	discretionary	infrastructure
14. interactive	tracking	proposition

The Beauty of the Inverted Pyramid

Journalistic writing style is the Flesch/Ylisela approach in action.

Reporters learn that words are precious and are not to be wasted. In their stories every word counts. If readers lose interest early, they're not likely to be around at the end of the story. That's where the inverted pyramid comes in. Newspaper story form is the opposite of that for a novel or short story. Whereas the climax of a novel comes at the end, the climax of a newspaper story comes at the beginning. A novel's important facts are rolled out as the plot thickens, but the critical facts in a newspaper story appear at the start. In this way, if readers decide to leave a news article early, they have already gained the basic ideas.

Generally, the first tier, or lead, of the story is the first one or two paragraphs, which include the most important facts. From there, paragraphs are written in descending order of importance, with progressively less important facts presented as the article continues—thus, the term *inverted pyramid*.

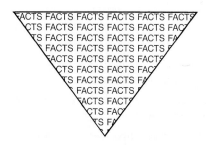

The lead is the most critical element, usually answering the questions concerning who, what, why, when, where, and occasionally how. For example, the following lead effectively answers most of the initial questions a reader might have about the subject of the news story.

> *Columbia Pictures announced today it had signed Britney Spears and Matthew McConaghey to a three-film deal for $60 million each.*

That sentence tells it all; it answers the critical questions and highlights the pertinent facts. It gets to the point quickly without a lot of extra words. In just about 20 words it captures and communicates the essence of what the reader needs to know.

After the lead, the writer must select the next most important facts and array them in descending order with the most important facts earlier in the story. In this way, the inverted pyramid style is more the *selection and organization* of facts than it is an exercise in creative *writing*.

This is the style of straightforward writing that forms the basis for the most fundamental, practical, ubiquitous, and easiest of all public relations tools: the news release.

The News Release

A valuable but much-maligned device, the news release is the granddaddy of public relations writing vehicles. The first recorded news release was issued by Ivy Lee in October of 1906, as a *"Statement from the Road"* offering an explanation from client Pennsylvania Railroad about that month's crash that killed 50 people. The release was published verbatim by *The New York Times* (perhaps the last recorded release to earn that status, alas!).

Most public relations professionals swear by the news release. Some editors and reporters swear about it. Indeed, PR Newswire, a paid wire service used by public relations people in 170 countries to distribute releases, issues more than 1,000 news releases—virtually all by email—every day.[4]

The reason is that everyone uses the release as the basic interpretive mechanism to let people know what an organization is doing. There is no better, clearer, more persuasive way to announce news about an organization, its products, and their applications than by issuing a news release.

A news release may be written as the document of record to state an organization's official position—for example, in a court case or in announcing a price or rate increase. More frequently, however, releases have one overriding purpose: to influence a publication to write favorably about the material discussed. Each day, in fact, professionals email releases to editors in the hope of stimulating favorable stories about their organizations.

Most news releases are not used verbatim, although there are occasional exceptions. Rather, they may stimulate editors to consider covering a story. In other words, the release becomes the point of departure for a newspaper, magazine, radio, or television story. Why, then, do some editors and others describe news releases as "worthless drivel"? The answer, according to researcher Linda Morton of the University of Oklahoma's Herbert School of Journalism, is threefold:

1. **Releases are poorly written.** Professor Morton found that most news releases are written in a more complicated and difficult-to-read style than are most newspaper stories. *"This could be the result of pressure from administrators as they review and critique press releases,"* she reasoned.

2. **Releases are rarely localized.** Newspapers focus largely on hometown or regional developments. The more localized a news release, the greater the

chance it has of being used. However, according to Professor Morton, *"Practitioners may not want to do the additional work that localization requires."* This is a bad decision because research indicates that a news release is 10 times more likely to be used if it is localized.

3. **Releases are not newsworthy.** This is the grand dilemma. An editor will use a public relations release only if he or she considers it news. If it's not newsworthy, it won't be used. What determines whether something is news?

Professor Morton suggests five requisites:

- *Impact:* a major announcement that affects an organization, its community, or even society.
- *Oddity:* an unusual occurrence or milestone, such as the one-millionth customer being signed on (see Figure 15-3).

FIGURE 15-3 **The Flattener.** Some may call it "odd," others may label it "practical," but whatever the case, the introduction of "Pound-It-Out" meat flattener was heralded in this news release. (Courtesy of Pound-It-Out LLC)

NEW KITCHEN GADGET MAKES MEAT FLATTENING EASY

April 22, 2008

Closter, New Jersey—Robert Limmer. President of Pound-It-Out LLC announces the introduction of Pound-It-Out®, The Incredible Meat Flattening Device. Limmer, the inventor of the patent pending device, intends to introduce the product at the upcoming Gourmet Housewares Show in Las Vegas, May 6-8, 2008.

The device makes the process of producing uniformly flattened meat a simple and efficient task, says Limmer and he adds that it is very cost effective when compared to the common practice of using plastic wrap or bags.

Made of high strength, unbreakable polypropylene, the device is sturdy as well as sanitary, cleaning up easily with soap and water or in the dishwasher.

Limmer says, "I own 6 different styles of meat mallets, yet, when a recipe called for flattened meat or poultry, I was reluctant to proceed as the use of plastic wrap or bags simply didn't thrill me, especially if I was preparing for a big group. I conceived the idea for Pound-It-Out out of this frustration and found my early prototype to be extremely functional. With that confidence I proceeded to develop and produce the version we are introducing to the Kitchen Accessory Market."

"Our target market is the home chef who currently owns a meat mallet", says Limmer. These cooking enthusiasts will appreciate the functionality as well as the results that they will achieve with Pound-It-Out®, The Incredible Meat Flattening Device. We took great care in designing a label that conveys the ease of use and are providing a Point of Sale display box for counter display as well as a built in hook for hanging. "I believe that our product will be received enthusiastically by retailers and consumers alike", says Limmer.

Contact Information:
Robert F. Limmer, President
Pound-It-Out LLC
201-805-8938
info@pound-it-out.com
www.pound-it-out.com

- *Conflict:* a significant dispute or controversy, such as a labor disagreement or rejection of a popular proposal.
- *Known principal:* the greater the title of the individual making the announcement—president versus vice president—the greater the chance of the release being used.
- *Proximity:* how localized the release is or how timely it is, relative to the news of the day.[5]

Beyond these characteristics, *human interest* stories, which touch on an emotional experience, are regularly considered newsworthy.

With this as a backdrop, it is not surprising that research indicates that in terms of the popular press, most news releases never see the light of print. Early studies, in fact, even before the exponential growth of releases, indicated that less than 10 percent of all news releases were published.[6] Nonetheless, each day's *Wall Street Journal, New York Times, USA Today,* CNN, Fox News, MSNBC, CNBC, Associated Press wire, Yahoo News, Google News, and other daily media around the nation and world are filled with stories generated from news releases issued by public relations professionals.

So the fact is that the news release—despite the harsh reviews of some—remains the single most important public relations vehicle.

News Release News Value

The key challenge for public relations writers is to ensure that their news releases reflect news. What is *news?* That's an age-old question in journalism. Traditionally, journalists said that when "dog bites man, it's not news, but when man bites dog, that's news." The best way to learn what constitutes news value is to scrutinize the daily press and broadcast news reports and see what they call news. In a general sense, news releases ought to include the following elements:

- Have a well-defined reason for sending the release.
- Focus on one central subject in each release.
- Make certain the subject is newsworthy in the context of the organization, industry, and community.

Talking Points Just the Facts

Writing in news release style is easy. It is less a matter of formal writing than it is of selecting, organizing, and arranging facts in descending sequence.

Here are 10 facts:

Fact 1: Supreme Court Chief Justice John Roberts will speak in Madison, Wisconsin, tomorrow.

Fact 2: He will be keynote speaker at the annual convention of the American Bar Association.

Fact 3: He will speak at 8 p.m. at the Kohl Center.

Fact 4: His speech will be a major one.

Fact 5: His topic will be capital punishment.

Fact 6: He will also address university law classes while in Madison.

Fact 7: He will meet with the university's chancellor while in Madison.

Fact 8: He became the 17th Chief Justice, replacing the late William Rehnquist in 2005.

Fact 9: He is a former practicing attorney.

Fact 10: He has, in the past, steadfastly avoided addressing the subject of capital punishment.

Organize these facts into an American Bar Association news release for tomorrow morning's Lansing newspaper. One right answer appears later in this chapter. Just don't peek.

- Include facts about the product, service, or issue being discussed.
- Provide the facts "factually"—with no puff, no bluff, no hyperbole.
- Rid the release of unnecessary jargon.
- Include appropriate quotes from principals but avoid inflated superlatives that do little more than boost management egos.
- Include product specifications, shipping dates, availability, price, and all pertinent information for telling the story.
- Include a brief description of the company (also called a "boilerplate") at the end of the release—what it is, and what it does.
- Write clearly, concisely, forcefully.

News Release Content

Again, the cardinal rule in release content is that the end product must be newsworthy. The release must be of interest to an editor and readers. Issuing a release that has little chance of being used by a publication serves only to crush the credibility of the writer.

When a release is newsworthy and of potential interest to an editor, it must be written clearly and concisely in proper newspaper style. It must get to the facts early and answer the six key questions. From there it must follow the inverted pyramid structure to its conclusion. For example, consider the following lead for the John Roberts news release posed in this chapter's Talking Points.

MADISON, WISCONSIN—Supreme Court Chief Justice John Roberts will deliver a major address on capital punishment at 8 p.m. tomorrow in the Kohl Field House before the annual convention of the American Bar Association.

This lead answers all the pertinent questions:

1. Who? Chief Justice John Roberts
2. What? a major address on capital punishment
3. Where? Kohl Field House
4. When? tomorrow at 8 p.m.
5. Why? American Bar Association is holding a convention

In this case, *how* is less important. Whether or not the reader chooses to delve further into the release, the gist of the story has been successfully communicated in the lead.

To be newsworthy, news releases must be objective. All comments and editorial remarks must be attributed to organization officials. The news release can't be used as the private soapbox of the release writer. Rather, it must appear as a fair and accurate representation of the news that the organization wishes to be conveyed.

And news releases—even email releases—must also be written in a certain professional style, even when the subject is tongue-in-cheek (see Figure 15-4).

News Release Style

The style of writing, particularly news release writing, is almost as critical as content. Alas, many in the public relations profession overlook the importance of proper writing style. Sloppy style can break the back of any release and ruin its chances for publication. Style must also be flexible and evolve as language changes.

News Release Essentials

Beyond the necessity of being newsworthy, news releases must include several time-honored essentials that will help get them considered for inclusion in print.

- **Rationale.** There must be a well-defined reasons for sending the release. Releases should answer the two critical questions. *What's new?* and *So what?* Stated another way, the subject matter of the release must be relevant to the readers or viewers of the target media. Lack of relevance should be enough to scuttle the release.

- **Focus.** Each release should speak about only one central subject. Lack of focus—that is, discussing many different things—is a guaranteed non-starter for a journalist.

- **Facts.** To a journalist, the *facts* about the product or service subject of the release are most important: the who, what, where, when, why, and how of the announcement. These should take precedent over the often gratuitous quotes that mark many releases.

- **No puffery.** Releases, to paraphrase Fox News commentator Bill O'Reilly, should be "puffery-free zones." Even mediocre reporters can sniff out hyperbole and puffiness, which may make them suspicious of the entire product. At all costs, avoid the taboo terms listed in the next Talking Points box.

- **Nourishing quotes.** Include quotes, but make them count. *"We think this is the best product of its type,"* doesn't add much. But, *"This product will add 20 percent to our annual revenue growth,"* advances the story by providing important projections that will help put the announcement in corporate context. The rule on quotes, then, is to avoid inflated superlatives that do little more than boost management egos.

- **Limit jargon.** Every industry, from banking to baking to rocket propulsion, has its own jargon. Reporters who cover the industry may understand the meaning of such jargon, but maybe they won't. And certainly, readers may not know the meaning of certain jargon-laden terms. Therefore, it is always a good idea to define, to the lowest sensible denominator, the terms you choose to use.

- **Company description.** Many reporters may not be familiar with a particular organization and what it does. Therefore, a succinct organizational description, commonly called boilerplate, is eminently appropriate to conclude a release by "positioning" the firm the way it wants to be recognized.

- **Spelling, grammar, punctuation.** Ask a journalist to describe the *quality* of the public relations releases he or she receives, and they'll invariably roll their eyes. If the most rudimentary writing principles of spelling, grammar, and punctuation aren't observed, how important can the release be? And how important can the reporter recipient be if the public relations writer doesn't even take the time to proofread?

- **Brevity.** A news release is not a book. It must be written as tweets or articles in *USA Today* are written: short and concise. Paragraphs should be short and varied; one-sentence paragraphs are encouraged. Words and sentences should be kept short. As to length of the entire release, the average news release runs about 500 words—no more than two and a half pages.

■ **Headlines.** Headlines summarize quickly to busy reporters what the release that follows is all about. Often, a reporter will make a snap judgment, based solely on the headline, as to whether the release merits being read further and ultimately used.

■ **Clarity, conciseness, commitment.** The best release from the best organizations are straightforward, understated, confident. Just like any other communications vehicle, a public relations news release can reveal much about the company that produces it.[7]

Talking Points News Release Taboo Terms

Back in the old days of 1978, the late comedian George Carlin found himself in deep turbulence for uttering seven "dirty words" that the Supreme Court found to be "patently offensive" to radio listeners. (Because this is a "family textbook," we will leave the seven words to your imagination or your next visit to the *Howard Stern Show* on satellite radio.)

In the 21st century, there is nothing more patently offensive to a reporter than a news release that contains the following taboo terms.

Leading. For example, "Goniff & Co., a *leading* public relations agency, today named 16 new vice chairpersons."

The problem is that everyone considers themselves "leading." Unless the agency is bigger, more profitable, or more highly recognized than others, the term is meaningless and, worse, embarrassing.

Going Forward. For example, "Gazbak said that *going forward* the company would rely more on generally accepted accounting principles in deriving earnings."

Can you ever go any other direction but "forward"? Answer: yes, but. . . . So "going forward," like "in the future," is one of those redundancies that means nothing and takes up space. Lose it.

Unique. For example, "Dr. Delaruprup's *unique* laser technology allows a patient to discard his eyeglasses."

C'mon. That ain't "unique." Lots of others may perform the same technological accomplishment. And that's the point. For something to be labeled as unique, you must be ready to demonstrate its individuality and distinctiveness. If you can't, don't use the word.

Breakthrough. For example, "Professor Kleinswort's *breakthrough* research proves conclusively that we are not alone."

Like "unique," it must be a demonstrable "breakthrough" to be labeled as such. Anybody can call his or her research or invention or product or process a breakthrough, but few can prove it. The overused word has become the worst of clichés.

Revolutionary. For example, "Sol Seymour's *revolutionary* hair-restoral method can grow a luxurious mane on a pomegranate."

Well, perhaps if it can do that, it *is* revolutionary. But like "unique" and "breakthrough," most new products or services or methods or models may in fact be "evolutionary" advancements of what came before, but they can't be fairly construed as revolutionary.

Cutting-Edge. For example, "Bilgebracket's *cutting-edge* radiology department keeps the hospital ahead of the curve in delivering health care services."

This one has really gotten out of hand in the press release business. Everything, it seems, is "cutting edge." But is what you're pitching really precedent-setting or original? If not, then it can't be considered cutting edge. Forget it.

State-of-the-Art. For example, "Poobah's *state-of-the-art* measurement system allows you to empirically evaluate the benefits of the publicity you attain."

See "Cutting-edge."

World-Class. For example, "Ms. Lung Lung, a *world-class* yodeler of immense proportions, has performed in concert with Shaggy and the Smyrna Philharmonic Orchestra."

Like "world-renowned" and "world-famous," this self-serving superlative should be reserved only for the most unique, revolutionary, and cutting edge of our society.

In writing a news release, then, forget these terms. Use some originality. Be more creative. Don't succumb to cheap and easy—and, as it turns out, journalistically suicidal—superlatives.

Mini-Case Bad Taste News Release

In the winter of 2001, the *Washington Post Magazine* took public relations firm Porter Novelli International to task for what the paper called a tasteless news release for client Chef America's Hot Pockets sandwiches.

Post columnist Gene Weingarten—no friend of the public relations industry—took dead aim at the firm for a release it sent in the wake of the 9/11 attacks. (Full disclosure: Weingarten, to whom this humble text is dedicated, was invited to be interviewed for this book but didn't have the courtesy to respond to two requests. So there!)

The Porter Novelli release in question said:

Although the last few weeks have been a challenging time for everyone both personally and professionally, I know that we are all striving to return to "normal."

In the coming weeks as you begin to return to your regular areas of focus, I want you to be familiar with Chef America, makers of HOT POCKETS brand sandwiches.

Weingarten proceeded to rip Weingar Porter Novelli for the release: *"This release cannot possibly be tasteless because it issues from no less distinguished a source than Porter Novelli International, a company that is, to quote its website, 'a world leader in the field of brand building and reputation management.'"*

Weingarten reasoned, *"People don't buy HOT POCKETS because they are grateful to the manufacturers for their humanitarian gestures. They buy HOT POCKETS because they're scared of Osama."*

Porter Novelli defended itself to Weingarten, contending it was not trying to capitalize on the terrorist attacks but rather *"trying to introduce the product to different people, and after September 11 less people are eating out."*

Question

1. Whose side are you on, Weingarten's or Porter Novelli's? Why?

Social Media News Releases

The Internet has revolutionized news releases and news release writing. Before the Internet, public companies would issue news releases only when they had newsworthy announcements to make. Today, companies regularly issue releases merely to be included on online databases—Google News, Yahoo News, MSN News, AOL News, etc.

Why? When consumers and investors read a verbatim release on line, it indicates to these important publics that the company is active and making progress. In issuing releases directly online, companies are, in effect bypassing traditional journalists to reach key constituents.

Going direct is particularly important in terms of social media—any online technology that people use to share content, opinion, insights, experiences, and perspectives. Examples of social media applications include social networking sites Facebook and MySpace, video sharing site YouTube, content sharing site Digg, video sharing site Flickr, etc.

Social media releases are designed to reach nontraditional journalists, such as bloggers and podcasters. Often, they use technological tools—video, audio, links, etc.—to mash up their own multimedia news stories (see Figure 15-5). Indeed, according to social media relations expert Todd Andrlik, vice president of marketing at Leopardo Companies, *"The purest form of a social media release is a blog post and the best solution for a social media news room is a blog engine."* In addition to directly reaching nontraditional journalists, so-called "old media" journalists are now fully adept in using the Internet for research.

In addition, many newswire services also offer social media releases or social media elements, such as RSS web feeds, Technorati tags to search blogs, Delicious social bookmarking to Web index copy, Digg shared links, etc.

Beyond disseminating a news release throughout the Web, social media news releases are best used at an organization's Web site to stimulate "conversation."

FIGURE 15-5 **Social media news release.** The blog-based corporate newsroom of Leopardo Companies, Inc., enlists all manner of social networking vehicles. (Courtesy of Leopardo Companies, Inc.)

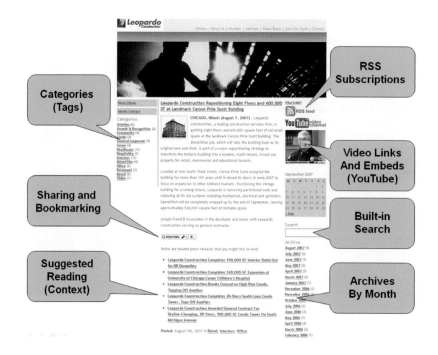

Writing Internet News Releases

The vast majority of journalists today prefer to receive news releases via email. In one survey of 400 journalists, seven of 10 reporters said they read every email release they received.[8]

In terms of news release writing for the Internet, brevity and succinctness are paramount. Reading from a computer screen is more difficult and tedious than extracting from paper. Therefore, Internet news release writing must conform to the following requisites:

- **One reporter per "To" line.** Nobody—least of all, reporters—likes to be lumped in with everybody else. That's why journalists despise press conferences. They want to be considered "special." So don't group journalists together on the "To" line of an email release. Listing one reporter per "To" line (online software programs exist to help accomplish this) will deliver the personalization that journalists prefer.

- **Limit subject line headers.** Most reporters are cursed with a daily email inbox that runneth over. They're swamped with email releases, just as their latter-day counterparts were swamped with print releases. Therefore, enticing them with a provocative subject line is a necessity if you want your release to be considered. You should limit subject headers to four to six words, no more.

- **Boldface "FOR IMMEDIATE RELEASE."** With this advisory on the first line of the release, right above the date and dateline, reporters will know instantly that this is news that can be used right away. As is true with print releases, "embargoing" news for later publication is rarely honored in a day of 24/7 breaking news and round-the-clock Internet publicity.

- **Hammer home the headline.** Email release headlines are as important as print headlines to attract immediate interest and subsequent coverage. Email headlines should be written in boldface upper- and lowercase and, as in all email writing, should be limited in length—to 10 words or less.

- **Limit length.** Email news releases should be shorter than print versions. PR Newswire reports that the average print release is 500 words. Email releases should generally be shorter than that.

- **Observe 5W format.** Email news releases should observe traditional news release style, leading with the 5W format, to answer the key questions of who, what, why, when, where, and even how. The limited length of the email—to say nothing of the attention span of the email reader—mandates that the writer get to the point immediately, right in the first paragraph.

- **No attachments.** Never. Never. Never. Journalists wish neither to face the risk of a virus nor take the time to download. So don't attach anything. Rather . . .

- **Link to the URL.** Accompanying information, such as photos, bios, backgrounders, and the like, should be linked in the email to the organization's URL. This negates the inconvenience of downloading and allows reporters the opportunity to link at their leisure.

- **Remember readability.** Email releases must balance information with readability. That means short paragraphs, varied paragraph length, bullets, numbers, lists—devices that make the release more eye-friendly and scannable.[9]

Importance of Editing

Editing is the all-important final touch for the public relations writer. You must edit your work. One error can sink a perfectly worthwhile release.

In a news release, a careful self-edit can save the deadliest prose. An editor must be judicious. Each word, phrase, sentence, and paragraph should be weighed carefully. Good editing will "punch up" dull passages and make them sparkle. For instance, *"The satellite flies across the sky"* is dead, but *"The satellite roars across the sky"* is alive.

In the same context, good editing will get rid of passive verbs. Invariably, this will produce shorter sentences. For example, *"George Washington chopped down the cherry tree"* is shorter and better than *"The cherry tree was chopped down by George Washington."*

A good editor must also be gutsy enough to use bold strokes—to chop, slice, and cut through verbiage, bad grammar, misspellings, incorrect punctuation, poorly constructed sentences, misused words, mixed metaphors, non sequiturs, clichés, redundancies, circumlocutions, and jargon. Redundant sentences such as *"She is the widow of the late Marco Picardo"* and *"The present incumbent is running for reelection"* are intolerable to a good editor.

Editing should also concentrate on organizing copy. One release paragraph should flow naturally into the next. Transitions in writing are most important. Sometimes it takes only a single word to unite two adjoining paragraphs.

Finally, editing must review one last time that a written document handles the necessary A's and B's of effective public relations writing:

- Avoid big words.
- Avoid extra words.
- Avoid clichés.
- Avoid Latin.
- Be specific.
- Be active.
- Be simple.
- Be short.

- Be organized.
- Be convincing.
- Be understandable.

Writing, like fine wine, should flow smoothly and stand up under the toughest scrutiny. Careful editing is a must.

Talking Points   The Sassy Style of the Internet

The Internet, of course, has a writing style all its own. In chat rooms, a correctly spelled word may be a sign of the inarticulate. Consider, for example, this conversation:

Wuzup?
n2m
well g/g c ya

The translation by anyone who spends eight to 10 hours a day texting or tweeting: Not too much is up with the respondent, and so the writer has got to go and will see his friend later.

Indeed, in terms of email vocabulary, the following shortened vernacular can be adjudged as "chat ready":

- please   pls
- feel free   flfre

- by the way   btw
- be right back   brb
- in real life   irl
- in my humble opinion   IMHO
- laughing out loud   lol
- rolling on the floor laughing   rotfl
- you are   u r
- information   info
- document   doc
- conversation   convo
- later   latr

Latr.

Last Word

Writing is the essence of public relations practice. The public relations professional, if not the best writer in his or her organization, must at least be one of the best. Writing is the communications skill that sets public relations professionals apart from others.

Or should.

The fact is that the most frequent complaint of employers is that "public relations people can't write." That's why any public relations student who "can write" is often ahead of the competition.

Some writers are born. But most are not.

Writing can be learned by understanding the fundamentals of what makes interesting writing; by practicing different written forms; and by working constantly to improve, edit, and refine the written product. When an executive needs something written well, one organizational resource should pop immediately into his or her mind: public relations.

Discussion Starters

1. What is the foremost technical skill of public relations professionals?"
2. What are several of the writing fundamentals one must consider?
3. What is the essence of the Flesch method of writing?
4. What are the cornerstone corporate writing fundamentals advocated by Jim Ylisela?
5. What is the inverted pyramid, and why does it work?
6. What is the essential written communications vehicle used by public relations professionals?
7. What are common purposes of news releases?
8. Should a news release writer try to work his or her own editorial opinion into the release?
9. What are the keys in writing releases for the Internet?
10. Why shouldn't public relations writers include attachments on email releases?

Top of

the Shelf Making Your Point / David Bartlett, New York, NY: St. Martin's
Press, 2008

This comprehensive book by an agency veteran covers every area of how to communicate more effectively in today's society—whether speaking to one person, delivering a speech to a small group, making a presentation to a client, or engaging in a media interview that may be seen or heard by millions of people.

The essence of Bartlett's wisdom is that effective communication depends on having a point to make, understanding why it is important, then knowing how to make it interesting and memorable, regardless of the circumstances. That's pretty wise.

Case Study   The Raina, Inc., News Release

Background: The Raina carborundum plant in Blackrock, Iowa, has been under pressure in recent months to remedy its pollution problem. Raina's plant is the largest in Blackrock, and even though the company has spent $5.3 million on improving its pollution-control equipment, black smoke still spews from the plant's smokestacks, and waste products are still allowed to filter into neighboring streams. Lately, the pressure on Raina has been intense.

- On April 7, J. K. Krafchik, a private citizen, called to complain about the "noxious smoke" fouling the environment.

- On April 8, Janet Greenberg of the Blackrock Garden Club called to protest the "smoke problem" that was destroying the zinnias and other flowers in the area.

- On April 9, Clarence "Smoky" Salmon, president of the Blackrock Rod and Gun Club, called to report that 700 people had signed a petition against the Raina plant's pollution of Zeus Creek.

- On April 10, WERS Radio editorialized that "the time has come to force area plants to act on solving pollution problems."

- On April 11, the Blackrock City Council announced plans to enact an air and water pollution ordinance for the city. The council invited as its first witness before the public hearing Leslie Sludge, manager of the Raina carborundum plant.

News Release Data

1. Leslie Sludge, manager of Raina's carborundum plant in Blackrock, appeared at the Blackrock City Council hearing on April 11.
2. Sludge said Raina had already spent $5.3 million on a program to clean up pollution at its Blackrock plant.
3. Raina received 500 complaint calls in the past three months protesting its pollution conditions.
4. Sludge said Raina was "concerned about environmental problems, but profits are still what keeps our company running."
5. Sludge announced that the company had decided to commit another $2 million for pollution-abatement facilities over the next three months.
6. Raina is the oldest plant in Blackrock and was built in 1900.
7. Raina's Blackrock plant employs 10,000 people, the largest single employer in Blackrock.

8. Raina originally planned to delay its pollution-abatement program but speeded it up because of public pressure in recent months.
9. Sludge said that the new pollution-abatement program would begin in October and that the company projected "real progress in terms of clean water and clean air" as early as two years from today.
10. Five years ago, Raina received a Presidential Award from the Environmental Protection Agency for its "concern for pollution abatement."
11. An internal Raina study indicated that Blackrock was the "most pollutant laden" of all Raina's plants nationwide.
12. Sludge formerly served as manager of Raina's Fetid Reservoir plant in Fetid Reservoir, New Hampshire. In two years as manager of Fetid Reservoir, Sludge was able to convert it from one of the most pollutant-laden plants in the system to the cleanest, as judged by the Environmental Protection Agency.
13. Sludge has been manager of Blackrock for two months.
14. Raina's new program will cost the company $2 million.
15. Raina will hire 100 extra workers especially for the pollution-abatement program.
16. Sludge, 35, is married to the former Polly Yurathane of Wheeling, West Virginia.
17. Sludge is author of the book *Fly Fishing Made Easy.*
18. The bulk of the money budgeted for the new pollution-abatement program will be spent on two globe refractors, which purify waste destined to be deposited in surrounding waterways, and four hyperventilation systems, which remove noxious particles dispersed into the air from smokestacks.
19. Sludge said, "Raina, Inc., has decided to move ahead with this program at this time because of its long-standing responsibility for keeping the Blackrock environment clean and in response to growing community concern over achieving the objective."
20. Former Blackrock plant manager Fowler Aire was fired by the company in July for his "flagrant disregard for the environment."
21. Aire also was found to be diverting Raina funds from company projects to his own pockets. In all, Aire took close to $10,000, for which the company was not reimbursed. At least part of the money was to be used for pollution control.
22. Aire, whose whereabouts are presently not known, is the brother of J. Derry Aire, Raina's vice president for finance.

23. Raina's Blackrock plant has also recently installed ramps and other special apparatus to assist employees with disabilities. Presently, 100 workers with disabilities are employed in the Raina Blackrock plant.
24. Raina's Blackrock plant started as a converted garage, manufacturing plate glass. Only 13 people worked in the plant at that time.
25. Today the Blackrock plant employs 10,000 people, covers 14 acres of land, and is the largest supplier of plate glass and commercial panes in the country.
26. The Blackrock plant was slated to be the subject of a critical report from the Private Environmental Stabilization Taskforce (PEST), a private environmental group. PEST's report, "The Foulers," was to discuss "the 10 largest manufacturing polluters in the nation."
27. Raina management has been aware of the PEST report for several months.

Questions

1. If you were assigned to draft a news release to accompany Sludge to the Blackrock City Council meeting on April 11, which items would you use in your lead (i.e., who, what, why, where, when, how)?
2. Which items would you avoid using in the news release?
3. If a reporter from the *Blackrock Bugle* called and wanted to know what happened to former Blackrock manager Fowler Aire, what would you tell the reporter?
4. How could Raina use the Internet to research public opinion of the pollution problem? How could the company use the Internet to communicate its position in advance of the Blackrock City Council meeting?

From the Top   An Interview with Hoa Loranger

Hoa Loranger is a User Experience Specialist at Nielsen Norman Group, specialists in communicating on the Web. She consults with many large, well-known companies in various industries such as entertainment, finance, technology, e-commerce, and government. She is a frequent speaker, conducts usability research worldwide, and has published reports on a variety of Web usability topics. She is coauthor of the book *Prioritizing Web Usability (2006)*. Ms. Loranger holds a masters degree in Human Factors and Applied Experimental Psychology from California State University, Northridge, and a BA in Psychology from University of California, Irvine.

What is the state of writing on the Web?
General Web site interaction design is getting better, but Web content is lagging behind. Organizations underestimate the role of effective writing in creating a successful Web site. In our studies, we often see people purposefully navigate to the correct areas of a site and be frustrated by verbose content. Companies are dumping information on Web sites without much thought of how usable it is. Employing shortcuts such as plastering content intended for printed material on the Web leads to disastrous outcomes. The traditional narrative writing style commonly used in printed media repels online readers. Unlike print, the Web is a user-directed medium, where people adopt information–seeking strategies to save time. People rely on visual cues to direct their attention to areas of interest and ignore everything else. People on the Web are impatient and expect to get answers quickly. Good Web sites design their content for the way people actually behave on the Web. Bad Web sites design their content the way they want people to behave.

What are the most common errors that Web writers make?
Writers often overwrite and choose hype over simplicity. Using sophisticated verbiage makes people work hard to find the information they need. Writers assume that their readers understand internal terminology or jargon. The terminology your organization or industry uses is not usually part of your user's vernacular. Simple language might not seem glamorous, but it is preferred by customers.

What are the most essential elements of writing for the Web?
Keep it short and sweet. Long rambling text frustrates audiences. People on the Web scan, and do not read text word for word. Nothing is more daunting on the Web than being confronted by a large wall of text. In general, the word count for Web content should be about half of that used in conventional writing. Conventional writing calls for complete sentences. Not so much online. If the same information can be conveyed effectively in fewer words, do it.

Start with key terms. Our eye-tracking studies show that people are extremely frugal with their gazes. Web pages are often packed with competing stimulus. Audiences develop selective attention to combat information overload; they notice little and ignore a lot. Headings that start with key terms get more attention than those that don't. For example, the link "Press Releases" is much more effective than "Click here to read press releases." Why? People focus on the first few words of headings while ignoring the rest. Saying "Click here" does not convey anything useful. So it's not good to save your information-carrying keywords for the end of the phrase.

Layer the content. Rather than overwhelm site visitors with extensive content, layer the information on different pages. Start with the key points first and then make it easy for people to drill down. Layering your content satisfies the needs of both casual browsers and serious researchers without sacrificing scannability and completeness. This approach facilitates people's nonlinear information-seeking behavior on the Web.

How important is writing in inverted pyramid style on the Web?
Start with the summary of key points, then reveal supporting facts is a technique adopted by many successful journalists. This structure gives readers the gist quickly and then lets them burrow into the details of they choose to read on. A long rambling introduction is a sure way to bore readers. People will more likely be captivated if the first part of an article is interesting and focused.

How important are bullets, fragments, white space, and brevity?
Formatting text for readability is essential in attracting and keeping people's attention. Proper Web-formatting techniques break up content into small chunks. Short paragraphs surrounded by white space or a bulleted list appear more approachable than a sold wall of text.

How does a public relations writer distinguish his news releases from those of others on the Web?
Have concise and descriptive titles. Titles that have descriptive keywords are important in garnering interest as well as for search engine optimization. Headlines and titles are often devoid of context, so sarcasm and word play can easily be misunderstood. The Web is truly a worldwide medium, and idioms don't translate easily across borders. Remember, your audience is coming to your site for direct content, not for cleverness.

Follow well-established Web-formatting techniques on all news releases. Repurposing a press release from print for the Web is lazy and should be avoided.

Public Relations Library

Aronson, Mary, Don Spetner, and Carol Ames. *The Public Relations Writer's Handbook*. New York, NY: Jossey-Bass, 2007. Authored by an executive recruiter, an agency professional, and a college instructor, this book provides a great practical resource in dealing with writing vehicles from news releases to financial documents to building Web sites.

Bivins, Thomas. *Public Relations Writing*, 4th Ed. Lincolnwood, IL: NTC/Contemporary Publishing Group, 2007. A popular text, updated to include all aspects of public relations writing, including writing for digital media.

Foster, John. *Effective Writing Skills for Public Relations*, 4th Ed. Philadelphia, PA: Kogan Page, 2008. Another solid writing text from a former journalist and public relations professional.

Newsom, Doug, and Jim Haynes. *Public Relations Writing*, 7th ed. Belmont, CA: Wadsworth, 2005. Outstanding and comprehensive writing manual.

Pacelli, Lonnie. *The Truth About Getting Your Point Across . . . and Nothing but the Truth*. Saddle River, NJ: Prentice-Hall, 2006. This is a guide to communicating in all settings—at meetings, presentations, interviews, and more.

Rhody, Ron, and Carol Ann Hackley. *Wordsmithing: The Art & Craft of Writing for Public Relations*, 2nd ed. United States: Ron Rhody and Carol Ann Hackley, 2006. This book, written by a corporate public relations veteran and experienced professor, offers a step-by-step guide to public relations writing.

Scott, David Meerman. *The New Rules of Marketing & PR*. Hoboken, NJ: John Wiley & Sons, Inc., 2007. This book primarily discusses the Internet and how such vehicles as news releases and blogs should be used.

Shapiro, Roger A. *Write Right*. Bloomington, IN: AuthorHouse, 2005. This paperback guide offers 26 tips that get down to the nitty-gritty, such as avoiding prepositions and being bold. Good primer.

Strunk, W., and E. B. White. *Elements of Style*. New York: Allyn & Bacon, 1999. A classic that *must* be in any public relations writer's library.

Treadwell, Donald, and Jill B.Treadwell. *Student Workbook for Public Relations Writing*. Thousand Oaks, CA: Sage Publishing Co., 2005. This presents an interesting approach to work for one hypothetical client, preparing all matter of public relations writing vehicles.

VandeVrede, Linda B. *Press Releases Are Not a PR Strategy*. United States: Linda B. VandeVrede, 2005. This book argues that editors and analysts are a public relations person's primary targets.

Weinbroer, Diana Roberts, Elaine Hughes, and Jay Silverman. *Rules of Thumb for Business Writers*, 2nd ed. New York: McGraw-Hill, 2005. The answers to every writing or grammar question that a business writer might have.

Whitaker, Richard W., Janet E. Ramsey, and Ronald D. Smith. *Media Writing: Print, Broadcast and Public Relations*. Mahwah, NJ: Lawrence Erlbaum Associates, Inc., 2004.

Zappala, Joseph M., and Ann R. Carden. *Public Relations Worktext*. Mahwah, NJ: Lawrence Erlbaum Associates, Inc., 2004. Solid introduction to public relations writing vehicles.

Chapter 16

Writing for the Eye
and Ear

FIGURE 16-1 Man in the middle. In 2009, Apple CEO Steve Jobs carefully explained that a treatable hormonal imbalance was responsible for his weight loss and gaunt look and not a recurrence of pancreatic cancer. (Photo: Newscom)

Writer beware.

That's the prevalent admonition of the 21st century, as it becomes increasingly dangerous to utter anything in public. Just ask United Airlines.

In the fall of 2008, an erroneous headline flashed across trading screens around the world, saying United had filed for a second bankruptcy. In less than an hour, United lost $1 billion in stock market value.

The only problem: The headline wasn't true.

United blamed an old *Chicago Tribune* article posted on a Web site and then picked up by a research firm, which then posted a link to it on a page on Bloomberg News, which sent a news alert based on the old article.[1]

As Bart Simpson would say, *"Ay caramba!"*

On the other hand, because of the Internet, sometimes you've just got to say something.

Like, for example, Apple CEO Steve Jobs, the subject of virulent Internet rumors, some claiming his cancer had recurred. For months in 2008, Apple stonewalled and refused to discuss its chief executive's health. This, of course, only fueled the blogo-sphere further and caused the Apple stock to plummet.

Finally, in January 2009 when Jobs canceled his annual keynote address at Macworld Expo, the company was forced to issue the following carefully crafted statement in the name of its CEO:

"My decision to have Apple's senior vice president of worldwide product marketing deliver the Macworld keynote set off another flurry of rumors about my health, with some even publishing stories of me on my deathbed.

"After further testing, my doctors think they have found the cause—a hormone imbalance that has been 'robbing' me of the proteins my body needs to be healthy. Sophisticated blood tests have confirmed this diagnosis. I will continue as Apple's CEO during my recovery"[2] (see Figure 16-1).

And while the Jobs statement didn't immediately quell the bloggers, it did drive Apple's stock up by $4. Apple continued to practice "cat and mouse disclosure" with its founder's health, as Jobs took a six-month leave from the company, returning in the summer of 2009 after undergoing a liver transplant.

Such is the power of the word.

Writing for reading and speaking is a hallmark of the practice of public relations.

Writing for reading emphasizes the written word. Writing for listening emphasizes the spoken word. The two differ significantly.

Writing for the eye traditionally has ranked among the strongest areas for public relations professionals. Years ago, most practitioners entered public relations through print journalism. Accordingly, they were schooled in the techniques of writing for the eye, not the ear. Today, of course, a background in print journalism is not necessarily a prerequisite for public relations work.

Just as important today is writing for the ear—writing for listening. The key to such writing is to write as if you are speaking. Use simple, short sentences, active verbs, contractions, and one- and two-syllable words. In brief, be brief.

This chapter will focus on two things: first, the most frequently used external communication vehicles designed for the eye, beyond the news release; and second, the most widely used methods for communicating through the ear, particularly speeches and presentations.

Today's public relations professional must be conversant in writing for both the eye and the ear.

Writing for the Eye

There are a myriad of external public relations writing vehicles, designed to be read. Among the most common are the following.

The Media Kit

Beyond the news release, the most ubiquitous written vehicle in public relations work is the media or press kit. In effect, the media kit serves as a "calling card" to introduce the organization to the media.

Media kits—in print or, more commonly today, online—incorporate several communications vehicles for potential use by newspapers and magazines. A bare-bones media kit consists of the following items, in addition to a news release:

- ■ **The Biography.** The biography, often called the biographical summary or just plain bio, is a necessity in the kit. The bio recounts pertinent facts about a particular individual. Bios can be written two ways:
  1. The **straight bio** lists factual information in a straightforward fashion in descending order of importance, with company-oriented facts preceding more personal details. For example, the straight biography of U.S. Vice President Joe Biden might begin this way:

     > *Joseph Robinette "Joe" Biden, Jr., is Vice President of the United States of America. On January 20, 2009, Joe Biden was inaugurated as Vice President of the United States of America.*
     >
     > *Prior to his election to Vice President in 2008, Biden was the senior U.S. Senator from Delaware. He was born in Scranton, PA, and lived there for 10 years before moving to Delaware. He became an attorney in 1969 and was elected to a county council in 1970.*
     >
     > *Biden was first elected to the Senate in 1972 and became the sixth-youngest senator in U.S. history. He was reelected to the Senate in 1978, 1984, 1990, 1996, 2002, and 2008.*

     This straight biography is written straightforwardly, a chronology of the subject's work history and accomplishments, with little editorializing.

2. The **narrative bio**, on the other hand, is written in a breezier, more informal way. This style gives spark and vitality to the biography to make the individual come alive. For example, in the case of Joe Biden, the narrative bio might read thusly:

> *Joe Biden was born in Scranton, PA, the first of four siblings in an Irish-Catholic family. The family later moved to a middle-class neighborhood in Delaware.*
>
> *At age 29, he became one of the youngest people ever elected to the United States Senate. Right after being elected, his first wife and daughter were killed in a car accident. People rallied around him, and for the next five years, he raised his two sons as a single parent, never forgetting family comes first.*
>
> *He never forgot where he came from. While most Senators live in Washington, he commuted home every night using public transportation to be with his wife of almost 30 years, Jill, a school teacher, and his now 89-year-old mother.*

The narrative bio, in addition to bringing the individual to life, doubles as a speech of introduction when that individual serves as a featured speaker. In effect, the narrative bio becomes a speech.

■ **The Backgrounder.** Background pieces, or backgrounders, provide additional information generally to complement the news release. Backgrounders can embellish the announcement, or they can discuss the institution making the announcement, the system behind the announcement, or any other appropriate topic that will assist a journalist in writing the story. In devising a backgrounder, a writer enjoys unlimited latitude. As long as the piece catches the interest of the reader/editor, any style is permissible (see Figure 16-2).

■ **Fact Sheets, Q&As, Photos, Etc.** Beyond bios and backgrounders, media kits may contain any other information that will help journalists tell a story. They want information in a hurry, without being delayed by voice mail or foot-dragging. Therefore, the following make great sense to include in media kits:

- *Fact sheets*, which compile the most relevant facts concerning the product, issue, organization, or candidate discussed in quick and easily accessible fashion (Figure 16-3).
- *Q&As*, which present the most probable questions posed about the subject matter at hand and then the answers to those questions. Again, this preempts a reporter having to ask questions of a live—and often unavailable—public relations person.
- *Photos*, which illustrate the subject. With photo editors now downloading from the Web, online color media kit photos are a necessity (see Figure 16-4). Although a detailed discussion of photographic terms and techniques is beyond the scope of this book, public relations practitioners should be relatively conversant with photographic terminology and able to recognize the attributes of good photos.

■ **Etc., etc., etc.** What other material should be included in media kits? Additional pertinent photos, advertising schedules and slicks, CDs, DVDs, speeches—there is no hard-and-fast rule. However, journalists have little patience for being overwhelmed with extraneous material. Therefore, as with news releases, in media kits, less is more.

PR Newswire Corporate Backgrounder

Company Overview:
PR Newswire Association LLC (http://www.prnewswire.com/) provides electronic distribution, targeting, measurement and broadcast services on behalf of tens of thousands of corporate, government, association, labor, non-profit, and other customers worldwide. Using PR Newswire, these organizations reach a variety of critical audiences including the news media, the investment community, government decision-makers, and the general public with their up-to-the-minute, full-text news developments.

Established in 1954, PR Newswire has offices in 14 countries and routinely sends its customers' announcements to outlets in more than 170 countries and in more than 40 languages. Utilizing the latest in communications technology, PR Newswire content is considered a mainstay among news reporters, investors and individuals who seek breaking announcements from the source. PR Newswire's leading services include ProfNet^{SM}, eWatch™, MEDIAtlas™, Search Engine Optimization, MediaRoom, MediaSense™, MultiVu™, U.S. Newswire, the preeminent policy newswire in the industry, Vintage Filings, the fastest growing Edgar filing company, and Hispanic PR Wire, LatinClips and Hispanic Digital Network, the foremost Hispanic communications services. PR Newswire is a subsidiary of United Business Media Limited, a leading global business media company that serves professional commercial communities around the world. For more information, go to www.unitedbusinessmedia.com.

About United Business Media Limited (www.unitedbusinessmedia.com)
United Business Media Limited (UBM) is a global media and marketing services company that informs markets and brings the world's buyers and sellers together at events, online, in print, and with the information they need to do business successfully. UBM serves professional and commercial communities, from IT professionals to doctors, from journalists to jewelry dealers, from farmers to pharmacists around the world. UBM employs more than 6,500 people in more than 30 countries. UBM's businesses operating in the US include CMPMedica, Commonwealth Business Media, Everything Channel, PR Newswire, RISI, TechInsights, TechWeb and Think Services. UBM is listed on the London Stock Exchange (UBM.L) and has a market capitalization of $2.5 billion.

Vice President of Public Relations:
Rachel Meranus, 201.360.6776 or
rachel.meranus@prnewswire.com

FIGURE 16-2
Backgrounder. All you need to know about PR Newswire, granddaddy of all media distribution services. (Copyright ©2009 PR Newswire Association LLC. All Rights Reserved. A United Business Media Company)

The Pitch Letter

The pitch letter is used to interest an editor or reporter in a possible story, interview, or event. Although letter styles run the gamut, the best are direct and to the point, while being catchy and evocative.

Pitch letters, like sales letters, may contain elements that seek to entice a reader's active participation in attending an event or covering a story. The vast majority today is sent via email and comprises a variety of types, among them:

■ The *"creative"* pitch.

> *Hello Fraser,*
>
> *A scrappy little PR agency is raking in the kind of results that make Madison Avenue anxious, and it's changing the way PR is done. While it has secured features for clients in nearly every major media outlet many times over, it's generated astounding results in just the past month, including getting clients featured on* Oprah, Montel Williams, the Early Show, Fox News, The New York Times, USA Today, Woman's World, and Child Magazine. *As a matter of fact, one of its very own is currently testing her skills as the first publicist ever selected for Donald Trump's* The Apprentice.
>
> *What's the secret?*

Quick Facts on PR Newswire

Headquarters: New York

History: Established in 1954 by Herbert Muschel

Number of employees: 1000+

Number of members: Tens of thousands worldwide including companies, agencies, organizations, governments, non-profits, associations and institutions

Audiences served:
Tens of thousands of traditional and non-traditional media points through digital, Internet, satellite, email and fax delivery, including those served through the media web site, PR Newswire for Journalists, http://www.prnewswire.com/media, plus the general public and millions of investment professionals through more than 4,000 websites, online databases and financial networks.

PR Newswire Executive Team:

Charles Gregson, Chief Executive Officer
Dave Wein, Chief Financial Officer
James Slattery, Chief Information Officer
Ken Dowell, Executive Vice President, Information Services
Scott Mozarsky, Executive Vice President and Chief Strategy & Global Development Officer
John M. Williams, Executive Vice President, Asia Markets
Angela Scalpello, Senior Vice President, Human Resources

Vice President, Public Relations:
Rachel Meranus, 201.360.6776 or
rachel.meranus@prnewswire.com

This is a perfect pitch letter. It sticks its neck out. It's gutsy. It's enthusiastic, without being boastful. Most of all, it lets "facts" do the talking. It isn't just posturing or rhetoric.

Rather, it's creative but fact-based and, therefore, newsworthy.

■ **The *"straight"* pitch.**

Dear Fraser:

I thought you might be interested in the recent staff additions to New Mexico–based public relations agency, Freddie J. Nanceman Public Relations. This news comes following a record increase in revenues and 30 percent growth for the agency.

There's nothing wrong with being straight. In fact, studies suggest that journalists appreciate receiving "just the facts."

In this case, not only is the pitcher straight with the facts, but she also cleverly incorporates sales points about the agency to further justify reporting on the promotions.

■ **The *"provocative question"* pitch.**

Hi Fraser,

— Why is unacceptable employee behavior as dooming to the entrepreneur as lack of money to run the business?

FIGURE 16-4 **Killer publicity photos.** One reason SeaWorld of California turned out the best publicity photos was that its star performer(s)—Shamu, the killer whale(s)—was (were) so photogenic. (Courtesy of SeaWorld of California)

— Why is dealing with employees an entrepreneur's greatest nightmare?

— How do you deal with an employee who is all "what's in it for me?"

TIME Magazine reports that "the average American office worker 'goofs off' for just over two hours a day—and that's not counting lunches or breaks." This might be acceptable for a mega-million dollar company flush with cash but it spells DISASTER for the entrepreneur.

Learn the dos and don'ts and tricks of the trade of managing even your worst nightmare of an employee with entrepreneurial expert, Frank Steph, author of Stop Killing My Business.

Questions in a pitch work beautifully—as long as they're pertinent, pointed, and provocative, like these. Would you be interested in meeting this author after this provocative pitch? Sure.

On the other hand, there is . . .

■ **The *"ho hum question"* pitch.**

Hi Fraser,

Would you be interested in how a professional services firm reinvented itself to great success and controversy?

After the economy turned in 2000, Stovepipe Group's "banner clients" like Microsoft and Intel took their PR business in-house. After struggling for a few years Stovepipe Group, a 12-year-old public relations firm, conducted a two-month formal and disciplined assessment of the company, its competition, and the marketplace.

How would you answer the question posed here? Would this query be enough to interest you? Probably not.

Granted, successful reinvention might, indeed, be interesting, but you need to tell us "why" it is in this case. The answer, as we find out, is that clients took their business in-house, thus forcing this agency to come up with a new plan.

So a better question to begin might be, *"What would you do if your top clients all of a sudden decided to fire you and perform your services in-house? Here's what we did . . . "*

Or something like that.

■ **The *"who cares"* pitch.**

Hi Fraser,

Y.O.Y. Consulting Group today announced its successful PR campaign with Wictionless Commerce to help the Bambridge, WY-based software company strengthen its leadership position in the enterprise sourcing market. Over the past nine months, Y.O.Y. Consulting has led an aggressive media relations and news management campaign aimed at increasing visibility for Wictionless' sourcing software and raising industry awareness around Enterprise Sourcing/Spend Management.

Why would any self-respecting reporter be interested in speaking with Y.O.Y. after this pitch? Who cares if the consultants have increased their client's visibility?

The one question that any pitch must answer is "Who cares?" If the answer is, "No one," then don't send the email.

■ **The *"what's new"* pitch.**

Dear Fraser,

I think I have a good little news piece for you about the relationship between consumer marketing and celebrities. We represent Offstage

> *Productions, the company that gives freebies to the celebrities at Awards Shows (we just did the Boomers Choice Awards on Sunday and have tons of photos).*
>
> *Whether you're selling toys, games, jewelry, clothing, or some other product, it always pays to have celebrities seen with your product.*

OK, fair enough. But what's new about this? We know celebrities help sell products. We may not like it, but we know it. So where's the new angle here? If the reporter isn't told early on, the story is a non-starter.

Therefore, the other question that any pitch must answer is, "What's new?" If the answer is, "Nothing" . . . well, you know the rest.[3]

Pitch letters that sell generally contain several key elements.

1. They open with a grabber, an interesting statement that impels the reader to continue reading.
2. Next, they explain why the story is relevant to the editor's readership, listenership, or viewership. That means it must allude to the scope and importance of the story.
3. Finally, pitch letters should be personally written to specific people rather than being addressed to "editor" (which is the journalistic equivalent of "occupant").

Related to the pitch letter is the "media advisory," a more straightforward listing of facts to interest an editor or news director, usually into attending an event. This format eschews the use of long paragraphs in favor of short, bulleted items highlighting the "5Ws" used by journalists: who, what, when, where, and why. The premise of the media advisory is that it "talks to the media in a language it has been trained to accept."

The Roundup Article

Let's say your organization is a small one and usually not considered for national publicity. Is national publicity possible? You betcha'.

Reporters get rewarded for two things in particular: scoops and trends. The former refers to breaking a story before anyone else. The latter concerns breaking a story that speaks of an emerging trend abroad in the land that is relevant to an industry.

Newspapers, magazines, TV programs, and online news services encourage articles that summarize, or "round up," the experiences of several companies within an industry. These trend articles may be initiated by the publications themselves or at the suggestions of public relations people.

Weaker or smaller companies, in particular, can benefit from being included in a roundup story with stronger, larger adversaries. Thoroughly researching and drafting roundup articles—generally in the form of a letter to a specific editor—is a good way to secure stories that mention the practitioner's firm in favorable association with top competitors.

So how can your small organization make the front page of the *Wall Street Journal?* By initiating a roundup article.

The Case History

Another popular and foolproof public relations writing vehicle to attract publicity is the case history.

The case history is frequently used to tell about a customer's favorable use of a company's product or service. Generally, the case history writer works for the company whose product or service is involved. Magazines, particularly trade journals, often welcome case histories, contending that one person's experience may be instructive to another.

Case histories generally follow a five-part formula:

1. They present a problem experienced by one company but applicable to many other firms.
2. They indicate how the dimensions of the problem were defined by the company using the product.
3. They indicate the solution adopted.
4. They explain the advantages of the adopted solution.
5. They detail the user company's experience after adopting the solution.

Trade book editors, in particular, are often willing to share a case that can be generalized—and is, therefore, relevant—to the broader readership. Done skillfully, such a case history is soft sell at its best: beneficial to the company and interesting and informative to the editor and readers.

The Byliner

The bylined article, or byliner, is a story signed and ostensibly authored by an officer of a particular firm. Often, however, the byliner is ghostwritten by a public relations professional.

In addition to carrying considerable prestige in certain publications, byliners allow corporate spokespersons to express their views without being subject to major reinterpretation by the publication.

Perhaps the major advantage of a byliner is that it positions executives as experts. The fact that an organization's officer has authored an informed article on a subject means that not only are the officer and the organization credible sources, but also, by inference, they are perhaps more highly regarded on the issues at hand than their competitors. The ultimate audience exposed to a byliner may greatly exceed the circulation of the periodical in which the article appears, because organizations regularly use byliner reprints as direct-mail pieces to enhance their image with key constituent groups.

The Op-Ed

Similar to the byliner, the op-ed article is an editorial written by an organizational executive and then submitted for publication to a leading newspaper or magazine. Most leading newspapers include a page opposite their editorial pages for outside opinions, thus "op-ed."

Being included on a publication's op-ed page is a prestigious publicity forum, and op-ed submissions are, therefore, plentiful. Thus op-ed pieces must be written in a style that attracts attention. According to writing counselor Jeffrey D. Porro, the good ones contain the following elements:

■ *Grabber*, which starts off the piece and "grabs" attention
■ *Point*, which hammers home the thesis of the article

- *Chain of evidence*, which gives the facts that support the argument
- *Summation*, which summarizes the argument
- *Good-bye zinger*, which leaves the reader with something to think about.[4]

The Standby Statement

Organizations often take difficult actions they anticipate will lead to media inquiries or even public protests. Such actions might include:

- Price increases
- Extraordinary losses
- Employee layoffs
- Age, sex, or other types of discrimination

In these cases, while the organization doesn't wish to make the actions public, it must be prepared to respond if there is public disclosure. Accordingly, firms prepare concise statements to clarify their positions should they be called upon to explain. Such *standby statements* generally are defensive—and certainly not meant to be volunteered.

They should be brief and unambiguous so as not to raise more questions than they answer. Most of the time—since few in an organization wish to raise bad news—it is the public relations professional who advances the discussion to confront the need for such standby statements. At any one time, a public relations professional, doing his or her job right, will have several standby statements at the ready should the dreaded call come.

The White Paper

Finally, public relations people are frequently called on to write "white papers," which often concern external dilemmas faced by the organization.

Written primarily for internal background purposes, white papers—or position papers—rigorously document the facts and assumptions that lead to a particular "position" that the organization is suggested to take.

White papers typically follow a five-part organization:

1. **Background**—a brief section that describes the pertinent historical perspective that has brought the organization to its current state. This allows the context for the decisions reached later in the paper.
2. **Statement of the challenge**—a simple statement that designates clearly the challenge that confronts the entity, to which proposed solutions will apply.
3. **Alternative solutions**—which briefly list the pros and cons of alternative paths the entity might take to deal with its challenge. (The first alternative is always "Do nothing.")
4. **Recommended solution**—which states clearly the one solution that the writer believes is the best one that can be adopted. This section should defend "why" one decision is preferable and why the alternatives are less good.

5. **Blueprint and "key messages" for action**—which first, describes the action plan of "next steps" that the entity should embrace to carry out the proposed solution, and second, lists the several key messages that will help ultimately to attain the desired public relations result.

Such white papers form the basis of review and discussion and ultimately serve as the nucleus for a corporate position. After such a position is ratified by management, a "sanitized" position paper may be made available for distribution to opinion leaders and the general public.

Writing for the Ear

Writing for listening differs from writing for the eye.

Listeners—whether watching video, listening to audio, or sitting in a presentation audience—need to be persuaded, motivated, stimulated. That requires a different writing style and approach than that required for writing for reading.

Often, effective oral presentation will read poorly. The trick for any writer composing a document for the ear is to "write like you speak." The two primary public relations-drafted documents designed for the ear are formal speeches and presentations. Here's the way these documents—indeed, all writing for the ear—should be approached.

The Speech

Some say that in the age of the Internet, speech writing is passé. Baloney. In terms of writing for the ear, the most important public relations vehicle is the external or internal speech.

Speechwriting has become one of the most coveted public relations skills. Increasingly, speechwriters have used their access to management to move up the organizational ladder. The prominence they enjoy is due largely to the importance government and business executives place on making speeches. Today's executives are called on to defend their policies, justify their prices, and explain their practices to a much greater degree than ever before. In this environment, a good speechwriter becomes a valuable—and often highly paid—asset.

A speech possesses five main characteristics:

1. *It is designed to be heard, not read.* The mistake of writing for the eye instead of the ear is the most common trap of bad speeches. Speeches needn't be literary gems, but they ought to sound good.

2. *It uses concrete language.* The ear dislikes generalities. It responds to clear images. Ideas must be expressed sharply for the audience to get the point.

3. *It demands a positive response.* Every word, every passage, every phrase should evoke a response from the audience. The speech should possess special vitality—and so, for that matter, should the speaker.

4. *It must have clear-cut objectives.* The speech and the speaker must have a point—a thesis. If there's no point, then it's not worth the speaker's or the audience's time to be there.

5. *It must be tailored to a specific audience.* An audience needs to feel that it is hearing something special. The most frequent complaint about organizational speeches is that they all seem interchangeable—they lack uniqueness. That's why speeches must be targeted to fit the needs of a specific audience.

Most of all, the speech has to get across the fact that the speaker "cares." If the speaker doesn't seem to have passion for the topic about which he or she is speaking, then the audience never will. Therefore, the most essential mandate for the speechwriter is to encourage the speaker to show that he or she "cares" about the topic.

Beyond adhering to these five principles and before putting words on paper, a speechwriter must have a clear idea of the process—the route—to follow in developing the speech.

The Speechwriting Process

The speechwriting process breaks down into four components: (1) preparing, (2) interviewing, (3) researching, and (4) organizing and writing.

Preparing

One easy way to prepare for a speech is to follow a 4W checklist: Answer the questions who, what, where, and when.

- **Who.** The "who" represents two critical elements: the speaker and the audience. A writer should know all about the speaker—manner of speech, use of humor, reaction to an audience, background, and personality. It's almost impossible to write a speech for someone you don't know. The writer should also know something about the audience. What does this audience think about this subject?

PR Ethics Mini-Case Blago's Back-'Em-into-the-Corner Speech

In the winter of 2008, they told him not to do it. But Blago would have none of it.

When Illinois Governor Rod Blagojevich was accused, through government wiretaps, of trying to peddle President-elect Barack Obama's U.S. Senate seat to the highest bidder, he was warned by his own Democratic Party not to "pull a fast one" and try to appoint a successor to Obama. Senate Majority Leader Harry Reid vowed that no person the defiant governor appointed would have a chance being seated as a U.S. senator.

That was all Blago needed to hear. It was like waving a red flag in front of a bull.

Sure enough, the embattled governor immediately held a news conference to announce that he had selected Illinois' first African American Attorney General, Roland Burris, as his choice to fill out the Obama term (see Figure 16-5).

Democrats were livid. But Blago, a master of the well-turned phrase, expressed his decision with carefully crafted poise and passion.

"The people of Illinois are entitled to have two U.S. Senators represent them in Washington, D.C.," he began the news conference.

FIGURE 16-5 Blago the orator. Embattled Illinois Governor Rod Blagojevich's impassioned press conference rhetoric about his Senate nominee Roland Burris had pundits buzzing and the U.S. Congress running for cover. (Courtesy of Fox News)

"As governor, I am required to make this appointment. If I don't make this appointment, then the people of Illinois will be deprived of their appropriate voice and voice in the U.S. Senate.

"Please don't allow the allegations against me to taint a good and honest man."

In light of such reasonable and resonant rhetoric, what could the U.S. Senate do?

You guessed it.

Sure enough, while the governor was ultimately impeached by the Illinois legislature, his choice as the next junior senator from Illinois, Roland Burris, was, indeed, seated as the successor to President Barack Obama.

And Gov. Blago, largely because of his dextrous rhetoric, wound up with the last laugh (even if he chortled it in the slammer!).

Questions

1. If you were Gov. Blagojevich's public relations advisor, how would you have suggested he respond to the seating of Roland Burris as senator?

2. How would you have suggested Gov. Blagojevich comport himself publicly, while the charges against him were pending?

- ■ **What.** The "what" refers to two things: (1) the "subject," the assigned topic of the talk, and (2) the "object," the speaker's intent to convince the audience to take some specific action.

- ■ **Where.** The "where" is the setting. A large hall requires a more formal talk than a roundtable forum. Often the location of the speech—the city, state, or even a particular hall—bears historic or symbolic significance that can enhance a message.

- ■ **When.** The "when" is the time of the speech. People are more awake in the morning and get sleepier as the day progresses. The "when" also refers to the time of year. A speech can always be linked to an upcoming holiday or special celebration.

Interviewing

Interviewing speakers in advance is essential. A good interview with a speaker often means the difference between a strong speech and a poor one.

In the interview, the speechwriter gets some time—from as little as 15 minutes to more than an hour—to observe the speaker firsthand and probe for the keys to the speech. The interview must accomplish at least three specific goals for the speechwriter:

1. *Determine the object of the talk.* Again, the object is the purpose of the speech— that is, what exactly the speaker wants the audience to do after he or she is finished speaking. This is the thesis of the speech. The interviewer's essential question must be "What do you want to leave the audience with at the conclusion of your speech?" Once the speaker answers this question, the rest of the speech should fall into place.

2. *Determine the speaker's main points.* Normally, an audience can grasp only a few points during a speech. These points, which should flow directly from the object, become touchstones around which the rest of the speech is woven.

3. *Capture the speaker's characteristics.* Most of all, during the interview, the writer must observe the speaker. How comfortable is the speaker with humor? How informal or deliberate is he or she with words? What are the speaker's pet phrases and expressions? The writer must file these observations away, recall them during the writing process, and factor them into the speech.

Researching

Like any writer, a speechwriter sometimes develops writer's block, the inability to come up with anything on paper. One way around writer's block is to adopt a formalized research procedure.

1. *Dig into all literature, books, pamphlets, articles, speeches, and other writings on the speech subject—especially those already written/uttered by the speaker.* A stocked file cabinet is often the speechwriter's best friend.

2. *Think about the subject.* Bring personal thoughts to bear on the topic. The writer should amplify the speaker's thoughts with his or her own.

3. *Seek out the opinions of others.* Perhaps the speaker isn't the most knowledgeable source within the organization about this specific subject. Outside sources, particularly politicians and business leaders, are often willing to share their ideas when requested.

Organizing and Writing

Once preparation, interviewing, and research have been completed, the fun part begins. Writing a speech becomes easier if, again, the speech is organized into its four essential elements: introduction, thesis, body, and conclusion.

Introduction. An introduction must grab the audience and hold its interest. An audience is alert at the beginning of a talk, and the writer's job is to make sure the audience stays there. Audience members need time to settle in their seats, and the speaker needs time to get his or her bearings on the podium and win audience rapport.

Thesis. The thesis, again, is the all important object of the speech—its purpose or central idea. A good thesis statement lets an audience know in a simple sentence where a speech is going and how it will get there. Without the thesis, there is no speech.

Body. The speech body is just that—the general body of evidence that supports the three or four main points. Although facts, statistics, and figures are important elements, writers should always attempt to use comparisons or contrasts for easier audience understanding.

Conclusion. The best advice on wrapping up a speech is to do it quickly. Net-oriented audiences won't sit through long speeches. As the old Texas bromide states *"If you haven't struck oil in the first 20 minutes, stop boring."* Put another way, the conclusion must be blunt, short, and to the point.

The Presentation

A business presentation is different from a speech. A presentation generally is designed to sell a product, service, or idea. Everyone, somewhere along the line, must deliver a presentation. Like any other speaking device, an effective presentation depends on following established guidelines.

1. *Get organized.* Before considering your presentation, consider the 4Ws of speechwriting. Who are you addressing? What are you trying to say? Where and when should something happen?

2. *Get to the point.* Know your thesis. What are you trying to prove? What is the central purpose of your presentation?

3. *Be logical.* Organize the presentation with some logic in mind. Don't skip randomly from one thought to another. Lead from your objective to your strategies to the tactics you will use to achieve your goal.

4. *Write it out.* Don't wing it. If Jay Leno, David Letterman, and Conan O'Brien write out their ad-libs, so should you. Always have the words right in front of you.

5. *Anticipate the negatives.* Keep carping critics at bay. Anticipate their objections and defuse them by examining and dismissing vulnerabilities in the presentation.

6. *Speak, don't read.* Sound as if you know the information. Practice before the performance. Make the presentation part of you. Reading suggests uncertainty. Speaking asserts assurance.

7. *Be understandable.* Speak with clarity and concreteness so that people understand you. If you want to make the sale, you must be clear.

8. *Use graphics wisely.* Audiovisual supports should do just that—support the presentation. Graphics should be used more to tease than to provide full information. They shouldn't be crammed with too much information. This will detract from the overall impact of the presentation. Because many audiovisual channels are available to a presenter, from PowerPoint projection to overheads, it may be wise to seek professional help in devising compelling graphics for a presentation.

9. *Be convincing.* If you aren't enthusiastic about your presentation, no one else will be. Be animated. Be interesting. Be enthusiastic. Sound convinced that what you're presenting is an absolute necessity for the organization.

10. *STOP!* A short, buttoned-up presentation is much more effective than one that goes on and on. At his inaugural, U.S. President William Henry Harrison delivered a two-hour, 6,000-word address into a biting wind on Pennsylvania Avenue. A month later, he died of pneumonia. The lesson: *When you've said it all, shut up!*

Last Word

Skillful writing lies at the heart of public relations practice. Basically, public relations professionals are professional communicators. Ergo, each person engaged in public relations work must be adept at writing.

In today's overcommunicated society, everyone from bloggers to newspaper editors to corporate presidents complains about getting too much paper. So, before a professional even thinks of putting thoughts on paper, he or she must answer the following questions:

1. *Will writing serve a practical purpose?* If you can't come up with a purpose, don't write.

2. *Is writing the most effective way to communicate?* Face-to-face or telephone communication may be better and more direct than writing.

3. *What is the risk?* Writing is always risky; just ask a lawyer. Once it's down in black and white, it's difficult or impossible to retract. And the risks have increased with the immediacy and pervasiveness of the Internet. So, think before you write.

4. *Are the timing and the person doing the writing right?* Timing is extremely important in writing. A message, like a joke, can fall flat if the timing is off. The individual doing the writing must also be considered. A writer should always ask whether he or she is the most appropriate person to write.

The pen—or, more likely, the PC or laptop or BlackBerry—is a powerful weapon. Like any other weapon, writing must be used prudently and properly to achieve the desired result.

Discussion Starters

1. What are the essential elements of a media kit?
2. What is the difference between a straight biography and a narrative biography?
3. What is a backgrounder?
4. What are the benefits of a roundup story?
5. When might an organization require a standby statement?
6. What are the essential characteristics of a speech?
7. What questions does one ask to begin the speechwriting process?
8. What are the elements that constitute an effective presentation?
9. What are the necessary four organizational components of a speech?
10. What are possible pitfalls that must be considered before writing anything?

Top of the Shelf   Public Speaking: A Student Guide / Katherine Pebley

O'Neal, San Luis Obispo, CA: Dandy Lion Publications, 2005

A great guide for students or anybody else challenged by turning a written composition into an oral presentation. The author takes speakers through the process of persuading listeners by weaving winning oral prose.

All the topics—from getting organized, to preparing a winning opening line, to involving the audience, and persuading with confidence—are covered here. Written in a simple, easygoing manner, this little gem may be all you need to become the next Barack Obama.

Case Study   Drafting the CEO's Speech

Congratulations.

You have been selected by your boss to draft the introduction to a speech your CEO will deliver before the 200 top officers of the organization.

You interview the CEO and find that she would like to address the general topic of *"The Key Challenges for Us in the Year Ahead."*

The object of her talk, according to the CEO, is to convince the officers that although this will be a difficult year, if everyone pulls together, it also can be a most successful one for our company.

Consequently, the CEO's thesis will be the following:

The year we face will be difficult. The environment, uncertain. The challenges, numerous. But if we all pull together in the several specific areas I'll describe, I'm confident that we will have a banner year.

This will form the basis of her remarks.

The CEO's views are based on the knowledge that the recessionary year just past was a tough one for the company, with profits down 7 percent year-to-year. To shore itself up, the organization has invested $15 million in new systems, adopted new bonus programs, and hired a dozen new executives from the outside.

With a 100-year heritage—the oldest firm in the industry—the company has always enjoyed a reputation for reliable products and quality service. It has traditionally ranked among *Fortune* magazine's "100 Best Companies to Work For." Indeed, in its 100 years, the company has never had to resort to any major layoff program.

The company's strong ethical streak emanates from a corporate mission that places integrity, product quality, and service as its three top values.

The setting of the CEO's speech is the annual officers' dinner of the corporation, held at the swankiest hotel in town.

The format calls for the chief operating officer to bang the gavel at around dessert time, say a few words of light spirited introduction, and bring on the CEO to deliver the "State of the Organization" speech.

The CEO desperately wants her important message to get across to all those in the room. So she hopes to begin strongly, soundly, and resoundingly.

Keep in mind the purposes of the introduction are to:

1. Ease the audience and the speaker into the speech.
2. Attract initial, favorable attention from the crowd.
3. Provide appropriate background to the audience on the subject.
4. Suit the occasion.

Question

1. What is the introduction you would write for your CEO?

Bonnie Grossman is an instructor in the School of Business, Department of Management and Entrepreneurship, at the College of Charleston in South Carolina. Prior to joining the faculty at the College of Charleston, Grossman worked 15 years in corporate public relations, including stints as manager of employee communications for medical manufacturer Hill-Rom Company and as public relations director for a community hospital.

How important is writing in public relations?

Writing skills are a career sifter in most fields—good writers move up and poor writers get passed up. But in public relations, good writing skills are absolutely crucial. A PR professional is expected to be the *best* writer in the organization. Knowing how to write for the media is only the first expectation.

PR people write, write, write. In the end, your ability to write is your key to access within your organization. When you can write well, you are trusted with information. Externally, the people you're writing *to* —the media—are all professional writers. If you send them bad writing, it shows. You lose credibility.

What's the caliber of public relations writing today?

There was a time when PR people came from the ranks of journalism and journalism schools. Their education and experience valued and practiced good writing skills. Sadly, that basic respect for language seems to be missing in much of today's PR writing. I see too many buzzwords devoid of meaning and too much rhetoric that is not reader friendly.

Are public relations writers "born," or can they be taught?

I wouldn't be a teacher if I thought I had no impact. I've taught journalism, business writing, and PR writing. Students who work to improve the mechanical aspects of their writing and then adapt their messages to particular audiences and styles develop the confidence they need to produce professionally acceptable written work.

Would we accept the idea that athletes are born and not taught? Skill is necessary for either writers or athletes, but coaching, training, and practice make the difference between good and great. I believe some writers are born with special talent, and for them, writing is an art. Words flow from their souls. But we don't each have to be able to produce a masterpiece of American literature. Just learn to write in plain English and be readable.

What's the secret to effective public relations writing?

Have something to say. Be newsworthy, be timely, and remember there are really *six* W's: *Who? What? When? Where? Why?* and *Who cares?* Just because your CEO has declared your newest initiative "news," doesn't mean it is. You must be prepared to show your reader why he or she should care about your news item.

Understand that you don't have control of the story. If you want control, buy an ad. The secret to *all* effective communications is to stop thinking about yourself as a writer and focus on your reader.

How important is writing in one's public relations career?

There is *no* time in one's PR career that writing becomes any less vital. Public relations practitioners understand the power of words. Occasionally, students enter my class with the perception that public relations is about event planning and taking people to lunch. They leave with a greater awareness of how pervasive, varied, and exciting our career field really is.

Public Relations Library

Altman, Rick. *The Most PowerPoint Presentations Suck*. Pleasanton, CA: Harvest Books, 2007. This book, from a computer expert, is worth the time for anyone who complements presentations with PowerPoint. And that's everyone!

Balshaw, Kevin. *Speech Maker's Bible*. Australia: National Library of Australia, 2008. A speechwriter from Down Under gives his prescription on how to author an effective speech.

Caplin, James. *I Hate Presentations: Transform the Way You Present with a Fresh and Powerful Approach*. Chichester, UK: Capstone Publishing Ltd., 2008. A look at presentations from the other side of the pond.

Davis, Ossie. *Life Lit By Some Large Vision*. New York, NY: Atria Books, 2006. A collection of impassioned speeches by social activist and actor Ossie Davis, collected by his wife, Ruby Dee.

Duarte, Nancy. *Slide:ology: The Art and Science of Creating Great Presentations*. Sebastopol, CA: O'Reilly Media, Inc., 2008. A Silicon Valley designer provides a graphic take on presentations.

Kador, John. *50 High Impact Speeches and Remarks*. New York, NY: McGraw-Hill, 2004. Interesting compilation of 50 mostly corporate speeches that served a specific purpose.

Koegel, Timothy J. *The Exceptional Presenter*. Austin, TX: Greenleaf Book Press Group, 2007. A presentation coach shares his secrets of creating a winning presentation.

Monarth, Harrison, and Larina Kase. *The Confident Speaker*. New York, NY: McGraw-Hill, 2008. How to confront your fears and deliver speeches that work.

Reynolds, Garr. *Presentation Zen*. Berkeley, CA: New Riders, 2008. A presentation, says the author, "is a journey." And this book certainly is!

Safire, William. *Lend Me Your Ears: Great Speeches in History*. New York, NY: The Cobbett Corporation, 2004. The New York Times columnist and public relations professional, who died in 2009, lists his all-time great rhetorical masterpieces, from Cicero to Lincoln to Churchill.

Speechwriter's Newsletter. Available from Ragan Communications, Inc. Ragan Communications, 316 North Michigan Ave., Suite 300, Chicago, IL 60601.

Walker, T.J. *Presentation Training A–Z*. New York, NY: Media Training Worldwide, 2005. The author traces what one need do to ensure the audience understands you, remembers what you said, and is motivated to tell others.

Weissman, Jerry. *Presenting to Win: The Art of Telling Your Story*. Upper Saddle River, NJ: Prentice-Hall, Inc., 2006. An experienced speech trainer shares his secrets.

Chapter 17

Integrated Marketing
Communications

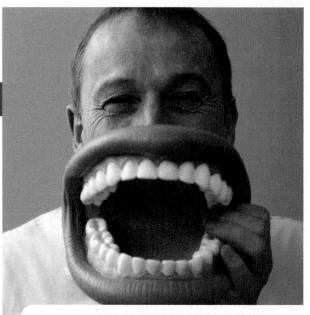

FIGURE 17-1 Big mouth marketing. Dr. Nick Daley of London demonstrates his contribution to integrated marketing, a novelty plastic mouth to promote his dental practice. (It worked!) (Photo: Newscom)

In these days of 24/7 media, social media networks, and uber-competition among products and services in every sector, it sure ain't "your mother's marketing" environment.

■ Today, when you hear that "the dentist will see you now," it may mean on YouTube! Dentists and other professionals have begun using the Web and all matter of public relations and marketing vehicles to differentiate their practices, with informational videos, demonstrations, and even props (see Figure 17-1).[1]

■ Cyber Monday, which started as a gimmick in 2005 to commemorate the kickoff of the "online shopping season" on the Monday after Black Friday following Thanksgiving Thursday (whew!), has become a monstrous shopping day, thanks to an enormous publicity offensive.[2]

■ Product placements—the insertion of marketing promotions in the middle of movies, TV shows, books, video games, etc.—have acquired a life of their own. In the 2008 season finale of *CSI:NY*, information about a shooting was shared on what was referred to as a "TelePresence screen." The unlikely—and unmentioned—supporting player in the episode was Cisco Systems, manufacturer of the TelePresence videoconferencing system, who paid for the prominent inclusion.[3]

■ And then there's the issue of "celebrity spokespersons," who tout products at every turn. In one of the most blatant uses, professional golfer Fred Couples is followed around the course by a gaggle of women paid to wear the name Bridgestone Golf, his sponsor.[4]

What's going on here?

Integrated marketing is the intersection of public relations and publicity, advertising, sales promotion, and marketing to promote organizations, products, and services. Creating YouTube videos, Internet publicity, using celebrities as spokespersons, inserting product placements in movies, sponsoring concerts, and a host of other publicity-seeking techniques are all examples of *integrated marketing communications*.

All are important to sell products and ideas.

While traditional advertising and marketing can build brand awareness, public relations establishes credibility and tells the brand story more comprehensively. Database marketing touches consumers one-on-one. Sales promotion motivates them to action.

The integration of these marketing techniques helps build a cohesive presence for a brand.

Some have suggested that advertising is dying and that public relations is taking over. That may be a bit overzealous.[5] Advertising isn't dead yet. Neither is marketing. But it is true that public relations and publicity integrated with these other disciplines are very much the rule in many organizations today.

Therefore, the need for *communications cross-training*—to learn the different skills of marketing, advertising, sales promotion, and public relations—becomes a requirement for all communicators.

Public Relations vs. Marketing vs. Advertising

What is the difference between marketing, advertising, and public relations?

Marketing, literally defined, is the selling of a service or product through pricing, distribution, and promotion. Marketing ranges from concepts such as free samples in the hands of consumers to buzz campaigns

Advertising, literally defined, is a subset of marketing that involves paying to place your message in more traditional media formats, from newspapers and magazines to radio and television to the Internet and outdoors.

Public relations, liberally defined, is the marketing of an organization and the use of unbiased, objective, third-party endorsement to relay information about that organization's products and practices.[6]

With so many media outlets bombarding consumers daily, most organizations realize that public relations can play an expanded role in marketing. In some organizations, particularly service companies, hospitals, and nonprofit institutions, the selling of both individual products and the organization itself are inextricably intertwined.

Stated another way, although the practices of marketing and advertising create a market for products and services and the practice of public relations creates a hospitable environment in which the organization may operate, marketing and advertising success can be nullified by the social and political forces public relations is designed to confront—and, thus, the interrelationship of the three disciplines.

In the past, marketers treated public relations as an ancillary part of the marketing mix. They were concerned primarily with making sure that their products met the needs and desires of customers and were priced competitively, distributed widely, and promoted heavily through advertising and merchandising. Gradually, however, these traditional notions among marketers began to change for several reasons.

- Consumer protests about both product value and safety and government scrutiny of the truth behind product claims began to shake historical views of marketing.
- Product recalls—from automobiles to tainted peanut butter, from toys to tuna fish—generated recurring headlines.
- Ingredient scares began to occur regularly.
- Advertisers were asked how their products answered social needs and civic responsibilities.

- Rumors about particular companies—from fast-food firms to pop-rock manufacturers—spread in brushfire manner.
- General image and specific financial problems of certain companies and industries—from oil to housing to banking—were fanned by a continuous blaze of media criticism.

The net impact of these challenges was that even though a company's products were still important, customers began to consider a firm's policies and practices on everything from air and water pollution to minority hiring. Beyond these social concerns, the effectiveness of advertising itself began to be questioned.

The increased number of advertisements in newspapers and on the airwaves caused clutter and placed a significant burden on advertisers who were trying to make the public aware of their products. In the 1980s, the trend toward shorter television advertising spots contributed to three times as many products being advertised on television as there were in the 1970s. In the 1990s, the spread of cable television added yet another multi-channeled outlet for product advertising. In the 2000s, the proliferation of cable TV and Internet advertising intensified the noise and clutter.

Against this backdrop, the potential of public relations as an added ingredient in the marketing mix has become an imperative. Indeed, marketing guru Philip Kotler was among the first to suggest more than a decade ago that to the traditional four Ps of marketing—product, price, place, and promotion—a fifth P, *public relations*, should be added.[7]

In the 21st century, Kotler's suggestion has increasingly become reality.

Product Publicity

To many, product publicity is the essence of the value of integrating public relations and marketing. In light of how difficult it now is to raise advertising awareness above the noise of so many competitive messages, marketers are turning increasingly to product publicity as an important adjunct to advertising. Although the public is generally unaware of it, a great deal of what it knows and believes about a wide variety of products comes through press coverage.

In certain circumstances, product publicity can be the most effective element in the marketing mix. For example:

- **Introducing a revolutionary new product.** Product publicity can start introductory sales at a much higher level of demand by creating more awareness of the product.
- **Eliminating distribution problems with retail outlets.** Often the way to get shelf space is to have consumers demand the product. Product publicity can be extremely effective in creating consumer demand.
- **Small budgets and strong competition.** Advertising is expensive. Product publicity is cheap. Often publicity is the best way to tell the story. That's why, as noted, Samuel Adams Boston Lager beer, became a household word—and a huge franchise—almost solely through publicity opportunities.
- **Explaining a complicated product.** The use and benefits of many products—particularly financial services—are difficult to explain to mass audiences in a brief ad. Product publicity, through extended news columns, can be invaluable.

■ **Tying the product to a unique representative.** Try as it might, the advertising industry can't escape the staying power of unique mascots who become tied inextricably to products. Consider the following:

- Morris the Cat was one answer to consumer disinterest in cat food for the 9 Lives Cat Food Company in 1968 and still appears today, well into middle age.
- The Jolly Green Giant has "ho ho ho'ed" so long at General Mills that he now has his own Green Giant Food Company and Web site.
- Burger King's "King" is back with a vengeance in the new century, cavorting on football fields and in other venues for a whole new generation.[8]
- But the real "king" is McDonald's standard bearer, Ronald McDonald, who first appeared in 1963 and has since starred on national television, at Academy Awards ceremonies, and around the world. No other iconic figure in history has become more synonymous with any company (see Figure 17-2).

Third-Party Endorsement

Perhaps more than anything else, the lure of third-party endorsement is the primary reason smart organizations value product publicity as much as they do advertising. Third-party endorsement, as noted, refers to the tacit support given a product by an "objective" third-party observer—a blog, newspaper, magazine, or broadcaster—who mentions the product as news.

Advertising often is perceived as self-serving. People know that the advertiser not only created the message but also paid for it. Publicity, on the other hand, which often appears in news columns, carries no such stigma. Editors, after all, are considered objective, impartial, indifferent, neutral. Therefore, publicity appears to be news and is more trustworthy than advertising that is paid for by a clearly nonobjective sponsor.

Editors, sensitive to the proliferating raft of product placements in the media, have become sensitive to mentioning product names in print. Some, in fact, have a policy of deleting brand or company identifications in news columns. Public relations counselors argue that discriminating against using product names does a disservice to readers or viewers, many of whom are influenced by what they read or see and may desire the particular products discussed. PR counselors further argue that journalists who accept and print public relations material for its intrinsic value and then remove the source of the information give the reader or viewer the false impression that the journalist generated the facts, ideas, or photography.

In recent years, one practice that has drawn journalistic scorn is that of organizations using well-known spokespersons to promote products without identifying that they are being paid for the endorsement. Journalists argue that such presentations are patently unethical paid endorsements designed to appear objective.[9] CNN, for one, imposed a strict policy on paid spokespersons after suffering an embarrassing incident with actress Kathleen Turner, who promoted drug company products without disclosing her financial relationship with the company.[10]

Understandably, editors and producers don't soon forgive firms that sponsor such devious spokespersons. One solution to achieve product recognition through the *endorsement* of objective authorities is to create events that are certain to attract publicity (see Figure 17-3).

FIGURE 17-3 **Balloons over Broadway.** To launch Snapple's White Tea, "the lightest tea on earth," Ruder Finn arranged for personal helium balloons to be the key to a sampling event that allowed passersby and media to ride up 100 feet in a personal balloon to get a unique view of New York City below. (Courtesy of O'Dwyerpr.com)

Building a Brand

The watchword in business today is branding—creating a differentiable identity or position for a company or product.

In more traditional times, it took years for brands like Pepsi, Coke, McDonald's, Hertz, FedEx, and Walmart to establish themselves. Today, with the advent of the World Wide Web, thriving Internet companies like Google, Yahoo!, Amazon, eBay, and Research in Motion have become household words in a historical nanosecond. Using integrated marketing communications to establish a unique brand requires adherence to the following principles.

- **Be early.** We remember the "first" in a category because of the *law of primacy*, which posits that people are more likely to remember you if you were the first in their minds in a particular category. Consequently, it is often better to be first than to be best. Don't believe it? Then who followed Charles Lindbergh as the "second" person to fly solo across the Atlantic? No, it wasn't Lindbergh flying back! (Actually, it was an Australian chap named Bert Hinkler, but you never heard of him!) Whether yours is really the "first" brand is less important than establishing primacy in the minds of consumers.

- **Be memorable.** Equally important is to fight through the clutter by creating a memorable brand. With hundreds of participants in categories from bottled water to bathing suits, a brand needs to stand out by distinguishing itself in some way—through uniqueness or advertising slogan or social responsibility or whatever. Creating brand awareness requires boldness.

- **Be aggressive.** A successful brand also requires a constant drumbeat of publicity to keep the company's name before the public. Potential customers need to become familiar with the brand. Potential investors need to become confident that the brand is an active one. Indeed, more and more, marketers are "taking to the streets" to spread their messages (see Figure 17-4). The

FIGURE 17-4 **Street cred.** Friendly Ice Cream Corporation took to the streets with free samples in an effort to reinforce brand recognition. (Courtesy of O'Dwyerpr.com)

new competitive economy leaves little room for demure integrated marketing communications.

- **Use heritage.** Baby boomers are old. Gen Xers are getting older. And *heritage* is very much in vogue. This means citing the traditions and history of a product or organization as part of building the brand. As consumers live longer, an increasing number of citizens long for "the good old days." As society longs for nostalgia, heritage works—to the point where the old reliables become "collector's items" that can be sold for cash on eBay (see Figure 17-5).

- **Create a personality.** The best organizations are those that create "personalities" for themselves. Who is number one in rental cars? Hertz. What company stands for overnight delivery? FedEx. What's the East Coast university that boasts the best and the brightest? Harvard. Or at least that's what most people think. The organization's personality should be reflected in all communications materials the organization produces.

As more and more companies each year attempt to bust through the advertising and marketing clutter by resorting to such marketing devices as banner ads, proprietary Web sites, free classified advertising, e-zines, and email marketing, the challenge to create a differentiable brand becomes that much more difficult.

Public Relations Advertising

Traditionally, organizations used advertising to sell products. In 1936, a company named Warner & Swasey initiated an ad campaign that stressed the power of America as a nation and the importance of American business in the nation's future. Warner & Swasey continued its ads after World War II and thus was born a unique type of advertising—the marketing of an image rather than a product. This technique became known variously as institutional advertising, image advertising, public service advertising, issues advertising, and ultimately public relations—or nonproduct—advertising.

In the 1980s, image advertising became *issues advertising*, which advocated positions from the sponsor's viewpoint. Often these concerned matters of some controversy. The practice was spearheaded by the outspoken Mobil Corporation— now, ExxonMobil. Indeed, ExxonMobil's practice of placing an issues ad on the op-ed page of *The New York Times* and other leading newspapers each Thursday, begun in the 1960s, is still going strong—although not every Thursday. Nonprofits, too, are often outspoken—and controversial—in the cause of such issues advertising (see Figure 17-6).

FIGURE 17-6 Advertising with attitude. Never one to back away from controversy, NBA star Ron Artest starred in this controversial ad for the People for the Ethical Treatment of Animals. (Courtesy of PETA)

Traditional public relations advertising—as opposed to image or issue positioning—is still widely used. Such advertising can be appropriate for a number of activities:

1. **Mergers and diversifications.** When one company merges with another, advertising provides a quick and effective way to convey this message.

2. **Personnel changes.** A firm's greatest asset is its employees. Presenting staff members in advertising not only impresses a reader with the firm's pride in its workers but also helps build confidence among employees themselves.

3. **Organizational resources.** The scope of a company's services also says something positive about the organization.

4. **Manufacturing and service capabilities.** The ability to deliver quality goods on time is something customers cherish. A firm that can deliver should advertise this capability.

5. **Growth history.** A growing firm, one that has developed steadily over time and has taken advantage of its environment, is the kind of company with which people want to deal. Growth history, therefore, is a worthwhile subject for nonproduct advertising.

6. **Financial strength and stability.** A picture of economic strength and stability—particularly in times of financial crisis—is one that all companies like to project. Advertisements that highlight the company's financial position earn confidence and attract customers and investors.

7. **Company customers.** Customers can serve as a marketing tool, too. Well-known personalities who use a certain product may be enough to win additional customers.

8. **Organizational name change.** With the proliferation of companies streamlining operations or merging with others, invariably names change—from Federal Express to FedEx; from Morgan Guaranty Trust/Chase Manhattan Bank to JPMorgan Chase; from Kentucky Fried Chicken to KFC. To burnish the new name in people's minds, a name change must be well promoted and well advertised. Only through constant repetition will people become familiar with the new identity.

9. **Trademark protection.** Companies such as Xerox, Kleenex, Google, and Coca-Cola, whose products are household names, are legitimately concerned about the improper generic use of their trademarks in the public domain. Such companies run periodic ads to remind people of the proper status of their marks.

10. **Corporate emergencies.** Occasionally, an emergency situation erupts—a labor strike, plant disaster, or service interruption. One quick way to explain the firm's position and procedures without fear of distortion or misinterpretation by editors or reporters is to buy advertising space.

Traditional Integrated Marketing

Among the more traditional public relations activities used to market products are article reprints, trade show participation, use of spokespersons, cause-related marketing, and in-kind promotions.

Article Reprints

Once an organization has received product publicity in a newspaper or magazine, it should market the publicity further to achieve maximum sales punch. Marketing can be done through article reprints aimed at that part of a target audience—wholesalers, retailers, or consumers—that might not have seen the original article. Reprints, included on a Web site and direct mailed, also help reinforce the reactions of those who read the original article.

As in any other public relations activity, use of reprints should be approached systematically, with the following ground rules in mind:

1. Plan ahead, especially if an article has major significance to the organization and you believe it might be positive. Ideally, reprints should be ordered before the periodical goes to press so that customers can receive them shortly after the article hits the newsstands.

2. Select target publics and address the recipients by name and title to ensure that the reprint reaches the most important audience.

3. Pinpoint the reprint's significance either by underlining pertinent information in the article, making marginal notes, or attaching a cover letter, so that the target audience readily understands your purpose.

4. Integrate the reprint with similar articles and information on the same or related subjects. Often several reprints can be combined into a single mailing or press kit.

Trade Show Participation

Trade show participation enables an organization to display its products before important target audiences. The decision to participate should be considered with the following factors in mind:

1. **Analyze the show carefully.** Make sure the audience is one that can't be reached effectively through other promotional materials, such as article reprints or local publicity. Also, be sure the audience is essential to the sale of the product.

2. **Select a common theme.** Integrate public relations, publicity, advertising, and sales promotion. Unify all organizational elements for the trade show to avoid any hint of interdepartmental rivalries.

3. **Make sure the products displayed are the right ones.** Decide well in advance exactly which products should be shown.

4. **Consider the trade books.** Often trade magazines run special features in conjunction with trade shows, and editors need photos and publicity material. Always know what special editions are coming up as well as their deadline schedules.

5. **Emphasize what's new.** Talk about the new model that's being displayed. Discuss the additional features, new uses, or recent performance data of the products displayed. Trade show exhibitions should reveal innovation, breakthrough, and newness.

6. **Consider local promotional efforts.** While in town during a trade show, an organization can enhance both the recognition of its product and the traffic at its booth by doing local promotions. This strategy involves visiting trade magazine editors and local media people to stir up publicity for the product during the show.

7. **Evaluate the worth.** Always evaluate whether the whole exercise was worth it. This involves counting, qualifying, and following up on leads generated as well as looking at other intangibles to see if marketing objectives were met.[11]

Spokespersons

In our celebrity-dominated culture, the use of spokespersons to promote products has increased. As noted, spokespersons shouldn't disguise the fact that they are advocates for a particular product.

Spokespersons must be articulate, fast on their feet, and thoroughly knowledgeable about the subject. When these criteria are met, the use of spokespersons as an integrated marketing tool can be most effective. As the music business has been hit by a barrage of negative factors, from recession to free downloads, rockers, in particular, have joined the ranks of spokespersons. The rock band Kiss was among the most prolific merchandisers, selling products ranging from condoms to musical toothbrushes to baby booties to the ever-fashionable "Kiss Kasket," a limited-edition coffin.[12]

In recent years, the use of spokespersons to promote products has become so crazed that in 2003, Coca-Cola signed high school basketball phenom LeBron James to a six-year, $12 million contract to promote Sprite. James hadn't even stepped foot onto an NBA court. Of course, at the time Coke signed him, the Ohio high schooler already had signed a shoe deal with Nike for a cool $100 million. And it all paid off for the sponsors, as King James has become one of the world's premier players and pitch men.[13]

Cause-Related Marketing

Public relations sponsorships tied to philanthropy are another effective integrated marketing device. In a down economy, with advertising costs cut back, companies turn to sponsorship of the arts, education, music, festivals, anniversaries, sports, and charitable causes for promotional and public relations purposes[14] (see Figure 17-7).

Cause-related marketing will continue to grow in the 21st century. Middle-aged baby boomers, in particular, are more concerned about issues that affect their lives, like protecting the environment and aiding the less fortunate. This change in itself will drive the creation of events and decision making by corporate sponsors.

In-Kind Promotions

When a service, product, or other consideration in exchange for publicity exposure is offered, it is called an *in-kind promotion*. Examples of in-kind promotions include:

1. Providing services or products as prizes offered by a newspaper or charity in exchange for being listed as a cosponsor in promotional materials.

2. Providing services or products to a local business in exchange for having fliers inserted in shopping bags or as statement stuffers.

3. Providing services or products to doctors' offices, auto repair shops, or other businesses in exchange for having brochures prominently displayed.

4. Providing samples and gifts of products and services, along with sales literature.

5. Providing point-of-purchase displays, literature, events, demonstrations, and samples at the point where the customer decides on purchasing the product or service.

6. Providing posters of the product or service at well-trafficked locations.

The point of in-kind promotions is to leverage the name and use of products and services, so that more potential buyers are exposed to the organization.

FIGURE 17-7 **Yes we can.** Cause-related marketing was very much on the mind of real estate executive and philanthropist Connie Milstein when her Connie's Bakery, dedicated to job training for low-income New Yorkers, baked and then gave away 20,000 brownies in Washington to celebrate the 2009 inauguration of President Barack Obama. (Courtesy of Connie's Bakery)

PR Ethics

Mini-Case   That's No Bomb Scare, It's "Harmless" Publicity

When terrorists struck the Pentagon, the World Trade Center, and a Pennsylvania field on September 11, 2001, it was an action and a day that no American would ever again forget.

Except maybe the chuckleheads who run Turner Broadcasting System's Cartoon Network.

On January 30, 2007, cable news networks interrupted regular programming with bulletins that bombs had reportedly been planted "all over Boston." Bomb squads were called in. Bridges and highways were shut down. The city, apparently, was under siege.

Or was it?

Well, not really.

As it turned out, the more than three dozen devices—planted in subway stations, bridges, and landmarks—were harmless, blinking electronic boards depicting a boxy cartoon character, the star of the Cartoon Network's new *Aqua Teen Hunger Force* (see Figure 17-8).

The faux bomb scare was intended as a harmless publicity stunt.

FIGURE 17-8 **Bad publicity.** Cable TV went wild when a Cartoon Network marketing stunt turned into a full-fledged terrorism scare. (Courtesy of Fox News)

But Boston authorities weren't laughing.

The police immediately arrested the two nitwits who planted the devices. Later, the national media grilled the two, who babbled on as their hapless lawyer stood dazed by their side.

A week later, Turner Broadcasting and its advertising agency agreed to pay $2 million in compensation for planting the devices. Two days after that, the president of Cartoon Network, a 13-year veteran of the company, tendered his resignation, saying, in part, *"I feel compelled to step down . . . in recognition of the gravity of the situation that occurred under my watch and to put this chapter behind us."** *

Questions

1. If you had been public relations director of the Cartoon Network, what would you have advised when apprised of the plans for the Boston marketing stunt?

2. How do you assess the reaction of Turner Broadcasting and its Cartoon Network to the public relations fallout?

*For further information, see Anthony Crupi, "Cartoon Net Chief Samples Resigns," *Mediaweek.com* (February 9, 2007); and Glen Johnson, "Firms to Pay $2M in Boston Bomb Scare," *Associated Press* (February 5, 2007).

21st Century Integrated Marketing

Beyond advertising, marketing, and public relations techniques, integrated marketing, too, must keep pace with the ever-changing world of promotional innovations to help sell products and services. Among them are television brand integration, infomercials, word-of-mouth marketing, television and movie product placement, and more.

Online Marketing

The fastest growing category of advertising in the 21st century is online. And the most rapidly emerging integrated marketing technique is using social media and the Web to create "buzz" for a product.

Traditional marketers from Coca-Cola to Kraft Foods to Procter & Gamble have all shifted significant marketing dollars to online marketing. In 2008, Pepsi-Cola went one step further by introducing a line of no-calorie carbonated beverages, with a campaign that bypassed altogether mainstream media like television and print. Even more unique, the beverages weren't aimed at social media-savvy younger consumers but rather at a demographic target of men and women ages 35 to 49.

Pepsi's fruit-flavored, caffeine free Tava line received a spirited send-off with its own Web site, banner ads, promotions, and offbeat buzz-building stunts like sampling events at popular shops and the delivery of free samples to the employees of prominent companies like Google and MTV.[15]

Television Brand Integration

The latest phenomenon in television is to integrate products into the fabric of what is being presented on the screen. When one of ABC's *Desperate Housewives* found herself hard up for cash, she donned an evening gown and extolled the virtues of a Buick Lacrosse at a car show. One of the stars of Warner Brothers' *What I Like About You* raved about Fruity Pebbles and competed to win a role in an Herbal Essences commercial.

Such product emphases were not just coincidence.

As technology and clutter blunt the effectiveness and reach of traditional 30-second commercials, more advertisers are paying to integrate their products directly into the action of a show or film.

The process of brand integration owed its start to CBS's *Survivor*, which financed itself largely through product tie-ins with advertisers whose products were mentioned in the course of the show. This was a far cry from serendipitous—that is, unpaid—product mentions, like Junior Mints and Pez on *Seinfeld*.[16]

Infomercials

Infomercials were greeted with universal catcalls in the 1980s when they were introduced as program-length commercials, shamelessly hawking products.

Even today, the infomercial remains the Rodney Dangerfield of marketing, accorded "no respect" for many reasons—state and federal investigations of infomercial producers, complaints about product performance, and most important, the belief, still, that a lengthy commercial disguised as a conventional program—like a talk show, complete with theme song and studio audience—unfairly masks an advertisement.

Nonetheless, infomercials remain strong for one reason: They work. Indeed, former boxing champion George Foreman's infomercial about his Lean Mean Fat-Reducing Grilling Machine reportedly earned him in excess of $137 million! Between $1 billion and $2 billion worth of merchandise is sold each year—from dicing and slicing kitchen utensils to exercise paraphernalia to psychic hot lines—despite condemnation and even lawsuits. Celebrities from Chuck Norris to Suzanne Somers to Donald Trump are staples among the growing parade of shameless infomercial hawkers.

Buzz Marketing

Also known as word-of-mouth, *buzz marketing* is another alternative to traditional advertising that enlists "influencers" or "trend setters" to spread the word about a particular product.

The practice began with teenagers, who appeared to be popular. Today, marketers have graduated to reaching out for "evangelists" who are already diehard fans of a particular product and persuading them to "spread the gospel." Its proponents hail word-of-mouth as the most honest and ethical of advertising media. *"People don't want to hurt their friends and family and colleagues with bad information,"* is the way one believer put it.[17]

Television and Movie Product Placements

As noted, product placements in novels, TV programs, movies, video games, and even cartoons have proliferated at a rapid—and to some, alarming—rate. As one watchdog put it, product placements are "a huge, out-of-control issue."[18]

We've come a long way since filmmaker Steven Spielberg first offered to link Reese's Pieces with the hero of his movie, *E.T.* In the 21st century, product placements—also known as *embedded advertisements*—have become a more integral part of movies and television shows.

- Advertisers from Dunkin' Donuts to Intel to Honda have all signed up with the publishers of game consoles to embed their messages in video games.[19]
- Comedy Central introduced its adult cartoon show, *Shorties Watchin' Shorties*, which prominently featured Domino's Pizza, Red Bull energy drink, and Vans sneakers.[20]

- General Motors, seeking new ways to market cars in a troubled economy, made its Camaro and Traverse brands central parts in the NBC series, *My Own Worst Enemy*. Unfortunately for GM, the show was canceled after only four episodes.[21]

- Also in 2008, TiVo, the Silicon Valley company that invented skipping over annoying commercials, reversed course completely. Teaming up with Amazon.com, TiVo introduced on-screen links to product ads for CDs, DVDs, and books that guests promote on talk shows like *The Oprah Winfrey Show* and *The Daily Show*.[22]

And according to one study, the proliferation of product placements in all forms of media—or *ad creep*. if you prefer—is just going to continue to grow around the world. Summarized the study's organizer, *"There's a new media order emerging, fueled by a fear of ad-skipping technology, doubts about traditional advertising's effectiveness, and, in some countries, a search for new revenue streams as government subsidies decline."*[23] Stated another way, product placements are here to stay.

You Name It

What other 21st century integrated marketing venues exist? How fertile is your imagination? Consider the following:

- **Song placements:** Marketers now compete to get brands mentioned in best-selling records. Thanks primarily to hip-hop luminaries like Jay-Z and Ludacris, brands such as Nike, Mercedes-Benz, Hennessy, Louis Vuitton, and Lamborghini all benefit from the "street cred" embodied in popular music. In 2005 alone, Nike was mentioned in 63 hip-hop songs.[24]

- **Sports teams:** It used to be that stadiums were named for the highest bidder. Today, the team itself takes on the name of the sponsor who pays for it. Venues like the St. Louis Cardinals' Busch Stadium and the Washington Redskins' FedEx Field have given way to teams like the New York Red Bulls, the Major League Soccer franchise named after the sports energy drink, which paid more than $100 million for the integrated marketing privilege. But when the New York Giants tried to sell stadium naming rights to a German insurance company linked to the Nazis, the franchise was forced to reverse field and shelve the $25 million-a-year bonanza.[25]

- **Whaaaa?** No space is too odd to integrate marketing messages. US Airways sells ads on airsickness bags. School districts sell ads on the outside of school buses. Hands down, the most bizarre 21st-century integrated marketing technique was the use of a person's body for marketing purposes. In 2008, a father looking for money to buy a new car sold rights to a permanent tattoo on his neck to Web-hosting company Globat. And if that wasn't enough, the same company purchased a temporary tattoo ad on the pregnant belly of a St. Louis woman— to promote its product (not the woman's baby).[26] Ridiculous? Perhaps. But if we're writing about it here—it worked!

Talking

Points The Ultimate Third-Party Endorser

And who are the Top 10 third-party endorsement superstars?

Well, according to *Fortune* magazine, the leading money makers among pro American athletes, endorsing all matter of merchandise are, in reverse order of their annual endorsement income (drumroll, please!):*

10. Dwayne Wade, NBA, $12 million

 9. Peyton Manning, NFL, $13 million

 7. (tie) Shaquille O'Neal, NBA, $15 million

 7. (tie) Jeff Gordon, NASCAR, $15 million

 6. Kobe Bryant, NBA, $16 million

 5. Michelle Wie, LPGA, $19.5 million

 4. Dale Earnhardt, Jr., NASCAR, $20 million

 3. LeBron James, NBA, $25 million

 2. Phil Mickelson, PGA, $47 million

 1. Tiger Woods, PGA, $100 million (see Figure 17-9)

*"The Top Ten Endorsement Superstars," *Fortune* (December 10, 2007): 108.

FIGURE 17-9 **The ultimate.** The reigning world champion third-party endorser is Tiger Woods, who earns nine figures a year from endorsement deals.   (Photo: Newscom)

Last Word

The key marketing question in the 21st century is, *How do we generate buzz?* How do we distinguish ourselves and get our voice heard in the midst of hundreds of thousands of competing voices?

To marketing expert Al Ries, who cut his teeth in the advertising industry, the answer was obvious. *"In the past, it may have been true that a beefy advertising budget was the key ingredient in the brand-building process. . . . Today brands are born, not made. A new brand must be capable of generating favorable publicity in the media or it won't have a chance in the marketplace."*[27]

In other words, said Ries, it is public relations and its attendant communications forms—not advertising alone—that differentiate an organization, product, or issue.

Perhaps more precisely stated, what is needed now is an integrated approach to communications, combining the best of marketing, advertising, sales promotion, and public relations with all forms of media from online to print to broadcast to face-to-face.

The clear marketing need for organizations and those who serve them is to build lasting client relationships. A successful communications professional must be knowledgeable about all aspects of the communications mix. Integrated marketing communications, then, becomes paramount in preparing public relations professionals for the challenges of the 21st century.

Discussion Starters

1. What is meant by *integrated marketing communications*?
2. Describe the differences among advertising, marketing, and public relations.
3. What is meant by *third-party endorsement*?
4. In what situations is product publicity most effective?
5. Describe the pros and cons of using a well-known individual as a spokesperson.
6. What is *cause-related marketing*?
7. How can integrated marketing help build a brand?
8. What are the purposes of public relations advertising?
9. What is the significance of Warner & Swasey and Mobil Oil in terms of public relations advertising?
10. What are several 21st century techniques of integrated marketing communications?

Top of the Shelf   The Fall of Advertising and the Rise of PR / Al Ries and Laura Ries, New York: HarperCollins, 2002

The cover of this book features a deflated sock puppet, symbolic of the failure of Pet.com's sock puppet ads, which in turn is symbolic of the limitations of advertising, especially compared with the fact that skillful public relations is what sells—at least according to these authors, father and daughter and advertising veterans.

The Ries and Ries writing team argues that public relations should be used instead of advertising to launch new brands.

Once a brand is established, advertising may then be used to maintain the brand in the consumer's mind. They cite a number of brands—Palm, Starbucks, the Body Shop, Walmart, and Red Bull—that have been built with virtually no advertising.

In fairness, it's probably premature to declare the death of advertising, but the Ries book, at the time of its release, generated lots of positive buzz about public relations.

Case Study   Resurrecting the Brand of Michael Vick

As the 2006 National Football League season began, Michael Vick stood as an integrated marketing whirlwind.

The top pick in the NFL's 2001 draft, the southpaw quarterback, who ran faster and threw further than most anyone else, had become a three-time, all-pro for the Atlanta Falcons. Vick's endorsement income from contracts from Nike, EA Sports, Coca-Cola, and other top corporations had earned him 33rd place on Forbes' list of *Top 100 Celebrities in 2005*. One magazine reported him as "one of the top 10 richest athletes in the United States."

Michael Vick was on top of the sports celebrity world.

Going to the Finger

But then during the 2006 season, Michael Vick's image began to take a hit.

In April, Vick settled a lawsuit by a woman who claimed the player knowingly gave her herpes.

In November, after a particularly disappointing game where his receivers dropped a boatload of passes, Vick was booed by the hometown Atlanta fans (see Figure 17-10). As he walked off the field after the 31-13 loss to the New Orleans Saints, Vick flashed two well-publicized fingers at the fans—a "double-barreled salute," as one reporter labeled it.

Vick issued a statement through the team Sunday night, saying, *"First and foremost, I would like to apologize for my inappropriate actions with fans today. I was frustrated and upset at how the game was going for my team, and that frustration came out the wrong way. That's not what I'm about. That's not what the Atlanta Falcons are about. I simply lost my cool in the heat of the moment. I apologize and look forward to putting this incident behind me."*

Vick paid a $10,000 team fine and donated another $10,000 to charity.

The issue was defused. But it was a sign of trouble to come.

In January 2007, Vick reluctantly surrendered a water bottle to security at Miami International Airport. The bottle smelled like marijuana and contained a substance in a hidden compartment. The police report characterized the substance as a residue that is "closely associated with marijuana."

Ten days later, Vick was exonerated, as no marijuana was found in the bottle.

Going to the Dogs

In April 2007, Michael Vick's reputation came crumbling down.

A report circulated that an elaborate, illegal dogfighting complex, owned by the Atlanta Falcons quarterback, was discovered

FIGURE 17-10 Hard landing. Michael Vick had a tough game against the New Orleans Saints and later took out his displeasure on the unsympathetic Atlanta fans. (Photo: Newscom)

in Surry County, Virginia. State and federal authorities were investigating.

In subsequent months, as details emerged about his "Bad Newz Kennels," Vick was considered a pariah by many, both animal lovers and non-animal lovers alike.

Reports from the complex were chilling.

Federal officials reportedly found equipment associated with dogfighting, blood stains on the walls of a room, and a blood-stained carpet stashed on the property. They reportedly removed more than 60 dogs.

In July, Vick and three associates were indicted on charges of conducting illegal dogfighting. The indictment alleged that Vick and his associates bought the property in 2001, expressly as the main staging area for housing and training pit bulls involved in dogfighting. They built "a fence to shield the rear portion of the compound from public view and multiple sheds used at various times to house training equipment, injured dogs, and organized fights."

Vick, himself, according to the indictment, was highly involved in the operation, attended fights, and paid off bets when his dogs lost.

Vick was also cited for being involved with "the execution of dogs that didn't perform well." The indictment reported that Vick and his colleagues "executed approximately eight dogs that did not perform well in 'testing' sessions by various methods, including hanging, drowning, and/or slamming at least one dog's body to the ground."

Although Vick was only accused—and not found guilty—of these frightening charges, his sponsors didn't hesitate. AirTran dropped him as a spokesperson for its airline. Nike, which at

first said it would "stand by" the standard bearer of its planned new Vick shoe, quickly reversed its stand and canceled the shoe and its multi-million dollar contract with Vick. Other sponsors quickly followed suit.

Going to the Slammer

At first, Vick seemed like he might fight the charges.

He immediately issued a statement apologizing to the people of Atlanta and Falcons' owner, Arthur Blank, *"who I love sincerely, I've put him though a lot. And you know it hurts me to put him through these situations."*

Vick refused to acknowledge his guilt, saying, *"There are a lot of things that needed to be worked out."*

By August 2007, Michael Vick had gotten religion—literally. He formally accepted a plea agreement from the federal government and held a press conference, at which he said he sought god's help to cure him. *"Dog fighting is a terrible thing. I reject it,"* he said at the press conference (see Figure 17-11).

Vick vowed to "redeem" himself and willingly serve his time in jail. His prison sentence was 23 months in Leavenworth, KA (where he played for the prison football team), with release in the summer of 2009.

Meanwhile, in 2008, Vick filed for personal reorganization bankruptcy protection, listing assets of $16 million and liabilities of $20 million. In 2009, Vick sued his former financial advisor for $2 million, claiming she used his money for her personal and business expenses.

Still a young man, not yet 30, Michael Vick hoped to return to football. As his attorney told the bankruptcy court in 2008,

FIGURE 17-11 **Doing time.** Michael Vick accepted his punishment in the fall of 2008, vowing to make a comeback after his time in the slammer. (Courtesy of Fox News)

"He has every reason to believe that upon his release, he will be reinstated into the NFL, resume his career, and be able to earn a substantial living."

Sure enough, in 2009 the NFL allowed Michael Vick to resume his career with the Philadelphia Eagles.

Questions

1. What do you think of Michael Vick's decision to accept jail time and hold a press conference?

2. If you were advising Vick, how would you suggest he comport himself now that he is back in the NFL? What should he do, in a public relations sense, when he is freed?

3. If you were advising the National Football League, how would you suggest it handle Vick's reinstatement?

4. If you were advising corporate sponsors, what would you suggest they do relative to Michael Vick, now that he is back in the NFL?

For further information, see Larry O'Dell, "Michael Vick Sues Former Financial Adviser," Associated Press (January 27, 2009); Mark Maske, "Falcons' Vick Indicted in Dogfighting Case," *Washington Post* (July 18, 2007); Michael S. Schmidt, "Vick Pleas Guilty in Dog-Fighting Case," *New York Times* (August 27, 2007); and "Michael Vick's Water Bottle Raises Suspicion at Miami Airport," *USA Today* (January 19, 2007).

From the Top An Interview with Marina Maher

Widely recognized as one of the nation's leading experts in marketing to women, Marina Maher is the principal of Marina Maher Communications, a New York public relations firm that she founded over 20 years ago. The agency specializes in building brand relationships for blue chip clients in the consumer products and health care categories. An early proponent of integrated communications programs, Maher has been instrumental in the creation of many award-winning campaigns that reflect her marketing mantra of "One Sight, One Sound, One Sell." She was named one of the 50 Most Influential Women in Public Relations by *PRWeek Magazine.*

How helpful can public relations be for a marketer?
PR is more than helpful—it's essential. In today's world of marketing, where consumers are bombarded with messages, hard to reach, and are skeptical, it's critical to create ways where consumers bond with a product. More than any other discipline in the marketing mix, public relations can build and nurture the relationship of a brand with its target by creating an emotional connection. Consumers who are emotionally linked become brand ambassadors, engaging other consumers in that brand.

How can public relations help build a brand?
Authenticity is an important word today, especially among younger consumers, when building and marketing a brand. By working through third parties (media, advocacy groups), public relations can facilitate endorsements. PR also excels at creating word-of-mouth, which is another important brand-building tool in today's marketplace of cynical consumers.

Is public relations more important than advertising in selling products?
The classic consumer marketing model is creating awareness, then interest, and finally, commitment. With a large enough

media buy (both offline and online), advertising can quickly build awareness. Public relations builds a dialogue and endorsement, which generates interest and awareness.

What are you most proud of in the work your agency has done?
I can't pick one campaign—there are too many great ones over 23 years! However, they all have a common denominator of which I am very proud: *We have no formulas.* Each campaign is based on fresh thinking grounded in solid strategy that is unique to the brand's marketing challenges. We challenge ourselves to create new and big ideas for each brand's needs.

What qualities do you look for in an employee?
I look for the passion gene—people who have a passion for their work, their clients, and MMC. I also place a premium on people who demonstrate a sense of ethics, have a team spirit, and have a sense of fun.

What employment path would you recommend to ascend to public relations management?
One, start as young as you can with internships—in media, at ad agencies, with online media and PR agencies. Nothing beats hands-on experience.

Two, start early developing the right side and the left side of the brain. Creativity is prized, and you also need to understand business.

Three, during your first five years in the public relations business, you'll get training on writing, media pitching, client management. Almost no one trains you on people management. Do whatever necessary to learn management from the day you start—find a mentor, take management classes on the outside. Learn conflict resolution, negotiation; take assertiveness training if necessary. These skills will prepare you for management and may even get you promoted earlier. And if nothing else, they are life skills as well!

Public Relations Library

Belch, George, and Michael Belch. *Advertising and Promotion, An Integrated Marketing and Communications Perspective,* Paperback New York, NY: McGraw-Hill, 2008.

Cone, Steve. *Steal These Ideas.* New York: Bloomberg Press, 2005. An experienced brand manager offers his version of the marketing concepts that are most compelling and memorable.

D'Vari, Marissa. *Building Buzz.* Franklin Lakes, NJ: Career Press, 2005. Concepts such as visualization and getting your name in the media are reviewed.

Gospe, Mike. *Marketing Campaign Development.* Silicon Valley, CA: Happy About, 2008. How a guerilla marketer might use integrated marketing.

Hanlon, Patrick. *Primal Branding.* New York, NY: Free Press, 2006. The author says there is a "primal code" that makes a product successful, all based on creating a "belief system" from your brand.

Percy, Larry. *Strategic Integrated Marketing Communications.* Oxford, England: Butterworth-Heinemann, 2008. Chapter and verse discussion of the roots and implementation of integrated marketing communications.

Rein, Irving, and Philip Kotler. *High Visibility.* New York: McGraw-Hill, 2006. What do Oprah Winfrey, Donald Trump, and Bill Gates have in common? The answer: high visibility, which the authors claim is necessary to succeed today.

Rostica, Christopher, with Bill Yenne. *The Authentic Brand: How Today's Top Entrepreneurs Connect with Customers.* Paramus, NJ: Noble Press, 2007. Case studies from the viewpoint of CEOs, whose companies stood apart from the competition.

Shiffman, Denise. *The Age of Engage: Reinventing Marketing for Today's Connective, Collaborative and Hyperinteractive Culture.* Ladera Ranch, CA: Hunt Street Press, 2008. This book charts a way to market on the Web and has a very long title.

Thompson, Harvey. *Who Stole My Customer?* Upper Saddle River, NJ: Prentice Hall, 2004. The main objective here is to help firms keep old customers and attract new ones.

Chapter 18

Public Relations
and Social Media

FIGURE 18-1 Twitter rescue assist. When a plane emergency landed in the freezing Hudson River in 2009, an observer in a nearby ferry "tweeted" the news to call for help for terrified passengers. (Photo: Newscom)

In the 21st century, the face of public relations is changing, largely due to the phenomenon of social media. To wit:

- President Obama, fresh off the most sophisticated use by a presidential candidate of the Internet to recruit campaign workers, share information, and raise money, created the first official White House blog shortly after taking the Oath of Office on January 20, 2009. The blog was the creation of Macon Phillips, the nation's first White House Director of New Media.[1]

- With advertising revenue sliding, *Business Week* magazine introduced *Business Exchange*, a Web site that combined all manner of social media—verticals, aggregation, user-generated content, popularity rankings, etc.—designed to attract new readers and funnel them into niches to attract new advertisers.[2]

- In January 2009, when a downed plane attempted an emergency landing in New York City's Hudson River (see Figure 18-1), the first reports of the floating airliner came from a nearby ferry passenger, who posted this message on Twitter:

  "There's a plane in the Hudson. I'm on the ferry going to pick up the people. Crazy."

  Within 30 minutes, the word had spread far and wide, and the original "tweeter" was interviewed live on MSNBC and CNN and would subsequently become a media star.

Such was the power of social media as a communications medium in the 21st century.

As companies tighten their spending in the face of worldwide financial challenges, inexpensive social media is clearly the next marketing and public relations frontier. As with any other phenomenon, social media offers enormous opportunities and also large pitfalls to be avoided.

While it is irrefutable that the Internet and social media have changed communications forever with newfound immediacy and pervasiveness, it isn't the case that the Internet has replaced human relationships as the essence of societal communications. Nor have the new techniques replaced human relationships as the essence of the practice of public relations.

The Internet and social media comprise important tools in the public relations arsenal. But it is important to remember, they are but "tools" nonetheless. In this chapter, we will explore how public relations professionals might harness these new technologies to more effectively communicate their messages.

Brief History of the Internet

What is the Internet? We all use it, but few of us know from whence it derived.

The Internet, technically, is a cooperatively run, globally distributed collection of computer networks that exchange information via a common set of rules. The Internet began as the ARPANET during the Cold War in 1969, developed by the Department of Defense and consultants who were interested in creating a communications network that could survive a nuclear attack.[3] It survived—even though there was, thankfully, no nuclear attack!—as a convenient way to communicate.

The World Wide Web, the most exciting and revolutionary part of the Internet, was developed in 1989 by physicist Tim Berners-Lee to enlarge the Internet for multiple uses. The Web is a collection of millions of computers on the Internet that contain information in a single format: HTML, or Hypertext Markup Language. By combining multimedia—sound, graphics, video, animation, and more—the Web has become the most powerful tool in cyberspace.

Without question, the Internet and the World Wide Web have transformed the way we work, the way we buy things, the way we entertain ourselves, the way business is conducted, and, most important to public relations professionals, the way we communicate with each other. The Internet phenomenon, pure and simple, has been a revolution.

By 2009, the Internet was used by nearly 24 percent of the world's people, more than 1.5 billion. In North America, 73 percent used the Internet. In Asia, more than 650 million logged on, and in Europe, 390 million.[4] Perhaps even more important, the so-called "digital divide" between haves and have-nots was closing rapidly. In the United States, while the sharpest growth in Internet access and use was among young people, blacks and other minority members were rapidly merging onto the digital information highway. One survey of people 18 and older indicated that 74 percent of whites go online, 61 percent of African Americans do, and 80 percent of English-speaking Hispanic Americans do as well.[5]

In terms of commerce, the first incarnation of the Internet in the 1990s carried great—and as it turned out, unattainable—promise, with the rise and fall of such phenomena as sock puppets, push technology, and B2B (business-to-business). Most of these "great high-tech concepts" crashed and burned along with the stock market in the initial years of the 21st century.

Today, not only the giant survivors of those early days—eBay, Yahoo!, and Amazon.com, among them—but many other Internet-oriented ventures have gotten their second wind and are thriving.[6] The dominator today, of course, is latter-day search engine Google, whose stock went public in 2005 at just under $90 a share and a year later was priced in excess of $400.

The new Internet explosion has taken new forms: blogs, social networks, podcasts, wikis, RSS feeds, and others. The pace of Internet change is so rapid and the addition of new communications vehicles so voluminous, in fact, that this summary of Web-based communications tools and tactics may be obsolete by the time you finish reading! Nonetheless, press on.

Public Relations and the Internet

The Internet has transformed the way that people communicate and make contact with each other. And the practice of public relations has responded accordingly.

Public relations departments now have interactive specialists and groups responsible for communicating via the Internet. Likewise, public relations agencies boast online departments that help clients access the Internet. Although the expansive number of Internet-oriented agencies that flourished in the late 1990s has declined, a handful of firms still specialize in Internet-related communications.

Journalists, meanwhile—still the primary customers for most in public relations—have also embraced the Internet as their primary source for research and reporting. Most reporters today are online and prefer email as their primary source of public relations correspondence. Nonetheless, personal contact with a journalist (i.e., building a relationship) is still the best way to ensure that your message will be heard.

Use of the Internet by public relations practitioners inevitably will grow as the century proceeds, for four reasons in particular.

- **The demand to be educated rather than sold.** Today's consumers are smarter, better educated, and more media savvy. They know when they are being hustled by self-promoters and con artists. Communications programs therefore must be grounded in education-based information rather than blatant self-promotion. The Internet is perhaps the world's greatest potential repository of such information.

- **The quest for conversation.** The Internet has enabled anyone to become a publisher, broadcasting views and opinions far and wide. In so doing, the Net has empowered users, by leveling the playing field between them and the organizations trying to reach them. The net result is that Internet dialogue is just that—a conversation—between supplier and consumer. And the more conversational and communications-savvy the organization, the more likely it will be to persuade prospects to buy its products, support its issues, and believe its ideas.

- **The need for real-time performance.** The wired world is moving quickly. Everything happens instantaneously and in real time. When insurgents in Iraq free an American captive held for months, her release is beamed immediately on the Internet around the world.[7] Public relations professionals can use this ability to their advantage to structure their information to respond instantly to emerging issues and market changes.

- **The need for customization.** There used to be three primary television networks. Today there are hundreds of television channels. Today's consumers expect more focused, targeted, one-on-one communications relationships. Increasingly, organizations must broadcast their thoughts to ever-narrower population segments. The Internet offers such narrowcasting to reporters, shareholders, analysts, opinion leaders, consumers, and myriad other publics.

For individual public relations practitioners then, familiarity with the Internet, mastery of it, and knowledge of its effective use have become frontline requisites of the practice. Consequently, it is important that practitioners are familiar with the primary areas of cyberspace communications.

Web Sites

Today virtually all organizations, from the largest corporation to the smallest nonprofit, have a Web site (see Figure 18-2). Perhaps the most familiar, broadly used, and oldest social media tool, Web sites provide organizations, individuals, and governmental agencies the ability to offer information to the public in an organized, consolidated manner.

Most of the time today, it is the Web site that serves as an organization's "first face" to the public. Web sites serve multiple functions, are commonly interactive, and afford

FIGURE 18-2 **First face.** More often than not in these days of Internet dominance, a Web site is the initial introduction to an organization. (Courtesy of King Pelican Coffee)

viewers the ability to browse for information and in many cases conduct business, create profiles, manage their accounts, and a plethora of other convenient options. Web sites permit an organization to speak in *its own voice*—unfettered and unadulterated by the media or other intermediaries.

Web site development is very much the province of public relations professionals. Public relations professionals need to be cognizant of the methods in which audiences prefer to receive information on Web sites. They need to make Web sites as navigable as possible, providing the necessary tools to facilitate ease of delivery of content. "Static," non–user friendly Web sites are more of a detriment than a tool. Web sites also must be "media friendly"; journalists should be able to navigate the Web site with ease. This means having a clearly identifiable "Media" icon and organized subsections, including a page for news and video clips, reports, and publications.

Another rapidly expanding use of the Internet by public relations professionals is the creation and maintenance of Web sites to profile companies, promote products, or position issues. A Web site gives an individual or institution the flexibility and freedom of getting news out without having it filtered by an intermediary. There are literally millions of Web sites, all of them open for visitors.

Developing a Winning Web Site

In many ways, the organization's Web site is its most important interface with the public. Today, journalists and others turn to the Web site first for an introduction to the organization.

The aim of any Web site is to provide information that visitors are looking for. The more you achieve that objective, the more "sticky" your site becomes. Stickiness is often measured by the amount of time visitors spend at a site and how many pages they view. For example, if visitors spend 10 minutes at the Web site and view five or more pages, you've achieved stickiness.[8]

How should you create a winning Web site? By first asking and answering several strategic questions.

1. **What is our goal?** To extend the business? Sell more products? Make more money? Win support for our position? Turn around public opinion? Introduce our company? Without the answers to these fundamental questions, the what

and how of a Web site are inconsequential. Just as in any other pursuit in public relations, the overriding goal must be established first.

2. **What content will we include?** The reason some Web sites are tedious and boring—and they are!—is because little forethought has gone into determining the content of a site. Simply cramming chronological news releases onto a Web site won't advance an organization's standing with its publics. Rather, content must be carefully considered, in substance and organization, before proceeding with a site.

3. **How often will we edit?** Often the answer to this question is "Not often enough." Stale news and the lack of updating are common Web site problems. Sites must regularly be updated. Another problem is overwriting. People seem to feel that because the Web is "free," they can write endlessly. Of course, they can. But no one will read it. So an editorial process to cull information down to its most essential parts is a necessity for a good Web site.

4. **How will we enhance design?** Like it or not, the style of the site is most important. If an organization's home page isn't attractive, it won't get many hits. Good design makes complicated things understandable, and this is essential in a Web site. The Web is a largely visual medium, so great care should be taken to professionally design a site.

5. **How interactive will it be?** Traditional communication is unidirectional, one way. You read or view it, and that's where the process stops. The great attraction of the Web, on the other hand, is that it can be bidirectional. Communication can be translated into an interactive vehicle, a game, an application, or an email chat vehicle. This is what distinguishes good sites from mediocre ones.

6. **How will we track use?** As in any other communications project, the use of a Web site must be measured. The most basic form of cyberspace measurement is the rough yardstick of hits to the site. But like measuring press clippings, this doesn't tell you whether your information is being appreciated, acted on, or even read. Measuring site performance, therefore, should be a multifaceted exercise that includes such analysis as volume during specific times of day, kind of access, specific locations on the site to which visitors are clicking first, and the sequencing through the site that visitors are following.

7. **Who will be responsible?** Managing a Web site, if it is done correctly, must be someone's full-time job. Companies may subordinate the responsibility to someone—occasionally in the public relations department—who has many other "more important" responsibilities. Or, as noted, the function may be a shared one. These are both wrong. It is much better is to treat the Web site as a first line of communication to the public, which requires full-time attention.

Email

Research suggests that more than 90 percent of adult Internet users surveyed said they "regularly use e-mail." But if you question how fast the Internet is moving, consider that in a survey of 935 teenagers, only 14 percent reported sending emails to their friends each day, making it the *least* popular form of social communication among teenagers. Much more highly rated were text messaging (36 percent), instant messaging (29 percent), and social network site messaging (23 percent).[9]

Email, technically, allows users connected to a network to exchange memoranda and files without having to be logged in at the same time. Users can compose, send, receive, forward, attach documents, or store messages in plain text or Hyper Text Mail Language (HTML). The latter allows the inclusion of images, audio, video, and other sophisticated technologies. This type of communication can be personal, business, informative, subscription-based, or unsolicited, that is, "spam."

More often than not today, email is transmitted via cell phones or other handheld devices.

Email has become a pervasive internal communications vehicle. In companies, schools, media institutions, and homes, email, delivered online and immediately, has replaced traditional print and fax technology as a rapid-delivery information vehicle.

Although many managers are reluctant to confront employees face to face, email tends to produce more honest and immediate feedback than traditionally had been the case. Because email is quick and almost effortless, a manager can deliver praise or concern without leaving the office. Thus, email has, by and large, improved organizational communications. That is not to say that face-to-face communication isn't always best. It is. But the ease and effectiveness of email make it a viable alternative.

Email Newsletters

Email has also supplanted the traditional employee print newsletter (see Figure 18-3).

Online newsletters are both more immediate and more interactive than print counterparts. Employees can "feed back" to what they've read or heard instantaneously. The organization, in turn, can apprise itself quickly of relevant employee attitudes and opinions. Such online vehicles also lend an element of timeliness that print magazines and newspapers often have a hard time offering.

Email newsletters for external use—to customers, investors, or the media—are equally popular and valuable. These differ from their print brethren in several important areas:

1. **No more than one page.** People won't read lengthy newsletters on the computer, so writers must write short newsletters.

2. **Link content.** Copy should be peppered with links to other material, such as teasers to full-length articles and product offers.

3. **Regular dissemination.** It is also important to send email newsletters at regular intervals so that recipients expect them.

Instant Messaging

Instant messaging—or "IM"—is an online, nonlinear, real-time form of communication that allows two or more users to exchange information quickly via text and to send small pictures any place in the world.

IM is more closely related to conversation. Today's technology allows IM users to send text or photos to email accounts in case other users are online but busy or away from their PCs or offline. Additionally, users are able to save online conversations that can be stored or sent by email. IM is especially popular among Generation Next, which includes Americans between the ages of 18 and 25.

FIGURE 18-3 **Email newsletter.** Naples Community Hospital CEO Allen Weiss keeps staff and the Florida community aware of recent developments through a weekly email newsletter. (Courtesy of Naples Community Hospital)

FIGURE 18-3 **Email newsletter.** Naples Community Hospital CEO Allen Weiss keeps staff and the Florida community aware of recent developments through a weekly email newsletter. (Courtesy of Naples Community Hospital)

Straight Talk NCH

A weekly update from management on the issues that matter most — NCH Healthcare System

February 12, 2009

Dear Friends and Colleagues:

There's a reason we have *two* ears and only *one* mouth – because communication is mostly *listening*!

So this week, let's "listen" to two of the many responses to last week's *Straight Talk* on **communications.**

Joe DeBellis, Director of Transportation, and a mentor to many, wrote:

> The news media communicate as much doom and gloom as possible. I find myself turning off the TV with disgust. I suggest, we "the team at NCH" spread the "good news," such as how many new employees we recently hired; how we have not cut anyone's hours and in some instances, due to need, some are getting more hours than they have in past years. Our medical benefits have been improved over the last couple of years, while some companies are doing away with them completely. We got a modest pay increase while some companies are asking employees to take pay cuts or work a shorter week. I think you get my drift. We need to remind everyone that we are in an industry that has its share of problems for sure, but we are way better off than most. That's my story and I'm sticking to it!

Bev Adams, an ever-enthusiastic and long-time NCH colleague, shared this:

> After reading your newsletter, I decided to take you up on communicating about our new and wonderful team of patient reps. We started this "Revenue Cycle" department last year. We had to apply for the position of Patient Representative and were all pretty scared of what was going to be expected.
> However, our supervisor, Sandy Nelson, kept us all upbeat and made us feel like we would become great collectors. (I personally thought she was crazy!) But she <u>has</u> made us into collectors.
> In October, when we just were getting our feet wet, we did about $40,000-$45,000 worth of collections. November was about $50,000-$55,000. Then everything seemed to start clicking. At the end of December, we collected $262,075. We were just so proud of that and our higher-ups were too. We just received our January collection total and it was $264,940 -- all from 10 reps (including Sandy). Anyways, I just wanted to let you know that this amount of money is above-and- beyond anything that is collected from the Business Office. And I thought you should know who we are: Downtown Naples – **Deborah Swilley, Linda Albanese, Dorothy Bailey, Jamie Miller, Lucille Bubnis, Bev Adams;** North Naples – **Pamela Hunt, Rosemarie Reilly, Jessica Burnside;** Supervisor **Sandy Nelson.**
>
> You're right Dr. Weiss, communication is important!

Amen, Bev. And thank you to everyone who took the time to write. Open communication helps reinforce the feelings of confidence and success we should all have as we work together to serve the community with quality care. So keep those emails coming. And we'll keep *listening*!

Respectfully,

Allen

Allen S. Weiss, M.D., President and CEO
P.S.: Feel free to share *Straight Talk* and ask anyone to email me at <u>allen.weiss@nchmd.org</u> to be added.

Texting

Another related messaging vehicle is text messaging or texting, the common term for sending short—160 characters or fewer—messages from cell phones, using the Short Message Service (SMS).

The most common application of the service is person-to-person messaging, but text messages are also often used to interact with automated systems, such as ordering products and services for mobile phones. There are some services available on the Internet that allow users to send text messages free of direct charge to the sender.

Text messaging started slowly but today is the most widely used mobile data service, with 35 percent of all cell phone users now texting.

In 2007, when a shooter killed 33 people on the Virginia Tech campus, the university was criticized for not notifying students more quickly. But later that year, when an ice storm swept over the University of Texas at Austin, administrators sent an urgent "alert" to its 67,000 students, faculty, and staff to "stay home tomorrow." Thanks to a state-of-art emergency communications system, students instantaneously received the alert as a text message on their cell phones and via email on their PCs. The next day, the campus was empty.[10]

The point? Texting works.

Blogs

A blog is an online diary, a personal chronological log of thoughts published on a Web page, sometimes referred to as Weblog or Web log.

Once used only by fringe media, blogs have now been embraced by professional communicators as well as mainstream print and broadcast media. Blogs are used to encourage as well as enhance dialogue among publics on subjects from politics to current events, from ethical issues to hobbies and sports. Blog sharing allows individuals to locate, share, and subscribe to blogs of interest.[11]

The blogosphere is immense. With more than 113 million blogs in operation by the end of 2008, Technorati, the search engine that searches blogs, catalogues 1.5 million blog postings per day—or 17 posts per second. According to Technorati:

- Nearly 1.5 new blog sites are created every second.
- There are also 11,000 spam blogs or splogs.
- It took 320 days for the blogosphere to grow from 35 to 75 million blogs.
- The number one blogging language is Japanese, accounting for 37 percent of all blogs; English is second at 33 percent; and Chinese is third at 8 percent.[12]

One reason for the proliferation of blogs is that audience preferences are shifting—many can see through a company's traditional "ad speak," and have begun to turn elsewhere for information and opinion. This phenomenon is important for public relations professionals in that it reflects the need for respected, third-party "endorsers" of products and services.

A blog gains respect thorough the support of what are called "sneezers"—or early adopters within a social group. These early adopters embrace a new trend and then spread, that is, "sneeze," the word by way of their own blogs.[13] An example is the advent of Gmail, Google's free email product. Instead of making Gmail available to the public, Google offered 1,000 invitation-only accounts to influential users, many of whom were high-profile bloggers in the search engine marketing industry. Google understood that these influential and respected third party bloggers would "sneeze" Gmail to their audiences. Faster than you could say "Gesundheit," the bloggers blogged, and Gmail was "sneezed" around the globe.

Among the most popular blogs are TMZ.com, a leading post for celebrity news and the latest salacious show biz gossip, and Huffingtonpost.com, a liberal-leaning news site begun by former conservative commentator Arianna Huffington.

The vast majority of blogs on the Internet attract little following and are hardly worth the attention of public relations practitioners. But the relatively few blogs that have earned credibility in certain sectors are as important to public relations professionals as traditional reporters. Therefore, public relations professionals must monitor,

identify, and build relationships with these influential bloggers, just as they have with reporters[14] (see Figure 18-4).

There is, of course, a downside to blogging, as many organizations are learning. Dell Computer suffered repeated and prolonged damage to its reputation from a blogging campaign that emphasized "Dell Hell" about the quality of the firm's computers. And when a Comcast technician was filmed falling asleep on the job, the subsequent YouTube video and blogging campaign sunk Comcast's reputation for customer service.[15] So monitoring the blogosphere is a front line public relations responsibility.

The real point with blogging, as noted by one veteran blogger, was that rather than focusing on the tool itself, organizations need to zero in on *"the principles behind social media that make it work, like participating in a larger community and not controlling the conversation."*[16]

CEO Blogs

The latest phenomenon to hit the blogosphere is CEO blogs, in which chief executives share their thoughts on a variety of subjects with their, well, "subjects."

CEO blogs have gotten mixed reviews. On the one hand, CEOs at companies like Sun Microsystems, Marriott International, and Pitney Bowes have received credit for blogging consistently in good and bad times. On the other hand, in many cases, *"blogs read like tired, warmed-over press releases . . . with companies yakking away about their companies and products, seemingly oblivious to whether their audience is listening or not."*[17]

When this happens, what might have been "positive public relations" turns negative in a hurry. To avoid such nonproductive communications, well-intentioned CEO bloggers should heed the advice of perhaps the most well-known and effective CEO blogger, Jonathan Schwartz of Sun, whose "Jonathan's Blog" was widely followed in and outside of the company, prior to Sun's purchase by Oracle in 2009. Says Mr. Schwartz:

"We all have choices in how we communicate—I use this format because it works for me, allows me to talk to a diversity of constituents (the open source community

is vastly larger than the investment community—even numerically, a stock market chat room would be a relatively inefficient forum to engage the market), and a blog is more affordable than the daily global town halls it supplants."[18]

In 2009, when the Marriott Hotel in Mumbai was struck by homicide bombers, Marriott International CEO Bill Marriott immediately blogged, expressing his and the company's sorrow at the tragic events. In true reportorial form, the 76-year-old CEO's "Marriott on the Move" blog began:

This Senseless Tragedy . . .
By: Bill Marriott
Posted: September 20, 2008
I am very sad to report a terrible tragedy at our Marriott hotel in Islamabad, Pakistan. At approximately 7:00 p.m. local time, a large truck pulled up to the security checkpoint of the heavily guarded hotel and exploded. The huge blast engulfed the front of the hotel and ruptured a gas line, which caused a large fire to break out.[19]

The CEO's comments were picked up worldwide, demonstrating how the CEO blog could serve as well as any public relations vehicle in disseminating news.

PR Ethics

Mini-Case That's the Way the Online Cookie Grumbles

What could be more wholesome than that classic American snack, the Girl Scout cookie?

Thin Mints. Trefoils. Peanut Butter Sandwiches. Do-Si-Dos. All yummy (see Figure 18-5).

But in the spring of 2009, the Girl Scouts of the USA were getting indigestion from them all, thanks to an industrious 8-year-old scout named Wild Freeborn.

Wild, a girl scout in Asheville, NC, set out to sell 12,000 boxes of cookies so that she could win a free week of Scout camp for her entire troop. Wild's father, a Web site developer, helped her advertise her mission online. So he promoted Wild's cookies on Facebook and Twitter. He even made a YouTube video of Wild bouncing on the couch. And the Asheville community "ate it up."

But then the Girl Scouts governing body got wind of Wild's Internet activity and blew the whistle, stating that Internet cookie sales were forbidden.

That's when the story—*8-year-old vs. the Girl Scouts*—went national.

The Girl Scouts argued that in addition to the dangers of the Web for an 8-year-old girl, there was a question of "fairness" in hitting the Internet for sales. Cookie sales, the Scouts argued, were designed for local communities and not to be promoted broadly on the Internet.

When the cyber dust settled, Wild had removed her online order form but still sold enough boxes to get her a free trip to Scout camp, although her sales fell short of getting her whole troop to go. And Wild's approach had gotten through to the Girl Scouts. Said a spokesperson, *"We need to find a way to come up with a program for girls to sell*

FIGURE 18-5 The battlefront.
The Girl Scout cookie that launched a national, online guerrilla war. (Photo: Newscom)

cookies that is safe and fair. Once we do, we will allow online sales."

Questions

1. Assess the ethics involved here, both from the standpoint of Wild Freeborn and of the Girl Scouts.

2. Do you think the Girl Scouts did the right thing in "going after" the organization's own member?

For further information, see Robbie Brown, "Girl Scouts Battle with One of Their Own," *New York Times* (March 19, 2009).

Social Networks

The theoretical concept of social networking stemmed from an article in a telecommunications journal by David Isenberg, a former employee of AT&T Labs Research. He described the Internet as a "stupid network"—a new type of data network that relied on "dumb transport in the middle, and intelligent user-controlled endpoints" and where information was provided "by the needs of the data, not the design assumptions of the network."[20] Isenberg contrasted his "stupid network" with the outmoded "intelligent network," which relied on a technological hierarchy dictated by others.

Thus was born the "dumb transport" of social networking sites, like MySpace and Facebook, that allows communities of participants, who share common interests, opinions, and activities, to interact with others to manage messaging, email, video, file sharing, blogging, discussion groups, and all other manner of Internet discussion.

While the network may, indeed, be "stupid," the end user becomes "smarter" as the dynamic, information-sharing technology improves.

The growth of social networks, also called "social software," "social computing," or "Web 2.0"—from the emergence of Netscape in the 1990s to the inception of MySpace in 2004 as a nexus for young people around the world to sites that attract a variety of age groups and interests—introduces expanding opportunities for public relations practice.

Indeed, in the 2008 U.S. presidential election, virtually every presidential nominee had his or her own MySpace or Facebook page. One obscure Texas Republican, Rep. Ron Paul, showed extraordinary strength on the Internet, organizing Internet-based "moneybomb" fundraising events and riding to the top of YouTube subscriptions and Web search terms—ranking right up there with Britney Spears and Lindsay Lohan! Another somewhat less obscure Illinois Democrat, Sen. Barack Obama, rode an unprecedented Web presence all the way to the White House.[21]

So on the one hand, as the 2008 political process underscored, the potential of spreading messages and persuading supporters via social networking is significant. But on the other hand, the use of social networks for public relations purposes is in its infancy. Therefore, as with any emerging technology, public relations practitioners must rigorously scrutinize the "value" of social networking to achieve communications objectives before embracing any one technology or network.

Social Networking Sites

As noted, social networking sites essentially began with young people reaching out to one another. The usage and growth of sites has increased in the 21st century. So, too, has the use of social networking sites by public relations practitioners. The most well-known sites include the following:

- **MySpace,** owned by the multinational Australia-based media giant, News Corporation, has more than 100 million members. As a consequence of this large member base, organizations such as Greenpeace and the American Civil Liberties Union have created MySpace accounts to keep in touch with and expand their own membership bases.

- **Facebook,** founded in 2004 by a Harvard sophomore named Mark Zuckerberg, passed MySpace in terms of visitors in 2009, with nearly 200 million active users worldwide. A number of media companies, including *The New York Times, The Wall Street Journal,* and *USA Today,* set up Facebook groups.

■ **Bebo,** owned by Time Warner, is a UK-based social network of 40 million users and the third largest social networking site. While 20 percent of Bebo's users are in the United Kingdom, the site is expanding throughout Europe.

■ **LinkedIn** is a business-oriented social networking site with 20 million members and popular with public relations practitioners. LinkedIn is used to connect like-minded professionals to discover new business or employment opportunities and to develop a network of contacts.

In addition to the social networking sites themselves, anti-social networking sites have also cropped up in satirical retaliation. Snubster is a site that allows members to focus on people and things that irritate them. Isolatr is a site that claims to help users find where other people aren't, so they can keep away from them. Introverster is a community "that prevents stupid people and friends from harassing you."

As to the use of social networking sites by public relations practitioners, a number of public relations areas, including marketing and issues management, seem to lend themselves to social media.

■ Edelman Public Relations, headed by social media advocate Richard Edelman (see *From the Top*, this chapter), has a division of Digital Integration, which actively markets the Internet to clients. To help market the Infiniti G35 series, Edelman researched online car communities, where it found fans of the G35. Using the data gleaned online, Edelman engaged the community with a YouTube auto show video, which became a valuable information resource on the G35.[22]

■ M+R Strategic Services is another agency that emphasizes social networking. In 2006, when South Dakota considered an abortion ban ballot initiative, M+R developed a MySpace profile for Planned Parenthood Federation of America that signed up 4,500 "friends" to join a campaign to help South Dakotans fight the initiative. The abortion ban was rejected.[23]

■ Ketchum Public Relations, another early social media adopter, created a blog for soft drink maker Dr. Pepper and connected it to rock group Guns N' Roses and its album, "Chinese Democracy" (see Figure 18-6). The agency stimulated fans and other bloggers to become involved and, in effect, created a "community" around the drink, the group, and the album.[24]

■ Meanwhile, the Obama administration, a vigilant advocate of new technology, barraged supporters through an elaborate social network built during a successful presidential campaign, to help pass budget and other legislation.[25]

FIGURE 18-6 Social networkers. Guns N' Roses guitarist Buckethead (right, with bucket on head) was a recipient of a Ketchum Public Relations–Dr. Pepper social networking campaign that helped promote the group's new album. Friend Bootsy Collins and unidentified hanging doll share the moment. (Photo: Newscom)

As the fragmentation of social networking sites continues—Beliefnet for spiritual and religious members, BlackPlanet.com for African-Americans, Masala.com for South Asians, Eons.com and Grandparents.com for senior citizens, and on and on—the opportunities for public relations people to interact with social networks will increase. Again, such sites should be approached with enthusiasm—and caution.

Twitter

By the end of the first decade of the 21st century, the hottest social-networking "flavor-of-the-month" was Twitter, the microblogging service that allows typing of short messages (140 characters maximum) to alert friends and followers "what you're doing now"—a multi-person text message service. Perhaps the final proof that Twitter was all the rage among Internet geeks and novices alike was the revelation in the spring of 2009 that Milwaukee Bucks basketball forward Charlie Villanueva had posted the following Twitter message—or *tweet*—from the locker room during the coach's halftime talk:

"In da locker room, snuck to post my twitt. We're playing the Celtics, tie ball game at da half. Coach wants more toughness I gotta step up."[26]

Villanueva's coach was not amused.

Twitter seemed to be catching on in the NBA, as none other than the league's leading ambassador, Shaquille O'Neal, tweeted far and wide about his on-and-off court antics, for example, "Schwww, tim Duncan was lucky i was tired," "Shaq a Claus makes an appearance," etc.[27] Indeed, sports stars, politicians, and celebrities eagerly jumped on the Twitter bandwagon (see Figure 18-7).

On the other hand, Twitter had its detractors, who suggested that it was little more than a passing fad for "people with nothing to say . . . writing for people with nothing to do." And while Twitter's prospects as a public relations vehicle were not at all clear, the field began taking advantage of the service in several ways. For one thing, journalists also began tweeting about stories they were considering covering. So public relations people could use Twitter in the same way they used to use "editorial calendars" to get the inside track on story ideas. Twitter was also used to direct fellow Twitterers to Web sites and even products, as a direct integrated marketing vehicle.[28]

FIGURE 18-7 Shaq Tweeter-in-Chief. The power behind the throne, responsible for her client Shaquille O'Neal's affinity to Twitter, was Kathleen Hessert, whose firm, Sports Media Challenge, led a tweeting revolution among athletes. (Courtesy of Sports Media Challenge)

Talking Points All That Twitters Is Not Tweet

The first thing to remember about Twitter—or for that matter, anything else you type or tweet or distribute on the Net—is that everything is searchable.

And that means, "everything."

Just ask a vice president of Ketchum Public Relations, who landed in Memphis to deliver a presentation to client FedEx at the latter's corporate headquarters. On arrival in beautiful downtown Memphis, the New York–based Ketchum employee jotted the following Twitter 'note to his pals:

"True confession, but I'm in one of those towns where I scratch my head and say, "'I would die if I had to live here!'"

Alas, it just so happened that a FedEx staffer happened to see the message and forwarded it to FedEx executives. In response, FedEx employees emailed FedEx management and said, in part:

"True confession: many of my peers and I don't see much relevance between your presentation this morning and the work we do in Employee Communications."

And what was the nit-tweet Ketchum vice president lecturing on in Memphis?

"The proper use of digital media."*

*For further information, see Oliver Marks, "Online Diplomacy: The Famous FedEx Twitter/Email Exchange," *ZDNet* (January 17, 2009); and Michael A. Stelzner, "The Dark Side of Twitter: What Businesses Need to Know, *HealthLeaders Media* (March 4, 2009).

Photo/Video Sharing

As the Internet has evolved, the importance of graphics and video has increased, particularly in sharing photos and videos through social networks.

■ Photo sharing sites allow users to upload, edit, print, and send their digital photos to others. Leading sites include Zoomr, Picasa, and Flickr. All three are free sites that allow users to organize, edit, and share photos, as well as create public relations materials, such as DVD slide shows, business cards, and other printed matter.

■ Video sharing has become a dominant communication form on the Internet, thanks to sites like Google Video, Revver, and particularly YouTube, a video sharing site that allows users to upload, view, and share video clips. YouTube was created in 2005 by three individuals, who supposedly were having trouble sharing videos on the Web. A year later, the three sold the company to Google for $1.65 billion. (Not bad!) YouTube has become an important destination for corporate and political messages to help promote products and sell ideas.

Additional Web-Based Communications Vehicles

Any discussion of communications vehicles available on the Internet is, by definition, obsolete as soon as it hits the page. Nonetheless, public relations practitioners should be knowledgeable of the full range of Web-based communications vehicles, most certainly including the following:

■ **Intranets** are a pervasive internal communications phenomenon. Generally defined, an intranet is an internal vehicle that integrates communication with workflow, process management, infrastructure, and all other aspects of completing a job. Intranets allow communicators, management, and employees to exchange information quickly and effectively, much more quickly and effectively than any similar vehicle. Intranets, in other words, are Internets for specific organizations, designed to provide the necessary proprietary information to improve productivity. Intranets may include blogs, online polling data, social networking, and a whole range of customized platforms to fit a particular organization.[29]

- **Extranets**, on the other hand, allow a company to use the Internet to communicate information to finely segmented external groups, such as the media, investors, vendors, key customers, left-handed female television producers, globe-trotting apartment-dwelling soccer players, blonde East Side artists' supermodels, whatever. In segmenting the information in such a focused fashion—and protecting its dissemination through a complex series of firewalls—the targeted audience is assured that the data will remain confidential. Only approved individuals can access the information by using an assigned ID and password, restricted to extranet users exclusively.

- **Wikis**, which derive from the Hawaiian word for "quick," are collaborative Web sites that combine the work of many authors. Similar to a blog in structure and logic, a wiki differs from a blog in that it allows anyone to edit, delete, or modify content that has been placed on the Web site, including the work of previous authors. The most prominent wiki derivative is Wikipedia, the free encyclopedia on the Web, to which anyone can contribute material, either pro or con—and often undocumented and suspect. (So don't necessarily believe it!)

- **Podcasting**, which gained its name and fame after Apple's iPod burst onto the scene in 2001, refers to the act of making audio programs available for download to any MP3 player (although Apple still controls about 80 percent of the market). Listeners already have an enormous selection of podcasts from which to choose—from amateur deejays hosting alternative radio programs to authors recording their own audio books to corporate public relations professionals promoting products. The "pod revolution" will be limited only by the supply of and demand for content.[30]

- **RSS**, which literally stands for *really simple syndication,* is an easy way to distribute content on the Internet, similar to a newsgroup. RSS feeds are widely used by the blog community, for example, to share headlines or full text. Major news organizations, including Reuters, CNN, PR Newswire, and the BBC, use RSS feeds to allow other sites to incorporate their "syndicated" news services. Companies also use RSS for delivery of news, replacing email and threatening the continued existence of that time-honored but increasingly obsolescent staple of the last century, the fax.

- **Second Life** is probably as bizarre a use of online communications techniques as any in the public relations arsenal. Second Life is a popular online universe launched in 2003 by Linden Lab, which is a 3-D world created entirely by its members or "residents." Not exactly a game, Second Life gives members a place to congregate, chat, explore, and even fly around. And as to whether this alternate universe has public relations application, consider that companies from IBM to Reebok have all flocked to Second Life to spread their messages.

These are but a sample of the Web-based communications vehicles available to public relations professionals. The important thing for public relations people is to stay aware of the changing nature of Internet communications vehicles. The Internet menu changes at lightning speed, and it's the responsibility of the communications professional to change right along with it.

The Darker Side of Online Communications

Google the name of the world's largest retailer, and you'll discover not only the Walmart Stores Inc. home page, but also links to message boards, blogs, wikis, and online communities attacking, shellacking, and vivisecting Walmart (see Figure 18-8). Welcome to the world of Internet sabotage, where no organization is immune from online attack.

As a consequence, monitoring the Internet is another frontline public relations responsibility. The World Wide Web is riddled with unhappy consumers spilling their guts, disgruntled stockholders badmouthing management in chat rooms, and rogue Web sites condemning this or that organization.

The Internet is free, wide open, international, and anonymous—the perfect place to start a movement and ruin an organization's reputation. And so it is imperative that public relations people monitor the Internet in consideration of the following.

- **Discussion groups and chat rooms** are hotbeds for discontented shareholders, unscrupulous stock manipulators, and disgruntled consumers. Any local or service provider message board that solicits public input about an organization is ripe for messaging contrary to the official position.[31] The Yahoo! finance boards, for example, are the source of continuing commentary about public companies from anonymous commentators, all using mysterious pseudonyms (see *Case Study*, this chapter). One will start with a cryptic message. Then another will add to it. And a third will chime in. This continuous commentary—called "the thread" on Wall Street—is the bane of many a company. The thread has become such a source of corporate discontent that monitoring firms have emerged to keep track of what is being said about companies in chat rooms and even lead "whisper campaigns" to incorporate positive information.

- **Rogue Web sites** must also be monitored by the organizations they attack. Rogue Web sites seek to confront an organization by:
  - Presenting negative information
  - Satirizing policy and management
  - Soliciting employees, current and former, to vent publicly
  - Serving as a gateway for complaints to regulators and media
  - Confusing the public regarding which Web site represents the real organization[32]

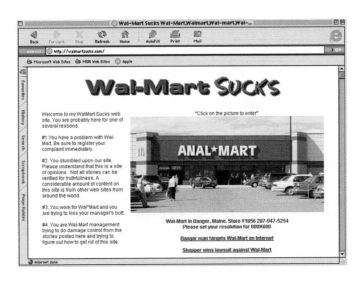

FIGURE 18-8
Walmart sucks.
This rogue Web site, designed to embarrass the mighty Walmart company, is typical of anticorporate sites on the Internet, all of which must be monitored.

A corporation's knee-jerk reaction—to call in the lawyers—hasn't resulted in great victory in battling the rogues. In perhaps the most celebrated case, Kmart sued www.kmartsucks.com, a Web site hosted by a disgruntled employee. The copyright infringement suit did succeed in forcing the site to change its name—to www.martsucks.com—but the considerable national media attention the suit received helped put the rogue Web site on the map. Eventually, the embattled Kmart launched its own "good news only" site, called Kmartforever.com, to combat the bashers.[33]

- **Urban legends** are yet another requisite for online monitoring. There is a growing body of corporate horror stories from bogus Internet rumors that have taken on legendary proportions. Most are spread by email at lightning speed across the country and the world. For example:
  - Upscale retailer Neiman Marcus was accused by an anonymous emailer of charging a $200 fee for its special cookie recipe. "Outrageous," cried the thousands who received the email. It's also completely untrue. Neiman Marcus doesn't have a cookie recipe.
  - Mrs. Fields also outraged the populace when an email dispatch reported that she had sent a batch of her famous cookies to O. J. Simpson after he won his infamous murder trial. This is also totally false.
  - In perhaps the most pervasive and pernicious urban legend of all, retailer Tommy Hilfiger was, according to the official-sounding email, evicted from *The Oprah Winfrey Show* by the lady herself when the clothes manufacturer admitted his garments weren't made for "African Americans, Hispanics, and Asians" (see Figure 18-9). The reality was that Tommy Hilfiger never met Oprah Winfrey, was never on her show, and certainly didn't design his clothing solely for white people. In the end, the false Internet legend proved so virulent that Oprah invited Hilfiger on her show to "clear the air" once and for all.

What should a proper public relations response be to such online efforts to derail the organization? Typical responses range from doing nothing to throwing money at an aggrieved party to engaging the aggrieved party to releasing the lawyers. The smartest organizations adopt "inoculation strategies" that establish clear communication channels on the Web, through which customers and employees can relay concerns to management, sometimes privately, before frustrations mount. Firms like IBM and McDonald's host secure, unedited sites where employees can openly and anonymously discuss corporate policies and strategies. Procter & Gamble sponsors an online forum, where customers can express their thoughts.[34] Such preemptive public relations make solid business sense.

The real lesson: Public relations professionals must constantly monitor the Web.

FIGURE 18-9 Stuff of legends. Urban legends like this email, discussing a bogus appearance by Tommy Hilfiger on *The Oprah Winfrey Show*, have become increasingly frequent as more people, some with questionable motives, access the Internet.

Subject: Tommy Hilfiger

MESSAGE:

I'm sure many of you watched the recent taping of the *Oprah Winfrey Show* where her guest was Tommy Hilfiger. On the show she asked him if the statements about race he was accused of saying were true. Statements like if he'd known African-Americans, Hispanics and Asians would buy his clothes he would not have made them so nice. He wished these people would *not* buy his clothes, as they are made for upper class white people. His answer to Oprah was a simple "yes". Where after she immediately asked him to leave her show.

Last Word

The Internet, as a popular communications medium, has been around only for two decades. In that short time, it has evolved into an indispensable marketing tool for organizations and a favored weapon for angry customers, disaffected employees, and consumer activists bent on attacking those same organizations.[35] As a consequence, mastering and monitoring the Internet have become a front-burner priority for public relations professionals.

In the 21st century, such new techniques as blogging for promotional product buzz, setting up "blog carnivals" to inform a community about a particular topic, creating search-friendly Web sites and search-optimal keywords, podcasting, videocasting, and orchestrating word-of-mouth marketing campaigns are all part of the public relations practitioner's online tool kit.[36]

As the number of the world's citizens using the Internet expands exponentially, it is urgent that public relations professionals understand the new technology and its capabilities and increase their competence in employing and monitoring it. Those who can blend the traditional skills of writing and media and communications knowledge with the online skills of the Internet will find a rewarding calling in the practice of public relations in the 21st century.[37]

Discussion Starters

1. What is the status of the Internet and World Wide Web in public relations today?
2. How has the Internet impacted journalism? Commerce? Internal communications?
3. How has email changed the way people and organizations communicate?
4. How has texting changed the way people look at email?
5. What are the characteristics that make up an effective email newsletter?
6. How have blogs influenced public relations practice?
7. What is the significance of Twitter relative to public relations practice?
8. What is the impact of the *thread* on public companies?
9. What is a *podcast*? A *wiki*? *Second Life*?
10. Why is meant by online *inoculation strategies*?
11. What is the difference between an intranet and an extranet?

Top of the Shelf PR 2.0 New Media, New Tools, New Audiences / Deidre Breakenridge, Upper Saddle River, NJ: Pearson Education, Inc., 2008

This is a terrific explanation of everything one needs to know about practicing public relations on the Internet. In common, understandable language, author Breakenridge demonstrates why she is one of the field's foremost Web practitioners. She provides practical examples on research methods to reach the influencers, creating interactive newsrooms, reaching audiences through social networking, and penetrating the mindset of the 2.0 journalist.

The author also examines the various online ways to achieve recognition for one's product or service, including the use of social media in all its glory. Best of all, the book is written *by* a public relations professional *for* public relations professionals.

If you need one book to navigate through the thicket of the Internet, this is the one.

Case Study — The Secret Life of an Organic CEO Blogger

Whole Foods Market CEO John Mackey prided himself on founding a company that offered nutritious products and contributed generously to all manner of charities (see Figure 18-10). Mr. Mackey founded the company as a 25-year-old college dropout, in Austin, Texas. When he and his co-founder (his 21-year-old girlfriend) were evicted from their apartment for storing food products in it, they decided to live at their small health foods store. Because it was zoned for commercial use, there was no shower stall, so they bathed using a water hose attached to their dishwasher.

Thus was born the world's foremost purveyor of healthy produce.

As Whole Foods increased its market share and became the nation's largest natural and organic grocer, its reputation as a model for corporate behavior grew as well.

With 270 locations in the United States, Canada, and the United Kingdom, Whole Foods Market produced all manner of wholesome produce—seafood, grocery, meat and poultry, bakery, prepared foods and catering, beer, wine, cheese, whole body, floral, pet products, and household products. The company was consistently ranked among the most socially responsible businesses and placed second on the U.S. Environmental Protection Agency's list of *Top 25 Green Power Partners.*

For many years, Whole Foods and its socially responsible CEO could do no wrong.

Right up until CEO Mackey's "secret blogging life" was exposed.

"Rahodeb, Is that You?"

On July 20, 2007, *The Wall Street Journal* reported that CEO Mackey was, for at least seven years, using the pseudonym, *"Rahodeb"* (an anagram of his wife's name, Deborah), to post to Yahoo! Finance forums opinions criticizing rival supermarket chain Wild Oats Market. The *Journal* reported that both the Federal Trade Commission and the Securities and Exchange Commission were investigating.

The anonymous CEO's postings painted a bleak future for Wild Oats Market, while predicting a bright one for Whole Foods.

An early *Rahodeb* posting posited the following:

"I think it is highly unlikely a conventional supermarket chain will buy OATS. Why not? What does OATS bring to the table?

"Good locations? No. For the most part they have poor real estate (based on the stores that I have seen). Their stores are also on average quite small—not the size stores that supermarket chains want to operate. Anyone that buys OATS is taking on huge operating lease liabilities from this poor real estate. OATS has many underperforming stores that should be written off."

Another *Rahodeb* posting proclaimed in 2006:

"The writing is on the wall. The end game is now underway for (Wild Oats) . . . Whole Foods is systematically destroying their viability as a business—market by market, city by city."

In another 2006 posting, *Rahodeb* warned:

"Bankruptcy remains a distinct possibility (for Wild Oats) if the business isn't sold within the next few years."

Anyone reading these dire anonymous warnings about the future of Wild Oats might have found it inconceivable that any company in its right mind would ever be interested in buying Wild Oats.

Who would be that gutsy or ignorant? The answer was a shocker.

Rahodeb Makes His Move

What *Rahodeb* aka Mackey didn't reveal in the anonymous postings was that his company, Whole Foods, planned to make an offer to buy Wild Oats. In February 2007, Whole Foods announced it intended to do just that at an aggregate price of $565 million—not

FIGURE 18-10 **Organic blogger revealed.** Whole Foods CEO John Mackey drew the wrath of the Federal Trade Commission by posting anonymous Internet messages about the competition. (Photo: Newscom)

bad for a firm that had been knocked so vociferously by the anonymous blogger.

Four months later, the Federal Trade Commission filed a lawsuit to block the proposed $656 million sale, on antitrust grounds, that it would hobble competition and increase prices to consumers. Whole Foods Market CEO John Mackey took the unusual step of initiating a blog on the subject to explain his opposition to the FTC's stance. Papers filed by the FTC revealed that for several years, CEO Mackey posted highly opinionated comments under the pseudonym *"Rahodeb"* on the Whole Foods Yahoo! investment message board, raising serious legal and ethical questions.

Additionally, the Securities and Exchange Commission began an investigation of the Mackey secret postings.

Whole Foods responded to the FTC complaint by saying its CEO posted comments under an alias *"to avoid having his comments associated with the company and to avoid others placing too much emphasis on his remarks."* Nonetheless, the company also decided to launch a board investigation of the postings and to restrict its CEO and other senior officers from posting future industry-related thoughts on the Internet.

And CEO Mackey, himself, mounted his own defense on his own blog, bashing the FTC and stating:

"The views articulated by rahodeb sometimes represent what I actually believed and sometimes they didn't.

Sometimes I simply played 'devil's advocate' for the sheer fun of arguing.

"All of rahodeb's posting also need to be understood in the context of the time that they were written. Because the competitive market has evolved so much in the last 5 years, older postings mean far less today than they did when they were written."

The FTC–Mackey/Whole Foods battle raged on for two years when, in 2009, the government settled with the company, forcing Whole Foods to sell the Wild Oats brand and 13 functioning stores, in order to keep another 19 outlets.

As a postscript, the SEC concluded in 2008 that it had decided to take "no action" on the anonymous CEO Web postings.

Questions

1. What are the ethical implications of the CEO's anonymous postings about the competition?

2. Would Mackey have been better off signing his name to the postings?

3. If you had been public relations director at Whole Foods, what would you have advised the CEO as to his Web postings and his blog?

For further information, see Diane Brady, "Who Advises John Mackey?" *Business Week* (July 13, 2007); Peter Kaplan, "John Mackey Panned Wild Oats on Web," Reuters (July 12, 2007); "Whole Foods 'Bans' Execs from Web," *Jack O'Dwyer's Newsletter* (November 14, 2007): 4; "Whole Foods CEO's Secret Identity," Associated Press (July 12, 2007); and "Whole Foods, FTC Settle on Wild Oats," CNNMoney.com (March 6, 2009).

From the Top   An Interview with Richard Edelman

Richard Edelman is president and CEO of Edelman, the world's largest independent public relations firm with 3,000 employees in 50 offices worldwide. Mr. Edelman is also the public relations executive most associated with the Internet and new technology. Under his leadership, Edelman has distinguished itself not only in traditional public relations areas but as a pioneer in the new media. A graduate of Harvard College and the Harvard Business School, Mr. Edelman is one of the only public relations executives to write his own blog.

How has the Internet changed the public relations business?
The Web has changed the PR business by giving us access to budgets that we never saw before . . . by allowing us to make each of our clients its own media company . . . by broadening our array of addressable media to include bloggers . . . to force us to have relationships with a whole new set of influencers who may not be at top magazines but are frequently posting content.

How proficient in terms of the Net should a public relations professional be today?
The PR person who does not read important blogs (for example, in DC you should read *Drudge Report,* Politico) is missing the game. You also must be posting comments to blogs that

matter. You need to be reading the mainstream media's blogs (for example, Andrew Ross Sorkin's blog at *NY Times—Deal Book*).

What are the primary online communications methods that you recommend to your clients?
Primary online methods are listening to the conversation by reading or viewing video blogs, making comments as appropriate, making relationships with key bloggers. For example, I had lunch the old-fashioned way with Laura Touby of Media Bistro, who was Twittering during our lunch about our conversation.

Why do you blog?
I blog because I enjoy writing, because I like to walk the talk about social media, because too few executives in PR agencies are willing to take a stand on issues.

Do you recommend that other CEOs blog internally?
I do recommend that other CEOs blog. I would rather have them make their blog posts accessible to the general public. But internal only is a good first step.

Do you recommend that clients get involved in online forums that are critical of them?
I believe that companies must participate in the horizontal axis of communications. You need to correct misinformation and to be part of the conversation. At least point people to alternative interpretations of the data on the company site or another site.

Who do you consider the leadership companies in terms of online communications?
Best companies are Walmart, GE, and GM. They offer access to mid-level staffers. Note, for example, the blog for Walmart which has buyers posting from around the world as they find new garments or electronics; also the GE research blog on future innovations.

What lies on the horizon for public relations use of the Web?
PR will have to improve the quality of its content. All of it must be ready for prime time—not as much selling mode as it will have to be conversational and factual. Also, it must include more visual content as words are no longer sufficient. We will be the means by which business can open up to conversation.

Public Relations Library

Baines, Paul, John Egan, and Frank Jefkins. *Public Relations Contemporary Issues and Techniques.* Burlington, MA: Elsevier Butterworth-Heinemann, 2004.

Bragman, Howard. *Where's My Fifteen Minutes?* New York, NY: Penguin, 2008. Ricki Lake's public relations counselor offers behind-the-scenes secrets to optimize publicity, including using the Internet.

Breakenridge, Deirdre, and Thomas J. DeLoughry. *The New PR Toolkit.* Upper Saddle River, NJ: Pearson Education, 2003. A good introduction for public relations professionals as to what works on the Internet.

Chase, Larry. *Larry Chase's Need-to-Know Marketing Sites: Web Digest for Marketers* (www.wdfm.com), 2002. Carefully selected and annotated directory of 400 marketing Web sites divided into 33 categories.

Gardner, Susannah. *Buzz Marketing with Blogs for Dummies.* Hoboken, NJ: John Wiley & Sons, 2005. This is the book tells you everything you need to know about blogging and bloggers.

Green, Andy. *Creativity in Public Relations,* 3rd Ed. London, England: Kogan Page, Ltd., 2008. This updated version includes creativity via the Internet.

Kelleher, Thomas. *Public Relations Online.* Thousand Oaks, CA: Sage Publications, Inc., 2007. This book offers a good explanation of relationship-based interactive public relations.

King, Janice M. *Copywriting that Sells High-Tech.* United States: WriteSpark Press, 2006. This book is for public relations writers who deal primarily with high-tech companies and products.

Lawson, Russell. *The PR Buzz Factor.* London, England: Kogan Page, Ltd., 2006. One way to create "buzz" is through a creative online presence and Web site, says this counselor.

Levine, John R., Margaret Levine Young, and Carol Baroudi. *The Internet for Dummies.* Hoboken, NJ: John Wiley & Sons, 2005. For anyone feeling left behind, this is your introduction to the Internet.

Levine, Michael. *Guerilla PR Wired.* New York, NY: McGraw-Hill, 2002. A noted street-fighting public relations consultant advises how the Web can provide an inexpensive mechanism for a winning publicity campaign.

Lynn, Jaqueline (ed.). *Start Your Own Public Relations Business.* New York, NY: Entrepreneur Media Inc., 2009. This provides a route—largely Internet-related—through which a practitioner might start his or her own public relations organization.

Scott, David Meerman. *The New Rules of Marketing and PR.* Hoboken, NJ: John Wiley & Sons, 2007. Marketing-oriented text emphasizes raising online visibility to enhance sales volume.

Sweeney, Susan, Andy MacLellan, and Ed Dorey. *3G Marketing on the Internet.* Gulf Breeze, FL: Maximum Press, 2006. It's third-generation time for the Internet, and this book provides business strategies for using the Internet today.

Vivian, John. *The Media of Mass Communications,* 4th ed. Boston: Allyn & Bacon, 2003.

Wong, Thomas. *101 Ways to Boost Your Web Traffic.* Intesync Web Professional Services, 2002. On the Internet, if you build it, they won't necessarily come. This book explains how to entice them.

Chapter 19
Crisis Management

"**A** *lie*," Mark Twain once said, *"can travel halfway around the world while the truth is still putting on its shoes."*

And he didn't even have access to the Internet! Consider the series of faux crises that occurred in one single week in September 2008:

- First, Apple Computer stock sunk like a stone after a CNN-sponsored citizen journalism site, ireport.com, published a false item reporting that Apple CEO Steve Jobs had been rushed to the emergency room (see *PR Ethics Mini-Case,* this chapter).

- Then United Airlines lost more than $1 billion in market value when traders treated a six-year-old announcement of a bankruptcy as a new development.

- Finally, the Drudge Report carried a false item that Oprah Winfrey had refused to host a show featuring Republican Party Vice Presidential nominee Sarah Palin. Later in the day, Oprah issued a statement denying the report—but not before the respected Tom Brokaw on NBC's *Meet the Press* asked Democratic Vice Presidential candidate Joe Biden, *"Do you think that some people will see that (Oprah's reported action) as an elitist position, that in some ways Democrats may be afraid of her, Sarah Palin?"*[1]

In the 21st century, thanks to the digital speed of the Internet and the pervasiveness of social media and viral communications, organizations and individuals are always one step away from crisis.

FIGURE 19-1 The monster of Wall Street. Bernard Madoff, guilty of defrauding investors out of $60 billion in the largest investor crisis in stock market history, met his "friends" in the media, at the start of his 150-year stay in the slammer. (Photo: Newscom)

And in recent years, the practice of public relations has become most well known for assisting those who find themselves in such crises.

Crisis, which public relations counselor James Lukaszewski once described as "unplanned visibility," can strike anyone at any time.[2] Indeed, in the new century, among the most well-regarded and highest-paid professionals in public relations are those who have achieved this status through their efforts in attempting to "manage" crises.

In a world of instantaneous Internet communications, round-the-clock cable news commentary, talk radio, tabloid news journalism, and exploding communications challenges, the number and depth of crises affecting business, government, labor, non-profits, and even private individuals have expanded exponentially.

No sector of society is immune from crisis.

- In *government,* the September 11, 2001, attacks on America opened the door to terrorist violence aimed at defenseless civilians, putting government officials at all levels on constant alert. Hurricane Katrina lack-of-preparedness in 2005 introduced yet another level of government crisis. And ever since, government scandals—from former New York Governor Elliot Spitzer's call girl fascination to former Illinois Governor Rod Blagojevich's impeachment to South Carolina Governor Mark Sanford's globe-trotting extramarital liaison on Father's Day 2009—have periodically dominated the news.

- In business, the outrageous ineptitude of the financial industry leading to the subprime lending crisis of 2008, complemented by the outrageous pay packages awarded failed CEOs at Citigroup, Merrill Lynch, Countrywide, and a host of lesser companies, enraged the nation and caused sweeping changes in government regulation of business in 2009.

- In *education,* a scandal at Duke University in 2006, involving bogus accusations of rape and racism among the college's lacrosse players, rocked the respected university.[3]

- In the *health care* sector, the CEO of giant HealthSouth, Richard Scrushy, was indicted in a government corruption case in 2006, after being ousted from the company he allegedly bilked for a personal fortune.[4]

- In the area of *religion,* the Catholic Church was still recovering from the shame of the pedophile priest scandals at the beginning of the decade.

- In the world of *charitable institutions,* in January 2009 universities and foundations across the nation discovered their investment portfolios savaged by the actions of one rogue investor, Bernard Madoff, a former chairman of the NASDAQ Stock Exchange. Madoff's actions caused a crisis of biblical proportions for charities, which suffered the brunt of the $60 billion he had reportedly bilked investors[5] (see Figure 19-1, on previous page). Shortly after Madoff's fraud was exposed, the revelation that Texas financier Robert Allen Stanford—or "Sir Allen," after he was knighted in Antigua—had bilked investors out of "a mere" $8 billion seemed like little more than "chump change."

- In *journalism,* a story created out of whole cloth by *Newsweek* in 2005, alleging that guards at the U.S. detention center at Guantanamo Bay flushed a copy of the Koran down a toilet, triggered Muslim world outrage and left as many as 17 dead and scores injured in Afghanistan.[6]

- In *public relations,* scandals in 2005 involving Ketchum Public Relations in a pay-for-play broadcaster scheme and Fleishman-Hillard in padding bills brought crisis to the crisis counselors themselves.

These are but the tip of the iceberg—a very few of the hundreds of small and large crises that afflict elements of society today in ever-expanding magnitude.

The list of such issues—and of the crises they often evoke—is unending. In the 21st century, society is flooded with front-burner issues that affect individuals and organizations. From war to peace, poverty to abortion, discrimination to downsizing, environmentalism to energy conservation, the domain of "issues management" has become increasingly important for public relations professionals.

Issues Management

In guarding against crisis, public relations professionals must constantly be aware of the primary issues that impact their organizations. The term *issues management* was coined in 1976 by public relations counselor W. Howard Chase, who defined it this way:

Issues management is the capacity to understand, mobilize, coordinate, and direct all strategic and policy planning functions, and all public affairs/public relations skills, toward achievement of one objective: meaningful participation in creation of public policy that affects personal and institutional destiny.[7]

Issues management is a five-step process that:

1. Identifies issues with which the organization must be concerned,
2. Analyzes and delimits each issue with respect to its impact on constituent publics,
3. Displays the various strategic options available to the organization,
4. Implements an action program to communicate the organization's views and to influence perception on the issue, and
5. Evaluates its program in terms of reaching organizational goals.

In sum, issues managers orchestrate the process whose goal is to help preserve markets, reduce risk, create opportunities, and manage image as an organizational asset for the benefit of an organization.

In specific terms, issues management encompasses the following elements:

- **Anticipate emerging issues.** Normally, the issues management process is about precrisis planning. It deals with an issue that will hit the organization a year later, thus distinguishing the practice from the normal crisis planning aspects of public relations.

- **Identify issues selectively.** An organization can influence only a few issues at a time. Therefore, a good issues management process will select several—perhaps 5 to 10—specific priority issues with which to deal. In this way, issues management can focus on the most important issues affecting the organization.

- **Deal with opportunities and vulnerabilities.** Most issues, anticipated well in advance, offer both opportunities and vulnerabilities for organizations. For example, in assessing higher oil prices, an insurance company might anticipate that fewer people will be driving and therefore there will be fewer accident claims. This would mark an opportunity. On the other hand, higher gas prices might mean that more people are strapped to pay their premiums. This would be a vulnerability that a sharp company should anticipate well in advance.

- **Plan from the outside in.** The external environment—not internal strategies—dictates the selection of priority issues. This differs from the normal strategic planning approach, which, to a large degree, is driven by internal strengths and objectives. Issues management is very much driven by external factors.

- **Bottom-line orientation.** Although many people tend to look at issues management as anticipating crises, its real purpose should be to defend the organization in light of external factors as well as to enhance the firm's business by seizing imminent opportunities.

- **Action timetable.** Just as the issues management process must identify emerging issues and set them in order, it must propose policy, programs, and an implementation timetable to deal with those issues. Action is the key to an effective issues management process.

- **Dealing from the top.** Just as a public relations department is powerless without the confidence and respect of top management, the issues management process must operate with the support of the chief executive. The chief executive's imprimatur is critical to the acceptance and conduct of issues management within a firm.

Risk Communication and Message Mapping

Risk *communication* is an outgrowth of issues management. Risk communication began as a process of taking scientific data related to health and environmental hazards and presenting them to a lay audience in a manner that is both understandable and meaningful.

Accordingly, use of risk communication replaced impulsive decision making with scientific principles. It is aimed to produce clear and concise messages.

Models of risk communication have been developed based on the position that *perception is reality*—a concept that has been part of public relations for years. Indeed, the disciplines of risk communication and public relations have much in common. Risk communication is based on behavioral scientific research, which shows how behavior changes when a person processes messages during high-stress situations. When stressed, the ability to hear, understand, and remember diminishes. Research indicates that in times of high stress, people can miss up to 80 percent of message content. Of the 20 percent they do hear, most messages are negative. In crisis, you must adjust for these effects to communicate effectively.

To confront this reality, risk communicators have developed a message-mapping process, based on seven steps.

1. Identify stakeholders.
2. Determine specific concerns for each stakeholder group.
3. Analyze specific concerns to fit underlying general concerns.
4. Conduct structured brainstorming with input from message-mapping teams.
5. Assemble supporting facts and proof for each key message.
6. Ask outside experts to systematically test messages.
7. Plan delivery of resulting messages and supporting materials.[8]

Message maps generally adhere to the following standard requirements:

- Three key messages.
- Seven to 12 words per message.
- Three supporting facts for each key message.

Like any other area of public relations, risk communication depends basically on an organization's actions. In the long run, deeds, not words, are what count in communicating risk.

Managing in a Crisis

The most significant test for any organization comes when it is hit by a major accident or disaster—that is, a *crisis.*

What is a crisis? According to the *Harvard Business Review,* "A crisis is a situation that has reached a critical phase for which dramatic and extraordinary intervention is necessary to avoid or repair major damage."[9]

How an organization handles itself in the midst of a crisis may influence how it is perceived for years to come. Poor handling of events with the magnitude of Exxon's *Valdez* oil spill, NASA's Challenger disaster, Denny's racial bias accusations, Wall Street's banking crisis, or Major League Baseball's steroids scandal can cripple an organization's reputation and cause it enormous monetary loss (see Figure 19-2). On the other hand, thinking logically and responding thoughtfully and quickly in a crisis, such as how Johnson & Johnson reacted to its Tylenol tablet poisoning episodes, can cement a positive reputation and establish enormous goodwill for an organization.

It is essential, therefore, that such emergencies be managed intelligently and forthrightly with the news media, employees, and the community at large.

As any organization unfortunate enough to experience a crisis recognizes, when the crisis strikes, seven instant warning signs invariably appear:

1. **Surprise.** When a crisis breaks out, it's usually unexpected. Often it's a natural disaster—a tornado or hurricane, for example. Sometimes, it's a human-made disaster—robbery, embezzlement, or large loss. Frequently, a public relations

FIGURE 19-2 **Ster-Rod walking.** In 2009, after admitting to taking steroids earlier in his career, New York Yankee Alex Rodriguez led his teammates on a slow walk to meet the media at spring training in Tampa. (Photo: Newscom)

professional first learns of such an event when the media calls and demands to know what immediate action will be taken.

2. **Insufficient information.** Many things happen at once. Rumors fly. Blogs come alive with wild stories. Wire services want to know why the company's stock is falling. It's difficult to get a grip on everything that's happening.

3. **Escalating events.** The crisis expands. The stock exchange wants to know what's going on. Will the organization issue a statement? Are the rumors true? While rumors run rampant, truthful information is difficult to obtain. You want to respond in an orderly manner, but events are unfolding too quickly.

4. **Loss of control.** The unfortunate natural outgrowth of escalating events is that too many things are happening simultaneously. Erroneous stories hit the Internet, the wires, and the airwaves.

5. **Increased outside scrutiny.** Bloggers, the media, stockbrokers, talk-show hosts, and the public in general feed on rumors. "Helpful" politicians and observers of all stripes comment to cable television on what's going on. Talk radio is abuzz with innuendo. The media want responses. Investors demand answers. Customers must know what's going on.

6. **Siege mentality.** The organization understandably feels surrounded. Lawyers counsel, "Anything we say will be held against us." The easiest thing to do is to say nothing. So, "No comment" is urged by the attorneys. But does that make sense?

7. **Panic.** With the walls caving in and with leaks too numerous to plug, a sense of panic pervades. In such an environment, it is difficult to convince management to take immediate action and to communicate what's going on.[10]

Talking Points The Lessons of *Valdez*

Remember the Exxon *Valdez* case discussed in Chapter 5? Because you've probably already dissected it thoroughly, it won't matter if we divulge here, courtesy of crisis expert Tim Wallace, how Exxon should have handled the situation.

1. **Develop a clear, straightforward position.** In a crisis, you can't appear to waffle. You must remain flexible enough to respond to changing developments, but you must also stick to your underlying position. Exxon's position seemed to waver.

2. **Involve top management.** Management must not only be involved, but it must also appear to be involved. In Exxon's case, from all reports, Chairman Lawrence Rawl was involved with the Gulf of Valdez solutions every step of the way. But that's not how it appeared in public. Rather, he was perceived as distant from the crisis. And Exxon suffered.

3. **Activate third-party support.** This support may come from Wall Street analysts, independent engineers, technology experts, or legal authorities. Any objective party with credentials can help your case.

4. **Establish an on-site presence.** This is what airline CEOs do when there is a plane crash. It's also what the CEO of Union Carbide did when a Carbide plant explosion killed thousands in Bhopal, India. His trip at least showed corporate concern. When Chairman Rawl explained that he "had better things to do" than fly to Valdez, Exxon effectively lost the public relations battle.

5. **Centralize communications.** In any crisis, a communications point person should be appointed and a support team established. It is the point person's job—and his or hers alone—to state the organization's position.

6. **Cooperate with the media.** In a crisis, journalists are repugnant; they're obnoxious; they'll stoop to any level to get the story. But don't take it personally. Treat the media as friendly adversaries and explain your side of the crisis. Making them enemies will only exacerbate tensions.

7. **Don't ignore employees.** Keeping employees informed helps ensure that the organization's business proceeds as normally as possible. Employees are your greatest ally. Don't keep them in the dark.

8. **Keep the crisis in perspective.** Often management underreacts at the start of a crisis and overreacts when it builds. The prevailing wisdom seems to be, "Just because we're paranoid doesn't mean they're not out to get us!" Avoid hunkering down. Exxon executives made this mistake, and it cost them dearly.

9. **Position the organization for the time when the crisis is over.** Concentrate on communicating the steps that the organization will take to deal with the crisis. Admit blame if it's due. Then quickly focus on what you are doing now rather than on what went wrong.

10. **Continuously monitor and evaluate the process.** Survey, survey, survey. Take the pulse of your employees, customers, suppliers, distributors, investors, and, if appropriate, the general public. Determine whether your messages are getting through. Constantly check to see which aspects of the program are working and which are not. Adjust accordingly.

Tim Wallace, "Crisis Management: Practical Tips on Restoring Trust," *The Journal of Private Sector Policy* (November 1991): 14.

Planning in a Crisis

The key to crisis management is being prepared. If there is one certainty in dealing with crisis, it is that all manner of accidents or disruptions make for spectacular headlines and sensational reporting. Reporters march to a different drummer. They consider themselves the guardians of the public trust and therefore may be quick to point fingers and ascribe blame in a crisis.

Thus, heightened preparedness is always in order, with five planning issues paramount.

- **First, for each potentially impacted audience, define the risk.** "The poison in the pill will make you sick." "The plant shutdown will keep you out of work." "The recall will cost the stockholders $100 million." The risk must be understood—or at least contemplated—before framing crisis communications.

- **Second, for each risk defined, describe the actions that mitigate the risk.** "Don't take the pill." "We are recalling the product." "We are studying the possibility of closing the plant." If you do a credible job in defining the risk, the public will more closely believe in your solutions. In 2006, for example, when a bird flu pandemic threatened the world, the parent of Kentucky Fried Chicken readied a consumer education and advertising program to reassure consumers that eating cooked chicken is perfectly safe.[11]

- **Third, identify the cause of the risk.** If the public believes you know what went wrong, it is more likely to accept that you will quickly remedy the problem. That's why people get back on airplanes after crashes. Moreover, if the organization helps identify the cause of the problem, the coverage of the crisis is likely to be more balanced.

- **Fourth, demonstrate responsible management action.** Most essential to the planning phase is to move toward fixing the problem—in other words, take proper action. Some managers make the mistake of thinking that crises are solved through "technique" and "intuition." Hogwash. Cosmetics are never the solution. Much more important is acting to correct the issue that got you in the soup in the first place.

- **Fifth, create a consistent message.** Agree on an official spokesperson who can disseminate one voice for the organization. The more serious the crisis, the higher up the organizational ladder you go to identify the appropriate spokesperson. Most of all, be honest, and never, ever cover up or lie. That just exacerbates the crisis.[12]

For example, in 2008 when New York Giants star receiver Plaxico Burress accidentally shot himself in the thigh during late night carousing, he enlisted a doctor and New York-Presbyterian Hospital personnel to allow him to check in anonymously. Officials at New York-Presbyterian Hospital didn't hesitate to take action. They immediately announced the suspension of the doctor for violating hospital policy and procedures in not reporting a gunshot wound to authorities (see Figure 19-3). The hospital won great credit for its immediate action.[13] And Burress was sentenced to a year in jail.

Letting people know that the organization has a plan and is implementing it helps convince them that you are in control. Defining the issues means both having a clear sense internally of what the focus of action should be and communicating that action into the marketplace to reach key constituents.

Simple but appropriate watchwords for any crisis plan are the following:

- Be prepared.
- Be available.
- Be credible.
- Act appropriately.

FIGURE 19-3
Conveying the facts on Plax. In 2008, when New York Giant star receiver Plaxico Burress enlisted a doctor to help him cover up the fact he accidentally shot himself, New York-Presbyterian Hospital won credit for immediately suspending the personnel involved for "violating our policies and procedures in not reporting a gunshot wound." (Photo: Newscom)

Mini-Case   Ailing Apple CEO "Jobs" the Media

Remember how Apple Founder and CEO Steve Jobs recovered so beautifully in Chapter 3 (*PR Ethics Mini-Case*) from missteps in pricing the Apple iPhone? Well what a difference 16 chapters makes!

No question that Steve Jobs is a genius who saved Apple Computer. Jobs built the company into colossus status. Then he left, and the company faltered. Then he returned, and the company regained its luster.

Jobs' performance at the helm of Apple was legendary, as was his ego. As *Fortune* once put it, *"Steve Jobs is considered one of Silicon Valley's leading egomaniacs."*

As a consequence, Jobs was equally legendary for being secretive about his physical condition. After a bout with pancreatic cancer in 2004, Jobs and Apple steadfastly refused to update the public on his health.

Some, including Jobs, wondered why the CEO's health was anybody else's business. The answer was that Jobs worked for the owners of his company, that is, his shareholders, who were entitled by law to be apprised of "material" information that might affect their holdings.

The most "material" information at Apple concerned Steve Jobs' health.

In the summer of 2008, when rumors circulated on the Internet that Jobs was dying, the CEO conducted an "off-the-record" telephone interview with respected *New York Times* columnist Joe Nocera. In that call, Jobs denied his cancer had recurred and told Nocera what ailed him. Unfortunately, the substance of the malady was "off-the-record," so Nocera couldn't reveal it. Nocera did write that the Apple CEO concluded his call to the *Times* by labeling reporter Nocera as a "slime bucket." (Never a good idea with the media!)

In January of 2009, however, Jobs admitted to a "hormone imbalance" and then days later, Apple announced the problems were "more complex" and that the CEO was leaving the company (see Figure 19-4). Apple's stock sank, as the information about the CEO's health dripped out to the public.

To complicate matters, Apple made little attempt to publicize other executives. In fact, it wasn't until three months before its CEO's abrupt departure that *Fortune* speculated that Apple's little-known chief operating officer Tim Cook might one day replace Jobs.

Sure enough, as Steve Jobs suddenly vamoosed, he was replaced as acting CEO by Tim Cook.

FIGURE 19-4 The CEO and the governor. A rail-thin Apple CEO Steve Jobs is inducted into The California Hall of Fame by Governor Arnold Schwarzenegger in December 2008. A month later, Jobs left the company because of mysterious health problems, returning in 2009 after a liver transplant. (Photo: Newscom)

Questions

1. What do you think of Apple's policy not to reveal information about its CEO's health?

2. If you were Apple's public relations director, what would you have counseled Steve Jobs in terms of communicating about his health?

For further information, see Fraser P. Seitel, "Ailing Apple CEO 'Jobs' the Media," odwyerpr.com (January 22, 2009).

Communicating in a Crisis

The key communications principle in dealing with a crisis is not to clam up when disaster strikes. Lawyers traditionally have advised clients to either (1) say nothing; (2) say as little as possible and release it as quietly as possible; (3) say as little as possible, citing privacy laws, company policy, or sensitivity; (4) deny guilt and act indignant that such charges could possibly have been made; or (5) shift or, if necessary, share the blame with others. A lawyer, correctly, is focused on defense in a court of law.

Public relations advice, on the other hand, is concerned about a different court—the court of public opinion—and therefore takes a different tack.

The most effective crisis communicators are those who provide prompt, frank, and full information to the media in the eye of the storm. Invariably, the first inclination of executives is to say, "Let's wait until all the facts are in." But as President Carter's press secretary, Jody Powell, used to say, *"Bad news is a lot like fish. It doesn't get better with age."*

In saying nothing, an organization is perceived as already having made a decision. Indeed, research sponsored by public relations agency Porter Novelli suggests that when most people—upwards of 65 percent—hear the words "no comment," they perceive the no-commenter as guilty. Silence angers the media and compounds the problem. On the other hand, inexperienced spokespersons, speculating nervously or using emotionally charged language, are even worse.

Most public relations professionals consider the cardinal rule for communications during a crisis to be *Tell it all and tell it fast!*

As a general rule, when information gets out quickly, rumors are stopped and nerves are calmed. There is nothing complicated about the goals of crisis management. They are (1) terminate the crisis quickly, (2) limit the damage, and (3) restore credibility. If this requires taking quick, remedial action, then that's what should be done.

The quickest way to end the agony and begin to build back credibility is to fix the action and communicate through the media.

Engaging the Media

Handling the media is the most critical element in crisis. Normally, treating the press as friendly adversaries makes great sense. But when crisis strikes, media attention quickly turns to "feeding frenzy." So dealing with the media in crisis demands certain "battlefield rules," among them:

- **Set up media headquarters.** In a crisis, the media will seek out the organizational soft spots where the firm is most vulnerable to being penetrated. To try to prevent this, organizations in crisis must immediately establish a media headquarters through which all authorized communication must flow.

- **Establish media rules.** In a crisis, the media are sneaky. Their goal is to unearth any salient or salacious element that will advance the story line of the crisis. In this respect, they are operating very much at cross-purposes with the organization, which is desperately trying to put the crisis behind it.

It is imperative, therefore, that the organization in the crucible set firm rules—which parts of the operation are off limits, which executives won't be available, and so on—for the media to follow.

■ **Media live for the "box score."** Crisis specifics make news—the grislier, the better.

- How many were fired?
- How many were displaced?
- What was the cost of the damage?
- How much was extorted?
- How many perished?

Stated another way, crisis is about numbers. And an organization in crisis must be ready to provide enough numbers to keep the media at bay.

■ **Don't speculate.** If you don't know the numbers or the reasons or the extent of the damage, don't pretend you do. Speculation is suicidal in crisis.

■ **Feed the beast.** The media in crisis are insatiable. Blogs, cable news, and wire services all must be fed 24/7. In the 21st century, with faux journalists blogging and tweeting round the clock, the media never sleep. "Nature abhors a vacuum," goes the old saying. And in crisis, any vacuum will be filled by your enemies.

So a smart organization in crisis will strive to keep the media occupied—even distracted—with new information that advances the story.

■ **Speed triumphs.** In crisis, the media mantra is speed first, accuracy second. This sad but true fact holds major implications for public relations people, who must monitor what is being wrongly reported so that it can be nipped quickly before others run with the same misinformation.

■ **Cable rules.** Cable television is a 21st-century phenomenon—CNN, MSNBC, Fox News Channel, CNBC, Fox Business, Bloomberg, and others. They compete vigorously with each other all the time—one of the last bastions of American reportorial competition. Which is good. What's not so good is that in a crisis, cable ratings spike, and the drumbeat of incessant hammering is relentless.

Once a crisis "victim" gets caught in the cable or talk radio spotlight, it is close to impossible to be extricated. Round the clock the skewering continues, on talk show after talk show, "expert" after "expert." So cable television, like talk radio, like the Internet, must be monitored scrupulously in crisis.[14]

As to what is said to the media, the following 10 general principles apply:

1. Speak first and often.
2. Don't speculate.
3. Go off the record at your own peril.
4. Stay with the facts.
5. Be open and concerned, not defensive.
6. Make your point and repeat it.
7. Don't wage war with the media.
8. Establish yourself as the most authoritative source.
9. Stay calm and be truthful and cooperative.
10. Never lie.

Talking Points When "No Comment" and "Comment" Are Equally Catastrophic

Normally, public relations crisis counselors advise avoiding "no comment" at all costs. White House press secretaries, working for administrations generally disdainful of the media's prying eyes, constantly have to parry reporters' questions with the dreaded phrase.

President George W. Bush's press secretary, Scott McClellan, for example, had to invoke the phrase repeatedly in the summer of 2005 when White House senior advisor Karl Rove was alleged to have identified Valerie Plame, the wife of an administration critic, as an undercover CIA officer.

McClellan's denials recalled the days of President Clinton's press secretary, Mike McCurry, who had to invoke a similar Kabuki-dancing strategy when his boss got mixed up with a White House intern and went public to adamantly deny the liaison (see Figure 19-5).

On the other hand, sometimes a comment is even worse than "no comment." This turned out to be the case in early 2006, when 12 miners were caught in a West Virginia mine explosion. After 41 hours underground, the miners, according to a statement by the mine's owner, were "found alive." The media communicated the news, and the nation rejoiced.

A day later, the earlier report was found to be mistaken—wishful thinking based on misunderstood communications. The CEO of the mine company apologized immediately and profusely, but the damage perpetrated by the false report had been done.

FIGURE 19-5 "I did not have sex with that woman." Well, I sorta' did. (Photo: Newscom)

Last Word

Although prevention remains the best insurance for any organization, crisis management has become one of the most revered skills in the practice of public relations. Organizations of every variety are faced, sooner or later, with a crisis. The issues that confront society—from energy and the environment, to health and nutrition, to corporate accountability and minority rights—will not soon abate.

The Internet, of course, with blogs and tweets and wikis banging about at all times, has added a new dimension of complexity to communicating in crisis. Nonetheless, research indicates that in time of crisis, consumers still turn to traditional media. Half of those polled turn to network television in times of crisis, followed by 42 percent, radio;

37 percent, newspapers; 33 percent, cable networks; and 25 percent, the Internet.[15]

All of this suggests that experienced and knowledgeable crisis managers who can skillfully navigate and effectively communicate, turning crisis into opportunity, will be valuable resources for organizations in the 21st century.

In the final analysis, communicating in a crisis depends on a rigorous analysis of the risks versus the benefits of going public. Communicating effectively also depends on the judgment and experience of the public relations professional. Every call is a close one, and there is no guarantee that the organization will benefit, no matter what course is chosen. One thing is clear: Helping to navigate the organization through the shoals of a crisis is the ultimate test of a

FIGURE 19-6
Posthumous crisis reassessment. When crisis-ridden entertainer Michael Jackson died in 2009, an emotional statement by his daughter, Paris, at Jackson's memorial service caused many of the millions viewing around the world to reassess their view of the young girl's father. Two weeks after his death, Jackson's solo albums sold 1.1 million copies, and 1.9 million Jackson songs were sold as digital downloads. (Photo: Newscom)

public relations professional. And crisis managers are very much in demand. Indeed, that's why, in April 2006, Wal-Mart cast its employment net to fill two critical public relations positions —one to handle "opposition research" and the other to "mobilize resources during crisis situations."[16]

In the years ahead, as the world continues to present new and more complex challenges, crisis management promises to be a *growth* area in the *growth* profession that is the practice of public relations (see Figure 19-6).

Discussion Starters

1. What is meant by the term *issues management?*
2. How can an organization influence the development of an issue in society?
3. What is meant by "message mapping"?
4. What is meant by the term *risk communications*?
5. What are the usual stages that an organization experiences in a crisis?
6. What are the principles in planning for crisis?
7. What are important rules in dealing with the media in crisis?
8. What is the cardinal rule for communicating in a crisis?
9. What are the keys to successful crisis communication?
10. What are likely to be the flashpoint crisis issues in the new century?

Top of the Shelf   Crisis Communication / Peter Anthonissen, London, England: Kogan Page, 2008

This book was written by members of the IPREX group of 64 worldwide, independent public relations agencies and offers a novel take on crisis communications in the 21st century.

The authors argue that the Internet has changed crisis communications to one of necessitating a "conversation" between publics and organization. Today's bloggers "are the new investigative reporters," it adds, saying "companies don't fear the camera crew at the front gate as much as a blogger posting insider information, a whistle-blower's allegations, non-attributed accusations, or the unleashing of unsubstantiated rumors." Consequently, advice is offered on properly dealing in crisis with blogs, podcasts, video, and RSS feeds.

Some may argue with the premise of the authors, but the book offers a clear 21st-century take on dealing with crisis.

Case Study JetBlue's Valentine's Day Massacre

More than any other business group, airlines must constantly be ready for crisis. Emergency landings, hijackings, and, most dreaded of all, crashes must constantly be considered by airline management and public relations personnel.

But little in the crisis manual could have prepared JetBlue Airways for what befell it one fateful Valentine's Day, February 14, 2007.

All Queued Up and No Place to Go

Since its founding in 2000 by airline veteran David Neeleman, JetBlue had distinguished itself as a unique, customer-friendly airline. Operating out of New York's JFK International Airport, JetBlue was a little airline that offered low-cost fares, TV at every seat, and satellite radio for all passengers. CEO Neeleman said that JetBlue's aim was "to bring humanity back to air travel."

And for most of the decade, that's precisely the reputation that JetBlue earned—right up until Valentine's Day, 2007.

On February 14, 2007, a vicious ice storm battered the northeast, much to the surprise of weather forecasters, who incorrectly predicted that the storm would be of the "passing" variety. It wasn't. And airline companies like JetBlue were literally caught with their flaps down.

At JFK, nothing seemed amiss when passengers boarded planes beginning at 8 a.m., most to head south for the warming sun of Florida. Nine flights, in all, boarded and left the gate, and queued up on the runway for de-icing and planned departure around 11 a.m. Meanwhile, planes were arriving at the busy airport from all over the world. This created a congestion problem at all gates.

As a consequence, when the ice storm intensified, passengers on the nine JetBlue queued-up planes were left stranded on the runway for six+ hours, with no way out.

Soldiering On . . . and On . . . and On . . .

With flights backed up at its New York hub, JetBlue officials had to make a decision: Did they cancel all flights connected to the New York delays or, conversely, did they soldier on, keep flights scheduled, and hope the New York mess would be reconciled sooner rather than later?

Alas, JetBlue chose to soldier on. And this proved to be a colossal error.

As JetBlue's Director of Corporate Communications Todd Burke, whose department handled the crisis on its own without outside assistance, put it, *"We were operating with a small-airline mentality. . . . We try to keep it feeling like a cute, little, hometown sort of airline. Well, our internal systems weren't prepared to deal with that kind of an issue."*

In other words, with all the delays and lack of clarity, JetBlue traffic schedulers didn't know where their pilots and flight attendants were. When they eventually found them, most had already worked their government-allotted hours and weren't permitted to serve further immediate duty.

What to do?

Over the next six days, JetBlue had no choice but to belatedly cancel 1,700 flights, inconveniencing passengers and creating a media firestorm.

YouTube Mea Maxima Culpa

The resultant media onslaught was as vicious as it was predictable.

- "JetBlue's Cancellation Blues"
- "JetBlue's Corporate Meltdown"
- "Chief 'Mortified' by JetBlue Crisis"

A blogger jumped in with jetbluehostage.com, to chronicle the experiences of miffed JetBlue customers. Even JetBlue employees couldn't immediately "fix" the crisis.

One thing JetBlue did do—too slowly perhaps for some, but soon enough—was communicate. Over the next week, the company issued seven news releases, updating the status of the airline. The public relations department fielded more than 5,000 media calls.

Meanwhile, CEO Neeleman conducted more than 20 broadcast interviews, apologizing in every one for "letting our customers down." The CEO's most memorable appearance was a YouTube video—suggested by a 25-year-old employee—in which a shirt-sleeved chairman looked directly into the camera and painfully described, in unscripted manner, "the most difficult time" in JetBlue's history. After outlining the steps JetBlue was taking to remedy the situation, CEO Neeleman promised his customers, *"The events that transpired over the past seven days will never happen again."*

The YouTube video was seen by millions and picked up by worldwide media, many of them sympathetic to CEO Neeleman's predicament and response.

Transparency Shall Set You Free

As JetBlue tried to return to normal, it picked up its communications offensive.

- JetBlue's public relations department made itself constantly available for all media inquiries. It sought full transparency, providing media with up-to-the-minute information.

FIGURE 19-7 **JetBlue apology.** JetBlue published this apology in full-page newspaper ads and included the signed letter from its CEO on the JetBlue Web site. (Courtesy of JetBlue)

- The company ran full-page ads addressed to JetBlue customers that began, *"We are sorry and embarrassed. But most of all, we are deeply sorry . . . "* (see Figure 19-7).
- JetBlue announced a "Customer Bill of Rights," which listed specific procedures to be followed during delays and compensation for effected customers (see Figure 19-8, next page).
- Public relations officials met with online pundits and influential bloggers, including Mr. jetbluehostage.com, to build better relationships.

The positive communications seemed to pay off, as positive stories began to appear, such as the one in *Aero News* about "How JetBlue Shook Off PR Crisis."

Ironically, a year after the Valentine's Day crisis, when a man sued JetBlue for allegedly making him give up his seat to a flight attendant and then forcing him to fly on the toilet for three hours—the airline quietly began to search for a crisis communications agency.

Questions

1. What do you think of JetBlue's response to its crisis?
2. What else could the airline have done on February 14?
3. How would you characterize the airline's positioning of its CEO?
4. What is the added JetBlue public relations challenge going forward?

JetBlue Airways' Customer Bill of Rights

Above all else, JetBlue Airways is dedicated to bringing humanity back to air travel. We strive to make every part of your experience as simple and as pleasant as possible. Unfortunately, there are times when things do not go as planned. If you're inconvenienced as a result, we think it is important that you know exactly what you can expect from us. That's why we created our Customer Bill of Rights. These Rights will always be subject to the highest level of safety and security for our customers and crewmembers.

INFORMATION
JetBlue will notify customers of the following:
- Delays prior to scheduled departure
- Cancellations and their cause
- Diversions and their cause

CANCELLATIONS
All customers whose flight is cancelled by JetBlue will, at the customer's option, receive a full refund or reaccommodation on the next available JetBlue flight at no additional charge or fare. If JetBlue cancels a flight within 4 hours of scheduled departure and the cancellation is due to a Controllable Irregularity, JetBlue will also issue the customer a $50 Voucher good for future travel on JetBlue.

DELAYS (Departure Delays or Onboard Ground Delays on Departure)
For customers whose flight is delayed 3 hours or more after scheduled departure, JetBlue will provide free movies on flights that are 2 hours or longer.

DEPARTURE DELAYS
1. Customers whose flight is delayed for 1-1:59 hours after scheduled departure time due to a *Controllable Irregularity* are entitled to a $25 Voucher good for future travel on JetBlue.
2. Customers whose flight is delayed for 2-4:59 hours after scheduled departure time due to a *Controllable Irregularity* are entitled to a $50 Voucher good for future travel on JetBlue.
3. Customers whose flight is delayed for 5-5:59 hours after scheduled departure time due to a *Controllable Irregularity* are entitled to a Voucher good for future travel on JetBlue in the amount paid by the customer for the oneway trip (or $50, whichever is greater).
4. Customers whose flight is delayed for 6 or more hours after scheduled departure time due to a *Controllable Irregularity* are entitled to a Voucher good for future travel on JetBlue in the amount paid by the customer for the roundtrip (or the oneway trip, doubled).

OVERBOOKINGS (As defined in JetBlue's Contract of Carriage)
Customers who are involuntarily denied boarding shall receive $1,000.

LAST UPDATED: 7/2008

ONBOARD GROUND DELAYS
JetBlue will provide customers experiencing an Onboard Ground Delay with 36 channels of DIRECTV®*, food and drink, access to clean restrooms and, as necessary, medical treatment. For customers who experience an Onboard Ground Delay for more than 5 hours, JetBlue will also take necessary action so that customers may deplane.

Arrivals:
1. Customers who experience an Onboard Ground Delay on Arrival for 1-1:59 hours after scheduled arrival time are entitled to a $50 Voucher good for future travel on JetBlue.
2. Customers who experience an Onboard Ground Delay on Arrival for 2 hours or more after scheduled arrival time are entitled to a Voucher good for future travel on JetBlue in the amount paid by the customer for the roundtrip (or the oneway trip, doubled).

Departures:
1. Customers who experience an Onboard Ground Delay on Departure after scheduled departure time for 3-3:59 hours are entitled to a $50 Voucher good for future travel on JetBlue.
2. Customers who experience an Onboard Ground Delay on Departure after scheduled departure time for 4-4:59 hours are entitled to a Voucher good for future travel on JetBlue in the amount paid by the customer for the oneway trip (or $50, whichever is greater).
3. Customers who experience an Onboard Ground Delay on Departure for 5 hours or more after scheduled arrival time are entitled to a Voucher good for future travel on JetBlue in the amount paid by the customer for the roundtrip (or the oneway trip, doubled).

In-flight entertainment:
JetBlue offers 36 channels of DIRECTV® service on its flights in the Continental U.S. If our LiveTV™ system is inoperable on flights in the Continental U.S., customers are entitled to a $15 Voucher good for future travel on JetBlue.

JetBlue Airways
118-29 Queens Blvd
Forest Hills, NY 11375

These Rights are subject to JetBlue's Contract of Carriage and, as applicable, the operational control of the flight crew, and apply to only JetBlue-operated flights.
*Available only on flights in the Continental U.S.

This document is representative of what is reflected in JetBlue's Contract of Carriage, the legally binding document between JetBlue and its customers, and its terms are incorporated herein.

For further information, see Kevin J. Allen, "JetBlue Managed Crisis from Inside Out," ragan.com (October 24, 2007); Todd Burke, "JetBlue's Social Media Success: YouTube Meets Crisis Communications," Ragan Communications Social Media Conference (September 28, 2007); Michael Bush, "JetBlue Seeks PR Shop to Help It Out of Toilet," AdAge.com (May 19, 2008); David Lazarus, "JetBlue Response Praised," *San Francisco Chronicle* (February 25, 2007); "Jet Blue: A Valentine's Day Hostage Crisis," jetbluehostage.com (August 7, 2007); and "JetBlue Bids to Recover from Snow Cancellations," National Public Radio Morning Edition (February 20, 2007).

the Top   An Interview with John Stauber

John Stauber is every public relations person's worst crisis. Mr. Stauber, who stepped down in 2009 after 16 years as executive director of the Center for Media and Democracy and the publisher of PRWatch.org., has made it his life's work to scrutinize the public relations business. Together with Sheldon Rampton, he authored *Toxic Sludge Is Good for You!, Mad Cow U.S.A.*, and *Trust Us, We're Experts!* Mr. Stauber is as "outspoken" a critic of the public relations industry as there is (as you will detect from his answers to the following questions). But despite that, he's a real good guy. So read on—if you've got the guts.

How would you describe the practice of public relations?
In a single word, and quoting the father of "spin" Edward Bernays, public relations is propaganda. PR is a multi-billion dollar business conducted by professionals trained in communications and politics and employed primarily by businesses and governments to strategically manage public perceptions, opinions, information, and policy.

How is public relations looked at by journalists?
Most media professionals seem to flatter and fool themselves that they are immune to PR manipulations, while using public relations professionals to further their journalistic goals.

How much influence does public relations exert on the media?
PR professionals have tremendous influence with the media although media professionals generally fail to admit or recognize this fact. Of course, it is in the interest of PR professionals to also downplay their influence with the media to preserve the public myths of vetted journalism and courageous, independent news reporting. Academic studies attempting to measure how much of the news results from PR have typically found that 40 percent or more of what is read, seen, and heard in mainstream media is the result of, or heavily influenced by, public relations. For example, most Americans get most of their news from television, yet every year thousands of Video News Releases (VNRs) are aired by TV news producers as if they were their own independent reporting, constituting the largest ongoing plagiarism scandal in U.S. history.

What is the proper relationship between a reporter and a public relations professional?
From the standpoint of the reporter, the relationship must be viewed as adversarial, although of course the PR professional generally strives to position him or herself as a helpful facilitator or gatekeeper for the reporter.

Were you a reporter, how would you approach your dealings with public relations professionals?
I *am* a reporter and I view my relationship with any PR professional as adversarial.

Do you think public relations professionals serve any purpose?
PR professionals make life much easier for lazy and compliant journalists, and they generally strive to protect their clients in government and business from scrutiny, criticism, and reform.

If you could "fix" the practice of public relations, what steps would you take?
Propaganda will always exist within a democracy, but it's a nemesis. I strive to fix and strengthen news reporting by educating and informing journalists, researchers, citizens, and policy-makers about the realities of PR and propaganda. PR works best when it is an invisible manipulator of public perceptions; my job is to spray paint that Invisible Man with a bright safety orange. Democracies function best without hidden persuaders.

Public Relations Library

Barton, Laurance. *Crisis Leadership Now*. New York, NY: McGraw-Hill, 2008. This book is written from the perspective of averting corporate disasters, from threats to sabotage to scandal.

Boin, Arjen, Paul t'Hart, Eric Stern, and Bengt Sundelius. *The Politics of Crisis Management*. Cambridge, England: Cambridge University Press, 2006. This is a treatise on major government crises, including 9/11 and the anthrax scare in the United States.

Coombs, W. Timothy. *Ongoing Crisis Communication*, 2nd ed. Thousand Oaks, CA: Sage Publications, 2007. This is a well-researched explanation, complemented by real-life case studies.

Devlin, Eric S. *Crisis Management Planning and Execution*. Boca Raton, FL: Auerbach Publications, 2007. This is a good compilation of case studies, emphasizing the planning aspects that go into crisis management.

Dezenhall, Eric, and John Weber. *Damage Control*. New York, NY: Penguin Group, 2007. The authors contend that "everything you learned about crisis communication is wrong." (Not quite.)

Fearn-Banks, Kathleen. *Crisis Communications: A Casebook Approach*, 2nd ed. Mahwah, NJ: Lawrence Erlbaum Associates, 2002. Recommends a plan for preventing and dealing with crises based on communication theories.

Friedman, Mark L. *Everyday Crisis Management*. Naperville, IL: First Decision Press, 2002. This book teaches thinking strategically, acting quickly, and responding decisively. (Sounds like the right approach.)

Gilpin, Dawn R., and Priscilla J. Murphy. *Crisis Management in a Complex World*. New York, NY: Oxford University Press, 2008. This book does a good job of tracing the roots and progression of crises, including the long, sad saga of Enron.

Giuliani, Rudolph W. *Leadership*. New York: Hyperion, 2002. Lessons from the man who took charge immediately of the greatest crisis contemporary America has known, the attacks of 9/11.

Glaesser, Dirk. *Crisis Management in the Tourism Industry*. Burlington, MA: Butterworth-Heinemann, 2003. With people falling overboard and other crises popping up in the tourism industry, this book is particularly timely.

Henry, Rene. *Communicating in Crisis*. Gollywobbler Productions, 2008. Leaning on his 40 years of experience in industry, sports, education, and government, the author warns, "Lawyers make little money preventing crisis and a lot resolving them."

Levick, Richard, and Larry Smith. *Stop the Presses,* 2nd ed. Ann Arbor, MI: Watershed Press, 2008. The authors contend that one important change in 21st-century crisis communication is the "sea change in Internet communications that now ties the world's most powerful corporations to the humblest public interest groups in an unholy dance of 'gotcha' and 'gotcha back.'"

Lewis, Gerald. *Organizational Crisis Management*. Boca Raton, FL: Auerbach Publications, 2006. This book focuses on crises involving personnel, premises, and the like, all affecting reputation.

Martin, Dick. *Tough Calls*. New York, NY: AMACOM, 2005. A former communications director of AT&T presents a riveting account of what led to that great firm's destruction as an independent company.

McCusker, Gerry. *Tailspin*. Sterling, VA: Kogan Page, 2005. This book covers some of the biggest public relations disasters in recent years, from 9/11 to Martha Stewart.

Mickey, Thomas J. *Public Relations Criticism*. Mahwah, NJ: Lawrence Erlbaum Associates, 2002.

O'Dwyer, Jack (Ed.). *Jack O'Dwyer's Newsletter* (271 Madison Ave., New York, NY 10016).

Rampton, Sheldon, and John Stauber. *The Best War Ever*. New York, NY: Penguin Press, 2006. Two industry critics offer a thorough trashing of the War on Terror, the Bush administration, and the entire public relations industry. (Look out below!)

Regester, Michael, and Judy Larkin. *Risk Issues and Crisis Management*, 3rd ed. London, UK: Michael Regester and Judy Larkin, 2005. Interesting dissertation on issues management and managing risk.

Smith, Denis, and Dominic Elliot. *Key Readings in Crisis Management*. New York, NY: Routledge, 2006. A series of essays on major international crises and how they were handled.

Ulmer, Robert Ray, Timothy L. Sellnow, and Matthew Wayne Seeger. *Effective Crisis Communication*. Thousand Oaks, CA: Sage Publications, 2007. This provides a good explanation of steps in crisis management, illustrated by famous cases.

Zdziarski, Eugene L., Norbert W. Dunkel, and J. Michael Rollo. *Campus Crisis Management*. San Francisco, CA: Jossey-Bass, 2007. This provides background on university crises, beginning with the University of Texas tower shootings in 1966 to the present.

Chapter 20

Launching a Career

In the old days, you got a job in public relations by "networking."

In the new days, you get a job in public relations by "networking" in social media.

At least that's how young David Murray found communications work in 2009.

- First, he reached out to followers on his Twitter account that he was officially "looking for work." He immediately received several prime leads.

- Second, he augmented these by entering keywords in Twitter Search, like "Hiring Social Media," "Online Community Manager," and "Blogging Jobs."

- Third, he pulled RSS feeds of his keyword conversations into Google Reader and checked his incoming mail every morning.

- Fourth, he followed up on promising leads by introducing himself via Twitter, inquiring about job leads, some of which hadn't been officially posted.

And before he knew it, voilà, he had landed a Web-based communications post at a Web site design firm.[1]

As Heather Huhman, author of the Entry Level Career pages for Examiner.com, put it, *"The Internet is changing just about everything—the internship/entry-level job search included. Gone are the days of printing out your cover letter and résumé on 'special' paper, sticking both in an envelope, and mailing the application package off. We are officially in the Job Search 2.0 era"* (see Figure 20-1).

FIGURE 20-1 PR career coach. Heather Huhman at http://heatherhuhman.com/?p=120, Generation Y author/columnist/mentor and social media expert, among other things, counsels public relations students and recent graduates about "breaking into" the practice of public relations. (Courtesy of Heather Huhman)

Finding a job in the practice of public relations—especially in times of economic downturn—is probably the most formidable task that an entry-level communicator faces. Once inside an organization, competence rises to the top. So if you're competent, you've got it made. But how do you get "through the door" in the first place? The challenge—the one we'll focus on in this final chapter—is "launching a career."

Public Relations in Economic Downturn

Traditionally, public relations jobs were the first to fall when economic times got rough. Not so much anymore.

Smart organizations today understand the critical importance of communications that are honest, candid, and transparent. CEOs, who by nature are tight-lipped, need only consider the carcasses of once-great companies laid to waste by arrogant or happy-talking leaders, who, in recent years, refused to level with the public about the state of their corporations.

- **American International Group (AIG)** was the world's largest insurance company, run by autocratic Hank Greenberg. When he was ousted in an accounting scandal, his successor as CEO, silent Martin Sullivan, flopped and was replaced by equally silent and ineffective Robert Willumstad. Today, the once mighty AIG company has become a ward of the U.S. taxpayers.

- **Washington Mutual (WaMu)** was the nation's largest savings and loan association, a high-flying stock market favorite, run by perpetually-selling CEO Kerry Killinger. WaMu, too, turned out not to be leveling with the facts. After Killinger was canned in 2008, the bank was seized by the U.S. government.

- **Countrywide Financial,** the nation's leading subprime mortgage lender, was founded by sharp-talking, sharp-dressing Angelo R. Mozilo, a fixture on CNBC and in the media. Again, Mr. Mozilo's confidence belied the fact that his company had made losing loans. When the firm's stock sank and the company was sold to Bank of America in 2008, its wealthy founder slunk away, having been named by CNN as one of its "10 Most Wanted Culprits of the 2008 U.S. Financial Collapse."[2] Sure enough, in 2009 the SEC charged Mozilo with insider trading and securities fraud.

- **Bear Stearns** and **Lehman Brothers** were two of the nation's most powerful investment banks, both run by CEOs who spurned revealing anything to the public. At Bear Stearns, CEO Alan Schwartz and his predecessor James Cayne did little publicly to stop the dismantling of their once-great firm. At Lehman, CEO Richard Fuld fumed and fulminated, all the way to the firm's bankruptcy in 2008 (see Figure 20-2).

The disastrous outcomes of these men and their firms helped remind remaining CEOs that "silence" is not "golden," nor is "happy talk," when it comes to public companies. The public, as Ivy Lee said 100 years ago, "must be informed."

FIGURE 20-2
Shame. Richard Fuld, CEO of bankrupt investment bank Lehman Brothers, was serenaded by protestors when he appeared before Congress in 2008, as a symbol of greed and arrogance in corporate board rooms. (Photo: Newscom)

As a consequence, the impact on the public relations industry of the economic downturn that afflicted the United States and the world at the end of the 21st-century's first decade was rather muted. A study of nearly 200 organizations by the University of Southern California indicated that public relations and communications functions of U.S. companies suffered only moderate decreases as the recession wore on. Instead of cutting staffs, as had been done in previous downturns, most companies opted to freeze or reduce staff compensation, rather than cutting headcount.[3]

While the practice of public relations isn't immune from cuts in bad times, it is no longer "the first to go." Most important, organizations today understand that especially in bad times, candid communications is a necessity.

Organizing the Job Search

Organizing a job search, in good times or bad, requires just that—"organization."

Just as in any assignment, public relations job seekers should follow a predetermined path to get them through the door to meet a person with a potential job offer. Again, it's getting *through* the door that's the problem.

As public relations practice has become more enticing to communications students, lawyers, journalists, and others, positions in the field have become more competitive.

As public relations salaries have increased, many public relations–focused executive search firms, which once helped entry-level practitioners find their way, today only entertain experienced professionals.

So what's an entry-level, fresh-eyed graduate to do as he or she commences the post-commencement job search?

According to experienced public relations executive and teacher Martin Arnold, the following ought to be considered:

- **First, consider what interests you, and start early.**
  Determine where, if you had your druthers, you would like to work. In sports? Fashion? Government? Big business? With a grassroots nonprofit? Where?

  The fact is that, today, everybody from mammoth corporations to do-good associations to the Pope have public relations people. So job seekers should investigate possibilities in their keenest areas of interest, determining key organizations—and the agencies that serve them.

  Also, build a database from Day 1 of neighbors, classmates, friends, family, workmates, bosses, just about everyone you know. Most jobs are gained through referrals.

- **Second, get a name.**
  Avoid writing blind to potential employers. Emails and letters that carry no addressee beyond the organization itself are destined never to be answered.

  To avoid the "dead letter response," network with colleagues to see if an associate might suggest a name at a target organization. Failing that, consult directories to discover the names of public relations professionals on staff. Failing that, call the organization directly and secure the name of the public relations director.

  Once you've got a real live (let's hope!) individual, you are ready to . . .

- **Third, dispatch a personal letter.**
  Write directly to the contact, requesting an interview. Explain in the note who you are, your rationale for choosing this organization as a target, and why

you're interested in speaking with the addressee. Make clear in the note that while "it would be great if your company had availabilities, securing a job at Oshkosh B'Gosh is less important to me than getting a chance to pick your brain."

In other words, don't make the interview contingent on job openings at the company in question. Even if no job is currently available—and most of the time that's the case—you still want to get through the door.

Tell the addressee you plan to call him/her in a week or so.

■ **Fourth, call.**
The sad truth is that few job applicants ever do.

They say in their letters they "plan to call," but rarely raise the gumption to follow through. Perhaps they fear rejection.

Pity.

While it's true that some potential employers—the nasty ones—refuse to be "bothered" by job seekers, most potential public relations employers are nicer than that. Some, in fact—the enlightened ones—will even allow you 30 minutes to come in and discuss opportunities.

The sadder truth is that few job applicants ever do.

■ **Fifth, prepare an elevator speech.**
Be prepared with a 30-second talk on who you are, what you are doing, and what you are trying to achieve. Memorize it and use it whenever you can. Most people will help if they know what you want.

The real point is that you'll never get a job without an interview, and you'll never get an interview without a call. So like it or not, following up letters with a call is obligatory for job seekers.[4]

Talking Points   Online Public Relations Job References

The Internet offers an expanding list of reference sites that access "public relations openings." Among them:

■ **Bulldog Reporter PR Job Mart**
Bulldog's PR Job Mart is an active, updated source for agency and corporate jobs at various levels. As with other free public relations sites, Bulldog's non-agency roster is flooded with hospitals, academic institutions, and nonprofits looking for public relations help. Bulldog also provides email updates of job openings each week to its subscriber list. (http://bulldogreporter.com/ME2/dirmod.asp)

■ **International Association of Business Communicators (IABC)**
The IABC's site lists 240 or so primarily internal communications openings at corporations and nonprofits. With its significant presence in Canada, IABC boasts the added advantage of listing Canadian job openings. (http://jobs.iabc.com/home/index.cfm?site_id=65)

■ **Media Bistro**
This site lists all manner of media jobs, from online and newspaper editors to broadcast journalists. It also includes a healthy sampling of public relations posts. (http://www.mediabistro.com/joblistings/)

■ **Monster**
Every day, approximately 20–50 "new" public relations positions are listed. Many are of the promotional/marketing cold call variety, but others are at legitimate public relations firms. Monster.com is a good source for "public relations" positions that often don't appear elsewhere. (http://jobsearch.monster.com/Browse.aspx)

■ **O'Dwyer**
Among its 70 or so availabilities, the inestimable Odwyerpr.com site generally lists higher level openings at firms, nonprofits, and companies. In addition to the high-level posts, O'Dwyer also lists a number of "intern" availabilities. (http://jobs.odwyerpr.com/home/index.cfm?site_id=258)

■ **PRNewsOnline**
PR News offers another excellent online source for corporate, nonprofit, and agency public relations positions. As with other sites, PR News offers a service for job seekers to post resumes for employers to peruse. (http://www.prnewsonline.com/resources/pr_jobs.html)

■ **PRSA Job Center**
The Public Relations Society of America site lists 1,700 job openings, many from agency members from around the nation. In addition, individual PRSA

chapters, like Cleveland and Houston, keep their own local job openings updated on a regular basis. (http://www.prsa.org/jobcenter/)

■ **PR Talent**
This service, begun by several public relations professionals, says that it "operates much like an entertainment talent agency, except that we identify and represent top full-time and freelance public relations and communications talent." (http://www.prtalent.com/jobSearch.aspx)

■ **Public Affairs Council**
The Public Affairs Council in Washington lists primarily lobbying, government relations, and government agency job openings, not only in the nation's capital but throughout the nation. (http://pac.org/jobs)

■ **Ragan Communications Career Center**
Ragan.com's 250 or so offerings span the gamut from internal to external positions, including public

relations posts at government agencies, such as the U.S. Coast Guard and the IRS. (http://www.ragan.com/jobadvice/)

■ **The Fry Group**
The Fry Group is a public relations executive search firm that lists some of its job searches on the Internet, where interested talent may inquire. Other search firms offer similar job quests in progress. (http://www.frygroup.com/listings.php)

Many of the job opening postings on these sites are redundant from one site to the next. Some are recurring month-to-month adverts designed to troll the waters to see what turns up. Still others are little more than low-level sales come-ons, looking for warm bodies.

Whatever.

All these site are worth a look from prospective public relations job seekers.

Remember, it only takes one.

Organizing the Job Interview

Once an applicant is fortunate enough to land an interview, he or she must understand that nine times out of 10, it is their responsibility to control the meeting agenda.

Stated another way, what one often finds once one is permitted entrée to the inner sanctum is that often people in public relations—just like people in many other pursuits—are less interested in you than you are, particularly if there are no specific openings at their firm, so they don't have much to say. You, therefore, must be the aggressor at the interview, asking them for information about availabilities and plans at their organization, advice, leads, contacts, colleagues at competitors with whom you might speak, etc.

This meeting is your chance—often your *only* chance—to find out the information you need about other firms and other individuals to keep your search progressing.

So walk in with a game plan and the "script" that will keep the interview going.

■ **First, take charge.**
To take your best shot, you have to—in a nice and subtle way—take charge of the interview.

So lead. Don't wait to be asked. Raise questions about the organization and the interviewer.
- How long have you been here?
- What's been the reaction to the acquisition?
- How has the change affected your job?

Demonstrate your interest in the organization and a job by taking charge of the interview.

■ **Second, lead with your knowledge and strength.**
Suggest through your questions and answers that you've done your homework on the organization. Show the interviewer that you've gone the extra mile by researching the firm and becoming knowledgeable about it.

Work into the conversation the fact that you've had experience in a variety of public relations capacities, that you enjoy writing and consider yourself a proficient scribe, and that you enjoy your work.

If you fail to leave these points with the interviewer—just because he or she never asks—you'll have left little impression that you deserve further consideration.

■ **Third, indicate what you'll add to the mix.**
Take the opportunity to allude to what that college training has afforded you, particularly in enhancing the expertise and scope of the department you'd love to join.

For example, all those social media tools that you took for granted in school—Facebook, MySpace, Twitter, Flickr, blogs, and all the rest—may reveal potential new avenues for an interviewer. Your facility with such social media may, therefore, suggest attractive possibilities to the interviewer.

Also, smile. As Professor Martin Arnold observes, "First and foremost people want to work with people they like."

■ **Fourth, get more names.**
This is your most important task at the interview.

Often, the interviewer is seeing you as a courtesy to a colleague. She or he doesn't mind talking, but there are no openings at the firm. No matter.

Use the interviewer to provide more names—advice, leads, contacts, colleagues at competitors with whom you might speak, etc. Don't walk out the door unless you have been given two or three other people you can call to continue the job search.

Eventually, one of them will hit.

■ **Fifth, follow up.**
Don't walk out the door with a "sayonara" but rather with a "see ya' later."

In other words, ensure that the interviewer won't mind if you "keep in touch," as situations with you and at the organization change. Once you've made the contact, you don't want to lose it.

So check back periodically—not to the point of becoming a nuisance, but rather as an occasional check on availabilities. Where most applicants lose hope and give up is the very area that can prove most fruitful—following up.

No question that looking for a job can, at times, be frustrating.

Many letters go unanswered. Some interviewers don't respond as quickly as you'd hope. And some executives, let's face it, can be real jerks. (Even in pubic relations!)

But a job seeker can't take any of it personally.

The reassuring point to keep always in mind is that as frustrating and maddening and ego-deflating as the job-seeking process sometimes seems to be, all it takes is one "You're hired" to start you on a lifelong career.[5]

Mapping a Career Path

Once a person lands a job in public relations, the next step is to begin to map a career path: determine a progression of accomplishment that will advance you up the chain of command.

Obviously, in public relations as in any field, career advancement is not a straight upwards line. Every career takes twists and turns. In fact, in public relations, it's important to gain experience in each of the field's major skills areas, so sometimes a "lateral move" to learn a new skill is the best course.

A typical corporate career path may take the following progression:

1. **Entry-level professional.**
   This is the typical "associate" job, which executes tasks and projects to achieve business results. It's important for entry-level professionals to build their knowledge base of the company and its industry. Entry-level associates build credibility by carrying out tasks effectively and developing relationships with communications team members and line managers.

2. **Professional manager.**
   Public relations managers typically manage the execution of tasks and projects, and may manage multiple people and third parties. Professional managers also participate in strategy development and business planning. Professional managers build credibility by completing assigned projects effectively and also by counseling management (see Figure 20-3).

3. **Senior professional director.**
   Senior public relations directors generally lead multiple, complex projects and teams of people. Public relations directors are usually skilled in all matter of communications skills and demonstrate product-specific expertise. Public relations directors build credibility as high-level implementers and senior management counselors (see Figure 20-4).

4. **Senior professional vice president.**
   Public relations vice presidents, first and foremost, serve as trusted advisors to senior business leaders. They are also responsible for setting the vision and strategic direction for the communications function, always aligning communications objectives with business goals. Public relations vice presidents should be as knowledgeable as any line manager about the organization, what it is and what it does (see Figure 20-5).

Ensuring Public Relations Success

For years, practitioners of the practice of public relations have searched for the "holy grail" to advise them on getting ahead.

How is it, they ask, that a relative few in this field have been able to ascend to high six-figure salaries, stock options, and bonuses, not to mention that most coveted of public relations goals, "gaining a seat at the management table"?

While many have speculated on achieving senior management success in public relations, a comprehensive study of 97 highest-level public relations leaders isolated the seven factors that can help pave the way to the top of the practice.

Recruiter William C. Heyman (see *From the Top* at the end of this chapter) and University of Alabama Professor Bruce Berger produced a study that pinpointed what it takes to pursue a successful career in public relations. They discovered seven keys—some expected, others counterintuitive—to a successful public relations career.

1. **Diversity of experience.**
   Traditionalists who counsel public relations people to "stay in a job to build credibility" may be all wrong, according to the Heyman-Berger study. While the executives polled averaged 23 years of experience, most indicated that it was "the accumulation of experiences over time" that forged the

MEDIA RELATIONS SPECIALIST

PURPOSE OF THIS JOB:

The Regional Communications Specialist (RCS) will assist the Regional Communications Manager (RCM) in **strategically positioning editorial communication of all marketing activity across all appropriate media channels across a Business Unit (BU) including print, television, radio and internet.** The RCS will assist in **generating media coverage** for select events, projects, teams and athletes in the BU—maximizing the impact of these initiatives via high profile and strategically placed media content. The RCS will also play a critical role in the **creation, collection and distribution of content** for all platforms. The RCS position supports the specific communication needs of the BU to ensure the delivery of an effective communication message that brings our brand image to life.

MAJOR ACTIVITIES TO ENSURE KEY RESULTS AND DELIVERABLES:

1. **Secure a solid brand relationship with local media outlets in close coordination with the RCM and HQ communications to guarantee best media output.**
    a. Maintain media lists for key metros; identify correct motorsports, culture, action sports, calendar editors, segment producers, Web/new media editors and bloggers, etc.
    b. Develop relationships with local news outlets and identify new editorial opportunities.
    c. Create relationships with local collegiate media outlets and Student Brand Managers to leverage our existing relationships within schools.
    d. Utilize events, athletes, and opinion leaders to create brand experiences for media.

2. **Support development of communication plans around select events and projects.**
    a. Brainstorm new and innovative ways to communicate events to the local market.
    b. Build momentum around each event to ensure maximum impact during key stages in their development and execution: from 'launch phase' coverage through to 'post-event' word-of-mouth.
    c. Incorporate all relevant media channels: new media, print, television, radio, and Web to ensure that we are as 'loud' as possible in reverberating each initiative's message and determine which channels work particularly well for the region and/or specific outlets within the region.
    d. Ensure BU initiative are properly represented on redbullusa.com.

3. **Develop a dynamic understanding of the brand and how our message can be translated to the regional media in a relevant way.**
    a. Attend and provide support at events to help translate our brand values to different target groups and to the media covering each event.
    b. Create and distribute communications tools such as media alerts and releases specific to each event which incorporate a local angle.

FIGURE 20-3
(continued)

   c. Stay current on local sports, athletes, culture, target groups, and industry trends.

   d. Regularly read and publish content on the Infonet to stay current on other regional, national, and international events.

   e. Attend periodic seminars and training sessions to strengthen writing, pitching, presentation, and project management skills.

   f. Continuously develop innovative ways for the brand's image to grow via media channels in the BU.

4. **Develop and share best practices.**

   a. Identify media opportunities unique to the market to impact the key consumers and provide communication strategies to address our business needs.

   b. Share results through comprehensive recaps and reports.

   c. Track developments in conventional and new media to ensure we are able to harness the latest techniques, tactics, and technologies.

5. **Administrative responsibilities.**

   a. Support the coordination of all content production (both video and interactive) within the BU.

   b. Assist in coordinating all media interviews, video, and photo shoots.

   c. Assist in writing press materials.

   d. Help maintain Media Contact database.

   e. Create and distribute post-event recap reports.

   f. Work with Insight to ensure all coverage is monitored.

   g. Publish new ideas and event information on the Infonet.

   h. Assist in writing and publishing web content.

   i. Staff BU events.

KNOWLEDGE, SKILLS, AND EXPERIENCE:

1. Minimum 2–3 years of related public relations experience.
2. Web/new media experience preferred.
3. Creative mind with a track record of putting new ideas into practice and analyzing results.
4. Strong writing and organization skills and a solid work ethic.
5. University—Bachelor's Degree preferred.
6. Travels 25%–40% and has flexibility to periodically work unusual hours.
7. Excellent communication skills, including personal presentation, email, and telephone interaction.
8. Ability to cultivate a team environment.
9. Must be proficient in Microsoft Word, Excel, PowerPoint, and Photoshop.

"tipping point" in their success. Study recipients clearly felt that focusing on one specialty throughout a career was counterproductive.

   "It takes three-to-five years to develop a skill set, but if you're unhappy, move on, diversify, and take a risk. Repeating the same job each year won't get you to the level of these senior professionals," Mr. Heyman said.

2. **Performance.**

Even its harshest critics acknowledge that effective public relations can't be delivered with smoke and mirrors. Successful public relations executives must deliver one tangible commodity—results. Survey respondents agreed that the power of performance—solving problems, meeting goals, providing counsel, and producing results—was an absolute requirement for success in public relations.

   What kind of performance?

   The executives said that performance constitutes more than "taking orders." Rather, they said, it means being creative, taking risks and challenging even the

FIGURE 20-4 **Public relations director.** Sample job description for a public relations director, with long-term experience in high-end retail communications.

Position Description

DIRECTOR, CORPORATE COMMUNICATIONS AND PUBLIC RELATIONS

SUMMARY:

The Director, Corporate Communications and Public Relations, at the direction of the Senior Vice President, Corporate Communications and Corporate Social Responsibility, will manage and execute communications and public relations programs in support of building brand awareness through media relations; writing press releases, speeches and other corporate communications; staging corporate media events for coverage (TV, radio, and print media); attend fashion store launches where brands are present; assist from a corporate perspective with product and brand launches; and assist with promotion and production of events. He/she will assist the SVP with the development of communications and corporate affairs strategy to position and brand the group in the U.S. and internationally with the media, as well as the public at large.

RESPONSIBILITIES:

- Create and implement strategic corporate communications, public relations and media relations programs aimed at enhancing the global corporate brand, the position of key company executives including its CEO, the organization's product brands, and its corporate social responsibilities efforts. This includes oversight over the planning, scheduling, and budgeting for multifaceted campaigns that include, but are not limited to, publications, advertising, promotional materials, publicity, direct mail, electronic mail, and the Internet.
- In conjunction with the SVP, the business unit communications teams, and functional staffs, develop a corporate public relations strategy that reflects the goals and objects for each business unit. Also, assist the SVP in identifying, researching, and cultivating opportunities for underrepresented brands to encourage involvement and participation by the media.
- Manage the corporate publicity strategy including actively engaging with members of the business and consumer media across all forms, creation and distribution of all press material, facilitation of press interviews and news conferences; act as corporate spokesperson, as necessary; maintain and update key media relations directory and coordinate company press archive.
- In consultation with business unit management, create and manage a two-way employee communications program that effectively relays key corporate messages to the company's global internal audience. Manage the production of print and online materials for internal distribution and for display at various company events.
- Oversee the company's corporate Web site and internal intranet content, working closely with members of the Web design team and other internal groups.
- Collaborate with the SVP on executive communications programs, which will include the original creation of speeches and talking points for the CEO and other key executives within

FIGURE 20-4
(continued)

the company; monitor and book appropriate engagements for speaking opportunities that will position the company and its management team as thought leaders within the industry.
- Assist with corporate social responsibility programs as needed, while developing appropriate communications strategies around such initiatives.
- Manage and work cooperatively with outside public relations counsel and internally with program and other internal teams; manage department's annual budget.

REQUIREMENTS:
- Bachelor's degree and a minimum of 8 to 10 years of progressively responsible corporate communications experience. Previous experience in fashion, jewelry, or consumer-focused environments is preferred.
- The ability to develop and implement creative, strategic, and successful communications programs—and a strong track record of accomplishments in planning, implementing, and directing results-oriented PR initiatives. Also, experience working with consumer trends research, market forecasting, and other analytical programs is preferred.
- Significant experience in managing high-profile program and communications issues.
- Superior written, verbal, presentation, and communication skills; the professional presence to represent the company well and act as a media spokesperson and to work directly with key members of the senior management team including the CEO.
- Experience consulting with and counseling executives to take advantage of external opportunities that elevate corporate image, mitigate risk, influence policy, and shape key business messages. The demonstrated ability to manage crisis communications.
- A track record of developing relationships and working well with fellow team members, management, news media representatives, and outside consultants.

senior most people in the organization. Once you begin to build a track record of results, more people will seek you out and believe in what you are advising.

3. **Communications skills.**
   Public relations practitioners are, at base, professional communicators. Therefore, highly honed technical communications skills, according to the study—from writing and design to the production of sophisticated communication materials—are imperative for public relations success.

   Communications skills, according to Prof. Berger, must be evident at every level of PR ascension.
   - Initially, at entry, it is the technical skills of writing, editing, and design that count.
   - At a second level, it is the more analytical skills of strategic planning that must be developed.
   - A third level tests the skills of interpersonal communication and building a network.
   - Finally, at the most sophisticated level of public relations counsel, the advocacy skills of dispensing advice and making decisions are key.

4. **Relationship building.**
   Common wisdom suggests that in public relations, "it's not what you know but who you know that counts." To a great degree, according to the study, common wisdom is correct.

   But while building *external* relationships—with the media, analysts, government, and others—is important, even more important, according to the executives surveyed, is "nurturing relationships inside the organization to gain influence and get ahead."

FIGURE 20-5
Public relations vice president. Sample job description for a public relations vice president, with long-term experience for health care communications position.

VICE PRESIDENT, COMMUNICATIONS

SUMMARY:

The Vice President, Communications will have primary responsibility for developing and guiding all media relations and internal communications for the system. From conception and strategy to implementation, this position oversees the system communications function. This position promotes the mission and vision of the organization, firmly establishing the system's identity with all internal and external audiences. Success in this position requires the confidence, trust, and close working relationships with the system's most senior managers, as the system undergoes a financial turnaround and integration of its principal units.

RESPONSIBILITIES:

- Conceptualize, develop, and implement all system level communications plans, strategies, programs, and services including crisis management, executive communications, internal communications, media relations, and system positioning.
- Ensure system communications integrate and reflect the mission and vision, firmly establishing the identity, as it goes through an integration and turnaround, of the organization with internal and external audiences.
- Serve as primary spokesperson for the system and its President/CEO. Manage the external communications program; develop strategic public relations plans and implement an effective media relations program. Establish and maintain relationships with key media to coordinate coverage and to improve communication of the organizational position.
- Provide internal consulting and thought leadership to other leaders at the system levels. Expand on the existing internal communications tools to maintain the promise of conveying management decisions to all 13,000 employees in a candid and transparent manner.
- Anticipate and identify which communications issues are most appropriately handled at the system level and provide consultation or seek collaboration with others as the situation dictates.
- Oversee the establishment of contingency plans for possible crises or special issues including development of core messages and position papers, identification of appropriate spokespersons and media training.
- Position the President/CEO as well as other system leaders within the community.
- Develop and maintain close working relationships with senior executives and turnaround consulting firms as needed.

REQUIREMENTS

- Bachelor's degree required; advanced degree preferred. Minimum of 10 years experience creating and implementing a comprehensive public and media relations strategic plan.

FIGURE 20-5
(continued)

- Proven track record of providing proactive leadership of the communications function in an organization with broad community visibility.
- Proven track record of working collegially with superiors, subordinates, and peers in a team-oriented environment.
- Outstanding strategic planning skills and solid business acumen.
- Ability to operate with a sense of urgency with rapid response capabilities.
- Capability of handling multiple projects on constricted timelines.
- Proven track record of cultivating and maintaining relationships with media.
- Adeptness at working with and meeting the needs of senior management; a willingness to provide counsel as well as listen and take direction.
- Excellent interpersonal and communications skills; a charismatic leader with the presence to introduce and influence ideas. Excellent and proven writing skills.
- Highly intelligent, articulate, fast-working individual, who works well under pressure, has integrity, is culturally sensitive, and is committed to a service ethic.

Nearly half of the executives, in fact, said the most valuable source of influence they possessed was relationships with senior executives, peers, and subordinates. Indeed, the findings hint that relationships may provide more power to professionals than their titles or formal positions in their organization.

5. **Proactivity and passion.**

   The executives said that public relations people must be go-getters, self-starters, risk-takers, opportunity-seekers with boundless energy, great curiosity, and passionate in their commitment to the practice. Or else, suggested the executives, you might get lost in the shuffle.

   According to Prof. Berger, *"Nobody in this field succeeds by going through the motions. You've got to get excited about what you're doing and why you're doing it."*

6. **Teamliness.**

   Most respondents agreed that achievement depended on three levels—the individual, organizational, and group or work unit, in that order.

   "Probably less than 10 percent of the jobs in this field depend solely on individual performance," stated Heyman. Most practitioners are in jobs where their contribution to the organization becomes a critical factor in their own individual success.

7. **Intangibles.**

   Chemistry. Likeability. Personality. Presence. Cultural fit.

   Do they really matter in determining ultimate success PR?

   You bet they do.

   In fact, nearly 90 percent of the executives polled cited positive personal character traits as the single most desired characteristic among job candidates.

   One disturbing aspect of their study, said the researchers, was that nearly half of those interviewed said the most significant limitation on public relations practice and influence was the "inaccurate or incomplete perceptions of the function's role and value," particularly among organizational executives.

   One way to upgrade that perception is for those who practice public relations—particularly young practitioners—to take seriously the list of successful attributes revealed in the Heyman-Berger study.[6]

Last Word

Public relations dialogue still revolves around finding that elusive "seat at the management table"; that is, convincing management that the public relations function is as imperative as legal or human resources or finance. Until the practice is accepted as a necessary management discipline, public relations will always be subject to the vicissitudes of economic change.

On the other hand, the financial services meltdown of the 21st century has triggered renewed calls for transparency and candor among corporate executives—in other words, of increased open and honest communications.

Consequently, employers will increasingly seek experienced and competent public relations professionals to help them communicate. How can entry-level professionals accommodate this Catch-22 need for "experience"? According to experienced counselor and public relations professor Barry Zusman, at least three specific courses should be considered:

- **Hone writing skills.** Says Prof. Zusman, *"While the current generation gets it as far as technology and digital media are concerned, we don't yet live in a world ruled by 140 Twitter characters."* Well-written content is still king.

- **Seize internships.** These are among the best ways to learn about the field with real-life experience. Although many internships are unpaid, they're still often worth it, since firms hire based on internship experience.

- **Join a professional communications organization.** And become involved in professional committees. Says Prof. Zusman, *"Listen and learn everything you can from the organization's members, who have been in the field and can serve as mentors."* [7]

To the Zusman principles, others suggest five additional keys to moving ahead in public relations.

1. **Use technology to your advantage.** You can often teach employers how to use social media for public relations value, so don't be shy.

2. **Pay attention to details.** Treat everything like a "big deal," using every opportunity to demonstrate your worth.

3. **Read, read, read.** The key to good writing, say veterans, is "good reading," so pick up newspapers, magazines, and books, and then *read* them.

4. **Be a student.** Just because you've graduated into the workplace doesn't mean you should stop *learning*. Learn constantly.

5. **Find a mentor.** Often, the old adage is right: It's not what you know but who you know that counts. So find someone or someones who can advise and help you as you proceed through the public relations profession.[8]

Public relations people remain divided on such issues as the value of a public relations degree vs. a degree in liberal arts or the importance of knowledge of digital media vs. traditional media or even the necessity of an education vs. on-the-job training. What most people don't disagree on is the importance to the field and the individuals within it of knowledge and judgement and, most of all, competence in the practice of public relations.

Top of the Shelf   PR: A Persuasive Industry? / Trevor Morris and Simon Goldsworthy, New York: Palgrave MacMillan, 2008

Finally, a popular book that doesn't trash the practice of public relations.

Authors Morris and Goldsworthy describe public relations as more gray than black and white, in terms of ethics. The authors describe public relations as "amoral," neither a tool for good nor bad but rather dependent on the specific ethic or motives of its professionals. They deride journalists who deride public relations, because without the field, "there would be little news."

The authors proclaim that public relations is growing by more than 30 percent annually in countries like China, Russia, and Turkey, and that "for a free press to function, PR is essential." All-in-all a positive and comprehensive analysis of the potential of public relations work in the free world.

Finally.

the Top   A Final Word to the Wise (Student): An Interview with Bill Heyman

Bill Heyman, founder, president, and CEO of Heyman Associates, has been the dean of public relations recruiters for more than two decades. He manages senior-level searches for blue-chip and emerging companies, leading public relations firms, nonprofit organizations, and government agencies. He is a board member of the Lagrant Foundation, which awards scholarships to minority students planning public relations careers. He is also an inaugural member of the advisory board for the Plank Center for Public Relations Studies in the College of Communication and Information Sciences at the University of Alabama. For additional information about Heyman Associates, log onto www.heymanassociates.com.

What is the employment outlook for public relations graduates today?
Public relations has become an essential business tool, not something that could be eliminated. On the whole, companies want to do a better job telling their stories. But, job seekers need to be realistic: The employment market is tied to the performance of capital markets. Those seeking jobs must recognize that salaries and perks will not match those of only a few years ago, when "new economy" companies ruled, and that more will be expected from them for lower initial salaries. It also is likely to take longer for most to earn their stripes—[that is, job seekers can expect to] rise more slowly within an organization, because organizations are smaller and leaner.

Where are the most attractive public relations employment skill areas?
The most employment opportunities today are in media relations, internal communications, issues management, financial public relations, branding and image development, and social responsibility. Each one of these specialties tends to target an audience that was underserved prior to corporations' rebuilding their images. Companies are no longer taking any audience for granted. Transparency is critical.

What are the most attractive industries for public relations employment?
The health care industry consistently looks at communications as an important way to deliver its message. Pharmaceutical and biotechnology companies lead the public relations job market. Almost on a level field is the financial services industry. Also, an increased number of the largest corporations are in the process of remaking their

images, especially those whose reputations have been challenged. With communications, they can demonstrate they are broad thinkers, technologically advanced, and contemporary.

What's the best preparation for public relations employment?
Become a strong writer. There is no greater need than having a strong writing ability. Key areas of employment today are in media relations and speechwriting, and both require strong writing skills.

Students must take as many writing classes as possible and intern (for pay or not) in places where they can get real-world experience (local newspapers, public relations agencies, companies, or philanthropic organizations).

And, because they must be increasingly well-rounded in their knowledge, they need to take a wide range of liberal arts classes (especially ethics) and meld that with exploring cultural experiences in the community (opera, theater, museums, etc.) and read, read, read newspapers, magazines, corporate Web sites, and books.

The most successful practitioners will be those that the CEO will want as a seatmate flying across the country or at a dinner table with the organization's most important client.

What is the ideal starting point for public relations beginners?
Often, an agency is the best training ground because of the diverse experiences. The broader the experience, the better it is. Corporate jobs, especially entry-level, tend to be more narrowly focused. Starting at a news organization enables people to learn up close what a reporter goes through and needs every day. Another area where people can consider working in the early stages of their career is a political campaign.

What are the public relations prospects in the nonprofit sector?
Public relations is becoming a valued commodity in the nonprofit sector, especially after 9/11. These jobs tend to have lower salaries, but the experience can be similar to that of a public relations agency and therefore a good training ground. Also, corporate foundations are doing more to articulate their specific business message and are looking for strong public relations executives.

What are the essential characteristics that public relations employers look for in potential employees?
There are five nontechnical characteristics that are most important: one, integrity; two, self-confidence; three, likeability (including respect for others); four, energy (including noticeable

enthusiasm); and five, intellect (including business knowledge and judgment).

Added to that are two technical characteristics: the ability to write and to present well. These seven criteria transcend communications posts and organizations.

What's the best way to find a public relations job?
There is no greater way to find a position than to develop a network from the earliest stages of your career.

- Contacting people, joining professional organizations, and being involved in volunteer work are all critical ways to meet other people.

- Conducting research and learning more about the companies you want to work for is key, as is finding a specific contact within each company.

- Learning about the alumni association at your college or university and who might be working within the field can help you start your career.

- During internships, reach out to anyone you meet.

- Always follow up with people, writing courteous notes asking for help. Two key characteristics in finding a job are to be courteous and tenacious. Always let people know how appreciative you are of any time they spend with you.

Public Relations Library

Aronson, Merry, Don Spetner, and Carol Ames. *The Public Relations Writer's Handbook*. San Francisco, CA: Jossey-Bass, 2007. This presents a good explanation of how the digital age has altered the requirements in the public relations field.

Careers in Advertising and Public Relations. San Francisco, CA: WebFeet Inc., 2005. This guide offers an analysis of whether an advertising or public relations firm is right for a writer.

Croft, A. C. *Managing a Public Relations Firm for Fun and Profit*. Binghamton, NY: Haworth Press, 2006. Once you've entered the field, prospered in it, and now are ready to become your own CEO, read this book to find out how to do it.

Feinglass, Art. *The Public Relations Handbook for Nonprofits*. San Francisco, CA: Jossey-Bass, 2003. This is a helpful handbook for nonprofits and also for those interested in going into nonprofit public relations.

Field, Shelly. *Career Opportunities in Advertising and Public Relations Rev. Ed*. New York, NY: Checkmark Books, 2005. This presents a full roster of jobs in the communications industry and what each requires.

Fitzpatrick, Kathy, and Carolyn Bronstein. *Ethics in Public Relations*. Thousand Oaks, CA: Sage Publishing, 2006. This offers a fresh approach on why public relations people should be "responsible advocates" for the views they represent.

Freitag, Alan R., and Ashli Quesinberry Stokes. *Global Public Relations*. New York, NY: Routledge, 2009. This presents the cross-border cultural impact of different societies on public relations practice.

Green, Andy. *Creativity in Public Relations*, 3rd ed. London, England: Kogan Page, 2007. The author emphasizes "creative thinking" as the road to inspired public relations.

Hall, Phil. *The New PR*. N. Potomac, MD: Larsten Publishing, 2007. Emphasis here is on how "experiential marketing strategies" will change the face of public relations.

Harris, Thomas L., and Patricia T. Whelan. *The Marketer's Guide to Public Relations in the 21st Century*. Mason, OH: Texere, 2006. The emphasis here is on marketing public relations.

Henderson, David. *Making News*. Lincoln, NE: iUniverse Star, 2006. This is an experienced look at how to effectively practice media relations.

Kelleher, Tom. *Public Relations Online*. Thousand Oaks, CA: Sage Publications, 2007. This is a fine explanation of the new technologies in public relations and how to use them.

Marconi, Joe. *Public Relations*. Hagerstown, MD: South-Western, 2004. This offers a marketing consultant's take on what public relations work requires.

Mogel, Leonard. *Making It in Public Relations,* 2nd ed. Mahwah, NJ: Lawrence Erlbaum Associates, 2002. This is a good, quick, soup-to-nuts approach on the business and how to secure a job in it.

Weiner, Mark. *Unleashing the Power of PR*. San Francisco, CA: Jossey-Bass, 2006. A measurement expert reminds practitioners that public relations measurement has become essential.

Yaverbaum, Eric. *Public Relations for Dummies,* 2nd ed. Hoboken, NJ: Wiley Publishing, 2006. A seasoned public relations professional talks about how "word of mouth" can move mountains.

Zappala, Joseph M., and Ann R. Carden. *Public Relations Worktext*. Mahwah, NJ: Lawrence Erlbaum, 2008. This is an excellent writing resource for the public relations professional.

Appendix A

PRSA Member Code of Ethics 2000

Approved by the PRSA Assembly October, 2000

Letter from the PRSA Board of Directors

It is with enormous professional pleasure and personal pride that we, the Public Relations Society of America Board of Directors, put before you a new Public Relations Member Code of Ethics for our Society. It is the result of two years of concentrated effort led by the Board of Ethics and Professional Standards. Comments of literally hundreds and hundreds of members were considered. There were focus groups at our 1999 national meeting in Anaheim, California. We sought and received intensive advice and counsel from the Ethics Resource Center, our outside consultants on the project. Additional recommendations were received from your Board of Directors, PRSA staff, outside reviewers, as well as District and Section officers. Extensive research involving analysis of numerous codes of conduct, ethics statements, and standards and practices approaches was also carried out.

In fact, this Member Code of Ethics has been developed to serve as a foundation for discussion of an emerging global Code of Ethics and Conduct for the practice of Public Relations.

This approach is dramatically different from that which we have relied upon in the past. You'll find it different in three powerfully important ways:
1. Emphasis on enforcement of the Code has been eliminated. But, the PRSA Board of Directors retains the right to bar from membership or expel from the Society any individual who has been or is sanctioned by a government agency or convicted in a court of law of an action that is in violation of this Code.
2. The new focus is on universal values that inspire ethical behavior and performance.
3. Desired behavior is clearly illustrated by providing language, experience, and examples to help the individual practitioner better achieve important ethical and principled business objectives. This approach should help everyone better understand what the expected standards of conduct truly are.

Perhaps most important of all, the mission of the Board of Ethics and Professional Standards has now been substantially altered to focus primarily on education and training, on collaboration with similar efforts in other major professional societies, and to serve an advisory role to the Board on ethical matters of major importance.

The foundation of our value to our companies, clients, and those we serve is their ability to rely on our ethical and morally acceptable behavior. Please review this new Member Code of Ethics in this context:

- Its Values are designed to inspire and motivate each of us every day to the highest levels of ethical practice.
- Its Code Provisions are designed to help each of us clearly understand the limits and specific performance required to be an ethical practitioner.
- Its Commitment mechanism is designed to ensure that every Society member understands fully the obligations of membership and the expectation of ethical behavior that are an integral part of membership in the PRSA.

This approach is stronger than anything we have ever had because:

- It will have a daily impact on the practice of Public Relations.
- There are far fewer gray areas and issues that require interpretation.
- It will grow stronger and be more successful than what we have had in the past through education, through training, and through analysis of behaviors.

The strength of the Code will grow because of the addition of precedent and the ethical experiences of other major professional organizations around the world.

Our new Code elevates our ethics, our values, and our commitment to the level they belong, at the very top of our daily practice of Public Relations.

PRSA Board of Directors

A Message from the PRSA Board of Ethics and Professional Standards

Our Primary Obligation

The primary obligation of membership in the Public Relations Society of America is the ethical practice of Public Relations.

The PRSA Member Code of Ethics is the way each member of our Society can daily reaffirm a commitment to ethical professional activities and decisions.
- The Code sets forth the principles and standards that guide our decisions and actions.
- The Code solidly connects our values and our ideals to the work each of us does every day.
- The Code is about what we should do, and why we should do it.

The Code is also meant to be a living, growing body of knowledge, precedent, and experience. It should stimulate our thinking and encourage us to seek guidance and clarification when we have questions about principles, practices, and standards of conduct.

Every member's involvement in preserving and enhancing ethical standards is essential to building and maintaining the respect and credibility of our profession. Using our values, principles, standards of conduct, and commitment as a foundation, and continuing to work together on ethical issues, we ensure that the Public Relations Society of America fulfills its obligation to build and maintain the framework for public dialogue that deserves the public's trust and support.

The Members of the 2000 Board of Ethics and Professional Standards

Robert D. Frause, APR, Fellow PRSA
Chairman BEPS
Seattle, Washington

Kathy R. Fitzpatrick, APR
Gainesville, Florida

Linda Welter Cohen, APR
Tucson, Arizona

James R. Frankowiak, APR
Tampa, Florida

James E. Lukaszewski, APR, Fellow PRSA
White Plains, New York

Roger D. Buehrer, APR
Fellow PRSA
Las Vegas, Nevada

Jeffrey P. Julin, APR
Denver, Colorado

David M. Bicofsky, APR, Fellow PRSA
Teaneck, New Jersey

James W. Wyckoff, APR
New York, New York

Preamble

Public Relations Society of America Member Code of Ethics 2000

- Professional Values
- Principles of Conduct
- Commitment and Compliance

This Code applies to PRSA members. The Code is designed to be a useful guide for PRSA members as they carry out their ethical responsibilities. This document is designed to anticipate and accommodate, by precedent, ethical challenges that may arise. The scenarios outlined in the Code provision are actual examples of misconduct. More will be added as experience with the Code occurs.

The Public Relations Society of America (PRSA) is committed to ethical practices. The level of public trust PRSA members seek, as we serve the public good, means we have taken on a special obligation to operate ethically.

The value of member reputation depends upon the ethical conduct of everyone affiliated with the Public Relations Society of America. Each of us sets an example for each other—as well as other professionals—by our pursuit of excellence with powerful standards of performance, professionalism, and ethical conduct.

Emphasis on enforcement of the Code has been eliminated. But, the PRSA Board of Directors retains the right to bar from membership or expel from the Society any individual who has been or is sanctioned by a government agency or convicted in a court of law of an action that is in violation of this Code.

Ethical practice is the most important obligation of a PRSA member. We view the Member Code of Ethics as a model for other professions, organizations, and professionals.

PRSA Member Statement of Professional Values

This statement presents the core values of PRSA members and, more broadly, of the public relations profession. These values provide the foundation for the Member Code of Ethics and set the industry standard for the professional practice of public relations. These values are the fundamental beliefs that guide our behaviors and decision-making process. We believe our professional values are vital to the integrity of the profession as a whole.

Advocacy
- We serve the public interest by acting as responsible advocates for those we represent.
- We provide a voice in the marketplace of ideas, facts, and viewpoints to aid informed public debate.

Honesty
- We adhere to the highest standards of accuracy and truth in advancing the interests of those we represent and in communicating with the public.

Expertise
- We acquire and responsibly use specialized knowledge and experience.
- We advance the profession through continued professional development, research, and education.
- We build mutual understanding, credibility, and relationships among a wide array of institutions and audiences.

Independence
- We provide objective counsel to those we represent.
- We are accountable for our actions.

Loyalty
- We are faithful to those we represent, while honoring our obligation to serve the public interest.

Fairness
- We deal fairly with clients, employers, competitors, peers, vendors, the media, and the general public.
- We respect all opinions and support the right of free expression.

PRSA Code Provisions

Free Flow of Information

Core Principle
Protecting and advancing the free flow of accurate and truthful information is essential to serving the public interest and contributing to informed decision making in a democratic society.

Intent
- To maintain the integrity of relationships with the media, government officials, and the public.
- To aid informed decision making.

Guidelines
A member shall:
- Preserve the integrity of the process of communication.
- Be honest and accurate in all communications.
- Act promptly to correct erroneous communications for which the practitioner is responsible.
- Preserve the free flow of unprejudiced information when giving or receiving gifts by ensuring that gifts are nominal, legal, and infrequent.

Examples of Improper Conduct Under this Provision
- A member representing a ski manufacturer gives a pair of expensive racing skis to a sports magazine columnist, to influence the columnist to write favorable articles about the product.
- A member entertains a government official beyond legal limits and/or in violation of government reporting requirements.

Competition

Core Principle
Promoting healthy and fair competition among professionals preserves an ethical climate while fostering a robust business environment.

Intent
- To promote respect and fair competition among public relations professionals.
- To serve the public interest by providing the widest choice of practitioner options.

Guidelines
A member shall:
- Follow ethical hiring practices designed to respect free and open competition without deliberately undermining a competitor.
- Preserve intellectual property rights in the marketplace.

Examples of Improper Conduct Under This Provision
- A member employed by a "client organization" shares helpful information with a counseling firm that is competing with others for the organization's business.
- A member spreads malicious and unfounded rumors about a competitor in order to alienate the competitor's clients and employees in a ploy to recruit people and business.

Disclosure of Information

Core Principle
Open communication fosters informed decision making in a democratic society.

Intent
- To build trust with the public by revealing all information needed for responsible decision making.

Guidelines
A member shall:
- Be honest and accurate in all communications.
- Act promptly to correct erroneous communications for which the member is responsible.
- Investigate the truthfulness and accuracy of information released on behalf of those represented.
- Reveal the sponsors for causes and interests represented.
- Disclose financial interest (such as stock ownership) in a client's organization.
- Avoid deceptive practices.

Examples of Improper Conduct Under this Provision
- Front groups: A member implements "grass roots" campaigns or letter-writing campaigns to legislators on behalf of undisclosed interest groups.
- Lying by omission: A practitioner for a corporation knowingly fails to release financial information, giving a misleading impression of the corporation's performance.
- A member discovers inaccurate information disseminated via a Web site or media kit and does not correct the information.
- A member deceives the public by employing people to pose as volunteers to speak at public hearings and participate in "grass roots" campaigns.

Safeguarding Confidences

Core Principle
Client trust requires appropriate protection of confidential and private information.

Intent
- To protect the privacy rights of clients, organizations, and individuals by safeguarding confidential information.

Guidelines

A member shall:

- Safeguard the confidences and privacy rights of present, former, and prospective clients and employees.
- Protect privileged, confidential, or insider information gained from a client or organization.
- Immediately advise an appropriate authority if a member discovers that confidential information is being divulged by an employee of a client company or organization.

Examples of Improper Conduct Under This Provision

- A member changes jobs, takes confidential information, and uses that information in the new position to the detriment of the former employer.
- A member intentionally leaks proprietary information to the detriment of some other party.

Conflicts of Interest

Core Principle

Avoiding real, potential, or perceived conflicts of interest builds the trust of clients, employers, and the publics.

Intent

- To earn trust and mutual respect with clients or employers.
- To build trust with the public by avoiding or ending situations that put one's personal or professional interests in conflict with society's interests.

Guidelines

A member shall:

- Act in the best interests of the client or employer, even subordinating the member's personal interests.
- Avoid actions and circumstances that may appear to compromise good business judgment or create a conflict between personal and professional interests.
- Disclose promptly any existing or potential conflict of interest to affected clients or organizations.
- Encourage clients and customers to determine if a conflict exists after notifying all affected parties.

Examples of Improper Conduct Under This Provision

- The member fails to disclose that he or she has a strong financial interest in a client's chief competitor.
- The member represents a "competitor company" or a "conflicting interest" without informing a prospective client.

Enhancing the Profession

Core Principle

Public relations professionals work constantly to strengthen the public's trust in the profession.

Intent
- To build respect and credibility with the public for the profession of public relations.
- To improve, adapt, and expand professional practices.

Guidelines
A member shall:
- Acknowledge that there is an obligation to protect and enhance the profession.
- Keep informed and educated about practices in the profession to ensure ethical conduct.
- Actively pursue personal professional development.
- Decline representation of clients or organizations that urge or require actions contrary to this Code.
- Accurately define what public relations activities can accomplish.
- Counsel subordinates in proper ethical decision making.
- Require that subordinates adhere to the ethical requirements of the Code.
- Report ethical violations, whether committed by PRSA members or not, to the appropriate authority.

Examples of Improper Conduct Under This Provision
- A PRSA member declares publicly that a product the client sells is safe, without disclosing evidence to the contrary.
- A member initially assigns some questionable client work to a non-member practitioner to avoid the ethical obligation of PRSA membership.

Resources

Rules and Guidelines
The following PRSA documents, available in The Blue Book, provide detailed rules and guidelines to help guide your professional behavior:
- PRSA Bylaws
- PRSA Administrative Rules
- Member Code of Ethics

If, after reviewing them, you still have a question or issue, contact PRSA headquarters as noted below.

Questions

The PRSA is here to help. Whether you have a serious concern or simply need clarification, contact Judy Voss at judy.voss@prsa.org.

PRSA Member Code of Ethics Pledge

I pledge:

To conduct myself professionally, with truth, accuracy, fairness, and responsibility to the public; to improve my individual competence and advance the knowledge and proficiency of the profession through continuing research and education; and to adhere to the articles of the Member Code of Ethics 2000 for the practice of public relations as adopted by the governing Assembly of the Public Relations Society of America.

I understand and accept that there is a consequence for misconduct, up to and including membership revocation.

And, I understand that those who have been or are sanctioned by a government agency or convicted in a court of law of an action that is in violation of this Code may be barred from membership or expelled from the Society.

_____

Signature

_____

Date

Public Relations Society of America
33 Irving Place
New York, NY 10003
www.prsa.org

Appendix B

PRIA Code of Ethics

The Public Relations Institute of Australia is a professional body serving the interests of its members. In doing so, the Institute is mindful of the responsibility which public relations professionals owe to the community as well as to their clients and employers. The Institute requires members to adhere to the highest standards of ethical practice and professional competence. All members are duty-bound to act responsibly and to be accountable for their actions.

The following Code of Ethics binds all members of the Public Relations Institute of Australia.

1. Members shall deal fairly and honestly with their employers, clients and prospective clients, with their fellow workers including superiors and subordinates, with public officials, the communications media, the general public and with fellow members of PRIA.
2. Members shall avoid conduct or practices likely to bring discredit upon themselves, the Institute, their employers or clients.
3. Members shall not knowingly disseminate false or misleading information and shall take care to avoid doing so inadvertently.
4. Members shall safeguard the confidences of both present and former employers and clients, including confidential information about employers' or clients' business affairs, technical methods or processes, except upon the order of a court of competent jurisdiction.
5. No member shall represent conflicting interests nor, without the consent of the parties concerned, represent competing interests.
6. Members shall refrain from proposing or agreeing that their consultancy fees or other remuneration be contingent entirely on the achievement of specified results.
7. Members shall inform their employers or clients if circumstances arise in which their judgment or the disinterested character of their services may be questioned by reason of personal relationships or business or financial interests.
8. Members practising as consultants shall seek payment only for services specifically commissioned.
9. Members shall be prepared to identify the source of funding of any public communication they initiate or for which they act as a conduit.
10. Members shall, in advertising and marketing their skills and services and in soliciting professional assignments, avoid false, misleading or exaggerated claims and shall refrain from comment or action that may injure the professional reputation, practice or services of a fellow member.
11. Members shall inform the Board of the Institute and/or the relevant State/Territory Council(s) of the Institute of evidence purporting to show that a member has been guilty of, or could be charged with, conduct constituting a breach of this Code.
12. No member shall intentionally injure the professional reputation or practice of another member.
13. Members shall help to improve the general body of knowledge of the profession by exchanging information and experience with fellow members.

14. Members shall act in accord with the aims of the institute, its regulations and policies.
15. Members shall not misrepresent their status through misuse of title, grading, or the designation FPRIA, MPRIA or APRIA.

Adopted by the Board of the Institute on November 5, 2001, this Code of Ethics supersedes all previous versions.

End Notes

Chapter 1

1. Robin Givhan, "Sanjaya's Idol Style: It's All in His Head," *Washington Post* (March 30, 2007): CO1.
2. Mark Trevelvan, "Bin Laden Video May Signal New Attacks," *Reuters* (September 8, 2007).
3. Bureau of Labor Statistics, U.S. Department of Labor, *Occupational Outlook Handbook, 2004–05 Edition*, Public Relations Specialists, www.bls.gov/oco/ocos086.htm.
4. "Executive, Congressional and Consumer Attitudes Toward the Media, Marketing and Public Relations Profession," sponsored by the Public Relations Society of America and Harris Interactive, November 10, 2005.
5. Kirk Hallahan, "Challenges Confronting PR Education," Public Relations Society of America Web site, www.prsa.org, November 2005.
6. www.Hoovers.com/public-relations.
7. "Company Expands Its Management Committee to Include Communicator," Ragan Report (September 19, 2005): 2.
8. "The Design for Undergraduate Public Relations Education," a study cosponsored by the public relations division of the Association for Education and Journalism and Mass Communication, the Public Relations Society of America, and the educators' section of PRSA, 1987, 1.
9. Cited in Scott M. Cutlip and Allen H. Center, *Effective Public Relations*, 6th ed. (Upper Saddle River, NJ: Prentice Hall, 1985): 5.
10. Edward L. Bernays, *Crystallizing Public Opinion* (New York: Liveright, 1961).
11. Rex F. Harlow, "Building a Public Relations Definition," *Public Relations Review 2*, no. 4 (Winter 1976): 36.
12. "About Public Relations," Public Relations Society of America Web site, www.prsa.org, November 2005.
13. John E. Marston, *The Nature of Public Relations* (New York: McGraw-Hill, 1963): 161.
14. "Denny Griswold, PRN Founder and Industry Luminary, Dies at 92," *Public Relations News* (March 12, 2001): 1.
15. Dr. Melvin L. Sharpe, professor and coordinator of the Public Relations Sequence, Department of Journalism, Ball State University, Muncie, IN 47306.
16. Sandra Sobieraj, "Senate Bans Company Loans to Officials," Associated Press (July 13, 2002).
17. John Dewey, *The Public and Its Problems* (Chicago: Swallow Press, 1927).
18. Linda P. Morton, "Segmenting Publics by Lifestyles," *Public Relations Quarterly* (Fall 1999): 46–47.
19. Dr. Melvin L. Sharpe, op. cit.
20. Timothy L. O'Brien, "Spinning Frenzy: P.R.'s Bad Press," *New York Times* (February 13, 2005): B1.
21. Derrick Jensen, "The War on Truth: The Secret Battle for the American Mind," interview with John Stauber, www.mediachannel.org (June 7, 2000).
22. "White House Official I. Lewis Libby Indicted on Obstruction of Justice, False Statement and Perjury Charges Relating to Leak of Classified Information Revealing CIA Officer's Identity," news release of Office of Special Counsel (October 28, 2005), www.usdoj.gov/usao/iln/osc.
23. "Heyman Associates Study Finds Critical Patterns for Public Relations Success," news release of Heyman Associates (June 28, 2004), www.heymanassociates.com.
24. Fraser P. Seitel, "Relax Mr. Stauber, Public Relations Ain't That Dangerous," www.mediachannel.org (June 7, 2000).
25. Abraham Lincoln, Lincoln–Douglas Debates, Ottawa, IL, August 21, 1858.

Chapter 2

1. Thomas Wagner, "Queen Elizabeth II Launches YouTube Channel," *Associated Press* (December 22, 2007).
2. World Internet Users December 2007, Internet World Stats: Usage and Population Statistics, www.internetworldstats.com, Miniwatts Marketing Group, 2008.
3. Scott M. Cutlip, Allen H. Center, and Glen M. Broom, *Effective Public Relations*, 8th ed. (Upper Saddle River, NJ: Prentice Hall, 2000): 102.
4. Fraser P. Seitel, "The Company You Keep," www.odwyerpr.com (July 22, 2002).
5. "Boston's Cardinal Law Resists Calls for His Resignation," CNN.com (April 12, 2002).
6. Harold Burson, speech at Utica College of Syracuse University, Utica, NY (March 5, 1987).
7. Ray Eldon Hiebert, *Courtier to the Crowd: The Story of Ivy L. Lee and the Development of Public Relations* (Ames: Iowa State University Press, 1966).
8. John E. Harr and Peter J. Johnson, *The Rockefeller Century: Three Generations of America's Greatest Family* (New York: Simon & Schuster, 1988): 130.
9. Interview with David Rockefeller, November 30, 2005.
10. Cited in Alvin Moscow, *The Rockefeller Inheritance* (Garden City, NY: Doubleday, 1977): 23.
11. Interview with Stuart Ewen, "Spin Cycles: A Century of Spin," CBC Radio (January 19, 2007).
12. Interview with Fraser Seitel, "Spin Cycles: A Century of Spin," CBC Radio (January 19, 2007).
13. Edward L. Bernays, "Bernays: 62 Years in Public Relations," *Public Relations Quarterly* (Fall 1981): 8.
14. Interview with Stuart Ewen, op. cit.
15. "Burson Hailed as PR's No. 1 Influential Figure," *PR Week* (October 18, 1999): 1.
16. Cited in Noel L. Griese, "The Employee Communications Philosophy of Arthur W. Page," *Public Relations Quarterly* (Winter 1977): 8–12.
17. Noel L. Griese, *Arthur W. Page: Publisher, Public Relations Pioneer, Patriot* (Tucker, GA: Anvil Publishers, 2001).
18. "An Afternoon with Peter Drucker," *The Public Relations Strategist* (Fall 1998): 10.
19. World Internet Users December 2007, op. cit.
20. Charles J. Hanley, "War Making Headlines But Peace Breaks Out," *Associated Press* (August 30, 2004).
21. Tim O'Reilly, "What Is Web 2.0?" oreillynet.com (September 30, 2005).
22. Enid Burns, "E-Commerce Equals Convenience, Risk to Consumers," clickz.com (February 15, 2008).
23. John L. Paluszek, "Public Relations Students: Today Good, Tomorrow Better," *The Public Relations Strategist* (Winter 2000): 27.
24. Bureau of Labor Statistics, U.S. Department of Labor, *Occupational Outlook Handbook, 2008-09 Edition*, Public Relations Specialists, www.bls.gov/oco/ocos086.htm.
25. Jack O'Dwyer (Ed.), *O'Dwyer's Directory of Corporate Communications* (New York: J. R. O'Dwyer Co., 2005).
26. Jack O'Dywer (Ed.), *O'Dwyer's Directory of Public Relations Firms* (New York: J. R. O'Dwyer Co., 2005).
27. Joseph Nocera, "Living in the Enron Dream World," *New York Times* (December 17, 2005): C1–12.

Chapter 3

1. Wikipedia: About wikipedia.org.
2. Noam Cohen, "After False Claim, Wikipedia to Check Degrees," *New York Times* (March 12, 2007).

3. Interview with Raymond Siposs, Director, Carnet Media, San Diego, CA (December 26, 2005).

4. Patrick Jackson, "The Unforgiving Era," *Currents* (October 1998).

5. Serge Moscovici, "Silent Majorities and Loud Minorities," *Communication Yearbook* 14 (1991): 298–308.

6. J. Delia, B. O'Keefe, and D. O'Keefe, "The Constructivist Approach to Communication," *Human Communication Theory* (New York: Harper and Row, 1982): 147–191. Also see E. Griffin, *A First Look at Communication Theory*, 4th ed. (New York: McGraw-Hill, 2000): 110–120; J. T. Wood, *Communication Theories in Action: An Introduction* (Belmont, CA: Wadsworth, 1997): 182–184.

7. W. B. Pearce and V. Cronen, *Communication, Action and Meaning: The Creation of Social Realities* (New York: Praeger, 1980). Also see G. Philipsen, "The Coordinated Management of Meaning: Theory of Pearce, Cronen, and Associates," *Watershed Research Traditions in Human Communication Theory*, Donald Cust and Branislave Kovocic, Eds. (Albany, NY: State University of New York Press, 1995): 13–43.

8. James E. Grunig and Todd Hunt, *Managing Public Relations* (New York: Holt, Rinehart and Winston, 1984): 21–27. See also Anne Lane, "Working at the Interface: The Descriptive Relevance of Grunig and Hunt's Theories to Public Relations Practices in South East Queensland Schools," http://praxis.massey.ac.nz/working_interface.html, 2003.

9. "McDonald's Launches Face-Saving Petition," *Bulldog Reporter's Daily Dog* (May 25, 2007).

10. Richard Lederer, "The Way We Word," *AARP Magazine* (March/April 2005): 86–93.

11. M. E. McCombs, D. L. Shaw, and D. L. Weaver, *Communication and Democracy: Exploring the Intellectual Frontiers in Agenda-Setting Theory* (Mahwah, NJ: Lawrence Erlbaum, 1997).

12. "Cigarette Smoking Drops to Lowest Level in 25 Year Trend." The Harris Poll, www.harrisinteractive.com (March 5, 2008).

Chapter 4

1. "Dunkin' Donuts Pulls Rachael Ray Ad," *CNNMoney.com* (May 29, 2008).

2. Mel Antonen, "Clemens: Steroids, HGH Injections, 'Never Happened,'" *USA Today* (January 7, 2008).

3. Michael S. Schmidt and Judy Battista, "Awaiting Sentence, Vick Speaks of Mistakes," *New York Times* (August 28, 2007).

4. David Crary, "Scandal Forces U.S. Red Cross to Ask Its New Leader to Resign," Associated Press (November 27, 2007).

5. "New Jersey Governor Quits, Comes Out as Gay," *CNNMoney.com* (August 13, 2004).

6. Cited in Edward L. Bernays, *Crystallizing Public Opinion* (New York: Liveright, 1961): 61.

7. Cited in Harwood L. Childs, *Public Opinion: Nature, Formation, and Role* (Princeton, NJ: Van Nostrand, 1965): 15.

8. James E. Grunig and Todd Hunt, *Managing Public Relations* (New York: Holt, Rinehart & Winston, 1984): 130.

9. Leon A. Festinger, *A Theory of Cognitive Dissonance* (New York: Harper & Row, 1957): 163.

10. Richard M. Perloff, *The Dynamics of Persuasion: Communication and Attitudes in the 21st Century*, 2nd ed. (Mahwah, NJ: Lawrence Erlbaum Associates, 2003). Ample discussion of social judgment theory, pioneered by Muzafer and Carolyn Sherif in 1967.

11. Abraham Maslow, *Motivation and Personality* (New York: Harper & Row, 1954).

12. R. E. Petty and J. T. Cacioppo. *The Elaboration Likelihood Model of Persuasion* (New York: Academic Press, 1986).

13. T. C. Brock and S. Shavitt, *Persuasion: Psychological Insights and Perspectives* (Chicago: Allyn & Bacon, 1999).

14. Saul D. Alinsky, *Rules for Radicals* (New York: Vintage Books, 1971): 81.

15. "President Pledges Assistance for New York in Phone Call with Pataki, Giuliani," White House news release, September 13, 2001.

16. Robert L. Dilenschneider, *Power and Influence* (New York: Prentice Hall, 1990): 5.

17. Hadley Cantril, *Gauging Public Opinion* (Princeton, NJ: Princeton University Press, 1972): 226–230.

18. D. T. Max, "The 2,988 Words That Changed a Presidency: An Etymology," *New York Times* on the Web (October 7, 2001).

19. Saad Abedine, "U.S. Death Toll in Iraq Reaches 2000," *CNN.com* (October 26, 2005).

20. Richard Benedetto, "Business News Alters Perceptions of Bush," *USA Today* (July 10, 2002): 6A.

21. "Senate GOP Planning Iraq PR Blitz to Counter 'Frustration' with Media Coverage of War," *Bulldog Reporter's Daily' Dog* (January 4, 2006).

22. Clifford Kraus, "Rockefeller Family Members Press for Change at Exxon," *International Herald Tribune* (May 26, 2008).

23. Randall Smith, "Greenberg's Pals Ship a Letter Rallying Support," *Wall Street Journal* (October 29, 2005): B1.

24. "Doorley Is Selling CEOs on the Value of Reputation," *PR Week* (November 18, 2002).

25. John Naisbitt and Patricia Aburdene, *Megatrends 2000* (New York: Morrow, 1990).

26. Philip Lesly, "How the Future Will Shape Public Relations—and Vice Versa," *Public Relations Quarterly* (Winter 1981–82): 7.

Chapter 5

1. Claudia H. Deutsch, "Chief Turns to Webcast to Pitch G.E.," *New York Times* (March 14, 2008).

2. James E. Grunig and Todd Hunt, *Managing Public Relations* (New York: Holt, Rinehart, & Winston, 1984): 89–97.

3. "Study Results Find Communications Competence Must Be Combined with Knowledge of the Business," study sponsored by Deloitte & Touche and IABC Research Foundation, June 14, 2001.

4. Internal Berkshire Hathaway memo from Warren Buffet, August 12, 1998, as quoted in *Business Week* (July 5, 1999): 62.

5. Stuart Z. Goldstein, "Building Reputation through Communication," *Strategic Communication Management* 8, no. 6 (October/November 2004): 23.

6. Scott Cutlip, Allen Center, and Douglas Broom, *Effective Public Relations*, Vol. 8 (Saddle Brook, NJ: Prentice-Hall, Inc., 2000): 340.

7. Lester R. Potter, "How to Be a Credible Strategic Counselor to Your Organization," delivered at IABC International Conference, Chicago, June 2002.

8. Stuart Z. Goldstein, "Information Preparedness," *Strategic Communication Management* 3, no. 1 (December/January 1999).

9. Norman R. Nager and T. Harrell Allen, *Public Relations Management by Objectives* (New York: Longman Publishing Group, 1984).

10. "American Legacy Foundation Board Names Arnold Communications for Multi-Million Dollar Anti-Tobacco Account," American Legacy Foundation news release, September 15, 1999.

11. Richard Virgilio, "Pay for Placement PR—The What, Why and How of No-Risk, Pay-for-Results Media Placements," *The Journal for Business Marketing & Advertising Professionals.*

12. "O'Dwyer's Director of Corporate Communications 2005" (New York: J. R. O'Dwyer Company, 2005): A5.

13. Remarks by Harvey Greisman, senior vice president/group executive global communications group, MasterCard Worldwide, May 15, 2007, Tarrytown, NY.

14. Karl Greenberg, "Survey Shows Strong Agency CEO Billing Rates," *PR Week* (July 31, 2006).

15. "2002 Public Relations Industry Revenue and Performance Data Fact Sheet," Council of Public Relations Firms, New York, NY, 2005.

16. "As Advertising Struggles, PR Steps into the Breach," *The Economist* (January 21, 2006).

17. Thomas Murray, "In Retreat from Excellence," *Ragan Report* (June 11, 2007): 1.

18. Pete Engardio and Michael Arndt, "What Price Reputation?" *Business Week* (July 9, 2007): 70.

19. Ken Wheaton, "NBA's Stern Gets It: Brand Image Is Key to Game Plan," *Advertising Age* (June 23, 2008).

20. "2002 Public Relations Industry Revenue and Performance Data Fact Sheet," op. cit.
21. "Salary Survey 2008," *PR Week* (February 25, 2008).
22. Fraser P. Seitel, "Reputation Management," odwyerpr.com (July 9, 2002).
23. "Salary Survey 2008," op. cit.
24. "Occupational Employment and Wages, May 2007," U.S. Department of Labor Bureau of Labor Statistics, www.bls.gov.
25. Anita Chabria, "2005 Salary Survey Reveals Growth in Wages and Hiring," *PR Week* (February 21, 2005): 1.
26. Richard Bailey, "A Glass Ceiling in PR?" *PR Studies* weblog from Leeds Business School at Leeds Metropolitan University, http://prstudies.typepad.com (April 2, 2005).
27. "Salary Survey 2008," *PR Week* (February 25, 2008): 19.
28. "Hot Careers for the Next 10 Years," *Fortune* (March 21, 2005): 131.
29. "Salary Survey 2005," *PR Week* (February 21, 2005).

Chapter 6

1. Brian Stelter and Sarah Lyall, "Prince Harry and the Secret Kept by Fleet Street," *New York Times* (March 1, 2008): 1.
2. Susan Schmidt and James V. Grimaldi, "Abramoff Pleads Guilty to 3 Counts," *Washington Post* (January 4, 2006): A1.
3. Alexei Barrionuevo and Vikas Bajaj, "At Enron Trial, 2 Sides Chart Widely Different Courses," *New York Times* (January 31, 2006): D1.
4. David Crary, "Red Cross President Ousted," *Associated Press* (November 27, 2007).
5. Rob Capriccioso, "Learning from American U's Mistakes," Insidehighered.com (October 28, 2005).
6. Frank Bruni, "Pope Tells Crowd of 'Shame' Caused by Abusive Priests," *New York Times* (July 29, 2002): A1–8.
7. "In Public Relations, 25% Admit Lying," *New York Times* (May 8, 2000): C20.
8. Jonathan Alter and Howard Fineman, "A Dynasty Dilemma," *Newsweek* (July 29, 2002): 24–29.
9. "Ethics: And Not a Moment Too Soon," *CFO Magazine* (January 2008): 17.
10. A. Larry Elliott and Richard J. Schroth. *How Companies Lie: Why Enron Is Just the Tip of the Iceberg* (New York: Crown Publishers, 2002).
11. Henry M. Paulson, Address to the National Press Club, Washington, DC (June 5, 2002).
12. "CSR, Ethics and the Board of Directors," *Ethisphere*, Q3 (2007): 8.
13. "Only 3% of Americans Fully Trust Congress," *Angus Reid Global Monitor* (May 29, 2006).
14. Tom Zeller, Jr., "For Bloggers Seeking Name Recognition, Nothing Beats a Good Scandal," *New York Times* (October 31, 2005): 6.
15. Jennifer Harper, "Supreme Court Justices Rank Highest in Credibility, Index Says," *Washington Times* (July 8, 1999): 20.
16. Fraser Seitel, "Public Relations Ethics," *O'Dwyer's PR Report* (April 2007): 36.
17. Teresa M. McAleavy, "Survey: Ethics Abuses on Rise," *The Record* (October 13, 2005): B1.
18. James Patrick Thompson, "Enforcing the Code of Conduct," *NYSE Magazine* (January 2006): 23.

Chapter 7

1. Jonathan D. Glater, "A Company Computer and Questions About E-Mail Privacy," *New York Times* (June 27, 2008): B1.
2. Gerhart L. Klein, *Public Relations Law: The Basics* (Mt. Laurel, NJ: Anne Klein & Associates, 1990): 1–2.
3. William Raspberry, "In the Plame Case, Losers All Around," washingtonpost.com (May 9, 2005).
4. Scott Shane and Eric Lichtblau, "Scientist Is Paid Millions by U.S. in Anthrax Suit," *New York Times* (June 28, 2008): 1.
5. Lara A. Bazelon, "Kozinski Disciplines Himself," *Los Angeles Times* (June 17, 2008).
6. Dennis L. Wilcox and Glen T. Cameron, *Public Relations Strategies and Tactics,* 8th ed. (Boston: Allyn & Bacon, 2002.): 265.

7. Thomas K. Grose, "$50 Million Lawsuit Against WSJ and Burrough May Make Some Authors-to-Be Think Twice," *TFJR Report* (April 1992): 3.
8. "Daughter of Egypt Nassar Loses Defamation Case," *Egypt News* (April 1, 2008).
9. "Judge Tosses Out NY Businessman's 'Borat' Lawsuit," *Associated Press* (April 2, 2008).
10. Denise Lavoie, "Media Troubled by Libel Ruling that Excludes Truth as Defense," *The Record* (March 8, 2009): A-10.
11. Constance L. Hays, "Aide Was Reportedly Ordered to Warn Stewart on Stock Sales," *New York Times* (August 6, 2002): C1–2.
12. Wil Deener, "Lights, Camera, Madness: Cramer Is CNBC's Best," *Dallas Morning News* (February 4, 2006).
13. Louis M. Thompson, Jr., "SEC Cites Investor Relations Officer for Insider Trading," National Investor Relations Institute release (July 2, 2002).
14. "Managing Tidal Wave of Corporate Disclosure," *Business Wire Newsletter* (April 2002): 2.
15. Joseph Nocera, "For All Its Costs, Sarbanes-Oxley Is Working," *New York Times* (December 3, 2005): C1.
16. Alix M. Freedman and Suein L. Hwang, "Brown & Williamson Faces Inquiry," *Wall Street Journal* (February 6, 1996): A1.
17. Kate Ackley, "McCain, Witnesses Weigh 'Indian Loophole' Fix," *Roll Call* (February 9, 2006).
18. Wilcox and Cameron, op. cit, *Public Relations Strategies and Tactics,* 271.
19. Harold W. Suckenik, "PR Pros Should Know the Four Rules of 'Fair Use,'" *O'Dwyer's PR Services Report* (September 1990): 2.
20. Saul Hansell, "The Associated Press to Set Guidelines for Using Its Articles in Blogs," *New York Times* (June 16, 2008).
21. Linda Greenhouse, "What Level of Protection for Internet Speech?" *New York Times* (March 24, 1997): D5.
22. Steven Levy, "U.S. v. the Internet," *Newsweek* (March 31, 1997): 77.
23. Linda Greenhouse, "Decency Act Fails," *New York Times* (June 27, 1997): 1.
24. "Government Seeks Google Records in Pornography Investigation," *Associated Press* (January 19, 2006).
25. Michael Liedtke, "Google's New Chinese Search Engine to Censor Results," *Associated Press* (January 25, 2006).
26. Chuck Kapelke, "Cyberlaw 101," *Continental* (May 2001): 42.
27. Kristi Heim, "Inside China's Teeming World of Fake Goods," *Seattle Times* (February 12, 2006).
28. "In Pursuit of Cybersquatters," *CFO Magazine* (November 1999): 16.
29. David Hanners, "Travelers in a Spat over Catty E-Chat," *St. Paul Pioneer Press* (March 13, 2008).
30. Kevin Lee, "Click Fraud: What It Is, How to Fight It," *ClickZ Experts* (February 18, 2005).
31. Greg Hazley, "PR, Legal Need to Play on Same Team," *O'Dwyer's PR Services Report* (December 2005): 1.
32. James E. Lukaszewski, "Managing Litigation Visibility: How to Avoid Lousy Trial Publicity," *Public Relations Quarterly* (Spring 1995): 18–24.

Chapter 8

1. "Internet's Broader Role in Campaign 2008," Pew Research Center for the People & the Press (January 11, 2008).
2. Katie Delahaye Paine, "Measuring Social Media, Can You Track the Wild West?" Address to Ragan Communications Conference (September 2007).
3. Jennifer Nedeff, "The Bottom Line Beckons: Quantifying Measurement in Public Relations," *Journal of Corporate Public Relations Northwestern University* (1996–1997): 34.
4. Walter K. Lindenmann, "Setting Minimum Standards for Measuring Public Relations Effectiveness," *Public Relations Review* (Winter 1997): 394–395.
5. Gary Holmes, "Nielsen Media Research Reports Television's Popularity Is Still Growing," Nielsen Media Research (September 21, 2006).

6. Tom Greenbaum, "The Gold Standard: Why the Focus Group Deserves to be the Most Respected of All Qualitative Research Tools," *Quirk's Marketing Research Review* (June 2003).
7. David J. Solomon, "Conducting Web-Based Surveys," *Practical Assessment, Research and Evaluation* (August 23, 2001).
8. Robin Lloyd, "Why Presidential Polls Are Wrong," *Live Science* (January 9, 2008).
9. Christine Bates, "Communications Audits and the Effects of Increased Information," *Technical Communication* (May 2003).
10. Katie Delahaye Paine, op. cit.
11. "Guidelines and Standards for Measuring and Evaluating PR Effectiveness," The Institute for Public Relations Commission on PR Measurement and Evaluation (2003).
12. Ibid.
13. Bill Zoellick, "Who, What, Why Important to Know about Web Visitors," *The Boulder County Business Reporter* (Summer 2000).
14. Katherine D. Paine and Beth Roed, "The Basics of Internet Measurement," *Ragan's Interactive PR* (March 1999): 7.
15. Clare Dowdy, "How to Measure the Value of Public Relations," *Financial Times* (June 20, 2006).
16. Fraser P. Seitel, "Strategic PR Research and Analysis," odwypr.com (January 26, 2004).
17. Jennifer Nedeff, op. cit.

Chapter 9

1. Angela Macropoulos, "A Misfired Memo Shows Close Tabs on Reporter," *New York Times* (April 2, 2007): C4.
2. Michael Sebastian, "Target Shuns Bloggers and Almost Pays the Price," *Ragan Report* (January 28, 2008): 4.
3. Seth Schiesel, "Author Faults a Game and Garners Flame Back," *New York Times* (January 26, 2008).
4. Interview with Ari Fleischer, for *The Practice of Public Relations*, 9th ed. (August 7, 2002).
5. "Associated Press, MSNBC and CNBC Seen as Having a Liberal Bias," Rasmussen Reports (July 22, 2007).
6. David T. Z. Mindich, "The New Journalism," *Wall Street Journal* (July 15, 1999): A18.
7. Satham Sanghera, "How Corporate PR Has Turned into the Art of Stonewalling," *Financial Times* (February 10, 2006).
8. "Annual Rankings of Top Media Available from Burrelles/Luce," Burrelles/Luce (May 14, 2008).
9. Timothy Egan, "Outposts," *New York Times* (July 2, 2008).
10. "The State of the News Media 2008," Project for Excellence in Journalism (2008).
11. Ibid.
12. Howard Kurtz, "Katie Couric's Future as CBS Anchor Under Discussion," *Washington Post* (April 10, 2008): C1.
13. "The State of the News Media 2008," op. cit.
14. Zev Chafets, "Late-Period Limbaugh," *New York Times* (July 6, 2008).
15. "The Top Talk Radio Audiences," *Talkers Magazine*, 2008 Talk Media Inc.
16. Richard Perez-Pena, "Washington Post Signals Shift with a New Editor," *New York Times* (July 8, 2008): 1.
17. Egan, op. cit.
18. "Newspapers Have Strong Showing, Drudge Tops Nielsen List Again," Newspaper Association of America (May 19, 2008).
19. Lee Berton, "Avoiding Media Land Mines," *Public Relations Strategist* (Summer 1997): 16.
20. Michael Hastings and Yepoka Yeebo, "Luxurious Reading," *Newsweek* (October 17, 2005): E24.
21. Steve O'Keefe, *Publicity on the Internet* (New York: John Wiley & Sons, 1997).
22. Fraser P. Seitel, "Preparing the CEO for a Print Interview," odwyerpr.com (July 11, 2001).
23. Adam Leyland, "Journalists Grudging Respect for PR Execs," *PR Week* (September 20, 1999): 1.
24. "Getting into the Times: How Andrews Views PR," *Across the Board* (August 1989): 21.

Chapter 10

1. Jamie Pietras, "United Pilots Launch Web Site to Oust CEO," ragan.com (August 21, 2008).
2. Kevin G. Hall, "Mounting Job Losses Point to More Economic Troubles," *McClatchey Newspapers* (August 1, 2008).
3. "U.S. Job Satisfaction Declines, The Conference Board Reports," The Conference Board (February 23, 2007).
4. Michael Sabastian, "CEO Blogs: What You Should Know," ragan.com (May 20, 2008).
5. Christine Kent, "Why Your Ceo's Blog Is Fading into Oblivion," ragan.com (August 7, 2008).
6. "CEOs Rely Most on Public Relations Professionals for Reputation Management," Burson-Marsteller news release (November 12, 2004).
7. Jeanne Sahadi, "CEO Pay: 364 Times More Than Workers," CNNmoney.com (August 29, 2007).
8. "Effective Employee Communication Linked to Stronger Financial Performance," Watson Wyatt news release (November 8, 2005).
9. Paul Dorf, "Is Turnover Back in Vogue?" Ezinearticles.com (November 2005).
10. "An Employee's Eye View of Business," *Ragan Report* (November 25, 1991): 1, 2.
11. "Management Failing to Connect with Employees at Almost Half of Companies," Right Management Consultants (October 11, 2005).
12. Fraser P. Seitel, "Rebuilding Employee Trust Through S-H-O-C," odwyerpr.com (July 11, 2005).
13. Jerry Stevenson, "How to Conduct a Self-Intranet Audit," *Ragan Report* (August 19, 2002): 7.
14. Kevin J. Allen, "Overhaul Your Intranet from A to Z," ragan.com (October 24, 2007).
15. "Two Ways to Pull People to the Intranet," *Ragan Report* (October 18, 1999): 6.
16. Steve Crecenzo, "How to Make Social Media Successful at Your Company," ragan.com (February 28, 2008).
17. "New Frontiers in Employee Communications: Current Practices and Future Trends," survey of Edelman Public Relations (2004).
18. Crecenzo, op. cit.
19. Scott Rodrick, "Use Intranets to Connect Employee Owners," *Interactive Investor Relations* (January 1997): 3.
20. "All Intranet, All the Time," *Ragan Report* (May 14, 2001): 6.
21. Jamie Pietrus, "Employee Networking: The Next Generation," *ragan.com* (October 2, 2008).
22. Allen, op. cit.
23. John R. Kessling, "Maintaining a Successful Intranet: The KGN Experience," *PR Tactics* (November 1999): 20.
24. "Kissing Off Your Print Publication," *Ragan Report* (October 11, 1999): 6.
25. John Guiniven, "Suggestion Boxes and Town Hall Meetings: Fix 'Em or Forget 'Em," *PR Tactics* (February 2000): 22.
26. Michael Sebastian, "Video 101 from the *New York Times'* Tech Critic," ragan.com (January 2, 2008).
27. Robert J. Holland, "Seven Ways to Use Face-to-Face Communication," ragan.com (August 7, 2008).
28. "Talking to the Troops," *Business Week* (July 5, 1999): 62.

Chapter 11

1. Chen May Yee, "Stiptease Clothing Drive Enrages Local Charities," *Minneapolis Star Tribune* (July 13, 2008).
2. Stephanie Strom, "Founder of a Nonprofit Is Punished by Its Board for Engaging in an Internet Ruse," *New York Times* (January 8, 2008): A21.
3. Stephanie Strom, "Hackers Cracked Charities' Addresses and Passwords," *New York Times* (November 27, 2007).

4. David Hinckler, "U.S. Minority Population Continues to Grow," America.gov (May 14, 2008).

5. Robert Bernstein, "U.S. Hispanic Population Surpasses 45 Million, Now 15 Percent of Total," U.S. Census Bureau (May 1, 2008).

6. Bernstein, op. cit.

7. "Urban, Spanish-Language Stations Dominate Major Radio Markets," Arbitron marketingcharts.com (October 7, 2008).

8. Steve Rubel, "Historically, Most Online Communities Haven't Stuck," micropersuasion.com (March 5, 2008).

9. Lynette Clemetson, "Latino Population Growth Is Widespread, Study Says," *New York Times* (July 31, 2002): A14.

10. Sharon Bond, "U.S. Charitable Giving Estimated to be $306.39 Billion in 2007," Giving USA Foundation (June 23, 2008).

11. "The Numbers," *Barron's* (January 16, 2006): 11.

12. "CEO Forum: Environmental Impact," *NYSE Magazine* (January/February 2006): 13.

13. Beckey Bright, "How More Companies Are Embracing Social Responsibility as Good Business," *Wall Street Journal* (March 10, 2008).

14. "Computer and Internet Use in the United States: 2003," U.S. Census Bureau (October 31, 2005).

15. Daniel Golden, "Time Warner to Buy Henry Gates's Africana.com," *Wall Street Journal* (September 7, 2000): B1–4.

16. Richard Perez-Pena, "Washington Post Starts an Online Magazine for Blacks," *New York Times* (January 28, 2008).

17. Emmanuel Legrand, "Live 8 Yields a Windfall," *Billboard* (November 5, 2005): Upfront News.

18. John Cook, "Charity Web Site Greatergood.com Shuts Down," *Seattle Post Intelligencer* (July 21, 2001).

19. Shelley Lowe, "One in Five Speaks Spanish in Five States," U.S. Census Bureau News (September 23, 2008).

20. Tom Martin, "A Few Good Men," *PR Week* (July 21, 2008).

21. "Reaching the Hispanic Audience," *fastforward* (Fall 1999): 1.

22. "The Hispanic Population," United States Census 2000, U.S. Census Bureau (May 2001).

23. "2002 U.S. Hispanic Market," Strategy Resource Corporation (June 2002).

24. "Hispanic Pubs Surge," *Jack O'Dwyer's Newsletter* (January 25, 2006): 3.

25. Robert Bernstein, op. cit.

26. Julia B. Isaacs, "Economic Mobility of Black and White Families," Brookings Institution (November 2007).

27. "Black Spending Power: $723 Billion," *Sacramento Observer* (August 11, 2004).

28. Jeremy Mullman, "*Ebony* Falls Short of Circulation Promise," *Crain's Chicago Business* (February 23, 2006).

29. Laurie Goodstein, "Start-Up Television Venture Is Aiming Its Programming at American Muslims," *New York Times* (November 29, 2004): C7.

30. "American TV Shows Depict Record Number of Gay Characters," www.pinnews.co.uk/news/article (September 26, 2008).

31. Claudia Eller, "Building an Empire of Gay Media," *Los Angeles Times* (June 29, 2008): C2.

32. "What's So Important about Diversity?" *Ragan Report* (August 9, 2004): 3.

33. Stephen Ohlemacher, "Gay Marriages Won't Count in 2010 Census," *The Huffington Post* (July 17, 2008).

34. Nicole Lewis, "Multiple Missions and a Thousand Ideas," *Chronicle of Philanthropy* (December 8, 2005): 37.

35. "Public Relations Society of America Launches National Diversity Initiative," Public Relations Society of America news release (September 14, 2004).

Chapter 12

1. Michael Luo, "Small Online Contributions Add Up to Huge Fund-Raising Edge for Obama," *New York Times* (February 20, 2008).

2. Katharine Q. Seelye, "Clinton Remark on Kennedy's Killing Stirs Uproar," *New York Times* (May 24, 2008).

3. Matt Bai, "Working for the Working-Class Vote," *New York Times* (October 19, 2008).

4. Adam Nagourney and Jeff Zeleny, "Obama Chooses Biden as Running Mate," *New York Times* (August 23, 2008).

5. David Murray, "PR Is Not the Problem—or the Solution," *Ragan Report* (November 24, 2003): 1.

6. Fraser P. Seitel, *The Practice of Public Relations*, 9th ed. (Upper Saddle River, NJ: Prentice-Hall, 2004): 341.

7. Karen De Young, "Bush to Create Formal Office to Shape U.S. Image Abroad," *Washington Post* (July 30, 2002): A1.

8. Sonya Ross, "White House Opens Office to Put a Better Face on U.S. Policy and Messages Abroad," *Associated Press* (July 30, 2002).

9. Fraser P. Seitel, "Words of Speech = Weapons of War," odwyerpr.com (October 15, 2001).

10. "GAO: Bush Administration Paid $200M for PR," *Jack O'Dwyer's Newsletter* (February 22, 2006): 2.

11. Alvin Snyder, "The Changing Voice of America," USC Center on Public Diplomacy (October 27, 2006).

12. "About VOA," Voice of America, Office of Public Affairs, 330 Independence Avenue, S.W., Washington, D.C. 20237.

13. David Barstow, "Behind TV Analysts, Pentagon's Hidden Hand," *New York Times* (April 20, 2008).

14. "Chertoff Blasts FEMA's Faux Press Conference," *Associated Press* (October 27, 2007).

15. Mark Hertsgaard, "Journalists Played Dead for Reagan—Will They Roll Over Again for Bush?" *Washington Journalism Review* (January–February 1989): 31.

16. "Give Him an 'F,'" *The Scudder Media Report* (October 1998): 1, 6.

17. "President Bush Overall Job Rating," CNN/Opinion Research Corp. (October 17, 2008).

18. Robert U. Brown, "Role of Press Secretary," *Editor & Publisher* (October 19, 1974): 40.

19. William Hill, "Nessen Lists Ways He Has Improved Press Relations," *Editor & Publisher* (April 10, 1975): 40.

20. William Safire, "One of Our Own," *New York Times* (September 19, 1974): 43.

21. Laurence McQuillan, "Ari Fleischer Warms Up for Grillings," *USA Today* (January 23, 2001): 6A.

22. Richard W. Stevenson, "Press Secretary on Trial in the Briefing Room," *New York Times* (November 3, 2005): A25.

23. Sheryl Gay Stolberg, "Bush's Press Secretary Is Out Raising Money, and Some Eyebrows," *New York Times* (October 16, 2006): A16.

24. Remarks by Mike McCurry, "A View from the Podium," New York, NY (May 5, 1999).

25. Michael J. Bennett, "The 'Imperial' Press Corps," *Public Relations Journal* (June 1982): 13.

26. Jeffrey H. Birnbaum, "The Road to Riches Is Called K Street," *Washington Post* (June 22, 2005): A01.

27. Hubert B. Herring, "$6 Million a Day to Whisper in Lawmakers' Ears," *New York Times* (January 9, 2005).

28. "Spending for Lobbyists Hits Record High in N.J.," *The Record* (February 26, 2006): A4.

29. Leslie Wayne, "John Ashcroft Sets Up Shop as a Well-Connected Lobbyist," *New York Times* (March 17, 2006): 1.

30. Fraser P. Seitel, "Lobbying Do's and Don'ts," *O'Dwyer's PR Services Report* (December 2005): 31.

31. Fraser P. Seitel, "Lobbying Part II: Making the Sale," *O'Dwyer's PR Services Report* (January 2006): 92.

32. Andy Sullivan, "Obama Launches Web Site to Fight Rumors," *Reuters* (June 12, 2008).

33. Robert Stacy McCain, "MoveOn.org: Don't Believe the Hype," *Ripon Forum* (Fall 2004): 16.

34. Adam Nagourney, "TV's Tight Grip on Campaigns Is Weakening," *New York Times* (September 5, 2002): A1–19.

Chapter 13

1. Sante J. Achilli, "World Statistics on the Number of Internet Shoppers," *Multilingual Search World Edition* (January 28, 2008).
2. Jena McGregor, "What Price Reputation?" *Business Week* (September 23, 2007).
3. Hillary Mayell, "As Consumption Spreads, Earth Suffers, Study Says," *National Geographic News* (January 12, 2004).
4. Landon Thomas, Jr., "Disney Says It Will Link Marketing to Nutrition," *New York Times* (October 17, 2006).
5. Nicholas Casey and Nicholas Zamiska, "Mattel Does Damage Control After New Recall," *Wall Street Journal* (August 15, 2007): B1.
6. Andrew Martin, "Burger King Shifts Policy on Animals," *New York Times* (March 28, 2007): C1.
7. "The General Electric Green Beijing Olympics, 2008," *Ecofuss,* www.ecofuss.com (August 11, 2008).
8. "Consumer-Generated Media Exceeds Traditional Advertising for Influencing Purchasing Behavior," *PR Newswire-Intelliseek* (September 26, 2005).
9. "Voice for the Consumer," *New York Times* (January 4, 2009).
10. Noam Cohen, "Doorstep Protest: Very Real, Very Virtual," *New York Times* (November 26, 2007): C3.
11. Jim Fitzgerald, "Consumer Reports' Flubs Relatively Few but Notable," *Associated Press* (January 21, 2007).
12. "Percentage of Internet Users in the U.S., 2008," infoplease.com (May 11, 2008).
13. *JetBlue Airways Customer Bill of Rights,* JetBlue Airways, Forest Hills, NY.
14. Steve Crescenzo, "One Way to Weather an Ice Storm," *Ragan Report* (February 26, 2007): 1.

Chapter 14

1. Elaine Sciolino and Souad Mekhennet, "Al Qaeda Warrior Uses Internet to Rally Women," *New York Times* (May 28, 2008).
2. Robert F. Worth, "A Living-Room Crusade via Blogging," *New York Times* (May 20, 2008).
3. David Brooks, "The Cognitive Age," *New York Times* (May 2, 2008).
4. Edward Wong, "China Leader Makes Debut in Great Wall of Facebook," *New York Times* (May 28, 2008).
5. Connor Digman, "Brand Builders vs. Flag Burners," *Ad Age Global* (December 2001): 4–5.
6. Heather Timmons and J. Adam Huggins, "New York Manhole Covers, Forged Barefoot in India," *New York Times* (November 26, 2007).
7. "Global Alliance for Public Relations Announces 2003 Executive Board," news release of the Global Alliance (July 16, 2002).
8. "Champions of Accountability Seek to Reclaim Their Crown," *London Sunday Herald* (June 5, 2002).
9. Lina Saigol and Jane Croft, "Blair's Son Puts a Different Spin on Image of the PR Business," *Financial Times* (January 16, 2006).
10. "Japan's Most Exclusive Clubs," *On the Media,* National Public Radio (December 12, 2008).
11. *Communicating: A Guide to PR in Japan,* Dentsu Public Relations (2005).
12. Carole Gorney, "China's Economic Boom Brings a PR Explosion," *The Strategist* (Spring 2005): 36.
13. Carole Gorney, "Why China Is Ripe for 'Professional' Public Relations," *International Review* (May 2000).
14. Keith Bradsher, "China Criticizes Google and Others on Pornography," *New York Times* (January 6, 2009).
15. "Top 5 China Stories of 2008," CBNnews.com (January 2, 2009).
16. Krishnamurthy Sriramesh, "The Models of Public Relations in India," *Journal of Communication Management 4,* No. 3 (2000): 229.
17. M. Krishnamoorthy, "PR Consultants Ready to Spread Wings Overseas," *The Star Online* (February 12, 2006).

18. Paolo Romero, "Palace Turns to PR Gurus to Improve GMA's Image," *Philippine Star* (January 24, 2006).
19. "Russia Spends Big to Polish Its Image," *Sydney Herald* (January 9, 2006).
20. Malcolm Cole, "Spin Doctor Numbers Surge," *Courier Mail* (January 9, 2006).
21. "PR Industry Growing, But Still Learning," *Zawya Business Monthly* (January 2006).
22. Hassan M. Fattah, "A New Al Jazeera with a Global Focus," *New York Times* (November 13, 2006).
23. "Muslim Scholars in Cartoon Talks," *BBC News* (March 23, 2006).

Chapter 15

1. Fraser P. Seitel, "PR Pros Are Horrible Writers," odwyerpr.com (March 5, 200)1.
2. Bill Moyers, "Watch Your Language," *The Professional Communicator* (August–September 1985): 6.
3. Jim Ylisela, "The Fundamentals of Good Writing," ragan.com (July 25, 2008).
4. Fraser P. Seitel, "Newsworthy News Releases," odwyerpr.com (March 13, 2001).
5. "How to Get Editors to Use Press Releases," *Jack O'Dwyer's Newsletter* (May 26, 1993): 3.
6. Linda P. Morton, "Producing Publishable Press Releases," *Public Relations Quarterly* (Winter 1992–1993): 9–11.
7. Fraser P. Seitel, "News Release Essentials," odwyerpr.com (July 18, 2001).
8. "Journalists Prefer E-Mail: Survey," *Jack O'Dwyer's Newsletter* (August 24, 2004): 3.
9. Fraser P. Seitel, "E-mail News Releases," odwyerpr.com (February 23, 2004).

Chapter 16

1. Micheline Maynard, "A Mistaken News Report Hurts United," *New York Times* (September 9, 2008).
2. Michael Sebastian, "Blogs Force Secretive Steve Jobs to Open Up," ragan.com (January 7, 2009).
3. Fraser P. Seitel, "Pitch Emails," odwyerpr.com (March 26, 2007).
4. Jeffrey D. Porro, Porro Associates, 1120 Connecticut Ave., Suite 270, Washington, D.C. 20036.

Chapter 17

1. Anne Eisenberg, "You've Had the Root Canal. Now See the Movie," *New York Times* (October 28, 2007).
2. Bob Tedeschi, "A Gimmick Becomes a Real Trend," *New York Times* (November 26, 2007).
3. Stephanie Clifford, "Product Placements Acquire a Life of Their Own on Shows," *New York Times* (July 14, 2008).
4. Laura Petrecca, "Product Placement—You Can't Escape It," *USA Today* (October 10, 2006).
5. Al Ries and Laura Ries, *The Fall of Advertising and the Rise of PR* (New York: Harper Business, 2002): 251.
6. Darren Press, "Getting Word Out Involves 3 Strategies," *Poughkeepsie Journal* (October 16, 2005).
7. Tom Harris, "Kotler's Total Marketing Embraces MPR," *MPR Update* (December 1992): 4.
8. Daniel Gross, "Ho Ho Ho Classic," *US Airways Magazine* (February 2006): 26.
9. James Bandler, "How Companies Pay TV Experts for On-Air Product Mentions," *Wall Street Journal* (April 19, 2005): A1.
10. "CNN Clamps Down on 'Stealth' Guests," *Jack O'Dwyer's Newsletter* (September 4, 2002): 3.
11. Kathy Burnham, "Trade Shows: Make Them Worth the Investment," *Tactics* (September 1999): 11.
12. Janet Morrissey, "If It's Retail, Is It Still Rock?" *New York Times* (October 28, 2007).

13. Chad Terhune and Brian Steinberg, "Coca-Cola Signs NBA Wunderkind," *Wall Street Journal* (August 22, 2003): B5.
14. Jessica Sidman, "20,000 Brownies for Obama," *Washingtonian* (January 16, 2009).
15. Stuart Elliott, "For a New Brand, Pepsi Starts the Buzz Online," *New York Times* (March 14, 2008).
16. Lorne Manly, "On Television, Brands Go from Props to Stars," *New York Times* (October 2, 2005): B1.
17. Julie Bosman, "Advertising Is Obsolete: Everyone Says So," *New York Times* (January 23, 2006): C7.
18. Clifford, op. cit.
19. Matt Richtel, "A New Reality in Video Games: Advertisement," *New York Times* (April 11, 2005).
20. Stuart Elliott, "Product Placement Moves to Cartoons," *New York Times* (October 21, 2004).
21. Brian Stelter, "Low Ratings End Show and a Product Placement," *New York Times* (November 14, 2008).
22. Brad Stone, "TiVo and Amazon Team Up," *New York Times* (July 22, 2008).
23. Stuart Elliott, "A Column on (Your Product Here) Placement," *New York Times* (August 16, 2006).
24. "The Age of Nikes, Cars and Guns—Not Roses," *Barron's* (January 16, 2006): 14.
25. Clyde Haberman, "Sell the Naming Rights and You May Sell Much More," *New York Times* (September 16, 2008).
26. Petrecca, op. cit.
27. Al Ries and Laura Ries, op. cit.

Chapter 18

1. Eric Benderoff, "Macon Phillips: Obama's New-Media Messenger," *Chicago Tribune* (March 9, 2009).
2. Richard Perez-Pena, "Topic Pages to be Hub of New BusinessWeek Site," *New York Times* (August 18, 2008).
3. "Facts and Figures," www.internetindicators.com.
4. "Internet Usage Statistics—The Big Picture," www.internetworldstats.com (December 31, 2008).
5. Michael Marriott, "Blacks Turn to Internet Highway and Digital Divide Starts to Close," *New York Times* (March 31, 2006): A1.
6. Dan Fost, "Festival Organizers Say Internet Bouncing Back with a Vengeance," *The Record* (March 11, 2006): A7.
7. Kirk Semple and Dexter Filkins, "Reporter Freed in Iraq, 3 Months After Abduction," *New York Times* (March 31, 2006): A1.
8. "Corporate Websites Still Coming Up Short," *The Holmes Report* (February 18, 2002): 1–2.
9. Rachel Leibrock, "Teens Treating E-mail as Too Old-Fashioned," *The Record* (July 8, 2008): A-7.
10. Li Yuan, Corey Dad and Paulo Prada, "Texting When There's Trouble," *The Wall Street Journal* (April 18, 2007).
11. Fraser P. Seitel, "Blog-Communications Weapon," *O'Dwyer's PR Services Report* (November 2005): 39.
12. Michael Sebastian, "April Showers Bring . . . Millions of Bloggers," *Ragan Report* (April 16, 2007): 4.
13. Seth Godin, "Unleash Your Ideavirus," *Fast Company* (December 19, 2007).
14. John Kelly, Carlos Manzano, and Stephanie Mattera, "The Changing Face of Public Relations," Practicum: New York University School of Continuing and Professional Studies (April 25, 2008).
15. Helio Fred Garcia and Laurel Hart, "CEO Advisory: Beware (and prepare for) the Blogosphere Era," *Strategy & Leadership 35*, No. 6 (2007): 51–53.
16. Beth Snyder Bulik, "Does Your Company Need a Chief Blogger?" *Advertising Age* (April 14, 2008): 24.
17. Chris Kent, "Why Your CEO's Blog Is Fading into Oblivion," *The Ragan Report* (December 2008): 9.
18. David Murray, "Rules for Blogging at Sun: 'Don't Do Anything Stupid,'" ragan.com (May 1, 2008).
19. Bill Marriott, "This Senseless Tragedy," Marriott on The Move blog (September 20, 2008).
20. D. Isenberg, "The Rise of the Stupid Network," *Computer Telephony* (August 1997): 16–26.
21. Jeffrey P. Maldonado, "People-Powered PR: Social Media in the 2008 Presidential Race," Capstone: New York University School of Continuing and Professional Studies (September 2008).
22. Kelly, Manzano, and Mattera, op. cit.
23. Marc Ruben, "The Ten Commandments of MySpace Advocacy," *O'Dwyer's PR Report* (December 2006): 8–9.
24. Kelly, Manzano, and Mattera, op. cit.
25. Helene Cooper and Carl Hulse, "Obama's Effort on Budget Echoes Fall Campaign," *New York Times* (March 18, 2009): A16.
26. "Tweet Leads to a Scolding," *New York Times* (March 18, 2009): B12.
27. Noam Cohen, "All a-Twitter About Stars Who Tweet," *New York Times* (January 5, 2009).
28. Christine Kent, "Is Twitter the Newest and Coolest Way to Pitch the Media," ragan.com (June 25, 2008).
29. Michael Sebastian, "10 Ways to Attract Employees to Your Intranet," *Ragan Report*.
30. Angelo Fernando, "Podcasting, Anyone?" *Communication World* (September–October 2005): 10.
31. Charles Pizzo, "Shield Your Company's Reputation from the Dark Side of Cyberspace," P.R., Inc., New Orleans, LA, P.O. Box 172846, Arlington, TX 76003-2846.
32. Charles Pizzo, op. cit.
33. "Where Do You Draw the Line?" *Ragan Report* (September 30, 2002): 1.
34. Christopher L. Martin and Nathan Bennett, "What to Do About Online Attacks," *Wall Street Journal* (March 10, 2008): R6.
35. Amelia Kassel, "Guide to Internet Monitoring and Clipping: Strategies for Public Relations, Marketing and Competitive Intelligence," www.cyberalert.com/whitepaper.html (1999–2000).
36. Gwendolyn Bounds, "How to Get Attention in a New-Media World," *Wall Street Journal* (September 25, 2006): R1.
37. Fraser P. Seitel, "Know Your Social Media," *O'Dwyer's PR Report* (November 2006): 34.

Chapter 19

1. Noam Cohen, "Spinning a Web of Lies at Digital Speed," *New York Times* (October 13, 2008).
2. Helio Fred Garcia, *Crisis Communications 1* (New York: American Association of Advertising Agencies, 1999): 9.
3. Ed Wiley III, "Duke Lacrosse Suspended Amid Rape Charges," BET.com (March 29, 2006).
4. Philip Rawls, "Magistrate Rejects Scrushy's Arguments of Prosecutor Misconduct," *Associated Press* (March 27, 2006).
5. Vernon Silver and David Glovin, "Madoff Scandal Ensnares Patron Saint for Moralists," *Bloomberg News* (February 13, 2009).
6. Richard Lacayo, "When a Story Goes Terribly Wrong," *Time* (May 22, 2005).
7. "Issues Management Conference—A Special Report," *Corporate Public Issues 7*, no. 23 (December 1, 1982): 1–2.
8. Richard C. Hyde, "In Crisis Management, Getting the Message Right Is Critical," *The Strategist* (Summer 2007): 32–35.
9. Richard K. Long, "Seven Needless Sins of Crisis (Mis)management," *PR Tactics* (August 2001): 14.
10. Fraser P. Seitel, "Spotting a Crisis," odwyerpr.com (March 20, 2001).
11. Kate MacArthur, "KFC Preps Bird-Glue Fear Plan," *Advertising Age* (November 7, 2005): 1.
12. Toddi Gutner, "Dealing with PR Crisis Takes Planning and Truth," *Wall Street Journal* (March 25, 2008).
13. John Branch, "Plaxico Burress Shoots Himself Accidentally," *New York Times* (November 29, 2008).
14. Fraser P. Seitel, "Crisis Management Lessons from the Astor Disaster," *O'Dwyer's PR Report* (December 2006): 30.

15. "Traditional Media Still Win in Crises," *Jack O'Dwyer's Newsletter* (October 9, 2006): 8.

16. Michael Barbaro, "Wal-Mart Begins Quest for Generals in P.R. War," *New York Times* (March 30, 2006): C3.

Chapter 20

1. David Meerman Scott, "How David Murray Found a New Job via Twitter," ragan.com (February 25, 2009).

2. Anderson Cooper, "Ten Most Wanted: Culprits of the Collapse," AC360 blog (October 29, 2008).

3. Lindsey Miller, "Recession Reprieve for Communicators," ragan.com (February 27, 2009).

4. Fraser P. Seitel, "Finding a PR Job," odwyerpr.com (June 13, 2005).

5. Fraser P. Seitel, "Finding a Job in Public Relations," odwyerpr.com (May 12, 2008).

6. Fraser P. Seitel, "The 7 Keys to Success in Public Relations," odwyerpr.com (July 15, 2004).

7. Interview with Barry Zusman (March 2, 2009).

8. Jessica Levco, "Veteran Communicators Share Advice with Newbies," ragan.com (March 16, 2009).

Index

Page numbers followed by *f* refer to figures and *t* refer to tables.